MASTER HANDBOOK OF MICROCOMPUTER LANGUAGES

SECOND EDITION

To the memory of my father,
Charles F. Taylor, Sr.,
who taught me the value of books.

No. 2893
$26.95

MASTER HANDBOOK OF MICROCOMPUTER LANGUAGES

SECOND EDITION

CHARLES F. TAYLOR, JR.

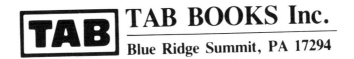

TAB BOOKS Inc.

Blue Ridge Summit, PA 17294

SECOND EDITION
FIRST PRINTING

Library of Congress Cataloging in Publication Data

Taylor, Charles F. (Charles Floyd), 1946—
Master handbook of microcomputer languages / by Charles F. Taylor,
Jr.—2nd ed.
p. cm.
Rev. ed. of: The master handbook of high-level microcomputer
languages. 1st ed. c1984.
Includes index.
ISBN 0-8306-0293-3   ISBN 0-8306-2893-2 (pbk.)
1. Microcomputers—Programming. 2. Programming languages
(Electronic computers) I. Taylor, Charles F. (Charles Floyd),
1946- Master handbook of high-level microcomputer languages.
II. Title.
QA76.6.T3925 1987   87-29024
005.26—dc19   CIP

Questions regarding the content of this book
should be addressed to:

Reader Inquiry Branch
Editorial Department
TAB BOOKS Inc.
Blue Ridge Summit, PA 17294

Contents

15 Microcomputer Languages Compared   483

Index   491

Introduction

This is a book about computer languages. More specifically, it is about high-level languages that are available for use on microcomputers. Twelve different languages are presented and described:

Ada	LISP
BASIC	Logo
C	Modula-2
COBOL	Pascal
Forth	PILOT
Fortran	Prolog

The purpose of the book is to provide in one location a description of each language, conveying the nature of each language along with its major features. Programming examples are interspersed liberally throughout. Along with the usual short examples, a longer, comprehensive sample program is provided at the end of each language chapter. You can thus see what a nontrivial program looks like in each language.

To make comparisons between languages easier, many of the programming examples are the same from language to language. You can thus see how the same problem can be solved in more than one language.

All of the languages presented in this book are available for microcomputers. The sample programs were run on either an Apple II Plus or a Zenith 150 (IBM PC compatible). Some were tested on both. The only ones of these languages that I haven't seen available for the Apple II series are Ada and Prolog. The only one of these languages I haven't seen for IBM PC compatibles is PILOT.

The typical reader of this book will probably know how to program in at least one high-level language (perhaps BASIC or Fortran), either on a microcomputer or on a larger machine. He or she can expect to learn what each of the various languages has to offer and will be in a better position to choose a language appropriate for a particular application.

It is of course impossible to cover every feature of every language in such a small space. I have attempted, however, to cover enough of the major features of each language so as to convey the essence of the language and to provide a valid basis for comparison. Features unique to a particular implementation of a language have been omitted when possible.

The first chapter addresses the question, "What is a high-level language?" The second chapter discusses in general terms the features commonly found in high-level languages. Its purpose is to provide a foundation for the chapters that follow and a basis for comparing languages. Chapters 3 through 14, the language chapters, form the heart of the book, with one chapter devoted to each language. The language chapters are presented in alphabetical order by the name of the language and may be read in any order. Chapter 15 provides a comparison of the various languages covered.

Changes from the first edition include the addition of Ada and Prolog. Some of the remaining chapters have been extensively revised, and others less so. Many of the examples have been converted or rewritten to run on an IBM PC compatible microcomputer, including all of the BASIC, C, COBOL, Modula-2, and Pascal programs.

1
What Is A High-Level Language?

Ada
BASIC
C
COBOL
Forth
Fortran
LISP
Logo
Modula-2
Pascal
PILOT
Prolog

At the heart of every microcomputer lies an integrated circuit called a *microprocessor*. This microprocessor makes up what is called the *central processing unit, or CPU,* of the microcomputer. All of the computation takes place in the CPU. In 1987, a microprocessor could be purchased for as little as $1.69 and was about the size of a man's thumb. Such a microprocessor contains as much computing power as the largest computers of 25 years ago. Such a computer then cost hundreds of thousands of dollars and occupied a large room. Times have changed.

Of course you cannot buy a microcomputer for $1.69, because a CPU is useless without such things as a power supply, input and output devices, memory, and various interface circuits. The total price is thus much higher, ranging from a few hundred dollars for the simplest microcomputers to over $10,000 for the more complex units. In 1987, a very powerful microcomputer could be purchased for one or two thousand dollars.

MACHINE LANGUAGES

Common microprocessors available today include the Intel 8086, 8088, 80286, and 80386, and the Motorola 68000 and 68020 chips. Earlier microprocessors, such as the Motorola 6800 and 6809, the Intel 8080 and 8085, the Mostek 6502, and the Zilog Z80, are all but obsolete, having been superceded by more powerful units.

Each microprocessor has its own *language*, or set of instructions that it understands, designed into the circuitry. Such a language is called a *machine language*. Machine languages are made up of 1s and 0s, or binary numbers. These binary numbers are often abbreviated as octal (base 8) or hexadecimal (base 16) numbers, but even so, they are dreadfully hard for humans to use. Worse yet, each microcomputer speaks a different machine language.

ASSEMBLY LANGUAGES

The next step above a machine language is an *assembly language.* In an assembly language a *mnemonic* is substituted for each machine language instruction. A mnemonic is made up of two or more letters and usually is an abbreviation for a phrase describing the action to be performed. Thus the mnemonic INX means "INcrement the X register" in 6502 assembly language. The machine language equivalent is binary 11101000 or hexadecimal E8.

In order for an assembly language program to work, it must be translated into machine language. Fortunately this can almost always be done by a computer program called an *assembler.*

While INX is a definite improvement over 11101000 or E8, there is still essentially a one-to-one correspondence between machine-language instructions and assembly-language instructions. Machine and assembly languages are often called *low-level languages.* What this means is that it takes a lot of instructions to do a little processing, and the programmer has to know and keep track of numerous minute details.

The term *low-level* refers to the distance between the programmer and the machine. With a low-level programming language, the programmer is right down at the machine level.

Low-level language programming is difficult. It takes a lot of effort to learn a low-level language. A program written in a low-level language for one computer may not work on another computer. In the early days of large computers, there was no choice but to program in a low-level language. The same was true in the early days of microcomputers. Today microcomputers are selling by the hundreds of thousands. People from every walk of life are buying and programming microcomputers. I think it is safe to say that this wouldn't be happening if only low-level languages existed today.

HIGH-LEVEL LANGUAGES

The term *high-level* implies that the programmer is above the machine level, separated from it by some distance. High-level languages were introduced on large computers in the mid to late fifties. Fortran and COBOL were among the first such languages to be introduced. Since then numerous other high-level languages have appeared. These include BASIC, LISP, and Pascal, to name but a few.

How does a high-level language differ from a low-level language? In several ways: Fundamental to the distinction is the fact that a high-level language programmer doesn't have to be aware of and keep track of so many minute details about the computer being used. High-level programmers need not get "down and dirty" with binary numbers and other such low-level details.

One statement in a high-level language is usually equivalent to many statements in a low-level language. The programmer can therefore accomplish much more with much less effort.

High-level languages are usually more-or-less machine-independent. A program written in COBOL to run on one computer can usually be made to run on another computer with only minor changes.

High-level languages are usually designed to be more readable than low-level languages. Suppose, for example that we wanted to add two numbers (A and B) together, giving a third number (C). In 6502 assembly language, this might look something like the following:

```
CLC            ;Clear the carry flag
LDA A          ;Load the accumulator with A
ADC B          ;Add B (with carry)
STA C          ;Store the result in location C
```

This example is short because I have assumed that the numbers in question, including the result, are integers between 0 and 255. If that were not true, the example would be much longer. In BASIC the example would look like this:

```
LET C = A + B
```

In COBOL it would look like this:

```
ADD A TO B GIVING C.
```

Even in this simple case, the high-level languages are much more readable. If I allowed the numbers to be much larger and included fractions, the assembly language example would become much more complex, while the high-level language examples would stay the same.

As is the case with assembly languages, high-level languages must be translated into machine language before a program can run. This is usually accomplished in one of two ways: with a *compiler* or with an *interpreter*. A compiler translates the program all at once. The result is a machine language program which can then be executed. An interpreter translates the program one line at a time, first translating the line and then executing it. The cycle is repeated for each line of the program.

Compiled programs usually run faster than interpreted programs. This is because each line of a compiled program is translated exactly once, regardless of how many times it is executed. A line of an interpreted program may have to be translated more than once if it is to be executed more than once (as in a loop). Interpreted languages, on the other hand, are sometimes easier to use because they do not require the extra compile step. Some languages, such as BASIC, are available on microcomputers in both interpreted and compiled versions. Most languages, however, are available only in one version or the other.

HIGH-LEVEL VERSUS LOW-LEVEL LANGUAGES

The primary advantage of low-level languages is execution speed. A program written in assembly language usually runs many times faster than a comparable program written in a high-level language.

Sometimes speed is critical, as in a program that will be executed many times in a production environment. In such cases, use of a low-level language may be advantageous. If a program is to be run only a few times, however, execution speed is less of a factor than development speed. In such cases, the value of the speed advantage is questionable. It usually takes much longer to write and test a program in a low-level language than in a high-level language.

Another advantage of low-level languages is that they provide easy access to the inner workings of a particular machine. This is an advantage when you are writing software such as compilers and operating systems.

High-level languages have advantages of their own. High-level languages are usually easier to learn and easier to use than low-level languages. The user need not be concerned about machine-specific details.

A programmer can usually be much more productive with a high-level language. The same operation usually requires fewer steps in a high-level language than in a low-level language. Studies have shown that programmers can usually produce the same number of lines of code per unit time, regardless of the level of language used. It therefore stands to reason that a programmer can effectively accomplish more in a given amount of time with a high-level language than with a low-level language.

Because a given high-level language is usually available on many different kinds of computers, large and small, programs written in high-level languages are more portable than programs written in low-level languages. In other words, a program written in a high-level language can usually be run on a variety of different computers. Recall that low-level languages usually will run on only one kind of computer.

Finally, high-level language programs are usually more readable than low-level language programs. This is especially important for programs that must be maintained or modified after they are written, whether by the same programmer or by someone else. Unfortunately, high-level language programs are sometimes so poorly written as to be difficult to read; nevertheless, the potential exists for high-level language programs to be much more readable than low-level language programs.

OBJECTIVES OF THIS BOOK

This book describes high-level languages from the point of view of the user. It discusses high-level languages in general in Chapter 2 and then discusses the particular features of various languages currently available for microcomputers. The emphasis is on portraying the "flavor" of each language, to provide the reader with an idea of what programming in each language is like. The strengths and weaknesses of each language are explored.

Emphasis has been placed on the features of each language that are common to most implementations. Machine-dependent features such as graphics have been ignored whenever possible. (The major exception to this rule is Logo, in which graphics play a central role.) For the same reason this book will not cover such details as how to create and run a program on a particular microcomputer. The user is referred to the instruction manual provided with the language for such details.

It is my firm conviction that there is not now, and probably never will be, a single language that is best for every application. Knowledge of more than one language can thus be an advantage because one language might be best for one application, another best for another application, and so on. What might be a long, convoluted program in one language might be trivial in another language. A programming language is a set of tools used to create computer programs. The programmer who limits himself or herself to only one programming language is a little like the carpenter who uses only a hammer and a saw; the job may get done, but it may not be done as well or as quickly as it might have been.

2

General Features of Computer Languages

The purpose of this chapter is to describe the various features common to computer languages in general, and so to provide a framework for examining individual computer languages. This will provide a convenient framework for making comparisons between the various languages available for use on microcomputers.

DATA REPRESENTATION

Computers are often referred to as electronic data processing machines. All computers process data in one form or another. It is useful to examine the ways in which that data can be represented in computer languages.

Constants

A *constant* is a data value that does not change. For example, the number 12 is a constant; it will always represent the same number.

At the lowest level, computers store data in the binary system (base 2), because the ones and zeros of the binary system correspond directly to the discrete states of digital electronic devices. When using a high-level computer language, the programmer need not be overly concerned with such details. What the programmer does need to know is that with some forms of data representation used by computer languages, numbers that can be represented exactly in the decimal system (base 10) cannot be represented exactly in the binary system (base 2). This can cause some unexpected results; the reasons therefor will be discussed below.

6

Two forms of number representation that rely internally on the binary system are *integer* values and *real* values. An integer is a whole number written without a decimal point, such as 1, 2, and −5. A real number is a number written with a decimal point and/or an exponent, such as 1.0, 3.1415926, −2.8, or 1.2E5. The last number in the preceding list is read as "1.2 times ten to the fifth power." The E is used to signify powers of ten, corresponding to the *scientific notation* of mathematics.

Integers are represented exactly in computers, but they often have limited ranges. On a microcomputer, integers can typically range between −32768 and +32767. Their range is limited by the amount of memory used for their storage (typically 16 binary digits, or *bits*) and by the form of their internal representation.

Real numbers are represented internally in two parts: an *exponent* and a *mantissa*. The number 1.234567890, as an example, would be represented internally as something like "0.123456E1." The "E1" is the exponent part and means "times ten to the first power." The "0.123456" is the mantissa. The last few decimal places were lost due to a restriction on the number of significant digits retained. The number of significant digits available is typically between six and seven and is a function of how much storage is allocated to storing the mantissa. The exponent can typically range between plus and minus 38. This is a function of the number of bits allocated to storage of the exponent.

Another reason that real numbers are not always represented exactly inside the computer has to do with the fact that the internal representation is binary. The number one tenth is easily represented in the decimal system as 0.1, using a finite number of digits. The number one third, however, would require an infinite number of digits for an exact representation in the decimal system (0.333333 . . . . .). In the binary system, neither number can be represented exactly using only a finite number of digits. The number one tenth, for example, would look something like 0.09999999 . . . . . .

Some implementations of high-level languages on microcomputers support what are often called *double-precision* real numbers. By allocating twice as much storage to such numbers, more significant digits (typically about 14) can be retained. This is often useful in statistical and other scientific applications.

For many applications of computers, integers and real or double-precision numbers are adequate. The exception is for financial applications. Accountants like to see their ledgers balance to the penny; they have little sympathy for excuses such as, ". . . . but my computer isn't that accurate." The solution is to use an encoding scheme that represents numbers internally as binary encoded decimal numbers rather than as ordinary binary numbers. This is done at a sacrifice in storage efficiency. In binary, eight bits can represent numbers between 0 and 255, but in decimal the same eight bits can only represent numbers from 0 to 99. The scheme by which this is accomplished is called *BCD*, for *b*inary *c*oded *d*ecimal. It permits the exact internal representation of decimal numbers. The first four bits represent a decimal digit between 0 and 9, as do the second four bits. As we shall see, this feature is supported in only a few of the popular high-level languages.

So far we have discussed only the representation of numbers. Computers must also represent the letters of the alphabet and other characters. This is most commonly done on microcomputers using *ASCII*, the *American Standard Code for Information Interchange*. The letter A in ASCII is represented by the number 65, the digit 7 by the number 55, and the character % by the number 37. These are all examples of what are referred to as *characters*. A sequence of characters is called a *character string*, or simply a *string*. This type of data is also often referred to as *alphanumeric* data.

Some computer languages also have a type of data called *logical* or *Boolean* (after George Boole, a nineteenth-century mathematician and logician). There are only two such data elements, *true* and *false*.

Variables

A variable in a computer language is often thought of as something mysterious out of a mathematical formula. A variable is not mysterious at all; it can simply be thought of as a place to store a data value. In fact, a variable is simply a name given to a particular place in the computer's memory where a value will be stored. The compiler or interpreter takes care of the details of setting aside and keeping track of the necessary memory for storing variables.

Variables are indispensable to all but the simplest computer programs. If it weren't for the availability of variables, you would have to write a new program for every different set of data you wanted to process. You would need a new program to balance your checkbook every month!

When a variable takes on a new value, it simply means that a new value has been stored in the place allocated to the variable, displacing whatever was there before.

In most languages a particular variable can hold only one *type* of data (real, integer, or string). Some languages require that the programmer specify in advance what variables he or she intends to use and what type each of these variables is to be. Other languages have default (assumed) types based on the first or last letter of a variable's name.

Computer languages that are very particular about variable types, how they are declared, and how they are used, are called *strongly typed* languages. Pascal is an example of a strongly typed language. Languages that are more lax about such matters are said to be *loosely typed*. BASIC is an example of a loosely typed language. There are advantages and disadvantages to each approach. Simply stated, loosely typed languages are more forgiving, but strongly typed languages provide better protection against careless mistakes.

THE ASSIGNMENT STATEMENT

An assignment statement is used to assign a particular value to a variable. As just discussed, this process can also be viewed as storing that value in a particular place in the computer's memory. Most languages denote this operation by a symbol called an *assignment operator*. Most languages use either the equals sign (=) or a colon followed by an equals sign (:=) for the assignment operator. For example, suppose you wish to assign the value 5.1 to a real variable X. In Pascal you would write

    X := 5.1;

in BASIC you would write either

    LET X = 5.1

or, simply,

X = 5.1.

One reason Pascal and some other languages do not use the simpler = for an assignment operator is that the assignment operator doesn't really indicate equality. Suppose, for example, that you want to add 1 to X and store the result back in X. In BASIC or Fortran you could write

X = X + 1.

But how can X "equal" X + 1? It can't. It is good practice to read the assignment operator as "is assigned the value of," regardless of what symbol is used. The above would thus be read, "X is assigned the value of X plus 1." An alternate way to read it would be, "X takes on the value of X + 1."

ARITHMETIC EXPRESSIONS

The easiest way to describe an arithmetic expression is to give examples. First of all, a constant such as 1.2 is an arithmetic expression. A numeric variable such as X can be an arithmetic expression. In most computer languages, an arithmetic expression followed by an arithmetic operator (+, −, etc.) followed by another arithmetic expression is also an arithmetic expression. Examples of this are X + 1, X + Y, and 2 ∗ X. (The ∗ means multiplication. The division operator is /.)

Arithmetic expressions can also contain parentheses. By repeated applications of the above rules, more complex arithmetic expressions can be formed, such as the following examples:

(X − Y)∗(X + Y)
2∗(3∗(X + 4)/(Y − 5))

Perhaps the key feature of arithmetic expressions is that they can be evaluated to a numeric value according to a given set of rules.

In the following arithmetic expression:

X + 2,

the X and the 2 are called *operands* and the + is called an *operator*. In most computer languages the operator goes between the operands. This is sometimes called *infix* notation. A few computer languages, such as LISP and Forth, use other forms of notation. LISP uses *prefix* notation (also called *Cambridge Polish* notation) in which the operator comes first, followed by the two operands. In LISP the above expression would be written as

(+ X 2),

OR

(PLUS X 2).

Forth uses *postfix* notation (also called *reverse Polish* notation) in which the two operands come first, followed by the operator. In this notation the above expression would be written as

    X 2 + .

The word *Polish* in the descriptions of the above two kinds of notation is in honor of the Polish mathematician Jan Lukasiewicz (1878-1956), who pioneered prefix notation.

The expression is one of the key features that distinguishes high-level languages from low-level languages. In a low-level language you can usually do only one thing at a time, that is one operation per statement. An arithmetic expression in a high-level computer language permits the programmer to accomplish many calculations with only one statement.

LOGICAL EXPRESSIONS

If an arithmetic expression evaluates to an arithmetic value, then you can rightly expect that a logical expression evaluates to a logical value, that is, true or false. The most common form of logical expression involves relational operators such as $>$, $<$, $=$, $< =$, $> =$, and $< >$. The last three operators are read as "less than or equal," "greater than or equal," and "not equal," respectively. Thus

    3 > 2

is a logical expression and evaluates to true.

If the variable X has the value 2 and the variable Y has the value 3, then the expression

    X + 2 = Y – 1

equates to false.

Computer languages also feature logical operators such as AND, OR, and NOT. The NOT operator changes the value of a logical expression from true to false or from false to true. The expression

    NOT (3 > 2)

evaluates to false, and

    NOT (2 > 3)

evaluates to true.

The other two logical operators, AND and OR, are a little more difficult to explain. First, note that each has two operands (NOT has only one). Each operand is a logical expression; one operand precedes and one follows the operator. The behavior of these operators is best described using truth tables. In the following truth tables, let A and B stand for logical expressions.

A	B	A AND B
TRUE	TRUE	TRUE
TRUE	FALSE	FALSE
FALSE	TRUE	FALSE
FALSE	FALSE	FALSE

From the table you can see that the logical expression A AND B is true if and only if A is true and B is true.

The following truth table describes the behavior of the OR operator.

A	B	A OR B
TRUE	TRUE	TRUE
TRUE	FALSE	TRUE
FALSE	TRUE	TRUE
FALSE	FALSE	FALSE

From this table you can see that the logical expression A OR B is false if and only if both A and B are false.

More complex logical expressions can be constructed by combining simpler logical expressions. The liberal use of parentheses is advisable in order to eliminate any possibility of ambiguity.

INPUT AND OUTPUT

Processing data would not be of much value if the results could not be printed out, either on a screen or on a printer. In most languages the statement that performs this function is called WRITE or PRINT or something similar. Most languages use the same or a similar statement whether the output device is a screen or a printer.

One way to give values to variables is, as we have seen, with the assignment statement. Another way is to read the values from the keyboard. In most languages the command to do this is called the READ statement or something similar. In BASIC, however, the appropriate command is called INPUT.

The various languages differ in how much control the user has over the format of the output. Useful formatting features include the ability to control the number of decimal places printed, the print field width, and so on.

Suppose you want a program to print, ''Enter Check Number:'' and then read the value into a variable called CKNR. In Pascal this would be accomplished as follows:

```
WRITE('Enter Check Number: ');
READLN(CKNR);
```

In BASIC the same thing could be accomplished this way:

```
INPUT "Enter Check Number:      ";CKNR
```

Other languages have similar facilities.

Most languages also have facilities for reading data from and writing data to disk files. These facilities are discussed under the heading File Handling.

CONTROL STRUCTURES

The natural flow of control through a program is sequential. That is, each statement is executed in the order in which it is found, beginning with the first statement in the program and ending with the last. For all but the simplest applications, sequential flow of control by itself is inadequate. For most programs, a more complicated control structure is needed.

Simple Selection: The IF-THEN-ELSE Statement

Consider, for example, a program that must calculate the pay of a worker. If that worker works 40 or fewer hours in a week, the pay is the number of hours worked times his/her wage rate. If the number of hours worked is more than 40, he/she is paid one-and-a-half times the regular wage rate for all hours in excess of 40. One way to do this is in Fortran 77 follows:

```
IF (HOURS .LE. 40) THEN
    PAY = HOURS * WAGE
ELSE
    PAY = 40 * WAGE + (HOURS - 40) *
            WAGE * 1.5
ENDIF.
```

(Note: .LE. stands for "less than or equal to.")

The beauty of the IF-THEN-ELSE construct is that what it does is almost self-explanatory. If the logical expression is true, it executes the statements following THEN and then passes control to the statement following ENDIF. Otherwise (ELSE) it executes the statements following ELSE. In either case, the next statement to be executed is the statement following ENDIF.

The IF-THEN-ELSE construct is extremely important in computer languages. It allows the program to handle basic decisions, yet what happens next is clear. You are cautioned to avoid whenever possible statements of the general form IF-THEN-GOTO. The reason for this injunction is that it is difficult to follow the flow of control in programs that contain this type of statement because it is not always clear what happens next.

The ELSE part of the construct is optional. For example, suppose that a program is computing tax refunds for the Internal Revenue Service and must set all amounts less than $1.00 to zero. This could be accomplished in Fortran 77 as

```
IF (AMT .LT. 1.00) THEN
    AMT = 0.0
ENDIF
```

or in the older versions of FORTRAN as

IF (AMT .LT. 1.00) AMT = 0.0.

Logically, this is equivalent to an IF-THEN-ELSE statement with an empty or null ELSE part.

The CASE Statement

The IF-THEN-ELSE statement allows two-way selection: the program selects one of two sets of statements to execute. Often it is necessary for the program to choose among more than two alternatives. The CASE statement provides a convenient way to do this.

CASE statements occur frequently in interactive programs. For example, suppose an educational program contained a multiple-choice question, such as, ''Who is buried in Grant's Tomb?'' In Pascal this could be programmed as follows:

```
WRITELN('Who is buried in Grant's Tomb?');
WRITELN('   1) Abraham Lincoln');
WRITELN('   2) General Grant');
WRITELN('   3) Groucho Marx');
WRITE('Select 1, 2, or 3: );
READLN(I);
CASE I OF
      1: WRITELN('Sorry, it was Grant.');
      2: WRITELN('Right!');
      3: WRITELN('Sorry, it was Grant.');
END;
```

In this case exactly one of the responses will be printed; which one depends on the value typed in for the variable I.

The GO TO Statement

The GO TO or GOTO statement allows program control to be transferred to any arbitrary place in a program. At first thought, this might seem to be a great convenience. Experience has shown, however, that indiscriminate use of the GO TO statement can lead to programs that are hard to read, hard to debug, and hard to modify. It is the author's firm conviction that the GO TO statement is to be avoided whenever possible. In some languages, however, it is needed in order to emulate control structures such as REPEAT-UNTIL (introduced below) that are not directly implemented. This is often necessary in BASIC and Fortran.

Loops

One thing that computers do especially well is repetition. If you asked a person to add up the populations of all cities in the United States with populations between 10,000 and 25,000, that person would likely become bored with the task quickly and make mistakes—but not so a computer. Provided the computer were programmed properly and given access to the raw data, it would complete the task quickly, accurately, and without complaint.

The control structure that performs repetitive tasks in a computer language is called a *loop*. There are two major types of loops in high-level computer languages, the counted loop and the conditional loop.

Counted Loops. In a counted loop, the statements within the body of the loop are repeated a specified number of times. Each counted loop has a counter variable. At the beginning of the loop the counter is set to a specified initial value. After the body of the loop has been executed, the counter is incremented and compared to its specified upper bound. If the upper bound has not been exceeded, the body of the loop will be executed again. If the upper bound has been exceeded, control passes to the statement following the end of the loop.

All of this is easier than it sounds. Here is a simple example in the BASIC language. The program prints out the numbers from 1 to 10:

```
10 FOR I = 1 TO 10
20    PRINT I
30 NEXT I
40 END
```

In this example I is the counter variable. At the beginning of the loop, I is set to 1. The body of the loop (the statements between the line beginning with FOR and the line beginning with **NEXT**) is then executed. In this case the body of the loop is simply line number 20, and the number 1 is printed. At line 30, the bottom of the loop, the counter I will be incremented to 2, then compared to the upper bound (in this case 10). Since 2 is less than 10, the body of the loop will be executed again and the number 2 will be printed. This cycle is repeated. When the number 10 is finally printed, the counter I will be incremented to 11. Because 11 is larger than 10 (the specified upper bound), execution will pass to statement 40, which terminates the program.

Conditional Loops. Another type of loop is the conditional loop, often called the *while* loop. Whereas the counted loop executes a group of statements a specified number of times, the conditional loop executes a group of statements as long as a specified condition is true.

Clearly, a conditional loop can do the work of a counted loop. Here is the above example repeated using a conditional loop:

```
10 I = 1
20 WHILE I < = 10
30    PRINT I
40    I = I + 1
50 WEND
60 END
```

(Note: some versions of BASIC, such as Applesoft, do not include the WHILE statement.)

In this case it took a few extra statements to do the same job with a conditional loop. This was a task better suited to a counted loop.

Suppose instead you want to read numbers from a keyboard until a zero or negative number is encountered and to add up the numbers. This requires a little planning, as the WHILE loop tests the condition before it executes the loop for the first time. That is why the first read is outside the loop. Here is how this example could be done in BASIC:

```
10 SUM = 0
20 INPUT "ENTER X:    ";X
30 WHILE X > 0
40     SUM = SUM + X
50     INPUT "ENTER X:";X
60 WEND
70 PRINT "SUM = ";SUM
80 END
```

In line 10, SUM is initialized to zero. In line 20 the first value of X is read. Line 30 checks to see whether or not the current value of X is greater than 0. If it is, statements 40 and 50 are executed. These statements add X to SUM and get the next X. The loop is repeated until an X less than or equal to 0 is encountered. When that happens, control passes to statement 70. Statement 70 prints the result, and statement 80 terminates the program.

A few languages offer a variant of the conditional loop in which the conditional testing takes place at the bottom of the loop rather than at the top, as is the case with the WHILE loop. In Pascal this variant is called the REPEAT-UNTIL loop. Here is the previous example in Pascal using REPEAT-UNTIL:

```
SUM := 0;
REPEAT
        WRITE('ENTER X:   ');
        READLN(X);
        SUM := SUM + X
UNTIL X < = 0;
WRITELN('SUM = ';SUM);
```

The problem with this example is that it doesn't work as intended. See if you can find the problem before reading on.

The above example initializes the variable SUM to 0 and then repeats the three statements between REPEAT and UNTIL until the variable X becomes negative. The intent is to add up all the numbers in a list, not including the negative number used to stop the loop. The problem is that the value of X is added to SUM before X is tested. When a negative number is entered to stop the loop, that number will be added to SUM before the loop is terminated.

Subroutines

Often it is convenient to divide programs into more-or-less self-contained segments or modules. Such modules are usually called *subroutines* or *procedures*. A subroutine or procedure is usually placed off by itself in a program, sometimes at the beginning of the program and sometimes at the end, depending on the language. Some languages permit the subroutines to be external to the program—that is, in a separate disk file.

Subroutines are activated or called by a *call statement.* A call statement causes the subroutine to be invoked, and when the subroutine has finished, program control reverts to the statement following the call statement. The format of call statements varies from language to language. Fortran uses the word **CALL** followed by the name of the subroutine; BASIC uses **GOSUB** followed by a line number. In most other languages a subroutine is invoked simply by writing its name.

There are several possible reasons for using a subroutine, including the following:

☐ The use of subroutines permits large tasks to be divided into smaller, more manageable tasks. This is sometimes called the "divide and conquer" strategy. It is a very important program design technique. Problems that seem otherwise unmanageable can often be handled easily when broken into appropriate modules.

☐ Because a call statement can occur as many times as necessary in a program, the use of subroutines can often save considerable typing. For example, suppose a sort needs to be done twice in a program. If a subroutine were not used, the sort routine would have to be typed into the program twice, once in each place it is needed. If a subroutine is used, the sort routine need be typed into the program only once; it can be called as often as it is needed from other parts of the program.

☐ If commonly used routines are programmed in the form of subroutines, they can be easily transported from one program to another. Suppose you have written a good sorting subroutine for one program and now you need a sorting subroutine in another program. Chances are you will be able to reuse the original sorting subroutine. Programmers often develop libraries of commonly used subroutines.

Subroutines usually use *parameters* and *arguments* to pass values back and forth between the subroutine and the calling program. Consider a subroutine designed to exchange the values of two numerical variables. Here is how such a subroutine might look in Fortran:

```
SUBROUTINE SWAP(X,Y)
      TEMP = X
      X = Y
      Y = TEMP
RETURN
```

The X and Y are called parameters of the subroutine. When the subroutine is called, the two variables to be exchanged might be named P and Q. Here is how a call to SWAP to exchange P and Q would look:

```
CALL SWAP(P,Q).
```

P and Q are referred to as arguments of the call statement. Later in the program, the variables R and S may need to be exchanged. The sort subroutine could be called again using R and S as arguments:

CALL SWAP(R,S).

Functions

Subroutines pass values using parameters and arguments, and are invoked with some form of call statement. Functions are similar to subroutines except in the manner in which they are invoked and in the manner in which values are returned to the invoking program.

Some functions are usually supplied as part of a language. These usually include functions for computing square roots, sines, cosines, and so on. Suppose you wanted to compute the square root of 4. In Fortran you would write

X = SQRT(4.0).

SQRT is the name of a function built into Fortran for this purpose. The argument is 4.0. Note that the function is invoked by writing its name in an expression as if it were simply another variable. The result, in this case 2.0, is returned and used in the expression as if it were the value of a variable named SQRT. In this case, the result is assigned to the variable X.

Functions can be defined by the user in much the same manner as subroutines are defined. One difference is that the name of the function is usually treated as if it were a variable within the body of the function definition. This is how the value to be returned by the function to the invoking routine is usually determined. As an example, suppose a function is needed in Fortran to return the larger of two integers. It might appear as follows:

```
FUNCTION MAX(I,J)
        IF I .GE. J THEN
            MAX = I
        ELSE
            MAX = J
        ENDIF
RETURN.
```

(Note: Older versions of Fortran do not include the IF-THEN-ELSE construct. The symbol .GE. stands for "greater than or equal to.")

The exact mechanism for passing the value of the function back to the calling program varies from language to language. The C language, for example, does not use the name of the function as a variable within the body of the function. It uses the return statement instead to return the value, as in the following:

```
return  MAX.
```

The differences between functions and subroutines will be explored more fully in the chapters on individual languages.

Recursion

Another method of controlling the flow of program execution is called *recursion*. A function or subroutine is said to be *recursive* if it calls or invokes itself. Some languages, such as Fortran and COBOL, do not permit recursion. In other languages, such as LISP and Logo, recursion is the most commonly used form of program control.

At first encounter, recursion seems mysterious to many beginning programmers— sort of like the snake that swallowed its own tail. Actually, recursion is simply another way of invoking repetition in a program. Of course the repetition would go on forever without some sort of escape mechanism. Recursive functions and subroutines must therefore check for termination conditions before invoking themselves again.

Certain applications are more naturally expressed using recursion rather than other forms of repetition. Computer language compilers are one example. Many other applications can be expressed either way. It is difficult to explain in a few words when recursion is most appropriate. Examples of recursive applications can be found in subsequent chapters.

DATA STRUCTURES

It is often convenient to be able to refer to a collection of related variables by a common name. For example, suppose you wanted to write a program to compute statistics describing the test scores of 26 students. You could use the letters A to Z, with each letter representing one score. The resulting program would be tedious to say the least.

Arrays

A better solution is to use an array. Suppose the array name is **SCORE**. Then **SCORE(1)** would refer to the score of the first student, **SCORE(2)** to the score of the second student, and so on. The numbers in parentheses are called *subscripts*. SCORE is an example of an array with one subscript (even though that one subscript can take on various values).

Suppose that you needed a data structure in which to record the number of points scored in each of 20 games by each of 10 basketball players. An easy way to handle this situation is to use an array with two subscripts. Suppose the name of this array were **POINTS**. Then **POINTS(1,3)** would contain the number of points scored by the first player in the third game; **POINTS(7,19)**, the number of points scored by the seventh player in the nineteenth game, and so on. Such an array is often called a *two-dimensional* array. In some languages arrays can have more than two dimensions if needed.

Arrays are often used in conjunction with loops. Suppose, for example, that you want to set all the elements of the two-dimensional array **POINTS** to zero. This can be done easily using a loop. Here is how it might look in BASIC:

```
10 FOR I = 1 TO 10
20    FOR J = 1 TO 20
30          POINTS(I,J) = 0
40    NEXT J
50 NEXT I
```

If the loop structure were not available, it could take 200 statements to accomplish the same thing.

The programmer must usually tell the compiler or interpreter in advance which variable names stand for arrays, how many subscripts each array has, and the range (permissible values) of each subscript. How this is done is peculiar to each language and will be covered for each language in the appropriate chapter.

Records

A limitation of arrays is that each element of the array must be of the same type, that is, integer, real, or alphanumeric (string). In the example above, **POINTS** was assumed to contain all integers. Suppose instead that you want to set up a grade book to keep track of the students in a class. You would need to record the name of each student and various numerical grades scored by that student. Note that the name is an alphanumeric variable, but each grade is numeric. It is useful in this situation to have the concept of a *record*.

A record is a collection of related information, where each element of the information may be of a different type. Suppose you wanted to set up a record called **STUDENT**, containing a student's name and his or her score on each of 20 tests. Each record should thus contain a string variable for the name, and an array with 20 numerical elements for the grades.

Some languages, such as Pascal and COBOL, implement records directly. How this is done is described in the appropriate chapters. With other languages, such as BASIC and Fortran, records must be simulated using *parallel arrays*.

In this example, two arrays would be needed: a string array called NAME and a numeric array called **GRADES**. NAME would be a one-dimensional array having as many elements as there were students. **GRADES** would be a two-dimensional array (similar to **POINTS** above), with the first subscript determining to which student the grade belongs, and the second subscript indicating on which test that grade was scored. If Bill Smith were the fifteenth student, and he scored a 90 on his third test, **NAMES(15)** would contain "Bill Smith" and **GRADES(15,3)** would contain 90.

Arrays Revisited

One advantage of an array is that any element of that array can be addressed directly, independently of all other elements of the array. You can refer to **NAME(2)** without referring to **NAME(1)**. This feature is often quite useful.

Arrays may have disadvantages in certain situations. Suppose, for example, you have an array called **NAME**, containing the first names of 10 men. Suppose NAME(1) is Al, NAME(2) is Bob, NAME(3) is Carl, and so on. You want to keep the names in alphabetical order. Now suppose you have to add a new name, Bill, to the list. Bill should fit between Al and Bob. The problem is that to do so requires that Bob, Carl, and all other names be moved down one place in the list to make room for Bill.

If **NAME** is part of a record (see the above example), then the rest of the record (in this example the array GRADES) would have to be adjusted accordingly.

An analogous situation occurs when you want to delete an element from an array.

The elements following the deleted element may need to be moved forward to close the gap.

Lists

You have just seen that arrays have the advantage that individual elements are accessible independently and the disadvantage that adding to or deleting from an ordered array may be difficult. In some instances you might be willing to give up independent access to elements (settling for sequential access) in exchange for ease in inserting and deleting elements. It turns out that there is a data structure called a *list* with just these properties.

The major properties of a list are that access is strictly sequential and that elements can be easily added to or deleted from the list. By allowing a list to be an element of another list, more complex data structures, such as trees, can be constructed. How this is done is beyond the scope of this book; you are referred to a book on data structures for more details.

In LISP and Logo, the list is the principle data structure. Some languages, such as Pascal, have facilities for the easy implementation of lists. With other languages, such as BASIC and Fortran, lists must be implemented using arrays. How this is done will be illustrated below.

In general, an element can be added to a list at the beginning, at the end, or anywhere in the middle. The same goes for retrieving or deleting an element from the list. (Of course accessing interior elements requires sequential access.) A list with the property that elements can be added or deleted only from the ends (one at a time) is called a *queue*. If additions and deletions can take place at only one end, the queue is called a *stack*, or a *last-in first-out* (LIFO) queue. In the Forth language, the stack is the most important data structure.

As an example of how a list might be used in a program, suppose you wish to maintain a list of names in alphabetical order. The list initially contains the name Bob, Ernie, and Jim, who all work in an office. Jerry joins the organization and needs to be added to the list between Ernie and Jim.

As described above, if you were to maintain the names in a simple array, you would need to move Jim to make room for Jerry. While this would work easily for such a short list, for longer lists it would be cumbersome. A better way would be to maintain the names as a linked list.

For this example, suppose that there can be a maximum of five names in the list. Several variables are needed to implement the list. An array of five elements is needed to hold the names themselves. Call this array **NAME**. Another array of five elements is needed to hold the links between names. Call this array **LINK**. Another name for a link is a *pointer*.

A pointer points to an element of an array if the value of the pointer is the value of the subscript of that element of the array. For example, if P is a variable being used as a pointer into array NAME and if it has the value 5, it points to array element NAME(5). A variable is needed to point to the (alphabetically) first name in the list. Call this variable **FIRST**. FIRST is used to store the subscript of the first name. Similarly, the variable **FREE** will be used as a pointer to the first free (unused) record in the list.

Once the list has been entered, each link points to the next name in the list. For example, suppose FIRST points to element 3. To find the name in the list that follows NAME(3) alphabetically, look at LINK(3). If LINK(3) has value 1, that means that NAME(1) follows NAME(3) alphabetically.

A value is needed to signal the end of the list. This value is usually 0 or -1, depending on the language. For languages with arrays that always begin with subscript 1 (such as Fortran and COBOL), the value 0 is usually used. For languages with arrays that begin with subscript 0 (such as BASIC and C), the value -1 is usually used. For this example, the value 0 will be used. If LINK(4) has the value 0, it means that there are no more names in the list to point to after NAME(4).

For our example, the list might initially look as follows:

FIRST   = 1
FREE   = 4

	NAME	LINK
1	Bob	2
2	Ernie	3
3	Jim	0
4		5
5		0

Following the links of the chain from FIRST, FIRST points to NAME(1), which is Bob. LINK(1) points to NAME(2), which is Ernie. LINK(2) points to NAME(3), which is Jim. LINK(3) has the value 0, meaning that NAME(3) is the end of the list.

Each element of the list is often called a *record*. Recall the discussion above about records as implemented by parallel arrays. A record in this case consists of a name and a link. The list of active records is sometimes called the *active list*.

There is another list called the *free list*. It is a chain of unused records. Following this chain from FREE, FREE points to record 4. LINK(4) points to record 5. Record 5 is the end of the free list, and is so designated because LINK(5) has the value 0.

Now let us consider what happens when Jerry is added to the list. His name is written in record 4, because record 4 was the first record in the free list. The other pointers are adjusted so as to add record 4 to the proper place in the active list and to remove record 4 from the free list. Here is how the updated list looks:

FIRST   = 1
FREE   = 5

	NAME	LINK
1	Bob	2
2	Ernie	4
3	Jim	0
4	Jerry	3
5		0

At first glance, the list now appears out of sequence. Following the chain from FIRST, however, you can see that FIRST points to Bob (FIRST = 1), Bob points to Ernie (LINK(1) = 2), Ernie points to Jerry (LINK(2) = 4), Jerry points to Jim (LINK(4) = 3), and Jim is the end of the list (LINK(3) = 0).

After some time, Ernie retires and needs to be removed from the list. Record 2, the record occupied by Ernie, then needs to be removed from the active list and added to the free list. This is done by manipulating the links. Here is the result:

```
FIRST   = 1
FREE    = 2
```

	NAME	LINK
1	Bob	4
2	Ernie	5
3	Jim	0
4	Jerry	3
5		0

Ernie appears to be still in the list. Following the active list from FIRST, however, reveals that he is not. Record 2 is now the first record in the free list. The fact that Ernie's name is still there is not a problem. The next name to be added will be written to the first record in the free list, which is now record 2. Ernie's name will then be overwritten.

Examples of the use of lists in various languages are included in the following language chapters. These examples show the details of how a record is added to and deleted from a list.

FILE HANDLING

If the amount of data to be processed by a program is small, it can be typed in from the keyboard whenever it is needed. In many computer applications, however, the data must be carried forward from one run of the program to the next run, and the quantity of data soon becomes too large to type in every time. For this situation data files are needed.

Computer programs used in business applications usually rely heavily on data files. Examples of such applications include general ledger, accounts receivable, accounts payable, inventory records, and so on. In selecting a language for such applications, the file handling features of the candidate languages should be examined closely.

Data files on microcomputers are most often kept on disk storage devices, either floppy disks or hard (fixed) disks. Floppy disks today usually come in the 5¼-inch size, but 3½-inch floppy disks are becoming more widely used. Floppy disks are convenient because they can be removed from the disk drive and stored in a safe place. Floppy disks typically hold from 100 kilobytes (a kilobyte is about one thousand characters) to 1.2 megabytes (a megabyte is about one million characters) of data.

Hard disks are not usually removable from the disk drive, but they provide faster access to the data, and each unit holds 20 megabytes or more. Hard disk drives also cost substantially more than floppy disk drives, although the cost of hard disk drives has come down significantly in the last few years.

Records

The concept of a record (discussed above) is very important in business and other applications that require file handling. It is very convenient to be able to read or write an entire record from or to the disk in a single operation. Consider, for example, a record that contains the name, address, and telephone number of an individual; to read such a record from the disk should require only one read operation.

COBOL was the first major language to deal conveniently with records in files. Among the languages that have come later, Pascal, C, Ada, and Modula-2 also provide facilities for dealing conveniently with records. Other languages make dealing with records less convenient.

Sequential-Access Files

A *sequential-access* file must be read (and written) sequentially from beginning to end. In other words, to read the thirty-second record in the file, the program must first read the first, then the second, and so on, until it reaches the thirty-second. In the earlier days of computing, when files were kept mainly on magnetic tapes, this was the only way files could be organized. It was a restriction imposed by the physical characteristics of the storage medium. That physical restriction does not exist for disk files, but it is still convenient in some cases to organize disk files sequentially. This is usually the case when every record in the file must be processed during a run.

Direct-Access Files

Any record of a *direct-access* file can be accessed directly, without previously accessing any other records in the file. For example, with a direct-access file, the program can access record 32 of a file without previously accessing records 1 through 31. Direct-access files are frequently also called *random-access* files. That is a slight misnomer, as most programmers prefer to access their files in specific rather than random locations.

To access a record in a direct-access file, the record number must be known. The programmer must have some means of keeping track of what information is in what record. This usually means maintaining an index of some sort.

Indexed Files

Most versions of COBOL provide for the automatic maintenance of an index for a file. This can relieve the programmer of a significant burden.

GRAPHICS

Some microcomputer languages have built-in graphics features. Unfortunately there is no standard way to handle graphics on large or small computers. Even among different versions of BASIC, there is no standard way to handle graphics. How a particular version of a language handles graphics (if it does) is usually a function of the microcomputer on which it is implemented. For that reason, the graphics features of high-level languages are not discussed in this book.

There is one exception to the above rule: Logo. All versions of Logo of which I am aware share the same basic graphic capabilities. Furthermore, graphics is an important part of the Logo language. Therefore the chapter on Logo includes a discussion of Logo's graphic capabilities.

SUMMARY

This chapter has explored in general terms the distinguishing features of high-level languages. Familiarity with these features will make the understanding of specific languages easier. The chapter on a specific language will describe in more detail how these features are implemented in that particular language. This chapter has attempted to establish a framework for examining individual languages and for comparing one language to another.

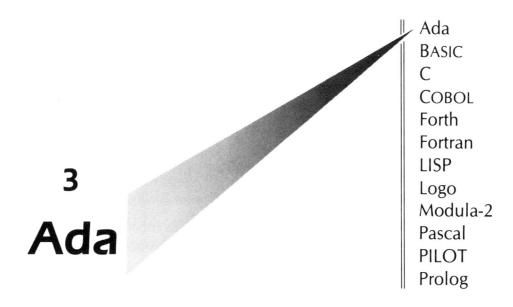

3

Ada

Ada is a relatively new language, developed in the late seventies and early eighties under the sponsorship of the U.S. Department of Defense (DoD).

In the early seventies, DoD recognized that software for embedded systems was being developed in many different specialized languages. An *embedded system* is a computer that is part of a larger system. The term excludes general-purpose standalone computer systems. An example of a military embedded system is the flight control system of a modern jet fighter. A civilian example of an embedded system is a microwave oven. One of the most complex embedded systems around is the onboard system that controls a space shuttle. An embedded system must be able to respond to real-time inputs from many sources, and it must be able to operate unattended. A programming language for such a system must meet a different set of requirements than most programming languages.

Ada was intended to become a standard language used for all embedded software systems developed for DoD. The idea was to issue a set of specifications in the form of a requirements document and solicit proposed language designs from private industry. The first version of the requirements document for Ada was published in 1975 under the name STRAWMAN. Succeeding iterations were called WOODENMAN (1975), TINMAN (1976), IRONMAN (1977), and finally STEELMAN (1978). An evaluation of 23 existing languages (including Pascal, Fortran, and COBOL) was conducted in 1976-77, and it was determined that no existing language would satisfy all of the DoD requirements.

CII Honeywell Bull of France was declared the winner of the language design competition in 1979. The winning design was developed by a team under the leadership of Dr. Jean Ichbiah. The standard reference document for Ada, *Reference Manual for the Ada Programming Language*, was published in 1983 as Military Standard (MIL-STD) 1815.

The Ada language was named after Ada, Countess of Lovelace, daughter of Lord Byron. She was an associate of Charles Babbage, a nineteenth-century English pioneer in the computer field, and is generally credited with being the world's first computer programmer.

Although developed primarily for programming embedded systems, Ada is broad enough in scope to be considered a general-purpose programming language. Ada is a very large language, with many powerful new features. It is well-suited for the development of large, complex programs in many fields, such as scientific applications and systems programming. Ada is a language for professional programmers; it requires a great deal of study to take advantage of its many advanced features. Beginners, however, can successfully use Ada if they select only the basic features of the language for use.

The programs of this chapter were compiled and tested on a Zenith 150 microcomputer (IBM PC compatible) using the Janus/Ada compiler by RR Software of Madison, Wisconsin. Because Ada is such a large language, it is a real challenge to implement it on a microcomputer. Janus/Ada implements a large subset of Ada, but it lacks support for some of the more advanced Ada features, such as tasks and generic procedures.

Because Ada is such a large language, the summary that follows is necessarily incomplete. The intention is to give an overview of the language, not to cover every language feature.

PROGRAM STRUCTURE

The basic unit of an Ada program is called a *compilation unit*. A compilation unit may be either a *subprogram* or a *package*. A package is similar to the module of Modula-2 and consists of one or more subprograms and associated variables.

A package allows related subprograms to be grouped and isolated from the rest of the program in order to prevent unwanted side effects or interference between different parts of a program. It can be thought of as an intermediate level of organization between the procedure level and the main program.

Subprograms can be procedures or functions. The main program is a procedure with no parameters. Compilation units can be all in one file, or they can be in separate files. Ada fully supports separate compilation. In other words, the various compilation units that make up an Ada program can be compiled one at a time or all at once.

A simple example of an Ada program is shown in Fig. 3-1. The line beginning with two hyphens (- -) is a comment. A comment in Ada can begin anywhere on a line and continues to the end of the line.

Ada has no input or output facilities built into the language itself. Such facilities are provided as separate packages. In this program I need a procedure to write a line of text to the screen. This procedure is called Put__Line and is found in the package called Text__IO. To gain access to this separately compiled package, the program must include the with Text__IO; clause. The use Text__IO; clause is optional, but without it, the call to Put__Line would have to be written as Text__IO.Put__Line.

The main program consists of a procedure called Ada__1. It has no parameters

```
       -- Figure 3-1:   A Simple Ada Program
       with Text_IO;
       use  Text_IO;

       Procedure ADA_1 is

       Begin

            Put_Line ("This is a test.");

       End ADA_1;
```

Fig. 3-1. A simple Ada program.

(otherwise it couldn't be a main program). Note the word "is" at the end of the procedure declaration.

The body of the procedure is contained between **Begin** and **End** ADA__1;. In this case the body of the procedure consists of a single statement, a call to the procedure **Put__Line**.

Because **Put__Line** is a procedure, it can handle only one character string at a time. To print two character strings would require two calls to **Put__Line**.

The call to **Put__Line** could have been replaced by the more general procedure **Put**. The difference is that **Put** does not print a carriage return after the string. A separate procedure called **New__Line** can be used to print the carriage return. The **Put__Line** call could have been replaced by the following:

```
Put ("This is a test.");
New__Line;
```

Put is more general than **Put__Line**. It can print characters and numbers as well as strings. Strictly speaking, there are several different versions of Put in Janus/Ada, one for each data type to be printed, and the compiler selects the correct one based on the data type of the item to be printed. This is called *overloading*.

Ada is not case-sensitive. "Put__Line," "PUT__LINE, and "put__line" are all equivalent.

The semicolon in Ada is a statement terminator (as in C), not a statement separator (as in Pascal). This means that a semicolon is *always* required at the end of a statement.

More features of Ada are discussed in the sections that follow.

DATA REPRESENTATION

The basic predefined data types of Ada are **Integer**, **Float**, **Character**, and **Boolean**. The **Float** type is for floating point numbers, often called real numbers in other languages. The **Boolean** type is for logical values, i.e., **True** and **False**.

Full implementations of Ada also include a data type called Long__Integer, which can represent numbers of greater magnitude than regular integers. A typical range is from −2,147,483,648 to 2,147,483,647.

Ada also includes a String data type, which is a special case of an array. Arrays are discussed later in this chapter.

Like Pascal and Modula-2, Ada includes a provision for defining new data types. A new data type can be derived from an existing data type (such as the integers from 1 to 100), or it can be a compound data type constructed from one or more existing types. An example of the latter would be a data type to contain the coordinates of a point in three-dimensional space.

Constants

Numbers are generally represented the same way in Ada as in other languages (see Chapter 2). In addition, the underscore character (__) can be used as a place holder, as in the following:

5__280

The underscore serves the same purpose as the comma in the U.S. (and the period in Europe) in separating thousands, millions, billions, and so on. The underscore is for readability only; it is ignored by the compiler.

Binary, octal, hexadecimal, and numbers in other bases can be easily represented in Ada. For example, the following numbers are all equivalent:

16#19#   hexadecimal (base 16)
8#31#   octal (base 8)
2#11001#   binary (base 2)
25   decimal (base 10, the default)

The number selected for the base can be any positive integer, but 16, 8, and 2 are the most commonly used (after base 10).

There are only two Boolean constants, True and False.

Character constants in Ada are enclosed by apostrophes, as in 'a', ''b'', and 'c'. String constants are enclosed by quotation marks, as in ''Hello!'' The quotation mark itself can be included in a string by typing it twice, as in the following:

"He said " "Hello" "."

Constants can be declared in programs as follows:

rate: Constant Float : = 0.08;

This statement declares a constant called rate and gives it the value 0.08. Strictly speaking, the Float is optional in the above, as the compiler can usually figure out the data type by inspection.

The use of constants is good programming practice, as it makes programs easier

```
-- Figure 3-2:   Illustrate A Constant Declaration
with Text_IO;
use   Text_IO;

Procedure ADA_2 is

PI:   constant FLOAT := 3.14159;

Begin

     Put ("PI = ");
     Put (PI, 2, 5, 0);
     New_Line;

End ADA_2;
```

Fig. 3-2. A constant declaration.

to understand and to modify. Because constants are defined at the beginning of a program, they are easy to find when their values must be changed (such as when new tax rates are published).

An example of the use of a declared constant in a program is given in Fig. 3-2. The program simply prints out the value of the constant. The first use of the procedure Put prints a string to label the constant. Because Put was used rather than Put__Line, the next Put starts printing on the same line. The second use of the procedure Put prints out the floating point constant PI. The numbers 2, 5, and 0 mean to allow two positions to the left of the decimal, five to the right, and no spaces for an exponent. The output will appear as follows:

PI = 3.14159

New__Line is used to print a carriage return to end the line.

Notice also that you must with and use the package Text__IO in order to gain access to Put and New__Line.

Ada also supports a special kind of constant called an *attribute*. These attributes are associated with the standard Ada types. For example, the following constants are the smallest (most negative) and largest integers:

Integer' First
Integer' Last

First and Last can also be used to get the smallest and largest subscripts of an array.

Variables

Variables in Ada are declared at the beginning of packages, procedures, and functions.

With one exception, all variables in an Ada program must be declared. The exception is the index variable of a for loop, which is discussed below.

Variables declared within a procedure or function are accessible or visible only inside that procedure or function. Variables declared at the beginning of a package are visible inside every procedure and function in that package. To gain access to a variable in another package, an Ada package must with and use that package.

A program illustrating variable declaration and use is shown in Fig. 3-3. The two variables used in the program are Area and Radius. The integer i is included for illustration purposes; it is not used elsewhere in the program.

This program assigns the value 5.0 to Radius and computes the area of a circle with that radius. It then prints out the values of Radius and Area, appropriately labeled. Each is written in a field with two places to the left of the decimal and five to the right; the total field width is eight, counting the decimal point.

Enumeration Types

Besides the usual data types such as Integer, Float, and Boolean, Ada allows the creation of *enumeration* types. (This feature is also found in Pascal and Modula 2.) Enumeration types are best described by example.

```
-- Figure 3-3:   Illustrate Variable Declarations
with Text_IO;
use   Text_IO;

Procedure ADA_3 is

PI:   constant FLOAT := 3.14159;

Area, Radius:   FLOAT;
i:              INTEGER;   -- not used

Begin

    Radius := 5.0;
    Area   := PI * Radius**2;

    Put ("Radius = ");
    Put (Radius, 2, 5, 0);
    New_Line;

    Put ("Area   = ");
    Put (Area, 2, 5, 0);
    New_Line;

End ADA_3;
```

Fig. 3-3. Variable declarations.

Suppose that your program needs to refer to the days of the week. A common way to handle this situation in most languages would be to define a mapping between the integers and the days of the week, where 1 stood for Sunday, 2 for Monday, 3 for Tuesday, and so on. In Ada, this is not necessary. You can simply define a new type such as the following:

```
type DayOfWeek is (Sunday,Monday,Tuesday,
        Wednesday,Thursday,Friday,Saturday);
```

A variable could then be declared as follows:

```
day:   DayOfWeek;
```

Once that is done, the following statements would be appropriate:

```
day: = Tuesday;
day: = DayOfWeek'Succ(Wednesday);—result is Thursday
Put(DayOfWeek'Image(day));        —prints "Thursday"
day : = DayOfWeek'First;          —Sunday
```

The use of enumeration types can make programs simpler to understand.

THE ASSIGNMENT STATEMENT

The assignment operator in Ada is a colon followed by an equals sign (: =), as in Pascal and Modula-2. The assignment statement computes the value of the expression to the right of the operator and stores it in the memory location represented by the name of the variable to the left of the assignment operator. The assignment statement is illustrated several times in Fig. 3-3.

The expression on the right side of an assignment station can be a variable, a constant, or a more complicated expression. The expression to the right of the assignment operator must be compatible in type with the variable on the left. For example they could be both Integers or both Floats. Arithmetic and Boolean expressions are discussed below.

When necessary, expressions can be converted from one type to another in order to avoid a conflict. Suppose i is an Integer, and x and y are Floats. The following assignment statement is perfectly legal in Ada:

```
i : = Integer (x/y);
```

It would divide x by y, truncate the result, convert it to Integer, and assign it to i.

ARITHMETIC EXPRESSIONS

Arithmetic expressions in Ada use conventional infix notation, as described in Chapter 2. Ada supports the following arithmetic operators:

+   addition
−   subtraction
*   multiplication
/   division
**   exponentiation
mod   modulus
rem   remainder
abs   absolute value

The **mod** and **rem** operators both produce the remainder after integer division. Both are defined only for integer operands. The difference is that **(A rem B)** has the sign of A, while **(A mod B)** has the sign of B. If both A and B have the same sign, then the two produce the same result.

The program in Fig. 3-3 uses an arithmetic expression to calculate the value of the variable **Area**.

BOOLEAN EXPRESSIONS

Boolean expressions were discussed in Chapter 2 under the name *logical expressions*. A Boolean expression evaluates to True or False. Ada supports the usual relational and logical operators discussed in Chapter 2, such as > (greater than) and **or**. The operator for "is not equal to" is /=, which differs from most other languages.

Ada also supports two additional logical operators called "short circuit forms." These are the operators **and then** and **or else**. With the ordinary logical operators **and** and **or**, both of their arguments are evaluated before the truth or falsity of the expression is determined. With the short circuit forms, the first operand is evaluated first, and if the truth or falsity of the expression can be determined at that point, the second operand is not evaluated. To illustrate this point, consider the following expression:

(n > 0) and ((m / n) > 5)

This would produce a "divide by zero" error if the variable **n** had the value zero. On the other hand, the expression

(n > 0) and then ((m / n) > 5)

would be correctly evaluated as false without an error. The fact that the first operand, (n > 0), evaluates to zero is sufficient to decide that the whole expression is false without attempting to evaluate the second operand, **and then**. The second operand need not be evaluated if the first operand is false. The operator **or else** operates similarly; the second operand is not evaluated when the first operand is true.

Three other languages described in this book, C, Modula 2, and Prolog, implicitly support this feature, but they do not offer the option of evaluating both operands first as in Ada. (I don't know why one would *need* that option, but Ada supports it.)

INPUT AND OUTPUT

As discussed above, input and output are implemented by means of procedures located in separate packages, such as Text__IO. The first three sample programs have shown the use of three such procedures, Put, Put—Line, and New—Line, to send output to the screen.

Programs must also be able to send output to a printer. Unfortunately many programming language texts do not cover this basic function. It would be convenient if Ada included a package called Print—IO that would take care of the details of setting up for printer output. Assume for the moment that such a package exists. I will show you how to create such a package later in this chapter.

The program in Fig. 3-4 shows how to use Print—IO to send output to a printer. Notice that the package must be referenced by **with** and **use** clauses. The procedure PrinterOn must be called before output can be sent to the printer. For a Put or Put—Line to send output to the printer, the variable Printer must be listed as the first argument of the procedure, as shown in the example. This variable is defined in the package Print—IO. The procedure PrinterOff is shown for completeness; it terminates the connection between the program and the printer. Most programs will work just as well without it.

The procedure New—Line will also work with Printer.

Figure 3-2 illustrated how to specify the field width when you were printing a Float number. You can also specify the field width when printing Integer numbers. For example, to print an integer called i in a field of width 4, you could use the following:

Put (i, 4);

The first argument of Put is the variable to be printed. The second is the field width, which is 4 in this example. (If you were printing to a printer, the variable to be printed would be the second argument, and the field width the third argument.)

If the field width specified is greater than the number requires, the field is padded on the left with blanks. If the field width specified is not wide enough to print the entire

```
-- Figure 3-4:  Test Printer Output
with Text_IO, Print_IO;
use  Text_IO, Print_IO;

Procedure ADA_4 is

Begin

    PrinterOn;

    Put_Line ("This goes to the screen.");
    Put_Line (Printer, "This goes to the Printer.");

    PrinterOff;

End ADA_4;
```

Fig. 3-4. Test printer output.

number, the field width is expanded to accommodate the number. If you want to allow just enough space for the number, but no more, specify a field width of 1.

If you do not specify a field width, the default for integers is six. This illustrates another feature of Ada: the ability to specify default values for procedure parameters. Any parameters not specified during the procedure call then revert to the default.

Just as New__Line causes a carriage return and line feed to be sent to the output device, New__Page causes a form feed to be output. It doesn't do any good to send a form feed to the screen, but it causes most printers to eject a page.

So far I have talked only of output, not of input. The counterparts of the standard output procedures Put and Put__Line are the standard input procedures Get and Get__Line. The program in Fig. 3-5 shows the use of Get__Line to read a string from the keyboard. Get is not available for string input. Get__Line reads a line of text into the specified string variable. It also returns the length of the string read into a second variable, called str__len in this example.

```
-- Figure 3-5:  Electronic Typewriter, Version 1
with Text_IO, Screen, Print_IO;
use  Text_IO, Screen, Print_IO;

Procedure ADA_5 is

    str:      String;
    str_len:  Natural;

Begin

    PrinterOn;
    ClearScreen;

    Put ("Welcome to your Electronic Typewriter.");
    New_Line;
    New_Line;
    Put ("Enter your text; <RETURN> at start of line to end.");
    New_Line;
    New_Line;
    loop
        Get_Line (str, str_len);
        exit when (str_len = 0);
        Put_Line (Printer, str);
    end loop;
    New_Line (Printer);

    PrinterOff;

End ADA_5;
```

Fig. 3-5. Electronic Typewriter, Version 1.

The program in Fig. 3-5 emulates a typewriter. Whatever you type at the keyboard is echoed to the printer, a line at a time. This allows you to make corrections to the current line as you type by backspacing over the errors before the text is printed.

This program references a procedure called **ClearScreen** from the package **Screen**, which does the obvious. Unfortunately this procedure does not come with Janus/Ada; I had to write it in assembly language.

This program uses the loop statement to repeat the statements between **loop** and **end loop**. The loop is terminated by the **exit when (strlen = 0);** statement, which transfers control to the statement following **end loop** when an empty string is read.

Another version of the Electronic Typewriter program is shown in Fig. 3-6. The principal difference between it and the previous example is that it reads the text from the keyboard a character at a time. Because **Get** ignores carriage returns, I had to use the function **End_of_Line** (from **Text_IO**) to determine when the program gets to the end of an input line so that it can send a carriage return and line feed to the printer using **New_Line**.

Another difference between this program and the previous one is the way it detects the end of the text input and exits the loop. In MS-DOS, the end-of-input character is Control-Z. If a program attempts to read past a Control-Z, it causes what is called an **END_ERROR** exception (trying to read past the end of the input). If this condition were ignored, it would cause the program to abort. Ada, however, provides a means of handling exceptions inside a program. This is done by the **exception** clause.

When an exception occurs, control is transferred to the exception clause to see whether or not provision for that kind of exception has been made. In this case, the exception clause checks for an **END_ERROR** exception and executes two statements, **null;** and **PrinterOff;**. The **null** statement is simply a placeholder and does nothing; the **PrinterOff** statement logically disconnects the printer. (The **null** statement is not essential in this case, but it would have been needed had the **PrinterOff** statement been left out.) This method of terminating an input loop is similar to the methods often used in Fortran and COBOL.

It should be clear by now that it is important to know what input and output procedures are available with your implementation of Ada. The best way to find out is to consult your documentation. It should provide a complete list of all procedures and functions provided in the various library packages.

LIBRARY PACKAGES: SEPARATE COMPILATION

The preceding programs assumed the existence of a package called **Print_IO**. This package did not come with the system; it was created and compiled separately. Once that was done, it could be used by any other program that accessed it with **with** and **use** clauses. This section explains how to create a separately compiled package.

There are a number of advantages to using separately compiled packages. The obvious one is that the procedures and functions in such packages can be made available to many different programs without going through the process of recompilation.

Separately compiled packages encourage modular programming. Large programs can be built in pieces. Once a given package is compiled correctly and tested, it need not be recompiled. In languages that do not support this feature, such as standard Pascal, every procedure in a program must be recompiled every time any other procedure is modified. (Some versions of Pascal have been extended to include separate compilation; Turbo Pascal, the version used in this book, does not support separate compilation.)

I mentioned earlier that the basic unit of an Ada program is the compilation unit. Compilation units can be packages or subprograms. The following discussion refers to packages, but it applies to subprograms (procedures and functions) as well.

There are two kinds of compilation units: *specifications* and *bodies*. Stand-alone compilation units, such as the programs in Figs. 3-1 through 3-6, are package bodies and do not require specification units. Any package that is to be accessed by another program, however, requires a separate specification unit to establish the interfaces between that package and the outside world.

Creation of a separately compiled package that is to be accessed by another package, then, requires the creation of both a specification unit and a package body.

```
    -- Figure 3-6:  Electronic Typewriter, Version 2

with Text_IO, Print_IO, Screen;
use  Text_IO, Print_IO, Screen;

Procedure ADA_6 is

    c:          Character;

Begin

    PrinterOn;
    ClearScreen;

    Put_Line("Welcome to your Electronic Typewriter, Version 2.");
    New_Line;
    Put_Line("Enter your text.");
    Put_Line("Follow each line by <Return>.");
    Put_Line("To exit, type <Control-Z> on a line by itself.");
    New_Line;

    loop
        Get(c);
        Put(Printer, c);
        if End_of_Line then
            New_Line(Printer);
        end if;
    end loop;

exception

    when END_ERROR =>
        null;
        PrinterOff;

End ADA_6;
```

Fig. 3-6. Electronic Typewriter, Version 2.

```
-- Figure 3-7:   Specification for the Package Print_IO
--
--        "PrinterOn" allows subsequent output to go to a printer,
--              using "Printer" as a destination file for "Put" or
--              "Put_Line".
--        "PrinterOff" disconnects the printer.
--
--        Example:
--                    with Print_IO, Text_IO;
--                    use  Print_IO, Text_IO;
--                    ...
--                    PrinterOn;
--                    Put_Line(Printer, "Hello!");
--                    ...
--                    PrinterOff;

with Text_IO;
use  Text_IO;

Package Print_IO is

     Printer:  File_Type;

     Procedure PrinterOn;

     Procedure PrinterOff;

End Print_IO;
```

Fig. 3-7. Specification for the package Print__IO.

The specification unit contains declarations and procedure/function headings for all data, types, functions, and procedures defined in the package body that are to be made available to other packages. With Janus/Ada running under MS-DOS, the file containing the specification unit is given the file extension, .LIB, while the file containing the package body is given the file extension .PKG. Except for the file extension, both are given the same filename.

The package specification for Print__IO is shown in Fig. 3-7. The filename used was Print__IO.LIB. The variable Printer is declared to be of type File__Type. This type is defined in the package Text__IO. Ada treats a printer just like a text file. You will learn more about file input and output later in this chapter.

The rest of the specification package simply gives the first line of each procedure declaration.

The package body for Print__IO is shown in Fig. 3-8. Note the presence of the word body in the package declaration. Note also that the variable Printer need not be redeclared, as it was already declared in the specification unit.

The rest of the package body consists of the definitions of the procedures PrinterOn and PrinterOff. The procedures Open and Close come from Text__IO and are the same procedures used to open and close files, as you will see later. In this case, Open

```
    -- Figure 3-8:   Body of the Package Print_IO

   Package Body Print_IO is

       Procedure PrinterOn is

       Begin

           Open(Printer, Out_File, "LST:");

       End PrinterOn;

       Procedure PrinterOff is

       Begin

           Close(Printer);

       End PrinterOff;

   End Print_IO;
```

Fig. 3-8. Body of the package Print-IO.

establishes the connection between the file variable Printer and the external device LST:, which is how MS-DOS refers to the standard system printer. Close merely terminates that connection.

In order to establish Print__IO as a separately compiled procedure, the specification of the package (Fig. 3-7) must be compiled before the body (Fig. 3-8). Once compilation is successfully done, the package can be referenced by other packages using the appropriate with and use clauses.

The order of compilation is significant. Ada has a number of rules that govern the proper order. The basic rule is that a package that depends on another package must be compiled *after* the specification unit of the subordinate package. For example, note that the program in Fig. 3-6 uses Print__IO. There are three packages involved: the packages in Fig. 3-6, Fig. 3-7, and Fig. 3-8. The specification unit, Fig. 3-7, must be compiled first. After that, Fig. 3-6 and Fig. 3-8 can be compiled in either order.

If you needed to make changes to the program in Fig. 3-6, there would be no need to recompile the packages shown in Fig. 3-7 or Fig. 3-8. If, on the other hand, you needed to make changes to the Print__IO package, and you changed Fig. 3-7, you would have to recompile Fig. 3-6 and Fig. 3-8. You could, however, change and recompile Fig. 3-8 without affecting Fig. 3-6.

The rules on the order of compilation tend to enforce version control between packages. They minimize the chance that a change in one part of a program will have unwanted side effects in another part of the program. Modula-2 has similar provisions for version control of modules.

CONTROL STRUCTURES

Ada provides a complete set of control structures. It provides the if statement, the case statement, the for statement, the generalized loop, the exit statement, and the goto statement.

Simple Selection: The IF Statement

The basic form of the if statement in Ada is as follows:

```
if <condition> then
   statement(s);
end if;
```

The condition can be any Boolean expression, as discussed earlier. There may be one or many statements between then and end if; end if is required no matter how many or how few statements there are after then. This syntax differs from that of Pascal and C, but is the same as that of Modula-2.

Suppose that you have two variables called month and year, and that you wish to increment month. Here is one way to do this using a simple if statement:

```
month := month + 1;
if month  > 12 then
   month := 1;
   year := year + 1;
end if;
```

This if statement determines whether or not month has been incremented past 12; if it has been, month is set back to 1 and year is incremented.

An if statement may also have an else part; the format is as follows:

```
if <condition> then
   statement(s);
else
   statement(s);
end if;
```

An if statement with an else can be used to accomplish the same task as in the previous illustration:

```
if month < 12 then
   month := month + 1;
else
   month := 1;
   year := year + 1;
end if;
```

The Ada if statement can also have an elsif clause to make it easier to have nested conditions. For example, consider the computation of a weekly payroll. If the hours worked do not exceed 40, payment is made at the standard rate. If more than 40 but fewer than 50 hours are worked, the hours in excess of 40 are paid at 1.5 times the standard rate. All hours in excess of 50 are paid at 2 times the standard rate. The following shows one way to handle the appropriate computations in Ada:

```
if hours < = 40.0 then
    pay := hours * rate;
elsif hours < = 50.0 then
    pay := 40.0 * rate +
      (hours – 40.0) * 1.5 * rate;
else
    pay := 40.0 * rate +
      10.0 * 1.5 * rate +
      (hours – 50.0) * 2.0 * rate;
end if;
```

This construct allows for three possible ways to compute weekly pay; only one of these ways will be executed for a given value of hours. The ordinary if statement allows for simple selection between two possibilities; with the elsif clause, it can allow selection between three or more possible actions.

Notice that some of the above statements are continued on more than one line. The end of a statement in Ada is determined by a semicolon, not the end of a line.

Multiple Selection: The CASE Statement

As mentioned in the previous section, the if statement can provide selection between two or more alternatives. Another way to provide selection between multiple alternatives is the case statement. (The case statement is only appropriate when the alternatives can be enumerated.)

An example of the use of a case statement is shown in Fig. 3-9. This program reads a month number from the keyboard and prints the name of and the number of days in the corresponding month. If the month number is not 1 through 12, an error message is printed.

The when clauses enumerate the various alternatives. Multiple alternatives are separated by vertical lines (|). The when others clause covers any cases not specifically enumerated. In this example such cases are errors.

Counted Loops: The FOR Statement

The basic counted loop in Ada is constructed using the for statement. Chapter 2 includes a simple program in BASIC to print out the integers from 1 to 10. The program in Fig. 3-10 does the same thing in Ada.

The format of the for loop in Ada is slightly different than in other languages. The clause i in 1 . . 10 in Ada means the same as I = 1 TO 10 in BASIC. The 1 . . 10 represents the sequence of integers from 1 to 10.

```
-- Figure 3-9:   The Calendar Program, Version 1
with Text_IO;
use  Text_IO;

Procedure Ada_9 is

    month, days, year:   Integer;
    reply:               Character;

Begin

    loop
        New_Line;
        Put("Enter the Month (1..12):   ");
        Get(month);
        case month is
            when 1 | 3 | 5 | 7 | 8 | 10 | 12 => days := 31;
            when 4 | 6 | 9 | 11             => days := 30;
            when 2 =>        Put("Enter the year:   ");
                             Get(year);
                             if (year mod 4 = 0) then
                                 days := 29;
                             else
                                 days := 28;
                             end if;
            when others => New_Line;
                           Put_Line("Sorry, month must be 1..12.");
                           days := 0;
        end case;
        Put("Month ");
        Put(month);
        Put(" has ");
        Put(days);
        Put_Line(" days.");
        New_Line;
        Put("Again?   ");
        Get(reply);
        Skip_Line;
        New_Line;
        exit when ((reply = 'N') or (reply = 'n'));
    end loop;

End Ada_9;
```

Fig. 3-9. The Calendar Program, Version 1.

Earlier in this chapter, I said that there was one exception to the rule that all variables must be declared before they are used in an Ada program. That exception is the counter variable in a **for** loop; in this case, it is the variable i.

When the **for** loop is first encountered, i is set to 1. A check is then made to see whether i is in the interval of one to 10. If so, the statements between loop and end loop are executed. The counter i is then incremented and tested to see whether it is still in the interval of one to 10. If it is, the statements between loop and end loop

```
-- Figure 3-10: Counted Loops: The FOR Statement.
with Text_IO;
use   Text_IO;

Procedure Ada_10 is

Begin

     for i in 1..10 loop
          Put(i);
          New_Line;
     end loop;

End Ada_10;
```

Fig. 3-10. Counted loops: The FOR statement.

are executed again. This process is repeated until i is no longer in the interval. At that time, control is passed to the statement following the **end loop**.

The interval 1 . . 10 could have been written as **a . . b** if **a** and **b** were integer variables. In that case, the loop would not be executed at all if **a** were greater than **b** in value. This is because the **for** loop does the test at the beginning of the loop. Suppose you were to write something like the following:

    for i in 2 . . 1 loop

The compiler would warn you that the interval is null (i.e., that the loop won't execute at all), but it would still compile without error.

Suppose that you want to print out the numbers from 1 to 10 in reverse order. The following **for** statement would accomplish the task:

    for i in reverse 1 . . 10 loop
       Put(i);
       New__Line;
    end loop;

Conditional Loops: The WHILE Statement

The counted loop is useful when a set of statements is to be executed a specified number of times. Sometimes, however, you need to execute a set of statements as long as a given condition is true. The **while** statement is useful for this situation.

The **while** statement repeats as long as the stated condition is true. The test is performed at the beginning of the loop, so a while statement may not be executed at all if the condition is initially false. The body of the loop must contain some logic such that the condition will eventually become false; otherwise the loop would repeat forever.

The program in Fig. 3-11 shows how a **while** loop can be used to perform the same

```
-- Figure 3-11:   Conditional loops:   The WHILE Statement.
with Text_IO;
use  Text_IO;

Procedure Ada_11 is

    i:   Integer;

Begin

    i := 1;
    while i <= 10 loop
        Put(i);
        New_Line;
        i := i + 1;
    end loop;

End Ada_11;
```

Fig. 3-11. Conditional loops: The WHILE statement.

function as the for loop in Fig. 3-10. Again, the program prints the numbers 1 to 10 on the screen. Several differences can be noted:

☐ The variable i must be declared explicitly.
☐ The variable i must be initialized before the while statement.
☐ The variable i must be explicitly incremented each time through the loop.

Recall that all of these things are taken care of automatically by a for loop. The trade off is that the while statement is more general; it can handle more complicated conditions.

An example of a while statement that handles a more complicated condition is shown in the program of Fig. 3-12. The program repeatedly reads in an integer until the sum of all integers read exceeds 100. It then prints out the sum and the number of integers read.

Notice that in this example the statement Get(num); occurs twice: once before the loop and once within the loop. This is necessary so that the condition can be checked both before the first pass and before each subsequent pass. Next you will see how to use a generalized loop statement to avoid this problem.

Generalized Loops: The LOOP Statement

When the for statement and the while statement are used, the test always takes place at the top of the loop. That means that there is only one place from which the loop can be exited. There are occasions when it is more convenient to exit the loop from the bottom or from somewhere other than the top or bottom.

In the last section I remarked that the Get(num); statement had to be written twice

```
-- Figure 3-12:   Another WHILE Statement Demonstration
with Text_IO;
use  Text_IO;

Procedure Ada_12 is

    num, count, sum:  Integer;

Begin

    count := 0;
    sum   := 0;
    New_Line;
    Put_Line("Enter a series of integers:");
    New_Line;

    Get(num);
    while (sum + num) <= 100 loop
        count := count + 1;
        sum   := sum + num;
        Get(num);
    end loop;

    New_Line;
    Put(count, 1);
    Put_Line(" numbers were read.");
    Put("They sum to ");
    Put(sum);
    Put_Line(".");

    Put("The number   ");
    Put(num);
    Put_Line(" was not counted.");

End Ada_12;
```

Fig. 3-12. Another WHILE statement demonstration.

in the example given, which used a while statement to read in a series of integers. This situation can be avoided by using a generalized loop statement, as shown in Fig. 3-13.

In a loop statement, the statements between loop and end loop are repeated indefinitely until an exit statement is encountered. In this case, the first statement inside the loop reads the number, and the second checks to see whether it is time to exit the loop. When the specified condition is met, control is transferred to the statement immediately following end loop. In this way it is necessary to include only one Get(num); statement.

Some other languages, such as Pascal, include a **repeat** . . . **until** loop in which the test takes place at the bottom of the loop. With the generalized **loop** statement, this situation can be handled easily by making **exit when** the last statement before **end loop**.

The GOTO Statement

Ada also includes a goto statement for completeness. Because of the flexibility of the other control statements of Ada, the goto statement is not often needed. This is

```
-- Figure 3-13:   The Generalized Loop
with Text_IO;
use   Text_IO;

Procedure Ada_13 is

    num, count, sum:   Integer;

Begin

    count := 0;
    sum   := 0;
    New_Line;
    Put_Line("Enter a series of integers:");
    New_Line;

    loop
        Get(num);
        exit when  (sum + num) > 100;
        count := count + 1;
        sum   := sum + num;
    end loop;

    New_Line;
    Put(count, 1);
    Put_Line(" numbers were read.");
    Put("They sum to ");
    Put(sum);
    Put_Line(".");

    Put("The number   ");
    Put(num);
    Put_Line(" was not counted.");

End Ada_13;
```

Fig. 3-13. The generalized loop.

fortunate, because recent studies of structured programming techniques have shown that **goto** statements are frequently a symptom of poor program organization.

Perhaps the best example of the use of a **goto** would be a situation in which it is necessary to escape from an error condition inside a nested loop. The following illustrates such a case:

```
loop
  loop
    . . .
    if z = 0 then
        goto label2;
    end if;
    . . .
  end loop;
end loop;
. . .
<<label2>> Put__Line ("Error! z = 0!");
```

Note the different bracketing symbols used for the label (the brackets are << and >>).

Procedures

Subroutines are discussed in Chapter 2. Procedures are a form of subroutine.

A program in Ada is a procedure without parameters. Other procedures can be defined to perform particular tasks. Procedures can be defined at the beginning of a program or in a separately compiled package. Examples of the latter are shown in Figs. 3-7 and 3-8.

The use of procedures makes it possible to build a complex program out of smaller, simpler components. This is done by first decomposing the task to be accomplished into successively simpler subtasks, each simple enough to be written as a procedure.

One use of a procedure is to eliminate duplicate coding in a program. As an example, consider a program that must exchange the values of two real numbers in different parts of the program. One way to do this would be to encode the algorithm to accomplish this exchange everywhere in the program that it is needed. A simpler way is to encode the algorithm in a procedure and then invoke the procedure wherever it is needed. This is what is done in the program in Fig. 3-14.

Two procedures are defined in the program in Fig. 3-14. The procedure **Swap** accomplishes the exchange of variables, and the procedure **Print2** prints two real variables. Note that these procedures are defined along with the variable declarations of the main procedure.

The procedure **Swap** has two parameters, u and v. These are declared inside the parentheses following the name of the procedure. When the procedure is called, as in the following statement,

Swap (p, q);

the value of p is substituted for the formal parameter u, and the value of q is substituted for the formal parameter v. This means that these values are passed to the procedure

```
-- Figure 3-14:   Demonstrate Use of Procedures

with Text_IO;
use  Text_IO;

Procedure Ada_14 is

    p, q, x, y:  Float;

    Procedure Swap(u, v: in out Float) is
        --Exchange the values of the two arguments.
        temp:  Float;
    Begin
        temp := u;
        u    := v;
        v    := temp;
    End Swap;

    Procedure Print2 (u, v: in Float) is
        --Print out and label two Float variables.
    Begin
        New_Line;
        Put ("First  Variable:   ");
        Put (u, 4, 6, 0);
        New_Line;
        Put ("Second Variable:   ");
        Put (v, 4, 6, 0);
        New_Line;
    End Print2;

Begin

    p := 1.0;   q := 2.0;
    Print2 (p, q);
    Swap (p, q);
    Print2 (p, q);

    x := 3.14159;   y := 2.71828;
    Print2 (x, y);
    Swap (x, y);
    Print2 (x, y);

End Ada_14;
```

Fig. 3-14. Demonstration of the use of procedures.

Swap and used wherever the names u and v appear. The variables p and q are called *arguments* of the procedure call.

The word in following a parameter declaration means that the value of that variable gets passed into the procedure. This is assumed if it is not explicitly stated. If only in appears, then the values of p and q (the arguments of the procedure call) in the main program cannot be changed by anything that happens in the procedure. That is acceptable for the procedure Print2 because it doesn't need to change the values of its arguments, but it would defeat the purpose of the procedure Swap.

The word out means that changes to the value of the parameters of the procedure are also reflected in changes to the values of the arguments of the procedure call in the main program. This is required in the case of Swap; otherwise the procedure would be useless.

The procedure Print2 is useful because the standard Put procedure can only handle one variable at a time. In this program there are four places where I need to print out two variables at a time, so it makes sense to write and use such a procedure.

What this program does is use Print2 to print out the values of two variables, use Swap to exchange the values, then use Print2 again to print out the new values. The process is repeated to illustrate that procedures can be used with different arguments, as long as they agree in type (Float, in this case).

Procedures may be called from the main program or from other procedures. As will be seen shortly, a procedure in Ada can also call itself.

Functions

A function is similar to a procedure. The main difference is that the name of the function has a value, and the function is invoked by using it in an expression. For example, the package STRLIB supplied with Janus/Ada contains a function called Length. This function can be used to find the length of a character string, as in the following example:

```
len := Length("Hello!");
```

The function computes the length of the character string. The assignment statement assigns that value to the variable len.

Recall that a procedure call, in contrast, stands by itself and is not used in an expression. See, for example, the way the procedure Swap is used in Fig. 3-14.

Because a function name has an associated value, it must also have a type. The type (Integer, Character, etc.) must be declared in the heading of the function. Consider, for example, a function that returns half of the value of its argument. Here is how such a function could be defined:

```
Function Half (x: in Float) return Float is
   Begin
      return x / 2.0;
   End Half;
```

The phrase return Float in the heading of the function declaration determines that the value returned will be of type Float. Ada insists that the parameters of a function

```
-- Figure 3-15:   Function Demonstration

with Text_IO;
use  Text_IO;

Procedure Ada_15 is

    i, j, k:      Integer;
    c:            Character;


    --Function returns the largest of its 3 inputs

    Function Max3 (x, y, z:   in Integer) return Integer is
        max:  Integer;
    Begin    --Max3
        if (x >= y) and (x >= z) then
            max := x;
        elsif (y >= x) and (y >= z) then
            max := y;
        else
            max := z;
        end if;
        return max;
    End Max3;

Begin --Ada_15

    loop
        New_Line; New_Line;
        Put_Line ("You will be asked to enter three integers.");
        Put_Line ("The program will then print the largest one.");
        New_Line;
        Put ("Enter an integer:   ");
        Get (i);
        Put ("Enter an integer:   ");
        Get (j);
        Put ("Enter an integer:   ");
        Get (k);
        New_Line;
        Put (Max3 (i,j,k), 1);
        Put_Line (" is the largest of the three.");
        New_Line;
        Put ("Again? (y/n):   ");
        Get (c);  Skip_Line;
        exit when (c /= 'y') and (c /= 'Y');
    end loop;

End Ada_15;
```

Fig. 3-15. Function demonstration.

be in parameters, so it is not possible for an Ada function to change the value of its own parameters (as can be done with out or in out parameters of procedures).

An example of how this function could be used is shown in the following statement:

y := Half(z);

The program in Fig. 3-15 shows a function used to return the value of the largest of its three inputs. The local variable max is used to compute the appropriate value, which is then sent back to the calling program by the return statement.

Recursion

A procedure or function that invokes itself is said to be *recursive*. Recursion is often useful as a means of controlling the flow of a program. Clearly there must be some means to terminate the recursion and make sure that the process is finite.

Recursion is a means of repeatedly invoking a process. Often there are other ways of doing so, such as with a loop. The decision as to whether or not to use recursion should usually be made on the basis of clarity: which way seems to make more sense? Sometimes, however, it is made on the basis of efficiency. Nonrecursive versions are usually more efficient.

A simple example of a recursive procedure is shown in Fig. 3-16. This program prints a character string, drops the first character, prints the string, and repeats the process until there are no more characters left. A typical result from this program would appear as follows:

HELLO
ELLO
LLO
LO
O

The recursive procedure is called PrintAndDrop. What makes it recursive is the fact that it calls itself, just before the end of the procedure. Note that the recursive call is within an if statement, so that the procedure is called recursively only if the length of the string is greater than zero. Because the length of the string decreases with each cycle, this guarantees that the process will terminate in a finite number of steps.

The Remove procedure, which deletes a character from the string, comes from the package STRLIB. This package is supplied with the compiler.

As alluded to earlier, this problem could have been solved as well with a loop. There are some problems, however, that lend themselves naturally to a recursive solution. One such problem is the computation of the factorial function, a problem from the field of mathematics.

The factorial of zero is defined as one. The factorial of a positive integer N is defined as N times the factorial of N − 1. The definition is itself recursive; that is, the function is defined in terms of itself.

The program in Fig. 3-17 shows the use of a recursive function to compute the factorial function. Each time the function is called, it either returns the number one for

```
-- Figure 3-16:   Demonstrate Recursive Procedure
with Text_IO, STRLIB;
use  Text_IO, STRLIB;

Procedure Ada_16 is

    s:   String;
    c:   Character;
    n:   Integer;

    Procedure PrintAndDrop (s:   in out String) is
        --Print a string; drop first character; repeat.
        Begin
            if Length(s) > 0 then
                Put_Line(s);
                -- Now remove 1 char at position 1
                s := Remove(s, 1, 1);
                -- Next is a recursive call
                PrintAndDrop(s);
            end if;
        End PrintAndDrop;

Begin --Ada_16

    loop
        New_Line;  New_Line;
        Put ("Type a string:  ");
        Get_Line (s, n);
        New_Line;
        PrintAndDrop (s);
        New_Line;  New_Line;

        Put ("Again?  (y/n):  ");
        Get (c);
        Skip_Line;
        exit when (c /= 'y') and (c /= 'Y');
    end loop;

End Ada_16;
```

Fig. 3-16. A recursive procedure.

zero factorial, or puts the computation on hold while it calls itself recursively to find the value of N − 1 factorial. When it finally gets down to zero factorial, all the computations that have been put on hold can be completed, starting with one factorial and working up successively to N factorial.

```
-- Figure 3-17:   Demonstrate Recursive Function

with Text_IO;
use  Text_IO;

Procedure Ada_17 is

    x:   Integer;
    n:   Long_Float;
    c:   Character;

    Function Factorial (n:   in Long_Float) return Long_Float is
        --Compute the factorial of a non-negative integer
        --Accurate to 15 digits, or n <= 17
        f:   Long_Float;
        Begin   -- Factorial
            if n < 0.0 then
                New_Line;
                Put_Line("Sorry, n must be greater than 0.");
                New_Line;
                f := 0.0;
            elsif n = 0.0 then
                f := 1.0;
            else
                f := n * Factorial (n - 1.0);
            end if;
            return f;
        End Factorial;

Begin   -- Ada_17

    loop
        New_Line;  New_Line;
        Put("Enter an integer >= 0:  ");
        Get (x);  Skip_Line;      -- Read as Integer
        n := Long_Float(x);       -- Convert to Long_Float
        Put (n, 1, 0, 0);
        Put (" factorial is ");
        Put (Factorial (n), 1, 0, 0);
        New_Line;  New_Line;

        Put ("Again?  (y/n):  ");
        Get (c);
        Skip_Line;
        exit when (c /= 'y') and (c /= 'Y');
    end loop;

End Ada_17;
```

Fig. 3-17. A recursive function.

The program was written using **Long Float** variables because the value of the factorial function gets very large very quickly, and the magnitude of **Integer** variables is limited. For simplicity, the input is read from the keyboard as an integer and then converted to a **Long Float** internally. This keeps the user from having to type a decimal point in input.

DATA STRUCTURES

Ada supports a wide range of data structures, including arrays and records. Ada records can be used to construct more complex data structures such as linked lists and trees.

Arrays

Ada uses parentheses to delimit the subscripts of arrays (unlike C, Pascal and Modula-2, which use square brackets). Arrays must be declared in advance.

Full Ada provides a great deal of flexibility in the way arrays can be specified and used. For example, it allows entire arrays to be used in assignment statements, as in the following example:

```
x, y: Array (1 . . 10) of Integer;
. . . .
x := y;
```

The example assumes that the elements of y have been assigned appropriate values between the declaration of y and its use.

Ada also allows access to subsets of arrays, called **slices**. The simplest way to explain what these mean is by example:

```
x(1 . . 3) := y(8 . . 10);
```

This example moves the values of the last three elements of y to the first three elements of x.

Ada allows quick access to the dimensions of an array. For example, if **Index** has been declared as an array of **Integer**, the following program segment could be used to initialize the array elements to zero:

```
for i in Index'First . . Index'Last loop
    Index(i) := 0;
end loop;
```

For short arrays, initialization can be taken care of by the array declaration. Assignment statements can also be used to assign multiple values to an array at one time. The following example illustrates these points:

```
Type Vector is array (1 . . 5) of Integer;
x: Vector := (0, 0, 0, 0, 0);
. . . .
x(2 . . 3) := (72, 18);
```

The declaration of x as a variable of type **Vector** includes the initialization of each element of the array to zero. The assignment statement that follows moves the integers 72 and 18 into the second and third elements of x, respectively.

One of the shortcomings of Pascal is the requirement to specify in advance the dimensionality of arrays used as parameters of procedures and functions. For example, if you want to write a procedure to sort an integer array, you have to decide in advance the largest size of array that you will ever need to sort. Ada solves this problem.

The following program uses a procedure to print out an array in reverse order:

```
with Text__IO;
use Text__IO;
Procedure Demo is
   Type Vector is array
      (Integer range < >) of Integer;
   a: Vector (1 . . 10);
   Procedure Reverse__It (a: Vector) is
      Begin
         for i in reverse a'range loop
            Put (a(i));
            New__Line;
         end loop;
      End Reverse__It;
   Begin  – – Demo
      for i in a'range loop
         a(i) := i;
      end loop;
      Reverse__It(a);
End Demo;
```

The expression a'range in this case is equivalent to 1 . . 10. In general, it stands for the range of the subscripts of the array a. Note how it is used in a for loop.

Janus/Ada, as of Version 1.5.2, does not implement all of these advanced features. In fact, it does not even implement arrays of more than one dimension. Multidimensional arrays can easily be simulated in Janus/Ada, however. The following shows how to declare a two dimensional array in full Ada and how to simulate the same thing in Janus/Ada:

```
Full Ada
   Matrix:        array (1 . . 5, 1 . . 10) of Integer;
Janus/Ada
   Mat1:          array (1 . . 10) of Integer;
   Matrix:        array (1 . . 5) of Mat1;
```

In full Ada, you would refer to the element in the second row, third column as Matrix (2, 3). In Janus/Ada, you would refer to the same element as Matrix (2)(3).

Figure 3-18 contains an example of the use of arrays in Ada to solve the Calendar problem. This problem was previously solved in Fig. 3-9 using a **Case** statement. The

```
-- Figure 3-18:   The Calendar Program, Version 2
with Text_IO;
use  Text_IO;

Procedure Ada_18 is

    month, days, year:  Integer;
    reply:   Character;
    DaysIn:  Array (1..12) of Integer;
    NameOf:  Array (1..12) of String;

Begin -- Ada_18

    DaysIn(1)  := 31;    NameOf(1)  := "January";
    DaysIn(2)  := 28;    NameOf(2)  := "February";
    DaysIn(3)  := 31;    NameOf(3)  := "March";
    DaysIn(4)  := 30;    NameOf(4)  := "April";
    DaysIn(5)  := 31;    NameOf(5)  := "May";
    DaysIn(6)  := 30;    NameOf(6)  := "June";
    DaysIn(7)  := 31;    NameOf(7)  := "July";
    DaysIn(8)  := 31;    NameOf(8)  := "August";
    DaysIn(9)  := 30;    NameOf(9)  := "September";
    DaysIn(10) := 31;    NameOf(10) := "October";
    DaysIn(11) := 30;    NameOf(11) := "November";
    DaysIn(12) := 31;    NameOf(12) := "December";

    loop
        New_Line;
        Put ("Enter the Month (1..12):  ");
        Get (month);  Skip_Line;
        if (month in 1..12) then
            days := DaysIn(month);
            if month = 2 then
                Put ("Enter the Year:  ");
                Get (year);  Skip_Line;
                if (year MOD 4) = 0 then
                    days := 29;
                end if;
            end if;
            Put (NameOf(month));
            Put (" has");
            Put (days, 3);
            Put_Line (" days.");
        else
            Put_Line ("Month must be in the interval 1..12.");
        end if;

        New_Line;
```

Fig. 3-18. The Calendar Program, Version 2.

```
        Put ("Again?   (y/n):   ");
        Get (reply);  Skip_Line;
        New_Line;
        exit when (reply = 'N') OR (reply = 'n');

    end loop;

End Ada_18;
```

array **DaysIn** stores the number of days in each month. The array **NameOf** stores, not surprisingly, the name of each month. Special arrangements are made to handle leap years. Special care is taken in the program to make sure that the subscripts of the arrays do not get out of the appropriate range (1 . . 12).

Records

Chapter 2 discussed an example in which it was convenient to have a record to hold the name and test scores of a student. A collection of such records might be used to make up a gradebook. Specifically, suppose you need to record up to 20 test scores for up to 30 students in a class.

This can be handled in Ada using an array of records. The following declarations would establish the appropriate data structure:

```
NrOfStudents:        constant Integer := 30;
NrOfTests:           constant Integer := 20;
type Entry is record
   Name:         String (25);
   Score:        array (1 .. NrOfTests) of Float;
end record;
Student:   array (1 .. NrOfStudents) of Entry;
```

First, constants defining the number of students and the number of tests are declared. Next, a record type called **Entry** is declared. Finally, an array of records called **Student** is declared. This is the required array of records.

Suppose that you need to print the name of the fourth student and the score that student received on the first test. The following would accomplish this task:

```
Put(Student(4).Name);
Put(" ");
Put(Student(4).Score(1));
```

The period or dot (.) is used to refer to individual elements in a record.

The sample programs in Figs. 3-19 and 3-20 later in this chapter demonstrate the use of records.

Linked Lists

Chapter 2 explained linked lists and showed one way that they can be implemented using arrays. Ada provides another way for linked lists to be implemented using *dynamic allocation* of storage space. Discussion of dynamic allocation of storage space is beyond the scope of this chapter.

This section shows how linked lists can be implemented in Ada using arrays of records. The methodology is essentially the same as that used in Chapter 2, except that an array of records is used instead of parallel arrays.

The following declarations establish an array of records that will support the example given in Chapter 2:

```
EndList:       Constant Integer : = 0;
MaxSize:       Constant Integer : = 5;
First, FirstFree:  Integer;
Type Item is Record
    Name:          String(15);
    Link:          Integer;
End Record;
List:   Array (1 . . MaxSize) of Item;
```

The following would print out the name part of the third record of the structure:

```
Put__Line(List(3).Name);
```

The subscript of the next record in the list can then be found in this element:

```
List(3).Link
```

The program in Fig. 3-20 at the end of the chapter illustrates the use of linked lists in a real program. The example shows how to add and delete records from a linked list, and how to follow the links from one record to the next.

FILE HANDLING

Many computer applications require the processing of data on a regular basis. For example, a program that maintains the accounting records of a company must record data for later retrieval and processing. This data is recorded in files, usually on disk. How a programming language handles disk files is an important factor in determining its suitability for such applications.

The Ada language does not have built-in file input and output. All input and output in Ada is accomplished by packages that are provided with the language. In order to handle files, an Ada program must **with** an appropriate library package.

There are three basic types of files commonly provided by Ada packages. The first is the *text* file. A text file is a sequence of characters. It can be accessed sequentially from start to finish. If a text file were copied to the console or to a printer, it would be readable to the human eye.

A printer is much like an output text file. In fact, the procedures for writing to a printer are simply a special case of those for writing to a file. The sample programs earlier in the chapter that sent output to a printer illustrate these procedures.

The second type of file usually supported by Ada implementations is the *sequential* file. A sequential file is a sequence of records. (Records were discussed in the previous section on data structures.) Records can be accessed one at a time, from the beginning of the file to the end. There is no way to access a record in the middle of a file except by first accessing all preceding records in sequence. There is a provision, however, to go back to the beginning of a text or sequential file.

A sequential file, unlike a text file, would usually be unreadable if copied to the console or a printer. This is because it is stored in binary form rather than text form.

The third type of Ada file is the *direct-access* file, sometimes called the *random-access* file. This type of file is also a sequence of records. The difference is that the records of the file can be accessed directly, in any sequence. Direct-access files are stored in binary form.

There are three file modes in Ada: In—File, Out—File, and InOut—File. In the In—File mode one can read from an existing file but not write to it. In the Out—File mode one can write to a new file but not read from it. (Opening an existing file in the Out—File mode causes that file to be overwritten.) In the InOut—File mode, you can both read from and write to a file.

Text and sequential files can be accessed in either the In—File or the Out—File mode, but not the InOut—File mode. In order to read from a sequential or text file you have just written to, you must first close it and reopen it in the In—File mode. Only direct-access files can be accessed in the InOut—File mode.

There appears to be one glaring omission in Ada's file-handling procedures: there is no easy way to append new data onto the end of an existing text or sequential file. Most languages support an access mode, usually called *append*, that allows a file to be opened for output in such a manner that the existing data in the file is preserved and new data is added at the end of the file. In Ada, you must open the existing file in In—File mode, open a new file in Out—File mode, and copy all the data from the existing to the new file before adding to the new file. After the new file has been closed, you can delete the old file and rename the new file. This is a lot of extra work for such a common process.

Operations common to all three kinds of files include **Create**, **Open**, and **Close**. There are actually three versions of each procedure, one for each type of file. In Janus/Ada, text files are supported by the package **Text—IO**, sequential files are supported by the package **Seq—IO**, and direct-access files by the package **RandIO**. Each of these three packages has its own version of **Create**, **Open**, and **Close**.

Consider a program that needs procedures in both **Text—IO** and **Seq—IO**. Given that any program that writes to the screen must use **Text—IO**, this is a common scenario. Recall that a program gains access to a package using a **with** clause. The **use** clause allows the program to refer to procedures in the package by name, without qualification, as long as there is no ambiguity. In the present scenario, ambiguity is guaranteed. The solution is to use qualification; for example,

Seq—IO.Open(f, In—File, file—name)

```
-- Figure 3-19:  Sequential File Demonstration
with Text_IO, Seq_IO;
use  Text_IO, Seq_IO;

Procedure Ada_19 is

    type FileRec is Record
        name:  String(20);
        age:   Integer;
    end record;

    R:  FileRec;
    f:  Seq_IO.File_Type;
    length:  Natural;

Begin --Ada_19

    Seq_IO.Create (f, Seq_IO.Out_File, "AGES.TXT");

    -- First read from keyboard and write to disk

    New_Line;  New_Line;
    Put_Line ("Enter Names and Ages:  Age 0 to quit.");
    loop
        New_Line;
        Put ("Name:  ");
        Get_Line (R.name, length);
        Put ("Age:    ");
        Get (R.age);  Skip_Line;
        Write (f, R);
        exit when R.age = 0;
    end loop;
    Seq_IO.Close (f);

    -- Now read the file back and display it on the screen

    Seq_IO.Open (f, Seq_IO.In_File, "AGES.TXT");
    New_Line;  New_Line;
    Put_Line ("Here are the contents of the file:");
    New_Line;
    loop
        Read (f, R);
        exit when R.age = 0;
        Put ("Name:   ");
```

Fig. 3-19. Sequential file demonstration.

```
            Put_Line (R.name);
            Put ("Age:    ");
            Put (R.age, 1);
            New_Line; New_Line;
      end loop;
      Seq_IO.Close (f);
      Put ("All Done...");

End Ada_19;
```

```
-- Figure 3-20:   Comprehensive Sample Program (Main Program)

--   A program to create and maintain a file of names and addresses.
--   The file is maintained in alphabetical order by name using an
--   index consisting of a linked list of pointers.  A linked list
--   of vacant (free) records is also maintained.

with File_IO, Print_IO, Lists, Scrn_IO;
use  File_IO, Print_IO, Lists, Scrn_IO;

--   File_IO      provides OpenFiles and CloseFiles.
--   Print_IO     provides PrinterOn and PrinterOff.
--   Scrn_IO      provides Menu.
--   Lists        provides Append, Review, ListFile, DumpFile.

Procedure Ada_20 is

    c:  Integer;

Begin                                        --Main Program

    OpenFiles;
    PrinterOn;

    loop
        Menu (c);
        case c is
            when 1 =>       Append;
            when 2 =>       Review;
            when 3 =>       ListFile;
            when 4 =>       DumpFile;
            when 5 =>       exit;            --Quit
            when others =>  null;            --Do nothing
        end case;
    end loop;

    PrinterOff;
    CloseFiles;

End Ada_20;
```

Fig. 3-20. Comprehensive sample program (main program).

refers to the version of **Open** from the package **Seq_IO**. It is sometimes convenient to omit the **use** clause and rely totally on explicit qualification.

Sequential Files

As mentioned above, a sequential file is a sequence of records, usually on disk, that is accessed one record at a time from start to finish. Records cannot be accessed out of sequence, except that you can usually start over at the beginning of the file.

An example of a program that uses a sequential file is shown in Fig. 3-19. The program prompts the user for a list of names and ages, then saves the data to a sequential file called **AGES.TXT**. After the file has been closed, it is reopened, read, and displayed on the screen, one record at a time.

The program declares a record type called **FileRec**. Each record of this type consists of a character string to hold the name, and an integer to hold the age. Notice that the file variable f is declared to be of type **Seq_IO.File_Type**. This is to distinguish it from **Text_IO.File_Type**, because both packages are visible to this program by way of **use** and **with** clauses. The same technique must be used with the **Open** and **Close** procedures.

The loop controls the input of data keys on the value of the variable **R.age**. This is a part of the record **R**, which is of type **FileRec**. When this variable is found to be zero, that is, when the user types in a zero age, the loop exits. A similar process is used to control the loop that reads the file back in from disk.

Direct-Access Files

As mentioned earlier, the records of a direct-access file can be accessed in any sequence. Direct-access files are implemented in Janus/Ada by the package **RandIO**. Because Janus/Ada is not full Ada and lacks a feature known as *Generic Packages*, the use of **RandIO** in Janus/Ada is something of a kludge (a quick fix). The package must be modified and recompiled for every different file type. The type of record that comprises the file must be defined and made known to **RandIO**, and the package must subsequently be recompiled.

Records in a direct-access file are numbered beginning with one. (In some languages the first record is record number zero.) The package **RandIO** defines a special subtype called **RandIO.Positive_Count**, which consists of the positive integers. Any variable used to access a record via **RandIO** must be of this specific type; an integer or another type consisting of the same elements won't do. This is an example of Ada's extremely strong type checking at work.

The package **RandIO** includes procedures called **Read** and **Write**, which read and write specified file records. The record number is a parameter of each procedure.

A program illustrating the use of a direct-access file is included as the comprehensive sample program later in this chapter.

GRAPHICS

The Ada language does not support graphics directly. This is consistent with the philosophy that excludes input and output details from the basic language, but permits their implementation via separately compiled packages. This is, of course, because the details of such packages tend to be implementation-dependent, and Ada eschews implementation dependencies.

There were no graphics packages supplied with the Janus/Ada compiler, but there is no reason why such packages could not be written and used with Ada programs.

THE COMPREHENSIVE SAMPLE PROGRAM

A program that illustrates many of the Ada features described in this chapter is shown in Figs. 3-20 through 3-27.

The main program is in Fig. 3-20. The basic data structure for the direct-access file used by the program is included by itself in Fig. 3-27. This is so that it can be referenced by the other packages that make up the program and by the RandIO package. There are three other packages that make up the program. Each consists of a specification and a body. The specifications are shown in Figs. 3-21, 3-23, and 3-25. The package bodies are shown in Figs. 3-22, 3-24, and 3-26.

A structure chart showing the hierarchy of the program is shown in Fig. 3-28. Beside the name of each procedure is the figure name of the package body that contains the procedure. Indented below each procedure are the names of any other procedures called by that procedure.

The purpose of the program is to maintain a file of names and addresses in alphabetical order by name, and to provide for adding records to the file, viewing the file, deleting records from the file, and listing the file on a printer. It also includes a provision for dumping the file to a printer in such a way that the index pointers are available for inspection.

The main program in Fig. 3-20 is very short. First, it calls procedures to open the disk files and turn the printer on. It then goes into the main loop. The main loop first calls a procedure to display a menu and read a response. It then uses a case statement to call the appropriate procedure, depending on which option was selected. All that remains after the main loop has been completed is to close the disk files and turn off the printer.

The program actually maintains two files: one to contain the data itself and one to contain the index. The data file, or address file as it is referred to, is maintained as a direct-access file using the package RandIO. The index file is maintained as a sequential file using the package Seq_IO.

Only one or two data records are kept in the computer's memory at a given time. Each record is written to disk as it is entered from the keyboard, and read from disk immediately before it is displayed. This makes it essential to be able to access these records as they are needed, in any order.

The index file, on the other hand, is small enough to be kept in memory in its entirety. At the end of the program it is written to a sequential file. At the beginning of the next session it is read into memory from that sequential file. While it is in memory, you can easily access whichever index record is needed, because it is stored in an array.

The indexing scheme used is based on a data structure called a *linked list*. Two linked lists are implemented within the array Index, declared in Fig. 3-21. Index(−1) is used to store the value of the subscript of Index that corresponds to ("points to") the first empty record of the file. Index(−1) is the beginning of a data structure called the *free list*.

Index(0) contains the value of the subscript of Index that points to the (alphabetically) first record of the file. Index(0) is the beginning of a data structure called the *active*

```
-- Figure 3-21:   Specification for the Package File_IO.
--                Used by the Comprehensive Sample Program.
with File_Def, Text_IO, RandIO;
use  File_Def, Text_IO;

Package File_IO is

    MaxRecords:  Constant Integer := 10;
    EndList:     Constant Integer :=  0;

    InBuf, OutBuf:  RecType;
    Console:        File_Type;

    Index:  Array (-1..MaxRecords) of Integer;

        --Note:  Index (-1) is subscript of first free record
        --       Index (0)  is subscript of first active record

    Procedure OpenFiles;
        --Opens Address and Index files; reads Index file

    Procedure CloseFiles;
        --Saves Index and closes Address and Index files

    Procedure GetRec (i:  in RandIO.Positive_Count; InBuf:  out RecType);
        --Reads record i of Address File into InBuf

    Procedure PutRec (i:  in RandIO.Positive_Count; OutBuf:  in RecType);
        --Writes OutBuf to file position i of Address File

    Procedure Pause;
        --Wait for a key to be pressed.

    --Note:  Body of File_IO opens Console for output

End File_IO;
```

Fig. 3-21. Specification for the package File_IO.

list. How these lists work is explained in the section on lists in Chapter 2.

The File_IO package of Figs. 3-21 and 3-22 takes care of opening and closing both files and manages all access to those files. It also establishes a file variable called **Console** so that the Text_IO package procedure **Put** can be used to write to the console or to the printer, depending on which is needed at a given time. This capability is needed by the procedure **ListFile** of the package **Lists**, which is defined in Figs. 3-25 and 3-26.

The package Scrn_IO is defined in Figs. 3-23 and 3-24. It takes care of the program menu and all other screen input and output. The procedures **ClearScreen** and **GoToXY** are not standard Ada because these functions are not provided by Janus/Ada. Implementing this program on another system would require replacing these functions with equivalent procedures. Other than that, the procedures in this package are straightforward.

The package **Lists**, shown in Figs. 3-25 and 3-26, contains the most complex logic in the program. It contains the procedures to administer data input, data storage, and index maintenance.

```
-- Figure 3-22:   Body of the Package FILE_IO.
--                Used by the Comprehensive Sample Program.
with Seq_IO, RText_IO;
use  RText_IO ;

Package Body File_IO is

    FName:  Constant String := "ADDRESS.FIL";
    IName:  Constant String := "INDEX.FIL";

    AddrFile:   RandIO.File_Type;
    IndexFile:  Seq_IO.File_Type;

    IndexBuf:   Integer range 0..MaxRecords;
    Counter:    RandIO.Positive_Count;

    Procedure Pause is
        --Pause until any key is pressed
        Begin
            New_Line;   New_Line;
            Put ("Press any key to continue....");
            loop
                exit when KeyPress;
            end loop;
        End Pause;

    Procedure Open_Addr is
        --Open Address File.
        --Create file and initialize if it doesn't already exist.
        blank:  Constant String := " ";
        Begin   --Open_Addr
            RandIO.Open (AddrFile, RandIO.InOut_File, FName);
            New_Line;
            Put_Line ("Address File is now open......");
            New_Line;
        Exception
            when RandIO.NAME_ERROR =>
                New_Line;
                Put_Line ("Creating Address File......");
                New_Line;
                RandIO.Create (AddrFile, RandIO.InOut_File, FName);

                OutBuf.name.last  := blank;
                OutBuf.name.first := blank;
                OutBuf.address    := blank;
                OutBuf.city       := blank;
                OutBuf.state      := blank;
                OutBuf.zip        := blank;
                OutBuf.phone      := blank;

                --Write blank records to initialize file
            for i in 1..MaxRecords loop
                Counter := RandIO.Positive_Count (i);
                RandIO.Write (AddrFile,OutBuf,Counter);
            end loop;

            RandIO.Close (AddrFile);
            Open_Addr;              --Recursive call to re-open

    End Open_Addr;
```

Fig. 3-22. Body of the package FILE_IO.

```
Procedure Open_Index (f:  In Out Seq_IO.File_Type; fn:   String) is
    --Open and read in index file.
    --Create file if it does not already exist.
    Begin
        Seq_IO.Open (f, Seq_IO.In_File, fn);
        for i in (-1)..MaxRecords loop
            Read (f, IndexBuf);
            Index(i) := IndexBuf;
        end loop;
        Seq_IO.Close (f);
        New_Line;
        Put_Line ("Index File has been read in......");
        New_Line;
    Exception
        when Seq_IO.NAME_ERROR =>
            New_Line;
            Put_Line ("Creating Index File......");
            New_Line;
            Seq_IO.Create (f, Seq_IO.Out_File, fn);
            IndexBuf := 1;        --First free record
            Write (f, IndexBuf);
            IndexBuf := EndList;
            Write (f, IndexBuf);
            --Now complete free list
            for i in 1..(MaxRecords-1) loop
                IndexBuf := i + 1;
                Write (f, IndexBuf);
            end loop;
            IndexBuf := EndList;
            Write (f, IndexBuf);
            Seq_IO.Close (f);
            Open_Index (f, fn);        --Recurse and read it in

    End Open_Index;

Procedure OpenFiles is
    --Open and read in files from disk.
    --Create files if they do not already exist.
    Begin
        Open_Addr;
        Open_Index (IndexFile, IName);
    End OpenFiles;

Procedure CloseFiles is
    --Write updated Index file to disk and close both files.
    Begin
        Seq_IO.Open (IndexFile, Seq_IO.Out_File, INAME);
        for i in -1..MaxRecords loop
            IndexBuf := Index(i);
            Write (IndexFile, IndexBuf);
        end loop;
        Seq_IO.Close (IndexFile);
        New_Line;
        Put_Line ("Index File written to disk and closed......");
        New_Line;
        RandIO.Close (AddrFile);
        New_Line;
        Put_Line ("Address File closed......");
        New_Line;

    End CloseFiles;
```

```
        Procedure GetRec (i:  in RandIO.Positive_Count; InBuf:  out RecType) is
           --Reads record i of AddrFile into InBuf
           Begin
               RandIO.Read (AddrFile, InBuf, i);
           End GetRec;

        Procedure PutRec (i:  in RandIO.Positive_Count; OutBuf:  in RecType) is
           --Writes OutBuf to file position i of AddrFile
           Begin
               RandIO.Write (AddrFile, OutBuf, i);
           End PutRec;

   Begin

      Open (Console, Out_File, "CON:");

   End File_IO;
```

Fig. 3-22. Body of the package FILE__IO. (Continued from page 65.)

Using the program requires selecting the desired action from a menu and filling in
a form on the screen when requested. The user can add a new record to the file, view
the file one record at a time, delete a record, or list the entire file on the screen or
on a printer.

When a record is deleted, it is added to the free list, which contains the record
numbers of all records not in use. When a record is to be added to the file, the first
record on the free list is used, and that record is added to the active list in the appropriate
position.

The dump option is provided as a learning tool. It is instructive to dump an empty
file, add a few records, dump it again, delete a few records, dump it again, and so on.
This lets you see how the program keeps track of the free list and the active list.

The program as shown is limited to handling a file of 10 records by the constant
MaxRecords, declared in Fig. 3-21. To accommodate a larger file, simply change the
value of that constant before compiling the package.

```
   -- Figure 3-23:  Specification for the Package SCRN_IO.
   --                 Used by the Comprehensive Sample Program.
 with Text_IO, File_Def, RandIO;
 use  Text_IO, File_Def;

 Package Scrn_IO is

     Procedure Menu (c:  Out Natural);
         --Display menu on screen and return selection as c

     Procedure GetEntry (r:  Out RecType; finished:  Out Boolean);
         --Read 1 record from console into record r

     Procedure PrintRec (f:  In File_Type; i:  In RandIO.Positive_Count);
         --Print record i of file f

 End Scrn_IO ;
```

Fig. 3-23. Specification for the package SCRN__IO.

```
-- Figure 3-24:   Body of the Package SCRN_IO.
--                 Used by the Comprehensive Sample Program.

-- Provides the Procedure Menu for the Address File Program.

with Screen, File_IO;
use  Screen, File_IO;

--   Text_IO (from Scrn_IO.LIB) provides Put and Get;
--   Screen  provides ClearScreen and GotoXY.

Package body Scrn_IO is

    Procedure NextField (col:  In Natural; row:  In Out Natural) is
        --Position cursor 2 rows down, same column
        Begin --NextField
            row := row + 2;
            GotoXY (col, row);
        End NextField;

    Procedure Menu (c:  Out Natural) is
        --Display the main menu and return selection
        row, col:  Natural;
        Begin
            ClearScreen;
            row := 5;    col := 5;
            GotoXY (col, row);
            Put ("1)  Add to File");
            NextField (col, row);
            Put ("2)  Review File on Screen");
            NextField (col, row);
            Put ("3)  List File to Screen or Printer");
            NextField (col, row);
            Put ("4)  Dump File to Printer");
            NextField (col, row);
            Put ("5) Quit");
            row := row + 2;
            col := 1;
            loop
                GotoXY (col, row);
                Put ("Select 1, 2, 3, 4, or 5:   ");
                Get (c);
                Skip_Line;
                exit when c in 1..5;
            end loop;
        End Menu;

    Procedure GetEntry (r:  Out RecType; finished:  Out Boolean) is
        --Read 1 record from console into record r
        row, col, start, length:  Natural;

        Procedure MarkOff (start, spaces:  In Natural) is
            --Mark off data input area with colons

        Begin
            GotoXY (start, row);
            Put (":");
```

Fig. 3-24. Body of the package SCRN__IO.

```
                for i in 1..spaces loop
                    Put (" ");
                end loop;
                Put (":");
            End MarkOff;

        Begin
            ClearScreen;
            --First display skeleton record
            start := 14;
            row := 5;  col := 1;
            GotoXY (col, row);
            Put ("Last Name:");
            MarkOff (start, 12);      NextField (col, row);
            Put ("First Name:");
            MarkOff (start, 12);      NextField (col, row);
            Put ("Address:");
            MarkOff (start, 20);      NextField (col, row);
            Put ("City:");
            MarkOff (start, 12);      NextField (col, row);
            Put ("State:");
            MarkOff (start, 2);       NextField (col, row);
            Put ("Zip:");
            MarkOff (start, 10);      NextField (col, row);
            Put ("Phone:");
            MarkOff (start, 14);      NextField (col, row);
            --Now read in each field
            row := 5;    col := 15;
            GotoXY (col, row);
            Get_Line (r.name.last, length);
            finished := (length = 0);    --True if length is 0
            if NOT finished then
                NextField (col, row);
                Get_Line (r.name.first, length);
                NextField (col, row);
                Get_Line (r.address, length);
                NextField (col, row);
                Get_Line (r.city, length);
                NextField (col, row);
                Get_Line (r.state, length);
                NextField (col, row);
                Get_Line (r.zip, length);
                NextField (col, row);
                Get_Line (r.phone, length);
            end if;
        End GetEntry;

    Procedure PrintRec (f:  In File_Type; i:  In RandIO.Positive_Count) is
        --Print record i of file f
        r:  RecType;

            Begin
                GetRec (i, r);
                Put (f, r.name.first);
                Put (f, " ");
```

```
            Put_Line (f, r.name.last);
            Put_Line (f, r.address);
            Put (f, r.city);
            Put (f, ", ");
            Put (f, r.state);
            Put (f, " ");
            Put_Line (f, r.zip);
            Put_Line (f, r.phone);
        End PrintRec;

End Scrn_IO;
```

Fig. 3-24. Body of the package SCRN__IO. (Continued from page 68.)

It is instructive to compare this program with the corresponding programs in the other language chapters. The Ada version corresponds most closely to the Modula-2 version.

ADVANTAGES AND DISADVANTAGES OF ADA

There is a lot more to Ada than has been discussed in this chapter. Space has permitted me to cover only the highlights. Among the topics omitted are asynchronous processes (*tasks*), generic procedures, limited private variable types, and pointer variables (*access* types). The reader interested in pursuing such advanced topics is referred to a book on Ada alone.

Ada has many advantages. It is an extremely powerful language, a rich language in the sense of having a wide range of features. The designers threw in every language feature except the kitchen sink, and I would have to read the fine print of the specification to make sure that it isn't in there too. In short, if it can be done on a computer, it can probably be done in Ada.

```
-- Figure 3-25:  Specification for the Package LISTS
--                Used by the Comprehensive Sample Program.

--   Performs list manipulation for the Address File Program.

Package Lists is

    Procedure Append;

    Procedure Review;

    Procedure ListFile;

    Procedure DumpFile;

End Lists;
```

Fig. 3-25. Specification for the package LISTS.

```
-- Figure 3-26:  Body of the Package LISTS.
--               Used by the Comprehensive Sample Program.

with Text_IO, RText_IO, File_IO, Scrn_IO, File_Def,
     Screen, Print_IO, RandIO;
use  Text_IO, RText_IO, File_IO, Scrn_IO, File_Def,
     Screen, Print_IO;

Package Body Lists is

    Function GetFree return Natural is
        --Get record number of next free record and
        --  remove it from the free list.
        free:  Natural;
        Begin
            free := Index(-1);            --First free record
            if free /= EndList then
                Index(-1) := Index(free);   --Update first free
            end if;
            Return free;
        End GetFree;

    Function Greater (a, b:  RecType) return Boolean is
        --Return TRUE if a.name > b.name
        Begin
            if (a.name.last > b.name.last) OR
              ((a.name.last = b.name.last) AND
               (a.name.first > b.name.first)) then
                    Return TRUE;
            else
                    Return FALSE;
            end if;
        End Greater;


    Procedure Insert (InBuf:  RecType) is
        --Insert a record in Index and write to Address File
        p, q, free:  Natural;
        TempBuf:      RecType;
        Begin
            free := GetFree;
            if free = EndList then
                Put_Line ("No room in the file....");
                New_Line;
                Pause;
            else
                PutRec (RandIO.Positive_Count (free), InBuf);
                p := Index(0);            --First record in use
                q := 0;
                loop
                    exit when p = EndList;
                    GetRec (RandIO.Positive_Count (p), TempBuf);
                    exit when NOT (Greater (InBuf, TempBuf));
                    q := p;
                    p := Index(p);
                end loop;
                Index(free) := p;         --Insert into linked list
                Index(q)    := free;
```

Fig. 3-26. Body of the package LISTS.

```
            end if;
     End Insert;

Procedure Append is
     --Add records to the file
     finished:  Boolean;
     Begin
         if Index(-1) = EndList then
             Put ("No room left in the file......");
             Pause;
         else
             loop
                 GetEntry (InBuf, finished);
                 exit when finished;
                 Insert (InBuf);
             end loop;
         end if;
     End Append;

Procedure Review is
     --Review records one at a time on screen.
     --Option to delete current record.
     subtype pos_links is integer range 0..MaxRecords;
     q, r:    pos_links;
     c:       Character;
     Buf:     RecType;
     okay:    Boolean;

     Procedure PutFree (r:  In pos_links) is
         --Put record r in the free list
         Begin
             Index (r)  := Index (-1);
             Index (-1) := r;
         End PutFree;

     Begin
         ClearScreen;
         r := Index (0);        --First record in linked list
         q := 0;
         outer:  loop
             exit outer when r = EndList;
             New_Line;
             PrintRec (Console, RandIO.Positive_Count(r));
             inner:  loop
                 New_Line;
                 Put ("G)et next record, D)elete this record, or Q)uit?  ");
                 Get (c);  Skip_Line;
                 New_Line;
                 case c is
                     when 'G' | 'g' =>   q := r;          --Get next
                                         r := Index (r);
                                         okay := True;
                     when 'D' | 'd' =>   Index (q) := Index (r);
                                         PutFree (r);    --Delete
                                         r := Index (q);
                                         okay := True;
                     when 'Q' | 'q' =>   exit outer;
                     when others    =>   okay := False;
                 end case;
                 exit inner when okay;
             end loop inner;
```

```
                 end loop outer;
        End Review;

    Procedure List (device:  In File_Type) is
        subtype links is integer range -1..MaxRecords;
        i:  links;
        j:  RandIO.Positive_Count;
        Begin
            i := Index (O);           --First record
            while i /= EndList loop
                New_Line (device);
                j := RandIO.Positive_Count(i);
                PrintRec (device, j);
                i := Index (i);
            end loop;
        End List;

    Procedure ListFile is
        --List file to Screen or Printer.
        a:  Character;
        Begin
            ClearScreen;
            GotoXY (5, 5);
            Put ("List to S)creen or P)rinter?  ");
            Get (a);  Skip_Line;
            New_Line;
            Case a is
                when 'S'| 's' =>  List (Console);
                when 'P'| 'p' =>  List (Printer);
                when others   =>  ListFile;          --Try again
            end case;
            Pause;
        End ListFile;

    Procedure DumpFile is
        --Print file and chain of pointers to printer
        --  for analysis.
        Begin
            Put_Line ("Dump file to printer....");
            New_Line;
                Put (Printer, "First Free Record:  ");
                Put (Printer, Index(-1), 1);
                New_Line (Printer);
                Put (Printer, "First Record in Use:  ");
                Put (Printer, Index(O));
                New_Line (Printer);
                for i in 1..MaxRecords loop
                    New_Line (Printer);
                    Put (Printer, "Record ");
                    Put (Printer, i, 1);
                    New_Line (Printer);
                    PrintRec (Printer, RandIO.Positive_Count (i));
                    Put (Printer, "Next Record:  ");
                    Put (Printer, Index(i), 1);
                    New_Line (Printer);
                end loop;

        End DumpFile;

End Lists;
```

Fig. 3-26. Body of the package LISTS. (Continued from page 71.)

```
-- Figure 3-27:    File Definition for the Comprehensive
                   Sample Program.
--                 Define the File Record for Random IO.

Package File_Def is

    Type NameType is record
        last, first:  String(15);
    end record;

    Type RecType is record
        name:         NameType;
        address:      String(20);
        city:         String(15);
        state:        String(2);
        zip:          String(10);
        phone:        String(14);
    end record;

End File_Def;
```

Fig. 3-27. File definition for the comprehensive sample program.

A major strength of the Ada language is the fact that it is backed by the United States Department of Defense (DoD). DoD has dictated that henceforth all embedded computer software developed for it will be developed in Ada. That is powerful economic incentive for software houses to get on the Ada bandwagon. It also means that a strict set of standards for the language will be maintained.

Ada was intended by DoD to facilitate the development of reliable embedded system software. Through Ada's ability to handle asynchronous tasks reliably and its strong type checking, Ada has gone a long way toward achieving that goal. An example of an embedded system developed in Ada might be the flight control software for a high-performance military jet aircraft. If I were a pilot whose life depended on the reliability of the flight control software, I would feel better having it written in Ada than, for example, in assembly language or C.

Another major strength of Ada is its modularity. The ability to construct programs out of separately compiled packages eases the development process and makes for programs that are more structured. The ability to group related procedures into packages is a useful concept (shared by Modula-2). Programs developed modularly tend to be more reliable. Ada's mechanism for making procedures and data elements in one module visible to other program units is too loose, however. One use clause makes the whole package visible. I prefer the Modula-2 method of exporting and importing specific elements of a package.

Ada's greatest strengths—its richness and its rigidity—are also its greatest shortcomings. Ada is overkill for many applications, particularly for small-computer applications. As of 1987, Ada is a language best suited for large applications developed on large computers. My opinion is that microcomputers aren't yet ready for Ada, and neither are the majority of microcomputer hobbyists.

```
Figure 3-28: Structure Chart for the Comprehensive Sample Program
Main Program              (Fig. 3-20)
    OpenFiles             (Fig. 3-22)
        OpenAddr          (Fig. 3-22)
        OpenIndex         (Fig. 3-22)
    PrinterOn             (Fig. 3-8)
    Menu                  (Fig. 3-24)
        NextField         (Fig. 3-24)
    Append                (Fig. 3-26)
        Pause             (Fig. 3-22)
        GetEntry          (Fig. 3-24)
            MarkOff       (Fig. 3-24)
            NextField     (Fig. 3-24)
        Insert            (Fig. 3-26)
            GetFree       (Fig. 3-26)
            PutRec        (Fig. 3-22)
            GetRec        (Fig. 3-22)
            Greater       (Fig. 3-26)
    Review                (Fig. 3-26)
        PrintRec          (Fig. 3-24)
            GetRec        (Fig. 3-22)
        PutFree           (Fig. 3-26)
    ListFile              (Fig. 3-26)
        List              (Fig. 3-26)
            PrintRec      (Fig. 3-24)
                GetRec    (Fig. 3-22)
    DumpFile              (Fig. 3-26)
            PrintRec      (Fig. 3-24)
                GetRec    (Fig. 3-22)
    PrinterOff            (Fig. 3-8)
    CloseFiles            (Fig. 3-22)
```

Fig. 3-28. Structure chart for the comprehensive sample program.

Personally, I found the sheer bulk of Ada to be awkward on a microcomputer, although I would love to have its power on a mainframe. I found the rigidity of its type checking to be extreme. It is frustrating to use data types that you know are identical but have the compiler "zap" you because the two were defined in different places.

In my judgment, Ada will not make a dent in the business data-processing area. The input and output facilities are just too awkward when compared to those of COBOL. In business data processing, most of what is done is input and output. In Ada, input and output are treated as something of a necessary annoyance, tacked onto the language as an afterthought.

A disadvantage that Ada shares with Modula-2 is the presence of procedures with the same names in different libraries. Examples include Get, Put, Open, and Close. The fact that they have the same names makes them harder to keep straight.

AVAILABILITY

Implementations of Ada for microcomputers are available from several companies. Artek has a version for $895. RR Software has three versions, selling for $900 (developer's package), $395 (educational package), and $95 (introductory package). Alsys has an Ada compiler that sells for about $3000, including the required four-megabyte memory expansion board. A new compiler recently announced is called Meridian Ada. A good place to find a source for these and other language compilers for microcomputers is in *Computer Language* magazine, published by CL Publications, Inc., San Francisco.

SUMMARY

Ada is a powerful, full-featured language that can handle nearly any computer programming project. It was designed to the specifications of the U.S. Department of Defense (DoD) as a standard language for the development of embedded computer systems such as a jet-aircraft flight-control system.

Ada is well-suited for its intended purpose. It also has application to many nonembedded computer programming situations, such as systems programming and scientific applications. It is less well-suited to business data processing applications.

The sheer bulk of Ada makes it an unlikely candidate for widespread use on microcomputers. Nevertheless, Ada is a very important language, not only because of its endorsement by DoD, but also because it is a showcase for so many state-of-the-art programming features. It will be interesting to see how many of these features turn out to be important enough to find their way into future languages.

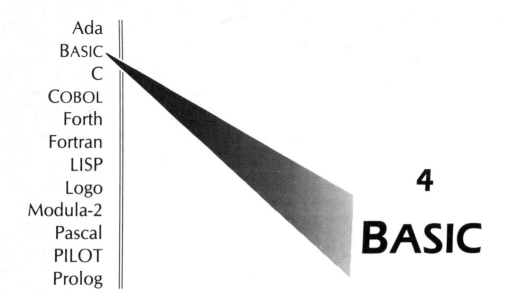

Ada
BASIC
C
COBOL
Forth
Fortran
LISP
Logo
Modula-2
Pascal
PILOT
Prolog

4

BASIC

The name BASIC is an acronym for *Beginner's All-purpose Symbolic Instruction Code*. The language was created in 1965 at Dartmouth College by John Kemeny and Thomas Kurtz. As the name suggests, it was intended as a simplified language, suitable for instructing beginners in computer programming.

BASIC is usually implemented as an interpretive language. This means that the program is translated into machine code a line at a time rather than all at once. The software that does this translation is called a BASIC *interpreter*. Interpreted languages are usually easier to use interactively than compiled languages, but the resulting programs usually run more slowly.

In the early days of microcomputers (before 1976), there were very few high-level languages available that would fit in the limited memory then available in microcomputers. Intel had a language called PL/M (written by Gary Kildall), but it was mostly suitable for systems programming. Gordon Eubanks had written the forerunner of a compiled version of BASIC, called CBASIC, as a masters' thesis project at the Naval Postgraduate School in Monterey. CBASIC later proved popular for business applications, but PL/M never really caught on for general use.

Because BASIC is a relatively simple language, it turned out to be possible to write a BASIC interpreter that occupied a very small amount of memory. This made BASIC an ideal candidate for use in microcomputers.

In 1976, William Gates and Paul Allen wrote a BASIC interpreter for the Altair microcomputer. Finally there was a high-level microcomputer language for the masses. With their BASIC interpreter as the foundation, Gates and Allen founded Microsoft, Inc., which is today a leading microcomputer software house. Since then, their original BA-

SIC interpreter has evolved into various versions known collectively as Microsoft BA-SIC. Microsoft BASIC and its various derivatives (including Applesoft BASIC, IBM PC BASIC, and GW-BASIC) have become the most widely used versions of BASIC in the marketplace.

Today, BASIC is by far the most popular high-level language in use on microcomputers. Many microcomputers, such as Apple, Tandy, and Commodore products, are sold with a BASIC interpreter in read-only memory (ROM). The IBM PC comes with BASIC partially in ROM and partially on disk. BASIC is also sold on disk for various computers, including those that run the MS-DOS and CP/M operating systems. Disk-based BASIC interpreters are usually more powerful than ROM-based BASIC interpreters.

Unfortunately, the various versions of BASIC available for microcomputers do not adhere to a common standard. The examples in this chapter were tested using Microsoft GW-BASIC Version 2, running under the MS-DOS operating system on a Zenith Z-150 microcomputer.

PROGRAM STRUCTURE

A BASIC program is simply a sequence of program statements. Each line of the program begins with a line number. A simple BASIC program that does nothing but print ''This is a test'' is shown in Fig. 4-1.

Line 10 of the program is a remark, or REM. It serves merely as a comment, used in this case to identify the program. Line 20 is present only for appearance. Line 30 does the actual printing, and line 40 stops the program—pretty simple.

Statements in BASIC usually occur one per line. Most versions of BASIC permit more than one statement per line, provided that the statements are separated by a special character, usually a colon (:). The default sequence of execution of a BASIC program is in order of increasing line numbers, regardless of the order in which the lines appear.

Some versions of BASIC permit remarks to occur on a line after the single quote symbol.

DATA REPRESENTATION

The more complete versions of BASIC support real, integer, double precision, and character-string data types. Some versions lack either the real or the integer type, and many versions lack the double-precision type.

Variables

Variable types in BASIC are usually distinguished by the last character of the variable name. If the last character of the variable name is a percent sign (%), then the variable

```
10   REM   Figure 4-1:   BASIC Test Program
20   REM
30   PRINT "This is a test."
40   END
```

Fig. 4-1. BASIC test program.

is an integer. If it is a dollar sign ($), the variable is a character string. If it is a pound sign (#), the variable is double precision. If it is an exclamation point (!) or anything else, the variable is assumed to be real.

Some versions of BASIC allow the default type of variables to be changed depending on the first letter of the variable name. For example, consider the following:

    10   DEFINT I

In a program, this would cause all variables beginning with the letter I to have a default type of integer in that program.

BASIC variables are initialized automatically to zero in the case of numeric variables and to the empty string in the case of character strings.

Constants

Numeric constants in a BASIC program can also have a specific type if they are followed by one of the symbols explained above, (%, #, or !). Character strings are surrounded by double quotation marks.

Although there is usually no explicit Boolean or logical type in BASIC, the value 0 usually means false, and the value −1 means true in the appropriate context. This is discussed in more detail in the section on logical expressions.

THE ASSIGNMENT STATEMENT

The assignment operator in BASIC is the equals sign (=). In the original version of BASIC, all assignment statements had to begin with the keyword LET, as in

    20   LET X = 5

In most versions of BASIC today, the LET keyword is optional and the following statement.

    20   X = 5

will accomplish the same thing.

BASIC freely allows assignment between the various numeric-variable types. The value of the expression on the right side of the assignment statement is automatically converted to the type of the variable on the left side before the assignment takes place. Common sense is the guide.

ARITHMETIC EXPRESSIONS

BASIC uses conventional infix notation (see Chapter 2) for its arithmetic expressions. The arithmetic operators are the usual symbols (+, −, *, and /) except for the symbol for exponentiation, which is the up-arrow or carat (^). Parentheses have the usual meaning.

LOGICAL EXPRESSIONS

BASIC uses the usual logical operators as listed in Chapter 2; for example, $<$ and OR. Logical expressions normally evaluate to the logical values true or false, but BASIC has no explicit logical values. Logical values in BASIC are represented by numerical values. The value 0 usually represents false and the value -1 represents true, although this convention can vary between versions of BASIC. The following logical expression

5 > 2

thus evaluates to -1.

INPUT AND OUTPUT

The **PRINT** statement of Fig. 4-1 outputs to the system console. To output to the system printer, the **LPRINT** statement is used instead. Figure 4-2 is a simple example of the use of the **LPRINT** statement. (Applesoft BASIC and several other forms of BASIC used on microcomputers do not have **LPRINT** statements. Users of these systems are referred to their BASIC manuals for instructions on using a printer.)

Whether or not a **PRINT** or **LPRINT** statement causes a carriage return and line feed to be appended to the output is determined by the punctuation used. The following statement

10   PRINT "Hello"

sends a carriage return and line feed to the screen. The statement below

10   PRINT "Hello";

does not. The difference is the semicolon at the end. The semicolon suppresses the carriage return and line feed.

Consider the following statement:

10   PRINT "Hello","Hello","Hello"

If repeated several times, it would print in three columns. The comma between items

```
10   REM   Figure 4-2:   Test Printer Output
15   REM
20   PRINT "This goes to the video screen."
30   LPRINT "This goes to the printer."
40   END
```

Fig. 4-2. Test printer output.

in the print list causes printing to continue in the next column. The width of each column depends on the implementation.

The LPRINT statement responds to punctuation in the same way as the PRINT statement.

The PRINT and LPRINT statements do not give the user very much control over the appearance of the output. For example, they do not allow the user to control the number of decimal places to be printed for real numbers. The better versions of BASIC, therefore, provide the PRINT USING and LPRINT USING statements. The LPRINT USING statement is equivalent to the PRINT USING statement except that it directs its output to the printer, so only the PRINT USING statement will be described.

The PRINT USING statement uses a character string enclosed in quotation marks to control the appearance of the output. For example, this statement:

```
10   X = 1/3
20   PRINT USING "##.###"; X
```

would print 0.333 on the screen. The pound symbol represents a numerical digit. The character string "##.###" means that the number is to be printed in a field six spaces wide (including the decimal point), and that three digits are to be printed to the right of the decimal point.

If X had the value 172.95, the printed result would have been %172.95. The percent sign in front of the number means that the number is too large to fit in the allotted number of spaces. (In this case, only two spaces were allotted to the left of the decimal point.)

The PRINT USING statement can use various other symbols in the character string to specify such things as a leading dollar sign, plus or minus signs, and so on.

Data is read from the keyboard by the INPUT statement. The INPUT statement also allows the programmer to specify a prompt message to be printed on the screen to tell the user when to enter data and what to enter. For example, the following statement:

```
10   INPUT "What is your name"; NAME$
```

would print What is your name? on the screen, then wait for the user to enter his or her name. The name would be stored in the string variable NAME$.

The question mark is automatically added when the prompt is followed by a semicolon, as above. If the prompt is instead followed by a comma, no question mark is printed.

The prompt is optional in the INPUT statement. The INPUT statement can also be used to enter more than one item, separated by commas. For example, the statement

```
10   INPUT X, Y, Z
```

would expect three numbers to be typed at the keyboard, separated by commas. If too many or too few items are entered, BASIC will respond with a message such as ?Redo from start. Because it is rather awkward to keep track of how many items to enter per line, it is usually better to ask for only one item per INPUT statement.

The program in Fig. 4-3 emulates an electronic typewriter, reading input from the keyboard and printing it on the system printer. It is included here to demonstrate the use of the INPUT statement and the LPRINT statement.

A useful feature of the INPUT statement is that it allows mistakes in the input to be corrected after they are typed (but before the Return key is pressed), using the backspace key.

This program has one major deficiency: it won't accept text with commas, unless the text is enclosed in quotation marks. That is because of the way the INPUT statement separates multiple input items, as discussed above. If a comma is entered in an unquoted line of text, the message ?Redo from start results.

Because BASIC lacks the REPEAT-UNTIL construct described in Chapter 2, a conditional GOTO was used in line 100 to emulate the REPEAT-UNTIL construct. The IF and GOTO statements are discussed in more detail below.

To get around the problem of not being able to enter text containing commas, the INPUT$ statement can be used. The INPUT$ statement reads data from the keyboard a character at a time. Version 2 of the Electronic Typewriter program makes use of this feature and is shown in Fig. 4-4.

Notice that in line 80 of the program, the INPUT$ is followed by a PRINT. If there were no PRINT, you would not be able to see what you were typing.

Notice that in Fig. 4-4, a character is sent to the printer before the next character is read. This implies that if the user types a character in error and tries to backspace over it to correct it, the error will have already gone to the printer. Thus, both the incorrect and the correct characters are sent to the printer.

Each program uses the backslash character (\) as a sentinel, to indicate the end of input. In the program of Fig. 4-3, the sentinel character must be entered as the first character of a line. In the program of Fig. 4-4 it can be anywhere in the input line.

Neither of these programs is complete enough to be very useful, but they do illustrate the behavior of the INPUT and INPUT$ statements. The interested user is encouraged to refine these programs to correct their deficiencies.

BASIC has a READ statement, but it differs from the READ statement of most other languages. For each READ statement, there must be a DATA statement in the program,

```
10   REM   Figure 4-3:   Emulate an Electronic Typewriter
20   REM
30   PRINT "Welcome to your Electronic Typewriter."
40   PRINT
50   PRINT "Enter your text, followed by a '\' in column 1."
60   PRINT
70   INPUT L$
80   LPRINT L$
90   INPUT L$
100  IF LEFT$(L$,1) <> "\" THEN GOTO 80
110  END
```

Fig. 4-3. Electronic Typewriter.

```
10   REM   Figure 4-4:   Emulate an Electronic Typewriter, Version 2
20   REM
30   REM
40   PRINT "Welcome to your Electronic Typewriter."
50   PRINT
60   PRINT "Enter your text, followed by a '\'."
70   PRINT
80   L$ = INPUT$(1):   PRINT L$;
90   IF L$ = "\" THEN GOTO 120
100  LPRINT L$;
110  GOTO 80
120  END
```

Fig. 4-4. Electronic Typewriter, Version 2.

and the **READ** statement takes its input from the **DATA** statement. For example,

```
10   DATA 3.14159, 2.71828
20   READ PI, E
```

would have the same effect as

```
10   PI = 3.14159
20   E = 2.71728.
```

CONTROL STRUCTURES

BASIC is a relatively simple language, having relatively few control structures. Some versions of BASIC have been extended to include such features as an **ELSE** clause in the **IF** statement and a **WHILE** statement. Other versions lack these features. The user who wishes to use the more complex control structures is often forced to emulate them using simpler control structures such as the **IF** statement and the **GOTO** statement.

Simple Selection: The IF Statement

The simplest forms of BASIC allow only IF statements of the following form:

```
40   IF X > 2 THEN 100.
```

If the condition is true, the next statement to be executed is statement number 100. Extensions to this form include the following:

```
50   IF X > 2 GOTO 100
60   IF X = 2 THEN GOTO 200
70   IF X < 2 THEN X = 2: GOTO 300.
```

Statements 50 and 60 do exactly the same thing as statement 40. The **THEN** introduced in statement 60 allows a statement to follow, which in this case happens to be a GOTO statement. In statement 70, two statements follow the THEN (an assignment statement and a GOTO statement) separated by a colon. If the condition is true, both of these statements will be executed; otherwise neither will be executed, and control will pass to the next statement after statement 70.

The next logical extension to the IF statement is the ELSE clause. In the IF-THEN-ELSE construct, either the statement (or statements separated by colons) following the THEN or the statement (or statements) following the ELSE are executed, depending on whether the condition is true or false. Then control is passed to the next statement in sequence. Under no conditions are both the THEN and the ELSE statements executed.

Here is a simple example:

```
80   IF DENOM = 0 THEN PRINT
     "Error—Division by Zero"
     ELSE PRINT NUM/DENOM
```

This statement prints out an error message if the proposed denominator is zero; otherwise it prints out the result of the division.

A drawback of the IF-THEN-ELSE construct in many implementations of BASIC on microcomputers is that the statements following THEN and ELSE cannot be indented so as to visually show the structure of the statement. This deficiency is even more of a problem with nested IF statements such as the following:

```
90   IF HOURS < = 40 THEN PAY = HOURS
     * RATE ELSE IF HOURS < = 50 THEN PAY
     = 40 * RATE + (HOURS – 40) * RATE * 1.5
     ELSE PAY = 40 * RATE + 10 * RATE * 1.5
     + (HOURS – 50) * RATE * 2.
```

The meaning of this statement can be ascertained after studying it carefully, but it is not immediately obvious. The ability to indent freely, as shown in Chapter 2, would allow BASIC programs to be made more readable.

Loops

The simpler forms of BASIC provide only one form of loop construct, the simple counted loop (the FOR statement). Many versions of BASIC also provide the WHILE statement, a form of conditional loop.

Counted Loops: The FOR Statement. The FOR statement of BASIC was described in Chapter 2 as an example of counted loops in general. An example was given there, so the FOR statement will not be discussed further here.

Conditional Loops: The WHILE Statement. The WHILE statement of BASIC was also described in Chapter 2 and two examples were given there. Note, however, that not all versions of BASIC include a WHILE statement.

Recall that a WHILE loop tests its condition at the top of the loop. The conditional loop that tests its condition at the bottom of the loop is called the REPEAT-UNTIL loop. Very few versions of BASIC include a REPEAT-UNTIL loop.

The GOSUB Statement

The closest that BASIC comes to allowing the use of subroutines or procedures is the GOSUB statement. Like a subroutine or procedure call, the GOSUB statement transfers control to another part of the program and enables it to return, but the GOSUB statement allows no parameters. All variables in a BASIC program are *global*, which means that they can be accessed from any place in the program. It also means that subroutines can have no local variables not accessible from elsewhere in the program.

To illustrate the disadvantage of not being able to use parameters in a subroutine, suppose that a subroutine is needed to sort an array. Suppose the subroutine calls that array X. Somewhere else in the program a subroutine is needed to sort the array Y. Because there is no way to pass parameters directly, the array Y must be copied into the array X, the sort subroutine called, then the resulting array copied back into array Y.

Figure 4-5 contains a simple BASIC program that uses a GOSUB statement. The purpose of the subroutine is to check the range of variables to be sure they are between 0 and 100. Variables less than zero are set to zero and variables greater than 100 are set to 100. The subroutine expects the variable to be checked to be named T. In order to check the variables X and Y, each is copied to T before the GOSUB and copied back from T afterward.

The GOSUB statement refers to the subroutine by the line number at which the subroutine begins, not by name. In this case, line 1000 is a REM (remark) that identifies

```
10    REM    Figure 4-5:    Demonstrate A Simple Subroutine
20    REM
30    REM
40    MIN = 0
50    MAX = 100
60    INPUT "Type a number between 0 and 100"; X
70    T = X                    'COPY
80    GOSUB 1000               'VERIFY RANGE
90    X = T                    'RECOPY
100   INPUT "Type another number between 0 and 100"; Y
110   T = Y                    'COPY
120   GOSUB 1000               'VERIFY RANGE
130   Y = T                    'RECOPY
140   PRINT                    'SKIP A LINE
150   PRINT "The two numbers are "; X; " and "; Y
160   END
170   REM
1000  REM    Subroutine to verify that T >= MIN and T <= MAX
1010  REM
1020  IF T < MIN THEN T = MIN ELSE IF T > MAX THEN T = MAX
1030  RETURN
```

Fig. 4-5. A simple subroutine.

the purpose of the subroutine. It is good practice to identify subroutines in this manner; otherwise it is not always obvious just where a subroutine begins and what it does.

Note that the main program ends at line 160. The **END** at line 160 is important; otherwise execution would "fall through" to the subroutine at the completion of the main program. The subroutine begins at line 1000 and ends at line 1030. Subroutines are always terminated by a **RETURN** statement, which returns control to the main program upon completion of the subroutine.

In this instance the amount of computation performed by the subroutine is small, and there is little obvious gain in doing this computation in a subroutine rather than "in line" in the main program. There is some gain in clarity, however. When the reader encounters the statement

    100   GOSUB 1000   'VERIFY RANGE

in a program, it is obvious that it is a call to a subroutine to check the range of the variable. The reader can then go on, concentrating on the main logic of the program. If the reader had instead encountered this statement:

    100   IF T<MIN THEN T=MIN ELSE IF
    T>MAX THEN T=MAX

there would be cause to stop and try to figure out first what that statement does, and second, how it fits into the main scheme of processing. There is a definite advantage to suppressing detail to subroutines.

Functions

The rules for using functions in BASIC are very different from those for using subroutines. First, a function must be defined before it is invoked; a subroutine can be defined anywhere in a program. Second, in most versions of BASIC a function is limited to one statement in length; a subroutine can be of any length. Third, a function is invoked by writing its name in an expression; a subroutine is invoked with a **GOSUB** statement. Fourth, a function may have parameters; a subroutine must rely on global variables.

The following is a simple BASIC function that computes the area of a circle of radius R:

    10   DEF FN AREA (R) = 3.14159 * R^2

The name of the function is **AREA**. Its parameter is R. The R in the function definition is independent of any other variable of the same or different name elsewhere in the program.

The function is invoked by writing its name together with a value for R in an expression, as in the following:

    50   PRINT FN AREA (4)
    60   PRINT FN AREA (6).

Statement 50 above will print the area of a circle with a radius of 4. Statement 60 will print the area of a circle with a radius of 6.

BASIC functions are sometimes useful in programs involving arithmetic computations, but in general, functions in BASIC are less useful than functions in other languages because of the limitations imposed on the use of functions in BASIC (as discussed above).

Recursion

BASIC does not officially support recursion, that is, a function or subroutine cannot invoke itself. Some implementations of BASIC, however, do support a limited degree of recursion, but recursion in BASIC is not dependable and therefore should be studiously avoided.

The ON . . . GOSUB Statement

BASIC does not have a CASE statement. (See Chapter 2 for a discussion of the CASE statement.) There are two statements in BASIC, however, that can be used to emulate the CASE statement. One is the ON . . . GOSUB statement. The other is the ON . . . GOTO statement, which is discussed later in this chapter.

The ON . . . GOSUB statement allows selection of exactly one subroutine out of several for execution. A simple illustration follows:

```
100   ON I GOSUB 1000, 2000, 3000, 4000, 5000
110   END
```

The numbers 1000, 2000, 3000, 4000, and 5000 are the line numbers of subroutines elsewhere in the program. The variable I is assumed to be an integer between 1 and 5 in this case, because exactly five subroutine line numbers are listed.

If I has the value 1, the subroutine at line 1000 will be executed because it is number 1 in the list of line numbers following the word GOSUB. If I has the value 2, the subroutine at line 2000 will be executed because it is number 2 in the list of line numbers, and so on. In any case, following execution of the appropriate subroutine, control will pass to line 110, which will end the program.

One common use of the ON . . . GOSUB statement is in interactive programs in which the user is given a menu of possible actions and must choose one. The program should check to be sure that the choice selected is within the appropriate range for the ON . . . GOSUB statement.

Figure 4-6 illustrates another use of the ON . . . GOSUB statement in a simple program that computes the number of days in a month.

Notice that in the program in Fig. 4-6 there are three subroutines. The subroutine at line 100 handles 31-day months, the subroutine at line 200 handles 30-day months, and the subroutine at line 300 handles February. The variable MONTH is read from the keyboard in line 30. Line 40 ensures that MONTH is between 1 and 12. The ON . . . GOSUB statement in line 50 calls the appropriate subroutine to print out the number of days in that month and returns control to line 60.

The logic of the program depends on the order of the line numbers in the ON . . . GOSUB statement. Suppose MONTH is 1 (January). The first line number in the list is line 100, so the program does a GOSUB 100. The subroutine at line 100 handles

```
10   REM   Figure 4-6:   The Calendar Program
20   REM
30   INPUT "ENTER THE MONTH (1..12):   ", MONTH
40   IF MONTH < 1 OR MONTH > 12 THEN GOTO 30
50   ON MONTH GOSUB 100, 300, 100, 200, 100, 200, 100, 100, 200, 100, 200, 100
60   PRINT "MONTH  ";MONTH;" HAS ";DAYS;" DAYS"
70   END
100 REM   SUBROUTINE FOR 31 DAY MONTHS
110 DAYS = 31
120 RETURN
130 REM
200 REM   SUBROUTINE FOR 30 DAY MONTHS
210 DAYS = 30
220 RETURN
230 REM
300 REM   SUBROUTINE FOR FEBRUARY
310 INPUT "ENTER THE YEAR:   ", YEAR
320 IF (YEAR MOD 4 = 0) THEN DAYS = 29 ELSE DAYS = 28
330 RETURN
```

Fig. 4-6. The Calendar Program.

31-day months, which is correct in this case. Suppose MONTH is 9 (September). The ninth line number in the list is 200, so the program does a GOSUB 200. The subroutine at line 200 handles 30-day months, which is again correct. The reader should verify that the program produces correct results in every case.

When month 2 (February) is selected, additional logic is required to determine whether the year is a leap year. The necessary logic is in line 320.

The GOTO Statement

The GOTO statement transfers the flow of execution to a specified location in the program. That specified location can be anywhere in the program. The form of the statement is as follows:

```
100   GOTO 250.
```

Following line 100, the next line to be executed will be line 250.

Unrestricted use of the GOTO statement in BASIC programs can result in programs that are difficult to read, difficult to understand, difficult to debug, and difficult to modify. The GOTO statement is often useful, however, as a means of emulating control statements not provided by BASIC. Some versions of BASIC, for example, do not provide a WHILE statement.

In Chapter 2 the WHILE statement was illustrated with a short program segment that reads and sums positive numbers, stopping when a negative number or zero is input. Here is the same program segment using a GOTO statement to emulate the WHILE statement:

```
10     SUM = 0
20     INPUT "ENTER X: "; X
```

```
25      REM Emulate WHILE loop
30      IF X < = 0 THEN GOTO 70
40      SUM = SUM + X
50      INPUT "ENTER X:"; X
60      GOTO 30
70      PRINT "SUM = "; SUM
80      END
```

In a similar manner, the REPEAT . . . UNTIL control structure can be emulated. Note the REM in line 25, which indicates that a WHILE loop is being emulated. This makes it obvious what is being done. In the absence of remarks, the purpose of a GOTO statement is not always obvious.

The ON . . . GOTO Statement

The ON . . . GOTO statement is much like the ON . . . GOSUB statement. The difference is that a GOTO rather than a GOSUB is performed to the appropriate line. In general, the ON . . . GOSUB statement is to be preferred to the ON . . . GOTO statement because with the former, the flow of the program must eventually return to the statement which follows. With the ON . . . GOTO, what will happen to program flow in the long run is not obvious.

DATA STRUCTURES

BASIC is rather limited in its support of data structures. The array is the only data structure directly supported. More complex data structures such as records must be simulated.

Arrays

Arrays in BASIC are declared using the DIM statement. The following statement declares a one-dimensional array named A:

```
10   DIM A(50)
```

In this case the array A has one subscript (i.e., it is one-dimensional), and that subscript can take on values from zero to 50. (Note that the lower bound is zero, not one.)

BASIC allows simple variables and arrays to have the same name. Thus, following the above declaration, you could refer to a nonsubscripted variable named A and to the array named A. BASIC would not confuse the two. *You* might, however.

Not all arrays need be declared in BASIC. Most versions of BASIC allow arrays to be used without being declared in a DIM statement, provided that the value of the subscript does not exceed 10. It is better form, however, to declare all arrays.

Arrays in BASIC can have more than one subscript; that is, be more than one-dimensional. An example is the following array, which has two subscripts:

```
20   DIM TABLE(5,10)
```

The array **TABLE** represents a two-dimensional table. The number of subscripts permitted in BASIC seems to vary from implementation to implementation. Applesoft BASIC claims to permit up to 88 subscripts. GW-BASIC, which is very similar to IBM PC BASIC, claims to support 255 dimensions, which is more than enough. When using more than two or three subscripts, memory availability can quickly become a problem on microcomputers.

Records

Records must be simulated in BASIC. This is usually done using parallel arrays. To see how this is done, consider an example.

In Chapter 2, I discussed a record containing a student's name and his or her scores on up to 20 tests. Suppose that there may be up to 30 students in the class. This scheme can be implemented in BASIC by using two arrays, a one-dimensional array of strings to contain the names and a two-dimensional array of real numbers to contain the scores. Their declarations in a BASIC program would look as follows:

```
10   DIM NAME$(30)
20   DIM SCORE(30,20)
```

Line 10 declares an array of 30 strings, one to contain the name of each student. Line 20 declares a two-dimensional array of 30 rows by 20 columns; each element of this array is a real number.

Each row of the array **SCORE** has an implicit relationship to an element of the array **NAME$**. The scores in row 10 of **SCORE**, for example, belong to the student whose name is in element 10 of the array **NAME$**, and so on. The arrays **NAME$** and **SCORE** are called parallel arrays. The tenth element of **NAME$** and the tenth row of **SCORE** together constitute one record.

Suppose that the name of student number 10 is John Jones, and that he scored 88 points on the fourth test of the period. Then **NAME$(10)** would have the value "John Jones" and **SCORE(10,4)** would have the value 88. To print these values, the following statement could be used:

```
100   PRINT NAME$(10), SCORE(10,4)
```

To print the scores on the fourth test for each of the students, the following could be used:

```
200   FOR I = 1 TO 30
210      PRINT NAME$(I), SCORE(I,4)
220   NEXT I
```

Linked Lists

BASIC arrays can also be used to simulate other advanced data structures such as linked lists, following the methodology outlined in Chapter 2.

In Chapter 2 the variable **FIRST** was used to point to the first record in the list, and the value 0 was used to indicate the end of the list. In BASIC, element 0 of the link array is available to point to the first record of the list, so the value −1 is used to indicate the end of the list. The value −1 of course cannot point to an actual array element.

Here are the initializations necessary to set up in BASIC the linked list described in Chapter 2, with modifications as described in the preceding paragraph:

```
10    EL = −1
20    REM End List marker
30    LL = 5
40    REM List Length
50    DIM NAME$(LL)
60    DIM LINK(LL)
70    REM LINK(0) points to the first
80    REM name in the linked list
90    FREE = 1
100   REM First Free element in list
110   LINK(0) = EL
120   REM List is initially empty
130   REM Now initialize free list
140   FOR I = 1 TO LL−1
150       LINK(I) = I + 1
160   NEXT I
170   LINK(LL) = EL
```

The comprehensive sample program at the end of the chapter shows the use of linked lists in an actual program. The algorithms for adding and deleting from linked lists are illustrated in that program.

FILE HANDLING

The use of statements that read from and write to disk files varies from one version of BASIC to another. The particular version discussed here is GW-BASIC. This version runs under the MS-DOS operating system and is very similar to the version of BASIC that comes with the IBM Personal Computer. Users of other versions of BASIC should consult their reference manuals for differences from the details given here. The concepts are the same.

File Records

A file in BASIC may be thought of as a sequence of records stored on disk. A record may be thought of as a set of related data items, such as the name and address of an individual.

Files in BASIC may be set up for sequential access or for direct (random) access. Direct-access files can also be accessed sequentially, but sequential-access files cannot be accessed directly. How file records are defined and manipulated varies between the two types of files in BASIC, so these topics will be covered in the appropriate section below.

Sequential Files

A file is called sequential if its records can be accessed only in sequence from beginning to end. Thus the second record of a sequential file can be accessed only after the first record. The file can be traversed only in the forward direction.

Figure 4-7 illustrates the use of a sequential file to store a list of names and ages on disk. The program prompts the user to enter the data from the keyboard, stores it on disk, and then reads it back and displays it on the video screen.

In line 40 of the program in Fig. 4-7, the O shows that the file is being opened for output (writing to the disk). The #1 is a reference number used within the program to indicate which file is being referenced. If another file were opened, it would be referred to as #2. AGES.TXT is the name to be given to the file. It will appear in the directory of the disk.

Line 90 writes a record to the file. Each record will be separated by a carriage return and line feed. In this case, each record will consist of a name and the corresponding age. Because they are both character strings, they will be written to the file surrounded by quotation marks.

The file is closed by line 110 after the user has finished entering names and ages. The file is reopened in line 130. The I means that it is to be opened for input (reading from the disk). When a sequential file is opened for input, the first record of the file read in will be the first record of the file. If the file were a tape, one would say that

```
10   REM   Figure 4-7:   Sequential File Illustration
15   REM
20   REM   Store a list of names & ages.
30   REM
40   OPEN "O", #1, "AGES.TXT":   REM Open file for output
50   PRINT "ENTER NAMES AND AGES; AGE 0 TO QUIT."
60   PRINT
70   INPUT "NAME:   ", N$
80   INPUT "AGE:    ", A$
90   WRITE #1, N$, A$:            REM Write to disk file
100  IF A$ <> "0" THEN GOTO 60
110  CLOSE #1
120  REM Now read the file back in and display the records.
130  OPEN "I", #1, "AGES.TXT":   REM Open file for input
140  PRINT:  PRINT
150  INPUT #1, N$, A$
160  IF A$ <> "0" THEN PRINT N$, A$: GOTO 150
170  CLOSE #1
180  PRINT
190  PRINT "All done..."
200  END
```

Fig. 4-7. Sequential file illustration.

the process of closing it (line 110) and reopening it (line 130), had caused the file to be "rewound" to its beginning.

Line 150 reads one record from the file. Line 170 closes the file after all records have been read from the disk and printed on the video screen.

In this context you should note that if an already-existing sequential file is opened for output, it is initially positioned at the first record of that file. Any write commands would overlay the previous contents of the file unless preventive action were taken. The usual procedure for avoiding this problem when adding data to a sequential file is as follows:

1. Open AGES.TXT for input (the I mode).
2. Open a second file (#2) called TEMP.TXT for output (the O mode).
3. Sequentially read in each record from AGES.TXT and write it to TEMP.TXT, thus coping the file.
4. Close AGES.TXT and delete it (the KILL command in GW-BASIC).
5. Add the new data to TEMP.TXT.
6. Rename TEMP.TXT as AGES.TXT using the BASIC NAME command.
7. Close the file.

Direct-Access Files

Recall that with sequential access, the records of a file must be accessed in sequence from beginning to end. It is often convenient to be able to directly access a particular record independently of all other records. As an example, the user may need the 99th record of a 100-record file. With a sequential file, the first 98 records would have to be read first; with a direct-access file, the 99th record could be read directly without any other records being read first.

The use of direct-access files is more complicated than the use of sequential files and requires learning several additional BASIC statements. These include the FIELD statement, the GET statement, the PUT statement, and the LSET statement. You must also learn several new BASIC functions including the MKI$, MKS$, MKD$, CVI, CVS, and CVD functions.

The program in Fig. 4-8 illustrates the use of a direct-access file to store a list of names and ages. The program stores the records on disk in the order in which they are entered from the keyboard, but it permits the records to be retrieved in any order.

Line 50 shows how the file is opened for direct access. The R (for Random) indicates the access mode. The 24 is the length of each record in bytes or characters. Unlike the records of sequential files, the records of direct-access files must all be of the same length. Note that a file opened in the R mode is available for either input or output.

The FIELD statement in line 60 defines the fields or components of the record. In this case there are two fields, F1$ and F2$. Note that both are and must be character strings. Twenty bytes are allocated for F1$ and four for F2$; the total is 24, which matches the record length in the OPEN statement. These two fields together comprise what is known as the *file buffer*. All input to and output from the file must move through this buffer.

The LSET statement is used to move data into the file buffer. In the case of line 140, the move is straightforward; LSET left-justifies the string N$ and pads it with blanks or truncates it, as appropriate, and moves it to F1$. In line 150, the MKS$ function

```
10 REM     Figure 4-8:  Direct-Access File Illustration
20 REM
30 REM     Store a list of names & ages.
40 REM
50 OPEN "R", #1, "DIRECT.TXT", 24
60 FIELD #1, 20 AS F1$, 4 AS F2$
70 RECNR = O
80 PRINT "ENTER NAMES AND AGES; AGE O TO QUIT."
90 PRINT
100       RECNR = RECNR + 1
110       INPUT "NAME:  ", N$
120       INPUT "AGE:   ", A
130       REM Move data into file buffer
140       LSET F1$ = N$
150       LSET F2$ = MKS$(A)
160       REM Now write to disk file
170       PUT #1, RECNR
180 IF A <> O THEN GOTO 90
190 REM
200 REM Now allow selective recall of records
210 PRINT
220 PRINT "YOU WILL NOW BE ABLE TO DISPLAY RECORDS IN ANY ORDER."
230 PRINT
240 PRINT "RECORD NUMBER MUST BE BETWEEN 1 AND "; RECNR; "."
250 PRINT "RECORD NUMBER = O CAUSES PROGRAM TO STOP."
260 PRINT
270 INPUT "RECORD NUMBER"; R
280     IF R < 1 THEN GOTO 390
290     IF R > RECNR THEN GOTO 270
300     REM Now get record R and fill buffer
310     GET #1, R
320     REM Now move from buffer into working variables
330     N$ = F1$
340     A  = CVS(F2$):  REM Convert from string to numeric
350     PRINT
360     PRINT N$, A
370     PRINT
380 GOTO 270
390 CLOSE #1
400 PRINT
410 PRINT "All done..."
420 END
```

Fig. 4-8. Direct-access file illustration.

must be used to convert the single-precision variable A to a string before it is moved to F2$ with the LSET statement.

Once the buffer has been filled, it is written to the file with the PUT statement, as shown in line 170. The #1 in line 170 relates to the #1 in the OPEN and FIELD statements. The variable RECNR is the record number of the file into which the contents of the buffer is to be placed.

Conversely, the contents of a record are read into the buffer by the GET statement, as shown in line 310. The variable R in line 310 indicates the number of the record that is to be read. The contents of the buffer are moved into other program variables in lines 330 and 340. In line 340, F2$ is converted back into single precision using the CVS function. Note that the records can be read in any order.

The file is closed in line 390, in the same way that a sequential file is closed. Note that the difficulties encountered in updating an already-existing sequential file do not arise with direct-access files, because the program can begin writing anywhere in the file.

The comprehensive sample program at the end of the chapter also illustrates the use of direct-access files.

GRAPHICS

Several versions of BASIC on microcomputers offer graphics. Unfortunately, there is little in common among implementations. Each graphics package is designed for a particular hardware configuration. As an example, the graphics commands of Applesoft BASIC are very different from those of IBM PC BASIC. For that reason, the graphics capabilities of the BASIC language will not be discussed further in this book.

THE COMPREHENSIVE SAMPLE PROGRAM

The purpose of the comprehensive sample program is to tie together in one program examples of the various BASIC constructs. In addition, it illustrates how a larger program ought to be organized. The previous programs in the chapter have been of such a size that the overall organization of the program has not mattered much. With larger programs, proper organization is essential.

The comprehensive sample program is shown in Fig. 4-9. The purpose of the program is to establish and maintain a file of names and addresses. The program provides the capability of adding and deleting records from the file and of listing the file on the video screen or on a printer. The file is always maintained in alphabetical order by name. It is never explicitly sorted, however; sorting is unnecessary because of the way the file is organized.

```
010 REM   Figure 4-9:   Comprehensive Sample Program
020 REM
100 REM   ***************************************************************
110 REM   ***                                                        ***
120 REM   ***   PROGRAM ADDRESS FILE                                 ***
130 REM   ***                                                        ***
140 REM   ***      Create and maintain a file of names and          ***
150 REM   ***      addresses.  The file is maintained in            ***
160 REM   ***      alphabetical order at all times, using an        ***
170 REM   ***      index of pointers.  The index is maintained      ***
180 REM   ***      as a linked list.  A linked list of vacant       ***
190 REM   ***      records called the "free list" is also           ***
200 REM   ***      maintained.                                       ***
210 REM   ***                                                        ***
220 REM   ***                                                        ***
230 REM   ***                                                        ***
240 REM   ***************************************************************
```

Fig. 4-9. Comprehensive sample program.

```
250 REM
260 MAXREC = 10                      :REM  FILE CAPACITY; MODIFY AS REQUIRED
270 FILEA$ = "ADDRESS.TXT"           :REM  FILE NAME
280 FILEI$ = "INDEX.TXT"             :REM  INDEX FILE NAME
290 ENDLIST = 0                      :REM  SENTINEL
300 DIM INDEX(MAXREC)
305 COLOR 6,0                        :REM  SET SCREEN COLORS
310 REM
320 REM            ***    MAIN PROGRAM    ***
330 REM
340 GOSUB 10000                      :REM OPEN FILES
350 GOSUB 12000                      :REM DISPLAY MENU
360 IF C = 5 THEN GOTO 400
370 ON C GOSUB 14000, 19000, 21000, 23000
380 REM APPEND, REVIEW, LIST FILE, OR DUMP FILE
390 GOTO 350
400 GOSUB 13000                      :REM CLOSE FILES
410 END
420 REM
9970 REM
9980 REM           ***       SUBROUTINES      ***
9990 REM
10000 REM          ***       OPEN FILES       ***
10010 REM
10020 OPEN "R", #1, FILEA$, 64
10030 FIELD #1, 12 AS F1$, 12 AS F2$, 20 AS F3$, 12 AS F4$, 2 AS F5$, 5 AS F6$
10040 REM
10050 ON ERROR GOTO 10500
10060 OPEN "I", #2, FILEI$
10070 ON ERROR GOTO 0
10080 INPUT #2, FREE, FIRST      :REM POINTERS TO FREE LIST, FIRST RECORD
10090 FOR I = 1 TO MAXREC        :REM READ IN INDEX
10100    INPUT #2, INDEX(I)
10110 NEXT I
10120 CLOSE #2
10130 RETURN
10140 REM
10500 REM *** ERROR RECOVERY ***
10510 GOSUB 11000                    :REM INITIALIZE FILES
10520 RESUME
10530 REM
11000 REM          ***        INITIALIZE FILES        ***
11010 REM
11020 REM INDEX FILE MUST BE INITIALIZED
11030 OPEN "O", #2, FILEI$
11040 FREE = 1
11050 FIRST = ENDLIST
11060 WRITE #2, FREE, ENDLIST
11070 FOR I = 1 TO MAXREC - 1
11080    WRITE #2, I + 1           :REM INITIALIZE FREE LIST
11090 NEXT I
11100 WRITE #2, ENDLIST
11110 CLOSE #2
11120 RETURN
11130 REM
12000 REM          ***       MENU       ***
12010 REM
12020 REM PRINT MENU AND RETURN CHOICE AS C
12030 CLS:   PRINT CHR$(12)
12040 ROW = 5
12050 COL = 5
12060 LOCATE ROW, COL
12070 PRINT "1)   ADD TO FILE"
12090 ROW = ROW + 2:  LOCATE ROW, COL
12100 PRINT "2)   REVIEW FILE ON SCREEN"
```

```
12110 ROW = ROW + 2:  LOCATE ROW, COL
12120 PRINT "3)  LIST FILE TO SCREEN OR PRINTER"
12130 ROW = ROW + 2:  LOCATE ROW, COL
12140 PRINT "4)  DUMP FILE TO PRINTER"
12150 ROW = ROW + 2:  LOCATE ROW, COL
12160 PRINT "5)  QUIT
12170 COL = 1
12180 ROW = ROW + 2:  LOCATE ROW, COL
12190 INPUT "SELECT 1, 2, 3, 4, OR 5:  ", C
12200 IF (C < 1) OR (C > 5) THEN GOTO 12190
12210 RETURN
12220 REM
13000 REM       ***     CLOSE FILES     ***
13010 REM
13020 REM WRITE INDEX FILE TO DISK AND CLOSE BOTH FILES
13030 OPEN "O", #2, FILEI$
13040 WRITE #2, FREE, FIRST
13050 FOR I = 1 TO MAXREC
13060    WRITE #2, INDEX(I)
13070 NEXT I
13080 CLOSE #2
13090 CLOSE #1
13100 RETURN
13110 REM
14000 REM       ***     APPEND RECORD TO FILE   ***
14010 REM
14020 GOSUB 15000                       :REM  GET ENTRY
14030 IF FINISHED THEN GOTO 14070
14040 GOSUB 16000                       :REM  INSERT
14050 IF FINISHED THEN GOTO 14070
14060 GOTO 14020
14070 RETURN
14080 REM
15000 REM       ***     GET ENTRY       ***
15010 REM
15020 REM READ 1 RECORD FROM KEYBOARD
15030 CLS                               :REM  CLEAR SCREEN
15040 START = 14
15050 ROW = 5:  COL = 1
15060 LOCATE ROW, COL
15070 PRINT "LAST NAME:";
15080 FLENGTH = 12
15090 GOSUB 25000                       :REM MARK OFF INPUT AREA
15100 ROW = ROW + 2:  LOCATE ROW, COL
15110 PRINT "FIRST NAME:";
15120 FLENGTH = 12
15130 GOSUB 25000                       :REM MARK OFF
15140 ROW = ROW + 2:  LOCATE ROW, COL
15150 PRINT "ADDRESS:";
15160 FLENGTH = 20
15170 GOSUB 25000                       :REM MARK OFF
15180 ROW = ROW + 2:  LOCATE ROW, COL
15190 PRINT "CITY:";
15200 FLENGTH = 12
15210 GOSUB 25000                       :REM MARK OFF
15220 ROW = ROW + 2:  LOCATE ROW, COL
15230 PRINT "STATE:";
15240 FLENGTH = 2
15250 GOSUB 25000                       :REM MARK OFF
15260 ROW = ROW + 2:  LOCATE ROW, COL
15270 PRINT "ZIP CODE:";
15280 FLENGTH = 5
15290 GOSUB 25000                       :REM MARK OFF
```

Fig. 4-9. Comprehensive sample program. (Continued from page 95.)

```
15300 ROW = 5:   COL = START + 1
15310 LOCATE ROW, COL
15320 INPUT "", LAST$
15330 FINISHED = (LAST$ = "")              :REM IF EMPTY
15340 IF FINISHED THEN RETURN
15350 ROW = ROW + 2:   LOCATE ROW, COL
15360 INPUT "", FIRST$
15370 ROW = ROW + 2:   LOCATE ROW, COL
15380 INPUT "", ADDRESS$
15390 ROW = ROW + 2:   LOCATE ROW, COL
15400 INPUT "", CITY$
15410 ROW = ROW + 2:   LOCATE ROW, COL
15420 INPUT "", STATE$
15430 ROW = ROW + 2:   LOCATE ROW, COL
15440 INPUT "", ZIP$
15450 RETURN
15460 REM
16000 REM        ***      INSERT        ***
16010 REM
16020 REM PLACE THE RECORD INTO THE INDEX AND WRITE IT TO DISK
16030 GOSUB 18000                     :REM GET FREE RECORD
16035 IF F = 0 THEN FINISHED = -1:  RETURN    :REM  NO MORE ROOM
16040 R = F
16050 LSET F1$ = LAST$                :REM MOVE TO FILE BUFFER
16060 LSET F2$ = FIRST$
16070 LSET F3$ = ADDRESS$
16080 LSET F4$ = CITY$
16090 LSET F5$ = STATE$
16100 LSET F6$ = ZIP$
16110 PUT #1, R                       :REM WRITE TO DISK
16120 REM NOW INSERT RECORD R INTO THE INDEX
16130 P = FIRST                       :REM FIRST RECORD IN USE
16140 Q = 0
16150 IF P = ENDLIST THEN GOTO 16250
16160    GET #1, P
16170    GOSUB 17000                  :REM COMPARE & FIND GREATER
16180    WHILE (P <> ENDLIST) AND (GREATER)
16190         Q = P
16200         P = INDEX(P)
16205         IF P=ENDLIST THEN GOTO 16230
16210         GET #1, P
16220         GOSUB 17000             :REM COMPARE
16230    WEND
16240 REM NOW INSERT INTO LINKED LIST
16250 INDEX(F) = P
16260 INDEX(Q) = F
16270 IF Q=0 THEN FIRST = F
16280 RETURN
16290 REM
17000 REM        ***      COMPARE       ***
17010 REM
17020 REM COMPARE FIRST$, LAST$ TO RECORD IN BUFFER
17030 GREATER = (LAST$ > F1$) OR ((LAST$ = F1$) AND (FIRST$ > F2$))
17040 RETURN
17050 REM
18000 REM        ***      GET FREE       ***
18010 REM
18020 REM RETURN THE NR OF THE NEXT FREE RECORD & REMOVE FROM FREE LIST
18030 F = FREE
18040 IF F=0 THEN INPUT "FILE IS FULL, <CR> TO CONTINUE...";AA$: RETURN
18050 FREE = INDEX(FREE)
18060 RETURN
18070 REM
19000 REM        ***      REVIEW         ***
19010 REM
```

```
19020 REM STEP THROUGH FILE, 1 RECORD AT A TIME.  ALLOWS DELETION.
19030 CLS:  PRINT CHR#(12)                    :REM CLEAR SCREEN
19040 R = FIRST
19050 Q = 0
19060 REM REPEAT UNTIL LOOP (SIMULATED)
19070 GET #1, R
19080    PRINT
19090    GOSUB 24000                         :REM PRINT RECORD R
19100    PRINT
19110    PRINT TAB(10) "1) GET NEXT RECORD"
19120    PRINT TAB(10) "2) DELETE THIS RECORD, OR "
19130    PRINT TAB(10) "3) QUIT?"
19135    PRINT
19140    REM REPEAT UNTIL LOOP (SIMULATED)
19150    INPUT "SELECT 1), 2), OR 3) ", C
19160         IF (C < 1) OR (C > 3) THEN GOTO 19150
19170    ON C GOTO 19180, 19210, 19240
19180    Q = R                               :REM GET NEXT RECORD
19190    R = INDEX(R)
19200    GOTO 19240
19210    INDEX(Q) = INDEX(R)                  :REM DELETE RECORD
19220    GOSUB 20000                          :REM PUT IN FREE LIST
19230    R = INDEX(Q)
19240    IF (R <> ENDLIST) AND (C <> 3) THEN GOTO 19070
19250 RETURN
19260 REM
20000 REM        ***     PUT FREE        ***
20010 REM
20020 REM PUT RECORD R BACK INTO THE FREE LIST
20030 INDEX(R) = FREE
20040 FREE = R
20050 RETURN
20060 REM
21000 REM        ***     LIST FILE       ***
21010 REM
21020 REM FIND OUT WHETHER TO LIST FILE TO SCREEN OR PRINTER
21030 REM THEN CALL LIST.
21040 CLS :  PRINT CHR#(12)                   :REM CLEAR SCREEN
21050 ROW = 5: COL = 10
21060 LOCATE ROW, COL
21070 PRINT "LIST TO"
21080 ROW = ROW + 2
21090 LOCATE ROW, COL + 5
21100 PRINT "1) SCREEN"
21110 ROW = ROW + 2
21120 LOCATE ROW, COL + 5
21130 PRINT "2) PRINTER"
21140 ROW = ROW + 2
21150 LOCATE ROW, COL
21160 INPUT "SELECT 1 OR 2:  ", D
21170 IF (D < 1) OR (D > 2) THEN GOTO 21160
21180 PRINT
21190 GOSUB 22000                            :REM LIST
21200 PRINT
21210 INPUT "TYPE <CR> TO CONTINUE",A#
21220 RETURN
21230 REM
22000 REM        ***     LIST            ***
22010 REM
22020 REM LIST ALL ACTIVE RECORDS IN ALPHABETICAL ORDER
22030 REM LIST TO SCREEN IF D = 1, TO PRINTER IF D = 2.
22040 R = FIRST
22050 WHILE R <> ENDLIST
```

Fig. 4-9. Comprehensive sample program. (Continued from page 97.)

```
22060    IF D=1 THEN PRINT: GOSUB 24000 ELSE IF D=2 THEN LPRINT:  GOSUB 26000 ELS
E PRINT "ERROR IN SUBROUTINE LIST.  D = ";D
22070    R = INDEX(R)
22080 WEND
22090 RETURN
22100 REM
23000 REM         ***     DUMP            ***
23010 REM
23020 REM DUMP ENTIRE FILE TO PRINTER, INCLUDING EMPTY RECORDS
23030 REM AND INDEX FILE ENTRIES.  USEFUL FOR LEARNING HOW
23040 REM PROGRAM WORKS.
23050 PRINT: PRINT
23060 PRINT "BE SURE PRINTER IS ON...."
23070 LPRINT "FIRST FREE RECORD:          ";FREE
23080 LPRINT "FIRST RECORD ALPHABETICALLY: ";FIRST
23090 FOR R = 1 TO MAXREC
23100    LPRINT
23110    LPRINT "RECORD         ";R
23120    GOSUB 26000                        :REM LPRINT RECORD R
23140    LPRINT "NEXT RECORD IS ";INDEX(R)
23150 NEXT R
23160 LPRINT
23170 RETURN
23180 REM
24000 REM         ***     PRINT RECORD    ***
24010 REM
24020 REM PRINT RECORD R ON THE SCREEN
24030 GET #1, R
24050 PRINT F2$;" ";F1$
24060 PRINT F3$
24070 PRINT F4$;" ";F5$;" ";F6$
24080 RETURN
24090 REM
25000 REM         ***     MARKOFF         ***
25010 REM
25020 REM MARK OFF DATA INPUT AREA
25030 LOCATE ROW, START
25040 PRINT ":";
25050 FOR J = 1 TO FLENGTH
25060    PRINT " ";
25070 NEXT J
25080 PRINT ":";
25090 RETURN
25100 REM
26000 REM         ***     LPRINT RECORD   ***
26010 REM
26020 REM PRINT RECORD R ON THE PRINTER
26030 GET #1, R
26050 LPRINT F2$;" ";F1$
26060 LPRINT F3$
26070 LPRINT F4$;" ";F5$;" ";F6$
26080 RETURN
26090 REM
60000 REM   ***************************************************************
60010 REM   ***                                                         ***
60020 REM   ***   DIRECTORY OF SUBROUTINES USED                         ***
60030 REM   ***                                                         ***
60040 REM   ***************************************************************
60050 REM
60100 GOTO 10000        :REM  OPEN FILES
60200 GOTO 11000        :REM  INITIALIZE FILES
60300 GOTO 12000        :REM  MENU
60400 GOTO 13000        :REM  CLOSE FILES
60500 GOTO 14000        :REM  APPEND
60600 GOTO 15000        :REM  GET ENTRY
```

```
60700 GOTO 16000        :REM   INSERT
60800 GOTO 17000        :REM   COMPARE
60900 GOTO 18000        :REM   GET FREE
61000 GOTO 19000        :REM   REVIEW
61100 GOTO 20000        :REM   PUT FREE
61200 GOTO 21000        :REM   LIST FILE
61300 GOTO 22000        :REM   LIST
61400 GOTO 23000        :REM   DUMP
61500 GOTO 24000        :REM   PRINT RECORD
61600 GOTO 25000        :REM   MARKOFF DATA INPUT AREA
61700 GOTO 26000        :REM   LPRINT RECORD
```

Fig. 4-9. Comprehensive sample program. (Continued from page 99.)

The file is organized as a linked list. The links are actually stored in a separate index file. As a record is added to the file, it is automatically placed in the proper place (alphabetically) in the index.

Notice that the main program is rather short, extending only to line number 410. Not counting remarks, declarations, or initializations, it consists of fewer than 10 lines. Most of the work is done in subroutines. A directory of subroutines is at the end of the program, beginning with line 60000. The subroutine to open files, for example, is found at line 10000. The directory uses the GOTO 10000 to indicate the location of the subroutine. The number 10000 could have been put in a REM statement, but when it is in a GOTO statement it will automatically be updated if the program is renumbered. The GOTO 10000 is never executed.

A structure chart showing the hierarchical organization of the program is shown in Fig. 4-10. The hierarchy is shown by indentation. For example, the main program calls those subroutines that are listed below it and are indented one level (Open Files, Display Menu, Append, Review, List File, Dump File, and Close Files). Similarly, the chart shows that the subroutine Append calls the subroutine Get Entry, which in turn calls the subroutine Mark Off. The numbers in parentheses are the line numbers where the subroutines are found in the program.

The main program provides overall control for the program. It uses the menu subroutine to determine what the user wants to do and then transfers control to the appropriate subroutine. The process is repeated until the user chooses to end the session.

By now it should be obvious that the program was designed and constructed in modules, with the modules being implemented as subroutines. Taken by itself, each module is relatively simple. Each one is relatively short and has a single purpose. The longest subroutine has fewer than 50 statements; most are much shorter. Modular design makes the program much easier to write, understand, and maintain.

Many of the modules could have been coded ''in line'' instead of as subroutines. The menu subroutine is a good example. It is needed only one place in the program. The body of the subroutine could have been incorporated into the main program at the appropriate place. The program is clearer, however, with the menu function as a separate subroutine. The main program is easier to read this way, provided an appropriate remark is present to indicate the purpose of the GOSUB.

Writing a program of this length without using subroutines is possible, but experience has shown that programmers can deal much more effectively with smaller pieces of program than with one large piece.

Getting back to specifics, there are several other features of the program in Fig. 4-9 that should be noted. First, note the subroutine called GET ENTRY, which begins at line 15000. The data input is set up so as to present the user with a form to fill out. The same function could have been accomplished with just a few INPUT statements, but extra effort to make the user interface more convenient often makes the difference between a mediocre program and a good program.

Second, note the manner in which the names are maintained in alphabetical order. This is a practical example of the use of linked lists, which were discussed earlier in the chapter. There are actually two linked lists in use; one is a list of records in alphabetical order, and the other is a list of unused records (the "free list").

The records themselves are kept in a direct-access file. The size of the file is established in line 260. It is set to 10 records for demonstration purposes. The user wishing to use this program for practical purposes should modify line 260 to establish a larger file.

The links that allow the maintenance of both linked lists are kept in a separate, sequential file. This file is kept in memory while the program is being run, and it is written back to disk at the end of the program. This is done for reasons of efficiency, but it

```
Figure 4-10:    Structure Chart for the Comprehensive Sample
                Program

   Main Program
        Open Files                    (10000)
            Initialize Files          (11000)
        Display Menu                  (12000)
        Append                        (14000)
            Get Entry                 (15000)
                Mark Off              (25000)
            Insert                    (16000)
                Get Free              (18000)
                Compare               (17000)
        Review                        (19000)
            Print Record              (24000)
            Put Free                  (20000)
        List File                     (21000)
            List                      (22000)
            Print Record              (24000)
            LPrint Record             (26000)
        Dump File                     (23000)
        Close Files                   (13000)

   Note:  The numbers in parentheses are line numbers.
```

Fig. 4-10. Structure chart for the comprehensive sample program.

has the disadvantage that if the program is interrupted (for example, by a power failure), access to all new records input during that session will be lost.

The interested reader might wish to add more features to this program. The modular structure makes this relatively easy to do. One suggestion is to add the ability to find the address of a particular individual and to display that address on the screen or write it to a printer.

The DUMP subroutine was included as a learning device. If you wish to understand more clearly how the program works, you should use this routine to print out the status of the file at various points during a session to see how additions to and deletions from the file are handled.

As an interesting aside, this program was originally written and tested using Microsoft BASIC Version 5.2 running on an Apple II+ under the CP/M operating system. The only changes required to make it run using GW-BASIC on a Zenith Z-150 under the MS-DOS operating system were to replace the functions that clear the screen and position the cursor.

ADVANTAGES AND DISADVANTAGES OF BASIC

The BASIC language was designed for students. It is a simple language that has a relatively small number of different instructions. It is therefore easy to learn all of the available instructions.

BASIC is usually implemented on microcomputers as an interpreted language. This makes program development simpler in the sense that it is easier to input a program and test it interactively than it would be if the language were implemented as a compiler. The user can enter the program, test, and correct errors all within the same environment. The result is a much friendlier programming environment.

With a compiled language, the user usually has to use a separate editor to input the text of the program, save the program to disk, and then invoke the compiler before he or she can test the program. Sometimes there are additional steps such as linking and loading. The result is a somewhat "user-hostile" environment. Two newer implementations of BASIC on microcomputers, QuickBASIC and Turbo BASIC, are actually compilers, but are packaged in a "user-friendly" environment.

On the negative side, most implementations of BASIC lack the full range of structured constructs such as the **CASE** statement, **REPEAT-UNTIL**, and so forth. These must often be emulated using **IF** and **GOTO** statements. BASIC also lacks local variables in subroutines and a means of passing parameters to subroutines.

Because BASIC is usually implemented as an interpreted language, BASIC programs usually run more slowly than equivalent programs in compiled languages. This is shown time and again in programming benchmarks. Again, newer compiled versions of BASIC have done much to overcome this shortcoming.

Most implementations of BASIC use binary-integer and floating-point arithmetic, which is fine for scientific and general applications, but inadequate for most business applications. As discussed in Chapter 2, BCD (decimal) arithmetic is desirable for business applications. Two versions of BASIC that do provide BCD arithmetic are CBASIC and Nevada BASIC.

In balance, BASIC is useful for writing relatively short programs for which execution speed is not of prime importance. Because of its user-friendliness, it is an excellent language for beginners.

AVAILABILITY

BASIC is the most widely available language for microcomputers. Most microcomputers sold today, including the most inexpensive, are distributed with the BASIC language. BASIC compilers are also available. An excellent combination is a BASIC interpreter for program development and a compatible BASIC compiler for compiling the program for production work.

BASIC compilers that feature a programming environment almost as friendly as an interpreter have recently been introduced. These include QuickBASIC by Microsoft of Redmond, Washington, and Turbo BASIC by Borland International of Scotts Valley, California.

SUMMARY

BASIC is the most popular language in use today for microcomputers. Its popularity is due in part to its wide availability and in part to its ease of use. It is easy to learn, yet sufficiently powerful for many applications. It is particularly well-suited for beginners.

Ada
BASIC
C
COBOL
Forth
Fortran
LISP
Logo
Modula-2
Pascal
PILOT
Prolog

5

C

The C programming language was designed and implemented in 1972 by Dennis Ritchie at Bell Laboratories in Murray Hill, New Jersey. It was based on the earlier languages BCPL by Martin Richards and B by Ken Thompson. C was originally designed for and implemented on the UNIX operating system on the Digital Equipment Corporation's PDP-11 minicomputer. C has since been implemented on numerous other computers, including microcomputers.

C is a general-purpose high-level language, but it includes many low-level features as well. The low-level features permit the bit-level manipulations often needed in writing systems software such as operating systems. In fact, the UNIX operating system is now written mostly in the C language. Before the advent of C, operating systems had been written almost exclusively in assembly or machine languages.

C is a very rich language, containing many operators (including operators for incrementing, decrementing, bit manipulation, and so forth, as well as the usual arithmetic operators). This richness provides for several alternative ways to accomplish a given task, often including several shortcuts. In the hands of an expert, C is a very powerful language. It is also a very subtle language. Along with the subtleties and shortcuts, there are pitfalls for the unwary.

The features of C tend to encourage a particular style of programming, one that takes advantage of the richness of the language. Unfortunately, programs written in that style tend to be difficult to read for the uninitiated. In fact, there is a book of C language puzzles on the market. The book highlights a number of obscure C programs and challenges the reader to figure out what they do. That does not mean, however, that understandable programs cannot be written in C. This chapter attempts to present the essential features of the C language clearly, while avoiding many of the more subtle and obscure idioms.

At the time of the first edition of this book (1984), there were relatively few books available on the C language compared to the number available for BASIC or Pascal. Since then, many other books on C have been published. The definitive reference remains *The C Programming Language*, by Brian W. Kernighan and Dennis M. Ritchie (Prentice-Hall, 1978). Newer books written at a more elementary level include *C Programming Guide*, by Jack Purdum (Que Corporation, 1983) and *The C Trilogy*, by Eric Bloom (TAB Books, Inc., 1987). There are many others.

One of the first implementations of C on a microcomputer was "Small C," published in *Dr. Dobb's Journal* in May 1980. Small C is a subset of C and is now in the public domain. In the early years of microcomputers, several companies produced enhanced versions of Small C for the CP/M-80 (eight-bit) environment. These versions usually lacked such features as floating point variables, direct-access files, and so on.

Today there are several full-featured implementations of the C language available for microcomputers ranging in price from $39.95 to $800 or so. The programs in this chapter were tested with the MIX-C compiler, available for $39.95 from Mix Software, Inc., Richardson, Texas.

PROGRAM STRUCTURE

A C program consists of one or more functions. One function must be called main( ). This corresponds to the main program of other languages. (C functions are discussed in more detail in the next sections.)

A simple C program that prints **This is a test.** is shown in Fig. 5-1. The first line is simply a comment identifying the program. In the next line, main( ) identifies the beginning of the main program. The parentheses are necessary because main( ) is actually a function, and function names in C must be followed by parentheses, even if the parentheses are empty. The body of the main program is enclosed by braces, { and }. Note that they are placed so as to be easy to locate.

The actual work is done in the line that begins with printf. The character string between the quotation marks is sent to the video screen by the standard library function printf( ). The only thing peculiar about this is the fact that the character string is terminated by the character pair \n (backslash-n, the *newline* character), which represents a carriage return and a line feed. One way to understand what is going on here is to note that two consecutive printf( ) functions without the newline character would print on the same line.

```
/*   Figure 5-1:   Simple C Program   */

main()
{
        printf("This is a test.\n");
}
```

Fig. 5-1. A simple C program.

Note that the printf( ) statement ends with a semicolon. In C the semicolon is a statement terminator, not a statement separator (as in Pascal), so every statement must end with a semicolon.

Wherever one statement can appear in C, so can a group of statements surrounded by braces. The braces correspond to the BEGIN and END of Pascal programs. The terseness of the C version is characteristic.

DATA REPRESENTATION

The C language supports the following simple data types: char (character), int (integer), float (floating point), and double (double precision). Additionally, the int type can be modified with the prefixes long, short, or unsigned. The exact number of bits in each variable type depends on the installation, but typically a char is eight bits, an int is 16 bits, a long int is 32 bits, a short int is 16 bits, a float is a 32-bit floating point number, and a double is a 64-bit floating point number. An unsigned int is always positive.

Constants

Integer constants in C follow the usual conventions discussed in Chapter 2, except that octal (base 8) and hexadecimal (base 16) constants can also be used. An octal constant is indicated by a leading zero. For example, the number 011 is an octal constant equal to the decimal constant 9. Similarly, hexadecimal constants are indicated by a leading 0x. The number 0x11, therefore, is the equivalent in hexadecimal of the decimal number 17. Some implementations also allow binary (base 2) constants, prefixed by 0b.

Floating point constants follow the conventions concerning real numbers described in Chapter 2.

Constants of the type char are single characters surrounded by single quotes, for example, 'a'. A character constant has a numeric value corresponding to the numeric value of that character in the character set of the machine in use (usually ASCII).

There are several special characters that can be represented by two-character sequences beginning with a backslash: \n is the newline character, \t is the tab character, and \0 is the null character (ASCII 00). An arbitrary character can be represented by preceding it with a backslash. The backslash character itself is represented by \ \ and the single quote by \' (backslash-single quote).

Arbitrary bit patterns can be represented by using the pattern '\ddd', where the ddd represents one to three octal digits. The ASCII linefeed, for example, would be represented as '\012'.

String constants are delimited with double quotes. A string in C is terminated with the null character (\0). The character 'c' is only one character in length, but the string "c" is two characters in length; the second (unseen) character is the null character. This extra character needs to be taken into consideration when declaring the length of a string.

Constants may be declared in C using #define. An illustration of the #define facility is given in Fig. 5-2. In this example the name of the constant is ENDLIST, and its value is −1. Everywhere that the name ENDLIST appears in the program text (except within quotation marks), the value −1 is substituted at the time the program is compiled. In

```
/*   Figure 5-2:   Illustrate Use of a Constant   */

#define   ENDLIST   (-1)

main()
{
    printf("The constant ENDLIST has value %d", ENDLIST);
}
```

Fig. 5-2. The use of a Constant.

this case the program merely prints out the value of ENDLIST. Note the %d within the character string in the printf( ) statement. This tells printf( ) to print the first item after the character string (in this case it is ENDLIST) at that place and to print that item as a decimal number. Notice that in this case the newline character (\n) was omitted; observe the difference in the behavior of the cursor on your screen as you run this program, compared to its behavior when you run the program in Fig. 5-1.

It is good form to use uppercase for the names of constants to make it easy to distinguish between constants and variables, which are almost always written in lowercase.

Variables

Variables in C are declared at the beginning of a program. Variables declared before the main( ) function are global to main( ) and all functions declared thereafter. Variables declared after the main( ) function heading are local to main( ). Declaring variables after the main( ) function heading is most common. Functions, discussed later in this chapter, may also have local variables not accessible from the main program or from other functions. A simple example of a variable declaration is shown in the example in Fig. 5-3. The program computes and prints the area and perimeter of a square.

Pointers

The name of a variable in C or any other language is a symbol that represents an actual physical address in the computer's memory. The connection between the name of the variable and the physical address is usually established by the compiler, unbeknownst to the programmer. The programmer usually doesn't care where in the computer's memory his or her variables are stored.

The C programming language provides a way to deal directly with these memory addresses. A variable whose value is a memory address is called a *pointer*. Pointers must be declared using an asterisk. The declaration tells the compiler what kind of a variable the pointer points to. Here is an example of the declarations of pointers to an integer and to a character:

```
int  *ip;
char *cp;
```

```
/*   Figure 5-3:   Illustrate Use of a Variable   */

main()
{
    int side, area, perim;

    side = 5;
    area = side * side;
    perim = side + side + side + side;
    printf("Area and perimeter of a square:\n\n");
    printf("Side:        %d\n", side);
    printf("Area:        %d\n", area);
    printf("Perimeter:   %d\n", perim);
}
```

Fig. 5-3. The use of a Variable.

The address of a variable can be extracted with the ampersand (&) operator. For example, if i is an integer, then &i refers to the location in memory where i is stored. That makes &i a pointer.

The asterisk (*) operator is used to access the value stored in memory at the location pointed to by a pointer. This is a form of indirect addressing and is sometimes called *dereferencing*. This is the sort of thing that is most familiar to assembly-language programmers.

The best way to illustrate how pointers work is by example. The program in Fig. 5-4 defines an integer variable, a character variable, and pointers to each. It initializes each variable and then prints out a table showing the address and value of each variable. (The %u, %c, and %d in the printf( ) statements tell C to print data as an unsigned integer, character, and decimal integer, respectively.) The program then illustrates an indirect assignment and its result. The output from one run of this program is shown below:

Variable	Address	Value
c	34808	a
cp	34809	34808
i	34811	1
ip	34813	34811

After assigning *ip = 29, i = 29. This happened because *ip points to i.

The numbers in the Address column represent the actual physical memory location that were used in my computer when I ran the program. If you ran the same program using another compiler on another computer, you would probably get different numbers.

The compiler starts assigning addresses at 34808. Because the variable c is of type char, it only takes up one memory location. The variable cp therefore begins at the next available location, 34809. Pointers in Mix-C take up two bytes, so the next available location is 34811, which is assigned to the variable i. Because the type int takes up two bytes also, the next available address is 34813, which is assigned to ip.

Note that the value of **cp** is the address of **c**. This was accomplished by the assignment statement

    cp = &cp;.

Likewise, the value of ip is the address of i.

The assignment statement *ip = 29; *indirectly* changes the value of i to 29. The computer is instructed to go to memory location 34813 (the address of ip), take what is stored there (34811), and use that value as the address at which to store the number 29.

At this point it is probably not clear why you would want to do such a thing. Later in the chapter you will see that the C language requires the use of pointers for certain applications, such as returning multiple data items from functions. The scanf( ) function for reading input from the console is a good example of a function that requires the use of pointers.

THE ASSIGNMENT STATEMENT

The assignment operator in C is the equals sign (=). The symbol used for testing equality is two equals signs (= =). The author of C decided that because the assignment

```
/*   Figure 5-4:   Demonstrate Pointers */

main()
{
     char   c, *cp;        /* "cp" is a pointer to a char   */
     int    i, *ip;        /* "ip" is a pointer to an int   */

     c   = 'a';
     c   = &c;             /* cp = the address of c          */
     i   = 1;
     ip = &i;              /* ip = the address of i          */

     /* Print a table with the address and value of each variable   */

     printf("Variable \t Address \t Value \n\n");

     printf("c          \t %u     \t %c    \n", &c,   c);
     printf("cp         \t %u     \t %u    \n", &cp, cp);
     printf("i          \t %u     \t %d    \n", &i,   i);
     printf("ip         \t %u     \t %u    \n", &ip, ip);

     /* Now demonstrate indirect access to i via a pointer          */

     *ip = 29;
     printf("\n\nAfter assigning *ip = 29 .......\n\n");
     printf("i   = \t %d\n\n", i);
     printf("This happened because *ip points to i.\n");
}
```

Fig. 5-4. The use of pointers.

operator is used more often than the symbol for testing equality, the assignment operator should consist of only one keystroke and the symbol for testing equality should consist of two.

Ironically, this means that the equals sign doesn't mean equality. This is not so unusual in the computer world (witness Fortran). The tradeoff is wholly consistent with the philosophy of C, which favors conciseness over other considerations. Pascal, on the other hand, favors clarity over conciseness, so the assignment operator takes two keystrokes, and the symbol for testing equality takes one keystroke.

The assignment operator in C is not very particular about data types. For example, it is common in C to assign a character value to an integer variable. This is what it means to say that C is a weakly typed language.

Figure 5-3 showed three examples of assignment statements.

ARITHMETIC EXPRESSIONS

C uses conventional infix notation (see Chapter 2) for its arithmetic expressions. It uses the usual arithmetic operators (+, −, *, /), plus a modulus operator (%). The modulus operator produces the remainder after integer division: 5 % 2 is 1, for example, and 10 % 4 is 2.

C, like Pascal, does not have an exponentiation operator. Exponentiation in C must be performed by using repeated multiplication or by using logarithms.

C has special operators for the common operations of incrementing and decrementing. The statement

```
i+ +;
```

is, for example, equivalent to the statement

```
i = i + 1;
```

and the statement

```
i− −;
```

is equivalent to the statement

```
i = i − 1;.
```

The incrementing and decrementing operators can also be placed before the variable. Compare the following two statements:

```
j = i+ +;      /* A */
j = + +i;      /* B */.
```

Suppose that i initially has the value 5. Following statement A, j would have the value 5 and i the value 6. The incrementing takes place after the value of i is used in the expression. If i again has the value 5 before statement B is executed, both i and j would end up with the value 6. In that case, i would be incremented before its value is used in the expression.

The C language allows another form of shortcut when the value of a variable is to be modified by other than simple incrementing or decrementing. Consider the following statements:

```
amount   + =   5;        /*  A1  */
amount   =   amount + 5;  /*  A2  */
sales    * =   2;         /*  B1  */
sales    =   sales * 2;   /*  B2  */.
```

Statements A1 and A2 are equivalent, as are statements B1 and B2. Similar statements can be constructed using other arithmetic operators.

LOGICAL EXPRESSIONS

The relational operators in C are = = (equals), != (not equals), >, > = (greater than or equals), <, and < = (less than or equals). The logical operators are && (AND) and II (OR).

The logical operators are evaluated from left to right, and evaluation stops as soon as it can be determined whether the expression is true or false. This is sometimes convenient, as in testing for zero before division.

The C language also contains logical operators for manipulating variables at the bit level. These operators are valid only for char or int variables. The following operators are provided: & (bitwise AND), I (bitwise OR), ^ (bitwise exclusive OR), ~ (one's complement), < < (shift left), and > > (shift right). The shift operators must be followed by an integer telling how many bit positions to shift.

Some printers expect to find the high-order bit of a character set high, and some expect it low. The following statement would set the high bit of the character c high:

```
c I= 0x80;
```

A bitwise OR is performed between the character c and the hexadecimal constant 0x80, which has all bits low (0) except the most significant bit, which is high (1). Note that this statement could also have been written as follows:

```
c = c I 0x80;
```

The following would ensure that the high bit of the character c is set low:

```
c &= 0x7f;.
```

A bitwise AND is performed between the character c and the hexadecimal constant 0x7f, which has the high-order bit low (0) and all other bits high (1).

CONDITIONAL EXPRESSIONS

A conditional expression evaluates to one of two values, depending on whether a given condition is true or false. It is a feature not often found in computer languages.

Suppose, for example, that you want a variable y to evaluate to the value of x or zero, whichever is larger. The following shows one way to accomplish this:

y = (x > 0) ? x : 0;.

If x is greater than zero, the value of the expression is x; otherwise it is zero. (The parentheses are optional.) The general form of the expression is

<log. exp.> ? <exp. 1> : <exp. 2>.

If the logical expression is true, the value of the expression is the value of expression 1, which follows the question mark. If the logical expression is false, the value of the expression is the value of expression 2, which follows the colon.

INPUT AND OUTPUT

You have already seen the printf( ) function in Figs. 5-1, 5-2, 5-3, and 5-4. Its purpose is, of course, to produce formatted output on the console (video screen). The C language has several other functions for sending output to the console or to a file.

Technically speaking, the C language has no input and output statements. This is not apparent to the user, however, because input and output are implemented using standard functions provided with the compiler (such as printf( )). These functions are actually in a library file, not in the compiler itself.

The advantage of this approach is that it makes C more portable; as the language is moved to another environment, all the input and output functions that might need to be changed are easily identifiable and easily accessible.

You should check the documentation provided with your C compiler to determine exactly which input and output functions are provided. Here is a typical list:

Input	Output
getchar( )	putchar( )
gets( )	puts( )
scanf( )	printf( )

Input and output functions that access files are discussed in a later section. Of the above functions, getchar( ), gets( ), and scanf( ) read from the console; printf( ), putchar( ), and puts( ) write to the console.

First let us look at the printf( ) function in more detail. The general form of the function is as follows:

printf (format, argument, argument, . . .)

The format is a character string containing text and possibly conversion specifications, which specify where and how the arguments are to be printed. In the following example, assume that a and b are integers:

```
printf("The sum of %d and %d is %d. \n", a,b,a+b);
```

The arguments in this case are a, b, and a+b. Each is associated by position with a %d conversion specification. This specification means to print the corresponding argument as a decimal integer. The output on the printer would look as follows, assuming a and b have the values 1 and 2, respectively:

```
The sum of 1 and 2 is 3.
```

Besides %d, there are several other permissible conversion specifications, as follows:

Specification	Format
%c	a single character
%s	a string
%u	an unsigned integer
%o	an octal integer
%x	a hexadecimal integer
%e	floating point, scientific notation
%f	fixed point notation
%g	fixed or floating point, whichever is shorter

Compilers that do not support floating-point numbers are not likely to support the %e, %f, or %g conversion specifications.

The counterpart of printf( ) for input is scanf( ). The general form of a scanf( ) function call is as follows:

```
scanf(format, argument, argument, . . .);
```

The format string is much like the format string of a printf( ) statement. Each component of the format string is a format specification such as %d, %s, or %c. Each argument must be a pointer to a variable of the appropriate type. (See the discussion of pointers earlier in the chapter.)

The program listed in Fig. 5-5 will read a name and a number from the console using scanf( ). A typical session with this program might print the following on the screen (with user input shown in boldface):

```
Enter a name and number
   separated by a space:  Joe 12
The name read was:   Joe
The number read was:  12
```

```
/*   Figure 5-5:   Demonstrate the scanf() function.   */

/*   The program reads a name and number              */
/*       from one input line.                         */

main()
{
    int n;
    char name[81];

    printf("\n\nEnter a name and number separated by a space:   ");
    scanf("%s %d", name, &n);

    printf("\nThe name read was:    %s\n", name);
    printf("The number read was:  %d\n", n);
}
```

Fig. 5-5. The scanf( ) function.

In C the name of a character string is also a pointer, so you don't need to use &
as a preface. You could, however, write &name[0], which is a pointer to the beginning
of the character string. The variable n is an integer, so &n is a pointer to an integer.

A character string read by scanf( ) with a %s format specification cannot contain
embedded spaces. The most common mistake in using scanf( ) is to forget to make an
argument a pointer.

The function printf( ) directs its output to the standard output device, which is usually
the video screen. To send output to the printer, you must use the function fprintf( ).
The fprintf( ) function directs its output to a specified file. You can specify the printer
as a special instance of a file. An example of how this is done is shown in Fig. 5-6.

The function fprintf( ) expects a pointer to a file as its first argument. To declare
such a pointer, you must first include a file called STDIO.H in the program. This is done
by the #include statement at the beginning of the program. This tells the compiler to
look in the named file and compile its contents also.

The variable prt is declared as the file pointer (FILE *prt;). Next, one must tell
the compiler which file to associate with that file pointer. This is done using the fopen( )
function, which associates prt with the file LPT1:, the designation of the printer in MS-
DOS. The "w" in the fopen( ) function tells the compiler that this file is to be opened
in the "write," or output, mode.

Once these details are taken care of, the rest of the program is simple. The printf( )
function sends its output to the screen and the fprintf( ) function sends its output to the
printer.

There are other output functions in C. The function puts( ) sends a string to the
console, followed by a carriage return and linefeed. The function putchar( ) sends a single
character to the console.

On the input side, the functions getchar( ) and gets( ) read a character and a string,
respectively, from the console.

Figure 5-7 contains a program that emulates an electronic typewriter. It illustrates
the use of the string input function gets( ) and the fprintf( ) function for printer output.

```
/*   Figure 5-6:   Demonstrate Screen and Printer Output */

#include      "STDIO.H"

main()
{
    int a, b, sum;
    FILE *prt;

    a = 2;
    b = 3;
    sum = a + b;

    /* First print to the console */
    printf("The sum of %d and %d is %d.\n\n", a,b,sum);

    /* Select Printer */
    prt = fopen("LPT1:", "w");

    /* Now send to the printer   */
    fprintf(prt, "The sum of %d and %d is %d.\n\n", a,b,sum);
}
```

Fig. 5-6. Screen and printer output.

```
/*   Figure 5-7:   Electronic Typewriter, Version 1   */

#define   MAXL            81
#include  "STDIO.H"

main()
{
    char str[MAXL];
    FILE *prt;

    /* Select Printer */
    prt = fopen ("LPT1:", "w");

    printf("Welcome to your Electronic Typewriter.\n\n");
    printf("Enter your text, followed by 'Control-Z'.\n\n");

    while (gets(str) != NULL) {
        fprintf(prt, "%s\n", str);
    }
    printf("\nThat is all....\n");
}
```

Fig. 5-7. Electronic Typewriter, Version 1.

(Note that the while construct was discussed in Chapter 2 and is discussed further later in this chapter.) This program reads in line after line until a line containing the Control-Z character is encountered. Each line is echoed to the printer.

For comparison, the program in Fig. 5-8 does essentially the same thing using the functions getchar( ) and putc( ), which input and output text a single character at a time. The getchar( ) function reads from the standard input device, usually the console. The putc( ) function, on the other hand, sends its output to the file specified by a file pointer. In this case the file pointer is prt, which points to the printer in the same way as explained above in the discussion of the fprintf( ) function.

Using the Mix-C compiler, the programs in Figs. 5-7 and 5-8 appear to the user to behave nearly identically. The author has seen other C implementations in which the program in Fig. 5-8 did not allow correction of errors by backspacing. This is because the erroneous characters had already been sent to the printer before the attempted correction. With Mix-C under MS-DOS, the input is buffered and handled a line at a time.

The following statement

```
c = getchar( );
```

in the program in Fig. 5-8 reads a character from the console and assigns that character to the variable c. Notice that the variable c is declared to be of type int rather than char. This is because the function getchar( ) returns (−1) when it encounters a control-Z, and (−1) is an integer, not a character.

```
/*   Figure 5-8:   Electronic Typewriter, Version 2   */

#include        "STDIO.H"

main()
{
    int c;
    FILE *prt;

    /* Select Printer */
    prt = fopen("LPT1:", "w");

    printf("Welcome to your Electronic Typewriter, Version 2.\n\n");
    printf("Enter your text, followed by 'Control-Z'.\n\n");

    c = getchar();
    while (c != EOF) {
        putc(c, prt);
        c = getchar();
    }
    putc('\n', prt);
    printf("\nThat is all....\n");
}
```

Fig. 5-8. Electronic Typewriter, Version 2.

CONTROL STRUCTURES

The C language has control structures comparable to that of Pascal, and many more control structures than languages such as BASIC, COBOL, and Fortran. Most of the control structures of C encourage compliance with the principles of structured programming. Certain features, however, such as the **break** statement, can easily be misused, violating the principle that a control structure should have a single entry point and a single exit point.

The formats of the various control statements call for a single statement in many places. Wherever one statement can appear in C, so can several statements grouped within the braces: { and }.

Simple Selection: if-else

The general format of the if statement in C is as follows:

```
if (expression)
    statement 1;
else
    statement 2;
```

The expression in parentheses is evaluated. If it is true (nonzero), then statement 1 is executed. If it is false (zero), then statement 2 is executed. In no case are both statements executed.

Because in C the semicolon is a statement terminator, the semicolon after statement 1 is required. This is contrary to the usage in Pascal.

As mentioned above, either statement 1 or statement 2 can be replaced by a group of statements within braces. Also, the **else** and statement 2 are optional.

Here is a simple if statement without an **else** part:

```
month++;
if (month > 12) {
    month = 1;
    year++;
}
```

This program segment increments the value of **month**, then resets it to 1 and increments **year** if **month** was incremented past 12.

Here is an if statement with an **else** part:

```
if (month == 12) {
    month = 1;
    ++year;
} else
    ++month;
```

This achieves the same result as the previous example, but in a slightly different way. Deciding which way is better is a matter of taste. There are two statements to be executed if the condition is true; they are enclosed between braces. There is only one statement to be executed if the condition is false.

Notice that the variable **year** in the if part and the variable **month** in the else part are incremented using the increment operator.

An if statement can be nested in C. Another way of saying this is to emphasize that statement 1 or statement 2 in the above skeleton format can be another if statement. Here is an illustration showing the computation of a weekly payroll:

```
if (hours < = 40)
    pay = hours * rate;
else if (hours < = 50)
    pay = 40 * rate + (hours – 40) *
       rate * 1.5;
else
    pay = 40 * rate + 10 * rate * 1.5 +
       (hours – 50) * rate * 2;
```

In this example, the employee is paid straight time for up to 40 hours per week, time-and-a-half for hours over 40 but under 50, and double time for hours over 50 per week. Notice that both the **else** parts are continued onto another line. This makes no difference.

Multiple Selection: The switch Statement

The if statement allows selection between two alternative courses of action. If the **else** part is missing, the second course of action is simply to do nothing. There are sometimes situations when it is desirable to choose among more than two different courses of action. Nested if statements will work, but they become cumbersome for more than three or four alternatives.

The C language offers the **switch** statement for multiple selection. It is roughly analogous to the **CASE** statement discussed in Chapter 2, but with an important difference. In the general **CASE** statement, each alternative is strictly mutually exclusive. There is no possibility for more than one alternative to be executed. This is not the situation in C. To make alternatives mutually exclusive in C, the **break** statement is needed. How the **switch** and **break** statements work together is illustrated in the program in Fig. 5-9.

The program in Fig. 5-9 reads in a number from 1 to 12, and then prints out the number of days in the corresponding month. The parentheses following the word **switch** contain an integer expression, in this case the variable **month**. Depending on the value of this expression, execution is passed to the appropriately labeled case. For example, if **month** has the value 11, control will be passed to the statement labeled **case 11:**. The statement **days** = 30; would then be executed. The next statement is the **break** statement. This causes execution control to pass to the statement following the end of the body of the **switch** statement, which in this case is a **printf( )** statement at the end of the program. Had the **break** not been there, the next statement to have been executed would have been the statement labeled **case 2:**.

```
/*   Figure 5-9:   The Calendar Program   */

main()
{
    int   month, days, year;

    printf("\nEnter the month (1..12):   ");
    scanf("%d", &month);

    switch (month) {
        case 1:
        case 3:
        case 5:
        case 7:
        case 8:
        case 10:
        case 12:  days = 31;
                  break;
        case 4:
        case 6:
        case 9:
        case 11:  days = 30;
                  break;
        case 2:   printf("\nEnter the year:   ");
                  scanf("%d", &year);
                  if ((year % 4) == 0)
                        days = 29;
                  else
                        days = 28;
                  break;
        default:  printf("\nSorry, month must be between 1 and 12.\n");
                  days = 0;
                  break;
    }
    printf("\n\nMonth %d has %d days.\n",month,days);
}
```

Fig. 5-9. The Calendar Program.

The **break** statement in general causes execution to pass the the statement following the end of the current construct, whether that construct is a **switch** statement or one of the looping statements discussed in the next section.

If **month** has value 3, for example, execution passes through to the **days = 31;** statement. If the value of **month** does not correspond to one of the labeled cases, execution is passed to the statement labeled **default**.

Note the use of the **scanf( )** function to read in the values of **month** and **year**.

Loops

The C language has three kinds of loops: the **for** loop, which is a counted loop, and the **while** and **do-while** loops, which are conditional loops.

Counted Loops: The for Statement. Chapter 2 contained a simple program in BASIC that printed out the integers from 1 to 10. The program of Fig. 5-10 accomplishes the same thing in C.

```
/*   Figure 5-10:   Demonstrate the for loop   */

main()
{
    int i;

    for (i=1; i <= 10; i++)
        printf("%d\n", i);
}
```

Fig. 5-10. The for loop.

The controlling parameters of a **for** loop are contained within parentheses following the word **for**. There are three parts within the parentheses, separated by semicolons. The first part is the initialization part, in this case, i = 1. The variable i starts with the value 1 on the first pass through the loop. The second part is the test part, in this case, i < = 10. This means that the condition i < = 10 must be true, or control will pass outside the loop. The third part is the reinitialization part, in this case i + +. This means that after each iteration of the loop, the variable i is incremented, the test condition is checked, and if the test condition is true, the body of the loop is repeated.

The body of the loop is, in this case, a single **printf( )** statement. In general it could be any statement, or a group of statements within braces.

Conditional Loops. A conditional loop repeats a statement or statements as long as a particular condition is true. The two kinds of conditional loops in C are the **while** loop and the **do-while** loop. The difference between them is that the **while** loop performs the test at the top of the loop, while the **do-while** performs the test at the bottom of the loop.

Because the **while** loop performs the test at the top, the body of the loop may not be performed at all if the condition is initially false.

```
/*   Figure 5-11:   Demonstrate the while loop   */

main()
{
    int i;

    i = 1;
    while (i <= 10) {
        printf("%d\n", i);
        i++;
    }
}
```

Fig. 5-11. The while loop.

Figure 5-11 shows how the task of the program in Fig. 5-10 can be performed using a while loop rather than a for loop. Notice that with the while loop, the initialization step (i = 1) must be performed outside the loop and the reinitialization step (i+ +) must be performed within the body of the loop. Only the test condition is contained within the parentheses following the word while.

In this situation, the for loop of Fig. 5-10 is more appropriate than the while loop of Fig. 5-11. There are other situations, however, where a while loop makes more sense. Suppose, for example, that a program is needed to read in integers from the console and sum these integers until their sum exceeds 100. The program must then print the sum and the number of integers that were included in the sum. The last integer read is not to be counted or summed. Such a program is shown in Fig. 5-12.

The variables count and sum are first set to zero. The first integer is read outside the loop. The while loop tests the termination condition, counts, sums, and reads in the next integer. The process is repeated as long as the sum is less than or equal to 100. After the loop terminates, the results are printed.

The same thing can be accomplished with a do-while loop, as shown in the program in Fig. 5-13. In this program some subterfuge is necessary to achieve the same result as in the previous program. Notice that count is initialized to −1 and then incremented back to zero on the first pass through the loop. There are several other minor differences.

```
/*   Figure 5-12:   Another while loop demonstration   */

/*   Read in numbers until their sum exceeds 100        */

main()
{
    int number, count, sum;

    count = 0;
    sum = 0;

    printf("Enter a series of numbers: \n");
    scanf("%d", &number);
    while ((sum + number) <= 100) {
        count++;
        sum += number;
        scanf("%d", &number);
    }

    printf("\n\n%d numbers were read.\n", count);
    printf("\nTheir sum is %d.\n", sum);
    printf("\nThe number %d was not counted.\n", number);
}
```

Fig. 5-12. Another while loop demonstration.

```
/*   Figure 5-13:  Demonstration of a do-while loop   */

/*   Read in numbers until their sum exceeds 100       */
/*   Version 2                                          */

main()
{
    int number, count, sum;

    count  = -1;
    sum    = 0;
    number = 0;

    printf("\nEnter a series of numbers:\n\n");
    do {
        count++;
        sum += number;
        scanf("%d", &number);
    } while (sum + number <= 100);

    printf("\n%d numbers were read.\n", count);
    printf("\nTheir sum is %d.\n", sum);
    printf("\nThe number %d was not counted.\n", number);
}
```

Fig. 5-13. Demonstration of a do-while loop.

In this case the **do-while** loop is less straightforward than the ordinary **while** loop. In other cases, the opposite is true. The form of the conditional loop that you should choose depends on the particular situation. Choose the form that results in the most straightforward solution.

Functions

There are no subroutines or procedures in C—there are only functions. Because a function in C can do everything that a subroutine can do in another language, this is not really a disadvantage.

A function is a more-or-less self-contained module that can be invoked from anywhere in a program. A function usually returns a value associated with the name of the function, as described in Chapter 2.

In C, a function can be invoked simply by writing its name; it can stand alone in a statement or it can be a part of an expression. In the stand-alone mode, it acts like a procedure; if it returns a value associated with its name, that value is simply ignored.

You have already seen several examples of functions in C, including printf( ), fprintf( ), gets( ), scanf( ), and getchar( ). These functions were furnished with the compiler. The documentation that comes with each C compiler includes a list of those functions furnished with the compiler together with a description of what they do.

Every C program contains at least one function, called main( ). This function corresponds to the main program of other languages. You can also write your own C functions. As a matter of fact, the use of functions to construct a C program in pieces is an excellent practice. Each function should perform a specific task or a group of related tasks. The idea is that it is easier to write a large program if it is broken up into pieces (functions) of a moderate size.

Several examples of C functions are shown in the program in Fig. 5-14. The purpose of the program is to read in two numbers, print them out, exchange their values, and print them out again. Three subtasks have been defined: reading in the numbers, printing them on the screen, and exchanging their values. A function was written to accomplish each of these subtasks.

Let's look at the function print2( ) first, as it is the simplest of the three. The function takes two integers passed to it by the calling function and prints them, appropriately labeled. In this case the calling function is main( ).

The function print2( ) receives the values to print using a method called *pass-by-value*. To understand what this means, it is necessary to look at the definition of the function:

```
print2(x,y)
int x,y;
```

The variables x and y are called *parameters* of the function. They are variables local to the function whose values are received from the calling function. When main( ) contains the following statement

```
print2(u,v);
```

the value of u is stored in the variable x and the value of v is stored in the variable y, while the function is executing. If the function contains the statement

```
x = 2*x;
```

the value of u would not be changed, because print2( ) is dealing with a copy of u, not with u itself.

In contrast to pass-by-value is *pass-by-reference*. This is illustrated by the function swap( ). The purpose of swap( ) is to actually exchange the values of the variables passed to it, so pass-by-value would not work. With pass-by-value, no matter what is done to the variables in the function swap( ), the variables in main( ) would remain unaffected.

Pass-by-reference works by passing a pointer to the function. As discussed above, a pointer is a variable that contains the actual physical address in the computer's memory where the variable pointed to is stored. When main( ) passes a pointer to swap( ), it is telling swap( ) where it can find the variable so that swap( ) can change it if necessary.

As mentioned, the address of a variable in C can be found by using the & operator.

```
/*    Figure 5-14:   Demonstrate functions.   */

/*    Read and swap two integers.            */

#define     MAXL            81
#include    "STDIO.H"

main()
{
    int u,v;
    char s[MAXL];

    do {
        clrscrn();
        u = input("Enter first  variable:  ");
        v = input("Enter second variable:  ");
        putchar('\n');
        print2(u,v);
        puts("Swapping....\n");
        swap(&u,&v);
        print2(u,v);
        printf("Again?  ");
        scanf("%s", s);
    } while ((s[0]=='y') || (s[0]=='Y'));
}

input(prompt)
char *prompt;
{
    int i;

    printf("%s", prompt);
    scanf("%d", &i);
    return i;

}

print2(x,y)
int x,y;
{
    printf("First  variable:        %d\n",  x);
    printf("Second variable:        %d\n\n",y);
}

swap(x,y)
```

Fig. 5-14. The use of functions.

```
int *x, *y;
{
    int temp;

    temp = *x;
    *x   = *y;
    *y   = temp;
}
```

Thus, the following statement

swap(&u,&v);

means that the addresses of the variables u and v are being passed to swap( ). C uses the asterisk (*) operator to reverse the process:

temp = *x;

means that **temp** is to receive the value pointed to by x. Consider the heading of swap( ):

swap(x,y)
int *x, *y;

The int statement means that x and y are pointers to variables of type int.

The function swap( ) uses the local variable temp to help carry out the exchange. Because pointers are being used, the function is actually exchanging the values of u and v in main( ). A pointer can be thought of as a form of reference, which makes the phrase pass-by-reference more meaningful.

Pass-by-value is the usual way that ordinary variables and constants are passed to functions unless explicit use is made of addresses and pointers, as discussed above. Character strings are an exception. Character strings are always passed by reference. This is because C treats the name of a character string (or any other array) as a pointer. This eliminates the overhead that would be required to make a copy of the string every time it is passed to a function.

When the compiler sees the following statement:

u = input("Enter first variable:");

in the program in Fig. 5-14, it stores the character string in a convenient place and passes a pointer to that string to the function input( ). No separate copy is made.

The first two lines of the function definition are as follows:

input(prompt)
char *prompt;

The variable prompt is called a parameter of the function. It is declared as a pointer to a character. This is in recognition of the fact that the function is receiving a pointer to a string from main( ).

The function input( ) prompts the user and then reads an integer. It operates much like the INPUT statement of BASIC. The prompt is supplied by main( ). The character string is printed on the video screen before the number is read using scanf( ).

I have not yet discussed how the value read in by input( ) is passed back to main( ). Note that this value is stored in the local variable i. The following statement:

```
return i;
```

causes the value of i to be passed back associated with the name of input( ). Thus, after the statement

```
v = input("Enter second variable:");
```

is executed v will have the value that was read within input( ) and passed to main( ) by return.

The program itself is straightforward. A main program often consists largely of a sequence of function calls; therefore if meaningful names are used for the functions, the program will be easy to read. Where meaningful names are not practical, appropriate comments should be included.

The function call

```
clrscrn( );
```

clears the screen. This particular function was provided with the Mix-C library. Other C compilers are likely to provide a similar function.

Most of the main program is enclosed in a do-while loop so that the demonstration can be repeated easily.

Recursion

As discussed in Chapter 2, a function is said to be recursive if it invokes itself. The program in Fig. 5-15 illustrates how this is handled in C. In this program, a recursive function is used to manipulate a character string.

The function takes a string of length N, then prints it N times, dropping the first letter each time, until there are no letters remaining. The result is a sort of triangle that can be read both horizontally and vertically. The function uses the standard C library function strlen( ), which returns the length of the string.

A function is also needed to delete the first character from a string. Because such a function does not exist in the standard library supplied with this C compiler, it is necessary to write it. Rather than write a function that serves only this purpose, a general-purpose delete function is written that will delete a specified number of characters beginning with a specified position in the string.

The recursive function is called triangle( ). When triangle( ) is called, the first thing it does is to check to make sure that the length of the string supplied to it is greater

```
/*   Figure 5-15:   Demonstrate recursion.   */

/*   The program manipulates a string recursively   */

#define    MAXL             81
#include   "STDIO.H"

main()
{
    char s[MAXL];
    int  i;

    clrscrn();
    puts("Type a string:\n");
    gets(s);
    puts("\n");              /*  Skip 2 lines (puts() includes 1 '\n') */
    triangle(s);

}  /* end main() */

triangle(s)      /* Print a string, drop first char, repeat */
char s[MAXL];
{
    if (strlen(s)>0) {
        puts(s);
        delete(s,1,1);
        triangle(s);
    }

}  /*  end triangle()  */

delete(s,i,n)    /* Delete n chars, starting with i-th char of s */
char s[MAXL];
int i,n;
{
    int j,k;
    char t[MAXL];

    strcpy(t,s);    /*  Copies s to t                        */
    i--;            /*  Adjust char # to array subscript */

    for(j=0; j<i; j++)         /*  Copy 1st part of string */
        s[j] = t[j];

    /*  Skip over deleted chars and copy the rest */
    for(k=i+n; k<MAXL-1 && t[k]!=NULL; j++, k++)
        s[j] = t[k];
    s[j] = NULL;               /*  Mark end of string */

}  /*  end delete() */
```

Fig. 5-15. The use of recursion.

than zero. If it is not, triangle( ) returns without doing anything. If it is, it prints the string, uses delete( ) to drop the first character, and then calls itself (triangle( )) again. After the last character has been deleted, strlen( ) will return zero, and the function will return to where it was last called. Because the recursive call is at the end of the function triangle( ), the function will keep returning until it finally returns to main( ). Because there is nothing left in main( ), the program terminates.

It is easier to understand how the program works after seeing it run. If you are still having trouble understanding the sequence of calls and returns, try adding the following:

```
puts("triangle( ) entered");
```

as the first statement of triangle( ) and the statement below:

```
puts("triangle( ) exited");
```

as the last statement of triangle( ).

For variety, the puts( ) function was used instead of the printf( ) function in this program. With some compilers, this can lead to a more compact program.

The delete( ) function includes a call to a function named strcpy( ). This function copies from one string to another and is a standard C function, provided with nearly all C compilers.

The goto Statement

The goto statement is not often needed in C because of the rich variety of other control statements available. In other languages, such as Pascal, the goto statement is sometimes used to escape from a loop before the loop has run its course. In C, the break statement can be used for that purpose.

The problem with the break statement is that it will cause an exit from only one level of nesting. If it is necessary to escape from more than one level of nesting, a goto is necessary. This situation sometimes arises when an irreparable error is discovered deep inside a program and a quick exit is needed.

Some of the earlier versions of C on microcomputers did not even support the goto statement, and it was not often missed. Nevertheless, for the record, I will discuss how it can be used in C.

A label must be defined to provide a destination for a goto. A label is simply an identifier followed by a colon. A label may precede any statement. A goto cannot jump out of a function; the target label must be in the same function as the goto that targets it. Here is a simple example of the use of a goto and the corresponding label:

```
/* Guessing game */
#define MAGIC    7

main( )
{
    int i;
```

```
start:   printf("Pick a number from 1 to 10");
         scanf("%d", &i);
         if ((i < 1) || (i > 10))
         goto start;
         if (i = MAGIC)
             printf("You win! \ n");
     else
             printf("You lose! \ n");
}
```

This program is rather simplistic and could have been programmed without the **goto** (by using **do-while**, for example), but serves to illustrate the basic mechanics of the statement.

DATA STRUCTURES

Up to this point, the C programs illustrated have used only integers, characters, pointers, and character strings. I will now introduce more advanced data structures, such as arrays, structures, and linked lists.

Earlier, in this chapter, I remarked that C is a rich language in that it provides a wide variety of control structures. C is also rich in its selection of data structures. The data structure called **structure** in C provides the user the ability to define new data structures of arbitrary complexity.

Arrays

Arrays in C are treated in nearly the same way as are character strings. Character strings are, in fact, a special case of character arrays, terminated with the null character ($\setminus 0$, or binary zero).

Array subscripts in C are delimited by square brackets. Subscripts in C arrays always begin with 0. To create an array of 10 integers in C, the following declaration would be used:

```
int test[10];
```

Subscripts for this array would run from zero to nine, not one to 10 as might be imagined. This peculiarity takes a little getting used to by programmers who have previously used other high-level languages, although it seems natural to assembly language programmers.

A two-dimensional array of 10 rows by 20 columns would be declared as follows:

```
int test2 [10] [20];
```

Notice that two sets of brackets are required.

Earlier, I mentioned that character strings are automatically passed to functions by reference rather than by value. The same is true for arrays.

Arrays can be accessed in C using pointers. The details of how this is done are omitted due to lack of space. The reader interested in pursuing how this is done is referred to a book devoted exclusively to C. Except for this use of pointers, the usage of arrays in C is similar to that in other languages. Examples showing the usage of arrays in C can be found in the following sections of this chapter.

Structures

In Chapter 2, I discussed an example in which a record containing a student's name and his or her scores on up to 20 tests was needed. Records in C are called *structures*. Suppose that there may be up to 30 students in the class. What is needed is an array of structures. Here is how the declaration would look:

```
structure {
    char name[26];
    int score[20];
} student[30];
```

This structure allows for the name to have up to 25 characters (plus the null terminator) and for each student to have up to 20 test scores (numbered zero to 19). If it is desired to have the test scores numbered from one to 20, the array must be dimensioned with 21 elements; element 0 can then simply be ignored.

The name of the fourth student and the score he or she received on the seventh test would be printed as follows:

```
printf("%s %d \n", student[3].name,
        student[3].score[6]);
```

Notice the placement of the square brackets and the use of the period (.) to refer to elements of a structure. Recall that element 3 is the fourth element of the array of students and that element 6 is the seventh element of the array of scores.

Linked Lists

This section discusses how linked lists can be implemented in C as arrays of structures. Another method involving dynamic allocation of storage and pointers exists, but it is beyond the scope of this book.

The methodology illustrated here for implementing linked lists in C is essentially the same as that discussed in Chapter 2, with several minor exceptions. Because array subscripts in C start with zero, the value -1 is used to mark the end of the list rather than the value 0. The first record of the list is stored as record 0 rather than as record 1. Also, rather than parallel arrays, one containing the name and the other the link, an array of structures is used.

The C declarations to set up the linked list are as follows:

```
#define EOL      (-1)
#define MAXLENGTH 5
#define NAMELEN    16
int first, free;
```

```
structure {
    char name[NAMELEN];
    int link;
} list[MAXLENGTH];
```

The constant **EOL** stands for end-of-list and is used to indicate that no more records follow in a list.

Following these declarations, the contents of record number 4 would be referred to as list[4].name and list[4].link.

The comprehensive sample program at the end of the chapter illustrates the use of linked lists in an actual C program, showing the details of how elements are added to and deleted from linked lists.

FILE HANDLING

A general-purpose high-level language must be able to write data to and read data from auxiliary storage devices. In the case of microcomputers, the most common form of auxiliary storage device is the magnetic disk, which can be either a floppy disk or a hard disk. A collection of data on a disk is called a *file*.

As mentioned earlier, the C language itself does not include any provision for input or output. Functions to handle input and output are customarily included in a function library provided with each C compiler. You have already seen functions that allow input from the console and output to the console and to a printer. In this section, functions to read from and write to disk files are discussed.

There is a de facto standard set of file input and output functions described in *The C Programming Language*, by Kernighan and Ritchie. Not every C compiler provides this standard set of file input and output functions, but most do. This book discusses the functions provided with the Mix-C compiler, which comply with the standard.

Each file in C has a *file pointer* associated with it. The special case of a file pointer to a printer was discussed earlier. Programs that access files must contain the following statement at the beginning of the program:

```
#include    "STDIO.H"
```

This tells the compiler to include and compile the text of the file **STDIO.H** into the program. The file pointer is declared this way:

```
FILE    *fp;
```

The file pointer can then be used to identify a particular file to the various input and output functions.

A file is opened using the **fopen( )** function. For example,

```
fp = fopen("test.txt", "w");
```

opens a file called **test.txt** in the *write* or output mode, and returns a file pointer for later use. This file pointer is assigned, in this case, to the variable **fp**. To open a file for input, the mode is r for *read*.

If an attempt is made to open a file in the **w** mode and that file already exists, a new file will be created and the previous version of the file will be lost. If the intent is to add on to the end of an existing file without overwriting that file, the file should be opened in the **a** or *append* mode.

If an **fopen( )** function fails for any reason, it returns NULL (binary zero) instead of a pointer. It is good practice to check for such an occurrence.

Files are closed using the **fclose( )** function. The correct usage is as follows:

```
status = fclose(fp);
```

where **status** is an integer and **fp** is a file pointer. The **fclose( )** function returns a status of 0 if successful or −1 if an error occurs.

When a character is sent to a file by a C function, an actual file output may not occur at that time. Instead, the character may go to a buffer, which usually consists of 128 or more characters. When that buffer is full, the actual physical write to disk takes place. Closing a file automatically writes any characters remaining in the buffer to disk.

Sequential Files

A sequential file is a sequence of characters on a disk that are accessed one character at a time, from beginning to end. Except for the first character, no character can be accessed unless its immediate predecessor in sequence has just been accessed. In other words, character 4 can be accessed only after character 3, character 3 after character 2, and so forth.

The function that writes a character to a file is called **putc( )**. For example,

```
a = putc(c, fp);
```

writes the character **c** to the file pointed to by **fp**. It returns and assigns to the variable **a** the character that was output if the write was successful; otherwise it returns EOF (end-of-file). (The value of EOF is defined in **STDIO.H**.)

The function that reads a character from a file is called **getc( )**. For example, the following statement:

```
c = getc(fp);
```

reads a character from the file pointed to by **fp** and assigns it to **c**. If the end of the file has been reached, **getc( )** returns EOF (−1). For that reason, **c** must be an integer, not a character, because a character could not hold the value of EOF.

Most C libraries also include a function called **ungetc( )**. This function puts a character back into a file after it has been read. It is sometimes useful when the program has read too far and needs to back up a character.

The program in Fig. 5-16 illustrates the use of sequential input and output. The program reads in a list of names and ages from the console and writes the list to a sequential file. It then reads the names back from the disk, displaying each one again on the console.

After the program clears the screen, it opens a file called **AGES.TXT** for output

```
/*   Figure 5-16:   Sequential file of Names and Ages.   */

#define          FN                   "AGES.TXT"
#define          FOREVER              (-1)
#define          INPUT                "r"
#define          OUTPUT               "w"
#define          MAXL                 81
#include         "STDIO.H"

main()
{
        char name[MAXL];
        int  age, status;
        FILE *fp;                              /* file pointer */

        clrscrn();
        fp = fopen(FN, OUTPUT);                /* open file for output */

        /* Read in names & ages from keyboard & write to file */
        printf("\nEnter Names and Ages; ");
        printf("<Ctrl-Z> <RETURN> to quit.\n\n");
        while (FOREVER) {
                printf("\nName:   ");
                status = scanf("%s", name);
                if (status == EOF) break;
                printf("Age:    ");
                status = scanf("%d", &age);
                if (status == EOF) break;
                fprintf(fp, "%s %d\n", name, age);
        }
        printf("\nInput complete; closing file %s.\n",FN);
        fclose(fp);

        /* Now read the file back and display on screen */
        printf("Reopening file %s.\n",FN);
        fp = fopen(FN, INPUT);

        printf("Here are the names and ages from the file.\n\n");
        while (fscanf(fp, "%s %d", name, &age) != EOF) {
                printf("%-10s %5d\n", name, age);
        }

        printf("\nClosing file %s.\n",FN);
        fclose(fp);

}   /* end main() */
```

Fig. 5-16. A sequential file of Names and Ages.

(mode w). Following this there appears to be an infinite loop (while(FOREVER)), where FOREVER has the logical value "true" (−1). This loop prompts the user to input a name and the corresponding age. If the user types Control-Z followed by a carriage return in place of a name, the scanf( ) function will return EOF, and the program will break out of the loop.

The string name and the integer age are read from the console with the scanf( ) function. This is quick and easy, but it has one disadvantage: only first names can be read, and no compound names, such as Mary Jo, can be read. This is because scanf( ) cannot read a string with an embedded space. The next example program shows how to get around this limitation.

A name and age pair is written to the sequential file by the fprintf( ) function. Recall that printf( ) outputs data in a form readable by people, i.e., as ASCII character strings suitable for display on a video screen. The fprintf( ) function does the same thing, except that it sends its output to the designated file. The format specifications are used to specify the required conversions and to insert a blank space between name and age, and a newline character after age.

Because of the way this file is formatted, i.e., as ASCII text, it can be easily read by using the MS-DOS TYPE command to list it on the screen.

After the last name and age pair are written to the file, the file is closed and reopened for input (mode r). Another while loop is used to read the data back in from the file and print it on the screen. Notice that when the file is opened for input, it is automatically positioned such that reading will start at the beginning of the file. The function fscanf( ) is used to read in a name and age pair from the file. This function returns EOF when the end of the file is encountered, thus terminating the loop.

The function fscanf( ) is similar to scanf( ) except that it reads from a file instead of from the console. It makes format conversions as specified by the format specifications, reversing the process of the fprintf( ) function.

Because name and age are to receive new values in the scanf( ) and fscanf( ) functions, they must be passed by reference, not by value. Because name is a character string, it is automatically passed by reference. Because age is an integer, it must receive special handling in order to be passed by reference. This means that a pointer to age rather than age itself must be passed to the function. Thus the function is called as follows:

```
fscanf(fp, "%s %d", name, &age);
```

Failure to follow the rules of passing variables by reference is a common error among beginning C programmers.

The final step is to close the file again.

Direct-Access Files

With a direct-access file, the program can access any record of the file independently of any other record. For example, record 2 can be accessed without first accessing record 1. An example might be a directory-assistance file that is used by a telephone operator to look up telephone numbers. It would be terribly inefficient if the file could only be accessed sequentially.

A direct-access file in C is treated as a sequence of bytes (or characters). The function fseek( ) is used to position the file at a particular place in the file. This position is measured relative to the beginning, the end, or the current position in the file. The offset is measured in numbers of characters. To use fseek( ), the programmer must be able to compute the position of the desired record in the file. This requires extra bookkeeping.

The offset used with the function fseek( ) is measured with a long integer. If it were measured with an ordinary or unsigned integer, it would be useful only with files of up to 65,535 characters, the largest value an unsigned integer can have in most C implementations.

Because details of direct-access input and output tend to vary from compiler to compiler, you should carefully check the documentation received with your compiler. It will cover, for example, the proper parameters to use for fopen( ).

Because direct-access files in C are character-oriented rather than record-oriented, it is less convenient to use direct-access files with C than with Pascal, Modula-2, Ada, COBOL, or Fortran. This deficiency can be overcome fairly quickly by creating functions that compute the location of a record in terms of characters, but with these other languages that function is handled by the language.

The comprehensive program at the end of this chapter illustrates the use of direct-access files in an actual C program.

GRAPHICS

The C language itself does not support graphics. There is no reason, however, why a particular implementation of C on a microcomputer with graphics capability could not include graphics functions. Because C supports low-level operations very well, the creation of such functions should be relatively easy.

THE COMPREHENSIVE SAMPLE PROGRAM

All the programs so far in this chapter have been relatively short and simple. Each has been intended to illustrate a particular feature of the language. The final program in this chapter is longer and more complex in order to portray more fully the nature of the language.

The comprehensive sample program in this chapter is similar to that in most other chapters of this book; it maintains a file of names and addresses in alphabetical order.

In this particular program the maximum size of the file is limited to 10 records by the constant MAXRECORDS. The reason for this will become clear later on. If the program is to be used for other than demonstration purposes, this upper limit can be changed easily.

The comprehensive sample program is shown in Fig. 5-17. It has the capability to add records to the file, to delete records from the file, to display the file one record at a time, and to list the entire file on the screen or on a printer.

The file is maintained in alphabetical order at all times. As each record is added to the file, it is inserted in its proper place, eliminating the need for an explicit sort.

The data structure that permits the file to be maintained in alphabetical order without sorting is the linked list. As discussed earlier in the chapter, a linked list facilitates the insertion and deletion of records while maintaining the order of the list.

```
/*   Figure 5-17:  Comprehensive Sample Program.  */

/**********************************************************/
/*                                                      */
/*   An Electronic Address Book.                        */
/*                                                      */
/*   This program maintains a direct-access file of     */
/*   names and addresses on disk.  A separate index     */
/*   file is used to access the names in                */
/*   alphabetical order.                                */
/*                                                      */
/*        Functions supported include:                  */
/*           - Add a record to the file                 */
/*           - Review records on screen with option     */
/*                to delete a record                    */
/*           - List file on screen or printer           */
/*           - Dump file, with pointers, to printer     */
/*                                                      */
/**********************************************************/

#include        "STDIO.H"
#define         EOL             (-1)      /* End Of List */
#define         FALSE           0
#define         TRUE            (-1)
#define         ANAME           "ADDR.TXT"
#define         INAME           "INDEX.TXT"
#define         BACKUP          "INDEX.BAK"
#define         INPUT           "r"
#define         OUTPUT          "w"
#define         APPEND          "a"
#define         MAXL            81
#define         MAXRECORDS      10        /* Increase as necessary */
#define         NEWLINE         '\n'
#define         RECLENGTH       72L       /* includes CR/LF at end */
#define         F1_LENGTH       13        /* 12 chars + NULL       */
#define         F2_LENGTH       13
#define         F3_LENGTH       22
#define         F4_LENGTH       13
#define         F5_LENGTH       3
#define         F6_LENGTH       6

struct filerec {
        char lname   [F1_LENGTH];
        char fname   [F2_LENGTH];
        char address [F3_LENGTH];
        char city    [F4_LENGTH];
        char state   [F5_LENGTH];
        char zip     [F6_LENGTH];
};

struct filerec RecBuf, TempBuf;                  /*   Record Buffers  */

int link[MAXRECORDS], first, free;

FILE *AddrFile, *IndexFile, *prt,
     *scrn;                                      /* file pointers    */
```

Fig. 5-17. Comprehensive sample program.

```
main()
{
    int c;
    openfiles();
    do {
        c = menu();
        switch (c) {
        case 1:
                append();
                break;
        case 2:
                review();
                break;
        case 3:
                listfile();
                break;
        case 4:
                dump();
                break;
        case 5:
                /* quit */
                break;
        default:
                break;
        }
    } while (c != 5);
    closefiles();

}   /* end main() */

openfiles()                 /* Open printer, address, and index files */
{
    int i;

    prt  = fopen("LPT1:", OUTPUT);      /* printer */
    scrn = fopen("CON:",  OUTPUT);      /* console */

    IndexFile = fopen (INAME, INPUT);
    if (IndexFile == NULL) {            /* indicates new file    */
        initfiles();
    }
    fscanf (IndexFile, "%d %d", &free, &first);
    for (i=0; i < MAXRECORDS; i++)
        fscanf(IndexFile, "%d", &link[i]);
    fclose(IndexFile);

    AddrFile = fopen(ANAME, APPEND);

} /* end openfiles() */

initfiles()
{                       /* Initialize IndexFile as a linked list of free  */
    int i;         /*    records and leave open                      */

    IndexFile = fopen (INAME, OUTPUT);
    free  = 0;       /* first free record    */
    first = EOL;     /* first active record */
    fprintf (IndexFile, "%d\n%d\n", free, first);
```

```
           /* Now complete the Free List */
           for (i=0; i<MAXRECORDS-1; i++)
               fprintf(IndexFile, "%d\n", i+1);
           fprintf (IndexFile, "%d\n", EOL);
           fclose (IndexFile);
           IndexFile = fopen (INAME, INPUT);

   }   /* end initfiles()    */

   menu()
   {
       int row, col, c;
       char s[MAXL];
       clrscrn();
       row = col = 5;
       poscurs(row,col);                   /* position cursor */
       puts("1) Add to file");
       row += 2;                           /* add 2 to row    */
       poscurs(row,col);
       puts("2) Review file on screen");
       row += 2;
       poscurs(row,col);
       puts("3) List file to screen or printer");
       row += 2;
       poscurs(row,col);
       puts("4) Dump file to printer");
       row += 2;
       poscurs(row,col);
       puts("5) Quit");
       col = 1;
       row += 2;
       do {
           poscurs(row,col);
           printf("Select 1, 2, 3, 4, or 5:  ");
           gets(s);                        /* scanf() leaves input */
           c = atoi(s);                    /* buffer cluttered     */
       } while ((c < 1) || (c > 5));
       return(c);

   }   /* end menu() */

   append()               /* add records to the file */
   {
       int i,c;
       i = getfree();
       if (i==EOL) return(EOF);
       while (getentry(i)!=EOF) {
           insert(i);
           i = getfree();
           if (i==EOL) break;
       }

   }   /* end append() */

   getfree()              /*  return rec nr of first free record */
   {
       int i;
```

Fig. 5-17. Comprehensive sample program. (Continued from page 137.)

```
    i = free;
    if (i==EOL) {
        warn();
        return(EOL);
    } else
        return(i);

}   /*  end getfree() */

insert(i)                /*  insert record into linked list in order */
int i;
{
    int p,q;
    if (free==EOL) {
        warn();          /*  no room to insert      */
        return;
    }
    free = link[i];      /*  delete from free list */
    p = first;
    q = EOL;
    getrec (AddrFile, &RecBuf, i);
    getrec (AddrFile, &TempBuf, p);
    while ((p!=EOL) && greater()) {
        q = p;
        p = link[p];
        getrec (AddrFile, &TempBuf, p);
    }
    link[i] = p;
    if (q==EOL)
        first = i;       /* new entry to head of list */
    else
        link[q] = i;

}   /*  end insert() */

getentry(i)              /* read record from keyboard into RecBuf */
int i;                   /* and write it to file as record i      */
{
    int row, col, start;
    char buffer[MAXL];
    clrscrn();
    start = 14;
    row = 5;
    col = 1;
    poscurs(row,col);
    printf("Last Name:");    markoff(start,row,12);
    row +=2;  poscurs(row,col);
    printf("First Name:");   markoff(start,row,12);
    row +=2;  poscurs(row,col);
    printf("Address:");      markoff(start,row,20);
    row +=2;  poscurs(row,col);
    printf("City:");         markoff(start,row,12);
    row +=2;  poscurs(row,col);
    printf("State:");        markoff(start,row,2);
    row +=2;  poscurs(row,col);
    printf("Zip Code:");     markoff(start,row,5);
    row = 5;  col = start + 1;
    poscurs(row,col);
    gets(buffer);
```

```
        if (buffer[0]==NULL) return(EOF);
        strcpy(RecBuf.lname,buffer);
        row +=2;  poscurs(row,col);
        gets(RecBuf.fname);
        row +=2;  poscurs(row,col);
        gets(RecBuf.address);
        row +=2;  poscurs(row,col);
        gets(RecBuf.city);
        row +=2;  poscurs(row,col);
        gets(RecBuf.state);
        row +=2;  poscurs(row,col);
        gets(RecBuf.zip);
        putrec (AddrFile, &RecBuf, i);
        return(0);

}  /*  end getentry() */

markoff(col,row,n)                    /*  delimit input field boundary */
int col,row,n;
{
    int i;
    poscurs(row,col);
    printf(":");
    for (i=0; i<n; i++)       /* n blank spaces */
        printf(" ");
    printf(":");

}  /*  end markoff() */

review()                  /* print records to screen 1 at a time */
                          /* allows deletion of current record    */
{
    int q,r;
    char c;
    clrscrn();
    if (first==EOL) return;
    r = first;
    q = EOL;
    do {
        putchar('\n');
        printrec(scrn, r);
        putchar('\n');
        do {
            printf("G)et next record, ");
            printf("D)elete this record, ");
            printf("or Q)uit?  ");
            c = getch();
            putchar('\n');
        } while ((c!='G') && (c!='g') &&
                 (c!='D') && (c!='d') &&
                 (c!='Q') && (c!='q'));
        switch (c) {
        case 'G':                      /* get next */
        case 'g':
                    q = r;
                    r = link[r];
                    break;
```

Fig. 5-17. Comprehensive sample program. (Continued from page 139.)

```
        case 'D':                    /* delete    */
        case 'd':
                    strcpy (RecBuf.lname, "Deleted");
                    strcpy (RecBuf.fname, "Record");
                    putrec (AddrFile, &RecBuf, r);
                    if (q==EOL) {
                        first = link[r];
                        putfree(r);
                        r = first;
                    } else {
                        link[q] = link[r];
                        putfree(r);
                        r = link[q];
                    }
                    break;
        case 'Q':
        case 'q':
                    break;
        }   /* end switch */
    } while ((r!=EOL) && (c!='Q') && (c!='q'));

}   /* end review() */

putfree(r)        /* put r in free list */
int r;
{
    link[r] = free;
    free = r;
}   /* end putfree() */

listfile()                /* list file to screen or printer */
{
    char c;
    int i;
    if (first==EOL) return;
    clrscrn();
    printf("List to S)creen or P)rinter?  ");
    c = getch();
    putchar('\n');
    switch (c) {
    case 'S':
    case 's':
                for (i=first; i!=EOL; i=link[i]) {
                    printrec(scrn, i);
                    fprintf (scrn, "\n");
                }
                break;
    case 'P':
    case 'p':
                for (i=first; i!=EOL; i=link[i]) {
                    printrec(prt, i);
                    fprintf(prt, "\n");
                }
                break;
    default:
                puts("Sorry, you must type 'S', 's', 'P', or 'p'.");
                putchar('\n');
                break;
    }
```

```
        pause();

}   /* end listfile() */

dump()                    /* dump file and pointers to printer */
{
    int i;
    fprintf(prt,"first active = %d , first free = %d \n",first,free);
    for (i=0; i<MAXRECORDS; i++) {
        fprintf(prt,"Record %d:\n",i);
        printrec(prt, i);
        fprintf(prt,"Link:  %d\n\n", link[i]);
    }

}   /* end dump() */

printrec(f, i)      /* print record i to file f          */
FILE *f;
int i;              /* where f is the screen or printer  */
{

    if (getrec(AddrFile, &RecBuf, i) == EOF) return;
    fprintf(f, "%s %s\n", RecBuf.fname, RecBuf.lname);
    fprintf(f, "%s\n",    RecBuf.address);
    fprintf(f, "%s, %s %s\n", RecBuf.city, RecBuf.state,
                              RecBuf.zip);

}   /* end printrec() */

closefiles()                /* write list to disk and close out */
{
    int i;
    rename (INAME, BACKUP);
    IndexFile = fopen(INAME, OUTPUT);

    fprintf(IndexFile, "%d\n%d\n", free, first);
    for (i=0; i<MAXRECORDS; i++)
        fprintf(IndexFile, "%d\n", link[i]);
    fclose(IndexFile);
    fclose(AddrFile);
    fclose(prt);

}   /* closefiles() */

greater()     /* return TRUE if RecBuf > TempBuf */
{
    int f1, f2;
    f1 = strcmp(RecBuf.lname,TempBuf.lname);
    f2 = strcmp(RecBuf.fname,TempBuf.fname);
    if (f1>0 || (f1==0 && f2>0))
        return(TRUE);
    else
        return(FALSE);

}   /*  greater() */

warn()
```

Fig. 5-17. Comprehensive sample program. (Continued from page 141.)

```
{
    fprintf(stderr, "\nWarning!!!  File is full!\n");
    pause();

}  /* end warn() */

getrec (f, p, i)            /* read in record i from file f */
FILE *f;                    /* into buffer p                */
struct filerec *p;
int i;
{
    long int offset, pos;
    int status;
    offset = ((long) i) * RECLENGTH;
    pos = fseek (f, offset, 0);
    if (pos == -1) {
        fprintf(stderr, "Seek error on record %d....\n", i);
        pause();
        return (EOF);
    }

    status = ffgets(f, p->lname,   F1_LENGTH);
    if (status == EOF) {
        return (EOF);
    }
    ffgets(f, p->fname,   F2_LENGTH);
    ffgets(f, p->address, F3_LENGTH);
    ffgets(f, p->city,    F4_LENGTH);
    ffgets(f, p->state,   F5_LENGTH);
    ffgets(f, p->zip,     F6_LENGTH);

}  /* end getrec() */

ffgets(f, s, n)         /* get string from fixed-field-length file */
FILE *f;
char *s;                /* string to read into                     */
int   n;                /* field length                            */
{
    int i, c;

    for (i=0; i<n; i++) {
        if ((c = getc(f)) != EOF) {
            s[i] = c;
        } else {
            return (EOF);         /* EOF encountered */
        }
    }
    return (0);                   /* successful      */

} /* end ffgets() */

putrec(f, p, i)             /* write record to file */
FILE *f;
struct filerec *p;
int i;
{
    long int offset;
    offset = ((long) i) * RECLENGTH;
    fseek (AddrFile, offset, 0);
```

```
        ffputs(f, p->lname,   F1_LENGTH);
        ffputs(f, p->fname,   F2_LENGTH);
        ffputs(f, p->address, F3_LENGTH);
        ffputs(f, p->city,    F4_LENGTH);
        ffputs(f, p->state,   F5_LENGTH);
        ffputs(f, p->zip,     F6_LENGTH);
        putc('\n', f);

}  /* end putrec() */

ffputs(f, s, n)        /* put string to fixed-length record field */
FILE *f;
char *s;
int   n;
{
    int i;
    char c;

    for (i=0; (i<n-1) && ((c = s[i]) != '\0'); i++)
        putc(c, f);
    while (i<n) {
        putc('\0', f);        /* pad with nulls */
        i++;
    }

}  /* end ffputs() */

pause()                /* wait for any key */
{
    fprintf(stderr, "\nPress any key to continue...");
    getch();
}
```

Fig. 5-17. Comprehensive sample program. (Continued from page 143.)

The data itself is stored in an array of structures. A separate array is used to store the links between records. (The links could as easily have been part of the structure.) A link points to a record by containing the value of that record's subscript.

The variable **first** is used to point to the first record in the file. It does so by holding the value of that record's subscript. The link corresponding to each record points to the next record in order. The corresponding link is the element of the array link with the same subscript as the record itself. A link value of -1 (**EOL**) indicates the end of the list.

Suppose that in a file that can hold 100 records, only 60 records are in use. Some way is needed to keep track of the unused records. One way to do this is to use a separate linked list called the *free list*. The variable **free** points to the first record in the free list; subsequent free records are linked in the same manner as are the records in the active list.

The process of adding a record to the list consists of finding a record in the free list, removing it from the free list, and inserting it in its proper place in the active list. During all of this, the record itself does not move; the list insertion and deletion is accomplished by manipulating the links.

The data are stored in a direct-access file called ADDR.TXT. The links are stored in a sequential file called INDEX.TXT at the conclusion of the program. The program always maintains a backup of the index file, called INDEX.BAK.

Notice that some of the variables in this program are declared outside of any function (before main( )). This makes these variables *global* in scope. In other words, these variables may be accessed from any function in the program. They need not be redeclared in each function; in fact any variable declared in a function with the same name as a global variable will prevent that global variable from being accessed in that function.

Global variables are useful for variables that must be referenced from several functions, such as the array of records and the array of links of this program. If they were not declared globally, they would have to be passed as arguments to each function that references them.

The overall structure of the program is illustrated by the structure chart in Fig. 5-18. In this chart, the names of functions that are called by another function are listed beneath and to the right of the calling function. For example, the functions openfiles( ), menu( ), append( ) are called by main( ). The functions getfree( ), getentry( ), and insert( ) are called by append( ); warn( ) is called by getfree( ), and so on.

To make the operation of this program more understandable, a function called dump( ) is included. This function prints each record of the file and the corresponding links in the order that they are stored in memory. To gain a better understanding of the data structures used in this program, you should enter several records, dump the file, and then add and delete several records, dumping the file between each action. (The dump( ) function as written requires a printer.) The reason that the constant MAXRECORDS was set to 10 was to keep the dump printout to a manageable size.

ADVANTAGES AND DISADVANTAGES OF C

The C language was written by a professional programmer for use by professional programmers. It can be used by advanced hobbyists, but is probably not a good choice for beginners. Power and conciseness were design considerations; clarity of expression was not.

C provides a wide variety of control structures, including a **for** statement that is considerably more powerful than the corresponding statement of other languages. An example of its power can be found in the way it is used to traverse a linked list in the function listfile( ) in the program in Fig. 5-17.

C also provides facilities for manipulating bits and bytes. These facilities are useful for systems programmers who must deal with operating systems and such.

C is particularly useful for programs that read and manipulate characters. Examples include text editors and filters that convert certain characters (for example a program to convert tab characters to blanks in a file).

C allows the definition of data structures of arbitrary complexity using the structure facility.

Because C is usually implemented as a compiled language, programs written in C usually execute much faster than equivalent programs written in BASIC.

Programs written in C can usually be transported easily from one computer to another computer, even if those computers are dissimilar. Several major microcomputer software houses now do all of their internal development in C, in part for this reason.

Software packages (including operating systems) written in C can be transported to new microcomputers as soon as a C compiler is available for that machine.

On the negative side, direct-access files are not as simple to use in C as in most other languages.

Most C compilers are relatively lax in their error-checking. For example, the compiler might not detect whether or not a function is being called with the proper number of

```
Figure 5-18:   Structure Chart for the Comprehensive
               Sample Program.


              main()
                   openfiles()
                        initfiles()
                   menu()
                   append()
                        getfree()
                             warn()
                                  pause()
                        getentry()
                             markoff()
                             putrec()
                                  ffputs()
                        insert()
                             warn()
                                  pause()
                             getrec()
                                  pause()
                                  ffgets()
                             greater()
                   review()
                        printrec()
                        putfree()
                   listfile()
                        printrec()
                             getrec()
                                  pause()
                                  ffgets()
                   dump()
                        printrec()
                             getrec()
                                  pause()
                                  ffgets()
                   closefiles()
```

Fig. 5-18. Structure chart for the comprehensive sample program.

arguments. Because C is a loosely typed language, the compiler might not notice errors in program logic caused by mixed-mode assignments or arithmetic operations. (*Mixed-mode* means involving data of different types, such as integer and floating point.)

The concept of pointers in C is a very powerful one, but it requires the programmer to have a more detailed understanding of the underlying machine than ought to be the case. In my opinion, a high-level language ought to insulate the programmer from the underlying machine more than C does. The author of C readily admits (in *The C Programming Language*) that C is not a very high-level language.

The misuse of pointers can cause errors that are extremely difficult to detect.

Like Pascal, C lacks an exponentiation operator.

Many implementations of C on microcomputers provide very slow compilation speeds. The process of writing and running C programs is therefore less convenient than the corresponding process for BASIC or a language that compiles more quickly. This has become less of a problem recently as faster compilers and more powerful microcomputers have become available.

AVAILABILITY

There are many implementations of C available to microcomputer owners. There are versions that run under IBM PC-DOS, MS DOS, CP/M, Apple DOS, CP/M-86, CP/M-68K, and Unix on various microcomputers. Some versions sell for as little as $39.95 and some for as much as $500.

The features of C compilers for eight-bit microcomputers vary greatly, so the potential buyer is cautioned to buy carefully. Some of these C compilers have floating point and long integers and some do not; some support direct-access files and some do not; some permit separate compilation of functions and some do not.

There are many excellent C compilers available for IBM PC and compatible microcomputers, and for Motorola 68000-based microcomputers such as the Apple Macintosh, Atari 1040ST, and Commodore Amiga. Among the companies that produce excellent C compilers are Microsoft, Lattice, Borland International, Mix Software, DeSmet, Ecosoft, Aztec, Computer Innovations, Mark Williams, and Wizard.

SUMMARY

C is a powerful language that is available for a wide variety of microcomputers. It is best suited for the intermediate to advanced programmer who already has a thorough understanding of the concepts of computers and computer programming and who needs the extra features provided by C.

C is an excellent choice for experienced assembly language programmers who wish to move to a higher-level language. It is also a good choice for an experienced BASIC or Pascal programmer who wants a more flexible language with more direct control over the underlying hardware. It is not a good choice as a first programming language for the beginner.

Ada
BASIC
C
COBOL
Forth
Fortran
LISP
Logo
Modula-2
Pascal
PILOT
Prolog

6

COBOL

The name COBOL stands for COmmon Business Oriented Language. It is by far the most widely used language today for business applications on large mainframe computers. A glance at the help-wanted advertisements in a major metropolitan newspaper will probably reveal many more jobs available for COBOL programmers than for all other programmers combined.

Despite its widespread use on mainframe computers, COBOL is relatively rarely used on microcomputers. Part of the reason is historic, in that BASIC was available on microcomputers before COBOL, and early business applications for microcomputers were written in BASIC. Nevertheless, COBOL is very well-suited to business applications and deserves a close look.

Just what does it mean for a language to be "business oriented?" The obvious answer is that a business-oriented language is a language that is suitable for business programs, but that just begs the question. How do business programs differ from other kinds of programs, and why aren't languages such as BASIC and Fortran suitable for business programs?

First, business programs are oriented toward data files stored on magnetic disk or tape. A language for business programs must have efficient file-handling facilities. It should be able to read and write data records simply, and it should handle both sequential and direct-access files.

Second, business programs must be able to handle dollars and cents exactly. Arithmetic must be exact. Floating-point arithmetic is unacceptable for most business uses, because it has limited precision (usually about seven decimal digits of precision). Integer arithmetic is exact and would be acceptable if it could handle larger numbers, but it cannot. Using integers to represent the number of cents, a 16-bit number could only handle amounts up to about $327.00. In short, a programming language should be able to perform exact decimal arithmetic involving large dollar amounts.

Most business programs involve storing, retrieving, and comparing data, with only simple arithmetic involved (addition, subtraction, multiplication, and division). A business programming language need not have advanced computational facilities.

Most general-purpose programming languages, such as BASIC, Fortran, Pascal, and C, provide excellent computational facilities. In fact these languages could be described as computationally oriented. COBOL is not computationally oriented, nor does it need to be.

The general-purpose languages have facilities for handling files that vary in sophistication, but none of them has file-handling facilities as advanced as a full-blown COBOL implementation.

The general-purpose languages usually provide only floating-point and integer arithmetic. COBOL provides decimal arithmetic. Some versions of BASIC and Pascal also provide decimal arithmetic, but they are in the minority.

In short, there is a whole class of problems for which the general-purpose programming languages are inadequate. This class of problems happens to be the largest group of problems that computers are called upon to solve. COBOL was designed for just this class of problems.

The roots of COBOL can be traced back to the work of Dr. Grace Murray Hopper in the early 1950s. Dr. Hopper was one of the first persons ever to program a large-scale digital computer, starting back in the early 1940s. She was long associated with the U.S. Navy, serving in both on active duty and in the Naval Reserve. She retired from the Navy in 1986 with the rank of rear admiral.

In the early days of computers, it was accepted as fact that computers had to be programmed in a very low-level language, using binary numbers (sometimes disguised as octal or hexadecimal numbers) and possibly a few symbols. To be able to program using decimal numbers was a goal. Dr. Hopper believed that a programmer ought to be able to program a computer in a language resembling English. She persisted in the face of much opposition, and one result was a language called Flow-Matic. Flow-Matic ran on a Univac computer beginning in 1956.

COBOL itself dates back to about 1960. Many of its principles were borrowed from Flow-Matic. Dr. Hopper is sometimes called the "mother of COBOL" for her role in its development.

The current version of COBOL was adopted by the American National Standards Institute (ANSI) in 1985. Several implementations of COBOL, ranging in price from $39.95 to over $3,000.00, are available for microcomputers. The implementation used for the examples in this chapter is the IBM Personal Computer COBOL Compiler, Version 1.00, by Microsoft. A current version of this compiler, sold by Microsoft, retails for $700.

PROGRAM STRUCTURE

The structure of a COBOL program is more rigidly defined than that of most other languages. For an example of a minimal COBOL program, see Fig. 6-1. This program simply prints the message This is a test. on the screen.

A COBOL program is made up of four divisions, the IDENTIFICATION DIVISION,

```
000010*FIGURE 6-1:   COBOL TEST PROGRAM.
000020*
000030*
000040 IDENTIFICATION DIVISION.
000050 PROGRAM-ID.     COBOL-1.
000060*
000070 ENVIRONMENT DIVISION.
000080 CONFIGURATION SECTION.
000090 SOURCE-COMPUTER.   ZENITH 150.
000100 OBJECT-COMPUTER.   ZENITH 150.
000110*
000120 DATA DIVISION.
000130*
000140 PROCEDURE DIVISION.
000150 BEGIN.
000160     DISPLAY "This is a test.".
000170     STOP RUN.
000180*
000190*END PROGRAM 6-1.
```

Fig. 6-1. COBOL test program.

the ENVIRONMENT DIVISION, the DATA DIVISION, and the PROCEDURE DIVISION. Most languages have the equivalent of the DATA DIVISION and the PROCEDURE DIVISION, though not so rigidly defined. The DATA DIVISION contains all the variable declarations and the PROCEDURE DIVISION contains all the action statements.

The IDENTIFICATION DIVISION is simply a place to put the name of the program, the author, the date written, and other documentary remarks. The ENVIRONMENT DIVISION contains information about the computer on which the program is to run and, when appropriate, information about external files.

One of the original design objectives of COBOL was portability from computer to computer. It was therefore decided to put all installation-specific information in one place near the beginning of the program. In theory, to convert this program to run on another computer, you would only have to change the ENVIRONMENT DIVISION and recompile on the new computer. In practice, it is more complicated than that, but COBOL programs do tend to be relatively easy to move from one computer to another.

COBOL programs were originally intended to be punched on cards for input to the computer via a card reader. Certain fields were intended to be punched in certain columns of the card. COBOL programs created using a text editor on a video display must still follow the same conventions. This is easily accomplished using the tab feature of most editors, but it is still a bit of a nuisance.

Columns 1 through 6 of a program contain sequence numbers. This is something of an anachronism and is optional on many modern COBOL compilers, including IBM

Personal Computer COBOL. In the early days of COBOL, sequence numbers could be punched into a deck of cards using the IBM 519 Reproducing Card Punch, which was programmed for the task using wires and a plug board (similar to an old-fashioned telephone switchboard). Today I use a simple COBOL program to do the same job, albeit using a disk file rather than a deck of cards. That program is shown later in the chapter as Fig. 6-13.

Column 7 is called the *indicator area*. An asterisk (*) in this column means the remainder of the line is to be taken as a comment or remark. A slash (/) serves the same purpose and additionally causes the program listing to skip to the top of the next page. A hyphen (-) in column 7 means that that line is to be interpreted as a continuation of the previous line. Columns 8-11 are called the *A-Field*, and columns 12-72 the *B-Field*. Certain statements must start in the A-Field and others must start in the B-Field. Anything beyond column 72 is ignored.

Notice that the COBOL programs in this book are written in uppercase (except for characters within quotation marks). This is also a legacy from the early days of the language. The old keypunch machines did not support lowercase. IBM Personal Computer COBOL supports both upper- and lowercase.

Examine the **DATA DIVISION** of the program in Fig. 6-1. It is empty because there are no variables in this program. The division heading must be present even if there is nothing in the division.

The **PROCEDURE DIVISION** is organized into paragraphs. A paragraph label starts in the A-Field, and the statements within the paragraph begin in the B-Field. This program contains only one paragraph, entitled **BEGIN**. The **PROCEDURE DIVISION** of a COBOL program must contain at least one paragraph. Several paragraphs can form a section.

The **DISPLAY** statement in line 000160 displays a character string on the video screen. The **STOP RUN** statement in line 000170 stops the program. The two lines that follow are comments.

COBOL uses periods at the ends of division, section, and paragraph headings; at the ends of variable declarations; and at the ends of sentences. In this program, each sentence contains only one statement, but in later programs you will note more than one statement per sentence. Statements within a sentence are separated by a space, a comma, a semicolon, or a carriage return. Punctuation in COBOL must be followed by at least one blank space.

All versions of COBOL of which I am aware are true compilers rather than interpreters. This means that COBOL programs are likely to run much faster than similar programs written in an interpreted BASIC.

DATA REPRESENTATION

Data representation in COBOL differs from that of most other languages. This is because of COBOL's business orientation. COBOL has alphabetic, alphanumeric, and numeric data types. Alphanumeric data corresponds to character strings in other languages. Alphabetic data is similar, except that it is limited to the letters of the alphabet and the space character.

Data types in COBOL are defined by **PICTURE** clauses in the **DATA DIVISION**. The **PICTURE** for alphabetic data is **A**. A **PICTURE** of **AAAAA** represents a string of five alphabetic characters. An equivalent representation is **A(5)**. The character **B** can also be included in an alphabetic PICTURE and represents a blank. Thus AAABAA represents a string of three alphabetic characters, a blank, and two more alphabetic characters.

The PICTURE for alphanumeric data is X. Thus, XXXXX or X(5) represents a string of five characters, each of which can be any ASCII character.

Numeric data can be classified by its usage, which is DISPLAY, COMPUTATIONAL, COMPUTATIONAL-0, or COMPUTATIONAL-3. This is indicated by a USAGE clause in the DATA DIVISION. A usage clause can be one of the following:

```
USAGE IS DISPLAY
USAGE IS COMPUTATIONAL
USAGE COMP
USAGE IS COMPUTATIONAL-3
USAGE COMP-3
USAGE COMP-0
```

USAGE COMP is short for USAGE IS COMPUTATIONAL and USAGE COMP-3 is short for USAGE IS COMPUTATIONAL-3. COMPUTATIONAL-0 data is stored internally in binary form, just like integers in most other languages. As such, there are limitations on the magnitude of numbers of this type. With IBM Personal Computer COBOL, those limits are from -32768 to 32767. COMPUTATIONAL-0 data should be used sparingly, preferably only when computational speed is important and when it is known that the magnitude of the numbers will be small.

COMPUTATIONAL-3 data is also called *packed decimal*. Each of the digits (zero to nine) can be represented in binary by four bits. Because there are eight bits to a byte, each byte can store two decimal digits.

There is some loss of efficiency with this method because one byte can store only 100 different numbers (zero to 99) instead of the 256 different numbers that can be stored in a single byte using ordinary binary notation. There are several advantages of using packed-decimal storage, however. First, it permits exact decimal arithmetic, which is important in business applications. Second, it permits the formation of numbers of arbitrarily large size by putting together packed-decimal bytes.

With COMPUTATIONAL and DISPLAY variables, numbers are stored one decimal digit per byte. If the USAGE clause is omitted for numeric data, DISPLAY is assumed. DISPLAY data is stored as a sequence of ASCII characters, very much like a character string. The PICTURE clause allows for an implicit or actual decimal point and for a sign. The following PICTUREs represent numeric data:

```
S9(5)V99
S99999V99
```

The two PICTUREs are equivalent. Each allows for a sign, five digits to the left of the (assumed) decimal point, and two digits to its right. Unless explicit provision is made for the sign, there is no sign. Without an S in the picture of numeric data, any negative sign will be lost. This is a frequent problem for programmers who have programmed in other languages before learning COBOL. The solution is to always use the S unless you are sure the numbers cannot be negative.

The programmer can specify as many digits of precision as may be required for the application with DISPLAY and with COMPUTATIONAL-3 data. This is a significant difference from other languages.

DISPLAY fields can also be edited. This is usually done in preparation for output. Here is an example:

    $Z(5).99 –

This PICTURE will cause the number to be preceded by a dollar sign. There will then be five digits to the left of the decimal point with leading zeros suppressed, an actual decimal point, two digits to the right of the decimal point, and a trailing minus sign if the number is negative. If the number is positive or zero, no sign will be printed. There are additional editing characters, which can be found in any COBOL manual or text.

Because DISPLAY data is stored in ASCII (on most computers), it is very portable from one computer to another. It is even very simple to convert display data from an ASCII computer to a computer that uses another character set such as EBCDIC.

The various forms of COMPUTATIONAL data are often implemented in different ways on different computers. (The same holds true for real and integer data types in other languages.) Sometimes those ways depend on hardware differences, such as the number of bits in a computer word. COMPUTATIONAL data is therefore much less portable than DISPLAY data. COMPUTATIONAL-3 data is more portable than either COMPUTATIONAL or COMPUTATIONAL-0 data.

COMPUTATIONAL-3 data is not a part of standard COBOL, but it is found in most COBOL implementations. Arithmetic involving COMP-3 data is faster than arithmetic with DISPLAY data, and COMP-3 takes up approximately half the storage space of DISPLAY. The tradeoff is between machine efficiency and portability.

In summary, COBOL programs should use DISPLAY data as a matter of course. If computational speed or storage space is critical, then COMPUTATIONAL-3 data should be used. Only rarely should COMPUTATIONAL-0 data be used.

Constants

COBOL does not support figurative constants in the same way as Pascal or C. It does, however, support the initialization of variables. This is done using the VALUE IS clause in the DATA DIVISION, as illustrated in the program in Fig. 6-2.

Within the DATA DIVISION is the WORKING-STORAGE SECTION, where independent variables are declared. (By independent variables, I mean those that are not part of a record.) The 77 in the A-Field of line 000140 is called the *level number*. Level 77 is used for independent variables. Other level numbers are considered later in this chapter. The name of the variable is CHAR-STRING, which starts in the B-Field. The variable is described by its PICTURE.

COBOL does support several symbolic constants such as ZERO, ZEROS, SPACE, and SPACES. The following declarations would initialize the variables A and B to zero and blank, respectively:

    77 A   PIC 9(5) VALUE ZERO.
    77 B   PIC X(5) VALUE SPACES.

```
000010*FIGURE 6-2:   ILLUSTRATE DATA INITIALIZATION.
000020*
000030*
000040 IDENTIFICATION DIVISION.
000050 PROGRAM-ID.      COBOL-2.
000060*
000070 ENVIRONMENT DIVISION.
000080 CONFIGURATION SECTION.
000090 SOURCE-COMPUTER.    ZENITH 150.
000100 OBJECT-COMPUTER.    ZENITH 150.
000110*
000120 DATA DIVISION.
000130 WORKING-STORAGE SECTION.
000140 77  CHAR-STRING     PICTURE IS X(30)
000150                     VALUE   IS "This is a character string.".
000160*
000170 PROCEDURE DIVISION.
000180 BEGIN.
000190      DISPLAY CHAR-STRING.
000200      STOP RUN.
000210*
000220*END PROGRAM 6-2.
```

Fig. 6-2. Data initialization.

Notice that **PICTURE IS** has been abbreviated to **PIC** and **VALUE IS** abbreviated to **VALUE**. Such abbreviation is common in COBOL programs.

Variables

As mentioned before, variables in COBOL must be declared in the **DATA DIVISION** before they are used. Several more examples of variable declarations are shown in the program in Fig. 6-3.

Note the **PICTURE** clauses in lines 000140 and following. The character 9 stands for any numeric digit. The variable **COST** consists of six numeric digits, and has an implied decimal point represented by **V**. Other commonly used descriptors include **X** for an alphanumeric character (letter, digit, or special character), and **A** for an alphabetic character or a space. These descriptors will be discussed more later in this chapter.

This program reads a dollar amount from the console, computes sales tax (at the rate of four percent, the current rate in Hawaii), and prints the result on the screen in edited format. How the **ACCEPT** and **DISPLAY** statements work is discussed later, in the section on input and output. The **MOVE** statement is discussed in the next section.

THE MOVE STATEMENT

The **MOVE** statement of COBOL corresponds roughly to the assignment statement of other languages. In some ways it is more powerful, and in other ways, less powerful.

As an example of the increased power of the **MOVE** statement, MOVEing an unedited numeric data item to an edited numeric field causes the appropriate editing to take place. This is illustrated in lines 000290, 000310, and 000330 in Fig. 6-3.

The MOVE statement can be used to move the figurative constants SPACE, SPACES, ZERO, and ZEROS to a variable when needed. This will set that variable to blanks or zero, as appropriate.

Another way that the MOVE statement is powerful is that it can have multiple destinations, as in the following:

MOVE ZERO TO A, B.

```
000010*FIGURE 6-3:  SIMPLE COMPUTATIONS WITH NUMERIC VARIABLES.
000020*
000030*
000040 IDENTIFICATION DIVISION.
000050 PROGRAM-ID.     COBOL-3.
000060*
000070 ENVIRONMENT DIVISION.
000080 CONFIGURATION SECTION.
000090 SOURCE-COMPUTER.   ZENITH 150.
000100 OBJECT-COMPUTER.   ZENITH 150.
000110*
000120 DATA DIVISION.
000130 WORKING-STORAGE SECTION.
000140 77  COST            PICTURE IS 9999V99.
000150 77  TAX-RATE        PICTURE IS 9V99
000160                     VALUE   IS 0.04.
000170 77  TAX-AMOUNT      PICTURE IS 9999V99.
000180 77  TOTAL-COST      PICTURE IS 9999V99.
000190 77  PRINT-LINE      PICTURE IS $ZZZ9.99.
000200*
000210 PROCEDURE DIVISION.
000220 BEGIN.
000230      DISPLAY (1, 1) ERASE.
000240      DISPLAY (1, 1) "COMPUTE SALES TAX."
000250      DISPLAY (5, 5) "ENTER COST:".
000260      ACCEPT   (5, 20) COST.
000270      MULTIPLY COST BY TAX-RATE GIVING TAX-AMOUNT ROUNDED.
000280      ADD COST, TAX-AMOUNT GIVING TOTAL-COST.
000290      MOVE COST TO PRINT-LINE.
000300      DISPLAY (7, 5) "COST:         ", PRINT-LINE.
000310      MOVE TAX-AMOUNT TO PRINT-LINE.
000320      DISPLAY (8, 5) "TAX:          ", PRINT-LINE.
000330      MOVE TOTAL-COST TO PRINT-LINE.
000340      DISPLAY (9, 5) "TOTAL:        ", PRINT-LINE.
000350 END-OF-JOB.
000360      STOP RUN.
000370*
000380*END PROGRAM 6-3.
```

Fig. 6-3. Simple computations with numeric variables.

This MOVE statement sets both A and B to zero.

Later in the chapter, you will see that the MOVE statement can be used to move groups of related data all at once.

On the negative side, the MOVE statement can handle only constants and variables; it cannot handle expressions. Arithmetic must be performed by the appropriate ADD, SUBTRACT, MULTIPLY, DIVIDE, or COMPUTE statement, not by a MOVE statement. These statements are discussed in the following section.

ARITHMETIC EXPRESSIONS

Most other languages use the symbols +, −, *, and / for addition, subtraction, multiplication, and division, respectively. The philosophy of COBOL is to make the program as much like the English language as possible, so COBOL uses the words ADD, SUBTRACT, MULTIPLY, and DIVIDE. COBOL also allows use of the symbols in the COMPUTE statement, which is illustrated later.

Line 000280 shows an example of an ADD statement. The equivalent statement in BASIC or Fortran would be something like the following:

TOTAL__COST = COST + TAX__AMOUNT.

Suppose you did not want to use another variable such as TOTAL-COST, but simply wanted to add TAX-AMOUNT to COST. This could be done as follows:

ADD TAX-AMOUNT TO COST.

Line 000270 shows an example of a MULTIPLY statement. Notice the ROUNDED clause. Rounding of numbers to the nearest penny is something that is required frequently in business-oriented problems, so the ROUNDED feature is included as a part of the language.

Not shown is the ON SIZE ERROR clause, which permits the program to check for a result too large for the receiving data field and to jump to an error routine.

The COMPUTE statement allows arithmetic to be performed using the usual arithmetic operators (+, −, and so on). The COMPUTE statement is illustrated later in the chapter, in lines 000650 and 000660 in Fig. 6-11.

LOGICAL EXPRESSIONS

The relational operators in COBOL are IS EQUAL TO, =, IS GREATER THAN, >, IS LESS THAN, <, IS NUMERIC, and IS ALPHABETIC. The English-language versions and the symbolic versions are equivalent; which to use is a matter of preference. The logical operators are AND, OR, and NOT.

Logical expressions in COBOL are used in much the same way as in other languages. The IS NUMERIC and IS ALPHABETIC expressions are not usually found in other languages, but their operation is predictable. They are often useful for editing input data. Here is an example:

IF MONTH IS NUMERIC
    ADD 1 TO MONTH.

COBOL handles compound conditions in two ways. One way is the same way as most other languages, for example

A > B) AND (A < C).

Another way that this could be handled in COBOL is as follows:

A > B AND < C.

This would be clearer in words:

A IS GREATER THAN B
AND LESS THAN C.

The first variable need not be repeated in each comparison if it does not change.

INPUT AND OUTPUT

You have already seen examples of the ACCEPT and DISPLAY statements for console input and output in Figs. 6-1, 6-2, and 6-3. The ACCEPT statement in line 000260 of the program in Fig. 6-3 requires a closer look.

The field into which data is being read is COST. The PICTURE for COST is 9999V99. COST is therefore a six-digit number (the implied decimal point doesn't count). The decimal point is not entered; it is understood. The input routines take care of the decimal point and allow for editing of typing errors.

The program in Fig. 6-4 illustrates how to handle printer output. Notice the INPUT-OUTPUT SECTION of the ENVIRONMENT DIVISION. This connects the local name PRT to the external device called PRINTER. This associates the printer with a pseudo-file called PRT. In other words, the program is made to think that the printer is a file. This is a common device in several other languages as well, including Pascal.

In the FILE SECTION of the DATA DIVISION, a file description (FD) is given for the file PRT. The format of this FD may vary slightly from compiler to compiler. Notice that the FD identifies a DATA RECORD called PRINT-LINE. This is analogous to a print buffer. PRINT-LINE is defined just below as a level 01 item with PICTURE X(80).

To the beginner, there is little apparent logic in how to set up for printer output. It varies from system to system and is best learned by rote. The easiest way is to find an example that works.

The actual output to the printer is accomplished in two steps. First the data to be output is MOVEd to PRINT-LINE; then the WRITE statement is used, as in line 000320. In this case alphanumeric data was moved to PRINT-LINE, which has PICTURE X(80). Numeric data can also be moved to alphanumeric fields such as PRINT-LINE, provided that the USAGE is DISPLAY. COMP and COMP-3 fields should first be moved to a numeric field with USAGE DISPLAY before being moved to PRINT-LINE.

The printer can be made to double space as follows:

WRITE PRINT-LINE
BEFORE ADVANCING 2 LINES.

```
000010*FIGURE 6-4:    USE OF A PRINTER.
000020*
000030*
000040 IDENTIFICATION DIVISION.
000050 PROGRAM-ID.        COBOL4.
000060*
000070 ENVIRONMENT DIVISION.
000080 CONFIGURATION SECTION.
000090 SOURCE-COMPUTER.   ZENITH 150.
000100 OBJECT-COMPUTER.   ZENITH 150.
000110 INPUT-OUTPUT SECTION.
000120 FILE-CONTROL.
000130      SELECT PRT ASSIGN TO PRINTER.
000140*
000150 DATA DIVISION.
000160 FILE SECTION.
000170 FD   PRT
000180      LABEL RECORD IS OMITTED
000190      DATA RECORD IS PRINT-LINE.
000200 01   PRINT-LINE     PICTURE IS X(80).
000210 WORKING-STORAGE SECTION.
000220 77   STRING-1        PICTURE IS X(80)
000230                      VALUE IS "This goes to the video screen.".
000240 77   STRING-2        PICTURE IS X(80)
000250                      VALUE IS "This goes to the printer.".
000260*
000270 PROCEDURE DIVISION.
000280 BEGIN.
000290      OPEN OUTPUT PRT.
000300      DISPLAY STRING-1.
000310      MOVE STRING-2 TO PRINT-LINE.
000320      WRITE PRINT-LINE.
000330 END-OF-JOB.
000340      CLOSE PRT.
000350      STOP RUN.
000360*
000370*END PROGRAM 6-4.
```

Fig. 6-4. Use of a printer.

For triple spacing, substitute 3 for 2, and so on. For printers with top-of-form capability, you can write the following:

```
WRITE PRINT-LINE
    BEFORE ADVANCING PAGE.
```

The DISPLAY statement allows output to be placed at a particular row and column of the screen. This was illustrated in lines 000230 and following in Fig. 6-3. Specifying the row and column turns off the automatic carriage return and linefeed that normally occurs at the end of a DISPLAY statement. If you simply want the output to go on the next line and the cursor to stay at the end of that line, type, for example,

DISPLAY (LIN) "Message".

LIN is a system variable that keeps track of the cursor line. Similarly, COL is a system variable that keeps track of the cursor column.

CONTROL STRUCTURES

COBOL has a fairly limited set of control structures compared to more modern languages such as Pascal. The user is forced to use the GO TO statement more frequently than would be necessary if the more advanced control structures were available.

Simple Selection: IF-ELSE

The general format for the IF statement in COBOL is as follows:

```
IF logical expression
   statement-1
ELSE
   statement-2.
```

Statement-1 can be a series of statements as long as they are separated by spaces, commas, semicolons, or carriage returns and not by periods. Statement-2 can also be a series of statements. The scope of the IF statement is determined by the placement of the final period following statement-2.

Statement-1 or statement-2 can also be NEXT SENTENCE, which is merely a placeholder. It means "go to the sentence following the IF statement." ELSE NEXT SENTENCE is redundant and may be omitted.

Here is a simple example of an IF statement without an ELSE part:

```
ADD 1 TO MONTH.
IF MONTH > 12
  MOVE 1 TO MONTH;
  ADD 1 TO YEAR.
```

Here is an example of an IF statement with an ELSE that accomplishes the same thing:

```
IF MONTH = 12
  MOVE 1 TO MONTH;
  ADD 1 TO YEAR;
ELSE
  ADD 1 TO MONTH.
```

Deciding which of the two examples is better is a matter of taste.

Multiple Selection

The COBOL equivalent of the CASE statement is the GO TO-DEPENDING ON statement discussed below.

Loops and Subroutines

COBOL has only one form of loop, the PERFORM statement. The PERFORM statement has several variants, however. The simple PERFORM statement is much like a subroutine call, most closely resembling the GOSUB of BASIC. PERFORM-TIMES repeats a fixed number of iterations, but without an iteration counter. PERFORM-UNTIL is like a conditional loop. PERFORM-VARYING-UNTIL is most like the counted loop of other languages.

Simple Subroutines: The PERFORM Statement. Earlier I pointed out that the PROCEDURE DIVISION of a COBOL program consists of a sequence of paragraphs. Each paragraph is identified by a paragraph name, which begins in the A-Field. The body of the paragraph begins in the B-Field. The end of one paragraph is marked only by the beginning of the next paragraph or by the end of the program.

Each paragraph in a COBOL program is a potential subroutine. A subroutine is invoked by a PERFORM statement as illustrated below:

```
PERFORM PARA-1.
```

In this example, PARA-1 is the name of a paragraph.

Another form of the PERFORM statement is as follows:

```
PERFORM PARA-1
    THRU PARA-3.
```

In this example, PARA-1, PARA-3, and all intervening paragraphs are treated as a single subroutine.

There is no explicit return statement in COBOL. The end of the subroutine is the end of the last-named paragraph.

There are no parameters in this simple form of subroutine in COBOL. All variables within the program are global in scope.

An example showing two simple subroutines is given in Fig. 6-5. The first subroutine prints the values of the variables X and Y along with their names, and the second subroutine exchanges the values of the two variables. The program processes two sets of values for the two variables. This illustrates that the subroutines can be used in more than one place in a program. Because all variables in COBOL are global, the data to be manipulated must first be MOVEd into the variables X and Y.

Notice the use of 01 and 02 levels in the WORKING-STORAGE SECTION of the DATA DIVISION. The 02 levels are subordinate to the preceding 01 level; if there were an 03 level, it would be subordinate to the preceding 02 level. One purpose of levels is to group related data together. Another is to permit multiple data elements to be MOVEd together. A MOVE of an 01 level item also MOVEs all subordinate levels.

```
000010*FIGURE 6-5:  USE OF THE PERFORM STATEMENT.
000020*
000030*
000040 IDENTIFICATION DIVISION.
000050 PROGRAM-ID.      COBOL-5.
000060*
000070 ENVIRONMENT DIVISION.
000080 CONFIGURATION SECTION.
000090 SOURCE-COMPUTER.   ZENITH 150.
000100 OBJECT-COMPUTER.   ZENITH 150.
000110*
000120 DATA DIVISION.
000130 WORKING-STORAGE SECTION.
000140 01   PRINT-LINE.
000150      02  PRINT-LABEL PIC     X(10).
000160      02  PRINT-VALUE PIC     ZZZZ9.
000170 77  X         PIC     9(5).
000180 77  Y         PIC     9(5).
000190 77  TEMP      PIC     9(5).
000200*
000210 PROCEDURE DIVISION.
000220 BEGIN.
000230      MOVE 1 TO X.
000240      MOVE 2 TO Y.
000250      PERFORM PRINT-2.
000260      PERFORM SWAP.
000270      PERFORM PRINT-2.
000280      DISPLAY SPACE.
000290*
000300      MOVE 27 TO X.
000310      MOVE 40 TO Y.
000320      PERFORM PRINT-2.
000330      PERFORM SWAP.
000340      PERFORM PRINT-2.
000350 END-OF-JOB.
000360      STOP RUN.
000370 PRINT-2.
000380      MOVE "X" TO PRINT-LABEL.
000390      MOVE   X  TO PRINT-VALUE.
000400      DISPLAY PRINT-LINE.
000410      MOVE "Y" TO PRINT-LABEL.
000420      MOVE   Y  TO PRINT-VALUE.
000430      DISPLAY PRINT-LINE.
```

Fig. 6-5. Use of the PERFORM statement.

```
000440 SWAP.
000450     MOVE X    TO TEMP.
000460     MOVE Y    TO X.
000470     MOVE TEMP TO Y.
000480*
000490*END PROGRAM 6-5.
```

There are occasions when elements of a group data item do not need to be accessed individually. These elements can be given the name FILLER. There can be multiple instances of FILLER data in a program. Looking ahead, there are examples in the WORKING-STORAGE SECTION of Fig. 6-14. These data items get their values through a VALUE IS clause or through a group MOVE.

The two subroutines in Fig. 6-5 are placed following the STOP RUN statement. The two lines following the subroutines have an asterisk in column 7 and are comment lines.

In this program each subroutine is PERFORMed twice. A subroutine can be PER-FORMed as often as needed, but it needs to be defined only once.

COBOL also supports separately compiled subroutines that are invoked by the CALL statement. This type of subroutine does support parameters. Separately compiled subroutines are considered to be an advanced topic, and space does not permit their consideration in this book.

Counted Loops: PERFORM-VARYING-UNTIL. In most languages, a loop consists of a control line (for example the FOR statement of BASIC or Pascal), a body of one or more lines, and possibly a terminal line (for example, the NEXT statement of BASIC). The body of the loop almost always follows the control line. COBOL is different. The body of the loop is a separate paragraph, possibly located elsewhere in the program. In fact, executing a loop in COBOL is akin to PERFORMing a subroutine multiple times.

An example of the PERFORM-VARYING-UNTIL loop is given in Fig. 6-6. This program simply prints the integers from one to 10 on the video screen.

Conditional Loops. Another form of the PERFORM statement provides the COBOL version of the conditional loop. The named paragraph is PERFORMed until a certain condition becomes true. If the condition is initially true, the paragraph will not be PERFORMed at all.

An example of the PERFORM-UNTIL statement is shown in Fig. 6-7. The program produces exactly the same output as the program in Fig. 6-6.

In this trivial example, there is little advantage to using the PERFORM-UNTIL rather than the PERFORM-VARYING-UNTIL. Another example, which better illustrates the utility of the simple PERFORM-UNTIL statement, is shown in Fig. 6-8.

The program in Fig. 6-8 reads a series of numbers until their sum exceeds 100. It then prints the count of the numbers included in the sum, the sum itself, and the number that would have made the sum go over 100.

The PERFORM-UNTIL statement is in line 000240. The body of the loop is the paragraph entitled TOTAL-IT. TOTAL-IT happens to call the subroutine READ-IT, using an ordinary PERFORM statement.

```
000010*FIGURE 6-6:   DEMONSTRATE A COUNTED LOOP.
000020*
000030*
000040 IDENTIFICATION DIVISION.
000050 PROGRAM-ID.     COBOL-6.
000060*
000070 ENVIRONMENT DIVISION.
000080 CONFIGURATION SECTION.
000090 SOURCE-COMPUTER.   ZENITH 150.
000100 OBJECT-COMPUTER.   ZENITH 150.
000110*
000120 DATA DIVISION.
000130 WORKING-STORAGE SECTION.
000140 77  COUNTER         PIC 9(5).
000150*
000160 PROCEDURE DIVISION.
000170 BEGIN.
000180     PERFORM PRINT-COUNTER VARYING COUNTER
000190               FROM 1 BY 1 UNTIL COUNTER > 10.
000200 END-OF-JOB.
000210     STOP RUN.
000220*
000230 PRINT-COUNTER.
000240     DISPLAY COUNTER.
000250*
000260*END PROGRAM 6-6.
```

Fig. 6-6. A counted loop.

Functions

The COBOL language does not support functions.

The GO TO Statement

The GO TO statement is needed rather more frequently in COBOL than in some other languages such as Pascal and C. Sometimes it is more convenient to simulate a while loop with its body in line than to use a PERFORM-UNTIL.

The program in Fig. 6-9 is a rewrite of the program in Fig. 6-8 using GO TO statements rather than a PERFORM-UNTIL. The coding is straightforward and needs little comment. Note that this method allows the structured loops of other languages to be emulated while keeping the bodies of the loops "in line" rather than in separate paragraphs.

As illustrated in this example, the object of a GO TO statement is a paragraph name.

```
000010*FIGURE 6-7:   DEMONSTRATE A CONDITIONAL LOOP.
000020*
000030*
000040 IDENTIFICATION DIVISION.
000050 PROGRAM-ID.      COBOL-7.
000060*
000070 ENVIRONMENT DIVISION.
000080 CONFIGURATION SECTION.
000090 SOURCE-COMPUTER.   ZENITH 150.
000100 OBJECT-COMPUTER.   ZENITH 150.
000110*
000120 DATA DIVISION.
000130 WORKING-STORAGE SECTION.
000140 77  COUNTER         PIC 99.
000150*
000160 PROCEDURE DIVISION.
000170 BEGIN.
000180     MOVE 1 TO COUNTER.
000190     PERFORM PRINT-IT UNTIL COUNTER > 10.
000200 END-OF-JOB.
000210     STOP RUN.
000220*
000230 PRINT-IT.
000240     DISPLAY COUNTER.
000250     ADD 1 TO COUNTER.
000260*
000270*END PROGRAM 6-7.
```

Fig. 6-7. A conditional loop.

The GO TO-DEPENDING ON Statement

The GO TO-DEPENDING ON statement permits the emulation of a Case statement, as described in Chapter 2. The program in Fig. 6-10 shows how this is done.

Between the GO TO (line 000280) and the DEPENDING ON (line 000400) is a list of paragraph names, each of which is the name of a month. Control is transferred to one of them based on its relative position in the list and on the value of the variable MONTH. If MONTH has value 1, control is transferred to the first paragraph named in the list (January); if MONTH has value 10, control is transferred to the tenth paragraph named in the list (October), and so on.

In this case, 12 paragraph names are listed. If MONTH is not between one and 12, control passes to the next statement, which in this instance is statement 000410. Statement 000420 then transfers control back to the beginning to read in another value for MONTH.

```
000010*FIGURE 6-8:   A MORE COMPLEX CONDITIONAL LOOP.
000020*
000030*
000040 IDENTIFICATION DIVISION.
000050 PROGRAM-ID.      COBOL-8.
000060*
000070 ENVIRONMENT DIVISION.
000080 CONFIGURATION SECTION.
000090 SOURCE-COMPUTER.   ZENITH 150.
000100 OBJECT-COMPUTER.   ZENITH 150.
000110*
000120 DATA DIVISION.
000130 WORKING-STORAGE SECTION.
000140 77   A-NUMBER        PIC S9(5).
000150 77   COUNTER         PIC 9(5).
000160 77   TOTAL           PIC S9(5).
000170 77   TEMP            PIC S9(5).
000180 77   D-LINE          PIC -----9.
000190*
000200 PROCEDURE DIVISION.
000210 BEGIN.
000220      MOVE ZERO TO COUNTER, TOTAL.
000230      PERFORM READ-IT.
000240      PERFORM TOTAL-IT UNTIL TEMP > 100.
000250      DISPLAY SPACE.
000260      MOVE COUNTER   TO D-LINE.
000270      DISPLAY D-LINE, " NUMBERS WERE READ.".
000280      MOVE TOTAL     TO D-LINE.
000290      DISPLAY "THEIR TOTAL IS ", D-LINE, ".".
000300      MOVE A-NUMBER TO D-LINE.
000310      DISPLAY "THE NUMBER     ", D-LINE, " WAS NOT COUNTED.".
000320 END-OF-JOB.
000330      STOP RUN.
000340*
000350 READ-IT.
000360      DISPLAY SPACE.
000370      DISPLAY (LIN) "Enter a Number:   ".
000380      ACCEPT A-NUMBER.
000390      ADD A-NUMBER, TOTAL GIVING TEMP.
000400 TOTAL-IT.
000410      ADD 1 TO COUNTER.
000420      ADD A-NUMBER TO TOTAL.
000430      PERFORM READ-IT.
000440*
000450*END PROGRAM 6-8.
```

Fig. 6-8. A more complex conditional loop.

```
000010*FIGURE 6-9:   DEMONSTRATE THE GO TO STATEMENT.
000020*
000030*
000040 IDENTIFICATION DIVISION.
000050 PROGRAM-ID.      COBOL-9.
000060*
000070 ENVIRONMENT DIVISION.
000080 CONFIGURATION SECTION.
000090 SOURCE-COMPUTER.   ZENITH 150.
000100 OBJECT-COMPUTER.   ZENITH 150.
000110*
000120 DATA DIVISION.
000130 WORKING-STORAGE SECTION.
000140 77   A-NUMBER           PIC S9(5).
000150 77   COUNTER            PIC 9(5).
000160 77   TOTAL              PIC S9(5).
000170 77   TEMP               PIC S9(5).
000180 77   D-LINE             PIC -----9.
000190*
000200 PROCEDURE DIVISION.
000210 BEGIN.
000220      MOVE ZERO TO COUNTER, TOTAL.
000230 LOOP.
000240      PERFORM GET-A-NUMBER.
000250      ADD A-NUMBER, TOTAL GIVING TEMP.
000260      IF TEMP > 100 GO TO PRINT-IT.
000270      ADD 1 TO COUNTER.
000280      MOVE TEMP TO TOTAL.
000290      GO TO LOOP.
000300 PRINT-IT.
000310      DISPLAY SPACE.
000320      MOVE COUNTER TO D-LINE.
000330      DISPLAY D-LINE, " NUMBERS WERE READ.".
000340      MOVE TOTAL   TO D-LINE.
000350      DISPLAY "THEIR TOTAL IS ", D-LINE, ".".
000360      MOVE A-NUMBER   TO D-LINE.
000370      DISPLAY "THE NUMBER      ", D-LINE, " WAS NOT COUNTED.".
000380 END-OF-JOB.
000390      STOP RUN.
000400*
000410 GET-A-NUMBER.
000420      DISPLAY SPACE.
000430      DISPLAY (LIN) "Enter a Number:   ".
000440      ACCEPT A-NUMBER.
000450*END PROGRAM 6-9.
```

Fig. 6-9. The GO TO statement.

There is a paragraph for each month. The paragraphs are listed in the **GO TO-DEPENDING ON** statement in order so that the appropriate paragraph is selected for each month. Within each paragraph the appropriate name is transferred to the character

```
000010*FIGURE 6-10:   THE CALENDAR PROGRAM, VERSION 1.
000015*
000020*ILLUSTRATES GO TO DEPENDING ON.
000030*
000040 IDENTIFICATION DIVISION.
000050 PROGRAM-ID.    COBOL-10.
000060*
000070 ENVIRONMENT DIVISION.
000080 CONFIGURATION SECTION.
000090 SOURCE-COMPUTER.   ZENITH 150.
000100 OBJECT-COMPUTER.   ZENITH 150.
000110*
000120 DATA DIVISION.
000130 WORKING-STORAGE SECTION.
000140 77    MONTH          PIC 99.
000150 77    DAYS           PIC 99.
000160 77    YEAR           PIC 99.
000170 77    MONTH-NAME     PIC X(10).
000180 77    REMAIN         PIC 9(5).
000190 77    QUOTIENT       PIC 9(5).
000200 77    TEMP           PIC 9(5).
000210 77    C              PIC X.
000220*
000230 PROCEDURE DIVISION.
000240 BEGIN.
000250     MOVE SPACES TO MONTH-NAME.
000260     DISPLAY (LIN, 1) "ENTER THE MONTH (1..12):   "
000270     ACCEPT MONTH.
000280     GO TO JANUARY,
000290          FEBRUARY,
000300          MARCH,
000310          APRIL,
000320          MAY,
000330          JUNE,
000340          JULY,
000350          AUGUST,
000360          SEPTEMBER,
000370          OCTOBER,
000380          NOVEMBER,
000390          DECEMBER
000400        DEPENDING ON MONTH.
000410 NONE-OF-THE-ABOVE.
000420     GO TO BEGIN.
000430 JANUARY.
```

Fig. 6-10. The Calendar Program, Version 1.

```
000440        MOVE "JANUARY"    TO MONTH-NAME.
000450        MOVE 31 TO DAYS.
000460        GO TO END-CASE.
000470 FEBRUARY.
000480        MOVE "FEBRUARY"   TO MONTH-NAME.
000490        DISPLAY (LIN, 1) "ENTER THE YEAR (00-99):    ".
000500        ACCEPT YEAR.
000510        DIVIDE 4 INTO YEAR GIVING QUOTIENT.
000520        MULTIPLY 4 BY QUOTIENT GIVING TEMP.
000530        SUBTRACT TEMP FROM YEAR GIVING REMAIN.
000540        IF REMAIN IS EQUAL TO 0
000550            MOVE 29 TO DAYS
000560        ELSE
000570            MOVE 28 TO DAYS.
000580        GO TO END-CASE.
000590 MARCH.
000600        MOVE "MARCH"      TO MONTH-NAME.
000610        MOVE 31 TO DAYS.
000620        GO TO END-CASE.
000630 APRIL.
000640        MOVE "APRIL"      TO MONTH-NAME.
000650        MOVE 30 TO DAYS.
000660        GO TO END-CASE.
000670 MAY.
000680        MOVE "MAY"        TO MONTH-NAME.
000690        MOVE 31 TO DAYS.
000700        GO TO END-CASE.
000710 JUNE.
000720        MOVE "JUNE"       TO MONTH-NAME.
000730        MOVE 30 TO DAYS.
000740        GO TO END-CASE.
000750 JULY.
000760        MOVE "JULY"       TO MONTH-NAME.
000770        MOVE 31 TO DAYS.
000780        GO TO END-CASE.
000790 AUGUST.
000800        MOVE "AUGUST"     TO MONTH-NAME.
000810        MOVE 31 TO DAYS.
000820        GO TO END-CASE.
000830 SEPTEMBER.
000840        MOVE "SEPTEMBER" TO MONTH-NAME.
000850        MOVE 30 TO DAYS.
000860        GO TO END-CASE.
000870 OCTOBER.
```

```
000880      MOVE "OCTOBER"   TO MONTH-NAME.
000890      MOVE 31 TO DAYS.
000900      GO TO END-CASE.
000910 NOVEMBER.
000920      MOVE "NOVEMBER"  TO MONTH-NAME.
000930      MOVE 30 TO DAYS.
000940      GO TO END-CASE.
000950 DECEMBER.
000960      MOVE "DECEMBER"  TO MONTH-NAME.
000970      MOVE 31 TO DAYS.
000980 END-CASE.
000990      DISPLAY MONTH-NAME, " HAS ", DAYS, " DAYS.".
001000      DISPLAY (LIN, 1) "AGAIN?   (Y/N):   ".
001010      ACCEPT C.
001020      IF C IS EQUAL TO "Y" OR EQUAL TO "y"
001030          GO TO BEGIN.
001040 END-OF-JOB.
001050      STOP RUN.
001060*
001070*END PROGRAM 6-10.
```

Fig. 6-10. The Calendar Program, Version 1. (Continued from page 168.)

string MONTH-NAME, and the appropriate number of days to the variable DAYS. At the end of each paragraph, except the last, is GO TO END-CASE, which ensures that only one of the paragraphs is executed for a particular value of MONTH.

For most months the action is simple. For February, however, action is required to determine whether or not the year is a leap year. The rule is that years divisible evenly by four are leap years.

In more complete implementations of COBOL, the remainder after division can be computed directly, as in the following:

```
DIVIDE 4 INTO YEAR GIVING QUOTIENT
   REMAINDER REMAIN.
```

In this program the remainder had to be computed indirectly.

DATA STRUCTURES

COBOL allows the construction of a wide variety of data structures. The relationships between the various elements of a data structure are determined hierarchically by the level numbers in more-or-less outline form.

Each element of a data structure is, of course, described by its PICTURE clause, which permits the construction of heterogeneous as well as homogeneous structures. In a homogeneous data structure, each data element has the same PICTURE. In a heterogeneous data structure, different elements can have different PICTUREs.

```
000010*FIGURE 6-11:  THE CALENDAR PROGRAM, VERSION 2.
000015*
000020*ILLUSTRATES TABLE USAGE
000030*
000040 IDENTIFICATION DIVISION.
000050 PROGRAM-ID.    COBOL-11.
000060*
000070 ENVIRONMENT DIVISION.
000080 CONFIGURATION SECTION.
000090 SOURCE-COMPUTER.  ZENITH 150.
000100 OBJECT-COMPUTER.  ZENITH 150.
000110*
000120 DATA DIVISION.
000130 WORKING-STORAGE SECTION.
000140 01   TABLE-1.
000150      02  FILLER     PIC X(10)       VALUE "JANUARY   ".
000160      02  FILLER     PIC X(10)       VALUE "FEBRUARY  ".
000170      02  FILLER     PIC X(10)       VALUE "MARCH     ".
000180      02  FILLER     PIC X(10)       VALUE "APRIL     ".
000190      02  FILLER     PIC X(10)       VALUE "MAY       ".
000200      02  FILLER     PIC X(10)       VALUE "JUNE      ".
000210      02  FILLER     PIC X(10)       VALUE "JULY      ".
000220      02  FILLER     PIC X(10)       VALUE "AUGUST    ".
000230      02  FILLER     PIC X(10)       VALUE "SEPTEMBER ".
000240      02  FILLER     PIC X(10)       VALUE "OCTOBER   ".
000250      02  FILLER     PIC X(10)       VALUE "NOVEMBER  ".
000260      02  FILLER     PIC X(10)       VALUE "DECEMBER  ".
000270 01   TABLE-2 REDEFINES TABLE-1.
000280      02  NAME       PIC X(10)       OCCURS 12 TIMES.
000290 01   TABLE-3.
000300      02  FILLER     PIC 99          VALUE 31.
000310      02  FILLER     PIC 99          VALUE 28.
000320      02  FILLER     PIC 99          VALUE 31.
000330      02  FILLER     PIC 99          VALUE 30.
000340      02  FILLER     PIC 99          VALUE 31.
000350      02  FILLER     PIC 99          VALUE 30.
000360      02  FILLER     PIC 99          VALUE 31.
000370      02  FILLER     PIC 99          VALUE 31.
000380      02  FILLER     PIC 99          VALUE 30.
000390      02  FILLER     PIC 99          VALUE 31.
000400      02  FILLER     PIC 99          VALUE 30.
000410      02  FILLER     PIC 99          VALUE 31.
000420 01   TABLE-4 REDEFINES TABLE-3.
000430      02  DAYS-IN    PIC 99          OCCURS 12 TIMES.
000440 77  MONTH          PIC 99.
000450 77  DAYS           PIC 99.
000460 77  YEAR           PIC 99.
000470 77  MONTH-NAME     PIC X(10).
000480 77  REMAIN         PIC 9(5).
```

Fig. 6-11. The Calendar Program, Version 2.

```
000490 77   QUOTIENT        PIC 9(5).
000500 77   C               PIC X.
000510*
000520 PROCEDURE DIVISION.
000530 BEGIN.
000540      DISPLAY (LIN, 1) "ENTER THE MONTH (01..12):   "
000550      ACCEPT MONTH.
000560*     VALIDATE INPUT.
000570      IF MONTH < 01 OR > 12 GO TO BEGIN.
000580*     TABLE LOOK-UPS.
000590      MOVE NAME    (MONTH) TO MONTH-NAME.
000600      MOVE DAYS-IN (MONTH) TO DAYS.
000610*     CHECK FOR LEAP YEAR IF MONTH IS FEBRUARY.
000620      IF MONTH NOT = 2 GO TO PRINT-RESULTS.
000630          DISPLAY (LIN, 1) "ENTER THE YEAR (00-99):     ";
000640          ACCEPT YEAR;
000650          COMPUTE QUOTIENT = YEAR / 4;
000660          COMPUTE REMAIN   = YEAR - 4 * QUOTIENT;
000670          IF REMAIN = 0 ADD 1 TO DAYS.
000680 PRINT-RESULTS.
000690      DISPLAY MONTH-NAME, " HAS ", DAYS, " DAYS.".
000700      DISPLAY (LIN, 1) "AGAIN?  (Y/N):   ".
000710      ACCEPT C.
000720      IF C IS EQUAL TO "Y" OR EQUAL TO "y"
000730          GO TO BEGIN.
000740 END-OF-JOB.
000750      STOP RUN.
000760*
000770*END PROGRAM 6-11.
```

Tables

Tables in COBOL correspond to arrays in other languages. Specifically, a table is a homogeneous array. Suppose you wished to construct a table containing the name of each of 30 students. An appropriate declaration in the DATA DIVISION would be as follows:

```
01   STUDENTS.
   02 NAME OCCURS 30 TIMES
      PIC X(20).
```

The name of the first student would be referred to as NAME (1), the name of the second student as NAME (2), and so on. Each name would be a character string of up to 20 characters.

More examples of tables are given in the program of Fig. 6-11. This is a rewrite of the program of Fig. 6-10, showing an alternative way of computing the number of days in a month. Each of the two programs produces exactly the same results.

The program in Fig. 6-11 shows a common COBOL technique for initializing tables. First, a structure called TABLE-1 is defined, with each element being FILLER with

PICTURE X(10). Each is initialized in turn to the appropriate month name.

Immediately following, in line 000270, is the statement, TABLE-2 REDEFINES TABLE-1. This means that TABLE-2 is another name that refers to exactly the same place in computer memory as does TABLE-1. Line 000280 states that NAME has a PICTURE of X(10) and OCCURS 12 TIMES. In TABLE-1 each element has a PICTURE of X(10), and there are 12 elements. The two tables therefore occupy exactly the same area of memory, and each element of NAME coincides with the appropriate element of TABLE-1. NAME (5) then has the value "MAY   ", NAME (9) has the value "SEPTEMBER" , and so on.

The same technique is used to initialize the table DAYS-IN with the appropriate number of days in each month.

The DATA DIVISION of this program is longer than that of the previous program; the overall program is shorter and the PROCEDURE DIVISION is much shorter. Most of the work is done with table look-ups in lines 000590 and 000600.

Additional computation is still needed to handle leap years. For variety, the COMPUTE statement was used to handle the necessary calculations. The result is more concise than the corresponding portion of the previous program.

In Chapter 2 I used a two-dimensional integer array called POINTS to record the number of points each of 20 students in a class scored on each of 10 tests. In COBOL this would be a two-dimensional table, declared as follows:

```
01 TWO-DIMENSIONAL-TABLE.
   02 STUDENT OCCURS 20 TIMES.
      03 POINTS OCCURS 10 TIMES
            PIC 999.
```

The score achieved by student number 15 on the third test would be referred to as POINTS (15, 3). Because COBOL requires a space after all punctuation, the space between the comma and the 3 is mandatory.

Although the declaration of tables in COBOL is quite different from the declaration of arrays in most other languages, their use is quite similar.

Records

In Chapter 2 I described a record containing a student's name and the scores achieved by that student on up to 20 tests. The basic record would be declared as follows:

```
01 STUDENT-RECORD.
   02 NAME      PIC X(20).
   02 SCORE     OCCURS 20 TIMES,
                PIC 999.
```

Now suppose that the equivalent of an array of 30 of these records were required. The declaration would change as follows:

```
01 STUDENT-RECORDS.
```

```
02 STUDENT OCCURS 30 TIMES.
   03 NAME        PIC X(20).
   03 SCORE       OCCURS 20 TIMES,
                  PIC 999.
```

The name of the 25th student would be referred to as NAME (25), and the score of the same student on the 5th test would be referred to as SCORE (25, 5).

Notice that this structure contains both names (PIC X(20)) and scores (PIC 999). It is therefore heterogeneous. The OCCURS clause must not appear in an 01 level or 77 level data item.

By using the appropriate level numbers and OCCURS clauses, data structures of arbitrary complexity can be defined in COBOL.

Linked Lists

The linked list is a useful data structure for maintaining ordered lists of data. Chapter 2 explained how a linked list can be implemented with parallel arrays. Linked lists can be implemented in COBOL using a table of records. The methodology is, however, quite similar.

The following COBOL DATA DIVISION declarations will support such a list:

```
01 TABLE-1.
   02 ELEMENT OCCURS 5 TIMES.
      03 NAME        PIC X(10).
      03 LINK        PIC 9.
77 FIRST          PIC 9.
77 FREE           PIC 9.
77 MAX-RECORDS    PIC 9
                  VALUE 5.
77 END-OF-LIST    PIC 9
                  VALUE 0.
```

For a list of more than nine records, the PICTUREs of the various pointers would have to be enlarged from nine to the appropriate size.

Because COBOL supports indexed files, to be described below, linked lists are less necessary in COBOL than in other languages. For that reason, the comprehensive sample program of this chapter will illustrate the use of indexed files rather than linked lists.

FILE HANDLING

Business applications usually involve the maintenance of files on external storage devices such as magnetic disks. A business-oriented language must therefore be able to handle files easily. File handling is in fact one of COBOL's great strengths.

COBOL provides four types of file organization: sequential, line sequential, relative, and indexed. Sequential file organization was discussed in Chapter 2. The only difference between a sequential file and a line-sequential file is that in the latter case, records are separated by a carriage return and a linefeed. In both cases, the size of individual records in the file may vary.

Relative file organization corresponds to direct-access file organization, as discussed in Chapter 2. A relative file provides access to any record in the file based on the relative position of that record in the file (i.e., the record number). All records in a relative file are fixed in length. Records in a relative file can be accessed in any order.

Records in an indexed file are also of fixed length and can be accessed in any order. The difference is that with an indexed file, access to a record of the file is based on the value of a *key field* within that record rather than the record's relative position in the file. COBOL maintains a separate index file for each indexed data file.

The ENVIRONMENT DIVISION of a COBOL program contains the declarations that distinguish between the various types of file organization. This chapter includes examples of the use of a sequential, a line-sequential, and an indexed file.

The record layout for each file must be declared in the DATA DIVISION of a COBOL program. Examples are given in the next section.

Files must be OPENed in the PROCEDURE DIVISION before they can be used. The OPEN statement must specify the mode of the file; that is INPUT, OUTPUT, or I-O. The first two categories are self-explanatory. When a file is opened for I-O, it is open for both input and output. Files must be CLOSEd at the end of a program.

Sequential Files

A program that uses a sequential file to maintain a list of names and ages is shown in Fig. 6-12. Notice that the basic parameters of the file are established in the INPUT-OUTPUT SECTION of the ENVIRONMENT DIVISION, lines 000130 to 000160. These statements give the file a name for use later in the program (AGE-FILE), assign it to disk, and establish its organization and access method (SEQUENTIAL).

The file is defined further in the FILE SECTION of the DATA DIVISION, lines 000200 to 000260. The external name of the file is established as AGES.TXT. This is the name you will see in the disk directory after the program has been run.

Line 000230 identifies the file buffer as ENTRY, which is defined in the following lines. This buffer may be thought of as both a place where data is stored on its way to and from the file, and as a template that defines the format of each file record. In this case each record consists of a character string called NAME, and a numeric variable called AGE. The record is 29 bytes long; NAME is 25 characters in length, AGE is 2 characters in length, and the system uses 2 bytes to store the length of the record.

There are no intervening characters between records of a sequential file.

The file is opened for output in line 000390. The data is read into the file buffer from the keyboard in line 000430, and written to the file in line 000450. The method of data input has not been previously discussed and requires explanation.

COBOL supports input by *screen*. The format of a screen is defined in the SCREEN SECTION of the DATA DIVISION. This follows the WORKING-STORAGE SECTION, if present. A screen may contain control fields, display fields, and input fields.

Line 000290 is an example of a control field; it specifies that the screen should be initially blank. A control field can also determine such attributes as foreground and background colors for color monitors.

Lines 000300 through 000330 are examples of display fields. They contain screen locations and the data to be displayed at those screen locations. The screen is displayed

```
000010*FIGURE 6-12:  SEQUENTIAL FILE USAGE.
000020*
000030*
000040 IDENTIFICATION DIVISION.
000050 PROGRAM-ID.    COBOL-12.
000060*
000070 ENVIRONMENT DIVISION.
000080 CONFIGURATION SECTION.
000090 SOURCE-COMPUTER.   ZENITH 150.
000100 OBJECT-COMPUTER.   ZENITH 150.
000110 INPUT-OUTPUT SECTION.
000120 FILE-CONTROL.
000130     SELECT AGE-FILE
000140         ASSIGN TO DISK,
000150         ORGANIZATION IS SEQUENTIAL,
000160         ACCESS IS SEQUENTIAL.
000170*
000180 DATA DIVISION.
000190 FILE SECTION.
000200 FD AGE-FILE,
000210     LABEL RECORDS ARE STANDARD,
000220     VALUE OF FILE-ID IS "AGES.TXT",
000230     DATA RECORD IS ENTRY.
000240 01  ENTRY.
000250     02  NAME              PIC X(25).
000260     02  AGE               PIC XX.
000270 SCREEN SECTION.
000280 01  NAME-SCREEN.
000290     02  BLANK SCREEN.
000300     02  LINE 06 COLUMN 20
000310         VALUE "Enter Name and Age; Blanks to Quit:".
000320     02  LINE 10 COLUMN 20 VALUE "NAME:".
000330     02  LINE 14 COLUMN 20 VALUE "AGE:".
000340     02  LINE 10 COLUMN 30 PIC X(25) TO NAME.
000350     02  LINE 14 COLUMN 30 PIC XX    TO AGE.
000360*
000370 PROCEDURE DIVISION.
000380 BEGIN.
000390     OPEN OUTPUT AGE-FILE.
000400 INPUT-LOOP.
000410     MOVE SPACES TO NAME.
000420     DISPLAY NAME-SCREEN.
000430     ACCEPT  NAME-SCREEN.
000440     IF NAME = SPACES GO TO END-INPUT-LOOP.
000450     WRITE ENTRY.
000460     GO TO INPUT-LOOP.
000470 END-INPUT-LOOP.
000480     CLOSE AGE-FILE.
000490*    NOW REOPEN & READ BACK, DISPLAYING EACH RECORD.
000500     OPEN INPUT AGE-FILE.
```

Fig. 6-12. Sequential-file usage.

```
000510      DISPLAY (1, 1) ERASE.
000520      DISPLAY "HERE ARE THE NAMES AND AGES FROM THE FILE.".
000530 OUTPUT-LOOP.
000540      DISPLAY SPACE.
000550      MOVE SPACES TO NAME.
000560      READ AGE-FILE RECORD AT END GO TO END-OF-JOB.
000570      DISPLAY ENTRY.
000580      GO TO OUTPUT-LOOP.
000590 END-OF-JOB.
000600      CLOSE AGE-FILE.
000610      STOP RUN.
000620*
000630*END PROGRAM 6-12.
```

as the result of a DISPLAY statement that references the screen name, as in line 000420 of Fig. 6-12.

Lines 000340 and 000350 are examples of input fields. An input field specifies a location on the screen, a data picture, and where to put the data when it is read. The actual data input occurs when the screen name is referenced by an ACCEPT statement, as in line 000430. Screen input allows the use of the usual editing keys on input, plus it allows the use of the back-tab key to back up to a previous data field to make corrections.

The use of screen input greatly simplifies the PROCEDURE DIVISION of a COBOL program, at the expense of a longer DATA DIVISION. The net result is usually a shorter program. Because the language does much of the work required to handle data input, the programmer can concentrate more on the logic of the program and less on data input.

Now let us return to the logical flow of the program in Fig. 6-12. After the requisite number of records have been written, the file is closed in line 000480. It is reopened for input in line 000500. The next READ statement in line 000560 will read the first record of the file, as the file is always "rewound" to its beginning by an OPEN statement.

After each record has been read in from the file and written out to the video screen, the file is closed again. The program as a whole is quite simple. It is important to note how the file is defined in the ENVIRONMENT DIVISION and DATA DIVISION. The details of how this is done can vary from compiler to compiler, so the compiler documentation should be carefully checked.

Line-Sequential Files

Earlier in the chapter I mentioned that I use a program to place sequence numbers in columns 1-6 of my COBOL programs. This program uses line-sequential file organization and is shown as Fig. 6-13.

Line-sequential file organization is appropriate in this case because it is the file organization most often used by text editor programs. Each line in the file is separated by a carriage return and a linefeed.

The only apparent difference between a program that uses line-sequential file organization and one that uses sequential file organization is the clause ORGANIZATION IS LINE SEQUENTIAL in the FILE-CONTROL SECTION of the ENVIRONMENT DIVISION. See line 000150 of Fig. 6-13.

```
000010*FIGURE 6-13:   RENUMBER COBOL SOURCE PROGRAMS.
000020*
000030*
000040 IDENTIFICATION DIVISION.
000050 PROGRAM-ID.    COBOL-13.
000060*
000070 ENVIRONMENT DIVISION.
000080 CONFIGURATION SECTION.
000090 SOURCE-COMPUTER.    ZENITH 150.
000100 OBJECT-COMPUTER.    ZENITH 150.
000110 INPUT-OUTPUT SECTION.
000120 FILE-CONTROL.
000130     SELECT PROG-FILE ASSIGN TO DISK;
000140     ACCESS MODE IS SEQUENTIAL;
000150     ORGANIZATION IS LINE SEQUENTIAL.
000160*
000170 DATA DIVISION.
000180 FILE SECTION.
000190 FD   PROG-FILE
000200     LABEL RECORDS ARE STANDARD
000210     VALUE OF FILE-ID IS F-NAME.
000220 01  PROG-LINE.
000230     02   SEQ-NR   PIC 9(6).
000240     02   FILLER   PIC X(66).
000250 WORKING-STORAGE SECTION.
000260 77  F-NAME       PIC X(12).
000270 77  COUNTER      PIC 9(6)  VALUE  ZERO.
000280 77  OUT-LINE     PIC X(72).
000290*
000300 PROCEDURE DIVISION.
000310 BEGIN.
000320     DISPLAY (1, 1)  ERASE;
000330     DISPLAY (1, 1)  "RENUMBER WHICH FILE?  ";
000340     ACCEPT  (1, 24) F-NAME.
000350     DISPLAY (3, 1)  ERASE.
000360     OPEN I-O        PROG-FILE.
000370 START-LOOP.
000380     READ PROG-FILE RECORD AT END GO TO END-OF-JOB.
000390     ADD 10 TO COUNTER;
000400     MOVE COUNTER TO SEQ-NR;
000410     MOVE PROG-LINE TO OUT-LINE;
000420     REWRITE PROG-LINE;
000430     DISPLAY OUT-LINE.
000440     GO TO START-LOOP.
000450 END-OF-JOB.
000460     CLOSE PROG-FILE.
000470     STOP RUN.
000480*
000490*END PROGRAM 6-13.
```

Fig. 6-13. Renumbering COBOL source programs.

The DISPLAY statement of line 000320 clears the screen from the designated point to the end of the screen. In this case, the designated point is the upper-left corner of the screen, so the entire screen is cleared.

Line 000340 reads the name of the file to be sequenced. Line 000360 opens the file in I-O mode. Line 000380 reads a line of text from the file. Lines 000390 through 000400 increment the sequence number and move it to the appropriate part of the file buffer. The REWRITE statement in line 000420 causes the modified file record to be written back to the same place in the file. Line 000410 moves the entire line to another output buffer for subsequent output to the screen.

Relative Files

As mentioned, relative file organization in COBOL corresponds to direct-access file organization as discussed in Chapter 2. The following shows how a relative file is declared in the ENVIRONMENT DIVISION of a COBOL program:

```
ENVIRONMENT DIVISION.
INPUT-OUTPUT SECTION.
FILE-CONTROL.
   SELECT FILE-1 ASSIGN TO DISK,
      ORGANIZATION IS RELATIVE,
      ACCESS MODE IS RANDOM,
      RELATIVE KEY IS FILE-1-KEY.
```

The WORKING-STORAGE SECTION of the DATA DIVISION must then contain an entry describing the file key, as in the following:

```
77 FILE-1-KEY   PIC 999.
```

To write something to the thirtieth record of the file, you could do the following:

```
MOVE "This goes in record 30"
   TO FILE-1-RECORD.
MOVE 30 TO FILE-1-KEY.
WRITE FILE-1-RECORD
   INVALID KEY DISPLAY
   "INVALID KEY: ", FILE-1-KEY.
```

Moving the value 30 to FILE-1-KEY causes the subsequent WRITE statement to write the contents of FILE-1-RECORD in record 30 of the file. The INVALID KEY clause is required, and in this case it causes a message to be displayed to the console if record 30 of the file does not exist.

The READ statement for a relative file works the same way: to read a particular record from a direct-access file, first MOVE the record number to the RELATIVE KEY field, and then use the READ statement.

Indexed Files

As mentioned, COBOL supports the use of indexed files. This type of file organization is sometimes called the Indexed Sequential Access Method, or *ISAM*, file organization. Newer mainframe COBOL compilers support a refinement of this method called the Virtual Sequential Access Method, or *VSAM*.

For each data file organized as an indexed file, COBOL creates and maintains a separate index file. This separate file serves as an index into the main data file. As a record is added to an indexed file, an entry is created in the file index. As a record in the main file is accessed by its key, the index file is first consulted to determine the actual location of the desired record. Internally, COBOL uses an indexing method called a *B-tree* for the index, and relative file organization for the data file.

The advantage of either ISAM or VSAM file organization is that compiler takes over much of the work of keeping track of individual file records, relieving the programmer of a significant burden. With an ISAM or VSAM file, the data records can be loaded in any sequence and then extracted either individually by the value of the record key, or sequentially in order of the key values. Listing the file in sequence does not require a separate, time-consuming, file sort.

Many business applications can take advantage of indexed files. The indexed file feature is one reason why COBOL is so successful for business applications.

The comprehensive sample program at the end of this chapter illustrates the use of an indexed file in a nontrivial application.

GRAPHICS

COBOL does not support graphics.

THE COMPREHENSIVE SAMPLE PROGRAM

The program in Fig. 6-14 maintains a computerized address book. It records names, addresses, and telephone numbers in an indexed file. The file is organized so that it is logically always in alphabetical order. No sorting is performed; the key of each record is recorded in the index as the record is added to the file. The program permits records to be added to the file, deleted from the file, displayed on the video screen, or listed on a printer.

The file is declared as an indexed file in the FILE-CONTROL clause of the INPUT-OUTPUT SECTION of the ENVIRONMENT DIVISION (lines 000150 to 000220). The key field is defined as part of the data record. In this case it is a field called AF-NAME.

The FILE STATUS field is something new. This field is identified as part of the file definition, and is declared in the WORKING-STORAGE SECTION. After each action on the file, the value of this variable indicates whether or not that action was successful, and if not, what went wrong.

Another new thing in this program is the LINAGE clause of the printer declaration. Using this, COBOL can be told to automatically skip over the perforations between printer pages—a nice touch that is unfortunately absent from most other languages.

The basic data file record is defined in lines 000380 through 000460. Note that the key field, AF-NAME, is a group name, consisting of the individual's last and first names, in that order. This facilitates indexing the file by last name first, then by first name.

Another feature that was not previously discussed is the use of *level 88*. Refer to the variable ERR-FLAG, declared in lines 000640 through 000660. It has two level 88

```
000010*FIGURE 6-14:   THE COMPREHENSIVE SAMPLE PROGRAM.
000020*
000030*
000040 IDENTIFICATION DIVISION.
000050 PROGRAM-ID.    COBOL-14.
000060*
000070*     DEMONSTRATE THE USE OF AN ISAM FILE TO MAINTAIN
000080*     A LIST OF NAMES, ADDRESSES, AND PHONE NUMBERS.
000090*
000100 ENVIRONMENT DIVISION.
000110 CONFIGURATION SECTION.
000120 SOURCE-COMPUTER.    ZENITH 150.
000130 OBJECT-COMPUTER.    ZENITH 150.
000140 INPUT-OUTPUT SECTION.
000150 FILE-CONTROL.
000160     SELECT PRT ASSIGN TO PRINTER.
000170     SELECT ADDRESS-FILE
000180           ASSIGN TO DISK
000190           FILE STATUS   IS AF-STATUS
000200           RECORD KEY    IS AF-NAME
000210           ACCESS MODE   IS DYNAMIC
000220           ORGANIZATION IS INDEXED.
000230*
000240 DATA DIVISION.
000250 FILE SECTION.
000260 FD   PRT
000270     LABEL RECORDS ARE OMITTED,
000280     LINAGE IS 55 LINES
000290           WITH FOOTING AT 55,
000300           LINES AT TOP     0,
000310           LINES AT BOTTOM 11,
000320     DATA RECORD   IS PRINT-LINE.
000330 01  PRINT-LINE          PIC X(80).
000340 FD   ADDRESS-FILE
000350     LABEL RECORDS ARE STANDARD,
000360     VALUE OF FILE-ID IS "ADDRESS.TXT",
000370     DATA RECORD IS ADDRESS-RECORD.
000380 01  ADDRESS-RECORD.
000390     02  AF-NAME.
000400         03  LAST-NAME    PIC X(15).
000410         03  FIRST-NAME   PIC X(15).
000420     02  ADDRESS          PIC X(24).
000430     02  CITY             PIC X(20).
000440     02  STATE            PIC X(2).
000450     02  ZIP              PIC X(10).
000460     02  PHONE-NR         PIC X(14).
000470 WORKING-STORAGE SECTION.
000480 01  PRINTER-FORMATS.
000490     02  LINE-1.
000500         03  PR-FIRST     PIC X(15).
000510         03  FILLER       PIC X    VALUE SPACE.
000520         03  PR-LAST      PIC X(15).
000530     02  LINE-2           PIC X(24).
000540     02  LINE-3.
```

Fig. 6-14. The comprehensive sample program.

```
000550            03    PR-CITY           PIC X(20).
000560            03    FILLER            PIC X     VALUE SPACE.
000570            03    PR-STATE          PIC X(2).
000580            03    FILLER            PIC X     VALUE SPACE.
000590            03    PR-ZIP            PIC X(10).
000600      02    LINE-4                  PIC X(14).
000610 77  AF-STATUS                      PIC XX    VALUE SPACES.
000620 77  CHOICE                         PIC X     VALUE SPACE.
000630 77  C                              PIC X     VALUE SPACE.
000640 77  ERR-FLAG                       PIC X     VALUE "N".
000650      88    NO-ERROR                          VALUE "N".
000660      88    AN-ERROR                          VALUE "Y".
000670 77  EOF-FLAG                       PIC X.
000680      88    AF-EOF                            VALUE "Y".
000690 SCREEN SECTION.
000700 01  OPENING-SCREEN.
000710      02    BLANK SCREEN FOREGROUND-COLOR O BACKGROUND-COLOR 7.
000720      02    LINE 10 COLUMN 15 "ADDRESS BOOK PROGRAM".
000730      02    LINE 13 COLUMN 15 "OPENING DISK FILE".
000740 01  MENU-SCREEN.
000750      02    BLANK SCREEN FOREGROUND-COLOR O BACKGROUND-COLOR 7.
000760      02    LINE 06 COLUMN 15 "1)    ADD TO FILE".
000770      02    LINE 08 COLUMN 15 "2)    RETRIEVE BY NAME".
000780      02    LINE 10 COLUMN 15 "3)    LIST FILE ON SCREEN".
000790      02    LINE 12 COLUMN 15 "4)    LIST FILE ON PRINTER".
000800      02    LINE 14 COLUMN 15 "5)    DELETE RECORD".
000810      02    LINE 16 COLUMN 15 "6)    QUIT".
000820      02    LINE 19 COLUMN 10 "SELECT 1, 2, 3, 4, 5, OR 6:  ".
000830      02    LINE 19 COLUMN 40 PIC X TO CHOICE.
000840 01  INPUT-SCREEN.
000850      02    BLANK SCREEN FOREGROUND-COLOR 1 BACKGROUND-COLOR 3.
000860      02    LINE 06 COLUMN 10 "LAST NAME:".
000870      02    LINE 08 COLUMN 10 "FIRST NAME:".
000880      02    LINE 10 COLUMN 10 "ADDRESS:".
000890      02    LINE 12 COLUMN 10 "CITY:".
000900      02    LINE 14 COLUMN 10 "STATE:".
000910      02    LINE 16 COLUMN 10 "ZIP CODE:".
000920      02    LINE 18 COLUMN 10 "PHONE NUMBER:".
000930      02    LINE 24 COLUMN 01 "ENTER DATA; BLANK TO EXIT.".
000940      02    LINE 06 COLUMN 25 PIC X(15) REVERSE-VIDEO TO LAST-NAME.
000950      02    LINE 08 COLUMN 25 PIC X(15) REVERSE-VIDEO TO FIRST-NAME.
000960      02    LINE 10 COLUMN 25 PIC X(24) REVERSE-VIDEO TO ADDRESS.
000970      02    LINE 12 COLUMN 25 PIC X(20) REVERSE-VIDEO TO CITY.
000980      02    LINE 14 COLUMN 25 PIC X(2)  REVERSE-VIDEO TO STATE.
000990      02    LINE 16 COLUMN 25 PIC X(10) REVERSE-VIDEO TO ZIP.
001000      02    LINE 18 COLUMN 25 PIC X(14) REVERSE-VIDEO TO PHONE-NR.
001010 01  DISPLAY-SCREEN.
001020      02    BLANK SCREEN FOREGROUND-COLOR 10 BACKGROUND-COLOR O.
001030      02    LINE 10 COLUMN 10 PIC X(15) FROM FIRST-NAME.
001040      02    LINE 10 COLUMN 26 PIC X(15) FROM LAST-NAME.
001050      02    LINE 12 COLUMN 10 PIC X(24) FROM ADDRESS.
001060      02    LINE 14 COLUMN 10 PIC X(20) FROM CITY.
001070      02    LINE 14 COLUMN 31 PIC X(2)  FROM STATE.
001080      02    LINE 14 COLUMN 34 PIC X(10) FROM ZIP.
001090      02    LINE 16 COLUMN 10 PIC X(14) FROM PHONE-NR.
001100      02    LINE 20 COLUMN 10 VALUE "PRESS <RETURN> TO CONTINUE ...".
001110      02    LINE 20 COLUMN 40 PIC X      TO   C.
```

```
001120 01    RETRIEVE-SCREEN.
001130      02   BLANK SCREEN FOREGROUND-COLOR 14 BACKGROUND-COLOR 1.
001140      02   LINE 05 COLUMN 05 VALUE "ENTER RECORD KEY".
001150      02   LINE 10 COLUMN 10 VALUE "LAST NAME:".
001160      02   LINE 12 COLUMN 10 VALUE "FIRST NAME:".
001170      02   LINE 10 COLUMN 25 PIC X(15) REVERSE-VIDEO TO LAST-NAME.
001180      02   LINE 12 COLUMN 25 PIC X(15) REVERSE-VIDEO TO FIRST-NAME.
001190*
001200 PROCEDURE DIVISION.
001210 BEGIN.
001220      DISPLAY OPENING-SCREEN.
001230      OPEN OUTPUT PRT.
001240      PERFORM OPEN-FILE.
001250      IF AF-STATUS NOT = "00"
001260            PERFORM FILE-ERROR,
001270            GO TO END-OF-JOB.
001280 MAIN-LOOP.
001290      DISPLAY MENU-SCREEN.
001300      ACCEPT  MENU-SCREEN.
001310      IF CHOICE = "1" PERFORM APPEND.
001320      IF CHOICE = "2" PERFORM RETRIEVE.
001330      IF CHOICE = "3" PERFORM LIST-SCREEN.
001340      IF CHOICE = "4" PERFORM LIST-PRINTER.
001350      IF CHOICE = "5" PERFORM DELETE-RECORD.
001360      IF CHOICE = "6" GO TO END-OF-JOB.
001370      GO TO MAIN-LOOP.
001380 END-OF-JOB.
001390      CLOSE PRT.
001400      CLOSE ADDRESS-FILE.
001410      STOP RUN.
001420*
001430 OPEN-FILE.
001440      OPEN I-O ADDRESS-FILE.
001450      IF AF-STATUS = "30" PERFORM INIT-FILE.
001460 INIT-FILE.
001470      OPEN OUTPUT ADDRESS-FILE.
001480      CLOSE ADDRESS-FILE.
001490      OPEN I-O ADDRESS-FILE.
001500 FILE-ERROR.
001510      MOVE "Y" TO ERR-FLAG.
001520      DISPLAY (LIN, 1) "FILE INPUT/OUTPUT ERROR ....".
001530      DISPLAY (LIN, 1) "STATUS CODE ", AF-STATUS.
001540      STOP "PRESS <RETURN> TO CONTINUE .....".
001550 APPEND.
001560      MOVE SPACES TO ADDRESS-RECORD.
001570      DISPLAY INPUT-SCREEN.
001580      ACCEPT  INPUT-SCREEN.
001590      IF AF-NAME NOT = SPACES
001600            WRITE ADDRESS-RECORD,
001610            GO TO APPEND.
001620 RETRIEVE.
001630      MOVE SPACES TO ADDRESS-RECORD.
001640      DISPLAY RETRIEVE-SCREEN.
001650      ACCEPT  RETRIEVE-SCREEN.
001660      READ ADDRESS-FILE
```

Fig. 6-14. The comprehensive sample program. (Continued from page 181.)

```
001670              INVALID KEY DISPLAY SPACES,
001680                      DISPLAY "INVALID KEY!".
001690      IF AF-STATUS = "00"
001700              DISPLAY DISPLAY-SCREEN,
001710              ACCEPT  DISPLAY-SCREEN,
001720      ELSE
001730              DISPLAY "RECORD NOT FOUND.",
001740              STOP "TYPE <RETURN> TO CONTINUE ....".
001750 LIST-SCREEN.
001760      MOVE LOW-VALUE TO AF-NAME.
001770      START ADDRESS-FILE KEY NOT LESS THAN AF-NAME.
001780      MOVE "N" TO EOF-FLAG.
001790      PERFORM READ-RECORD UNTIL AF-EOF OR AN-ERROR.
001800 LIST-PRINTER.
001810      MOVE LOW-VALUE TO AF-NAME.
001820      START ADDRESS-FILE KEY NOT LESS THAN AF-NAME.
001830      MOVE "N" TO EOF-FLAG.
001840      PERFORM PRINT-RECORD UNTIL AF-EOF OR AN-ERROR.
001850      MOVE SPACES TO PRINT-LINE.
001860      WRITE PRINT-LINE BEFORE ADVANCING PAGE.
001870 DELETE-RECORD.
001880      PERFORM RETRIEVE.
001890      DISPLAY (22, 10) "TYPE 'Y' TO DELETE RECORD ...".
001900      ACCEPT  (22, 40) C.
001910      IF C = "Y" OR = "y" DELETE ADDRESS-FILE RECORD.
001920 READ-RECORD.
001930      READ ADDRESS-FILE NEXT RECORD,
001940              AT END MOVE "Y" TO EOF-FLAG.
001950      IF AF-STATUS NOT = "00" AND NOT AF-EOF
001960              PERFORM FILE-ERROR
001970      ELSE IF NOT AF-EOF
001980              DISPLAY DISPLAY-SCREEN,
001990              ACCEPT  DISPLAY-SCREEN.
002000 PRINT-RECORD.
002010      READ ADDRESS-FILE NEXT RECORD,
002020              AT END MOVE "Y" TO EOF-FLAG.
002030      IF AF-STATUS NOT = "00" AND NOT AF-EOF
002040              PERFORM FILE-ERROR
002050      ELSE IF NOT AF-EOF
002060              MOVE FIRST-NAME TO PR-FIRST,
002070              MOVE LAST-NAME  TO PR-LAST,
002080              WRITE PRINT-LINE FROM LINE-1
002090                      BEFORE ADVANCING 1 LINE,
002100              WRITE PRINT-LINE FROM ADDRESS
002110                      BEFORE ADVANCING 1 LINE,
002120              MOVE CITY  TO PR-CITY,
002130              MOVE STATE TO PR-STATE,
002140              MOVE ZIP   TO PR-ZIP,
002150              WRITE PRINT-LINE FROM LINE-3
002160                      BEFORE ADVANCING 1 LINE,
002170              WRITE PRINT-LINE FROM PHONE-NR
002180                      BEFORE ADVANCING 2 LINES.
002190*
002200*END PROGRAM 6-14.
```

sublevels. The field NO-ERROR is defined to have the value "N", and the field AN-ERROR is defined to have the value "Y". The result is best illustrated by the following examples:

```
MOVE "N" TO ERR-FLAG.
IF NO-ERROR GO TO PARA-7.
```

This would result in a jump to PARA-7. In other words, NO-ERROR is true if ERR-FLAG has the value "N". Similarly,

```
MOVE "Y" TO ERR-FLAG.
IF AN-ERROR GO TO PARA-9.
```

would result in a jump to PARA-9.

Five different screens are defined in the SCREEN SECTION. Note the use of various foreground and background colors and the use of reverse video.

The main program portion of the PROCEDURE DIVISION is very short. The program opens the disk file and the printer file; it then repeatedly displays the menu screen and performs the appropriate action. When choice 6 is selected, the program closes the files and terminates.

The program first attempts to open the address file in I-O mode. If a status code of 30 is returned, that means the file did not previously exist. In that case the file is opened in OUTPUT mode to create it, then closed and reopened in I-O mode.

The actions to add a record to the file, list the file, and delete a record are performed in the various subroutines, each of which is very short. Two that are worth discussing are the RETRIEVE subroutine because it retrieves a record by its key, and the LIST-SCREEN subroutine, because it traverses the file in sequence.

The RETRIEVE subroutine uses a screen to read a name from the keyboard. Recall that the last and first names together form the record key. The screen called RETRIEVE-SCREEN puts the name into the key field. The READ statement in line 001660 then reads the appropriate record from the disk. If a record matching that key is not found, an appropriate message is displayed.

The LIST-SCREEN subroutine begins by placing the COBOL constant LOW-VALUE into the key field. The START statement in line 001770 then positions the file pointer to a record that is not less than the record key field, which has the value LOW-VALUE. This value is defined such that it will be less than any possible record key, so the effect is to place the file pointer at the logical beginning of the file, so that a subsequent READ statement will read the record with the smallest key value. The subroutine READ-RECORD then reads each record in sequence until the end of the file is detected.

It is worth noting that, because of the power of the screen input and indexed file capabilities of COBOL, this program is significantly shorter than the comparable program in other languages such as C, Pascal, Ada, and Modula-2. (Refer to the appropriate chapters for comparison.)

The organization of the program of Fig. 6-14 can be seen more easily by consulting the structure chart shown in Fig. 6-15. This chart shows by indentation which subroutines call which other subroutines.

The program as it stands can be useful for maintaining a list of names and addresses

```
MAIN PROGRAM
    OPEN-FILE
        INIT-FILE
    FILE-ERROR
    APPEND
    RETRIEVE
    LIST-SCREEN
        READ-RECORD
            FILE-ERROR
    LIST-PRINTER
        PRINT-RECORD
            FILE-ERROR
    DELETE-RECORD
        RETRIEVE
```

Fig. 6-15. Structure chart for the comprehensive sample program.

to be printed out. Addition of the capability to search the file based on name, city, or other field would make the program even more useful.

ADVANTAGES AND DISADVANTAGES OF COBOL

The early examples in this chapter are longer and wordier than their counterparts in other languages. COBOL does not appear to be very concise. It is tempting to criticize COBOL because of its wordiness. In the comprehensive sample program, however, COBOL showed some of its true power, resulting in a program significantly shorter than the corresponding programs of most other languages represented in this book, including C, a language known for its conciseness.

The two major strengths of COBOL are its ability to handle data in a wide variety of forms and structures (including screens), and its ability to handle files.

The importance given by COBOL to data is symbolized by the fact that COBOL has a separate **DATA DIVISION**. There is an increasing recognition in the data processing industry that the data to be processed is more important than the algorithms with which it is processed. Most other computer languages were designed for ease of expressing algorithms; COBOL was designed for ease of describing data.

The importance of data requires that much of it be stored in files, and the facilities that COBOL provides for file handling are excellent. Full COBOL implementations also provide a built-in file-sorting facility.

Although the **DATA DIVISION** of COBOL programs tends to be larger than the corresponding portion of programs in other languages, this often results in shorter and more concise algorithms in the **PROCEDURE DIVISION**. The comprehensive sample program is an excellent example of this phenomenon, as will be seen by comparing the COBOL comprehensive sample program with the corresponding program in other languages.

The **MOVE** statement of COBOL is very powerful when compared to the assignment statement of other languages. Whole structures can be **MOVE**d in one statement. Data can also be converted from **COMPUTATIONAL** to **DISPLAY** format with a **MOVE** statement.

On the negative side, COBOL is notably weak in its control structures. To emulate a while statement requires a PERFORM statement with the body of the loop stored elsewhere or a GO TO statement.

COBOL handles basic arithmetic very well, but it has problems with more complicated mathematics such as exponentiation and trigonometry. Simple arithmetic, however, is all that is needed in most business applications.

Also on the negative side, all variables in a COBOL program are global, with the exception of variables used in separately compiled subroutines invoked by the CALL statement. (The CALL statement was not discussed in detail in this chapter.) A subroutine invoked by a PERFORM statement must rely only on global variables.

AVAILABILITY

COBOL implementations for computers running the CP/M-80, PC-DOS, and MS-DOS operating systems are widely available at costs ranging from $39.95 to over $3000. Most are priced in the $500 to $700 range. At the low end, a version called *Utah COBOL* is available from Ellis Computing of Reno, Nevada, for $39.95. *Microsoft COBOL*, by Microsoft Corporation of Redmond, Washington, lists for $700. *Realia COBOL*, by Realia, Incorporated, of Chicago, Illinois, lists for $995. *Micro Focus Level II COBOL*, by Micro Focus, lists for $1500. *Micro Focus Professional COBOL* lists for $3000. Advertisements and current prices can be found in *Byte* or *Computer Language* magazines.

SUMMARY

COBOL is the most widely used computer language on large computers. It has powerful facilities for the handling of data and data structures, both within a program and in external files.

All in all, COBOL is an excellent language for its intended purpose, business-oriented data processing. Programmers who write business applications in BASIC or C are working too hard. COBOL is not suitable for applications that require extensive mathematical calculations.

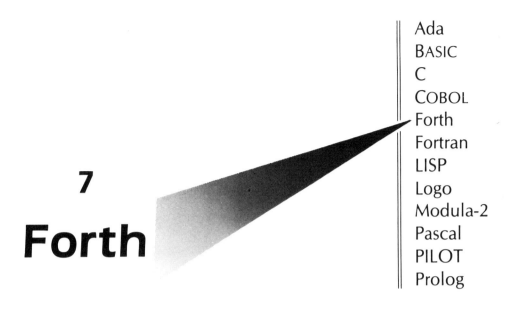

7

Forth

The language called Forth was developed by Charles H. Moore in the late 1960s and early 1970s. That makes it of about the same vintage as C, Logo, Pascal, Prolog, and PILOT. Forth is very popular among a small but enthusiastic group of microcomputer users.

The name Forth has an interesting derivation. Programming languages are sometimes categorized by generation. The first generation of programming languages consists of machine languages. Assembly languages is the second generation. Machine and assembly languages are computer-specific and are collectively called *low-level languages.* The third generation of programming languages includes Fortran, COBOL, Pascal, and most other popular programming languages, including Ada. They are also called *high-level languages.*

Moore thought that his new language was so much superior to earlier languages that it should be classified as a ''fourth-generation language.'' He wanted to call it ''Fourth,'' but the computer on which he was working (an IBM 1130) permitted only five characters in a word. He therefore truncated ''Fourth'' to ''Forth.''

Forth is many things:

☐ a high-level language
☐ a low-level language
☐ an operating system
☐ a programming philosophy

One of the distinguishing characteristics of a high-level language is that it is not machine-specific. A Pascal program written for one computer will (at least in theory) run on any other computer that has a Pascal compiler. In that sense, Forth is a high-level language; implementations of Forth are available for most microcomputers powerful enough to support a disk drive, and for many minicomputers.

Another, related, characteristic of a high-level language is that the programmer need not be concerned with the architecture of the computer on which the program is executed. By the architecture of the computer I mean such details as stacks, registers, and the computation of addresses for array elements. While it is true that the Forth programmer does not have to worry about the computer's stacks and registers, he or she does have to contend with the architecture of "the Forth Machine," and does have to worry about the Forth Machine's stacks and about the computation of addresses for array elements.

The Forth Machine is a *virtual* machine, that is, it is the image of how the computer appears to the Forth programmer. It exists in software, and stands between the programmer and the actual physical machine. The problem is that the Forth programmer must be concerned with nearly the same level of detail concerning the Forth Machine as an assembly-language programmer must be concerning an actual physical machine. In that sense Forth is a low-level language.

The Forth Machine consists of the following:

- [ ] the parameter stack
- [ ] the return stack
- [ ] the dictionary
- [ ] secondary (disk) storage

I have left out several predefined areas, but the point is that there are specific places for most things in the Forth Machine, and it is up to the programmer to keep track. Each of these parts of the Forth Machine will be discussed in turn in the pages that follow.

Forth is an operating system in the sense that it performs a number of tasks within the language that are normally performed by the operating system. The most obvious of these is disk file management. The Forth disk file management scheme is very simple; in fact it doesn't even include a disk directory. The disk is divided into blocks of 1024 bytes each. Each block has a number. It is up to the user to keep track of what is in each block and to load and save blocks by number.

Some newer implementations of Forth implement the Forth disk management scheme within a file under the host operating system (e.g., MS-DOS). The disk file becomes a *virtual disk* organized as if it were a Forth disk.

Forth is also a programming philosophy, perhaps even a state of mind. The Forth philosophy is that computer memory and computer time are scarce resources, and that the programmer should go out of his or her way to conserve those resources. Forth is designed to afford the user maximum control over those resources. The Forth philosophy encourages the use of programming tricks that save computer time or memory. Sometimes this cleverness comes at the expense of clarity. The Forth philosophy encourages mental gymnastics; Forth programmers are fond of showing each other one- or two-line programs and issuing the challenge, "I'll bet you can't figure out what this does!"

The following comment was observed on the COMPUSERVE network in March 1987:

"What Forth programs are usually not is *readable*. Like survivors of some Japanese Great Depression, Forth programmers have developed a horror of wasted space, and try to compress as much code into as little space as possible. My theory is that this is a legacy of the days when there were no systems that supported both hard disk and Forth. Regardless of the cause, the source and sample code supplied with most Forth implementations looks like a Tokyo commuter train: little capsules of code containing the syntactically required minimum of white space."

Forth is often used in industrial control applications; that is, it is used for programming small microprocessors that control machines in real time. These machines might be household appliances or industrial robots. For these applications at least, time and memory are often at a premium, so the Forth philosophy is appropriate.

Forth is a controversial language. Forth divides people into three groups:

- [ ] those who love Forth
- [ ] those who hate Forth
- [ ] those who have never heard of Forth

It is difficult to know anything about Forth and remain indifferent about it. There are a number of books about Forth on the market. All were written by those who love Forth. (Why would anyone who hates Forth bother to write a book about it?) I have tried to remain objective in this chapter; you can be the judge of whether I have succeeded.

The programs in this chapter were written and tested on an Apple computer using MVP-FORTH, a product of Mountain View Press. MVP-FORTH complies with the FORTH-79 Standard.

PROGRAM STRUCTURE

The basic structural unit in Forth is the *word*. A word in Forth corresponds to a function or procedure in other languages. Even the basic operators such as +, −, and so on are implemented as Forth words.

A Forth program is made up of one or more Forth words. The usual procedure is to break a task up into smaller and smaller pieces until each is manageable and then to implement each piece as a Forth word. The interactive nature of Forth facilitates implementing and testing each word independently.

A simple Forth program that prints This is a test on the screen is shown in Fig. 7-1. This program is implemented as the Forth word TEST. A detailed analysis of this

```
SCR #1
  0  ( Figure 7-1:   Simple Test Program )
  1
  2  : TEST     CR  ." This is a test."  CR ;
  3
```

Fig. 7-1. A simple test program.

word definition follows. Because of the significance of spaces and quotation marks in Forth, individual words will be delimited by braces, { and }, within the text. The braces are not part of the Forth words being presented.

Comments in Forth are delimited by parentheses. Note that the left parenthesis is separated from the rest of the text by a space. This is necessary because the left parenthesis is actually a Forth word. All Forth words, including punctuation marks, must be separated from each other and from other text by one or more spaces. The comment for this program serves to identify the example.

The initial colon { : } is itself a Forth word and is used to initiate the definition of another Forth word. The definition is terminated by the semicolon { ; } at the end of the line. Notice that the colon and semicolon are separated from the adjacent words by a space.

A Forth program is compiled in one of two ways. It can be entered interactively at the keyboard, or it can be created using the Forth editor, stored on a disk as a Forth *screen,* and compiled as it is loaded from the disk. If a Forth program is entered interactively at the keyboard, no record is kept of the source listing; only the compiled program is stored. For that reason it is usually preferable to create Forth programs using the editor and to store them on disk before compiling them.

A Forth screen is a block of 16 lines of text, each 64 characters in length. Its total size is 1024 characters. Most of the figures in this chapter show all or part of Forth screens, with the lines numbered from 0 to 15. The line numbers are not part of the screen, but are supplied by the Forth editor. Each screen has a screen number. The screens are stored on disk in order according to screen numbers. The program in Fig. 7-1 occupies screen #1 (lines 4 through 15 of the screen were omitted from the figure). It is loaded and compiled by typing 1 LOAD at the console. { LOAD } is of course a Forth word. The 1 represents the screen number.

The name { TEST } is the name given to the word. To execute the word after it has been defined, simply type

TEST

at the terminal. The { CR } emits a carriage return and causes the output to appear on a line by itself. The Forth word { ." } initiates the printing of the following character string. Because it is a Forth word, it is separated from the text by a space. The character string is terminated by the next quotation mark { " }. The quotation mark that terminates a character string is a delimiter, not a Forth word, and therefore does not need to be separated from the preceding text by a space.

After a Forth word has been successfully compiled, it is entered into the Forth Dictionary. The Forth Dictionary contains the definitions of all Forth words, whether they were furnished with the system or supplied by the user. When a Forth word is compiled, it is added to the end of the dictionary. When Forth searches the dictionary for a word, it starts at the end and searches sequentially toward the beginning. If a word is defined more than once in the dictionary, only the most recent definition will be found. The names of the words in the Forth dictionary can be viewed on the screen by typing the word { VLIST }.

One consequence of the way words are added to the dictionary is that during the development cycle, when a word is being developed, several versions of the word may be compiled. If the word has been compiled six times, it will appear in the dictionary six times. Of course only the most recent definition will be found, but the earlier definitions become garbage. Forth therefore provides the { EMPTY } word, which deletes all user-defined words from the dictionary, leaving only predefined words. It is good practice to include { EMPTY } at the beginning of a program so that earlier versions of the program can be deleted before the new version is added.

A typical Forth program consists of a series of word definitions. The lower-level definitions appear first so that they can be incorporated in the higher-level definitions that follow. The highest-level definition appears last. This corresponds to the main program of most other languages.

DATA REPRESENTATION

The basic data types in Forth are characters (eight-bit), normal integers (16-bit), unsigned integers (16-bit), and double-precision integers (32-bit). The logical data type does not exist as such, but zero is recognized as false and anything else as true in the appropriate context.

The range of normal integers is from -32768 to $+32767$. Unsigned integers can range from 0 to 65535. Double-precision integers can range from $-2,147,483,648$ to $+2,147,483,647$.

The FORTH-79 standard does not support floating-point numbers, but some Forth implementations do. (MVP-FORTH does not.) Some Forth enthusiasts will argue that it is an advantage not to support floating-point numbers because floating-point arithmetic is much slower than fixed-point (integer) arithmetic, and anything that is worth doing can be done in one way or another with fixed-point arithmetic anyway (possibly with double precision). While this is true, it often requires more effort on the part of the programmer.

Although Forth supports the data types described above, there is no such thing as a type declaration. Forth is very loosely typed; it is up to the programmer to keep track of what type of data his or her program is dealing with.

The Parameter Stack

Data in most languages is stored in memory locations called variables. While Forth supports variables, they play only a secondary role. Data in Forth programs is most often stored on a *stack*.

A stack is a *last-in*, *first-out* (LIFO) list. It can be likened to one of the spring-loaded plate dispensers found in many cafeterias. A plate is placed on top of the stack, and those below sink beneath its weight. Only the plate on top of the stack is accessible at a given time. When a plate is removed from the stack, the next plate rises to the top of the stack and becomes accessible.

There are no springs in Forth stacks; it is all done with pointers, but the effect is the same. Only the number at the top of the stack can be accessed. Numbers come off of the stack in the reverse of the order in which they go on. If you placed the numbers 1, 2, and 3 on the stack in that order, they would come off as 3, 2, and 1.

There are two stacks in the Forth Machine, the *parameter stack* (often called simply "the stack") and the *return stack*. Each stack element has 16 bits, and is usually a 16-bit integer, although it could be a character (padded to 16 bits) or half of a 32-bit integer.

The parameter stack is so called because it is used as a means for passing parameters to a Forth word. (Recall that a Forth word corresponds to a function or subroutine in other languages.) The parameter stack has other uses as well. The top of the stack is used in much the same way as an accumulator is used in assembly languages. It is the site for processing arithmetic expressions and a conduit for data on its way to or from such places as memory, the video screen, the return stack, the printer, and disk files.

A number is placed on the stack simply by typing it, whether directly from the keyboard or within a program. The Forth word { . } (a period, pronounced "dot" by Forth programmers) removes a number from the top of the stack and prints it on the screen. If you typed { 3 4 . } at the keyboard, Forth would respond, { 4 OK }. (OK is the system's signal that it has successfully processed your command and is awaiting another.) The 3 and the 4 would be placed on the stack; the { . } word would then remove the 4 and print it. If you then typed { . }, Forth would respond with { 3 }.

A way to see what is on the stack without removing anything is to use the Forth word { .S }. This word is useful during the program development process, because it is important to keep track of what each Forth word does to the stack. The Forth community has even developed a special notation for documenting how a particular word affects the stack. As an example, the stack effects of the word { . } can be described as follows:

(n —)

The n on the left of the — indicates that { . } expects to find a number on the top of the stack. The fact that there is nothing to the right of the — indicates that that number is removed from the stack.

Several stack manipulation words are worth discussing here. These words and their stack effects are listed below:

```
.R        ( n1 n2 — )
SWAP      ( n1 n2 — n2 n1 )
DUP       ( n — n n )
ROT       ( n1 n2 n3 — n3 n2 n1 )
OVER      ( n1 n2 — n1 n2 n1 )
DROP      ( n — )
```

The { .R } prints the number n1 right-justified in a field n2 characters wide. The {SWAP} simply exchanges or swaps the two top elements of the stack. Before the execution of {SWAP}, n2 was on top of the stack; after execution, n1 is on top. The {DUP} simply duplicates the value of the top element on the stack. The {ROT} exchanges the values of the first and third elements of the stack. The {OVER} duplicates the value of the second item on the stack and places it on the top of the stack. The {DROP} simply discards the top element of the stack.

The Return Stack

The other stack in the Forth Machine is the return stack. Forth words are stored in the dictionary. When a Forth word is executed, control passes to that word in the dictionary. The system must keep track of where to return to find the next word to execute in the program. The system uses the return stack for this purpose.

The system also uses the return stack to keep track of loop counter variables. In addition, the return stack is available to the programmer for temporary storage of data. Because of the other uses of the return stack, the programmer must be careful not to leave data on the return stack too long (not past the end of the execution of a word) and to be extra careful within the body of a loop.

The Forth word { >R } moves the top element of the parameter stack to the top of the return stack. The complementary word { R> } moves the top element of the return stack to the top of the parameter stack. Both of these words remove the element from the source stack. By contrast, { R@ } copies the top of the return stack onto the parameter stack without removing the element from the return stack.

Constants

Forth supports the use of named constants. These are useful for storing data that doesn't change during the course of a program. Programs that use named constants are easier to read, because a meaningful name can be used, and easier to modify, because the value appears only once in the program.

Suppose that a program needs to refer to the minimum age for voting. A constant called V.AGE can be declared and initialized for this purpose as follows:

18 CONSTANT V.AGE

Notice that the value comes before the word { CONSTANT }. This is typical of Forth and occurs because 18 is a parameter of the word { CONSTANT } and is passed to { CONSTANT } via the parameter stack.

Constants are stored in the dictionary. Once a constant has been declared, its value is retrieved and placed on the stack whenever its name appears. Also, once a constant has been declared, its value can never be changed.

Variables

Variables must also be declared in Forth, and they are also stored in the Forth Dictionary. The primary difference between a variable and a constant is that the value of a variable can be changed as often as needed in a program.

Suppose that a variable called **SUM** is to be used. It is declared as follows:

VARIABLE SUM

Data is assigned to a variable using the *store* word { ! }. To set the value of **SUM** to zero, one would write the following:

0 SUM !

When the Forth interpreter encounters the number 0, it places it on the stack. The interpreter next looks up the address of the variable SUM and places it on the stack. The interpreter then passes control to the word { ! }, which uses the address at the top of the stack (the address of SUM) to store the next value on the stack (in this case, zero).

To recall the value of the variable SUM, the word *fetch* { @ } is used, as in the following:

SUM @

The address of SUM is placed on the stack; then { @ } retrieves the value stored at that address.

Double Precision

As mentioned earlier, Forth supports double-precision (32-bit) data. Double-precision numbers can be either signed or unsigned. Because they take up 32 bits, they are stored on the stack as if they were two single-precision numbers. The low-order 16 bits go first, with the high-order 16 bits following on top.

There are separate stack operators for double-precision numbers. Some of these words and their stack effects are listed below:

D.	(d —)
D.R	(d n —)
DDROP	(d —)
D@	(addr — d)
D!	(d addr —)
DCONSTANT	(d —)
DVARIABLE	(—)
DSWAP	(d1 d2 — d2 d1)
DOVER	(d1 d2 — d1 d2 d1)

These words are similar in operation to their single-precision counterparts and therefore need no further explanation.

There is also a class of words that begin with 2. These words are similar in operation to the above-listed words, but they are used to manipulate the top two elements of the stack even when they are two separate single-precision numbers. These words include the following:

2!	(d addr —)
2@	(addr — d)
2CONSTANT	(d —)
2VARIABLE	(—)
2DROP	(d —)
2DUP	(d — d d)
2OVER	(d1 d2 — d1 d2 d1)
2SWAP	(d1 d2 — d2 d1)

Again, the operation of these words is analogous to the operation of their single-precision counterparts.

ARITHMETIC EXPRESSIONS

Forth uses *reverse Polish* notation, sometimes called *postfix* notation, for arithmetic expressions. (See Chapter 2 for a discussion of the various forms of notation.) In postfix notation the numbers to be operated on come first, followed by the operator. For example, the numbers 2 and 3 would be added as follows:

2 3 +

Here is what happens as this expression is evaluated: first the number 2 is placed on the top of the stack; then the number 3 is placed on the stack. The two top elements on the stack are then 2 and 3, with 3 on top. The { + } operator adds the two top elements of the stack and leaves the result at the top of the stack. As indicated by the notation, the operator { + } is a Forth word and is stored in the dictionary like other Forth words.

Other Forth arithmetic operators include { – }, { * }, { / }, and { MOD }. These operators perform subtraction, multiplication, integer division, and the modulus operations (remainder after integer division), respectively. The operator { /MOD } provides both the integer dividend and the remainder. Each of these operators take the top two elements of the stack as operands and leave the result at the top of the stack. In the case of { /MOD }, both results are left on the stack.

Figure 7-2 illustrates the use of arithmetic expressions in Forth. Two words are defined in Fig. 7-2. Each word expects to find a number on the stack. That number is

```
SCR #2
   0   ( Figure 7-2:    Arithmetic  Expressions  in  Forth )
   1   (                3X**2 + 5*X + 1                     )
   2
   3   VARIABLE X
   4   3 CONSTANT  A
   5   5 CONSTANT  B
   6   1 CONSTANT  C
   7
   8   : FN1       DUP A * B + * C + . ;
   9
  10   : FN2       X !
  11               X @ DUP * A *
  12               X @ B * +
  13               C +
  14               . ;
  15
```

Fig. 7-2. Arithmetic expressions in Forth.

taken as X in the expression, "A times the square of X plus B times X plus C," where A is 3, B is 5, and C is 1. Each word prints the result on the screen.

The constants A, B, and C in the expressions are declared explicitly in lines 4, 5, and 6. This makes the functions themselves easier to read and makes the program easier to modify.

The first word, FN1, is written in the usual Forth style. No variables are used; all data is stored and manipulated using only the stack. The expression was factored into a simpler form before being programmed. This is consistent with Forth style: the premise is that the programmer should factor the problem into the form most convenient for Forth so that the resulting program will be compact and efficient.

First a duplicate is made of X and left on the stack. Next the X on top of the stack is multiplied by A and B is added. At this point the result of the expression A*X + B is on top of the stack, and the duplicate value of X is right underneath it. Then the top two elements of the stack are multiplied, leaving the result A*X**2 + B*X on the stack. Finally C is added and the result printed.

The second word, FN2, is programmed in a style more often found in programs written in languages such as BASIC, Fortran, and Pascal. A variable, which is declared in line 3, is used. The word FN2 itself is defined in lines 10 through 14. The first step is to store the value found on the stack in the variable X. In line 11, X is retrieved, squared, and multiplied by A. In line 12, X is again retrieved, multiplied by B, and added to the previous result. In line 13, C is added. The result is printed in line 14.

A separate set of Forth words exist for performing arithmetic operations involving double-precision numbers. These include the following:

D+	(d1 d2 — d3)
D–	(d1 d2 — d3)
DABS	(d1 — d2)

In the case of { D+ }, the double-precision number d3 is the sum of the double-precision numbers d1 and d2. In the case of { D– }, d3 is the difference rather than the sum. { DABS } produces the absolute value of a double-precision number.

LOGICAL EXPRESSIONS

A logical expression produces the value true or false, which are represented in Forth by 1 and 0, respectively. In the appropriate context, any nonzero value is taken as representing true.

Like arithmetic expressions, logical expressions in Forth are written using postfix notation. For example, to test whether three is greater than two, you would write the following:

    3 2 >

Like arithmetic operators, relational operators such as { > } are Forth words and take their operands from the stack. The above expression is thus testing whether the next-to-the-top element of the stack (3) is greater than the top element (2). Because this is true, { > } will leave the truth value (1) on top of the stack.

The relational operators in Forth include the following:

>	greater than
<	less than
=	equal
0=	zero equal
0<	zero less than
0>	zero greater than

Notice that there are special operators for making comparisons with zero. These operators require only one operand from the stack. The first three operators listed require two operands from the stack. Each of the six leaves 0 (false) or 1 (true) on the stack.

The logical operators in Forth are { AND }, { OR }, and { NOT }. The { AND } and { OR } each require two operands. The { AND } produces a 1 (true) if and only if both operands are nonzero; otherwise it produces a 0 (false). The { OR } produces a 0 (false) if and only if both operands are zero; otherwise it produces a 1 (true). The { NOT } requires only one operand. If that operand is zero, { NOT } returns a 1 (true); if the operand is nonzero, { NOT } returns a 0 (false). The { NOT } is equivalent to { 0= }.

You might have noticed the absence of operators to test for less than or equal, greater than or equal, and not equal. The test for greater than or equal has the same meaning as not less than, and could be accomplished as in the following example:

5 4 < NOT

This example would leave a one at the top of the stack because five is greater than or equal to (not less than) four.

If the above procedure seems awkward, you can define a new Forth word to accomplish the same thing as follows:

: >=   < NOT ;

The new word { > = } will then behave exactly as if it were built into the language. Similarly, you can define words to test less than or equal and not equal as follows:

: <=   > NOT ;
: <>   = NOT ;

These are good examples of the extensibility of Forth.

There are also separate words for use in logical expressions involving double-precision numbers. These include the following:

D>	greater than
D<	less than
D=	equal to
D0=	equal to zero

Their usage is analogous to that of their single-precision counterparts. Each leaves a 0 (false) or 1 (true) on the stack.

INPUT AND OUTPUT

This section discusses how Forth programs read data from the keyboard and write data to the terminal (or video screen) and the printer. Disk file input and output is discussed in the section on File Handling.

You have already seen two Forth words for terminal output, { . } and { ." } (pronounced "dot" and "dot-quote," respectively). The { . }, of course, prints the number at the top of the stack to the terminal, followed by a space. The number is removed from the stack as it is printed. The { ." } prints all characters up to the next quote, as shown in Fig. 7-1.

Other simple output words include the following:

Word	Stack Effect
CR	(—)
EMIT	(n—)
BL	(—32)
SPACE	(—)
SPACES	(n—)
TYPE	(addr n—)

The { CR } simply outputs a carriage return and line feed. The { EMIT } outputs the character whose ASCII value is at the top of the stack. To output the bell character for example (Control-G), type the following:

```
7   EMIT
```

The { BL } places the ASCII equivalent of a blank on the stack. The { SPACE } outputs a single blank. The same result could be achieved by the following sequence:

```
BL EMIT
```

The { EMIT } in this case takes as its input the ASCII blank left on the stack by { BL }. The { SPACES } outputs the number of spaces indicated by the number at the top of the stack.

The operation of { TYPE } is more complicated. It expects to find a number (n) at the top of the stack and an address (addr) below that. The { TYPE } outputs n characters beginning at address **addr**. The { TYPE } is used in conjunction with number formatting commands, as described below.

The most common formatting words are { <# }, { # }, { #S }, { HOLD }, and { #> }. { <# }, pronounced variously as "bracket-number" or "less-sharp," marks the beginning of a formatting sequence, and { # > } marks the end of the sequence. Here is a simple example of a formatting sequence:

```
< # # # 46 HOLD #S #>  TYPE
```

This sequence prints a number with two decimal places. The number to be printed is taken from the stack and is expected to be a double-precision unsigned number. It is first converted to a character string, then printed by { TYPE }. The formatting operators leave the proper arguments on the stack for { TYPE }.

A double-precision number can be put on the stack in several ways, including the following:

```
1,250
1250.
1250  0
```

Inclusion of a punctuation mark such as a period (.), comma (,), slash (/), minus (−), or colon (:) marks a number as double-precision. The third example causes the high-order part of the number to be set to zero. As mentioned earlier, a double-precision number can be printed directly from the stack by using the word { D. }.

The number is converted to a character at a time, right to left. The first two occurrences of { # } convert the digits that are to the right of the decimal. The 46 is the decimal representation of the ASCII value for the period. The { HOLD } inserts that character into the character string being created. The { #S } converts the remaining digits to the left of the decimal.

A more complicated character conversion is shown in the program in Fig. 7-3. The Forth word { .$ } expects to find a double-precision number on the stack. That number can be positive or negative. The { .$ } prints out that number with a leading minus sign if the number is negative (no sign if it is positive), a dollar sign, and two decimal places. The sign is handled by the word { SIGN }, which, incidentally is at the end of the definition. Recall that digits are converted from right to left.

There are no explicit commands that send output to the printer. How this is done depends on the implementation. In the Apple version of MVP-FORTH, the { PR# } word is used to activate and deactivate the printer. The expression

```
1 PR#
```

activates the printer, provided that the printer interface card is plugged into the Apple slot #1. The printer is deactivated by the following expression:

```
0 PR#
```

```
SCR #3
  0  ( Figure 7-3:  Print Dollars and Cents. )
  1
  2  : .$        SWAP OVER DABS
  3              <#  # #  46 HOLD  #S  36 HOLD  ROT  SIGN #>
  4              TYPE SPACE ;
  5
```

Fig. 7-3. Printing dollars and cents.

```
SCR #4
   0   ( Figure 7-4:   Use of the Printer in Forth. )
   1
   2   : PRINT
   3         1 PR#
   4         CR  ." This goes to the printer."  CR
   5         3 PR#
   6         CR  ." This goes to the screen."  CR
   7         ;
   8
```

Fig. 7-4. Use of the printer in Forth.

If an 80-column display card is plugged into the Apple slot #3, then the expression

  3 PR#

serves to deactivate the printer. The use of the printer is illustrated in the program in Fig. 7-4.

Forth contains words for the input of characters and character strings. Input of a number requires first reading in a character string and then converting that character string to a number. A program that demonstrates this process is shown in Fig. 7-5. This program reads in two numbers from the keyboard and prints out their sum.

The word { QUERY } reads in a string of up to 80 characters and places it in a special area called the *terminal input buffer*. The word { WORD } has as its input the blank character. It scans the terminal input buffer until it finds the blank and transfers the substring ending with the blank to a safe place in memory. It leaves the address of that place on the stack. The word { NUMBER } uses the address on the stack to find that substring and converts it to a double-precision number, which it places on the stack.

```
SCR #5
   0   ( Figure 7-5:   Demonstrate Input Commands. )
   1
   2   : ADD2
   3         CR  ." Enter First   Number:   "
   4         QUERY BL WORD NUMBER
   5         CR  ." Enter Second Number:   "
   6         QUERY BL WORD NUMBER
   7         D+
   8         CR  ." The Total is:        "
   9         D. ;
  10
```

Fig. 7-5. The use of input commands.

```
SCR #6
  0  ( Figure 7-6:   Demonstrate Text Input. )
  1
  2  : HELLO
  3        CR   ." What is your first name?    "
  4        QUERY BL TEXT
  5        CR   ." Hello,  "
  6        PAD COUNT TYPE
  7        ." !  It is a pleasure to meet you."
  8        CR ;
  9
```

Fig. 7-6. Text Input.

This process is repeated, so two double-precision numbers will be put on the stack. The word { D+ } adds them, and { D. } prints the result.

An example of simple character input is shown in Fig. 7-6. A typical exchange using this program follows:

HELLO	(User)
What is your first name?	(Forth)
MARY	(User)
Hello, MARY! It is a pleasure to meet you.	(Forth)

The word { QUERY } in this program functions in the same way as in the previous program. This time { TEXT } is used instead of { WORD }. Note that { TEXT } also takes the blank character as a delimiter. It transfers the substring to a special location called the *PAD*. This is a scratch pad area and is guaranteed to be at least 64 bytes long. The word { PAD } puts the address of this area on the stack. The word { COUNT } counts the number of characters and sets up the stack for the word { TYPE }, which types the name at the console.

Notice that handling input and output in Forth requires a fairly detailed understanding of the inner workings of the Forth machine.

CONTROL STRUCTURES

Forth supports a wide variety of control structures. Forth supports IF statements, various kinds of loops, the equivalent of functions and procedures, and recursion. The only significant omission is a CASE statement. (See Chapter 2 for a discussion of the CASE statement.) Forth in particular encourages a modular approach to program structure and design.

Forth control structures rely heavily on the parameter stack for inputs and in many cases on the return stack for intermediate operations. How the stacks are used will be discussed in the following paragraphs.

Simple Selection: IF-ELSE-THEN

The general format for this statement is as follows:

```
condition IF
      statement(s)
ELSE
      statement(s)
THEN
```

The Forth format differs from the format most often found in high-level languages in several ways. First, the condition *precedes* the word { IF }. This is to be expected, as { IF }, like other Forth words, takes its arguments from the stack. The other major difference is the use of the word { THEN } to mark the end of the construct. Some implementations of Forth also accept the word { ENDIF } as a synonym for { THEN }.

The above illustration shows the IF construct properly indented in order to clearly show the structure. There is an unfortunate tendency among some Forth programmers to compress such constructs into a single line.

A program to demonstrate an IF statement is shown in Fig. 7-7. The program computes and prints the gross weekly wages of a worker when the overtime rate is one-and-a-half times the basic rate for between 40 and 50 hours per week, and double the basic rate for work in excess of 50 hours per week.

There are several points to note about this program. First, the basic pay rate of $8.00 per hour is stored as 800, an integer constant. Second, there are several new words introduced. { M* } takes two 16-bit numbers as arguments, multiplies them, and

```
    SCR #7
       0   ( Figure 7-7:   Compute Weekly Pay. )
       1
       2   800 CONSTANT RATE
       3
       4   : HOURS   DUP
       5       40 < IF
       6            RATE M*
       7       ELSE DUP 50 < IF
       8            40 - RATE 3 2 */ M*
       9            40 RATE M* D+
      10       ELSE
      11            50 - RATE 2* M*
      12            RATE 3 2 */ 10 M* D+
      13            40 RATE M* D+
      14       THEN THEN
      15       CR  ." Weekly Pay is "  .$  CR ;
```

Fig. 7-7. Computing weekly pay.

produces a 32-bit result. Double precision is needed in this problem because weekly pay can exceed $327.67, which would be stored as 32767 pennies.

Because the number 1.5 cannot be represented directly as an integer, some other way must be used to compute 1.5 times the basic pay rate. One way is to multiply by 3, then divide by 2. This can be done all at once, using the word { */ } as in the following expression:

RATE 3 2 */

This is the expression used in line 8 of Fig. 7-7.

The other word in this example that has not been used before is { 2* }. This is merely a shorthand for the expression { 2 * }.

The word { HOURS } expects to find the number of hours worked on the stack. Here are a few sample results:

30 HOURS	Weekly pay is $240.00
40 HOURS	Weekly pay is $320.00
45 HOURS	Weekly pay is $380.00
50 HOURS	Weekly pay is $440.00
55 HOURS	Weekly pay is $520.00

The program uses nested IF statements. The various branches of the IF statements leave the result on the stack as a double-precision number. The result is converted to a dollars-and-cents representation using the { .$ } word shown in Fig. 7-3. This is a good example of how Forth words are often reused in the definition of other Forth words.

Counted Loops

Forth supports counted loops with the DO-LOOP structure. The format of this structure is as follows:

```
limit start DO
    statement(s)
LOOP
```

A simple example is shown in the program in Fig. 7-8. This program prints the numbers from one to ten.

The loop counter I is maintained on the return stack. The Forth word { I } copies the value of the loop counter to the parameter stack. The initial value of the loop counter is taken from the top of the parameter stack, and the upper limit for the loop counter is taken as the next item on the parameter stack. These are represented by start and limit, respectively, in the format illustration above.

The loop counter is incremented by one at the end of each pass through the loop. The loop counter is compared to the upper limit, and if it is strictly less than the upper limit, the body of the loop is executed again. If the loop counter equals or exceeds the upper limit, control is passed to the first statement following the end of the loop. Because the test is performed at the bottom of the loop, a DO loop is always executed at least once.

```
SCR #8
   0  ( Figure 7-8:   The DO Loop. )
   1
   2  : 1TO10
   3        11 1 DO
   4             CR  I .
   5        LOOP ;
   6
```

Fig. 7-8. The DO loop.

Notice that two Forth words, { DO } and { LOOP }, make up the counted loop construct just described. They work as a team. Notice also that the loop counter is incremented by one at the end of each iteration. If desired, the word { +LOOP } can be substituted for { LOOP }. When this is done, the loop counter is incremented by whatever value is on the stack when { +LOOP } is encountered. The following variation of the program in Fig. 7-8 will count from 2 to 10 in increments of 2:

```
: SKIP
    11 2 DO
    CR I .
    2 +LOOP ;
```

Conditional Loops

There are two basic forms of conditional loop in Forth: the BEGIN . . . UNTIL loop and the BEGIN . . . WHILE . . . REPEAT loop. The BEGIN . . . UNTIL loop is very similar to the REPEAT . . . UNTIL loop of Pascal, and the BEGIN . . . WHILE . . . REPEAT loop is much like the WHILE loop of Pascal and other languages.

Each of these loop forms is controlled by a condition left on the stack. That condition is the result of a logical expression, such as those discussed earlier in this chapter. In the case of the BEGIN . . . UNTIL loop, it is the { UNTIL } word that looks for the condition. The loop is repeated as long as the condition is false. In the case of the BEGIN . . . WHILE . . . REPEAT loop, it is the { WHILE } word that looks for the flag. If the condition is false (zero), control is immediately passed to the statement following the REPEAT. Otherwise, the { REPEAT } word causes the loop to repeat.

Figure 7-9 contains two programs. Each counts to 10, as did the program in Fig. 7-8. One uses a BEGIN . . . UNTIL loop and the other uses a BEGIN . . . WHILE . . . REPEAT loop.

Unlike the program in Fig. 7-8, these two programs do not use the return stack. As a result, the { I } word cannot be used to obtain the loop index. All of the counting has to be done within the loop. Notice that each program ends with the word { DROP }. The process of testing a Forth word should include checking to see what is left on the stack after the word is executed, in order to avoid unintentionally leaving extraneous data on the stack.

```
      SCR #9
        0   ( Figure 7-9:   Conditional Loops. )
        1
        2   : RLOOP
        3         1 BEGIN
        4             CR DUP .
        5             1+ DUP
        6             11 =
        7         UNTIL DROP ;
        8
        9   : WLOOP
       10         1 BEGIN
       11             CR DUP .
       12             DUP 10 <
       13         WHILE
       14             1+
       15         REPEAT DROP ;
```

Fig. 7-9. Conditional loops.

The process of counting to 10 is done more easily with a counted loop than with a conditional loop. There are many other situations, however, in which a conditional loop is more natural. An example of this situation was given in Chapter 2.

The word { LEAVE } causes a loop to be exited before the next iteration. This is similar to the **break** command of the C language. When used, it is almost always found within the body of an IF statement.

Recursion

A Forth word is recursive if it refers to itself in its definition. Recursion can be a useful control structure in certain types of programs. A common example is the calculation of the factorial function.

The factorial of a positive integer is a mathematical function that is defined recursively. The factorial of zero is defined as 1. The factorial of a number N is defined as the product of that number and the factorial of $N-1$. Thus the factorial function is defined in terms of itself.

Different versions of Forth implement recursion in different ways. The MVP-FORTH implementation requires a little subterfuge. There is a flag in the dictionary definition of each Forth word called the *smudge bit*. When a Forth word is being defined, this smudge bit is set to indicate that the word has not yet been successfully compiled until it actually has been. This prevents incorrectly defined words from being found in the dictionary. As a result, when the recursive word is being defined, it cannot find itself in the dictionary. The Forth word { SMUDGE } is used to toggle the smudge flag so that the recursive word can in fact find itself.

The { SMUDGE } must be enclosed between brackets so that it will be executed during compilation rather than compiled as part of the word definition. Because the flag has been toggled, it must be toggled again after the word has been successfully defined in order to return it to its normal state. All of this is illustrated in the program in Fig. 7-10.

The program is used as follows:

```
4 FACTORIAL        (User)
24 OK              (Forth)
```

The argument precedes the name of the function, as is usual in Forth. The program first takes the absolute value of its argument to protect against negative arguments. The factorial of a negative number is not defined, and without this safeguard, an attempt to calculate the factorial of a negative number could result in an infinite loop.

The IF-ELSE-THEN construct checks to see whether the argument is 0. What happens then is best explained by example. Suppose that the original number is 3. Because 3 is not equal to 0, the ELSE branch is taken. This branch tries to multiply 3 by 2 factorial. This invokes FACTORIAL again, because the factorial of 2 is not yet known. In a similar manner, the function tries to calculate the factorial of 2 in terms of the factorial of 1. The factorial of 1 is calculated in terms of the factorial of 0. This time around, the function can finally calculate a value directly; it returns 1. Now 2 factorial can be calculated. Given 2 factorial, 3 factorial can be calculated, and the process is finished.

The program in Fig. 7-10 is of limited usefulness as it stands. The factorial function increases rapidly; the factorial of 8 is too large to fit in a 16-bit integer. A useful exercise for the reader would be to convert the program to double-precision.

DATA STRUCTURES

Forth provides support for advanced data structures such as arrays, lists, and so

```
SCR #10
   0  ( Figure 7-10:  Recursive Factorial Function. )
   1
   2  EMPTY
   3  : FACTORIAL
   4         ABS
   5        DUP 0= IF
   6                    DROP 1
   7                ELSE
   8                    DUP 1-
   9                    [ SMUDGE ] FACTORIAL
  10                    *
  11                THEN ;
  12  SMUDGE
  13
  14
  15
```

Fig. 7-10. A recursive factorial function.

forth, but at a rather primitive level. It is true that complex data structures can be programmed in Forth, but the same can be said of assembly language. Like assembly language, Forth makes the programmer do most of the work.

Arrays

One-dimensional arrays can be implemented in Forth without too much difficulty. With the addition of a few user-defined words, it is fairly easy.

The Forth word { VARIABLE } associates a variable name with a storage location in the Dictionary and allocates two bytes of storage. The word { ALLOT } is used to add more storage space to the most recently defined variable. For example, suppose that an array called WEEK is needed, and that it must have room for seven 16-bit integers. It would be declared as follows:

```
VARIABLE WEEK
12 ALLOT
```

Fourteen bytes of storage are needed for seven 16-bit integers. The { VARIABLE } word provides two of the 14 bytes. The { ALLOT } word provides the remaining 12.

This method of allocating space for arrays forces the user to count bytes. It would be better if the user could simply indicate how many elements the array should contain. With a little work, a new Forth word that will allow such declarations can be created.

One way to improve matters is to define a Forth word as follows:

```
: DIMENSION  1 -  2* ALLOT ;
```

This word expects to find the number of elements the array is to contain on the stack. The number of bytes to allot is computed by subtracting one and multiplying by two. Using this new word, the array WEEK could be declared as follows:

```
VARIABLE WEEK
7 DIMENSION
```

This spares the programmer from having to figure out how many bytes to allot.

When a variable name appears in a Forth program, it causes the address of the appropriate memory location to appear on the stack. The seven elements are usually thought of in Forth as being numbered from 0 to 6. The addresses of the seven elements of the array WEEK can be visualized as follows:

Element	Address
0	WEEK
1	WEEK + 2
2	WEEK + 4
3	WEEK + 6
4	WEEK + 8
5	WEEK + 10
6	WEEK + 12

To retrieve the value of the fourth element of WEEK (element number 3), you could write the following:

    6 WEEK + @

The process of computing the addresses of array elements can be simplified considerably by creating a new Forth word:

    : ADDR   SWAP 1– 2* + ;

With this word, you no longer have to number the items 0 to 6; you can use the more natural 1 to 7 numbering scheme. With this new word, the fourth element of WEEK can be retrieved as follows:

    4 WEEK ADDR @

The word { ADDR } can also be used to compute the address for storing data into the array. For example, the following would store the number 10 in the second element of the array WEEK:

    10 2 WEEK ADDR !

The use of arrays in Forth is made much easier using the new words { DIMENSION } and { ADDR }. There is another, simpler, way to accomplish the same thing using the word pair { CREATE } and { DOES> }. With this method you can create a new defining word called ARRAY, which can then be used to declare any number of arrays. How this is done is shown in Fig. 7-11.

The word { ARRAY } can be used to declare the array WEEK as follows:

    7 ARRAY WEEK

```
SCR #11
  0   ( Figure 7-11:   Array Handling Words. )
  1
  2   : DIMENSION    1– 2* ALLOT ;
  3
  4   : ADDR         SWAP 1– 2* + ;
  5
  6   : ARRAY
  7          CREATE 2*   ALLOT
  8          DOES>       ADDR ;
  9
 10
```

Fig. 7-11. An array handling words.

If another array called **MONTH** is required, it could be declared by the following:

    30 ARRAY MONTH

No separate **VARIABLE** declaration is needed when { **ARRAY** } is used.
The following would retrieve the fourth element of the array **WEEK**:

    4 WEEK @

The method for storing 7 in the fifth element of WEEK is as follows:

    7 5 WEEK !

As you may have deduced, the code between { **CREATE** } and { **DOES>** } is used at the time the array is declared; it allocates the appropriate number of bytes of storage. The code following { **DOES** } is executed when the name of the array is used in an expression. In this case I simply used the previously defined word { **ADDR** } to calculate the appropriate address.
If you have access to Forth on a computer, you can use the words { **FILL** } and { **DUMP** } to experiment with arrays. The expression

    1 WEEK 14 0 FILL

will fill the array **WEEK** with zeros. The contents of the array can be displayed on the screen by typing the following:

    1 WEEK 14 DUMP

This sequence displays the contents of memory for 14 bytes beginning with the first element of **WEEK**. If you zero-fill an array and then dump it after performing a store operation, it will be easy to see the results.

Character Strings

The arrays discussed above have all consisted of 16-bit data elements. Forth can also handle arrays consisting of eight-bit data elements. These are useful for storing characters. Arrays of characters are commonly called character strings.
Forth character strings are usually stored with the length of the string in the first byte. This means that Forth character strings can hold up to 255 characters.
The Forth word to store an eight-bit character is { **C!** }. The word to retrieve an eight-bit character to the top of the stack is { **C@** }. If you adopt the convention that the length of a character string is in element 0 of the array, and that the nth character is in element n, then the array will have n + 1 elements. Using techniques similar to those used above for integer arrays, you can define a word to create character arrays as follows:

    : CARRAY

```
CREATE 1+ ALLOT
DOES> SWAP
+ ;
```

Using this word, a character array called **STRING** capable of holding 80 characters would be created as follows:

```
80 CARRAY STRING
```

The following would retrieve the tenth character in STRING:

```
10  STRING  C@
```

To store the letter A in the first character position of **STRING**, you would type the following:

```
65 1 STRING C!
```

The number 65 is the ASCII representation for A. The following sequence would retrieve the letter A from STRING and print it as a character:

```
1 STRING C@ EMIT
```

The word { EMIT } converts the number 65 back to the letter A and prints it.

Forth provides several words that make the manipulation of character strings easier. One useful function initializes a character string to all blanks. This can be done as follows:

```
0 0 STRING C!
1 STRING 80 BL FILL
```

The first line sets the character count to zero. The first 0 is the value that is stored, and the second zero is the subscript of the character array **STRING** that indicates where the character count resides. The second line stores 80 blanks beginning with the address **STRING** + 1. Some versions of Forth have a word called { BLANK } or { BLANKS }, which could be used to accomplish the same task in a slightly simpler way:

```
0 0 STRING !
1 STRING 80 BLANK
```

The word { CMOVE } can be used to move characters from one string to another. Suppose you have two character strings, 1STRING and 2STRING. The contents of 1STRING can be copied into 2STRING as follows:

```
0 1STRING
0 2STRING
81 CMOVE
```

The expression { 0 1STRING } leaves the address of the beginning of the first string on the stack. Similarly, { 0 2STRING } puts the address of the second string on the stack. The number 81 is the number of characters to move.

The word { COUNT } can be used to separate the character count from the rest of the string, setting up the stack for other commands that require the character count to be on the stack. Its action can be summarized by the following:

(addr — addr + 1 n)

Before { COUNT } is executed, the address on the stack is the address of the count byte. After { COUNT } is executed, the address of the first character is in the second position of the stack and the count is on the top of the stack.

A word that requires the stack to be set up in this manner is { TYPE }. The contents of STRING can be displayed on the screen in the following manner:

0 STRING COUNT TYPE

Another word that requires the stack to be set up the same way is { – TEXT }. The sequence

0 1STRING COUNT
0 2STRING COUNT – TEXT

will compare the two strings. If they are equal, a zero will be left on the stack. If the contents of { 1STRING } is less than the contents of { 2STRING }, a negative number will be left on the stack. Otherwise, a positive number will be left on the stack. The ''–'' at the beginning of { – TEXT } stands for not. It is used to indicate that it returns zero (false) for a positive (true) result.

Two-Dimensional Arrays

Forth has no direct provision for arrays with more than one dimension. Two-dimensional arrays can be handled, but it is left up to you to take care of the details.

The handling of two-dimensional arrays can be greatly simplified by creating a Forth word to take care of the necessary details. Such a word, called { 2ARRAY }, is shown in Fig. 7-12.

The word { 2ARRAY } allows a two-dimensional array to be declared, as in the following:

3 5 2ARRAY TABLE

This creates a three-row by five-column array of integers named TABLE. The number of columns is stored in a variable called NC, because it will be needed in the computation of addresses for individual array elements. (Because a single variable is used, all arrays declared using 2ARRAY within a given program must have the same number of columns.)

The { DOES> } portion of the word { 2ARRAY } expects to find the subscripts and the name of the array on the stack. The two { ROT } words move the subscripts ahead of the array name on the stack. The displacement in bytes from the beginning of the array is computed using the algorithm shown in lines 10 through 14 in Fig. 7-12. Note the use of the number of columns in the computation.

Suppose the array **TABLE** has been declared to be a three-by-five array as described above. The following sequences would first store the number 10 in row 2, column 3 of the array and then retrieve and print it:

```
10 2 3 TABLE !
2 3 TABLE ?
```

The word { ? } retrieves and prints the integer stored at the address on top of the stack.

Figure 7-13 shows the use of nested **DO** loops in conjunction with the two-dimensional array **TABLE**. The word { TFILL } fills each element of the array with the product of its row and column numbers. The word { TPRN } prints out the contents of the array in a tabular format. Note the use of the words { I } and { J } in the inner loops. The word { I } returns the value of the current loop counter from the return stack. The word { J } returns the value of the next outer loop counter from the return stack. The expression { 5 .R } causes the top of the stack to be printed right-justified in a field five characters wide.

Records

Chapter 2 illustrated the concept of a record with the need to record a student's name and his or her scores on up to 20 tests. If there are 30 students in the class, this information will be needed for each. One instance of name and scores constitutes a *record*.

```
SCR #12
   0  ( Figure 7-12:    Two-Dimensional Array Setup. )
   1
   2  VARIABLE   NC
   3
   4  : 2ARRAY
   5        CREATE              ( ROW COL 2ARRAY NAME )
   6              DUP NC !      ( SAVE NR OF COLUMNS   )
   7              * 2* ALLOT    ( ALLOCATE SPACE       )
   8        DOES>
   9              ROT ROT
  10              1- SWAP       ( COLUMN DISPLACEMENT )
  11              1- NC @ *     ( ROW     DISPLACEMENT )
  12              +             ( TOTAL   DISPLACEMENT )
  13              2*            ( 2 BYTES PER INTEGER )
  14              + ;           ( ADD TO BASE ADDRESS )
  15
```

Fig. 7-12. Two-dimensional array setup.

```
SCR #13
   0  ( Figure 7-13:   Use of Two-Dimensional Arrays. )
   1
   2  3 5 2ARRAY TABLE
   3
   4  : TFILL   4 1 DO
   5                    6 1 DO
   6                         J I * J I TABLE !
   7                    LOOP
   8              LOOP ;
   9
  10  : TPRN    4 1 DO CR
  11                    6 1 DO
  12                         J I TABLE @
  13                         5 .R
  14                    LOOP
  15              LOOP CR ;
```

Fig. 7-13. Use of two-dimensional arrays.

Forth does not directly support the concept of a record. Forth does, however, provide the means to define records of various kinds. It is left up to the programmer to figure out how.

The first step is to decide on a record layout. One possibility is the following:

Name	Positions 1-30
Scores	Positions 31-70

The name field would allow for up to 30 characters. A count byte is not necessary for the name field because it will always be of the same fixed length, padded with trailing blanks if necessary. Because each score is assumed to be a 16-bit (2-byte) integer, and there are up to 20 scores, 40 bytes are needed for scores. The record length is therefore 70 bytes.

To be able to use records conveniently, three capabilities are needed:

☐ the capability to allot the required memory
☐ the capability to access the desired record
☐ the capability to access the desired field within a record

Forth words to carry out each of these tasks can be defined using many of the techniques illustrated in the preceding sections of this chapter. The details are omitted here, but they will be shown in the comprehensive sample program at the end of the chapter.

Linked Lists

As with other advanced data structures, linked lists are not directly supported in

Forth. Because of the flexibility provided by Forth, there are several ways that a linked list could be implemented. Perhaps the simplest way is to implement a linked list as an array of records, with one field of each record used as a link or pointer.

Suppose the first record should point to the third record. This would be accomplished by setting the link field of the first record to 3. This way of implementing a linked list was explained in more detail in Chapter 2.

The comprehensive sample program at the end of this chapter illustrates the use of linked lists, showing the details of how records are added to and deleted from linked lists.

FILE HANDLING

One of the things that computers do well is store data. Because of the limited amount of memory in most computers, external storage is required in order to store an appreciable amount of data. On microcomputers the external storage medium is usually a magnetic disk.

A collection of data stored on a disk is called a *file*. One of the measures of the usefulness of a high-level language is how well it handles the storage of data in files. This section will describe how Forth handles files.

Forth treats a disk as if it were an extension of regular memory. The disk is conceptually divided up into *blocks* of 1024 bytes each. How many blocks there are on a disk depends on the system: with MVP-FORTH on an Apple II, there are 140 blocks per disk. Forth maintains two or more *buffers* in memory, each large enough to hold one block. The Forth program acts as if it is writing directly to a block on disk, but it is really writing to a buffer in memory. The Forth system takes care of moving data between a buffer and the disk. The programmer has three responsibilities in this area:

☐ To specify which block number is being addressed.
☐ To use the { UPDATE } word after a block has been modified, so the system will know that the buffer must be saved.
☐ To use the { SAVE-BUFFERS } word before changing the disk or turning off the system, so Forth will be sure that all buffers have been saved to disk.

Blocks in Forth are addressed by number, not by name. The programmer must keep track of which blocks comprise which files. The equivalent of an **OPEN** command is either the { BUFFER } or the { BLOCK } command, depending on whether the file to be opened is a new file or an existing file. The command

30 BUFFER

opens a new file; it establishes a buffer in memory associated with block number 30, but it does not read in any data from the disk. The command

30 BLOCK

on the other hand, not only establishes a buffer associated with block number 30, it also reads the contents of that block into the buffer.

The equivalents of the **CLOSE** command are the { **UPDATE** } and { **SAVE-BUFFERS** } words discussed above.

All Forth files are direct-access files. The program can access any byte of any file at any time. Direct-access files can be addressed sequentially if desired.

File Records

A file consists of logical units called *records*. A record can consist of a single byte, or it can consist of a sequence of bytes that contain related information. A record can be of fixed or variable length; this chapter will discuss only fixed record lengths.

Forth leaves the organization of records to the programmer. All details associated with writing records to disk and reading records from disk must be handled by the programmer.

Sequential File Access

A file is said to be accessed sequentially if the records of the file are accessed in sequence from beginning to end. Figure 7-14 contains an example of a program that creates a file of names and ages and then reads the file back from disk and displays it on the screen.

The program consists of four Forth words. Three are executed directly from the keyboard, and one is treated as a subroutine. The word { **INIT** } initializes the file to all blanks. The word { **MAKE** } prompts the user for keyboard input and creates the file. The word { **PRINT** } reads the file back from disk and prints its contents on the screen. The word { **GETREC** } computes the address of a given record and is used as a subroutine.

Three constants are declared: **ADDR** is set to 50, which is the block number in which this file is stored. Each record is 32 bytes in length; 30 bytes are allocated to the name and 2 bytes to the age. There is room for a maximum of 32 records of 32 bytes in length in a block of 1024 bytes, so the constant **MAXREC** is set to 32. The constant **EOL** is set to 13, the ASCII representation of the carriage-return character.

A program of this complexity requires a detailed, almost line-by-line explanation. Line 0 of Screen #14 is simply a comment that identifies the program. Line 2 causes Screen #15 to be loaded. Before discussing the word { **MAKE** } in Screen #14, let's discuss the words { **INIT** } and { **GETREC** } in Screen #15.

The word { **INIT** } in Screen #15 initializes the file to all blanks. The sequence { **ADDR BUFFER** } puts the address of the buffer for the block number on the stack. The sequence { **1024 BLANK** } causes 1024 blanks to be stored beginning at that address. This fills the buffer.

The word { **GETREC** } at line 7 of Screen #15 expects to find the record number on the stack. (Record numbers range from 0 to 31.) Its purpose is to compute the address of the first byte of that record. It does this by multiplying the record number by the record length (32) and adding the starting address of the block (**ADDR BLOCK**). The word { **GETREC** } leaves the record address on the stack for use by other routines.

Now let's return to the word { **MAKE** }, which begins in line 4 of Screen #14. Line 5 is the beginning of a **DO** loop, which counts from 0 to 31, the range of possible record numbers. Line 6 prompts the user to type in a name. That name is read by the { **QUE-**

```
SCR #14
   O  ( Figure 7-14:   Sequential Name and Age File. )
   1
   2  15 LOAD
   3
   4  : MAKE                    ( Read from KBD & Write File )
   5          MAXREC O DO
   6                  CR ." Enter Name:   "
   7                  QUERY EOL TEXT
   8                  PAD C@ O= IF LEAVE ELSE
   9                      PAD 1+ I GETREC PAD C@ CMOVE
  10                      CR ." Enter Age:    "
  11                      QUERY BL WORD NUMBER DROP
  12                      I GETREC 30 + !
  13                  THEN
  14          CR LOOP
  15          UPDATE SAVE-BUFFERS ;

SCR #15
   O  ( Part of Figure 7-14 )
   1
   2  50 CONSTANT ADDR        ( BLOCK NUMBER        )
   3  32 CONSTANT MAXREC      ( MAX NR OF RECORDS )
   4  13 CONSTANT EOL         ( END-OF-LINE CHAR   )
   5
   6  : INIT     ADDR BUFFER 1024 BLANK ;
   7  : GETREC   32 * ADDR BLOCK + ;
   8  : PRINT    CR
   9            MAXREC O DO
  10                CR I GETREC DUP DUP
  11                C@ BL = IF LEAVE ELSE    ( DONE?    )
  12                    30 TYPE
  13                    30 + @ 3 .R          ( GET AGE )
  14                THEN CR
  15            LOOP ;
```

Fig. 7-14. A sequential name and age file.

RY } of line 7. The sequence { EOL TEXT } transfers the text from the input buffer
to the PAD, using the end-of-line character (carriage return) as an end-of-text marker.

Line 7 checks the first character of the PAD to see if it is zero. If it is, the character
count is zero. That means that the user typed an immediate carriage return instead of
a name in response to the name prompt. This causes the word { LEAVE } to be executed,
which in turn causes an exit from the loop before the next iteration. If the character
count is not zero, lines 9 through 12 are executed.

In line 9, the word { CMOVE } moves the name from the PAD to the appropriate location in the file buffer. The source address is PAD + 1. The destination address is computed by passing the loop counter (which is the record number) to { GETREC }. The number of bytes to move is retrieved from the count byte at location PAD.

Line 10 prompts the user to type the age. Line 11 reads in the age using { QUERY }. The sequence { BL WORD NUMBER } converts the number from a character string to a double-precision number and places the result on the stack. The word { DROP } converts the number back to single precision. The sequence { I GETREC } of line 12 computes the address of the beginning of the record. Adding 30 computes the address of the age field within the record. The { ! } word stores the age at the appropriate buffer location.

Line 13 marks the end of the IF statement, and line 14 the end of the DO loop. Line 15 marks the block as having been updated ({ UPDATE }) and then causes the contents of the buffer to be written to disk ({ SAVE-BUFFERS }).

The word { PRINT }, which begins at line 8 of Screen #15, can be used to print the contents of the file on the screen. The DO loop between lines 9 and 15 again spans the range of possible record numbers, with provision for an early exit ({ LEAVE }) if the end of the file is found.

Line 10 computes the address of the beginning of record I; it then makes two extra copies of the address and leaves them on the stack. The first copy of this address is used to retrieve the first character of the record. This character is checked to see whether or not it is blank, which would indicate the end of the file. (Recall that the file was initialized to all blanks.) If it is not blank, the next copy of the record address is used in conjunction with { 30 TYPE } to print the contents of the name field of the record to the screen.

Line 13 uses the final copy of the record address from the stack, adds 30 to compute the start of the age field, retrieves the age from the buffer, and prints it right-justified in a 3-character field. Lines 14 and 15 terminate the IF statement and DO loop, respectively.

This program created a file which was confined entirely to one block of the disk. Files can span more than one block, but at the expense of more program overhead to keep track of the various blocks. The comprehensive sample program at the end of the chapter illustrates the use of a file that spans more than one block.

Direct-Access Files

The file described in the previous section was accessed sequentially, even though Forth files all have direct-access capability. The sequence was controlled by the DO loop, which counted in record-number sequence. The record number was fed to { GETREC }, which calculated the starting address of the appropriate record. There is nothing to stop { GETREC } from computing the starting address of any record in any sequence. { GETREC } functions like the SEEK procedure of some other languages.

The comprehensive sample program at the end of the chapter will illustrate the use of a direct-access file by a Forth program.

GRAPHICS

Forth itself does not support graphics. Because Forth is so easily extended, and because of the ease with which Forth can handle low-level data (bits and bytes), adding a graphics capability to Forth is relatively simple. The MVP-FORTH implementation for the Apple II series includes high-resolution graphics. Because graphics are not "native" to Forth, they will not be discussed further here.

THE COMPREHENSIVE SAMPLE PROGRAM

The examples in this chapter have been relatively short; each has been intended to illustrate some facet of the language. In order to portray more accurately the nature of the Forth language, a longer, more complex example is needed. Such a program is shown in Fig. 7-15.

The program in Fig. 7-15 maintains an address book on disk, or more precisely, a disk file containing names, addresses, and telephone numbers. The program provides the capability to create a new file, to add records to a file, to delete records from a file, and to display the contents of the file on the video screen or on a printer.

The program maintains the file in alphabetical order by name. A record, as it is added, is physically placed in the next available place in the file. The logical order of the file is maintained using pointers to implement a linked list. No sorting is required; each record is linked in the proper place in the list as it is added to the file.

Each record is 80 characters in length. The first 78 characters make up the actual data; that is the name, address, and so forth. These data are stored as ASCII characters. The last two positions of the record hold the link field, which is stored as an integer. Each record has a logical record number. If record 4 is linked to record 7, then the link field of record 4 has the value 7. This is the method of implementing linked lists that was explained in more detail in Chapter 2.

Each disk block in Forth consists of 1024 characters. There is therefore room for 12 records of 80 characters each, with some space left over. The extra space in the first block is used to store the two pointers **FIRST** and **FREE**, which point to the first active and the first free record of the file, respectively. The program as written allows for 15 records, enough to span two blocks. The word **RECORD** is used to translate from a logical record number (0,1,2, . . .) to a physical disk address (block number and displacement within the block).

The details of file length, record length, and field length within a record are all defined in the constant declarations near the beginning of the program. To change any of these parameters, it is only necessary to change the appropriate constants and recompile.

The program is loaded by typing { 16 33 THRU }. To run the program, type { BOOK }. The program is completely menu driven. To initialize a file, select menu item 1. To open a previously existing file, select 2. To close a file that has been modified, select 7. The other options are similar. There are built-in safeguards to keep you from listing a file that has not been opened and making other such illogical selections.

The organization of the program is illustrated by the structure chart shown in Fig. 7-16. The main program is the word called **BOOK**. A word that serves as a subroutine is shown indented below the word that calls it. BOOK calls **MENU, OPEN, APPEND, REVIEW, LISTFILE, DUMPFILE,** and **CLOSE**; REVIEW calls **PRINTREC** and **PUTFREE**, and so on.

The **DUMP** option allows the user to examine the structure of the file, including pointers. By using this option after various add and delete scenarios, the operation of the program can be more easily understood.

```
SCR #16
   0  ( Figure 7-15:    Comprehensive Sample Program. )
   1
   2  ( This program maintains a list of names, addresses,   )
   3  ( and telephone numbers in a disk file.                )
   4
   5  ( To load, type 16 33 THRU                             )
   6
   7  ( To run, type BOOK                                    )
   8
   9  ( Initial configuration:                               )
  10  (        15 Record maximum                             )
  11  (        80 Character records                          )
  12
  13  ( To reconfigure, modify the appropriate constants.    )
  14
  15

SCR #17
   0  ( Part of Figure 7-15:    Declarations                 )
   1   13 CONSTANT   EOL          ( END OF LINE CHARACTER     )
   2   -1 CONSTANT   NIL          ( PTR TO END OF LIST        )
   3  110 CONSTANT   ADDR         ( 1ST BLOCK IN ADDR FILE    )
   4   80 CONSTANT   RLEN         ( RECORD LENGTH             )
   5   12 CONSTANT   RPB          ( RECORDS PER BLOCK         )
   6   15 CONSTANT   MAXREC       ( MAX # OF RECORDS IN FILE  )
   7    0 CONSTANT   LNAME        ( DISPL OF LAST NAME FIELD  )
   8   12 CONSTANT   LNL          ( LENGTH OF LAST NAME FIELD )
   9   12 CONSTANT   FNAME        ( DISPL OF FIRST NAME FIELD )
  10   12 CONSTANT   FNL          ( LENGTH OF FIRST NAME FIELD)
  11   24 CONSTANT   STREET       ( DISPL OF STREET ADDR FIELD)
  12   20 CONSTANT   STRL         ( LENGTH OF STREET FIELD    )
  13   44 CONSTANT   CITY         ( DISPL OF CITY FIELD       )
  14   12 CONSTANT   CITL         ( LENGTH OF CITY FIELD      )
  15   56 CONSTANT   STATE        ( DISPL OF STATE FIELD      )

SCR #18
   0  ( Part of Figure 7-15:    Declarations                 )
   1    2 CONSTANT   STAL         ( LENGTH OF STATE FIELD     )
   2   58 CONSTANT   ZIP          ( DISPL OF ZIP CODE FIELD   )
   3    6 CONSTANT   ZIPL         ( LENGTH OF ZIP CODE FIELD  )
   4   64 CONSTANT   PHONE        ( DISPL OF PHONE NR FIELD   )
   5   14 CONSTANT   PHOL         ( LENGTH OF PHONE NR FIELD  )
   6   78 CONSTANT   LINK         ( DISPL OF LINK FIELD       )
   7 1000 CONSTANT   FRP          ( DISPL OF 1ST RECORD PTR   )
   8 1002 CONSTANT   FFP          ( DISPL OF 1ST FREE REC PTR )
   9  VARIABLE OPEN?              ( FILE OPEN INDICATOR       )
  10  VARIABLE FIRST              ( PTR TO 1ST RECORD IN FILE )
  11  VARIABLE FREE               ( PTR TO 1ST FREE RECORD    )
  12  VARIABLE FLAG               ( GENERAL PURPOSE FLAG VAR  )
  13  VARIABLE P                  ( TEMPORARY POINTER         )
  14  VARIABLE Q                  ( "                "        )
  15  VARIABLE R                  ( "                "        )
```

Fig. 7-15. Comprehensive sample program.

```
SCR #19
   0  ( Part of Figure 7-15:  Word Definitions              )
   1  : RECORD                    ( RECORD_NR -- ADDR        )
   2     RPB  /MOD
   3     ADDR + BLOCK             ( COMPUTE BLOCK NR         )
   4     SWAP RLEN * + ;          ( ADDR OF RECORD           )
   5
   6  : INIT                      ( INITIALIZE FILE          )
   7     MAXREC 0 DO
   8         I RECORD DUP RLEN BLANK ( BLANK FILL REC I      )
   9         LINK +              ( ADDR OF LINK FIELD        )
  10         I 1+ SWAP ! UPDATE  ( PTR TO NEXT FREE REC      )
  11     LOOP
  12     MAXREC 1- RECORD LINK +  ( LAST LINK                )
  13     NIL SWAP ! UPDATE        ( PTR TO END OF LIST       )
  14     NIL FIRST !  0 FREE !    ( INITIALIZE POINTERS      )
  15     1 OPEN? ! ;              ( MARK FILE OPEN           )

SCR #20
   0  ( Part of Figure 7-15:  Word Definitions              )
   1
   2  : OPEN                      ( OPEN FILES               )
   3     ADDR BLOCK DUP
   4     FRP + @ FIRST !          ( READ PTRS FROM FILE      )
   5     FFP + @ FREE  !          ( AND STORE AS VARIABLES)
   6     1 OPEN? ! ;              ( MARK FILE OPEN           )
   7
   8  : CLOSE                     ( CLOSE FILE & SAVE PTRS)
   9     ADDR BLOCK DUP
  10     FRP + FIRST @ SWAP !
  11     FFP + FREE  @ SWAP !
  12     UPDATE
  13     SAVE-BUFFERS
  14     0 OPEN? ! ;              ( MARK FILE CLOSED         )
  15

SCR #21
   0  ( Part of Figure 7-15:  Word Definitions              )
   1
   2  : CLEARSCREEN               ( FOR APPLE II+            )
   3     12 EMIT ;                ( WITH ALS SMARTERM II     )
   4
   5  : GOTOXY                    ( POSITION CURSOR          )
   6     30 EMIT                  ( X Y -- )
   7     SWAP 32 + EMIT
   8     32 + EMIT ;
   9
  10  : GETNUM                    ( READ INTEGER & LEAVE     )
  11     QUERY                    (   ON STACK               )
  12     BL WORD NUMBER
  13     DROP ;                   ( CONVERT TO SINGLE        )
  14                              (    PRECISION             )
  15

SCR #22
```

Fig. 7-15. Comprehensive sample program. (Continued from page 219.)

```
   0  ( Part of Figure 7-15:   Word Definitions                    )
   1
   2  : MENU                               ( DISPLAY MENU; LEAVE     )
   3     CLEARSCREEN                       (    CHOICE ON STACK      )
   4     5 5 2DUP                          ( INITIAL SCREEN COORDS )
   5     GOTOXY           ." 1) Initialize new file"
   6     2+ 2DUP GOTOXY ." 2) Open existing file"
   7     2+ 2DUP GOTOXY ." 3) Add to file"
   8     2+ 2DUP GOTOXY ." 4) Review file on screen"
   9     2+ 2DUP GOTOXY ." 5) List file on screen or printer"
  10     2+ 2DUP GOTOXY ." 6) Dump file and pointers on printer"
  11     2+ 2DUP GOTOXY ." 7) Close file"
  12     2+       GOTOXY ." 8) Quit"
  13     CR CR
  14     ." Select 1, 2, 3, 4, 5, 6, 7, or 8:   "
  15     GETNUM ;

SCR #23
   0  ( Part of Figure 7-15:   Word Definitions                    )
   1
   2  : WARN
   3     CR ." Warning!!!  File is full!"  CR
   4     CR ." Press <SPACE> to continue..."
   5     KEY DROP ;
   6
   7  : MARKOFF                       ( COL ROW N -- )
   8     >R GOTOXY ." :"
   9     R> SPACES ." :" ;
  10
  11  : GETFREE                       ( RETURNS FIRST FREE    )
  12     FREE @ DUP                   (    RECORD NR          )
  13     NIL = IF
  14         WARN DROP NIL
  15     THEN ;

SCR #24
   0  ( Part of Figure 7-15:   Word Definitions                    )
   1
   2  : PAINTSCREEN
   3     CLEARSCREEN
   4     1 5 2DUP GOTOXY ." Last Name:"  14 OVER LNL  MARKOFF
   5     2+   2DUP GOTOXY ." First Name:" 14 OVER FNL  MARKOFF
   6     2+   2DUP GOTOXY ." Address:"    14 OVER FNL  MARKOFF
   7     2+   2DUP GOTOXY ." City:"       14 OVER FNL  MARKOFF
   8     2+   2DUP GOTOXY ." State:"      14 OVER FNL  MARKOFF
   9     2+   2DUP GOTOXY ." Zip:"        14 OVER FNL  MARKOFF
  10     2+   2DUP GOTOXY ." Phone:"      14 OVER FNL  MARKOFF
  11     2DROP
  12  ;
  13
  14
  15

SCR #25
   0  ( Part of Figure 7-15:   Word Definitions                    )
   1
```

```
 2  : READSCREEN                    ( R -- R )
 3     DUP RECORD DUP >R RLEN 2 - BLANK
 4     15 5 2DUP GOTOXY R> DUP LNAME + DUP LNL EXPECT C@
 5     0= IF DROP 2DROP DROP NIL ELSE >R
 6        R@ LINK + @ P !
 7        2+ 2DUP GOTOXY R@ FNAME  + FNL  EXPECT
 8        2+ 2DUP GOTOXY R@ STREET + STRL EXPECT
 9        2+ 2DUP GOTOXY R@ CITY   + CITL EXPECT
10        2+ 2DUP GOTOXY R@ STATE  + STAL EXPECT
11        2+ 2DUP GOTOXY R@ ZIP    + ZIPL EXPECT
12        2+ 2DUP GOTOXY R@ PHONE  + PHOL EXPECT
13        P @ R> LINK + !
14        UPDATE
15     THEN ;

SCR #26
 0  ( Part of Figure 7-15:  Word Definitions                )
 1
 2  : GREATER                       ( R1 R2 -- FLAG)
 3     ( FLAG =T 1 IF REC 1 > REC 2, OTHERWISE 0            )
 4     DUP 0< IF 1 FLAG ! ELSE 0 FLAG !
 5        RECORD SWAP RECORD SWAP ( GET BUFFER ADDRESSES  )
 6        LNL FNL + 0 DO
 7           2DUP
 8           I + C@ SWAP I + C@ SWAP      ( GET CHARS TO  )
 9           2DUP                         (   COMPARE     )
10           > IF 1 FLAG !  LEAVE  THEN
11           < IF 0 FLAG !  LEAVE  THEN
12        LOOP
13     THEN
14     2DROP
15     FLAG @ ;

SCR #27
 0  ( Part of Figure 7-15:  Word Definitions                )
 1
 2  : INSERT                        ( R -- )
 3     ( INSERT REC R IN LINKED LIST                        )
 4     DUP R !
 5     RECORD LINK + @ FREE !       ( REMOVE FROM FREE LIST )
 6     FIRST @ P !  NIL Q !
 7     BEGIN P @ NIL = NOT  R @ P @ GREATER AND WHILE
 8        P @ Q !  P @ RECORD LINK + @ P ! UPDATE
 9     REPEAT
10     P @ R @ RECORD LINK + ! UPDATE
11     Q @ NIL = IF
12        R @ FIRST !
13     ELSE
14        R @ Q @ RECORD LINK + ! UPDATE
15     THEN ;

SCR #28
 0  ( Part of Figure 7-15:  Word Definitions                )
 1
```

Fig. 7-15. Comprehensive sample program. (Continued from page 221.)

```
   2   : APPEND                       ( ADD RECORDS TO FILE   )
   3      MAXREC 0 DO
   4         GETFREE DUP NIL = IF
   5            DROP LEAVE
   6         ELSE
   7            PAINTSCREEN
   8            READSCREEN
   9            DUP NIL = IF
  10               DROP LEAVE
  11            ELSE
  12               INSERT
  13            THEN
  14         THEN
  15      LOOP ;

SCR #29
   0  ( Part of Figure 7-15:  Word Definitions            )
   1.
   2  : PUTFREE                      ( R -- )
   3     FREE @ OVER RECORD LINK + !
   4     FREE ! UPDATE ;
   5
   6  : PRINTREC                     ( R -- )
   7     CR RECORD
   8     DUP FNAME   + FNL  -TRAILING TYPE SPACE
   9     DUP LNAME   + LNL  TYPE CR
  10     DUP STREET  + STRL TYPE CR
  11     DUP CITY    + CITL -TRAILING TYPE SPACE
  12     DUP STATE   + STAL TYPE SPACE
  13     DUP ZIP     + ZIPL TYPE CR
  14     PHONE       + PHOL TYPE CR
  15     CR 10 EMIT ;

SCR #30
   0  ( Part of Figure 7-15:  Word Definitions            )
   1
   2  : PRINTER    1 PR#
   3               9 EMIT ." 80N"
   4              30 EMIT ;
   5  : OFF        3 PR# ;
   6  : LISTFILE
   7     CLEARSCREEN
   8     ." List to S)creen or P)rinter?  "
   9     KEY DUP 80 = SWAP 112 = OR IF PRINTER THEN
  10     10 EMIT
  11     FIRST @ P !
  12     MAXREC 0 DO
  13        P @ DUP DUP NIL = IF DROP DROP LEAVE
  14        ELSE PRINTREC RECORD LINK + @ P ! THEN
  15     LOOP OFF ;

SCR #31
   0  ( Part of Figure 7-15:  Word Definitions            )
   1
   2  : REVIEW
   3     CLEARSCREEN
```

```
  4        FIRST @ NIL = NOT IF
  5            FIRST @ R !      NIL Q !
  6            BEGIN R @ PRINTREC
  7                ." G)et next record, D)elete this record, or Q)uit?  "
  8                KEY SPACE CR DUP DUP DUP 68 = SWAP 100 = OR IF
  9                    Q @ NIL = IF
 10                        R @ RECORD LINK + @ FIRST !
 11                        R @ PUTFREE      FIRST @ R !
 12                    ELSE  R @ RECORD LINK + @ Q @ RECORD LINK + !
 13                        R @ PUTFREE    Q @ RECORD LINK + @ R ! THEN
 14                ELSE R @ Q !    R @ RECORD LINK + @ R ! THEN
 15            81 = SWAP 113 = OR R @ NIL = OR UNTIL THEN ;

SCR #32
  0  ( Part of Figure 7-15:  Word Definitions              )
  1
  2  : DUMPFILE
  3     PRINTER
  4     MAXREC 0 DO
  5         ." RECORD " I .
  6         ." LINK " I RECORD LINK + ?
  7         I PRINTREC
  8     LOOP ;
  9
 10

SCR #33
  0  ( Part of Figure 7-15:  Main Program                  )
  1
  2  : BOOK                   ( THIS IS THE MAIN PROGRAM  )
  3     0 OPEN? !             ( MARK FILE CLOSED          )
  4     BEGIN    MENU DUP 8 = NOT WHILE
  5         DUP 1 = IF INIT ELSE
  6         DUP 2 = OPEN? @ NOT AND IF OPEN ELSE
  7         DUP 3 = OPEN? @ AND IF APPEND    ELSE
  8         DUP 4 = OPEN? @ AND IF REVIEW    ELSE
  9         DUP 5 = OPEN? @ AND IF LISTFILE ELSE
 10         DUP 6 = OPEN? @ AND IF DUMPFILE ELSE
 11         DUP 7 = OPEN? @ AND IF CLOSE
 12         THEN THEN THEN THEN THEN THEN THEN CR CR
 13         ." PRESS <SPACE> TO CONTINUE...." KEY DROP DROP
 14     REPEAT DROP CR CR ;
 15
```

Fig. 7-15. Comprehensive sample program. (Continued from page 223.)

The program is modular in nature, with no one module exceeding 16 lines in length. Some of the modules, such as **PAINTSCREEN**, are simple and straightforward in nature. Others, such as **REVIEW**, are complex and difficult to read. There is not room here to discuss the operation of each module in detail.

ADVANTAGES AND DISADVANTAGES OF FORTH

Perhaps the most striking advantage of Forth is its extensibility. Forth comes with

```
Figure 7-16:    Structure Chart for the Comprehensive Sample
                Program
        BOOK
            MENU
                GETNUM
            OPEN
            APPEND
                GETFREE
                    WARN
                PAINTSCREEN
                    MARKOFF
                READSCREEN
                INSERT
                    GREATER
            REVIEW
                PRINTREC
                PUTFREE
            LISTFILE
                PRINTREC
            DUMPFILE
                PRINTREC
            CLOSE

        Common-use subroutines:

        PRINTER          RECORD
        OFF              GOTOXY
        CLEARSCREEN
```

Fig. 7-16. Structure chart for the comprehensive sample program.

a basic library of operations in the dictionary, but if additional operations are needed, they can easily be added.

Forth encourages modular programming; that is, it encourages the decomposition of a complex task into a series of simpler tasks. This makes the process of program development go much faster.

Another feature that makes the process of programming go faster is the interactive nature of Forth. Individual Forth words can easily be tested interactively and independently before they are incorporated into a larger program.

Forth programs produce code that is very fast and very compact, sometimes even more compact than the equivalent assembly-language code. This can be important in many applications.

Forth provides low-level control at the bit and byte level. This is important for many machine-control applications.

Forth has been implemented on many different microcomputers. Forth programs can be programmed on one microcomputer and executed on another, sometimes much smaller, microcomputer, such as a computer built into a robot.

On the negative side, Forth programming is at a very low level for a high-level language. The programmer must be concerned with many low-level details such as the contents of the stack and the physical location of files on a disk. Most other high-level languages insulate the programmer from such details. It has been said by detractors of Forth that the Forth compiler leaves many of the details of compilation to the programmer.

Forth requires the programmer to think in terms of postfix or reverse Polish notation. Most people find this somewhat awkward. It is certainly a workable notation, but it requires the programmer to adapt to the language rather than vice versa.

Forth programs tend to be dense and hard to read. Understanding a Forth program written by someone else often requires a great deal of tedious effort to track stack effects and so on. Some would call Forth a "write only" language.

Because of the complexity of Forth, many people find it more difficult to learn than languages such as BASIC, Pascal, and Logo.

Because Forth is its own operating system, it is difficult to pass data files between Forth and non-Forth programs. If a text editor were written in Forth, for example, it would be difficult to pass files created by that editor to, say, a Pascal compiler running under the MS-DOS operating system.

The editor that comes with many versions of Forth is rather primitive and inflexible. It works with "screens" of 1024 characters each, and it is inconvenient to write Forth words that span more than one screen using this editor.

Because Forth is so different than most other computer languages, it is difficult to switch between programming in Forth and programming in other languages. Forth is probably not a good choice if you intend to program in more than one language.

AVAILABILITY

Forth is available in versions for many different kinds of microcomputers, large and small. The language itself is in the public domain. Implementations of Forth are available through the Forth Interest Group (FIG) of San Carlos, California, and Mountain View Press (MVP) of Mountain View, California. Current addresses for these and other Forth suppliers can be found in magazines specializing in microcomputers.

SUMMARY

Forth is a compact but powerful language. It is a very flexible language that can be adapted to a wide variety of applications, including machine control. Forth is a controversial language; it has many advantages and many disadvantages. Its supporters and opponents are quite vocal.

Programs written in Forth run quite fast, usually much faster than programs written in BASIC. In addition, programs written in Forth tend to be very compact.

Forth tends to require more programming effort than other high-level languages because it requires the programmer to keep track of many low-level details. This is partially offset by the ease with which program modules can be interactively tested in Forth.

Forth is especially popular among programmers who enjoy dealing with the low-level details of microcomputers. Many Forth programmers are former assembly-language programmers.

Forth was designed to provide fast, compact code with both high-level and low-level features. It is best suited for applications in which speed, compactness, and low-level features are needed. Forth is an excellent alternative to assembly-language for such applications.

Ada
BASIC
C
COBOL
Forth
Fortran
LISP
Logo
Modula-2
Pascal
PILOT
Prolog

8
Fortran

The Fortran language has been in widespread use longer than any other computer language. It was produced by a team at IBM headed by John W. Backus during the period 1954 to 1957. Backus and his team were asked to develop a compiler for the IBM 704 computer. The IBM 704 computer has long since become obsolete, but the Fortran language endures.

The name Fortran is short for FORmula TRANslator. Fortran has long been the language of choice of the scientific and engineering community, just as COBOL has long been the language of choice of the business community. As the name suggests, Fortran is particularly suited to manipulating of formulas and performing of various mathematical calculations.

Although there are other languages today that have similar capabilities and add other features besides, Fortran remains firmly entrenched among nonbusiness users of large computers. Part of the reason is tradition; since the late 1950s, most scientific computing has been done in Fortran. Because it is widely used, it is widely taught in universities. And because it is widely taught in universities, it is widely used.

There is a wide body of scientific software that has been created in Fortran and that is widely available in computer subroutine libraries in universities and in industry. These subroutines are easily incorporated into Fortran programs; doing so can save much programming effort.

There are two versions of Fortran in wide use today, Fortran IV and Fortran 77. Fortran IV is the name usually used to refer to the version adopted by the American National Standards Institute (ANSI) in 1966. Fortran 77 is the 1977 ANSI standard. The main enhancements added with the 1977 standard are improved character handling and the IF-THEN-ELSE control structure. Fortran 77 has not completely displaced Fortran IV, probably because its additional features do not provide a significantly greater capability than that of Fortran IV.

Fortran has not been widely accepted by microcomputer users. In the microcomputer world BASIC has been available longer than Fortran. BASIC is therefore more popular on microcomputers than Fortran for much the same reasons as those that make Fortran so popular on large computers. Also, BASIC is often furnished at no extra cost with a microcomputer, whereas Fortran invariably costs extra.

Fortran has several advantages over BASIC, however, as will be seen below. Because it is almost always implemented as a compiled language rather than an interpreted language, Fortran programs usually run much faster than BASIC programs. Fortran has a reputation for speed.

Fortran also has its limitations, as will also be seen in this chapter. Nevertheless, a language with such a long history of successful use deserves a close look.

The programming examples in this chapter were written and tested using the Nevada Fortran compiler by Ellis Computing running on an Apple II Plus microcomputer under the CP/M 80 operating system.

PROGRAM STRUCTURE

A Fortran program is a sequence of Fortran statements. The usual rule is one statement per line. In earlier days, a line was synonymous with a card, and the usual rule was stated as ''one statement per card.'' Today you will still hear Fortran (and COBOL) programmers talk about cards and card columns even when their programs are created and stored electronically. The tendency is to think of a line as a *card image.*

Each Fortran statement must follow a prescribed structure. The statement itself can be anywhere between columns 7 and 72, inclusive. A C in column 1 means that the rest of the line will be treated as a comment or remark.

Statement numbers, when present, may be anywhere between columns 1 and 5. Statement numbers are needed only in certain circumstances, such as to mark the target of a GO TO statement. When they appear, statement numbers do not need to be in any particular order, so long as each is unique.

Column 6 is reserved for a continuation indicator. Normally this column is left blank. Any character (except zero or blank) in column 6 means that the line is to be considered as a continuation of the previous line. Otherwise, a statement is assumed to end at the end of a line. No punctuation is needed to terminate or separate statements.

Columns 73-80 are ignored by the compiler. This practice dates back to the days of cards, when sequence numbers were often punched in these columns. This facilitated reassembling a card deck using a mechanical sorter after the cards had been dropped on the floor. Those of you who missed the days of punched cards and keypunch machines are fortunate.

A simple Fortran program is shown in Fig. 8-1. This program simply prints out the message This is a test. The first two lines are comments, as indicated by the letter C in column 1. The printing is done by the WRITE statement. The (1,*) in the WRITE statement sends the output to the screen in a standardized format; this will be explained in more detail in the section on input and output.

The STOP statement causes the program to stop executing and to transfer control

```
C       Figure 8-1:   Minimal FORTRAN Program.
C
        WRITE (1,*) 'This is a test.'
        STOP
        END
```

Fig. 8-1. A minimal FORTRAN program.

back to the operating system. It is usually near the last statement of the program, but it can technically be anywhere in the program. The END statement tells the compiler that it has come to the end of the program; it must be the last statement of the program. In short, the difference between the two statements is that the STOP statement does its job at run time (when the program is run) and the END statement does its job at compile time (when the program is compiled).

DATA REPRESENTATION

The basic data types in Fortran are REAL, DOUBLE PRECISION, COMPLEX, INTEGER, and LOGICAL. DOUBLE PRECISION numbers are floating-point numbers with twice the storage allocation of REAL numbers; they are sometimes needed for scientific calculations. A COMPLEX variable is stored as an ordered pair of real numbers. (If you have to ask what a complex number is, you don't need to know! Complex numbers are used by mathematicians, physicists, and engineers.)

Fortran 77 also includes the CHARACTER data type, but Fortran IV does not. Character strings exist in Fortran IV, but they must be stored in arrays of type INTEGER. How this is done will be described in the section on arrays.

Nevada Fortran supports the REAL, INTEGER, and LOGICAL data types. DOUBLE PRECISION data is permitted, but is treated exactly like REAL data.

Constants

Numerical constants in Fortran follow the usual conventions, as described in Chapter 2. Literal constants can be handled in one of two ways. The simplest is to enclose the literal within single quotation marks, as in the following:

'Literal'

The older and less convenient way is to write it as follows:

7HLiteral

This is called a *Hollerith constant*, after the inventor of the character encoding system used on punched cards. The 7H means that the seven characters following the letter

H are to be taken as a literal constant. This is awkward and seldom used any more because it requires the programmer to count characters.

The **LOGICAL** constants are .TRUE. and .FALSE.. The periods preceding and following the words are part of the constant.

Fortran does not support named constants, as do Pascal, C, and some other languages.

Variables

Variable names in Fortran may consist of one to six letters or digits. The first character must be a letter. Standard Fortran does not permit lowercase letters to be used in variable names or Fortran key words. Some implementations do permit lowercase letters, however. For the sake of standardization, the examples in this chapter will use lowercase letters only in literal constants.

Fortran permits **REAL** and **INTEGER** variables to be declared by default. If a variable is not explicitly declared, it is assumed to be an **INTEGER** variable if the first letter of its name is I, J, K, L, M, or N. Otherwise, it is assumed to be of type **REAL**. It is good programming practice, however, to declare all variables.

Figure 8-2 shows the declaration of three **REAL** variables called PI, AREA, and RADIUS. It also shows the declaration of an integer variable called I, even though it is not used later in the program.

Figure 8-2 also shows how a variable can be initialized using the **DATA** statement. In this case PI is initialized to the value 3.14159.

The program in Fig. 8-2 simply computes and prints the area of a circle with a radius of 5.

THE ASSIGNMENT STATEMENT

Fortran uses the equals sign (=) for the assignment operator. The example in Fig. 8-2 shows two examples of its use.

```
Figure 8-2:    Area of a Circle.

REAL PI, AREA, RADIUS
INTEGER I
DATA PI/3.14159/

RADIUS = 5.0
AREA    = PI * RADIUS**2
WRITE (1,*) 'RADIUS = ',RADIUS
WRITE (1,*) 'AREA    = ',AREA
STOP
END
```

Fig. 8-2. The area of a circle.

ARITHMETIC EXPRESSIONS

Fortran uses conventional infix notation (see Chapter 2) for its arithmetic expressions. It uses the usual arithmetic operators, as shown below:

Operator	Meaning
+	Addition
−	Subtraction
*	Multiplication
/	Division
**	Exponentiation

The statement in the program in Fig. 8-2 that calculates the area of a circle has an arithmetic expression on the right-hand side of the assignment operator.

Parentheses should be used freely in the construction of arithmetic expressions to eliminate any possible ambiguity.

LOGICAL EXPRESSIONS

Logical expressions evaluate to .TRUE. or .FALSE.. They are constructed using the relational and logical operators shown below:

Operator	Meaning
.GT.	Greater than
.GE.	Greater than or equal to
.EQ.	Equal to
.NE.	Not equal to
.LE.	Less than or equal to
.LT.	Less than
.AND.	Logical AND
.OR.	Logical OR
.NOT.	Logical NOT

The periods are integral parts of the operator names and cannot be omitted. The meanings of these operators are as discussed in Chapter 2.

Parentheses should be used freely in the construction of logical expressions to reduce the probability that an expression could be misinterpreted.

INPUT AND OUTPUT

Figures 8-1 and 8-2 contain examples of the use of the WRITE statement in Fortran. A more general form of the WRITE statement is as follows:

WRITE (N1, N2) <OUTPUT LIST>

Here N1 refers to the unit number to which the output should be directed. In Nevada Fortran, unit number 1 means the system console or video screen. Thus in Fig. 8-1, the statement

WRITE (1,*) 'This is a test.'

wrote its message to the video screen.

Unit number 0 in Nevada Fortran is reserved for console input. Other unit numbers can be assigned as needed for a printer and disk files. An example of how to redirect output to a printer in Nevada Fortran is given in Fig. 8-3. The technique of establishing the linkage to the external device may vary from compiler to compiler, but the principle of using a different unit number will stay the same.

The N2 above can be an asterisk (*) or the statement number of a FORMAT statement. Use of the asterisk invokes what is called *format-free* output. In format-free output, the compiler decides what the output should look like. If you have been running the example programs, you may have noticed that the numbers printed out by the program in Fig. 8-2 were printed in scientific notation. Often, however, the user wishes to control the format of the output, as with the PRINT USING statement of BASIC. This is accomplished in Fortran by using the FORMAT statement.

Figure 8-4 shows two examples of formatted output. The program does exactly the same as the program in Fig. 8-2; only the form of the output is different.

Two FORMAT statements are used in this example, one for each WRITE statement. The first WRITE statement references FORMAT statement number 200 and the second references FORMAT statement 210.

The purpose of a FORMAT statement is to describe the appearance of the output. The F10.5 in statements 200 and 210 is called a *field descriptor*. The F stands for *fixed point* and means a number with a decimal point but no exponent. The 10 means that field is to be 10 spaces wide (counting the decimal point and the sign, if any), and the 5 means that there are to be 5 digits to the right of the decimal point.

A list of some of the more common field descriptors follows. The letter w stands for the width of the field, the letter d for the number of decimal places, and the letter n for the number of times the field is to be repeated.

```
C       Figure 8-3:   Demonstrate Printer Output.
C
        CALL OPEN (2, 'LST:')
C
C       Note:  'LST:' is the CP/M list device (printer)
C
        WRITE (1,*) 'This goes to the video screen.'
C
        WRITE (2,*) 'This goes to the printer.'
C
        STOP
        END
```

Fig. 8-3. Printer output.

```
C         Figure 8-4:   Illustrate Formatted Output.
C

          REAL PI, AREA, RADIUS
          INTEGER I
          DATA PI/3.14159/
C
C         Compute Area of a Circle
C

          RADIUS = 5.0
          AREA   = PI * RADIUS**2
          WRITE (1,200) RADIUS
          WRITE (1,210) AREA
          STOP
     200  FORMAT (' RADIUS = ', F10.5)
     210  FORMAT (' AREA   = ', F10.5)
          END
```

Fig. 8-4. Formatted output.

Descriptor	Definition
Iw	Integer
nFw.d	Fixed point
nEw.d	Floating point (scientific notation)
nAw	Alphanumeric (character) data
nLw	Logical (prints T or F)
nGw.d	General
nX	Blank spaces
Tw	Tab to column w

Most of these are more-or-less self-explanatory. The A format will be discussed in more detail in a later section, and the G format will be presented in the following paragraphs.

Field descriptors are matched with items in the output list by position, except for X and T descriptors, which may be interspersed between other descriptors without a corresponding item in the output list. Additionally, literal constants (such as ' RADIUS = ') may be inserted between field descriptors. In the example in Fig. 8-4, the variable RADIUS is associated with the field descriptor F10.5 by position. The variable is the first item in the output list, and the field descriptor is the first in the FORMAT statement, not counting the literal constant.

Field descriptors and literals are separated by a comma or a slash (/). When descriptors are separated by a slash, a new output line is started.

Data elements (variables or constants) in the output list must agree with the corresponding field descriptor by type. An F or E descriptor expects a data element of type REAL or DOUBLE PRECISION. An I descriptor expects a data element of type

INTEGER, an L descriptor expects a data element of type LOGICAL, and an A descriptor expects an alphanumeric literal. The exception is the G descriptor, which can handle an INTEGER or a REAL data element. In the case of an INTEGER, Gw.d acts the same as Iw. In the case of a REAL, how it acts depends on the value of the number. If the number will fit, Fw.d is used. If the number is too large or too small for Fw.d, then Ew.d is used.

Technically a FORMAT statement can be almost anywhere in a Fortran program; the connection between the WRITE statement and the FORMAT statement is established by the statement number. In fact, two or more WRITE statements can reference the same FORMAT statement. A convenient place to group all FORMAT statements is between the STOP and END statements. This removes formatting details from the main flow of processing. Some programmers prefer to place each FORMAT statement immediately after the appropriate WRITE statement. Deciding which way is better is a matter of individual preference.

The FORMAT statement provides the programmer with a great deal of flexibility in formatting output. It does require some effort to use, however. More examples of FORMAT statements will be found in the remaining programs of this chapter.

Input is handled by the READ statement. The general format for the READ statement is as follows:

READ (N1, N2) <INPUT LIST>

N1 is the unit number and N2 is an asterisk or a statement number. Nevada Fortran has reserved unit number 0 for console input. If N2 is an asterisk, no FORMAT statement is needed. FORMAT statements are not usually needed for console input. The field descriptors described above are applicable, except that the d describing the number of places to the right of the decimal is overridden when an actual decimal point is entered.

The program in Fig. 8-4 is of limited use, as it can compute the area of only one size circle. The program in Fig. 8-5 adds a READ statement to get the radius of the circle from the console. The program can then be used to compute the area of a circle with another radius.

If the radius is so large that the area of the circle no longer fits in an F10.5 format, 10 asterisks will be printed instead. That is Fortran's way of telling you that you need a wider field descriptor.

CONTROL STRUCTURES

Fortran has fewer control structures than more recent languages such as Pascal. Traditionally, Fortran programmers have relied heavily on the GO TO statement in a rather unstructured way. There is no reason, however, why well-structured programs cannot be written in Fortran.

Simple Selection: IF-THEN-ELSE

The IF-THEN-ELSE statement is found in all Fortran 77 implementations and in some ANSI 1966 Fortran IV implementations. In versions of Fortran that lack the IF-THEN-ELSE construct, the logical IF can be used. The logical IF is described below.

```
C        Figure 8-5:   Illustrate the READ Statement.
C
         REAL PI, AREA, RADIUS
         INTEGER I
         DATA PI/3.14159/
C
         WRITE (1,*)  'COMPUTE THE AREA OF A CIRCLE.'
         WRITE (1,*)
         WRITE (1,*)  'ENTER RADIUS: '
         READ  (0,*) RADIUS
         AREA   = PI * RADIUS**2
         WRITE (1,200) RADIUS
         WRITE (1,210) AREA
         STOP
     200 FORMAT (' RADIUS = ', F10.5)
     210 FORMAT (' AREA   = ', F10.5)
         END
```

Fig. 8-5. The use of the READ statement.

The **ELSE** part of the **IF-THEN-ELSE** statement is optional. Here is a simple example with the **ELSE** part omitted:

```
MONTH = MONTH + 1
IF (MONTH .GT. 12) THEN
    MONTH = 1
    YEAR = YEAR + 1
ENDIF
```

There can be as many statements as desired between the **THEN** and the **ENDIF**. These statements should be indented as shown to visually indicate the scope of the statement. This makes programs much easier to read. The parentheses surrounding the conditional expression (**MONTH .GT. 12**) are mandatory.

The same task can be accomplished in another way, using an **ELSE** part:

```
IF (MONTH .LT. 12) THEN
    MONTH = MONTH + 1
ELSE
    MONTH = 1
    YEAR = YEAR + 1
ENDIF
```

Again, note the pattern of indentation.

The GO TO Statement

A GO TO statement requires a label as a destination. A label in Fortran is a statement number. Statement numbers in Fortran must be placed between columns 1 and 5 of a statement. Figure 8-6 shows a common use of a GO TO statement in Fortran, to implement a simple conditional loop. The program does exactly the same computations as the program in Fig. 8-5, except that it allows multiple computations within a single run.

The Logical IF Statement

When there is no ELSE part, and when there is only one statement to be conditionally executed, the logical IF statement may be used. Suppose, for example, that a number must be set to zero if it is negative. The following statement:

IF (X .LT. 0) X = 0

will do the job. The single statement may be a GO TO statement.

In some versions of Fortran (prior to Fortran 77), the IF- THEN-ELSE statement is not available. In that case, the logical IF can be used to emulate the IF-THEN-ELSE. The example in the previous section can be emulated as follows:

```
IF (MONTH .LT. 12) GO TO 20
    MONTH = 1
    YEAR = YEAR + 1
    GO TO 30
```

```
C      Figure 8-6:  The GO TO Statement.
C
       REAL PI, AREA, RADIUS
       INTEGER I
       DATA PI/3.14159/
C
       WRITE (1,*)   'COMPUTE THE AREA OF A CIRCLE.'
    10 WRITE (1,*)
       WRITE (1,*)   'ENTER RADIUS:  (0 TO QUIT)'
       READ  (0,*) RADIUS
       IF (RADIUS .EQ. 0.0) GO TO 99
       AREA   = PI * RADIUS**2
       WRITE (1,200) RADIUS
       WRITE (1,210) AREA
       GO TO 10
    99 STOP
   200 FORMAT (' RADIUS = ', F10.5)
   210 FORMAT (' AREA   = ', F10.5)
       END
```

Fig. 8-6. The GO TO statement.

```
20  CONTINUE
          MONTH = MONTH + 1
30  CONTINUE
```

The structure of the construct is made obvious by proper indentation.

The **CONTINUE** statement in the example above is merely a place holder, a convenient place to attach a label.

The program in Fig. 8-6 contains an example of a logical **IF** statement with a **GO TO** used to implement a conditional loop. The logical **IF** statement with a **GO TO** is a combination encountered so often that it deserves a name of its own; the *Conditional GO TO* statement is an appropriate name.

The Arithmetic IF

Fortran provides another form of **IF** statement called the *arithmetic IF* statement. Its format is as follows:

```
IF (<integer expression>) n1, n2, n3
```

The <integer expression> is evaluated. If its value is negative, control is transferred to statement number n1. If its value is zero, control is transferred to statement n2. If it is positive, control is transferred to statement n3.

The arithmetic **IF** is an idea whose time has come and gone. Its use can lead to confusing programs. Its use is therefore not recommended.

Multiple Selection

The **IF-THEN-ELSE** statement is fine when there are precisely two alternatives. If there are more than two possible alternative actions, **IF** statements can be nested. A simple example, which shows the computation of a weekly payroll, is shown in Fig. 8-7.

The example shows that pay for up to 40 hours is paid at the normal rate; pay for work between 40 and 50 hours is paid at one-and-one-half times the normal rate; pay for work in excess of 50 hours is paid at twice the normal rate.

Fortran does not have a **CASE** statement, as discussed in Chapter 2. The **CASE** statement can be emulated using a Computed **GO TO** statement. An example is shown in Fig. 8-8.

The sample program reads in an integer between 1 and 12 and then prints out the number of days in the corresponding month. The Computed **GO TO** statement jumps to one of the statement numbers contained within the parentheses, depending on the value of the integer **MONTH**. If **MONTH** is 1, the destination is the first-listed statement number, which is 101. If **MONTH** is 2, the destination is statement number 102, and so on. The numerical value of the statement number is not significant; it is the relative position of the statement number within the parentheses that matters.

Note that conditional **GO TO** statements preceding the computed **GO TO** keep the value of **MONTH** from straying beyond the proper bounds.

Recall that a **CONTINUE** statement does nothing but hold a place. **GO TO 101** will therefore have the same result as **GO TO 112**, which is to set **DAYS** to 31. **GO**

```
C       Figure 8-7:  Multiple Selection with Nested IF.
C
C       Compute Weekly Pay
C
        REAL HOURS, PAY, RATE
        DATA RATE/10.00/
C
        WRITE (1,*) 'COMPUTE PAY:'
    10  WRITE (1,*)
        WRITE (1,*) 'ENTER NUMBER OF HOURS WORKED (0 TO HALT):'
        READ  (0,*) HOURS
        IF (HOURS .LE. 0.0) GO TO 99
        IF (HOURS .LE. 40.0) THEN
            PAY = HOURS * RATE
        ELSE
            IF (HOURS .LE. 50.0) THEN
                PAY = 40.0*RATE + (HOURS-40.0)*1.5*RATE
            ELSE
                PAY = 40.0*RATE + 10.0*RATE*1.5 + (HOURS-50.0)*2.0*RATE
            ENDIF
        ENDIF
        WRITE (1,200) HOURS
        WRITE (1,210) RATE
        WRITE (1,220) PAY
        GO TO 10
    99  STOP
   200  FORMAT ('HOURS WORKED:   ', F10.2)
   210  FORMAT ('NORMAL RATE:    ', F10.2)
   220  FORMAT ('GROSS PAY:      ', F10.2)
        END
```

Fig. 8-7. Multiple selection with nested IF.

TO 120 is needed to ensure that only the appropriate case is chosen.

In the case of February, additional action is required to determine whether or not the desired year is a leap year. The MOD function computes the modulus, or the remainder after integer division.

Loops

Fortran provides only one kind of loop, the DO loop. The DO loop is a counted loop. Conditional loops must be emulated using the GO TO statement.

Counted Loops: The DO Statement. The DO statement, commonly called the *DO loop,* is a workhorse in Fortran programs. The basic format of a DO loop is as follows:

```
DO 10 I = N1, N2, N3
    <statements>
10  CONTINUE
```

The 10 immediately following the word DO is the statement number of the last statement in the loop. The last statement of the loop can be any statement, but it is best to make it a CONTINUE statement. The I following the 10 is the loop counter. At the beginning

```
C       Figure 8-8:   The Calendar Program, Version 1.
C
C       Demonstrate the Computed GO TO Statement.
C
        INTEGER MONTH, DAYS, YEAR
C
   10 WRITE (1,*)
      WRITE (1,*) 'ENTER THE MONTH (1..12):   (0 TO HALT)'
      READ  (0,*) MONTH
      IF (MONTH .LE. 0)  GO TO 999
      IF (MONTH .GT. 12) GO TO 10
C     EMULATE CASE STATEMENT
      GO TO (101,102,103,104,105,106,107,108,109,110,111,112), MONTH
C             31-DAY MONTHS
  101         CONTINUE
  103         CONTINUE
  105         CONTINUE
  107         CONTINUE
  108         CONTINUE
  110         CONTINUE
  112         CONTINUE
                DAYS = 31
                GO TO 120
C             30-DAY MONTHS
  104         CONTINUE
  106         CONTINUE
  109         CONTINUE
  111         CONTINUE
                DAYS = 30
                GO TO 120
C             FEBRUARY
  102         CONTINUE
                WRITE (1,*) 'ENTER THE YEAR:'
                READ  (0,*) YEAR
                IF (MOD(YEAR,4) .EQ. 0) THEN
                        DAYS = 29
                ELSE
                        DAYS = 28
                ENDIF
                GO TO 120
C     END CASE
  120 CONTINUE
      WRITE (1,*)
      WRITE (1,200) MONTH, DAYS
      GO TO 10
  999 STOP
  200 FORMAT (' MONTH ', I2, ' HAS ', I2, ' DAYS.')
      END
```

Fig. 8-8. The Calendar Program, Version 1.

of the loop, I is initialized to N1. After the first iteration of the loop, N3 is added to N1. If the result is less than or equal to N2, another iteration is performed. If not, control is transferred to the statement following statement number 10.

If N3 is omitted, the loop counter is incremented by 1 at each iteration. A Fortran DO loop always performs at least one iteration, regardless of the relative values of N1 and N2. That is because the testing of the value of N1 versus N2 is done after, rather than before, each iteration.

N1, N2, and N3 may be integers or integer variables. In either case, their value must be one or greater. Zero and negative values are not permitted.

The value of I is technically undefined after the loop has completed. In most versions of Fortran it will have the value N2 + 1, but the programmer should not rely on its value once the loop has terminated.

Chapter 2 contained a simple example in BASIC of a program that printed out the integers from 1 to 10. Figure 8-9 contains a Fortran program that does the same thing. Notice that the body of the loop is indented. This makes it easy to see at a glance the extent of the loop.

There is another form of the DO loop in Fortran, called the *implied DO loop*. It can be used only in READ and WRITE statements. The DO loop in Fig. 8-9 could be programmed as one line using an implied DO loop as follows:

WRITE (1,*) (I, I = 1,10)

The I = 1,10 follows the same rules as the corresponding part of an ordinary DO loop. Implied DO loops are also useful for handling arrays and will be illustrated further following the discussion of arrays.

Conditional Loops. Fortran does not provide conditional loops such as the WHILE or REPEAT-UNTIL loops of Pascal. When the situation calls for such a loop, it must be emulated using the logical IF and GO TO statements.

As you will recall, a WHILE loop repeats as long as a condition is true, and the test is performed at the top of the loop. Because the test is at the top, the body of the loop may be executed zero times if the condition is initially false. The program in Fig. 8-10 shows how a WHILE loop can be emulated in Fortran. Comments are used to show what is being emulated.

```
        C       Figure 8-9:   The DO Loop.
        C

                INTEGER  I
        C

                DO  10  I  =  1, 10
                    WRITE  (1, *)  I
        10  CONTINUE
            STOP
            END
```

Fig. 8-9. The DO loop.

```
C       Figure 8-10:   The WHILE Loop Emulated.
C
        INTEGER I
C
        I = 1
C       WHILE (I .LE. 10) DO
     10 IF (I .GT. 10) GO TO 20
            WRITE (1,*) I
            I = I + 1
            GO TO 10
     20 CONTINUE
C       END WHILE
        STOP
        END
```

Fig. 8-10. The WHILE loop emulated.

This program does exactly the same thing as the program in Fig. 8-9. In this particular case the **DO** loop of Fig. 8-9 is more appropriate. The **DO** loop takes care of initializing and incrementing the loop counter I.

There are other situations, however, in which the **WHILE** loop is more appropriate. Consider the case in which a program needs to read numbers from the console until their sum exceeds 100. The program needs to report the actual sum and a count of how many numbers were included in the sum. A **DO** loop would not be appropriate, because a **DO** loop executes a predetermined number of times. A **WHILE** loop is better suited to situations when the number of iterations is not known in advance.

Figure 8-11 shows the program described above. The emulated **WHILE** loop is labeled with comment lines. Note again that the body of the loop is indented to make it easy to see the scope of the loop at a glance.

Another type of conditional loop is the **REPEAT-UNTIL** loop with the test at the bottom of the loop. This type of loop is repeated until a certain condition becomes true. Figure 8-12 shows how the previous problem could be programmed another way using the **REPEAT-UNTIL** structure. The emulated structure is described with comment lines.

In this example the variable **COUNT** was initiated to −1 so that it will be incremented to zero on the first pass through the loop. This is slightly unnatural. The **WHILE** loop would probably be the better choice in this situation.

Subroutines

A subprogram is a self-contained module that can be referenced from a program or from another subprogram. Subroutines and functions are the two types of subprograms available in Fortran. Subprograms in Fortran are placed after the **END** statement of the main program. Many versions of Fortran also allow subprograms to be defined in separate files.

```
C       Figure 8-11:   Another WHILE Loop Emulation.
C
        INTEGER NUM, COUNT, SUM
C
        COUNT = 0
        SUM   = 0
        WRITE (1,*) 'ENTER A SERIES OF INTEGERS:'
        READ  (0,*) NUM
C       WHILE ((SUM + NUM) .LE. 100) DO
     10 IF ((SUM + NUM) .GT. 100) GO TO 20
            COUNT = COUNT + 1
            SUM   = SUM + NUM
            READ (0,*) NUM
            GO TO 10
     20 CONTINUE
C       END WHILE
        WRITE (1,*)
        WRITE (1,*) COUNT, ' NUMBERS WERE READ.'
        WRITE (1,*) 'THEIR SUM IS ', SUM
        WRITE (1,*) 'THE NUMBER ', NUM, ' WAS NOT COUNTED.'
        STOP
        END
```

Fig. 8-11. Another WHILE loop emulation.

```
C       Figure 8-12:   A REPEAT-UNTIL Loop Emulation.
C
        INTEGER NUM, COUNT, SUM
C
        COUNT = -1
        SUM   = 0
        NUM   = 0
        WRITE (1,*) 'ENTER A SERIES OF INTEGERS:'
C       REPEAT
     10 CONTINUE
            COUNT = COUNT + 1
            SUM   = SUM + NUM
            READ (0,*) NUM
        IF ((SUM + NUM) .LE. 100) GO TO 10
C       UNTIL ((SUM + NUM) .GT. 100)
        WRITE (1,*)
        WRITE (1,*) COUNT, ' NUMBERS WERE READ.'
        WRITE (1,*) 'THEIR SUM IS ', SUM
        WRITE (1,*) 'THE NUMBER ', NUM, ' WAS NOT COUNTED.'
        STOP
        END
```

Fig. 8-12. A REPEAT-UNTIL loop emulation.

As discussed in Chapter 2, subroutines have several advantages. Most importantly, they facilitate the breakup of large, unwieldy programs into modules of manageable size. Other potential benefits include the elimination of duplicate coding.

A sample program that contains two subroutines is shown in Fig. 8-13. One subroutine simply prints out the value of two variables, suitably labeled. The second subroutine

```
C       Figure 8-13:   Demonstrate SUBROUTINE Usage.
C
C       Exchange two variables
C
        REAL P, Q, X, Y
C
        P = 1.0
        Q = 2.0
        CALL PRINT2 (P, Q)
        CALL SWAP   (P, Q)
        CALL PRINT2 (P, Q)
C
        X = 3.14159
        Y = 2.71828
        CALL PRINT2 (X, Y)
        CALL SWAP   (X, Y)
        CALL PRINT2 (X, Y)
C
        STOP
        END
C
        SUBROUTINE PRINT2 (U, V)
C          PRINT THE VALUE OF U, V
           REAL U, V
           WRITE (1, 200) U, V
           RETURN
    200    FORMAT ('FIRST  VARIABLE:   ', F15.5 /
                   'SECOND VARIABLE:   ', F15.5)
        END
C
        SUBROUTINE SWAP (U, V)
C          EXCHANGE THE VALUES OF U AND V
           REAL U, V, TEMP
           TEMP = U
           U    = V
           V    = TEMP
           RETURN
        END
```

Fig. 8-13. SUBROUTINE Usage.

exchanges the value of two variables. The program prints two variables, exchanges them, and then prints them again. The process is repeated with different variables to show the ability of Fortran subroutines to handle different variables. The first time the subroutine SWAP is invoked, it exchanges the values of P and Q; the second time it exchanges the values of X and Y. This is a capability not found in BASIC.

Note that a subroutine in Fortran is invoked using the CALL statement. Following the word CALL is the name of the subroutine and a list of arguments to be passed to the subroutine in parentheses.

A subroutine is defined by writing the word SUBROUTINE followed by the name of the subroutine and a list of parameters in parentheses. These parameters, plus any other variables to be used in the subroutine, should be declared within the subroutine. Any variables used in the subroutine, except the parameters, are strictly local to the subroutine and are independent of all other variables in other parts of the program, whether or not they have the same name.

Parameters in Fortran are passed by reference. The result is that any changes made to a parameter within the subroutine are also made to the corresponding argument in the CALL statement in the calling program or subprogram. This is how data is passed back to the main program. Care must be exercised, however, to avoid unintentionally altering the value of a variable in the main program.

Control is passed from the subroutine back to the calling program or subprogram by the RETURN statement. The RETURN statement in the subroutine takes the place of the STOP statement of the main program. Each subroutine also requires an END statement.

Note that the body of each subroutine is indented. This makes it clear at a glance where a subroutine begins and ends.

In this example the advantage gained by using subroutines is marginal. The purpose of the example was to illustrate the mechanics of defining and using subroutines. In the comprehensive sample program at the end of the chapter, subroutines are used to much better advantage. In fact, it is typical for large, well-written programs to consist mainly of subroutines and to have a very short main program.

A subroutine in Fortran may CALL another subroutine, but it may not call itself, either directly or indirectly. In other words, if subroutine A calls subroutine B, subroutine B may not call subroutine A.

Functions

A function is another form of subprogram. Like a subroutine, a function is a stand-alone module that can be invoked from the main program or from another subprogram. The primary differences between a subroutine and a function are in how each is defined and invoked, and in how each returns data to the calling program or subprogram.

Fortran has numerous built-in functions. You have already seen one such function, the MOD function, in Fig. 8-8. Other common built-in Fortran functions include functions to calculate square roots, sines, cosines, and other numerical and trigonometric functions.

User-defined functions are defined following the END statement of the main program along with the subroutines. Subroutines and functions may be defined in any order. The heading of a function contains the word FUNCTION, preceded by the type of value to be returned (e.g., REAL) and followed by the function name and argument list. An example of a function definition is shown in Fig. 8-14.

The function, called MAX3, returns the largest of its three arguments. A function is invoked by writing its name in an expression (as in BIG = MAX3 (X, Y, Z)). The value returned is attached to the name of the function. In fact, the name of the function is treated as if it were a variable within the body of the function. It *must* be given a value somewhere within the body of the function.

In this case the value to be returned is of type REAL. Therefore the function is declared to be of type REAL, both in its heading *and* in the main program. If the programmer neglected to declare MAX3 as REAL in the main program, the main program would assume the result to be an integer because the default type for variables beginning with the letter M is INTEGER.

In other ways a function is like a subroutine. They both require a RETURN and an END statement. Neither can invoke itself recursively, directly or indirectly. The parameters and arguments of each are treated the same way. The body of the function has been indented in the example to show clearly the beginning and end of the function.

```
C       Figure 8-14:  Demonstrate a Function.
C
C       Find the largest of three numbers.
C
        REAL X, Y, Z, MAX3, BIG
C
        WRITE (1,*) 'ENTER THREE NUMBERS:'
        WRITE (1,*) 'FIRST  NUMBER:'
        READ  (0,*) X
        WRITE (1,*) 'SECOND NUMBER:'
        READ  (0,*) Y
        WRITE (1,*) 'THIRD  NUMBER:'
        READ  (0,*) Z
        BIG = MAX3 (X, Y, Z)
        WRITE (1,200) BIG
        STOP
    200 FORMAT (F10.5, ' IS THE LARGEST OF THE THREE')
        END
C
        REAL FUNCTION MAX3 (X, Y, Z)
C          RETURN THE LARGEST OF THE THREE ARGUMENTS
           REAL X, Y, Z
           MAX3 = X
           IF (Y .GT. MAX3) MAX3 = Y
           IF (Z .GT. MAX3) MAX3 = Z
           RETURN
        STOP
        END
```

Fig. 8-14. A sample function.

Recursion

As mentioned above, the Fortran language does not support recursive subroutine or function calls.

DATA STRUCTURES

So far, the Fortran programs in the examples have used only variables of type **INTEGER** and **REAL**. More advanced data structures, such as arrays, records, and linked lists, are introduced in this section. In addition, how to handle character strings using **INTEGER** variables and arrays is described.

Arrays

The subscripts of Fortran arrays are enclosed within parentheses. The lower bound for Fortran array subscripts is always one. The upper bound is specified in a **DIMENSION** statement. The following shows the declaration of a **REAL** array with 100 elements:

```
REAL X
DIMENSION X(100)
```

The same result could be obtained by the following abbreviated declaration:

```
REAL X(100)
```

The use of arrays in Fortran is much like that in other languages. An example is given in Fig. 8-15, to be discussed in the following section on character strings.

Character Strings

Until Fortran 77, there was no explicit provision in Fortran for character strings. Because not all versions of Fortran available today have the character-handling facilities of Fortran 77, an explanation is included here of how to handle character strings in Fortran using **INTEGER** variables and arrays.

INTEGER variables in various implementations of Fortran are stored in two, four, six, or some other number of bytes. Nevada Fortran uses six bytes. You might recall that a character will fit in one byte. An **INTEGER** variable in Nevada Fortran will therefore hold from one to six characters. Character strings longer than six characters may be stored in **INTEGER** arrays.

If individual characters in a character string need to be accessed or manipulated, it is best to store the character string in an array with one character per array element. Although this is wasteful (up to six characters could go in each element), it is sometimes the only convenient way to operate.

There are three ways that a variable can receive a character value. It can receive a character value via a **READ** statement using an A format, it can receive a character value initially from a **DATA** statement, or it can receive a character value by assignment from another variable. A variable cannot receive a character value by assignment from

```
C       Figure 8-15:   The Calendar Program, Version 2.
C
C       Demonstrate Arrays.
C
        INTEGER MONTH, NUMBER, YEAR, DAYS(12), NAME(12), PROMPT(6)
        DATA DAYS/31,28,31,30,31,30,31,31,30,31,30,31/
        DATA NAME/'JAN','FEB','MAR','APR','MAY','JUN',
     1           'JUL','AUG','SEP','OCT','NOV','DEC'/
        DATA PROMPT/'ENTER THE MONTH (1-12), 0 TO QUIT:  '/
C
     10 CONTINUE
        WRITE (1,*)
        WRITE (1,200) PROMPT
        READ  (0,*) MONTH
        IF (MONTH .LE. 0)  GO TO 999
        IF (MONTH .GT. 12) GO TO 10
        NUMBER = DAYS(MONTH)
C       CHECK FOR LEAP YEAR IF MONTH IS FEBRUARY
        IF (MONTH .EQ. 2) THEN
            WRITE (1,*) 'ENTER THE YEAR:'
            READ  (0,*) YEAR
            IF (MOD(YEAR,4) .EQ. 0) THEN
                NUMBER = NUMBER + 1
            ENDIF
        ENDIF
        WRITE (1,210) NUMBER, NAME(MONTH)
        GO TO 10
    999 STOP
    200 FORMAT (6A6)
    210 FORMAT ('THERE ARE ', I2, ' DAYS IN ', A3, '.')
        END
```

Fig. 8-15. The Calendar Program, Version 2.

an alphanumeric literal. In other words,

    A = 'HELLO'

is *illegal* in Fortran.

Figure 8-8 contained a program that computed the number of days in a given month using the Computed **GO TO** statement. The program in Fig. 8-15 shows how to accomplish the same task using numeric and character arrays.

Three arrays of type **INTEGER** are declared in the program in Fig. 8-15, and each is used in a different way. The array **DAYS** is used in the conventional way and is initialized via a **DATA** statement to contain the number of days in each month.

The array **PROMPT** is used to store a single character string. It is also initialized using a **DATA** statement. The characters are stored six characters per array element.

The WRITE statement that prints it out simply refers to it by name, without any subscripts.

The array NAME is used to store the names of the months. Because each array element can store at most six characters, only the first three letters of each month name are used. The array is initialized with a DATA statement.

The program itself is very simple. The month is read as an integer between 1 and 12; then the number of days in that month and the name of that month are determined by consulting the arrays DAYS and NAMES, respectively. Additional processing is required for February to check for leap year.

Records

In Chapter 2, I discussed the desirability of having a record containing the name of a student and his or her scores on up to 20 tests. There are 30 students in the class. Fortran does not support records directly, but they can be simulated using the concept of *parallel arrays*. Using this concept, the corresponding elements of several arrays together comprise a record. The correspondence is by subscript, so the third record consists of the elements with subscript 3 from the arrays that make of the record.

Here is how the arrays comprising the record for the example of Chapter 2 would be declared in Fortran:

```
INTEGER NAME(30,5)
REAL SCORE(30,20)
```

The first subscript of each array corresponds to the student number (recall that there are 30 students in the class). The second subscript of the INTEGER array NAME is 5. This array will be used to hold the student names, and with six characters per array element, there will be room for up to 30 characters in each student's name.

Suppose you wish to write the name of the fourth student and his or her score on the first test. Reading or writing a student's name presents an interesting problem. The solution is to use an implied DO loop. The required information is written as follows:

```
      WRITE (1,200) (NAME(4,J), J = 1,5),
    1      SCORE(4,1)
  200 FORMAT (5A6, F6.2)
```

This will write the desired information, all on one line.

Initializing a two-dimensional array such as NAME with a DATA statement should not be attempted. Fortran stores its arrays by columns, so the DATA statement would have to first list the first 6 characters of the first name, the first 6 characters of the second name, and so on. The array is best initialized with a READ statement.

The last two programs of this chapter contain actual examples of the usage of records in Fortran programs.

Linked Lists

The concept of linked lists was discussed extensively in Chapter 2. This section discusses how linked lists can be implemented in Fortran using parallel arrays. The implementation is nearly the same as described in Chapter 2, except that a two-dimensional array is needed to hold the names. This array is manipulated as discussed in the preceding section.

The Fortran declarations to set up the linked list are as follows:

```
    INTEGER EOL, NAME(5,3), FIRST, FREE,
1       LINK(5)
    DATA EOL/0/
```

This allows for five names in the list. **EOL** stands for End-Of-List and is used to indicate that no more records follow in the list.

The comprehensive sample program at the end of the chapter illustrates the use of linked lists in an actual Fortran program and shows the details of how elements are added to and deleted from a linked list.

FILE HANDLING

Microcomputer programs are frequently required to store data in files on floppy disks. Fortran does well in this regard, except for the difficulties of character handling, as discussed above.

Standard Fortran handles only sequential files, but most implementations, including Nevada Fortran, have provision for direct-access files as well. Unfortunately these provisions vary between implementations.

A file in Fortran is a sequence of records. The extent of a record is determined by the **FORMAT** statement used to write to the file. Each record is separated by a carriage return/line feed pair.

Although it is possible to create binary or unformatted files in Fortran, most files are formatted. A formatted file is written under the control of a **FORMAT** statement; all numbers are converted to characters before being written to the file.

Each Fortran file has associated with it a *unit number.* Earlier you saw that unit numbers 0 and 1 are reserved for console input and output, respectively. Other unit numbers are available for printer and file output. Nevada Fortran supports unit numbers 0 to 7. Other versions of Fortran may support more unit numbers.

A unit number is associated with an external file by the **OPEN** subroutine. (In some versions of Fortran, **OPEN** is a Fortran statement, not a subroutine.) The following would open the file **TEST.TXT** as unit 4:

```
    CALL OPEN (4, 'TEST.TXT')
```

If the user wishes to check for an error in opening the file, a third parameter is needed. Suppose **IERR** is an integer variable. Then following

```
    CALL OPEN (4, 'TEST.TXT', IERR)
```

would be the call. Following this call, an examination of the value of **IERR** would reveal whether or not the file was opened successfully. The value 0 means a successful open, and the values 1 through 7 indicate various kinds of errors. (Such details are found in the language manual that accompanies a compiler.)

After a file has been opened and written to, the **ENDFILE** command is used to mark the end of the file, as in

    ENDFILE 4

which puts an end-of-file mark (Control-Zs in CP/M) in the unit 4 file. The file is closed by the following:

    CALL CLOSE (4)

File Records

Earlier, I mentioned that a **FORMAT** statement determines the extent of a Fortran file record. Suppose that you wish to create a file consisting of the name and age of several individuals. Allow space for 24 characters in the name and three digits in the age. The **FORMAT** statement for reading and writing such a file would look as follows:

    200 FORMAT (4A6, I3)

The **4A6** file descriptor allocates 24 spaces—six for each of four integer variables.

The following declarations would define appropriate variables:

    INTEGER NAME(4), AGE

A statement to write to the file might look like this:

    WRITE (4, 200) NAME, AGE

This **WRITE** statement would output one record. The record length would be 29 characters: 24 for **NAME**, three for **AGE**, and two for the carriage-return/line-feed pair at the end.

Sequential Files

Now suppose you wish to create a sequential file consisting of the names and ages of several individuals. The file will be sequential because the records will be written in sequence, one after another, and retrieved the same way. The previous section has already shown how each record of the file can be laid out.

The basic steps to be followed in creating the file are to open the file, write out the records, write an end-of-file mark, and close the file.

The program in Fig. 8-16 demonstrates the use of such a file. The file is created using data from the keyboard. It is then closed and reopened for input. The data is read back from the file in sequence.

```
C       Figure 8-16:   Create a Sequential File of Names and Ages.
C
        INTEGER NAME(4), AGE
C
        CALL OPEN (2, 'B:AGES.TXT')
        WRITE (1,*) 'ENTER NAMES & AGES; <RETURN> TO QUIT:'
   10   WRITE (1,*)
C       GET DATA FROM KEYBOARD
        WRITE (1,*) 'NAME:'
        READ  (0,210) NAME
        IF (NAME(1) .EQ. '        ') GO TO 20
        WRITE (1,*) 'AGE:'
        READ  (0,*) AGE
C       WRITE ONE RECORD TO THE FILE
        WRITE (2,200) NAME, AGE
        GO TO 10
   20   CONTINUE
C       CLOSE FILE AND REOPEN FOR INPUT
        ENDFILE 2
        CALL CLOSE (2)
        CALL OPEN (2, 'B:AGES.TXT')
        WRITE (1,*)
        WRITE (1,*) 'HERE ARE THE NAMES AND AGES FROM THE FILE.'
        WRITE (1,*)
C       READ IN RECORDS IN SEQUENCE
   30   READ (2,200,END=40) NAME, AGE
C       DISPLAY ON SCREEN
        WRITE (1,200) NAME, AGE
        GO TO 30
   40   CONTINUE
        CALL CLOSE (2)
        STOP
  200   FORMAT (4A6, I3)
  210   FORMAT (4A6)
        END
```

Fig. 8-16. Creating a sequential file of names and ages.

In the keyboard input section, the program checks for a blank name (signifying that the user entered a carriage return when prompted for a name), and terminates keyboard input when it is found.

The loop used to read the file back in deserves closer scrutiny. In the statement numbered 30 in Fig. 8-16, the END = 40 parameter causes a GO TO 40 to be executed when the program tries to read past the end of the file. It is a convenient way to implement loops for input from a file. The structure of the loop resembles that of a WHILE loop.

Direct-Access Files

Often it is convenient to have direct access to specific records of a file without having to read the file sequentially. As mentioned earlier, standard Fortran does not provide for direct-access files, but most implementations of Fortran do. The method of handling direct-access files discussed in this chapter is that implemented in Nevada Fortran. Direct-access files may be handled differently in different versions of Fortran.

Nevada Fortran uses the SEEK subroutine to implement direct access. The following is a sample call to SEEK:

```
CALL SEEK (UNIT, DISPL)
```

The UNIT parameter is the unit number associated with the file when it was opened. The DISPL parameter is the relative displacement from the beginning of the file in bytes or characters. Note that this is different from the Pascal SEEK command, which computes the displacement in terms of records, not characters.

In order to use SEEK, it is necessary for the program to keep track of the position in the file of each record. Suppose that a file record is defined by the following FORMAT statement:

```
200 FORMAT (21A6)
```

The record length for this file record is 128 bytes. This is computed as $(21 * 6 = 126)$ plus an allowance for the carriage return and line feed.

Suppose DISPL, RECLEN and RECNR have been declared as integers. The following sequence will compute the displacement for record number (RECNR) 5 of the file:

```
RECLEN = 128
RECNR = 5
DISPL = (RECNR – 1) * RECLEN
```

Notice that the displacement for the first record of the file is zero.

It is convenient, though not always necessary, to allocate space for a direct-access file by writing the file initially as a sequential file, possibly with blank records. This practice is illustrated in the program in Fig. 8-17, which sets up the files for the comprehensive sample program a little later in the chapter.

The direct-access file to be set up is called B:ADDRESS.TXT. The other file created by this program will be discussed later.

Use of a direct-access file in an actual program is illustrated in the comprehensive sample program which follows.

GRAPHICS

Fortran does not support graphics.

THE COMPREHENSIVE SAMPLE PROGRAM

The sample programs thus far in this chapter have been relatively short. Each has been intended to illustrate a particular idea, such as how to use a counted loop in Fortran.

```
C       Figure 8-17:   Initialize a File for Direct Access.
C
C       Set up for the Address Book Program
C
        INTEGER NREC, C, I, EOL
        DATA EOL/0/
C
        WRITE (1,*) 'WARNING:  THIS PROGRAM INITIALIZES B:ADDRESS.TXT.'
        WRITE (1,*) 'IT WILL DESTROY AN EXISTING B:ADDRESS.TXT.'
        WRITE (1,*)
        WRITE (1,*) 'DO YOU WISH TO CONTINUE? (Y/N)'
        READ  (0,100) C
        IF ((C .NE. 'Y      ') .AND. (C .NE. 'y      ')) GO TO 999
        WRITE (1,*) 'HOW MANY RECORDS SHOULD BE ALLOCATED?'
        READ  (0,*) NREC
        CALL OPEN (2, 'B:ADDRESS.TXT')
        DO 10 I = 1, NREC
C           OUTPUT A DUMMY RECORD
            WRITE (2,200)
     10 CONTINUE
        ENDFILE 2
        CALL CLOSE (2)
C       NOW CREATE THE INDEX FILE
        CALL OPEN (3, 'B:INDEX.TXT')
C       WRITE INDEX OF FIRST ACTIVE RECORD (EOL = END OF LIST)
        WRITE (3,210) EOL
C       WRITE INDEX OF FIRST RECORD IN FREE LIST
        I = 1
        WRITE (3,210) I
C       BUILD THE CHAIN OF FREE RECORDS (FREE LIST)
        DO 20 I = 2, NREC
            WRITE (3,210) I
     20 CONTINUE
C       MARK THE END OF THE FREE LIST
        WRITE (3,210) EOL
C       MARK THE END OF THE INDEX FILE
        ENDFILE 3
        CALL CLOSE (3)
    999 STOP
    100 FORMAT (A1)
    200 FORMAT (102X)
    210 FORMAT (I4)
        END
```

Fig. 8-17. Initializing a file for direct access.

Short programs are well-suited for that purpose; in fact, short programs are all that are found in many programming texts. Unfortunately, short programs do not convey adequately the flavor of real Fortran programs.

Real Fortran programs, that is, Fortran programs written for other than instructional purposes, tend to be longer than those seen so far in this chapter, and they tend to contain numerous subroutines. Because the primary purpose of this chapter is to illustrate the flavor of the Fortran language, a longer programming example is appropriate.

This longer program maintains an ordered file of names and addresses on disk. It functions as an electronic address book, providing the ability to add, display, and delete names. Names may be displayed on the video screen or listed on a printer.

This program is perhaps not the best choice to demonstrate the strengths of Fortran, because it involves string manipulation and not much numerical computation. It does, however, provide an excellent example of the construction of a long, complex application from a series of relatively short subroutines. In addition, it provides a good means for comparing Fortran to other languages, as a similar program is included in most of the other language chapters.

The basic data structure used to maintain the names in alphabetical order is the linked list. This data structure was described extensively in Chapter 2. The program uses a direct-access file to store the names and addresses and a sequential file to store the links.

A separate program, shown in Fig. 8-17, is used to initialize these files. The address file itself is initialized to blank records, while the index file is initialized to contain the appropriate pointers for an empty list. Note that the address file is initialized using sequential access, even though it will be used as a direct-access file later.

When the setup program is run for the first time, the user should respond ''10'' when asked how many records to allocate. This will match the initial configuration of the following program, as discussed below.

The comprehensive sample program itself is shown in Fig. 8-18. A structure chart that shows the hierarchical organization of the program is given in Fig. 8-19. In this chart the subroutines called by the main program are listed below the main program at the first level of indentation. Subroutines called by another subroutine are indented another level and listed below the calling subroutine.

Notice that the main program is relatively short. Its primary function is to call the subroutines in the proper sequence. It uses system subroutines to open the files; then it reads the index file into memory. The main loop calls the menu subroutine and then passes control to the appropriate subroutine, depending on the menu item selected. When the user chooses the QUIT option, the address file is closed, and the index file is saved to disk and closed.

As described in Chapter 2, active records in the file are maintained in order using a linked list called the *active list,* and inactive records are maintained in a linked list called the *free list.* As mentioned earlier, the links are read into and maintained in main memory while the program is running. When the program terminates, the links are written back to a sequential file. The names and addresses themselves are maintained in the direct-access file, not in main memory. This makes possible the maintenance of a much longer file than would be possible if the names and addresses were all maintained in main memory.

The free list is maintained using a method that is slightly different than the one discussed in Chapter 2 and implemented in the other chapters. Records deleted from the file are not automatically returned to the free list. The subroutine PUTFRE, which would ordinarily perform this function, has been modified to do nothing by making most of its statements into comments (C in column 1). The reason for this is that a bug in the Nevada Fortran compiler causes damage to the file during direct-access writes to other than the last active record of the file.

To permit the eventual reutilization of deleted records, a subroutine called REORG

```
C       Figure 8-18:  Comprehensive Sample Program.
C
C
CCCCCCCCCCCCCCCCCCCCCCCCCCCCCCCCCCCCCCCCCCCCCCCCCCCCCCCCCCCCCCCCCC
C                                                                C
C    PROGRAM:  ADDRESS BOOK                                      C
C                                                                C
C       Maintains an ordered file of names and addresses.  The program  C
C       in Figure 8-17 must be run to initialize the files before       C
C       this program is run for the first time.                 C
C                                                                C
C       File size is now set to 0010 records.  To expand, you must      C
C       modify the value of MAXREC and the dimension of the array       C
C       LINK.                                                    C
C                                                                C
CCCCCCCCCCCCCCCCCCCCCCCCCCCCCCCCCCCCCCCCCCCCCCCCCCCCCCCCCCCCCCCCCC
C
        INTEGER MAXREC, RECLEN, LINK(10), FIRST, FREE, EOL, RECNR,
     1    C, I, P, Q, R, F1(3), F2(3), IER
        DATA MAXREC /10/, EOL /0/, F1 /'B:ADDRESS.TXT     '/,
     1    F2 /'B:INDEX.TXT       '/, RECLEN /104/
C
        CALL CLEAR
        WRITE (1,*) 'WELCOME TO YOUR ADDRESS BOOK.'
        WRITE (1,*)
        WRITE (1,*) 'INITIALIZING...'
C       OPEN FILES AND INITIALIZE PRINTER
        CALL OPEN (2, F1)
        CALL OPEN (4, 'LST:')
C       OPEN AND READ IN INDEX FILE
        CALL GETINX (LINK, MAXREC, FIRST, FREE, F2)
C       MAIN LOOP
C       REPEAT
      5 CONTINUE
          CALL MENU (C)
          IF ((C .LT. 1) .OR. (C .GT. 6)) GO TO 5
C         EMULATE CASE STATEMENT
          GO TO (10, 20, 30, 40, 50, 60), C
     10   CONTINUE
            CALL APPEND (FIRST, FREE, RECLEN, LINK, MAXREC, EOL)
            GO TO 70
     20   CONTINUE
            CALL REVIEW (FIRST, EOL, MAXREC, LINK, RECLEN, FREE)
            GO TO 70
     30   CONTINUE
            CALL LIST (FIRST, EOL, MAXREC, LINK, RECLEN)
            GO TO 70
     40   CONTINUE
            CALL REORG (FIRST, FREE, EOL, MAXREC, LINK, RECLEN, F2)
            GO TO 70
     50   CONTINUE
            CALL DUMP (FIRST, FREE, MAXREC, LINK, RECLEN)
            GO TO 70
     60   CONTINUE
            WRITE (1,*) 'CLOSING FILES....'
     70   CONTINUE
```

Fig. 8-18. Comprehensive sample program.

```
C         END CASE
          IF (C .NE. 6) GO TO 5
C         UNTIL (C .EQ. 6)
C         CLEAN UP
          CALL CLOSE (2)
C         SAVE AND CLOSE INDEX FILE
          CALL SAVINX (LINK, MAXREC, FIRST, FREE, F2)
          STOP
          END
C
      SUBROUTINE GETINX (LINK, N, FIRST, FREE, FN)
C         READ INDEX FILE
          INTEGER N, LINK(N), FIRST, FREE, FN(3), I
          CALL OPEN (3, FN)
          READ (3, 200) FIRST
          READ (3, 200) FREE
C         NOW READ IN THE ARRAY LINK
          I = 1
   10     READ (3, 200, END=99) LINK(I)
              I = I + 1
              IF (I .GT. (N + 1)) THEN
                  WRITE (1,*) 'WARNING... INDEX FILE TOO BIG.'
                  GO TO 99
              END IF
              GO TO 10
   99     CONTINUE
          CALL CLOSE (3)
          RETURN
  200     FORMAT (I4)
      END
C
      SUBROUTINE SAVINX (LINK, N, FIRST, FREE, FN)
C         SAVE INDEX FILE
          INTEGER N, LINK(N), FIRST, FREE, FN(3), I
          CALL OPEN (3, FN)
          WRITE (3, 200) FIRST
          WRITE (3, 200) FREE
          DO 10 I = 1, N
              WRITE (3, 200) LINK(I)
   10     CONTINUE
          ENDFILE 3
          CALL CLOSE (3)
          RETURN
  200     FORMAT (I4)
      END
C
      SUBROUTINE MENU (C)
C         DISPLAY MENU AND RETURN CHOICE
          INTEGER C, ROW, COL
          CALL CLEAR
          ROW = 5
          COL = 5
          CALL GOTOXY (COL, ROW)
          WRITE (1,*) '1)  ADD TO FILE'
          ROW = ROW + 2
          CALL GOTOXY (COL, ROW)
          WRITE (1,*) '2)  REVIEW FILE ON SCREEN'
          ROW = ROW + 2
          CALL GOTOXY (COL, ROW)
```

```
                 WRITE (1,*) '3)   LIST FILE TO SCREEN OR PRINTER'
                 ROW = ROW + 2
                 CALL GOTOXY (COL, ROW)
                 WRITE (1,*) '4)   REORGANIZE FILE'
                 ROW = ROW + 2
                 CALL GOTOXY (COL, ROW)
                 WRITE (1,*) '5)   DUMP FILE TO PRINTER'
                 ROW = ROW + 2
                 CALL GOTOXY (COL, ROW)
                 WRITE (1,*) '6)   QUIT'
                 ROW = ROW + 2
                 COL = 1
       10        CALL GOTOXY (COL, ROW)
                 WRITE (1,*) 'SELECT 1, 2, 3, 4, 5, OR 6:'
                 READ  (0,*) C
                 IF ((C .LT. 1) .OR. (C .GT. 6)) GO TO 10
                 RETURN
           END
C
           SUBROUTINE APPEND (FIRST, FREE, RECLEN, LINK, N, EOL)
C          ADD RECORDS TO THE FILE IN THE PROPER ORDER
                 INTEGER LNAME(2), FNAME(2), ADDR(4), CITY(3), STATE,
        1            ZIP(2), PHONE(3), FIRST, FREE, N, LINK(N), EOL,
        2            ROW, COL, RECNR, RECLEN
       10        CALL CLEAR
                 IF (FREE .EQ. EOL) THEN
                       WRITE (1,*) 'NO ROOM REMAINING IN THE FILE....'
                       CALL WAIT
                       GO TO 99
                 ENDIF
C          DISPLAY SKELETONIZED FORM ON SCREEN
                 ROW = 5
                 COL = 1
                 CALL GOTOXY (COL, ROW)
                 WRITE (1,*) 'LAST NAME     :              :'
                 ROW = ROW + 2
                 CALL GOTOXY (COL, ROW)
                 WRITE (1,*) 'FIRST NAME    :              :'
                 ROW = ROW + 2
                 CALL GOTOXY (COL, ROW)
                 WRITE (1,*) 'ADDRESS       :                  :'
                 ROW = ROW + 2
                 CALL GOTOXY (COL, ROW)
                 WRITE (1,*) 'CITY          :                :'
                 ROW = ROW + 2
                 CALL GOTOXY (COL, ROW)
                 WRITE (1,*) 'STATE         :  :'
                 ROW = ROW + 2
                 CALL GOTOXY (COL, ROW)
                 WRITE (1,*) 'ZIP CODE      :           :'
                 ROW = ROW + 2
                 CALL GOTOXY (COL, ROW)
                 WRITE (1,*) 'PHONE NR      :               :'
C          READ DATA FROM SCREEN
                 ROW = 5
                 COL = 15
                 CALL GOTOXY (COL, ROW)
```

Fig. 8-18. Comprehensive sample program. (Continued from page 257.)

```
                     READ (0,200) LNAME
                     IF (LNAME(1) .EQ. '        ') GO TO 99
                     ROW = ROW + 2
                     CALL GOTOXY (COL, ROW)
                     READ (0,200) FNAME
                     ROW = ROW + 2
                     CALL GOTOXY (COL, ROW)
                     READ (0,200) ADDR
                     ROW = ROW + 2
                     CALL GOTOXY (COL, ROW)
                     READ (0,200) CITY
                     ROW = ROW + 2
                     CALL GOTOXY (COL, ROW)
                     READ (0,200) STATE
                     ROW = ROW + 2
                     CALL GOTOXY (COL, ROW)
                     READ (0,200) ZIP
                     ROW = ROW + 2
                     CALL GOTOXY (COL, ROW)
                     READ (0,200) PHONE
C          FIND FREE RECORD AND WRITE TO DISK
                     CALL GETFRE (RECNR, FREE, LINK, N)
                     CALL PUTREC (RECNR, RECLEN, LNAME, FNAME, ADDR, CITY,
      1                   STATE, ZIP, PHONE)
C          INSERT IN INDEX
                     CALL INSERT (LNAME, FNAME, RECNR, RECLEN, N, LINK,
      1                   EOL, FIRST)
                     GO TO 10
   99          RETURN
  200          FORMAT (4A6)
         END
C
      SUBROUTINE GETFRE(RECNR, FREE, LINK, N)
C          FIND NEXT FREE RECORD AND REMOVE FROM FREE LIST
               INTEGER RECNR, FREE, N, LINK(N)
               RECNR = FREE
               FREE =  LINK (FREE)
               RETURN
         END
C
      SUBROUTINE INSERT (LNAME, FNAME, RECNR, RECLEN, N, LINK,
      1          EOL, FIRST)
C          INSERT RECNR IN INDEX IN PROPER ORDER
               INTEGER LNAME(2), FNAME(2), RECNR, N, LINK(N), EOL, FIRST,
      1            LNB(2), FNB(2), DA(4), DC(3), DS, DZ(2), DP(3), I,
      2            P, Q, RECB, RECLEN
               LOGICAL FLAG
C          LNB, FNB ARE BUFFERS FOR TEMPORARILY STORING LNAME, FNAME
C          DA, DC, ETC. ARE DUMMY VARIABLES FOR HOLDING ADDR, CITY, ETC.
C
C          MOVE NAMES TO BUFFERS
               DO 10 I = 1, 2
                     LNB(I)  = LNAME(I)
                     FNB(I)  = FNAME(I)
   10          CONTINUE
               RECB = RECNR
C          FIND PROPER PLACE IN LIST AND ADJUST LINKS
               IF (FIRST .EQ. EOL) THEN
C                    LIST WAS PREVIOUSLY EMPTY
```

```
                        LINK(RECB) = EOL
                        FIRST      = RECB
                        GO TO 99
                ELSE
                        P = FIRST
                        Q = EOL
                ENDIF
      20        CALL GETREC (P, RECLEN, LNAME, FNAME, DA, DC, DS, DZ, DP)
                CALL COMPAR (LNAME, FNAME, LNB, FNB, FLAG)
C               RETURNS .TRUE. IF LNAME,FNAME .LT. LNB, FNB
                IF (FLAG) THEN
                        Q = P
                        P = LINK(P)
                        IF (P .NE. EOL) THEN
                                GO TO 20
                        ENDIF
                ENDIF
C               AT THIS POINT, Q POINTS TO PREDECESSOR OF BUFFER NAME
C                       AND P POINTS TO ITS SUCCESSOR
                LINK(RECB) = P
                IF (Q .EQ. EOL) THEN
                        FIRST = RECB
                ELSE
                        LINK(Q) = RECB
                ENDIF
      99        RETURN
        END
C
        SUBROUTINE COMPAR (LNAME, FNAME, LNB, FNB, FLAG)
C               RETURN .TRUE. IF NAME .LT. BUFFER NAME.
C               USES SYSTEM-SUPPLIED SUBROUTINE COMP, WHICH
C               RETURNS -1, 0, 1 DEPENDING ON WHETHER FIRST
C               STRING IS .LT., .EQ., OR .GT. SECOND STRING.
                INTEGER LNAME(2), FNAME(2), LNB(2), FNB(2), RESULT
                LOGICAL FLAG
C
                RESULT = COMP (LNAME, LNB, 12)
                IF (RESULT .EQ. 1) THEN
                  FLAG = .FALSE.
                ELSE
                  IF (RESULT .EQ. -1) THEN
                    FLAG = .TRUE.
                  ELSE
                    RESULT = COMP (FNAME, FNB, 12)
                    IF (RESULT .EQ. 1) THEN
                      FLAG = .FALSE.
                    ELSE
                      FLAG = .TRUE.
                    ENDIF
                  ENDIF
                ENDIF
                RETURN
        END
C
        SUBROUTINE REVIEW (FIRST, EOL, N, LINK, RECLEN, FREE)
C               REVIEW RECORDS ON THE SCREEN, 1 AT A TIME.
                INTEGER FIRST, EOL, R, Q, UNIT, C, N, LINK(N), RECLEN,
```

Fig. 8-18. Comprehensive sample program. (Continued from page 259.)

```
      1          FREE
           CALL CLEAR
           WRITE (1,*) 'REVIEWING FILE...'
           WRITE (1,*)
           IF (FIRST .EQ. EOL) THEN
                  WRITE (1,*) 'NO RECORDS TO REVIEW...'
                  GO TO 99
           ENDIF
           UNIT = 1
C          UNIT 1 IS THE SCREEN
           R = FIRST
           Q = EOL
C          REPEAT
   10      CONTINUE
                  CALL PRTREC (UNIT, R, RECLEN)
                  WRITE (UNIT,*)
                  WRITE (UNIT,*) 'SELECT'
                  WRITE (UNIT,*) '    1) GET NEXT RECORD'
                  WRITE (UNIT,*) '    2) DELETE THIS RECORD'
                  WRITE (UNIT,*) '    3) QUIT'
                  READ  (0,*) C
                  IF (C .EQ. 1) THEN
C                         GET NEXT RECORD
                          Q = R
                          R = LINK (R)
                  ELSE
                          IF (C .EQ. 2) THEN
C                                 DELETE THIS RECORD
                                  IF (Q .EQ. EOL) THEN
                                          FIRST = LINK(R)
                                          CALL PUTFRE (R,LINK,N,FREE)
                                          R = FIRST
                                  ELSE
                                          LINK(Q) = LINK(R)
                                          CALL PUTFRE (R,LINK,N,FREE)
                                          R = LINK(Q)
                                  ENDIF
                          ENDIF
                  ENDIF
           IF ((R .NE. EOL) .AND. (C .NE. 3)) GO TO 10
C          UNTIL ((R .EQ. EOL) .OR. (C .EQ. 3))
   99      CALL WAIT
           RETURN
      END
C
      SUBROUTINE PUTFRE (R, LINK, N, FREE)
C         PUT RECORD BACK IN THE FREE LIST.
C         THIS SUBROUTINE DISABLED BECAUSE OF A BUG IN THE
C         NEVADA FORTRAN COMPILER WHICH DOES NOT ALLOW REUSE
C         OF DELETED RECORDS IN THE MIDDLE OF THE FILE.
C
C         INTEGER R, N, LINK(N), FREE
C         LINK(R) = FREE
C         FREE    = R
          RETURN
      END
C
      SUBROUTINE LIST (FIRST, EOL, N, LINK, RECLEN)
          INTEGER FIRST, EOL, C, UNIT, N, LINK(N), RECLEN
```

```
C              LIST ALL RECORDS TO THE SCREEN OR PRINTER
               CALL CLEAR
               IF (FIRST .EQ. EOL) THEN
                   WRITE (1,*) 'NO RECORDS IN FILE TO LIST...'
                   GO TO 99
               ENDIF
      10       WRITE (1,*) 'LIST FILE TO 1) SCREEN OR 2) PRINTER?'
               READ (0,*) C
               IF ((C .LT. 1) .OR. (C .GT. 2)) GO TO 10
               IF (C .EQ. 2) THEN
                   UNIT = 4
C                  PRINTER
               ELSE
                   UNIT = 1
C                  SCREEN
               ENDIF
               R = FIRST
C              REPEAT
      20       CONTINUE
                   WRITE (UNIT, *)
                   CALL PRTREC (UNIT, R, RECLEN)
                   R = LINK (R)
               IF (R .NE. EOL) GO TO 20
C              UNTIL (R .EQ. EOL)
               WRITE (UNIT, *)
      99       CALL WAIT
               RETURN
        END
C
        SUBROUTINE REORG (FIRST, FREE, EOL, MAXREC, LINK, RECLEN, F2)
C           REORGANIZE FILES TO ELIMINATE DELETED RECORDS.
C           REORG USES IMPLEMENTATION-SPECIFIC SUBROUTINES.
            INTEGER FIRST, FREE, EOL, MAXREC, LINK(MAXREC), N,
     1          F2(3), R, RECLEN, DISPL, I, LNAME(2),
     2          FNAME(2), ADDR(4), CITY(3), STATE, ZIP(2), PHONE(3)
C         COPY FILE IN SEQUENCE TO A SCRATCH FILE, THEN BACK TO ITSELF
            CALL OPEN (5, 'SCRATCH.TXT')
            R = FIRST
      10    IF (R .EQ. EOL) GO TO 20
                DISPL = (R - 1)*RECLEN
                CALL SEEK (2, DISPL)
                READ  (2,100,END=20) LNAME,FNAME,ADDR,CITY,STATE,ZIP,
     1                PHONE
                WRITE (5,100) LNAME,FNAME,ADDR,CITY,STATE,ZIP,PHONE
                R = LINK(R)
                GO TO 10
      20    CONTINUE
            ENDFILE 5
C         REINITIALIZE LINKS
            FREE = 1
            FIRST = EOL
            N = MAXREC - 1
            DO 30 I = 1, N
                LINK(I) = I + 1
      30    CONTINUE
            LINK(MAXREC) = EOL
C         COPY BACK TO THE ORIGINAL FILE & RE-INSERT IN INDEX
```

Fig. 8-18. Comprehensive sample program. (Continued from page 261.)

```
            REWIND 5
   40       READ (5,100,END=50) LNAME,FNAME,ADDR,CITY,STATE,ZIP,PHONE
               CALL GETFRE (R, FREE, LINK, MAXREC)
               CALL PUTREC (R, RECLEN, LNAME, FNAME, ADDR, CITY,
     1                 STATE, ZIP, PHONE)
               CALL INSERT (LNAME, FNAME, R, RECLEN, MAXREC, LINK,
     1                 EOL, FIRST)
               GO TO 40
   50       CONTINUE
            CALL CLOSE (5)
            CALL DELETE ('SCRATCH.TXT')
C        SAVE INDEX
            CALL SAVINX (LINK, MAXREC, FIRST, FREE, F2)
            RETURN
  100       FORMAT (2A6, 2A6, 4A6, 3A6, A6, 2A6, 3A6)
        END
C
        SUBROUTINE DUMP (FIRST, FREE, N, LINK, RECLEN)
            INTEGER LNAME(2), FNAME(2), ADDR(4), CITY(3), STATE,
     1            ZIP(2), PHONE(3), FIRST, FREE, N, LINK(N),
     2            RECLEN, I
            CALL CLEAR
            WRITE (1,*) 'DUMPING FILE TO PRINTER...'
            WRITE (4,200) FIRST, FREE
            WRITE (4,*)
            DO 10 I = 1, N
               WRITE (4,210) I
               CALL PRTREC(4, I, RECLEN)
               WRITE (4,220) LINK(I)
               WRITE (4,*)
   10       CONTINUE
            RETURN
  200       FORMAT ('FIRST ACTIVE RECORD: ', I4,
     1            ' FIRST FREE RECORD:  ', I4)
  210       FORMAT ('RECORD NUMBER: ', I4)
  220       FORMAT ('LINK: ', I4)
        END
C
        SUBROUTINE PRTREC (UNIT, RECNR, RECLEN)
C          PRINT RECORD RECNR TO CONSOLE OR PRINTER, DEPENDING ON
C          THE VALUE OF "UNIT".  GETS THE RECORD FROM DISK.
            INTEGER UNIT, RECNR, LNAME(2), FNAME(2), ADDR(4), CITY(3),
     1            STATE, ZIP(2), PHONE(3), RECLEN
            CALL GETREC(RECNR, RECLEN, LNAME, FNAME, ADDR, CITY,
     1            STATE, ZIP, PHONE)
            WRITE (UNIT, 200) FNAME, LNAME, ADDR, CITY, STATE,
     1            ZIP, PHONE
  200       FORMAT (2A6, 1X, 2A6 / 4A6 / 3A6, 1X, A2, 1X 2A6 /
     1               3A6)
            RETURN
        END
C
        SUBROUTINE GETREC (RECNR, RECLEN, LNAME, FNAME, ADDR,
     1      CITY, STATE, ZIP, PHONE)
C          READS RECORD NUMBER RECNR FROM FILE
            INTEGER RECNR, RECLEN, LNAME(2), FNAME(2), ADDR(4),
     1            CITY(3), STATE, ZIP(2), PHONE(3), IER, DISPL
            DISPL = (RECNR - 1)*RECLEN
            CALL SEEK (2, DISPL, IER)
```

```
              IF (IER .NE. 0) THEN
                    WRITE (1,*) 'WARNING:  SEEK ERROR IN GETREC.'
                    WRITE (1,*) 'IER   = ', IER
                    WRITE (1,*) 'RECNR = ', RECNR
                    STOP
              ENDIF
              READ (2,200) LNAME, FNAME, ADDR, CITY, STATE, ZIP, PHONE
              RETURN
    200       FORMAT (2A6, 2A6, 4A6, 3A6, A6, 2A6, 3A6)
C             SAME AS FORMAT (17A6)
        END
C
        SUBROUTINE PUTREC (RECNR, RECLEN, LNAME, FNAME, ADDR,
      1       CITY, STATE, ZIP, PHONE)
C             WRITES RECORD NUMBER RECNR TO FILE
              INTEGER RECNR, RECLEN, LNAME(2), FNAME(2), ADDR(4),
      1           CITY(3), STATE, ZIP(2), PHONE(3), IER, DISPL
              DISPL = (RECNR - 1)*RECLEN
              CALL SEEK (2, DISPL, IER)
              IF (IER .NE. 0) THEN
                    WRITE (1,*) 'WARNING: SEEK ERROR IN PUTREC.'
                    WRITE (1,*) 'IER   = ', IER
                    WRITE (1,*) 'RECNR = ', RECNR
                    STOP
              ENDIF
              WRITE (2,200) LNAME, FNAME, ADDR, CITY, STATE, ZIP, PHONE
              RETURN
    200       FORMAT (2A6, 2A6, 4A6, 3A6, A6, 2A6, 3A6)
        END
C
        SUBROUTINE CLEAR
C             CLEAR THE SCREEN (MACHINE-DEPENDENT)
C             PUT OUTPUTS A CHARACTER TO THE SCREEN GIVEN ITS ASCII VALUE
C             THIS SEQUENCE IS (ESC) "*"
              CALL PUT (27)
              CALL PUT (42)
              RETURN
        END
C
        SUBROUTINE GOTOXY (COL, ROW)
C             POSITION CURSOR AT NAMED COL & ROW (MACHINE-DEPENDENT)
C             THE LEAD-IN CHARACTERS ARE (ESC) "="
              INTEGER COL, ROW, X, Y
              CALL PUT (27)
              CALL PUT (61)
              Y = 31 + ROW
              X = 31 + COL
              CALL PUT (Y)
              CALL PUT (X)
              RETURN
        END
C
        SUBROUTINE WAIT
C          WAIT FOR (RETURN) FROM KEYBOARD
           INTEGER C
           WRITE (1,*) 'PRESS (RETURN) TO CONTINUE...'
           READ (0,200) C
```

Fig. 8-18. Comprehensive sample program. (Continued from page 263.)

```
      RETURN
200   FORMAT (A1)
      END
```

has been added to the list of options in the program menu. This subroutine reorganizes the file so that all active records are contiguous and in the proper order at the beginning of the file and so that all remaining records are in the free list. This is accomplished by first copying the active records in order (using the links) to a scratch file and then copying them back, using the appropriate subroutines to recreate the links. If you are using a different version of Fortran or a corrected version of Nevada Fortran, the reorganization option will not be necessary, provided that you remove the C in column 1 of the appropriate lines of the subroutine PUTFRE.

The subroutine COMPAR requires some comment. Because ANSI 1966 Fortran does not support character strings directly, the results of comparisons between character strings cannot always be predicted. It depends on the particular implementation. Accordingly, the designers of Nevada Fortran have provided a built-in function called COMP, which compares a specified number of characters of two character strings and returns -1, 0, or 1, depending on whether the first string is less than, equal to, or greater than the second string. Users of other versions of Fortran should check their documentation, because other versions might provide different solutions to this problem.

The program as written will only support a file of 10 records. This limitation was imposed in order to keep the output from the DUMP option to a reasonable length. This option has been provided in order to make it easy for the user to see the effects of adding and deleting records. If the user then wishes to expand the capacity of the file, it is necessary to do three things:

1. Run the program in Fig. 8-17 again to allocate more file space.
2. Change the dimension of the array LINK at the beginning of the main program of Fig. 8-18.
3. Change the value of the variable MAXREC in the DATA statement near the beginning of the main program.

Once these three things have been done, the program may be used to maintain an actual file of addresses.

ADVANTAGES AND DISADVANTAGES OF FORTRAN

The major strength of Fortran is the facility with which it handles numerical computations. It is particularly well-suited for scientific and engineering programs.

Fortran has a reputation for speed. While the speed might vary from implementation to implementation, a compiled Fortran program is virtually guaranteed to run much faster than the equivalent interpreted BASIC program.

Fortran is widely taught in colleges and universities. People who have learned Fortran on large computers will find the transition to Fortran on microcomputers easy.

A large volume of mathematical software has been written in Fortran and is available in the form of subroutine libraries in many large computer centers.

```
Figure 8-19:   Structure Chart for the Comprehensive Sample
               Program.

MAIN PROGRAM

     GETINX
     MENU
     APPEND
          GETFRE
          PUTREC
          INSERT
               GETREC
               COMPAR
     REVIEW
          PRTREC
          PUTFRE
     LIST
          PRTREC
               GETREC
     REORG
          GETFRE
          PUTREC
          INSERT
          SAVINX
     DUMP
          PRTREC
               GETREC
     SAVINX


Common Use Subroutines

     CLEAR
     GOTOXY
     WAIT
```

Fig. 8-19. Structure chart for the comprehensive sample program.

Modular programming is easy in Fortran because of the presence of subroutines and functions. It is easy to break large Fortran programs down into smaller pieces.

On the negative side, versions of Fortran prior to Fortran 77 lack direct support for character strings. Although character strings can be handled using **INTEGER** variables, as seen in the example programs, it is awkward to do so.

Some versions of Fortran lack the **IF-THEN-ELSE** construct. This construct was officially added effective with Fortran 77.

Fortran is notably weak in the area of control structures. It lacks a **WHILE** statement (conditional loop with the test at the top), a **REPEAT-UNTIL** statement (conditional loop with the test at the bottom), and a **CASE** statement. Although each of these constructs can be simulated using other Fortran statements, their absence is a disadvantage.

Fortran also lacks the ability to handle recursive subroutines and functions.

AVAILABILITY

Several versions of Fortran are available for microcomputers that run the MS-DOS or PC-DOS operating system. These include Microsoft Fortran ($450), by Microsoft Inc. of Redmond, Washington; RM/Fortran ($595), by Ryan-McFarland of Rolling Hills Estates, California; F77L (Lahey Fortran) ($477), by Lahey Computer Systems of Incline Village, Nevada; and Utah Fortran ($39.95), by Ellis Computing of Reno, Nevada. Offerings for the CP/M operating system include versions by Ellis Computing (Nevada Fortran) and Microsoft.

SUMMARY

Fortran is the oldest of high-level languages in wide use today. Its use is largely confined to minicomputers and mainframes. The reasons for this include the earlier availability of BASIC on microcomputers and the wide availability of more modern languages such as Pascal and C. There are a large number of applications, however, in which Fortran can be used to good advantage. These include applications involving intensive numerical computations, particularly when fast execution is required.

Fortran is similar enough in form to BASIC to make it easy for BASIC programmers to learn Fortran as a second language.

The fact that Fortran has been used so successfully by so many for so long is reason enough for it to warrant consideration for use on microcomputers.

Ada
BASIC
C
COBOL
Forth
Fortran
LISP
Logo
Modula-2
Pascal
PILOT
Prolog

9

LISP

The LISP language was developed about 1960 by a group headed by Professor John McCarthy at the Massachusetts Institute of Technology. LISP is about the same age as COBOL; of the languages in general use today, only Fortran is older than LISP and COBOL. That these languages have survived for so long is a tribute to the farsightedness of their progenitors.

Some interesting details about the original design of LISP can be found in an important paper describing LISP entitled ''Recursive Functions of Symbolic Expressions,'' published by Professor McCarthy in the April 1960 issue of *Communications of the Association for Computing Machinery* (CACM). That article relates that LISP (like Fortran) was originally designed for the IBM 704 computer and that (again like Fortran) certain of its characteristics can be traced to the hardware details of the IBM 704 computer. For example, two of the most commonly used LISP functions are called **CAR** and **CDR**. **CAR** stands for Contents of the Address part of the Register. **CDR** stands for Contents of the Decrement part of the Register. What these functions do will be described in detail in the appropriate section of this chapter; it is by no means obvious outside the context of the IBM 704.

The name ''LISP'' is a blend that stands for LISt Processor. LISP was developed for use in research in the area of artificial intelligence, and it is still the principal language of choice in that field in the United States. In recent years, Prolog has also become an important language in the area of artificial intelligence, particularly in Europe and in Japan.

Professor McCarthy has since moved to Stanford University. It is no coincidence that two of the world's most advanced centers for research in artificial intelligence are located where Professor McCarthy has done most of his work, at Stanford and at MIT.

The field of artificial intelligence is beyond the scope of this book. This chapter will attempt to portray the nature of LISP in other contexts.

LISP tends to divide people into two groups: insiders and outsiders. To the insiders, LISP is the greatest language ever conceived. To the outsiders, it is mysterious at best. Some of the aura of mystery stems from the unusual vocabulary of LISP which, as you have seen, includes some historical anachronisms. LISP is also very different from the more conventional languages such as Fortran, BASIC, and Pascal. Once you get beyond appearances, however, LISP is really a very simple and consistent language. Once a few basic concepts are mastered, the language is easy to learn.

LISP is at its best in applications that require the manipulation of symbols, whether they be words, numbers, sentences, or whatever. It supports data structures of arbitrary complexity, facilitating the organization of information for easy retrieval. It also has the capability of performing numerical computations, but it is clearly not the language of choice for such applications.

LISP was originally designed as a batch language. Programs were to be entered into the computer via punched cards and the output received via printout. The design of the language, however, is much better suited to today's interactive environment. LISP functions can be entered directly via the keyboard and results received via the video screen.

LISP is usually implemented as an interpreted language. The language is easily extended and modified. As a result, several dialects of LISP have grown up and come into common use. The programs in this chapter were tested on an Apple II Plus microcomputer (with Z80 Softcard) using the MuLISP interpreter once distributed by Microsoft, Incorporated. (MuLISP is now distributed by Soft Warehouse of Honolulu, Hawaii.) Several of the keywords were modified so as to more closely resemble "standard" LISP.

LISP PROGRAMS AND FUNCTIONS

The basic building blocks of LISP are data, expressions, and functions. The subject of data will be covered in detail in a later section.

LISP uses functions instead of procedures or subroutines. All functions return a value, whether that value is needed or not. If it is not needed by the calling function, the returned value can simply be ignored. (It is interesting to note that the C language adopted this same scheme a decade later.)

There is no clear distinction between LISP programs and LISP functions. Any LISP function can stand alone and be invoked from the keyboard, or it can be invoked by another function. A program can be thought of as a collection of one or more functions that exist simultaneously in the computer's memory in an area that I will call a *workspace*. Subject to space limitations, any number of functions can exist in a workspace at a given time. The workspace can also contain any data needed by the functions.

In the MuLISP environment, a workspace can be saved to and retrieved from disk. LISP functions can also be created using a separate text editor and read into a workspace.

LISP recognizes both upper- and lowercase characters, but it distinguishes between them. Because the built-in functions and commands were defined in uppercase in MuLISP, they cannot be invoked in lowercase. It is therefore good practice to do MuLISP programming in all capital letters except when lowercase letters are needed in text. (Warning:

Some other LISP interpreters require the use of *lowercase* for built-in functions and commands.)

Two simple LISP functions are shown in Fig. 9-1. The first one, called DEMO1, prints a simple message on the screen. To execute this function, the following is typed:

(DEMO1)

Note the parentheses. LISP uses lots of parentheses. In fact, all commands you type in must be enclosed in parentheses, together with any arguments. Some dialects of LISP would have you type DEMO1 ( ) instead. In either case, the system displays the following in response:

This is a test.
This is a test.

Why is the message printed twice? The first copy comes from the PRINT function. The second copy of the message is the value returned by the function DEMO1. DEMO1 must return something, and that something is the value of the last expression evaluated, which is the PRINT function. When a function such as DEMO1 returns a value and the user doesn't say what to do with that value, LISP simply prints it out.

Let us now look at the form of the function DEMO1. Notice that the function definition begins with the word DEFINE and the name of the function, and that the whole definition is enclosed in parentheses. Next comes the word LAMBDA followed by empty parentheses. The LAMBDA function is used by LISP to define the parameters of a function. In this case there are no parameters, which is why the parentheses are empty. The word LAMBDA was borrowed from a book entitled *The Calculi of Lambda-Conversion*, by A. Church (Princeton University Press, Princeton, NJ, 1941)—another unfortunate anachronism.

LISP function parameters bound by LAMBDA are passed according to the *call-by-value* scheme discussed in Chapter 2. In other words, the actual arguments are evaluated and their values passed to the function. LISP also permits *call-by-name*, in which the names of the arguments themselves are passed for use within the function. This is invoked by using the word NLAMBDA instead of LAMBDA. Fortunately, this is rarely needed in LISP except by those who write language compilers and such.

```
        Figure 9-1:   Minimal LISP Functions.


    (DEFINE DEMO1 (LAMBDA  ()
        (PRINT "This is a test.") ))


    (DEFINE DEMO2 (LAMBDA  ()
        (DEMO1) ))
```

Fig. 9-1. Minimal LISP functions.

Some dialects of LISP make the use of the word **LAMBDA** optional. Unfortunately, MuLISP is not among them.

Once the name of the function and the parameters are defined, the body of the function can follow. The body of the function consists of a series of expressions. In this case there is only one, the **PRINT** function. Following the last function, all that remains is to close all open parentheses.

The use of parentheses in function definitions is something that must be learned. The entire definition is enclosed by one set, and the part that begins with **LAMBDA** by another set. Each expression in the body of the function must also be enclosed by parentheses.

The function **DEMO2** is included in Fig. 9-1 to show that a function can be invoked from another function. **DEMO2** simply invokes **DEMO1** and produces exactly the same results.

DATA TYPES

A data element in LISP can be an *atom* or a *list*. Each of these kinds of data is discussed in detail in the following paragraphs.

Atoms

An atom is another of those unfortunate names used in LISP. An atom can be thought of simply as a basic data element. Atoms can be one of two principle subtypes, numeric and nonnumeric.

Numeric atoms can be either integer or floating point. MuLISP does not support floating-point numbers, but integers can be of almost infinite precision (would you believe 256 raised to the 256th power?).

Nonnumeric atoms are more interesting. Each has a name, a value, and a property list. To illustrate, consider the following session at the console. The $ is the MuLISP prompt, and the computer's output is shown in bold.

```
$  JOHN          (User)
JOHN             (LISP)
```

When the user types an atom name, LISP responds with its value. Here LISP hasn't been given any other value, so it responds with the name.

```
$  (SETQ JOHN OLD)      (User)
OLD                     (LISP)
```

The **SETQ** function, to be discussed in more detail later, gives the atom **JOHN** a value, which is echoed by LISP.

```
$  JOHN          (User)
OLD              (LISP)
```

Now when the user types the name of the atom, LISP responds with its new value.

```
$  (QUOTE JOHN)            (User)
   JOHN                    (LISP)
```

The name of the atom is still accessible using the QUOTE function.

```
$  (PUT JOHN AGE 72)       (User)
   72                      (LISP)
```

Here the user has started to create a *property list* for the atom **JOHN**. The function **PUT** (called **PUTPROP** in some dialects of LISP) establishes a property called **AGE** for **JOHN** and sets its value to 72. If the property **AGE** had already existed, its previous value would have been overwritten.

```
$  (PUT JOHN HEALTH GOOD)       (User)
   GOOD                         (LISP)
```

Here another property is established. The properties can be retrieved from the property list using the **GET** function, which is shown below:

```
$  (GET JOHN AGE)          (User)
   72                      (LISP)
$  (GET JOHN HEALTH)       (User)
   GOOD                    (LISP)
```

Lists

A *list* is a sequence of elements, each of which may be an atom or another list. Each list element is separated by a blank. The list is enclosed in parentheses. Here is a simple example of a list:

```
(THIS IS A LIST)
```

Here is an example of a list that contains another list:

```
((A LIST) IN A LIST)
```

Lists can also include numeric atoms, as in the following:

```
(1 2 3 4 5)
```

A special case of a list is the empty list, which can be written as ( ) or as **NIL**. You shall see examples of its use later in the chapter.

Lists can be used to implement more complex data structures. This is discussed in more detail in the section on data structures.

List Manipulation

LISP provides a number of functions for the manipulation of lists. These functions provide for access to individual elements of a list. They also allow lists to be constructed.

Functions that allow access to individual elements of lists are called *selector functions*. The two principle selector functions are called **CAR** and **CDR**. (How these functions got their names was discussed earlier in the chapter.) **CAR** returns the first element of a list. **CDR** returns everything but the first element. Here are a few examples:

```
$   (CAR (THIS IS A LIST))          (User)
THIS                                (LISP)
$   (CDR (THIS IS A LIST))          (User)
(IS A LIST)                         (LISP)
$   (CAR ((A LIST) IN A LIST))      (User)
(A LIST)                            (LISP)
```

Elements other than the first element of a list can be retrieved by repeated application of **CAR** and **CDR**. For example, the second element of a list could be retrieved by the following:

```
$   (CAR (CDR (THIS IS A LIST)))    (User)
IS                                  (LISP)
```

Because this is such a common occurrence, LISP provides a shortcut:

```
$   (CADR (THIS IS A LIST))         (User)
IS                                  (LISP)
```

As a matter of fact, LISP provides a whole family of shortcuts of the form **CxxR** and **CxxxR**, where any of the x's can be either **A** or **D**. Where there is an A, a **CAR** is done, and where there is a D, a **CDR** is done. How this works is easier to show by example than to explain in words. You have already seen how **CADR** works. The following example shows how to retrieve the third elements of a list using this notation:

```
$   (CADDR (THIS IS A LIST))        (User)
A                                   (LISP)
```

This is equivalent to the following:

```
$   (CAR (CDR (CDR (THIS IS A LIST))))    (User)
A                                         (LISP)
```

Here is another example:

```
$   (CDAR ((A LIST) IN A LIST))     (User)
(LIST)                              (LISP)
```

This example was a little trickier. In stages, here is what it did:

```
$   (CAR ((A LIST) IN A LIST))      (User)
(A LIST)                            (LISP)
```

```
$  (CDR (A LIST))            (User)
(LIST)                       (LISP)
```

Functions that are used to construct lists are called *constructor functions*. The principle constructor functions are CONS, APPEND, LIST, and REVERSE.

CONS takes two arguments. The first argument may be a list or an atom, but the second argument must be a list. (CONS X Y) returns a list in which X has been inserted as the first element of list Y. Here are some simple examples:

```
$  (CONS A (B C D))          (User)
(A B C D)                    (LISP)
$  (CONS A ( ))              (User)
(A)                          (LISP)
$  (CONS (A B) (C D))        (User)
((A B) C D)                  (LISP)
```

APPEND takes two arguments, both of which must be lists. It returns a list that combines the original two lists. Here is a simple example:

```
$  (APPEND (A B) (C D))      (User)
(A B C D)                    (LISP)
```

The effect of LIST is a little more complicated. It can take any number of arguments and produces a list. Each argument may be an atom or a list. LIST evaluates each argument before adding it to the list. What gets added to the list is not the name of the argument, but its value. This is illustrated by the following examples:

```
$  (LIST A B C D)            (User)
(A B C D)                    (LISP)
$  (LIST JOHN MAN RIVER)     (User)
(JOHN MAN RIVER)            (LISP)
$  (SETQ JOHN (QUOTE OLD))   (User)
OLD                          (LISP)
$  (LIST JOHN MAN RIVER)     (User)
(OLD MAN RIVER)             (LISP)
```

When first used, an atom such as JOHN evaluates to itself. Thus LIST produced no surprises until JOHN was given a different value. Then LIST caused JOHN to be evaluated to OLD before adding it to the list. This evaluation can be stopped by the QUOTE function, as illustrated below:

```
$  (LIST (QUOTE JOHN) MAN RIVER)        (User)
(JOHN MAN RIVER)                        (LISP)
```

It takes practice to become comfortable with the distinction between CONS, APPEND, and LIST. Here is an illustration showing how each of the three functions deals with the same arguments:

```
$   (CONS (A B) (C))          (User)
((A B) C)                     (LISP)
$   (APPEND (A B) (C))        (User)
(A B C)                       (LISP)
$   (LIST (A B) (C))          (User)
((A B) (C))                   (LISP)
```

The REVERSE function is straightforward. It produces a list that consists of the same elements but in reverse order. Here is a simple example:

```
$(REVERSE (JOHN MAN RIVER))       (User)
(RIVER MAN JOHN)                  (LISP)
```

One use of REVERSE is to aid in the selection of the last element of a list. The following example shows how this can be done easily:

```
$   (CAR (REVERSE (THIS IS A LIST)))       (User)
LIST                                       (LISP)
```

REVERSE caused the list to be reversed, and CAR extracted the first element of the reversed list.

Now suppose you need all but the last element of a list. REVERSE is needed twice in this case:

```
$ (REVERSE (CDR (REVERSE (THIS IS A LIST))))
(THIS IS A)
```

Without the additional REVERSE, the result would have been (A IS THIS).

If you anticipate needing these two operations frequently, you could define them as LISP functions, perhaps called LAST and BUTLAST.

Character Manipulation

Although the atom is supposedly the smallest component of matter and of LISP data, both physics and LISP recognize the existence of subatomic particles. In LISP these are characters.

LISP does not provide functions for dealing directly with characters, but it does provide functions for expanding the characters of an atom into a list and for compressing a list into an atom. Here are some examples:

```
$   (EXPLODE BOMB)        (User)
(B O M B)                 (LISP)
$   (EXPLODE 123)         (User)
(1 2 3)                   (LISP)
```

```
$  (COMPRESS (A I R))          (User)
AIR                            (LISP)
$  (COMPRESS (12 34 56)        (User)
123456                         (LISP)
```

In some dialects of LISP, the EXPLODE and COMPRESS functions are called UNPACK and PACK, respectively.

Variables

As you have already seen, an atom can have a value. This value can be an atom (numeric or nonnumeric), or it can be a list. The value of a numeric atom is the number itself. Technically you can give a numeric atom a different value, but such an action is strongly discouraged.

When an atom is typed at the keyboard, its value is returned. As you have seen, evaluation of an atom can be suppressed with the QUOTE function. Here are some simple examples that assume that the value of the atom A has been previously assigned to be 10 and the value of B is the list (1 2 3):

```
$  A                (User)
10                  (LISP)
$  (QUOTE A)        (User)
A                   (LISP)
$  B                (User)
(1 2 3)             (LISP)
```

The EVAL function, on the other hand, causes evaluation to be carried one step further. Consider the following sequence of operations:

```
$  (SETQ JOHN (QUOTE OLD))     (User)
OLD                            (LISP)
$  (SETQ OLD 80)               (User)
80                             (LISP)
$  JOHN                        (User)
OLD                            (LISP)
$  (EVAL JOHN)                 (User)
80                             (LISP)
```

When the EVAL function is applied to JOHN, JOHN is evaluated to OLD, and OLD is in turn evaluated to 80.

Variables in LISP may be *bound* or *free*. A *bound* variable is a variable that is listed as a parameter of a function. It is local to that function. Any action taken upon that variable or its name within the function does not affect any variable with the same name that may exist outside of that function. (This of course assumes the usual call-by-value, as discussed above.) When the function terminates, so does the existence of the bound variable.

A free variable, on the other hand, is not listed as a parameter of a function. It is something like a global variable in other languages. It may be used within a function or outside of a function (as, for example, in an expression typed at the keyboard). If the value of a free variable is changed within a function, the new value outlives that function and is available to other functions. Free variables have an existence separate from any functions. If a workspace is saved to disk, all of the free variables within the workspace are saved with it.

The Equivalence of Programs and Data

A striking feature of LISP is that programs and data are equivalent in form. A program can be manipulated as data, and data can be executed as a program. This is possible because programs, functions, and expressions are all stored as lists. That is why you have to use so many parentheses when entering expressions.

As a simple example, consider the expression used above:

```
$  (EVAL JOHN)          (User)
80                      (LISP)
```

You can treat this expression as data, as in the following:

```
$  (CAR (EVAL JOHN))       (User)
EVAL                       (LISP)
```

Here the list (EVAL JOHN) is treated first as an expression and then as data.

Now consider going the other direction, treating data as an expression. The following illustrates this:

```
$  (SETQ Q (QUOTE (EVAL JOHN)))     (User)
(EVAL JOHN)                         (LISP)
$  Q                                (User)
(EVAL JOHN)                         (LISP)
$  (EVAL Q)                         (User)
80                                  (LISP)
```

Here you have seen the list (EVAL JOHN) treated first as data (a character string), then as an expression.

THE ASSIGNMENT FUNCTION: SETQ

You have already seen several examples of the use of the assignment function SETQ. The name SETQ is actually an abbreviation for SET QUOTE. The following two assignment functions are equivalent:

```
(SETQ X 12)
(SET (QUOTE X) 12)
```

You want the value 12 to be assigned to the name of the atom X, so you need the QUOTE function. With SETQ, the QUOTE function is understood. SETQ is used much more often than SET.

SET can have unexpected results if it is not used properly. Consider the following sequence:

```
$  (SETQ X (QUOTE Y))        (User)
Y                            (LISP)
$  (SET X 12)                (User)
12                           (LISP)
$  X                         (User)
Y                            (LISP)
$  Y                         (User)
12                           (LISP)
```

Here you see that when you typed (SET X 12), X was evaluated to Y before the assignment took place. The QUOTE is needed to prevent the evaluation of X. Of course when SETQ is used, the QUOTE is understood and need not be repeated.

Care must also be taken to use the QUOTE function with the second argument of the SET or SETQ function if its name and not its value is desired. It is easy to get careless in this area because the initial value of an atom is the name of the atom. Unless care is taken, the value of an expression can depend unnecessarily on the order of execution. Consider the following sequence:

```
$  (SETQ X Y)                (User)
Y                            (LISP)
$  (SETQ Y 15)               (User)
15                           (LISP)
$  X                         (User)
Y                            (LISP)
$  Y                         (User)
15                           (LISP)
```

No surprises there. Now suppose the order of the assignments is reversed:

```
$  (SETQ Y 15)               (User)
15                           (LISP)
$  (SETQ X Y)                (User)
15                           (LISP)
$  X                         (User)
15                           (LISP)
$  Y                         (User)
15                           (LISP)
```

In the expression (SETQ X Y), Y was evaluated before the assignment took place, so X was assigned the value 15 rather than the value Y. If you assume that it was the user's intention for X to have the character value Y, the use of (SETQ X (QUOTE Y)) would have prevented the mixup.

Variables that are created using an assignment function at the keyboard are free variables. (See the above section on variables for a discussion of the meaning of the term *free variable*.)

ARITHMETIC EXPRESSIONS

Arithmetic expressions in LISP use a form of prefix notation called *Cambridge Polish notation*. (See Chapter 2 for a discussion of the various types of notation.) In other words, the arithmetic operator comes before the operands. To add 2 and 3, for example, you would type the following in LISP:

```
$  (PLUS 2 3)          (User)
5                      (LISP)
```

The sequence for multiplying these numbers would be as follows:

```
$  (TIMES 2 3)         (User)
6                      (LISP)
```

Prefix notation takes some getting used to, but it is perfectly consistent. Most of us are used to a mixture of infix and prefix notation, as in the following BASIC expressions:

```
2 + 3          (infix)
SQR (9)        (prefix)
```

The following arithmetic functions are normally available in LISP:

(MINUS X)	Unary minus; returns $-X$
(PLUS X Y)	Returns $X + Y$
(DIFFERENCE X Y)	Returns $X - Y$
(TIMES X Y)	Returns $X * Y$
(QUOTIENT X Y)	Returns X/Y (integer division)
(REMAINDER X Y)	The remainder after integer division (the modulus function)
(DIVIDE X Y)	Returns X/Y (real division, or in MuLISP, returns the integer quotient and remainder.)
(ADD1 X)	Returns $X + 1$
(SUB1 X)	Returns $X - 1$
(ABS X)	Returns absolute value of X

Various dialects of LISP may include additional arithmetic functions.

LISP was not designed for applications that require extensive numerical computations.

It can easily handle the basics, however.

A simple LISP program that computes the area of a square, or, equivalently, the square of a number, is shown in Fig. 9-2.

LOGICAL EXPRESSIONS (PREDICATES)

Logical expressions in LISP are called *predicates*. A predicate tests an expression and returns T for true or NIL for false. (ZEROP N) is a simple logical expression that will return T if N is equal to zero, or NIL otherwise.

The names of most LISP predicates end in the letter P, but there are exceptions. Here is a list of some of the common LISP predicates and the conditions under which each returns T. Each one returns NIL under all other conditions.

(ATOM X)	T if X is an atom
(NUMBERP X)	T if X is a number
(NAME X)	T if X is a name
(NULL X)	T if X is an empty list
(MINUSP X)	T if X is negative
(PLUSP X)	T if X is positive
(EVEN X)	T if X is an even number
(ZEROP X)	T if X is zero
(EQ X Y)	T if X and Y are identically equal. Used for names and numbers.
(EQUAL X Y)	T if X and Y are equal. Used for more complicated objects.
(MEMBER X Y)	T if X is an element of the list Y.
(GREATERP X Y)	T if X and Y are numbers and X > Y.
(LESSP X Y)	T if X and Y are numbers and X < Y.
(NOT X)	T if X has the value NIL
(AND X Y Z . . .)	T if all the arguments are T

```
    Figure 9-2:   Square of a Number.


        (DEFINE SQUARE (LAMBDA (X)

           (TIMES X X) ))
```

Fig. 9-2. Calculating the square of a number.

(OR X Y Z ...)	T if any of the arguments are T
(FLAGP X Y)	T if the attribute Y is on the property list of object X

Note that the AND and OR predicates can have any number of arguments. For these two functions, any value other than NIL is considered the same as a T value.

As indicated, all predicates use prefix notation. As with all other LISP expressions, the entire expression, including the operator, must be enclosed within parentheses. The use of predicates will be illustrated by example later in this chapter.

INPUT AND OUTPUT

Input and output operations in LISP are simple. There are functions to print and functions to read. There are ways to select input from either the keyboard or a disk file, and to direct output to the video screen, a disk file, or a printer.

The READ function reads a list. Its use can be illustrated by this simple session:

$ (READ)	(User)
(Hello"," how are you?)	(User)
(Hello, how are you?)	(LISP)

Notice that the input to READ had to be typed as a list (with parentheses) and was returned as a list. The quotation marks are needed for special characters such as commas and periods.

The idea that READ is a function and returns a value is illustrated by the following:

$ (SETQ L (READ))	(User)
(Hello"," how are you?)	(User)
(Hello, how are you?)	(LISP)
$ L	(User)
(Hello, how are you?)	(LISP)

The value of the list was assigned to the atom L.

The function RATOM reads an atom instead of a list. Here are a few examples:

$ (RATOM)	(User)
Hello	(User)
Hello	(LISP)
$ (RATOM)	(User)
"Hello, how are you?"	(User)
Hello, how are you?	(LISP)

Notice that a single word can be read without quotation marks, but to read more than one word and store it as an atom rather than a list, quotation marks are necessary.

The PRINT function prints the value of an expression. For example, the following statement

(PRINT X)

prints the value of X and also returns the value of X. You saw how this worked in Fig. 9-1. PRIN1 works the same way, except that it does not output a carriage return and line feed after printing, as does PRINT. Note that the value of X can be an atom (numeric or nonnumeric) or a list.

To output only a carriage return and line feed, use the function TERPRI. The SPACES function outputs a specified number of blank spaces.

In addition to the basic input and output functions, there are functions for modifying the effects of the input and output functions. For example the WRS (WRite Select) function can be used to redirect output between the screen and a disk file. The command below

(WRS X Y Z)

redirects output to file Z:X.Y, i.e., file X.Y on drive Z.

There is a control variable called LPRINTER, which controls printer output. If LPRINTER has any value other than NIL, the output goes to a printer in addition to its regular destination (e.g., the video screen or disk file). An example of how this is done is shown in Fig. 9-3. The program in Fig. 9-3 writes a message to the printer and then to the screen.

The RDS (ReaD Select) function can be used to select input from the keyboard or from a disk file. Disk file input and output are discussed in more detail later.

CONTROL STRUCTURES

LISP has relatively few control structures compared to other languages. The most widely used control structures are the conditional statement COND and recursion. LISP is sufficiently flexible, however, so that additional control structures can be added to the language by the user if needed.

```
Figure 9-3:   Printer Demonstration.


      (DEFINE PRINTER (LAMBDA ()
          (SETQ LPRINTER T)
          (PRINT (THIS GOES TO THE PRINTER))
          (SETQ LPRINTER NIL)
          (PRINT (THIS GOES TO THE SCREEN)) ))
```

Fig. 9-3. A printer demonstration.

Simple and Multiple Selection: COND

The COND function can handle both simple and multiple selection. Its format is as follows, where L1, L2, and L3 are lists.

(COND L1 L2 ... L3)

The COND function consists of the word COND followed by a sequence of one or more lists. The CAR of each list is evaluated until one is found with a non-NIL value. The CDR of that list is executed. Suppose L2 is the first list in which a non-NIL CAR is found. COND would then execute the CDR of L2 and return the last value obtained. COND returns as soon as one list is found with a non-NIL CAR, and the CDR of that list is executed. If the CDR of a list is empty, the value of the CAR is returned.

The operation of COND is best explained by example. Consider the following IF statement in BASIC:

IF X < 0 THEN X = 0

The LISP version of this statement would be as follows:

(COND ((MINUSP X) (SETQ X 0)))

The list following COND is the following:

((MINUSP X) (SETQ X 0))

The CAR of this list is the predicate (MINUSP X), which returns T if X is less than 0. If this is the case, then the CDR of the list, (SETQ X 0) is executed. This sets X to zero and returns the value zero.

Now consider the following IF-THEN-ELSE statement in Fortran:

```
IF (MONTH .EQ. 12) THEN
   MONTH = 1
   YEAR = YEAR + 1
ELSE
   MONTH = MONTH + 1
ENDIF
```

The equivalent statement in LISP would be as follows:

```
(COND
  ((EQ MONTH 12)
    (SETQ MONTH 1)
    (SETQ YEAR (ADD1 YEAR)) )
  (T
    (SETQ MONTH (ADD1 MONTH))) )
```

Notice that the second list begins with T. This is how LISP handles the **ELSE** part. If **MONTH** is equal to 12, the **COND** function returns after the remainder of that list is executed. If **MONTH** is not equal to 12, the proper action is to add 1 to **MONTH**. Starting the next list with T guarantees that the **CDR** of the next list will be executed.

To illustrate multiple selection using **COND**, consider the problem of finding the number of days in a month. A LISP solution of this problem is shown in Fig. 9-4. Here is a sample session showing this function in action:

```
$   (CALENDAR JANUARY)        (User)
31                            (LISP)
$   (CALENDAR FEBRUARY)       (User)
(ENTER THE YEAR)              (LISP)
1984                          (User)
29                            (LISP)
$   (CALENDAR TUESDAY)        (User)
NIL                           (LISP)
```

```
Figure 9-4:   The Calendar Program, Version 1.


(DEFINE CALENDAR (LAMBDA (M)
  (COND
     ((EQ M (QUOTE JANUARY)) 31)
     ((EQ M (QUOTE FEBRUARY) (FEB) )
     ((EQ M (QUOTE MARCH)) 31)
     ((EQ M (QUOTE APRIL)) 30)
     ((EQ M (QUOTE MAY)) 31)
     ((EQ M (QUOTE JUNE)) 30)
     ((EQ M (QUOTE JULY)) 31)
     ((EQ M (QUOTE AUGUST)) 31)
     ((EQ M (QUOTE SEPTEMBER)) 30)
     ((EQ M (QUOTE OCTOBER)) 31)
     ((EQ M (QUOTE NOVEMBER)) 30)
     ((EQ M (QUOTE DECEMBER)) 31) ) ))


(DEFINE FEB (LAMBDA ()
   (PRINT (ENTER THE YEAR))
   (SETQ YR (RATOM))
   (COND
      ((EQ (REMAINDER YR 4) 0) 29)
      (T 28) ) ))
```

Fig. 9-4. The Calendar Program, Version 1.

Notice that if the argument is not the name of a month, CALENDAR returns NIL. If the month is February, a special function is called to query the user for the year. If the year is evenly divisible by 4 (i.e., if (REMAINDER YR 4) is zero), FEB returns 29; otherwise it returns 28. The COND function of FEB is a good example of a simple if-then-else statement in LISP.

Later in the chapter you will see two more versions of the Calendar program.

Functions

Because of the lack of a clear distinction between functions and programs, functions have already been discussed in this chapter. A few more comments on functions are in order at this point.

It is important to realize that functions provide an important means of controlling the flow of execution. A good example of this was shown in Fig. 9-4. When the function CALENDAR was given FEBRUARY as an argument, it invoked the function FEB to interrogate the user for the year and to do the necessary calculations.

Note also that the arguments of a function can be atoms or lists. A function can return one atom or one list. If multiple atoms need to be returned, they can always be put in a list and returned that way.

Recursion

Recursion is the primary means of implementing repetitive actions in LISP. As discussed in Chapter 2, a function is said to be recursive if it invokes itself. Recursion is very useful in processing lists, and much programming in LISP consists largely of processing lists.

The classic example of recursion is the *factorial* function. The factorial of a positive integer N is defined to be N times the factorial of N – 1. The factorial of zero is defined to be 1. The factorial function is thus defined in terms of itself. A version of the factorial function is shown in Fig. 9-5.

The first thing the function FACTORIAL does is to check its argument to be sure it isn't being erroneously asked to compute the factorial of a negative number. If it is, it returns NIL. It next checks to see whether N is zero. If so, it returns the value 1. Otherwise, it applies the rule that the factorial of N is N times the factorial of N-1. To compute the factorial of N-1, the function FACTORIAL calls itself recursively.

```
        Figure 9-5:   Recursive Factorial Function.


  (DEFINE FACTORIAL (LAMBDA (N)
     (COND
       ((MINUSP N) NIL)
       ((ZEROP N) 1)
       (T (TIMES N (FACTORIAL (SUB1 N)))) ) ))
```

Fig. 9-5. A recursive factorial function.

This is like saying, for example, "I could compute the value of 2 factorial if only I knew the value of 1 factorial." The function would then call **FACTORIAL** with argument 1. The next step would be to say, "I could compute the value of 1 factorial if only I knew the value of 0 factorial." Using the argument 0, the function calls to find 0 factorial. This time, the function knows that 0 factorial is 1, so it returns that value. Once 0 factorial is known, 1 factorial can be computed. Once 1 factorial is known, 2 factorial can be computed. The process is then complete.

A nonnumeric example of recursion is the word-triangle program. This program takes a word as input, and then prints it repeatedly, dropping the first letter each time until there are no more letters. The LISP version of this program is shown in Fig. 9-6.

The function **TRIANGLE** operates by printing its argument (**WORD**) and then calling itself with an argument one character shorter. The function removes the first character of its argument by using the function **EXPLODE** to convert **WORD** to a list, **CDR** to drop the first element, and **COMPRESS** to compress the list back into an atom. The **COND** function is used to check for the termination condition, which occurs when there are no more letters left in **WORD**.

Here is a sample interchange with the function TRIANGLE:

$ (TRIANGLE HELLO)	(User)
HELLO	(LISP)
ELLO	(LISP)
LLO	(LISP)
LO	(LISP)
O	(LISP)

The word "HELLO" can be read horizontally or vertically.

Another example of a program that uses recursion is version 2 of the calendar program, shown in Fig. 9-7. This program operates in a very different manner than version 1 of the calendar program, which was given in Fig. 9-4. It uses a list called **MLIST** to store the number of days in each month except February. (February is handled by a separate function called **FEB**, which was also used in Fig. 9-4.) To compute the number of days in a month, say March, the function **CALENDAR** does a table lookup.

CALENDAR takes two arguments: the name of the month for which the number of days is to be found and the list **MLIST**. It operates by comparing the name in the

```
Figure 9-6:   The Word Triangle Program in LISP.


(DEFINE TRIANGLE (LAMBDA (WORD)
   (PRINT WORD)
   (COND
      ((NULL (CDR (EXPLODE WORD))) (TERPRI) )
      (·T (TRIANGLE (COMPRESS (CDR (EXPLODE WORD))))) ) ))
```

Fig. 9-6. The Word Triangle Program in LISP.

```
Figure 9-7:  The Calendar Program, Version 2.


(DEFINE CALENDAR (LAMBDA (M MLIST)
  (COND
    ((EQ M (QUOTE FEBRUARY)) (FEB) )
    ((NULL MLIST) NIL)
    ((EQ M (CAAR MLIST)) (CADAR MLIST) )
    (T (CALENDAR M (CDR MLIST))) ) ))


(DEFINE INIT (LAMBDA ()
  (SETQ MLIST ((JANUARY 31)
               (MARCH 31)
               (APRIL 30)
               (MAY 31)
               (JUNE 30)
               (JULY 31)
               (AUGUST 31)
               (SEPTEMBER 30)
               (OCTOBER 31)
               (NOVEMBER 30)
               (DECEMBER 31))) ))


(DEFINE FEB (LAMBDA ()
  (PRINT (ENTER THE YEAR))
  (SETQ YR (RATOM))
  (COND
    ((EQ (REMAINDER YR 4) 0) 29)
    (T 28) ) ))
```

Fig. 9-7. The Calendar Program, Version 2.

argument to the first name in the list. If there is a match, it returns the number of days from the list. If there is not, CALENDAR calls itself with the same month name but with the CDR of MLIST. If the month is not found, CALENDAR returns NIL. February is of course handled as a special case.

Here is a sample session with this program:

```
$  (INIT)                        (User)
$  (CALENDAR APRIL MLIST)        (User)
30                               (LISP)
$  (CALENDAR JULIUS MLIST)       (User)
NIL                              (LISP)
```

The function INIT is used to initialize MLIST. When CALENDAR was called with the erroneous name JULIUS, CALENDAR correctly returned NIL.

Three short functions are shown in Fig. 9-8. The function SUM adds up the numbers in a list. The function COUNT counts the elements in a list (numbers or otherwise). The function AVERAGE uses SUM and COUNT to compute the average of the numbers in a list.

SUM works as follows: If the list L is empty (NULL), it returns 0. If the list is not empty, it returns the first element of the list plus the sum of the remaining elements. Eventually the recursion reaches the empty list, so the recursion terminates and the sum is calculated.

The function COUNT works similarly. If the list L is empty (NULL), it returns 0. If the list is not empty, it returns 1 plus the number of elements in the CDR of the list. Because each recursive call involves the CDR of the list, eventually the empty list is returned and the recursion terminates. The elements in the list L need not be numbers in order for COUNT to work. Note that COUNT counts only top-level entries. (COUNT (1 (2 3))) would return 2, as there are only two top-level entries in the list, the atom 1 and the list (2 3).

The function AVERAGE shows again how LISP functions, such as SUM and COUNT, can be easily used as building blocks for more complex functions.

Here are a few examples of the use of these functions:

```
$  (SUM (2 6 4))          (User)
12                        (LISP)
$  (COUNT 2 6 4))         (User)
3                         (LISP)
```

```
Figure 9-8:   The SUM, COUNT, and AVERAGE Functions.


(DEFINE SUM (LAMBDA (L)
   (COND
     ((NULL L) 0)
     (T (PLUS (CAR L) (SUM (CDR L)))) ) ))


(DEFINE COUNT (LAMBDA (L)
   (COND
     ((NULL L) 0)
     (T (PLUS 1 (COUNT (CDR L)))) ) ))


(DEFINE AVERAGE (LAMBDA (L)
   (DIVIDE (SUM L) (COUNT L)) ))
```

Fig. 9-8. The SUM, COUNT, and AVERAGE functions.

$ (AVERAGE (2 6 4))   (User)
(4 . 0)   (LISP)

MuLISP does not support noninteger arithmetic, so the output of the DIVIDE function in AVERAGE is the integer quotient (4) and the remainder (0), which just happens to be the same as 4.0.

The GO Statement

MuLISP does not support the GO statement, but most other versions of LISP do. The GO statement is implemented in conjunction with the PROG function, which defines subprograms with local variables. I will not go into much detail about this facility, but here is how the function COUNT in Fig. 9-8 might look using the GO statement:

```
(DEFINE COUNT2 (LAMBDA (L)
  (PROG (N)
    (SETQ N 0)
  LOOP
    (COND
      ((NULL L) (RETURN N)))
    (SETQ N (ADD1 N))
    (SETQ L (CDR L))
    (GO LOOP)) ))
```

In this example, N is a local variable used to keep a tally of the number of elements of the list as they are processed. The value of N is returned when there are no more elements to count.

The GO function is not really necessary. Nearly always there is a way to accomplish the task using recursion, as in the case of the COUNT function. Why then have a GO function? The answer is efficiency. Recursion has a certain amount of overhead associated with it. With each recursive call, LISP must keep track of the status of the function and its variables. When the recursion is deep, the overhead in extra storage requirements and processing time can be appreciable. Iterative loops using the GO function require much less overhead and can be processed faster. For simple functions such as are illustrated in this book, the difference is not significant.

Loops

LISP does not provide directly for any kind of looping other than recursive looping and looping using the GO statement. MuLISP, however, does provide a powerful iterative looping construct to compensate for the lack of the GO function. This function is called LOOP and is a very general and very powerful form of conditional loop.

The MuLISP function consists of the word LOOP followed by a series of lists. Each list is called a *task*. At least one of these tasks must begin with a predicate (conditional expression). A task is said to begin with a predicate if the CAR of the CAR of the task is an atom. The tasks within the body of the loop are evaluated consecutively until a task with a non-NIL predicate is found, as in a COND function. The difference is that if all the predicates evaluate to NIL, execution starts again with the first task in the LOOP function.

An example of the LOOP function is shown in Fig. 9-9. The COUNT3 function counts the number of top-level elements in a list, just as the function COUNT in Fig. 9-8 and the function COUNT2 shown above. Note that COUNT3 has an extra argument (N) following LAMBDA. That is MuLISP's way of providing for local variables within a function. This local variable N is initialized to zero at the beginning of the function.

The LOOP function in COUNT3 contains only one predicate, which checks to see whether or not the list L is empty. If it is (i.e., if (NULL L) has value T), LOOP returns the current value of N. If it is not, one is added to the value of N and L is set to its CDR. Eventually L will be empty; this will occur just as the last element of L has been counted.

The natural question to ask at this point is, "When should I use recursion and when should I use iteration?" If efficiency is not an issue, then you should use whichever seems easier. If efficiency is important for an application, and if all that you need to do is to step through the elements of a list one at a time, then iteration is to be preferred.

DATA STRUCTURES

The building blocks for data structures in LISP are atoms, lists, and property lists. From these can be constructed data structures of arbitrary complexity. Advanced data structures, such as queues and trees, are easily implemented using lists. The use of advanced data structures is, however, beyond the scope of this book.

Arrays

LISP does not directly support arrays. An array can be readily emulated in LISP, however, using a list. You have already seen that CAR retrieves the first element of a list, CADR the second element, and CADDR the third element. A function can easily be written to retrieve the Ith element of a list. The function RETRIEVE shown in Fig. 9-10 is such a function. RETRIEVE retrieves the Ith element of the list A. I therefore corresponds to the subscript of the array.

```
Figure 9-9:   The MuLISP LOOP Function.


(DEFINE COUNT3 (LAMBDA (L N)
   (SETQ N 0)
   (LOOP
      ((NULL L) N)
      (SETQ N (ADD1 N))
      (SETQ L (CDR L)) ) ))
```

Fig. 9-9. The MuLISP LOOP function.

```
Figure 9-10: Function to Retrieve the Ith Item From a List.


(DEFINE RETRIEVE (LAMBDA (I A)
   (COND
     ((EQ I 1)
       (CAR A) )
     (T (RETRIEVE (SUB1 I) (CDR A))) ) ))
```

Fig. 9-10. A function to retrieve the Ith item from a list.

Association Lists

It is not terribly useful to emulate arrays in LISP. There is usually another data structure that can do the job as well or better. One such data structure is the *association list*.

In an array, the value of an element is associated with a subscript. If X(1) has the value 13, the value 13 is associated with the subscript 1. It is often simpler to associate a value with a name, which I will call a *key value*. In this case suppose that X(1) represents the age of a person named Nat. You can associate the name Nat and the value 16 together in a list, such as (NAT 16). You could also add in some other value, such as a gender indicator (M or F). Suppose there is another person named Heather, who is 12 years old, and another named Cindy, who is three years old. You can now form an association list as follows:

```
((NAT 16 M)
(HEATHER 12 F)
(CINDY 3 F) )
```

LISP provides the built-in function ASSOC to retrieve data from association lists. Suppose the above list is called ALIST. ASSOC can be used to retrieve the sublist that has the key value NAT. Here is how:

```
$  (ASSOC NAT ALIST)        (User)
(NAT 16 M)                  (LISP)
```

The key value is always the CAR of a sublist. In this case, Nat's age can be retrieved with CADR, and his gender with CADDR. If there were more elements in the sublist, the function RETRIEVE in Fig. 9-10 could be used.

If desired, association lists could also be used within each sublist. Here is an example:

```
((NAT        (AGE 16)     (SEX M))
(HEATHER     (AGE 12)     (SEX F))
(CINDY       (AGE 3)      (SEX F))  )
```

If this list were called BLIST, you could retrieve Nat's age by typing the following:

```
$  (ASSOC AGE (ASSOC NAT BLIST))        (User)
(AGE 16)                                (LISP)
```

Again, CADR could be used to extract the age itself.

Version 2 of the calendar program, shown in Fig. 9-7, is a good example of the use of recursion in LISP, but it would have been easier to use the function ASSOC. The list MLIST in Fig. 9-7 is organized as an association list. The month name is the key value, and the number of days in the month is the associated value.

Once MLIST is in existence (recall it was created by the function INIT), values can be retrieved from it as follows:

```
$  (ASSOC SEPTEMBER MLIST)       (User)
(SEPTEMBER 30)                   (LISP)
$  (CADR (ASSOC JULY MLIST))     (User)
31                               (LISP)
```

ASSOC returned the first sublist of MLIST whose CAR was the name of the month. To extract the number of days in that month, the CADR function was used.

Figure 9-11 shows still another version of the calendar program, this time using the ASSOC function. Note that this version of the calendar program is nonrecursive. Also note that only one argument is needed, as in the following:

```
$  (CALENDAR JULY)       (User)
31                       (LISP)
```

Property Lists

Earlier in this chapter I discussed property lists in LISP. You may be wondering why the things I did in the previous section using association lists couldn't have been done with property lists. The answer is that I could easily have used property lists.

Consider the example of the age and gender of an individual. You could type the following to establish these values:

```
(PUT NAT AGE 16)
(PUT NAT GENDER M)
```

The following could then be used to retrieve these values:

```
$  (GET NAT AGE)         (User)
16                       (LISP)
$  (GET NAT GENDER)      (User)
M                        (LISP)
```

You have thus seen that some functions can be served by either a property list or

```
Figure 9-11:   The Calendar Program, Version 3.


(DEFINE CALENDAR (LAMBDA (M)
  (COND
    ((EQ M (QUOTE FEBRUARY))
      (FEB) )
    ((NULL MLIST) NIL)
    ((CADR (ASSOC M MLIST))) ) ))


(DEFINE FEB (LAMBDA ()
  (PRINT (ENTER THE YEAR))
  (SETQ YR (RATOM))
  (COND
    ((EQ (REMAINDER YR 4) 0) 29)
    (T 28) ) ))


(DEFINE INIT (LAMBDA ()
  (SETQ MLIST ((JANUARY 31)
               (MARCH 31)
               (APRIL 30)
               (MAY 31)
               (JUNE 30)
               (JULY 31)
               (AUGUST 31)
               (SEPTEMBER 30)
               (OCTOBER 31)
               (NOVEMBER 30)
               (DECEMBER 31))) ))
```

Fig. 9-11. The Calendar Program, Version 3.

an association list. Which to use is largely a matter of preference. I find property lists slightly easier to use.

Records

In Chapter 2, I discussed the concept of a record. A record contains related information, such as the name and age of an individual, or the name of a month and the number of days in that month. You have already seen examples of the use of records in LISP. Lists provide a convenient means of grouping related information into records.

Chapter 2 discussed the example of a structure of records, each containing the name of a student and that student's scores on a series of tests. Conventional languages, such as BASIC or Pascal, require that such structures be defined rigidly in advance. The number of records and the number of test scores must be specified. In LISP, this is not necessary because of the flexibility of lists as building blocks for more complex data structures.

The following LISP expression creates a structure containing the names and test scores of two students:

```
(SETQ CLASS (((JOHN DOE)
             (95 87 100 93))
 ((MARY SMITH) (98 85 95 88))))
```

The various elements of this structure can be retrieved in an *ad hoc* fashion as in the following examples:

$ (CAR CLASS)	(User)
((JOHN DOE) (95 87 100 93))	(LISP)
$ (CADR CLASS)	(User)
((MARY SMITH) (98 85 95 88))	(LISP)
$ (CAAR CLASS)	(User)
(JOHN DOE)	(LISP)
$ (CDAAR CLASS)	(User)
(DOE)	(LISP)
$ (CAR (REVERSE	
(CAAR CLASS)))	(User)
DOE	(LISP)
$ (CAR (CADAR CLASS))	(User)
95	(LISP)

This last example is the first test score of the first student.

While the above examples are certainly illustrative, retrieving information in that manner would get tedious rather quickly. Imagine what you would have to write to get the fourth test score of the fourteenth student in a larger class. A better way is needed.

A better way is to write LISP functions to do the work. A set of basic functions would include the following:

1. A function to print out a class roster.
2. A function to print out a classbook, including names and test scores.
3. A function to retrieve the Ith record of the list.
4. A function to retrieve the record which matches a given student name.
5. A function to retrieve the test scores of the Nth student.
6. A function to retrieve the Ith test score of the Nth student.

The function **RETRIEVE** in Fig. 9-10 will take care of requirement number 3. The built-in function **ASSOC** will take care of requirement number 4. Functions to take care of requirements 1, 2, 5, and 6 are shown in Fig. 9-12.

To obtain a roster of the class, type the following:

```
(ROSTER CLASS)
```

```
Figure 9-12:   The Classbook Program.


(DEFINE ROSTER (LAMBDA (CLASS)
  (PRINT (CAAR CLASS))
  (COND
     ((NOT (NULL (CDR CLASS)))
        (ROSTER (CDR CLASS)) ) ) ))


(DEFINE CLASSBOOK (LAMBDA (CLASS)
  (COND
     ((NULL CLASS) NIL)
     (T (PRINT (CAR CLASS)) (CLASSBOOK (CDR CLASS))) ) ))


(DEFINE SCORES (LAMBDA (N)
  (CADR (RETRIEVE N CLASS)) ))


(DEFINE TEST (LAMBDA (I N)
  (RETRIEVE I (SCORES N)) ))
```

Fig. 9-12. The Classbook Program.

The function will print out the names in order, followed by NIL, which signifies the end of the list. To obtain a classbook, type the following:

(CLASSBOOK CLASS)

The following sequence illustrates the use of the functions to satisfy requirements 5 and 6:

$ (SCORES 1)	(User)
(95 87 100 93)	(LISP)
$ (TEST 2 1)	(User)
87	(LISP)

The first example retrieves the scores of the first student. The second example retrieves the score on test number 2 of student number 1.

Ordered Lists

Chapter 2 showed how ordered lists could be implemented using arrays in a language such as BASIC, which does not directly support linked lists. Because the list is an integral feature of LISP, it is not necessary to emulate linked lists. Neither is it necessary to worry about the links between list elements nor any special end-of-list indicator; these functions are handled by LISP without direct involvement by the user.

The list illustrated in Chapter 2 consisted of first names. Initially the list contained the names Bob, Ernie, and Jim. The following expression would create such a list in LISP:

    (SETQ L (BOB ERNIE JIM))

Recall that the list is to be maintained in alphabetical order. Functions are needed to insert and delete names from the list. These functions are shown in Fig. 9-13.

The basis for ordering the names in the list is the ability to determine whether or not one name comes before another alphabetically. The LISP functions **LESSP** and **GREATERP** cannot be used directly, because they must have numeric arguments. The ASCII function must be used to convert a name to a number so that **LESSP** and **GREATERP** can be used. ASCII returns the numeric code that corresponds to the first letter in a name.

The process of comparing two names for alphabetic precedence is more difficult than it might seem. The function **LTEQ** in Fig. 9-13 provides this capability. It returns **T** if its first argument is Less Than or EQual to its second argument, and **NIL** otherwise. If the first letters of each word are different, the process is easy. If they are the same, you must first check to see whether they are the only letters in each word. If they are, the words are equal and **T** is returned. Otherwise, the function drops the first letter of each word and calls itself recursively.

The process of dropping a letter from a word is accomplished by the separate function **DROP1**, also shown in Fig. 9-13.

With these preliminaries out of the way, I can discuss the functions **INSERT** and **DELETE**, which are also shown in Fig. 9-13. INSERT inserts the name given as its first argument into the list given as its second argument. There are three possible cases for **INSERT**. In the first case, the list is empty, so **INSERT** returns the name in the form of a list. In the second case, the name comes before the first name of the list, so **CONS** is used to put the name first in the list. In the third case, **CONS** is used to combine the **CAR** of the list with the results of recursively applying **INSERT** to the **CDR** of the list.

DELETE is quite similar. If the name to be deleted is not a member of the list, the list is returned intact. (Note: **MEMBER** is a primitive LISP function.) This also covers the case in which the list is empty. If the name is equal to the **CAR** of the list, the **CDR** of the list is returned. Otherwise, **CONS** is used to combine the **CAR** of the list with the results of recursively applying **DELETE** to the **CDR** of the list.

Here are a few examples of the use of these functions. You should note that the list must be created with **SETQ** before anything is inserted to or deleted from it. Setting it to **NIL** is sufficient.

```
$  L                         (User)
(BOB ERNIE JIM)              (LISP)
$  (INSERT JERRY L)          (User)
(BOB ERNIE JERRY JIM)        (LISP)
```

```
Figure 9-13:   Insertion and Deletion with an Ordered List.


(DEFINE INSERT (LAMBDA (NAME L)
  (COND
    ((NULL L)
      (LIST NAME) )
    ((LTEQ NAME (CAR L))
      (CONS NAME L) )
    (T (CONS (CAR L) (INSERT NAME (CDR L)))) ) ))


(DEFINE DELETE (LAMBDA (NAME L)
  (COND
    ((NOT (MEMBER NAME L)) L)
    ((EQ NAME (CAR L))
      (CDR L) )
    (T (CONS (CAR L) (DELETE NAME (CDR L)))) ) ))


(DEFINE LTEQ (LAMBDA (A B)
  (COND
    ((LESSP (ASCII A) (ASCII B)) T)
    ((GREATERP (ASCII A) (ASCII B)) NIL)
    ((AND
        (EQ (ASCII A) (ASCII B))
        (AND
          (EQ 1 (LENGTH A))
          (EQ 1 (LENGTH B)) ) ) T)
    (T (LTEQ (DROP1 A) (DROP1 B))) ) ))


(DEFINE DROP1 (LAMBDA (WORD)
  (COMPRESS (CDR (EXPLODE WORD))) ))
```

Fig. 9-13. Insertion and deletion with an ordered list.

$ L	(User)
(BOB ERNIE JIM)	(LISP)
$ (SETQ L (INSERT JERRY L))	(User)
(BOB ERNIE JERRY JIM)	(LISP)
$ L	(User)
(BOB ERNIE JERRY JIM)	(LISP)
$ (SETQ L (DELETE ERNIE L))	(User)
(BOB JERRY JIM)	(LISP)

Notice that a LAMBDA (call by value) function does not change its arguments. To make the insertion "permanent," I had to use SETQ.

FILE HANDLING

MuLISP allows the reading and writing of sequential text files and system files. There is no provision for direct-access disk files.

Sequential disk files are created by using the **WRS** (WRite Select) function to divert to disk text that would ordinarily go to the screen. These files can be read in by using the **RDS** (ReaD Select) function to take input from a disk file rather than from the keyboard. A file that is to be read in from disk should have ''(RDS)'' as the last record of the file. Without this, the system will attempt to continue to read from the disk file rather than from the keyboard.

The following causes a file to be read in from disk:

(RDS X Y A)

Data that is read in from disk is evaluated as if it were being typed from the keyboard. It is therefore easy to read in function definitions, but it is difficult to read in data and associate the data with a variable. Advanced LISP programmers could write a special evaluation function for this purpose. Another way to store and retrieve data would be to store it as a function that, when evaluated, assigns the value of the data to the appropriate variable name. Both of these methods are beyond the scope of this book.

MuLISP uses the concept of a *workspace*. All the functions that are created or are read in during an interactive session reside in the system memory in an area called a workspace. Free variables (such as the list L in the preceding example) also reside in the workspace. Anything that resides in the workspace is accessible to an interactive user.

A workspace can be saved intact as a system file using the **SAVE** function. It can be reloaded intact using the **LOAD** function. This file includes functions and free variables. The MuLISP user therefore does not need to read or write text files, as both programs and data can be stored as system files. The classbook program in Fig. 9-12 could be used to maintain records, and the records could be saved as part of the workspace at the end of each session.

GRAPHICS

LISP has no inherent graphics capabilities. The Apple version of MuLISP provides access to the Apple's low-resolution graphics, but not its high-resolution graphics. In keeping with the intention of this book to avoid machine-dependent functions as much as possible, this topic will not be pursued further.

THE COMPREHENSIVE SAMPLE PROGRAM

The sample programs shown thus far in this chapter have been rather short. While they convey how individual features of LISP are used, they do not adequately convey how larger, more complex LISP programs are put together. For that reason, a comprehensive sample program is included in the chapter.

The comprehensive sample program maintains a list of names and addresses in alphabetical order by name. It functions as an electronic address book. The program permits records to be added to the list, deleted from the list, reviewed on the screen, and listed to a printer. The program is shown in Fig. 9-14.

The data for this program is not stored in a separate file, as in the corresponding programs in most of the other languages presented in this book. The data is instead stored in a free variable called ALIST. The data is saved on disk as part of the workspace by the function SAVE. It is reloaded as part of the workspace by the function LOAD. The user must therefore remember to save the workspace at the end of each interactive session. A disadvantage of this method is that the amount of data that can be handled by the program is limited by the amount of computer memory available.

This program does not include a DUMP function. The DUMP function was included in the corresponding programs in some of the other languages in order to permit the user to see and examine the linkages between records. This is unnecessary in LISP for two reasons: First, there are no visible linkages in LISP data structures because LISP takes care of such details out of sight of the user. Second, because the data resides in the workspace, the user can interactively print the data out for inspection without the assistance of a program.

You might have noticed that this program is much shorter than the corresponding program in BASIC, Pascal, and most of the other languages represented in this book. This is due largely to the fact that the basic data structure of the program is the list, and LISP was designed for processing lists. The language takes care of most of the housekeeping details that must be taken care of by the programmer when other languages are used.

Earlier I pointed out as a disadvantage of LISP the fact that the user has to remember to save the workspace at the end of a session in which the data is updated. A compensating advantage of LISP is that the programmer does not have to specify the length of each data field in advance. In Pascal, for example, the programmer would have to specify that the street address field could not exceed 20 characters in length. If a particular street address required more than 20 characters, the user would have to abbreviate or be out of luck. Not so with LISP. Because each data field is a list, it can be as long or as short as needed.

There are a few limitations in the way that MuLISP handles input and output that limit the usefulness of this sample program. First, MuLISP requires that lists read in from the keyboard be delimited with parentheses. Because this is inconvenient for the user who must type in the data to the program, an alternate solution is desirable. One solution is to read in individual words as atoms and assemble them into a list. Because the input functions do not recognize carriage returns at the end of an input line, some sort of delimiter is still needed. My solution was to write the function RLIST, which requires that each line of text be terminated with the / character.

The second limitation is that leading zeros in numeric atoms are suppressed. A zip code such as 01234 is printed as 1234. A telephone number such as 123-0987 is printed as 123-987.

The hierarchical structure of the address book program is shown in the structure chart in Fig. 9-15. The main program is the function called BOOK. The functions called

```
Figure 9-14:  Comprehensive Sample Program.

(DEFINE BOOK (LAMBDA ()
  (COND
    ((ATOM AB)
      (SETQ AB NIL) ) )
  (SETQ BLANK " ")
  (SETQ C (MENU))
  (COND
    ((EQ C 1)
      (ADDREC) )
    ((EQ C 2)
      (REVIEW AB) )
    ((EQ C 3)
      (LISTFILE AB) ) )
  (COND
    ((EQ C 4) EXIT)
    (T (BOOK)) ) ))


(DEFINE MENU (LAMBDA ()
  (CLEARSCREEN)
  (PRINT "1)   ADD TO FILE")
  (TERPRI 1)
  (PRINT "2)   REVIEW FILE ON SCREEN")
  (TERPRI 1)
  (PRINT "3)   LIST FILE TO SCREEN OR PRINTER")
  (TERPRI 1)
  (PRINT "4)   QUIT")
  (TERPRI 2)
  (PRIN1 "SELECT 1, 2, 3, OR 4: ")
  (SETQ C (RATOM))
  (COND
    ((NOT (NUMBERP C))
      (MENU) )
    ((LESSP C 1)
      (MENU) )
    ((GREATERP C 4)
      (MENU) )
    (T C) ) ))


(DEFINE ADDREC (LAMBDA ()
  (CLEARSCREEN)
  (WLIST (ADD RECORDS TO THE FILE))
  (TERPRI 1)
  (WAIT)
  (GETRECS) ))


(DEFINE GETRECS (LAMBDA (R)
  (SETQ R (GETENTRY))
  (COND
    ((NOT (NULL R))
```

Fig. 9-14. Comprehensive sample program.

```
            (SETQ AB (INSERT R AB))
            (GETRECS) ) ) ))


(DEFINE INSERT (LAMBDA (R AB)
  (COND
    ((NULL AB)
      (LIST R) )
    ((LTEQ (CONCATKEY R) (CONCATKEY (CAR AB)))
      (CONS R AB) )
    (T (CONS (CAR AB) (INSERT R (CDR AB)))) ) ))


(DEFINE GETENTRY (LAMBDA ()
  (CLEARSCREEN)
  (WLIST (FOLLOW EACH ENTRY WITH """/""" <RETURN>))
  (WLIST ("""/""" AT THE BEGINNING OF ANY ENTRY TERMINATES INPUT))
  (SETQ COL 1)
  (SETQ ROW 5)
  (GOTOXY COL ROW)
  (PROMPT ((LAST NAME:) (FIRST NAME:) (ADDRESS:) (CITY:) (STATE:) (ZIP:)
      (PHONE:)))
  (SETQ COL 15)
  (SETQ INCR 2)
  (READLIST L 7 COL ROW INCR) ))


(DEFINE PROMPT (LAMBDA (L)
  (COND
    ((NULL L) NIL)
    (T (WLIST (CAR L)) (TERPRI 1) (PROMPT (CDR L))) ) ))


(DEFINE READLIST (LAMBDA (L N COL ROW INCR TL)
  (COND
    ((ZEROP N) L)
    (T (GOTOXY COL ROW)
      (SETQ TL (RLIST TL))
      (COND
        ((NULL TL) NIL)
        (T (READLIST (REVERSE (CONS TL (REVERSE L)))
            (SUB1 N) COL (PLUS ROW INCR) INCR))))
    ) ))


(DEFINE LTEQ (LAMBDA (A B)
  (COND
    ((LESSP (ASCII A) (ASCII B)) T)
    ((GREATERP (ASCII A) (ASCII B)) NIL)
    ((AND
        (EQ (ASCII A) (ASCII B))
        (AND
          (EQ 1 (LENGTH A))
          (EQ 1 (LENGTH B)) ) ) T)
    (T (LTEQ (DROP1 A) (DROP1 B))) ) ))


(DEFINE CONCAT (LAMBDA (N1 N2)
  (COMPRESS ((CAR N1) BLANK (CAR N2))) ))
```

```
(DEFINE CONCATKEY (LAMBDA (R)
  (CONCAT (RETRIEVE 1 R) (RETRIEVE 2 R)) ))


(DEFINE REVIEW (LAMBDA (L)
  (COND
    ((NULL L)
      (WAIT) )
    (T (TERPRI 1)
       (LISTREC (CAR L))
       (TERPRI 2)
       (PRINT ("1:" GET NEXT RECORD))
       (PRINT ("2:" DELETE THIS RECORD))
       (PRINT ("3:" QUIT))
       (TERPRI 1)
       (PRIN1 (SELECT 1 2 OR "3:"))
       (SETQ C (RATOM))
       (COND
         ((EQ C 1)
           (REVIEW (CDR L)))
         ((EQ C 2)
           (SETQ AB (DELREC (CAR L) AB)) (REVIEW (CDR L)))
         ((EQ C 3) NIL)
         (T (REVIEW L))))
  ) ))


(DEFINE LISTREC (LAMBDA (R)
  (TERPRI 1)
  (WLIST (LIST (CAADR R) (CAAR R)))
  (WLIST (RETRIEVE 3 R))
  (WLIST1 (RETRIEVE 4 R))
  (WLIST ((CAR (RETRIEVE 5 R)) BLANK (CAR (RETRIEVE 6 R))))
  (WLIST (RETRIEVE 7 R)) ))


(DEFINE LISTFILE (LAMBDA (F)
  (SETUP)
  (LISTF F)
  (SETQ LPRINTER NIL)
  (TERPRI 1)
  (WAIT) ))

(DEFINE LISTF (LAMBDA (F)
  (COND
    ((NULL F) NIL)
    (T (LISTREC (CAR F)) (LISTF (CDR F)) ) ))


(DEFINE SETUP (LAMBDA ()
  (CLEARSCREEN)
  (PRINT (SEND OUTPUT TO SCREEN OR PRINTER?))
  (PRIN1 (TYPE """S""" FOR SCREEN OR """P""" FOR PRINTER:))
  (SETQ C (RATOM))
  (COND
    ((EQ C P)
```

Fig. 9-14. Comprehensive sample program. (Continued from page 301.)

```
         (SETQ LPRINTER T) )
      (T (COND ((NOT (EQ C S)) (SETUP)))) ) ))


(DEFINE DELREC (LAMBDA (R L)
  (COND
    ((NULL L) L)
    ((EQUAL R (CAR L))
      (CDR L) )
    (T (CONS (CAR L) (DELREC R (CDR L)))) ) ))


(DEFINE RLIST (LAMBDA (L W)
  (SETQ W (RATOM))
  (COND
    ((EQ W (QUOTE /)) L)
    (T (RLIST (REVERSE (CONS W (REVERSE L))))) ) ))


(DEFINE WLIST (LAMBDA (L)
  (COND
    ((ATOM (CAR L))
      (PRIN1 (CAR L))
      (SPACES 1) )
    (T (WLIST (CAR L))) )
  (COND
    ((NULL (CDR L))
      (TERPRI)
      BLANK )
    (T (WLIST (CDR L))) ) ))


(DEFINE WLIST1 (LAMBDA (L)
  (COND
    ((NULL L) BLANK)
    (T (PRIN1 (CAR L)) (SPACES 1) (WLIST1 (CDR L))) ) ))


(DEFINE CLEARSCREEN (LAMBDA ()
  (PRIN1 (ASCII 27))
  (PRIN1 (ASCII 42))
  BLANK ))


(DEFINE GOTOXY (LAMBDA (COL ROW)
  (PRIN1 (ASCII 27))
  (PRIN1 (ASCII 61))
  (PRIN1 (ASCII (PLUS 31 ROW)))
  (PRIN1 (ASCII (PLUS 31 COL)) BLANK) ))


(DEFINE PUTXY (LAMBDA (MSG COL ROW)
  (GOTOXY COL ROW)
  (PRIN1 MSG)
  BLANK ))


(DEFINE DROP1 (LAMBDA (WORD)
  (COMPRESS (CDR (EXPLODE WORD))) ))
```

```
(DEFINE RETRIEVE (LAMBDA (I A)
   (COND
      ((EQ I 1)
        (CAR A) )
      (T (RETRIEVE (SUB1 I) (CDR A))) ) ))


(DEFINE WAIT (LAMBDA ()
   (PRIN1 (PRESS ANY LETTER AND <RETURN> TO CONTINUE))
   (RATOM) ))
```

Fig. 9-14. Comprehensive sample program. (Continued from page 303.)

by BOOK are MENU, ADDREC, REVIEW, and LISTFILE, as indicated by the fact that the names of the functions are indented one level from BOOK. Functions called by these functions are indicated by further indentation.

Several commonly used utility functions are listed at the bottom of the chart. These include the functions CLEARSCREEN and GOTOXY, which handle machine-specific screen manipulation; WAIT, which holds the display in place until the user responds; and several list utilities. RETRIEVE returns the Ith element of a list. RLIST reads in a list terminated by a slash (/). WLIST writes out a list without the parentheses. It can handle nested lists, printing each on a separate line, and it is perhaps the most complex function shown in this chapter. WLIST1 is a simpler version of WLIST that does not output a carriage return after printing the list.

The function BOOK is rather simple. If the data list AB is an atom (because it has not yet been established as a list), it is initialized as the empty list. The constant BLANK is initialized. The function MENU is called to prompt the user to select the desired function. A COND function is used to invoke the selected function. Another COND is used to determine whether or not the QUIT option was selected. If it was, BOOK returns the word EXIT; otherwise it invokes itself recursively.

The MENU function is straightforward. Note that it validates its input so that it cannot return an invalid menu selection.

The ADDREC function takes care of adding records to the file. This it does by calling the function GETRECS. GETRECS in turn calls GETENTRY, to read in a record, and INSERT, to place that record in its proper place in the list.

The function GETENTRY is responsible for creating the user input screen and reading in the input. This rather tedious task is simplified considerably by the functions PROMPT and READLIST.

PROMPT merely prints a series of list elements on the screen in a column. These form the user prompts. READLIST reads a specified number of user inputs into a list. These two functions are coordinated to work together in presenting a unified input screen. This is a good illustration of how programs can be made simpler by properly breaking down tasks into simpler subtasks.

INSERT relies on the functions CONCATKEY and LTEQ to compare names in order to determine the proper place in a list for a record. CONCATKEY concatenates (joins together) last and first names, separated by a blank. To do this it uses the subfunction CONCAT. The concatenated names are passed to LTEQ, which determines whether its first argument is alphabetically Less Than or EQual to its second argument.

```
Figure 9-15:   Structure Chart for the Comprehensive Sample
               Program.


BOOK
     MENU
     ADDREC
          GETRECS
               GETENTRY
                    PROMPT
                    READLIST
               INSERT
                    CONCATKEY
                         CONCAT
                    LTEQ
                         DROP1
     REVIEW
          LISTREC
          DELREC
     LISTFILE
          SETUP
          LISTF
               LISTREC


Common-Use Functions:

     CLEARSCREEN        WAIT
     GOTOXY             WLIST
     RETRIEVE           WLIST1
     RLIST
```

Fig. 9-15. Structure chart for the comprehensive sample program.

LTEQ requires the subfunction DROP1, which returns the name of an atom, less its first letter. (Note: LTEQ was previously used in Fig. 9-13.)

The function REVIEW permits the data file to be reviewed on the video screen a record at a time. After each record is displayed, the user is given the choice of going to the next record, deleting the current record, or returning to the main menu. If the user chooses to delete the record, the function DELREC is called. (The function DELREC is similar in operation to the function DELETE in Fig. 9-13.)

Individual records are displayed by REVIEW, which calls the function LISTREC. LISTREC accomplishes such mundane tasks as printing the first name before the last name and putting city, state, and zip code all on the same line. The functions WLIST and RETRIEVE are used to accomplish these tasks.

LISTFILE allows the file to be listed in its entirety to either the video screen or to an attached line printer. The function **SETUP** prompts the user for a selection of output devices. If the printer is selected, the variable **LPRINTER** is set to **T**. **LISTFILE** sets it back to NIL to deselect the printer before exiting.

LISTFILE calls **LISTF** to take care of the actual listing of the file. **LISTF** uses **LISTREC** to print individual records; then it calls itself recursively until there are no more records left to list.

Notice that each function that makes up the address book program is quite short. The interactive nature of LISP allows these functions to be developed and tested independently. The intelligent decomposition of a program into subfunctions can greatly facilitate program development.

ADVANTAGES AND DISADVANTAGES OF LISP

Before looking at the advantages and disadvantages of LISP, you need to consider that LISP was developed for a specific purpose: research in the area of artificial intelligence. It was not intended to serve as a general-purpose language. Some of the disadvantages listed below relate to its limitations as a general-purpose language, which is perhaps unfair. It is, however, in keeping with the purpose of this book to point out limitations where they exist.

The principle strength of LISP is the ease with which it handles complex data structures. You have seen how LISP handles lists, association lists, and property lists, but LISP also supports trees, queues, and other advanced data structures. This ability to easily handle complex data structures is important in many applications, including those applications that require the organization of large amounts of knowledge. Such applications are often called expert systems.

Another strength of LISP is its suitability for interaction. Commands can be executed interactively from the keyboard, outside of a program. Program modules can be developed and tested independently and then easily linked together as a system. Programs developed in this manner are relatively easy to maintain and modify.

On the negative side, LISP has relatively primitive facilities for input and output. A list that is to be read from a file or from the keyboard requires delimiters. LISP cannot easily handle input of data from a sequential file (unless the data is embedded within LISP functions). LISP has no facilities for handling direct-access files. (Note: some implementations of LISP may have extensions that correct these deficiencies.)

Although LISP can handle simple calculations, numeric computation is not among its strengths. Its use of prefix notation is an annoyance to many.

Because LISP functions are stored as lists, LISP is rife with parentheses. The difficulty of matching so many parentheses is another minor annoyance.

LISP provides no built-in features for the formatting of output, such as the **PRINT USING** statement of BASIC or the **FORMAT** statement of Fortran.

LISP is an interpreted language, and as such it can be expected to produce programs that execute more slowly than equivalent programs written in a compiled language.

AVAILABILITY

Several versions of LISP are available for microcomputers that run the MS-DOS operating system, including Golden Common Lisp by Gold Hill Computers of Cambridge,

Massachusetts; IQLISP and IQCLISP by Integral Quality of Seattle, Washington, and PC Scheme by Texas Instruments. MuLISP from Soft Warehouse of Honolulu, Hawaii, is available for both MS-DOS and CP/M.

SUMMARY

LISP is a very powerful language, intended primarily for use in artificial intelligence research. It is also useful for applications that require extensive symbol manipulation (such as symbolic differential calculus) or the organization and application of knowledge (expert systems).

Although LISP is very different from conventional programming languages, it has a simple syntax and is remarkably consistent. Programming in LISP requires the understanding of a few basic concepts, such as prefix notation, recursion, and list manipulation. Once these concepts are mastered, programming in LISP is very simple.

Not all applications are suitable for programming in LISP. For an appropriate application, however, a LISP program will likely be much simpler to write than a program in a more conventional language such as BASIC or Pascal. LISP deserves a place in a programmer's bag of tricks.

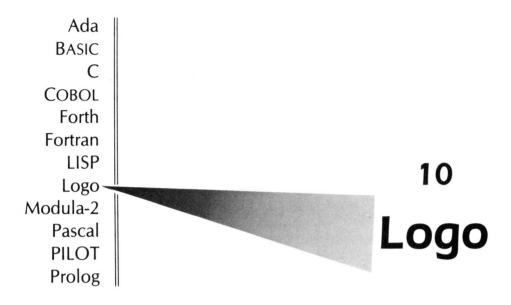

Ada
BASIC
C
COBOL
Forth
Fortran
LISP
Logo
Modula-2
Pascal
PILOT
Prolog

10

Logo

The Logo language was developed in 1968 by W. Feurzeig, S. Papert, M. Bloom, R. Grant, and C. Solomon at Bolt, Beranek and Newman, Inc., in Cambridge, Massachusetts. Their work was sponsored by the National Science Foundation. Further work on Logo has been done at the Massachusetts Institute of Technology in the Artificial Intelligence Laboratory and in the Division for Study and Research in Education.

The name "Logo" is not an acronym; it was coined by Feurzeig and is derived from the Greek word meaning "word" or "thought."

Logo is based on the earlier language LISP. (See the previous chapter for a discussion of the LISP language.) In fact, Logo is considered by some to be a dialect of LISP.

LISP was created for use in artificial intelligence research. Logo was created for use in introducing young children to computers and computer programming. The intent was to create a programming environment that would encourage learning.

The creators of Logo have succeeded admirably in designing a language suitable for children. Much effort has gone into the user interface, into making the language "friendly" and easy to use. An innovative graphics package with the engaging name Turtle Graphics has been included. An entire programming environment has been developed to support Logo.

The success Logo has achieved with children has led many to believe that it is a toy language, not suitable for use by adults. Nothing could be further from the truth! Underneath the friendly user interface lies the power of LISP, which is very much a serious language. Logo has many serious applications, as I will attempt to illustrate in this chapter. Besides, we adults can use a little friendliness now and then. A language needn't be difficult to use to be powerful.

Because Logo is so different in form from more conventional languages such as BA-SIC and Pascal, the topics in this chapter are presented in a somewhat different order than the topics in most of the other chapters of this book.

The examples in this chapter have been tested on an Apple II Plus using the Logo implementation by Terrapin, Inc., of Cambridge, Massachusetts.

LOGO PROGRAMS AND PROCEDURES

Logo commands can be executed directly, outside of any program. For example, typing the following:

PRINT [HELLO]

at the keyboard will cause the system to print HELLO on the screen. In this way, Logo resembles BASIC.

Logo statements can also be combined into Logo *procedures*. Logo procedures are modules that can stand alone or be invoked by other procedures. A Logo procedure is invoked by typing its name followed by any required arguments.

These procedures can be thought of as building blocks from which larger units can be built. What is different about Logo is that these procedures exist more or less independently in what is called a *workspace*. A workspace consists of whatever procedures and variables have been defined during a session. It is saved to disk as a unit and read back in from disk as a unit. Subject to space limitations, any number of Logo procedures can be in a workspace, whether or not they are related.

The distinction between a Logo program and a Logo procedure is not clear. The same module can serve both as an independent program and as a subprocedure of another program. For purposes of discussion, one could say that a program is a module that is invoked by the user, whereas a procedure is a module invoked by a program or another procedure. It is impossible to distinguish the two, however, except by context. The term procedure will therefore be used in this chapter to refer to both Logo programs and Logo procedures.

All Logo commands, procedures, and so forth must be written in uppercase. Logo does not support lowercase, even in character strings.

A simple Logo procedure (program) is shown in Fig. 10-1. All that this procedure does is print THIS IS A TEST. on the screen. The first line, TO DEMO1 is the procedure heading. Conceptually, it can be thought of as saying, "To execute the procedure called DEMO1, do the following." The next line, which begins with a semicolon (;), is a comment line and serves only to document the procedure. The last line (END) serves to terminate the procedure. The body of the procedure consists only of the PRINT statement.

This procedure is executed by simply typing its name, DEMO1, at the console. A procedure can also be executed from within another procedure, as shown in Fig. 10-2. This procedure invokes the procedure in Fig. 10-1.

DATA TYPES

The basic data elements in Logo are numbers, words, and lists. Each is discussed in detail in the paragraphs that follow.

```
;    Figure 10-1:   Minimal Logo Program.

TO DEMO1
     PRINT [THIS IS A TEST.]
END
```

Fig. 10-1. A minimal Logo program.

Numbers

Logo numbers can be integers or floating-point numbers. Integers can range between approximately plus two billion and minus two billion. Floating-point numbers can range in magnitude from approximately 10^{-38} to 10^{38}. Floating-point numbers are accurate to about seven digits.

Floating-point constants can be written with or without an exponent. Here are several examples:

    3.14159
    −2.3E2
    2.5N1

The first two numbers are written in the same manner as they are in most other languages. The E in the second number indicates a positive power of 10; that number could also be written as follows:

    −230.

The N in the third number indicates a negative power of 10; that number could also be written as:

    0.25.

Logo numbers are weakly typed. In other words, there is no strong distinction between integers and floating-point numbers. They may be used more or less

```
;    Figure 10-2:   Procedure Call Demonstration.

TO DEMO2
     ;   This procedure calls DEMO1
     DEMO1
END
```

Fig. 10-2. A procedure call demonstration.

interchangeably within the appropriate ranges. Logo converts freely between integer and floating-point numbers as necessary in arithmetic expressions.

Words

A *word* in Logo is a string of characters. A word is written with a leading quotation mark; for example, the following:

"HELLO

is a word. A word is terminated by a space or a square bracket; no final quotation mark is required. In fact, the statement

PRINT "HELLO"

will produce

HELLO"

on the screen.

It is possible to have embedded spaces in a word, but it is not common, because the same effect can be achieved using a list. Here is an example, however, of a word with embedded spaces:

"'THIS IS A WORD WITH EMBEDDED SPACES'

The single quotation marks serve as delimiters.

Logo has commands that allow the individual characters of a word to be manipulated. They are FIRST, BUTFIRST, LAST, and BUTLAST. FIRST produces the first character of a word. Thus, the following statement:

PRINT FIRST "LOGO

will print the letter L. BUTFIRST produces the word consisting of all but the first character of the word. The statement below:

PRINT BUTFIRST "LOGO

will print OGO.

Similarly, LAST produces the last character, and BUTLAST the word consisting of all but the last character. Thus, the following:

PRINT LAST "LOGO
PRINT BUTLAST "LOGO

will produce O and LOG, respectively.

Access to the interior letters of a word is gained indirectly. Procedures for doing so are discussed later in the chapter.

So far I have discussed numbers and words. There is a relationship between the two: a number is a word, but a word is not necessarily a number. Anywhere a word can appear, so can a number. The commands that are used to manipulate words also manipulate numbers in the same way. Not surprisingly, however, arithmetic operations cannot be performed with words that are not numbers.

The words "TRUE and "FALSE have special meaning in Logo, as discussed in the section on logical expressions later in this chapter.

The empty word is indicated by a quotation mark alone, so

PRINT "

will print nothing.

Lists

The remaining type of data element is the *list*. A list is a sequence of words, separated by blanks. It is delimited by square brackets, as in the following example:

[TODAY IS SUNDAY]

One difference between a word and a list is that while a word is manipulated character by character, a list is manipulated word by word. Quotation marks are not needed for the words in a list. A list may include numbers.

There is only one space between the words in a list; if you try to put multiple spaces between the words in a list, the system will eliminate them. Multiple spaces must be embedded within a word, as discussed in the section on words.

A list may also contain another list, as in the following:

[[A LIST] IN A LIST]

In this example, the list contains four elements, one of which is a list and three of which are words. The innermost list contains two words. This is a powerful concept, which can be used to build more complex data structures. It is discussed in more detail in the section on data structures.

Individual elements of a list can be manipulated by the FIRST, BUTFIRST, LAST, and BUTLAST commands. When used with lists, these commands operate on the elements of the list, which are usually words. Thus, the command:

PRINT FIRST [TODAY IS SUNDAY]

produces TODAY, and the command:

PRINT FIRST [[A LIST] IN A LIST]

produces A LIST. Similarly, the statement:

PRINT LAST [TODAY IS SUNDAY]

produces SUNDAY, and the following:

PRINT BUTLAST [[A LIST] IN A LIST]

produces [A LIST] IN A.

The empty list is written as [ ].

Procedures for manipulating lists to get at interior elements are discussed in later sections of this chapter.

Other Word and List Operations

You have already seen the operation of the FIRST, BUTFIRST, LAST, and BUTLAST commands. In this section you will learn about the WORD, LIST, SENTENCE, FPUT, and LPUT commands.

The WORD command takes two or more words as inputs and combines them into a single word. Here is an example with two inputs:

PRINT WORD "ONE "TWO

It produces the following:

ONETWO

on the screen. Parentheses must be used with more than two inputs. The parentheses must contain the command as well as its arguments. Here is an example with three inputs:

PRINT (WORD "ONE 2 "THREE)

It produces the following on the screen:

ONE2THREE

This example emphasizes that a number is also a word and that a quoted word must be followed by a space before a parenthesis.

The LIST command also takes two or more inputs, but each input may be a word or a list. The result is a single list. If an input is a list, that list will remain intact as an element of the new list. Here is a simple example:

PRINT (LIST "ONE [TWO THREE] 4)

It produces the following on the screen:

ONE [TWO THREE] 4

The SENTENCE operation is similar to LIST, but it strips one level of brackets off arguments that are lists. Thus the statement

    PRINT (SENTENCE "ONE [TWO THREE] 4)

will produce this:

    ONE TWO THREE 4

Applying the same logic to an example with nested lists, the command:

    PRINT (SENTENCE [THIS] [IS] [[A LIST] IN A LIST])

will produce this on the display screen:

    THIS IS [A LIST] IN A LIST

FPUT and LPUT each require exactly two inputs. The first input of each may be a word or a list, but the second must be a list. The result is a list, with the first input inserted into the second input (which was a list to begin with). With FPUT, the first input is inserted at the beginning of the list, and with LPUT it is inserted at the end.

Distinguishing between the actions of LIST, SENTENCE, and LPUT can be confusing at first. The following table attempts to illustrate the distinctions by example:

COMMAND	RESULT
LIST [A B] [C]	[[A B] [C]]
SENTENCE [A B] [C]	[A B C]
FPUT [A B] [C]	[[A B] C]
LIST [A B] "C	[[A B] C]
SENTENCE [A B] "C	[A B C]
FPUT [A B] "C	*
LIST [[A]] [B]	[[[A]] [B]]
SENTENCE [[A]] [B]	[[A] B]
FPUT [[A]] [B]	[[[A]] B]

The asterisk indicates that an error would result because the second input of FPUT must be a list, not a word.

Mastering these operations is not difficult, but it takes practice.

Variables

Variables in Logo can have values that are numbers, words, or lists. Variables do not need to be explicitly declared.

A variable name can be any legitimate Logo word. To refer to the name of a variable, the leading quotation mark is used. The value of a variable can be obtained in two different ways. Suppose the variable "X has the value 2. The Logo function THING can be used to get at this value. Thus, the statement below:

    PRINT THING "X

will print out 2. Because this is such a common operation, there is another, abbreviated, way to accomplish the same thing:

PRINT :X

The colon is usually called *dots* in Logo.

The following would print out the variable name itself:

PRINT "X

This, of course, is the same as printing the word "X, emphasizing that the variable name is a word.

THE ASSIGNMENT STATEMENT: MAKE

The **MAKE** command is used in Logo to assign a value to a variable. When you assign a value to a variable, you are really associating the variable name and a value. Accordingly, the two arguments required by **MAKE** are a variable name and a value. Here are several examples of assignment statements in Logo:

MAKE "X 2
MAKE "Y "HELLO
MAKE "Z [TODAY IS SUNDAY]
MAKE "W :X

These examples illustrate several points. The first argument of **MAKE** is the variable name, written with leading quotation mark. The second argument is the value to be assigned. That value may be a number, a word, a list, or the value of another variable. Recall that to obtain the value of that other variable, you precede its name with "dots."

To print out the value of these four variables, you could write the following:

PRINT :X
PRINT :Y
PRINT :Z
PRINT :W

The results would be, respectively:

2
HELLO
TODAY IS SUNDAY
2

Logo variables may be local to a particular procedure, or they may be global. Global variables in Logo are called *free variables*. A free variable has an existence of its own in a workspace and is accessible from within any Logo procedure in that work space. A free variable keeps its value from one execution of a procedure to the next. When a workspace is saved, the values of all free variables are saved with it. Typing the following statement:

MAKE "X 2

outside of a procedure in Logo creates X as a free variable.

ARITHMETIC EXPRESSIONS

Most arithmetic expressions in Logo use conventional infix notation. (See Chapter 2 for a discussion of infix notation.) The arithmetic operators provided are +, −, *, and /. An example illustrating an arithmetic expression is shown in Fig. 10-3. This example also illustrates the use of an assignment statement in an actual program.

The procedure in Fig. 10-3 is called **AREA**. It calculates and prints the area of a circle. Notice that the procedure heading includes an argument (:**RADIUS**). This permits the procedure to be used to compute the areas of circles of differing radii. Typing this:

AREA 5

would result in the printing of the area of a circle of radius 5, while the following:

AREA 10

would result in the printing of the area of a circle of radius 10.

The division operator (/) produces real results (as opposed to integer results); that is, the statement:

PRINT 5/2

will print 2.5. When integer division is desired, the operator **QUOTIENT** is available. This operator uses prefix notation. Thus, to find the integer quotient of five and two, you would write the following:

PRINT QUOTIENT 5 2

```
;   Figure 10-3:   Numerical Computations in Logo.

TO AREA   :RADIUS
    ;  Calculate area of a circle.
    ;  Illustrate Assignment and Arithmetic Expressions.
    MAKE "PI 3.14159
    MAKE "A  :PI * :RADIUS * :RADIUS
    PRINT A
END
```

Fig. 10-3. Numerical computations in Logo.

The result would be 2. Similarly, the remainder can be found by typing the statement:

PRINT REMAINDER 5 2

This result would be 1.

Another operator provided by Logo is RANDOM. The following statement:

PRINT RANDOM 5

will print a random integer between zero and four. If desired, the random number generator can be reinitialized using the RANDOMIZE command.

LOGICAL EXPRESSIONS (PREDICATES)

Logical expressions in Logo are called predicates. The result of a predicate in Logo is either "TRUE or "FALSE. Thus, the statement:

PRINT 2 > 1

would print TRUE, and the following:

PRINT 2 < 1

would print FALSE.

The basic logical operators in Logo are <, >, and =, which have the usual meanings. The operator NOT also has the usual meaning.

Other logical operators provided by Logo include the following:

ALLOF
ANYOF
NUMBER?
WORD?
LIST?
THING?

Each of these uses prefix notation. ALLOF corresponds to a logical AND, while ANYOF corresponds to a logical OR. Each has a default number of two arguments, as in the following:

ALLOF (2 > 1) (:X > :Y)

and

ANYOF (2 > 1) (2 > 3).

If either operator is to have more than two arguments, the entire expression, including the operator, is enclosed in parentheses. For example, the statement:

PRINT (ALLOF (2 > 1) (3 > 2) (4 > 3))

would print TRUE. Note carefully the placement of parentheses.

The operator NUMBER? returns "TRUE if its argument is a number. Similarly, WORD? and LIST? return "TRUE if their arguments are words or lists, respectively. The operator THING? outputs "TRUE if its argument is a variable that has some value associated with it.

INPUT AND OUTPUT

Input and output operations in Logo are rather simple. You have already seen examples of the PRINT statement. PRINT usually takes one argument, whether it be a number, a word, or a list. It can take multiple arguments when the command and its arguments are enclosed by parentheses. The two following PRINT statements will produce identical results:

PRINT [THIS IS A TEST]
(PRINT "THIS "IS "A "TEST)

Note that in the former statement, PRINT has but one argument, which is a list. In the latter statement, PRINT has four arguments, each of which is a word. Note carefully the placement of parentheses. Note that the last parenthesis is separated from the preceding word by a space; otherwise Logo would think that the word was TEST) and wouldn't be able to find the closing parenthesis.

The PRINT statement always causes a carriage return and line feed to be output after its arguments. If this is not desired, the PRINT1 statement can be used. Otherwise, the two statements are identical. The PRINT1 statement is useful for labeling output, as in the following example:

PRINT1 [THE ANSWER IS]
PRINT :X

In this example, THE ANSWER IS and the value of X will both appear on the same line of the display.

A procedure may also cause a result to be output using the OUTPUT statement. Here is a simple example:

TO DOUBLE :X
    OUTPUT 2 * :X
END

If the user types DOUBLE 2, Logo will respond RESULT: 4. The OUTPUT statement also causes an immediate exit from the procedure, regardless of its position within the procedure.

In a later section you will see how the OUTPUT statement can be used to pass data from a procedure to the procedure that called it.

Output can be redirected from the screen to a printer. Unfortunately, the technique for doing so is implementation dependent. For Terrapin Logo running on an Apple, the command that redirects output is called OUTDEV. For an Apple with a printer interface card in slot number 1, the following command:

OUTDEV 1

turns printer output on and the command:

OUTDEV 0

turns printer output off. When printer output is on, the output of a PRINT statement appears on the printer and on the screen. When printer output is off, the output of a PRINT statement appears only on the screen. An example program is shown in Fig. 10-4.

Logo provides two commands for input from the keyboard. REQUEST reads an input line and returns the result as a list, and READCHARACTER reads a single character and returns it as a word. A common error in Logo is to fail to recognize the form of the input. If a number is desired as an input, a list must be read and the number extracted from the list. This process is illustrated in the program of Fig. 10-5.

This program is a rewrite of the program in Fig. 10-3. It also calculates the area of a circle, but it prompts the user to input the radius from the keyboard. The command REQUEST returns a list from the keyboard, and FIRST REQUEST extracts the first word from that list, which happens to be a number. The MAKE command assigns the value of this number to the variable RADIUS. This form of input takes some getting used to by programmers with experience in more conventional languages such as BASIC or Pascal.

An example of the use of READCHARACTER is illustrated in a later section. It is used much less frequently than REQUEST by most Logo programmers.

CONTROL STRUCTURES

Logo has relatively few control structures when compared to some other languages,

```
;   Figure 10-4:   Printer Output.

TO OUTDEMO
    ; Demonstrate output to screen and printer.
    PRINT [THIS GOES TO THE SCREEN]
    OUTDEV 1
    PRINT [THIS GOES TO THE PRINTER]
    OUTDEV 0
END
```

Fig. 10-4. Printer output.

```
    :   Figure 10-5:   Console Input.

 TO CIRCLE
      ; Illustrate use of REQUEST
      ;    for console input.
      PRINT []
      PRINT1 "'ENTER RADIUS '
      MAKE "RADIUS FIRST REQUEST
      MAKE "A 3.14159 * :RADIUS * :RADIUS
      PRINT []
      PRINT [THE AREA OF A CIRCLE]
      ( PRINT1 "'WITH RADIUS ' :RADIUS "' IS ' :A )
      PRINT []
      PRINT []
 END
```

Fig. 10-5. Console input.

such as Pascal. Other than simple selection (the IF statement), the most widely used control structure in Logo is recursion. The counted loop (REPEAT) is primitive, and there is no conditional (while) loop nor case statement.

The absence of these structures can be misleading. It does not mean that Logo is less powerful than languages with these structures. First, the need for more advanced looping structures can be replaced by recursion. Second, the power of Logo is such that if a new control structure (such as a while loop or a more powerful counted loop) is needed, it can be created using the Logo RUN command.

Simple Selection: IF-THEN-ELSE and TEST

The format for the IF-THEN-ELSE statement is as follows:

IF predicate THEN s1 ELSE s2

Recall that a predicate in Logo is equivalent to a conditional or logical expression in other languages. The symbols s1 and s2 each stand for one or more statements. If the predicate is true, the statement(s) marked s1 are executed; if the predicate is false, the statement(s) marked s2 are executed.

Here is a simple example of an IF-THEN-ELSE statement in Logo:

```
IF :MONTH = 12 THEN
     MAKE "MONTH 1
     MAKE "YEAR :YEAR +1
ELSE
     MAKE "MONTH :MONTH + 1
```

The major problem with this structure is that the entire IF-THEN-ELSE construct must be typed as one line, as in most versions of BASIC. (It may wrap around to the next line; here it was split into several lines for clarity.) This restriction tends to make the structure hard to read, especially compared to the equivalent statements in Pascal or C.

Because of this problem, Logo offers another way to achieve the same result. Here is the same example using the TEST, IFTRUE, and IFFALSE statements:

```
TEST :MONTH = 12
IFTRUE MAKE "MONTH 1
    MAKE "YEAR :YEAR + 1
IFFALSE MAKE "MONTH :MONTH + 1
```

It should be obvious what this sequence of statements does.

By this time, you should be getting accustomed to the quotes and dots of Logo. Recall that preceding a name by quotes indicates that you are referring to the name of the variable, while preceding a name by dots indicates that you are referring to the value of the variable.

Loops: The REPEAT Statement

The only type of loop built into Logo is the REPEAT statement. The form of this statement is as follows:

```
REPEAT :N [statement(s)]
```

The :N may be either a variable or a constant. The statement or statements within the square brackets are repeated the appropriate number of times. There is no automatic incrementing of a counter variable as in the FOR statement of BASIC or Pascal, nor is there any conditional testing, as in a while statement.

A simple example of a REPEAT statement is given in the program in Fig. 10-6. The program prints the integers from one to 10 on the screen.

Procedures and Functions

Procedures were discussed in an earlier section because of their similarity to Logo

```
;   Figure 10-6:   A Counted Loop in Logo.

TO COUNT
     ; Count to 10
     MAKE "I 1
     REPEAT 10 [PRINT :I MAKE "I :I + 1]
END
```

Fig. 10-6. A counted loop in Logo.

programs. One point that needs to be discussed in more detail, however, is the manner of passing data to procedures.

A Logo procedure, like a procedure in most languages, has a list of arguments. Most languages, however, enclose the list of arguments in parentheses. Logo does not. The arguments are simply written after the name of the procedure, separated by blanks. Arguments of Logo procedures may be numbers, words, or lists.

Logo does not make a clear distinction between functions and procedures. A procedure that contains the OUTPUT statement behaves in Logo the same way as a function behaves in other languages and will be called a function in this chapter. The OUTPUT statement was discussed above in the section on input and output.

Logo provides the usual built-in functions, such as SQRT. To find the square root of 25, you would type the following:

```
SQRT 25.
```

If that value were to be assigned to the variable X, you would type this:

```
MAKE "X SQRT 25.
```

The point is that the value returned by the function SQRT can be used in an arithmetic operation.

Suppose you wanted a simple function to divide a number by two. It could be defined as follows:

```
TO HALVE :X
    OUTPUT :X / 2
END
```

This function could then be used in exactly the same way as the built-in function SQRT.

Recursion

As mentioned in Chapter 2, a procedure or function is recursive if it calls or invokes itself. The use of recursion is very common in Logo. Recursion is a powerful technique for the processing of lists and can also be used for looping.

An example of a recursive procedure is shown in Fig. 10-7. The procedure permits a computer with a printer to be used as an electronic typewriter. Because Logo does not support lowercase, neither does this electronic typewriter. Also, depending on the printer, it may not output anything until a carriage return is typed; then it will print the whole line.

The program reads a character from the keyboard, turns the printer on, prints the character, turns the printer back off, and then calls itself. When the procedure calls itself, the process starts over, repeating the same actions.

There are several features about this procedure that deserve comment. For one thing, it is much shorter than the corresponding program in other chapters. For another thing, it has no provision for stopping itself. Logo programs can be stopped from the

```
;    Figure 10-7:   Logo Electronic Typewriter, Version 1.

TO TYPE
    ; Emulate a typewriter; requires a printer.
    MAKE "C READCHARACTER
    OUTDEV 1
    PRINT1 :C
    OUTDEV O
    TYPE
END
```

Fig. 10-7. Logo Electronic Typewriter, Version 1.

keyboard, usually by typing Control-G. It is therefore common to deliberately include infinite loops in Logo programs; it makes programs simpler.

A recursive procedure can also be used in much the same way as a conditional loop would be in another language. Consider, for example, a procedure to count backwards from a given number to zero. Such a program is given in Fig. 10-8.

Notice that the first line of the program (after the comment) is a test for termination. This is not an infinite loop; it terminates as soon as the termination condition is met.

Next, let us consider a recursive function. The factorial of a positive integer is a mathematical function that is defined recursively. The factorial of zero is defined as one. The factorial of a positive integer N is defined as N times the factorial of $N-1$. This definition is recursive because it is defined in terms of itself. A recursive implementation of the factorial function is shown in the program of Fig. 10-9.

Recursive functions can also be used to advantage to process words and lists. Figure 10-10 contains a program called **TRIANGLE**. It accepts a word as an argument and then prints the word repeatedly, dropping the first letter of the word after each iteration. When there are no more letters remaining, the procedure stops. The result looks something like a word triangle that can be read horizontally and vertically.

```
;    Figure 10-8:    Recursion in Logo:   Count Down.

TO COUNTDOWN :N
    ; A recursive program to count in Reverse
    IF :N < O THEN STOP
    PRINT :N
    COUNTDOWN :N - 1
END
```

Fig. 10-8. Recursion in Logo: count down.

```
;    Figure 10-9:    The Factorial Function.

TO FACTORIAL :N
     ; Compute N Factorial
     IF :N = O THEN OUTPUT 1
     OUTPUT :N * FACTORIAL :N - 1
END
```

Fig. 10-9. The Factorial Function.

Consider the problem of summing a list of numbers when it is not known in advance how many numbers there are in the list. The numbers may have been read in from the keyboard or put in the list by another procedure. This process is easy to handle in Logo. A recursive procedure that sums the numbers in the list is shown in Fig. 10-11.

To sum a list of numbers using this procedure, you could type the following:

SUM [5 2 1 7 9 6]

Logo would print out the result, which is 30.

Getting accustomed to using recursion as a matter of routine often takes some time for programmers who first learned to program with a nonrecursive language such as BASIC. Most find, however, that it is well worth the effort.

The GO Statement

The GO statement of Logo corresponds to the GO TO statement of most other languages. It is not often needed, but it occasionally can be used to advantage.

Consider again the electronic typewriter program in Fig. 10-7. The program in Fig. 10-12 is a rewrite of this program, this time using a GO statement rather than recursion for looping.

DATA STRUCTURES

The basic Logo data types of numbers, words, and lists support the construction of some very sophisticated data structures. The key to this flexibility is that a list can include other lists as members.

```
;    Figure 10-10:    The Word Triangle.

TO TRIANGLE :W
     PRINT :W
     IF NOT BUTFIRST :W = "    TRIANGLE BUTFIRST :W
END
```

Fig. 10-10. The Word Triangle.

```
;   Figure 10-11:   Sum the Numbers in a List.

TO SUM :L
    IF BUTFIRST :L = [] THEN OUTPUT FIRST :L
    OUTPUT ( FIRST :L ) + SUM BUTFIRST :L
END
```

Fig. 10-11. Summing the numbers in a list.

Arrays

One data structure that Logo does not support is the array. Its place is taken by the list. It is quite simple to write a procedure to retrieve a particular element from a list (say the third element) as if that list were an array. Here is such a procedure, called GET:

```
TO GET :I :A
    IF :I = 1 THEN OUTPUT FIRST :A
    OUTPUT GET (:I − 1) BUTFIRST :A
END
```

The first parameter of the function, :I, is equivalent to the subscript of the array. The second parameter, :A, is the list itself.

```
;   Figure 10-12:   Logo Electronic Typewriter, Version 2.

TO TYPEGO
    ; Illustrate GO Statement
    PRINT [WELCOME TO YOUR ELECTRONIC TYPEWRITER]
    PRINT []
    PRINT [ENTER YOUR TEXT, ]
    PRINT [FOLLOWED BY <CONTROL-C>]
    PRINT []
    OUTDEV 1
    LOOP:  MAKE "C READCHARACTER
    IF :C = CHAR 3 THEN PRINT [] OUTDEV 0 STOP
    PRINT1 :C
    GO "LOOP
END
```

Fig. 10-12. Logo Electronic Typewriter, Version 2.

Records

Chapter 2 discussed the need for records. The example given was that of a record containing the name of a student and his or her scores on up to 20 tests. You can represent the name of the student by a list, and the test scores by another list. These two lists form the first and second elements of another list, which corresponds to the record. Because I am using lists instead of arrays, I need not specify in advance how many test scores there might be.

Because Logo does not require the advance declaration of data structures, this structure is illustrated by example. The following creates a structure containing the records of two students:

```
MAKE "CLASS
   [ [ [JOHN DOE]
         [95 87 100 93] ]
   [ [MARY SMITH]
         [98 85 95 88] ] ]
```

(This must be entered as one line.)

The following illustrates the organization of this data structure: If you type the following:

```
FIRST :CLASS
```

the result is this:

```
[ [JOHN DOE] [95 87 100 93] ]
```

This is the first record of the data structure. If you type the following:

```
LAST :CLASS
```

the result is below:

```
[ [MARY SMITH] [98 85 95 88] ]
```

This is the last record of the data structure. Each record consists, as expected, of a name and several test scores.

Now suppose you wish to extract the name from the first record. This can be accomplished by typing this:

```
PRINT FIRST FIRST :CLASS
```

The following will extract the last name of the first student:

```
PRINT LAST FIRST FIRST :CLASS
```

Similarly, the first test score for this student can be retrieved by the following command:

PRINT FIRST LAST FIRST :CLASS

As you may have noticed, this can get a bit tedious, even if you fully understand what is going on. Imagine what you would have to write in order to print the third test score of the seventeenth student in a larger class. There must be a better way.

As a matter of fact, there is a better way. Logo procedures can be written to take care of all the busy work involved in retrieving records and elements of records from the data structure. Figure 10-13 shows several such procedures, including procedures to do the following:

☐ Print out all the student names.
☐ Retrieve the Ith record in the list.
☐ Retrieve the record that matches a given student name.
☐ Retrieve the scores from a given record (as a list).
☐ Retrieve the Ith test score from a list of scores.

These procedures can be used singly or in combination to handle most requirements for record retrieval. Another set of procedures could be written to handle update requirements. Notice that each procedure is quite short.

To print out all the names, such as for a class roster, type the following:

ROSTER :CLASS

To print out the name and scores of the second student, type this:

PRINT GET 2 :CLASS

To print out the record of John Doe, type this:

PRINT GETNAME [JOHN DOE] :CLASS

The scores are separated from the rest of the record using GETSCORES. Individual test scores are retrieved from a list of scores using GETTEST. For example, to print the score received by John Doe on the third test, type the following:

PRINT GETTEST 3 GETNAME [JOHN DOE] :CLASS

This illustrates how Logo procedures can be combined, with the output of one procedure becoming the input to another procedure.

Linked Lists

Chapter 2 showed how linked lists could be implemented using arrays in a language such as BASIC, which does not directly support linked lists. Because the list is supported directly in Logo, it is not necessary to emulate linked lists. Neither is it necessary to

```
;   Figure 10-13:   Logo Gradebook Program.

TO ROSTER :CLASS
    PRINT FIRST FIRST :CLASS
    IF NOT BUTFIRST :CLASS = [] THEN ROSTER BUTFIRST CLASS
END

TO GET :I :A
    IF :I = 1 THEN OUTPUT FIRST :A
    OUTPUT GET ( :I - 1 ) BUTFIRST :A
END

TO GETNAME :NAME :CLASS
    ; Return the record of :NAME
    IF :CLASS = [] THEN PRINT [NOT FOUND] OUTPUT [] STOP
    IF :NAME = FIRST FIRST :CLASS THEN OUTPUT FIRST :CLASS
    OUTPUT GETNAME :NAME BUTFIRST :CLASS
END

TO GETSCORES :NAME :CLASS
    IF :CLASS = [] THEN PRINT [NOT FOUND] OUTPUT [] STOP
    IF :NAME = FIRST FIRST :CLASS THEN OUTPUT FIRST
        BUTFIRST FIRST :CLASS
    OUTPUT GETSCORES :NAME BUTFIRST :CLASS
END

TO GETTEST :I :RECORD
    ; Retrieve the Ith test score from :RECORD
    IF :I = 1 THEN OUTPUT FIRST :RECORD
    IF BUTFIRST :RECORD = [] PRINT [THERE AREN'T THAT
        MANY TESTS] OUTPUT [] STOP
    OUTPUT GETTEST ( :I - 1 ) BUTFIRST :RECORD
END

TO CLASSBOOK :CLASS
    PRINT FIRST :CLASS
    IF NOT BUTFIRST :CLASS = [] THEN
        CLASSBOOK BUTFIRST :CLASS
END
```

Fig. 10-13. Logo Gradebook Program.

deal directly with the links or an end-of-list indicator, as these are taken care of by the language, safely out of sight of the user.

The list illustrated in Chapter 2 consisted of first names. Initially the list consisted of the names Bob, Ernie, and Jim. The list could be created as follows in Logo:

    MAKE "L [BOB ERNIE JIM]

Procedures for adding and deleting names from this list are shown in Fig. 10-14. Using the procedure INSERT, Jerry could be added to the list as follows:

    MAKE "L INSERT "JERRY :L

Ernie could be deleted from the list by typing the following:

    MAKE "L DELETE "ERNIE :L

Logo does not provide directly for the comparison of characters or words. The < and > operators work only with numbers. (The = works with numbers and words.)

```
;   Figure 10-14:   List Insertion and Deletion.

TO INSERT :NAME :L
    ; Insert a name in a list
    IF :L = [] THEN OUTPUT SENTENCE :NAME :L
    IF LTEQ :NAME FIRST :L THEN OUTPUT FPUT :NAME :L
    OUTPUT ( SENTENCE FIRST :L INSERT :NAME BUTFIRST :L )
END

TO LTEQ :A :B
    ; Determine whether :A is less than or equal to :B
    IF ASCII FIRST :A < ASCII FIRST :B THEN OUTPUT "TRUE
    IF ASCII FIRST :A > ASCII FIRST :B THEN OUTPUT "FALSE
    IF BUTFIRST :A = " THEN OUTPUT "TRUE
    IF BUTFIRST :B = " THEN OUTPUT "FALSE
    OUTPUT LTEQ BUTFIRST :A BUTFIRST :B
END

TO DELETE :NAME :L
    ; Delete a name from a list
    IF :L = [] THEN OUTPUT :L
    IF :NAME = FIRST :L THEN OUTPUT BUTFIRST :L
    OUTPUT SENTENCE FIRST :L DELETE :NAME BUTFIRST :L
END
```

Fig. 10-14. List insertion and deletion.

The INSERT procedure requires word comparison so that the name can be inserted into its proper position alphabetically. A new procedure had to be written to carry out this comparison.

The procedure LTEQ compares its two inputs and determines whether or not its first input is less than or equal to its second input (alphabetically). The comparison is done a letter at a time and uses the ASCII function to convert the letter to its numeric representation. The procedure first attempts to make the comparison based on the first letters of each word. If the first letters are equal, it checks to see whether one of the words has no more letters. (This would distinguish B from BE, for example.) If not, the procedure is called recursively with the remaining letters of each word.

The logic of the INSERT and DELETE procedures may take some study to understand. Neither is very long, however. Short procedures such as these can be used as building blocks for longer, more complicated procedures.

FILE HANDLING

Logo does not provide facilities for the reading and writing of disk files from within programs. Logo relies instead on the concept of a workspace, as discussed above.

If a Logo program needs to maintain a set of data from one session to the next, it does not need to create a separate disk file. It can instead store the data in free variables within the workspace. Then when the workspace is saved, the free variables are saved along with any procedures that happen to be in the workspace.

You have already seen an example of maintaining data in a free variable in the preceding section on linked lists. The list L is a free variable and can be saved from session to session by saving the workspace along with the procedures INSERT, LTEQ, and DELETE.

The command to save a workspace in Terrapin Logo is as follows:

    SAVE "WSNAME

where WSNAME is the desired name for the workspace. The workspace can be read back in by typing the following:

    READ "WSNAME

GRAPHICS

In the beginning of this chapter, I stated that Logo was designed for children and has been used extensively by them. At this point you might be wondering why children find list insertion and deletion so fascinating. The fact is, they don't. What attracts children to Logo is the graphics. What keeps their interest is the friendly, interactive environment. Lists, recursion, and the other features of Logo are simply means to an end.

The graphics package provided with Logo is called *Turtle Graphics.* It is very similar to the graphics package of the same name provided as part of the Apple implementation of UCSD Pascal. The main difference is that in Logo, unlike UCSD Pascal, graphics commands can be executed directly from the keyboard.

The central metaphor of Turtle Graphics is the turtle. The turtle is an imaginary creature who can be moved about the screen. He carries with him a pen, which can

```
;   Figure 10-15:   Logo Turtle Graphics Program.

TO PATTERN :N
     TRI
     RIGHT 360 / :N
     PATTERN :N
END

TO TRI
     REPEAT 3 [FORWARD 80 RIGHT 120]
END

TO SETUP
     DRAW
     LEFT 30
     HIDETURTLE
END
```

Fig. 10-15. Logo Turtle Graphics Program.

be "down" so that it leaves a trail, or "up" so that it does not leave a trail. The pen can write with different colors of ink, depending on the capabilities of the computer and video display.

Because a turtle has a head, he is always heading in a single direction. The turtle can be moved forward or backward a given number of steps, or he can be turned to the right or left a specified angle (in degrees). Using combinations of these movements, the turtle can be made to trace out any shape.

The details of turtle graphics may vary slightly from implementation to implementation. The discussion in this section is based on the Terrapin implementation of Logo on the Apple microcomputer.

The graphics mode is entered with the command DRAW. This command clears the screen and displays the turtle as a small triangle in the center of the screen. With the turtle thus displayed, its position and heading are readily observed. The turtle can be hidden from view, if desired, with the command HIDETURTLE.

The main commands for moving the turtle and changing its direction are FORWARD, BACKWARD, RIGHT, and LEFT. Each command is followed by a number. In the case of FORWARD and BACKWARD, the number represents the number of steps to be taken in the specified direction. In the case of RIGHT and LEFT, the number represents the number of degrees to turn.

Some interesting designs can be made using just these simple commands. Figure 10-15 contains three short Logo procedures which were used to create the patterns shown in Figs. 10-16, 10-17, and 10-18.

The procedure SETUP in Fig. 10-15 is used to clear the screen and initialize the turtle. The procedure TRI draws a single equilateral triangle. The procedure PATTERN creates a pattern consisting of multiple equilateral triangles.

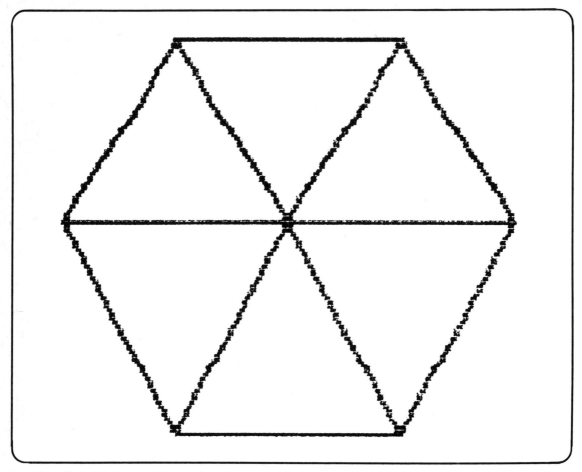

Fig. 10-16. Sample turtle graphics output.

PATTERN calls TRI to draw a triangle, turns the turtle to the right, and then calls itself recursively. The only way to stop the procedure is by typing Control-G. The parameter :N of PATTERN is used to determine how many triangles to draw in one complete revolution. The design in Fig. 10-16 was created with the following commands:

```
SETUP
PATTERN 6
```

Following the drawing of each triangle, the turtle was turned 360/6 = 60 degrees to the right. There are therefore 6 triangles visible in the pattern.

The design in Fig. 10-17 was created with the following commands:

```
SETUP
PATTERN 12
```

In this case the turtle turned 360/12 = 30 degrees between triangles.

The design in Fig. 10-18 was created with the following:

SETUP
PATTERN 18

In this case the turtle turned 20 degrees between triangles.

One of the fascinating things about turtle graphics in Logo is that a few short procedures can be used to create such a variety of designs. Given a few short procedures, a child (or even an adult!) can create variation upon variation on the basic theme.

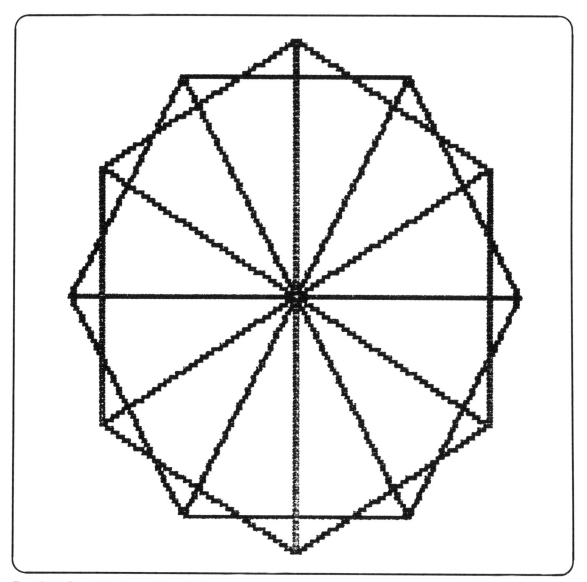

Fig. 10-17. Sample turtle graphics output.

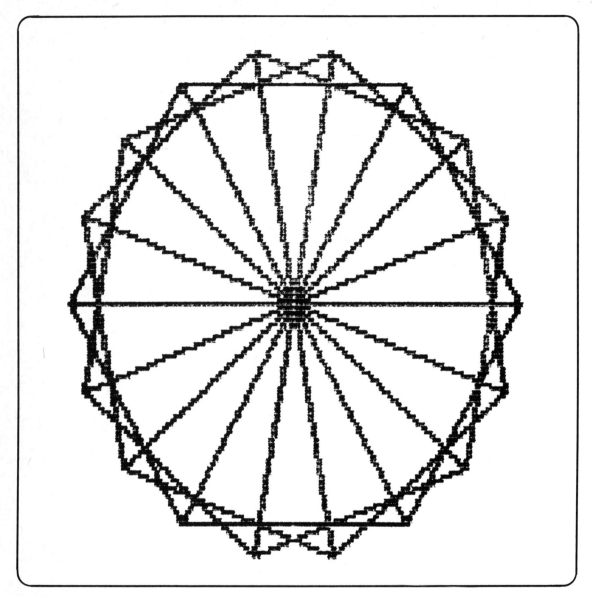

Fig. 10-18. Sample turtle graphics output.

Turtle graphics procedures are easy to write in Logo. It would be a simple matter to write a procedure to create a square instead of a triangle and then to substitute it for TRI in the procedure PATTERN. This would permit the creation of a whole new family of designs. From there, a short procedure could be written to create any regular polygon (triangle, square, pentagon, hexagon, etc.) for incorporation into the PATTERN procedure.

I have only touched on the power of turtle graphics in Logo. My intent has been to convey a little of their flavor and a hint at their potential. More extensive coverage of graphics in Logo may be found in almost any of the available books on Logo. A particularly excellent book on Logo is *Logo For the Apple II* by Harold Abelson (Byte/McGraw-Hill, Peterborough, NH, 1982).

THE COMPREHENSIVE SAMPLE PROGRAM

The sample programs shown so far in this chapter have been rather short. You can gain a better appreciation for Logo by examining a longer example, one that does something useful.

The comprehensive sample program of this chapter maintains a list of names and addresses in alphabetical order by name. The program permits records to be added to the list, deleted from the list, reviewed on the screen, and listed to a printer. The program is shown in Fig. 10-19.

The list itself is stored in a free variable called **AB**. The list is not stored in a separate disk file as in the corresponding programs of other chapters. It is instead saved as part of the workspace along with the Logo procedures that comprise the program. The user must therefore remember to save the workspace at the end of a session in which records have been added or deleted. (A Logo user should consult the documentation that came with his or her system for procedures to save and retrieve workspaces.) The disadvantage of this technique is that the size of the address list is limited by the amount of computer memory available.

One feature that this program lacks that is found in the corresponding programs in other chapters is the dump feature. It is not necessary in the Logo version because all the links are hidden from the user. A user who wants to examine the structure of the list can do so interactively.

The most striking feature of this program is that it is only about one third the length of the corresponding programs in most of the other chapters. This is attributable to the fact that Logo directly supports the list as a data structure, making the emulation of a list using arrays and pointers unnecessary. The system takes care of all the housekeeping functions that are taken care of by the program in languages such as BASIC and Pascal.

An advantage of the Logo program over most of the other versions of this program is that the lengths of the individual fields do not have to be specified in advance. This is because each field is a list, and lists can be of any length. In languages such as Pascal and C, the programmer has to specify in advance the length of each field (for example 12 characters for a last name) and reserve the appropriate amount of space. Space allocation is handled by the system in Logo.

The structure of the program is illustrated by the structure chart in Fig. 10-20. The main program is called **BOOK**. It consists of a control loop, which calls the appropriate procedure depending on the option selected interactively. **BOOK** uses a primitive emulation of a **case** statement to handle the choices.

The procedure **APPEND** uses the procedure **GETENTRY** to read a name and address record from the console and the procedure **INSERT** to add the record to the list in the proper position. The logic used in the **INSERT** procedure is similar to that used in the insert procedure in Fig. 10-14. Before doing alphabetic comparisons of names, the first names are concatenated to the end of the last names using the Logo primitive **WORD**.

Both the **REVIEW** and the **LISTFILE** procedures use the procedure **LISTREC** to

```
;   Figure 10-19:   Comprehensive Sample Program.

TO BOOK
    ;   Maintain a list of names, addresses, and
    ;    telephone numbers in alphabetical order
    ;    by name.
    ;   The list is in the free variable "AB.
    ;
    IF NOT THING? "AB THEN MAKE "AB []
    LOOP:   MAKE "CASE MENU
    IF :CASE = 1 THEN APPEND GO "LOOP
    IF :CASE = 2 THEN REVIEW :AB GO "LOOP
    IF :CASE = 3 THEN LISTFILE GO "LOOP
    IF :CASE = 4 THEN STOP
    IF :CASE < 1 THEN GO "LOOP
    IF :CASE > 4 THEN GO "LOOP
END

TO MENU
    ; Display menu and return selection
    ;
    CLEARTEXT
    PRINT [1)   ADD TO FILE]
    PRINT []
    PRINT [2)   REVIEW FILE ON SCREEN]
    PRINT []
    PRINT [3)   LIST FILE TO SCREEN OR PRINTER]
    PRINT []
    PRINT [4)   QUIT]
    PRINT []
    PRINT []
    PRINT1 [SELECT 1, 2, 3, OR 4:  '  ']
    OUTPUT FIRST REQUEST
END

TO APPEND
    ; Add records to the file
    ;
    CLEARTEXT
    PRINT [ADD RECORDS TO THE FILE]
    PRINT []
    WAIT
    LOOP:   MAKE "E GETENTRY
    IF :E = [] THEN STOP
    MAKE "AB INSERT :E :AB
    GO "LOOP
END
```

Fig. 10-19. Comprehensive sample program.

```
TO NEXT :COL :ROW
    MAKE "ROW :ROW + 2
    CURSOR :COL :ROW
END

TO GETENTRY
    ; Prompt user and return a record
    ;
    CLEARTEXT
    MAKE "ROW 5
    MAKE "COL 1
    CURSOR :COL :ROW
    PRINT1 [LAST NAME:]
    NEXT :COL :ROW
    PRINT1 [FIRST NAME:]
    NEXT :COL :ROW
    PRINT1 [ADDRESS:]
    NEXT :COL :ROW
    PRINT1 [CITY:]
    NEXT :COL :ROW
    PRINT1 [STATE:]
    NEXT :COL :ROW
    PRINT1 [ZIP CODE:]
    NEXT :COL :ROW
    PRINT1 [PHONE:]
    MAKE "ROW 5
    MAKE "COL 15
    CURSOR :COL :ROW
    MAKE "E []
    MAKE "E FPUT REQUEST :E
    IF FIRST :E = [] THEN OUTPUT []
    REPEAT 6 [NEXT :COL :ROW MAKE "E LPUT REQUEST :E]
    OUTPUT :E
END

TO INSERT :ENTRY :AB
    ; Insert an entry in the address book in
    ;   alphabetical order by name.
    ;
    IF :AB = [] THEN OUTPUT FPUT :ENTRY :AB
    IF BEFORE ( WORD ( FIRST FIRST :ENTRY )
        ( FIRST FIRST BUTFIRST :ENTRY ) )
        ( WORD FIRST FIRST FIRST :AB )
        ( FIRST FIRST BUTFIRST FIRST :AB ) )
        THEN OUTPUT FPUT :ENTRY :AB
    OUTPUT FPUT FIRST :AB INSERT :ENTRY BUTFIRST :AB
END

TO BEFORE :A :B
```

```
      ; Determine whether :A comes before :B
      IF ASCII FIRST :A < ASCII FIRST :B THEN OUTPUT "TRUE
      IF ASCII FIRST :A > ASCII FIRST :B THEN OUTPUT "FALSE
      IF BUTFIRST :A = " THEN OUTPUT "TRUE
      IF BUTFIRST :B = " THEN OUTPUT "FALSE
      OUTPUT BEFORE BUTFIRST :A BUTFIRST :B
END

TO REVIEW :L
      ; Print records to screen 1 at a time.
      ; Allows deletion of current record.
      ;
      IF :L = [] THEN PR [] WAIT STOP
      PR []
      LISTREC FIRST :L
L1:   PR []
      PR []
      PRINT [1)  GET NEXT RECORD]
      PRINT [2)  DELETE THIS RECORD]
      PRINT [3)  QUIT]
      PRINT []
      PRINT1 [SELECT 1, 2, OR 3:  '  ']
      MAKE "C FIRST REQUEST
      IF ANYOF ( :C < 1 ) ( :C > 3 ) THEN GO "L1
      IF :C = 1 THEN REVIEW BUTFIRST :L
      IF :C = 2 THEN MAKE "AB DELETE FIRST :L :AB
         REVIEW BUTFIRST :L
END

TO LISTREC :ENTRY
      ; Display a single record.
      ;
      PRINT []
      ; First the name.
      PRINT1 GET 2 :ENTRY
      PRINT1 "'   '
      PRINT GET 1 :ENTRY
      ; Now the address.
      PRINT GET 3 :ENTRY
      ; Now the city, state, and zip code.
      PRINT1 GET 4 :ENTRY
      PRINT1 "', '
      PRINT1 GET 5 :ENTRY
      PRINT1 "'  '
      PRINT GET 6 :ENTRY
      ; Now the phone number.
      PRINT GET 7 :ENTRY
END
```

Fig. 10-19. Comprehensive sample program. (Continued from page 337.)

```
TO DELETE :E :L
    ; Delete element :E from list :L
    IF :L = [] THEN OUTPUT :L
    IF MATCH :E FIRST :L THEN OUTPUT BUTFIRST :L
    OUTPUT FPUT FIRTS :L DELETE :E BUTFIRST :L
END

TO MATCH :A :B
    ; Compares two list elements
    OUTPUT ALLOF ( ( GET 1 :A ) = ( GET 1 :B ) )
       ( ( GET 2 :A ) = ( GET 2 :B ) )
END

TO LISTFILE
    ; List file to screen or printer.
    SETUP
    LISTF :AB
    OUTDEV 0
    PR []
    WAIT
END

TO SETUP
    CLEARTEXT
    L1:   PRINT1 [LIST FILE TO S)CREEN OR P)RINTER? ]
    MAKE "C FIRST REQUEST
    IF :C = "P THEN OUTDEV 1 ELSE IF NOT :C = "S THEN GO "L1
END

TO LISTF :F
    IF :F = [] STOP
    LISTREC FIRST :F
    LISTF BUTFIRST :F
END

TO WAIT
    PRINT1 [PRESS <RETURN> TO CONTINUE...]
    MAKE "C REQUEST
END

TO GET :I :A
    ; Retrieve the Ith record of :A
    IF :I = 1 THEN OUTPUT FIRST :A
    OUTPUT GET ( :I - 1 ) BUTFIRST :A
END
```

Fig. 10-19. Comprehensive sample program. (Continued from page 338.)

```
    Figure 10-20:   Structure Chart for the
                    Comprehensive Sample Program.


        BOOK
            MENU
            APPEND
                GETENTRY
                INSERT
                    BEFORE
            REVIEW
                LISTREC
                DELETE
                    MATCH
            LISTFILE
                SETUP
                LISTF
                    LISTREC



        Common-Use Procedures:

            WAIT
            GET
```

Fig. 10-20. Structure chart for the comprehensive sample program.

print a single record. LISTREC in turn relies on the procedure GET to extract individual elements of the record. GET was first seen in Fig. 10-13.

The REVIEW procedure provides the option of deleting a record by calling the DELETE procedure. The logic for deletion is similar to that seen in Fig. 10-14.

The LISTFILE procedure provides the option of sending the names to a printer as well as seeing them on the screen. This is accomplished by the subprocedure SETUP.

Each of the procedures in this program is quite short. The longest is GETENTRY, but it is not involved—only tedious. Its length is governed by the amount of data to be read in from the console and by the need to format the input screen. The substantive procedures, such as INSERT and DELETE, are only a few lines long.

ADVANTAGES AND DISADVANTAGES OF LOGO

One of the main advantages of Logo is its ease of use. Even young children can learn to program in Logo, almost as soon as they can learn to read. Logo is designed for interactive use with the user seated at the keyboard. Most other languages (including Fortran, COBOL, Pascal, and even BASIC) were designed for batch use, with the user interacting by means of keypunch, card reader, and printer.

Logo easily supports data structures of many kinds, including lists, queues, and trees. These data structures are well-suited for the organization of knowledge. The available control structures are well-suited for manipulating these data structures. The result is a language that can accommodate the development of programs that rely upon accumulated knowledge and upon decision making based on that knowledge. In other words, Logo is well-suited for programs in the field of artificial intelligence.

Logo can handle symbols as well as numbers. It is excellent for those sorts of problems that require the manipulation of words, characters, and other symbols. One such potential application would be symbolic differential calculus.

Another of Logo's principal strengths is in the area of graphics. Complex graphic images are easily created in Logo using turtle graphics.

Another plus is the way that Logo procedures can be developed and defined separately, and then interact together. This means that when a single procedure is modified, the other procedures in the program do not have to be redefined. This greatly speeds the development of complex programs, such as the program in Fig. 10-19.

On the negative side, Logo does not directly support the reading and writing of data files from within programs. Because Logo is an interpretive language, Logo programs are relatively slow in execution.

Although Logo can handle simple calculations, numeric computation is not its main strength. It lacks an exponentiation function, although one can easily be defined.

AVAILABILITY

Versions of Logo are available for several popular microcomputers including the Apple II series, the IBM Personal Computer, the Radio Shack Color Computer, the Commodore 64, and the Texas Instruments TI 99/4A.

SUMMARY

Logo is a very powerful and easy-to-use language. It is well-suited for many applications, including graphics, symbol manipulation, artificial intelligence, and general programming.

Logo is easy to learn. Programming in Logo tends to be quite different than programming in BASIC, Pascal or one of the other common languages. This is largely due to the prevalence of recursion as a control structure and to Logo's ability to handle data in lists.

Logo is an excellent choice for both children and adults. It deserves to be much more widely used than it is at present.

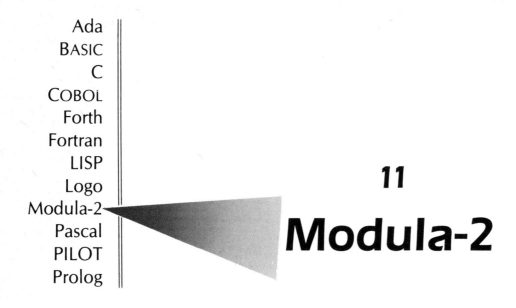

11

Modula-2

Modula-2 is one of the newest of the languages presented in this book; of these languages, only Ada is newer. Modula-2 was developed by Niklaus Wirth of the Eidgenossische Technische Hochschule (Federal Institute of Technology), Zurich, Switzerland, and first implemented in 1979. It was first made available to the public in 1981.

Niklaus Wirth is perhaps better known as the creator of the Pascal language. After creating Pascal, Wirth developed an experimental language called Modula. Modula has some interesting features, but it was never intended for widespread use. Modula-2 is the direct descendant of both Pascal and Modula. It could as easily have been called Pascal-2, but Wirth chose Modula-2 because its syntax more closely resembles that of Modula. In any event, programmers who are familiar with Pascal will find many similarities between Pascal and Modula-2.

Modula-2 also has roots in the language Mesa, which Wirth encountered while on sabbatical leave in 1976 at the Xerox Palo Alto Research Center, Palo Alto, California.

The name Modula is short for MODUlar LAnguage. The name is customarily written as "Modula-2" rather than "MODULA-2," so that custom will be followed in this book. Modula-2 is often referred to simply as "Modula."

Modula-2 is a general-purpose language; it is suitable for most programming applications, including scientific applications, business applications, and systems programming applications. It is particularly well-suited to large, complex applications. The example programs of this chapter were tested on a Zenith Z-150 microcomputer using the Modula-2 compiler by Interface Technologies Corporation (ITC) of Houston, Texas. This version is referred to as ITC Modula-2 herein and runs on most IBM PC-compatible microcomputers.

PROGRAM STRUCTURE: THE MODULE CONCEPT

The feature that most distinguishes Modula-2 from other languages is the *module*. The structure of a Modula-2 program is defined in terms of modules. The program module corresponds to the main program of other languages. Other modules can be defined to support the program module. A module usually consists of a group of related procedures (subroutines). The module thus provides a level of organization between the main program and the procedure.

A module can be thought of as a fence around a segment of a program. This fence allows selected variables and procedures to be isolated from the remainder of the program. This reduces the chance of interference between different parts of the program. Data and access to procedures can be passed explicitly from one module to another using the **EXPORT** and **IMPORT** statements. These will be described shortly.

A major feature of Modula-2 is that modules can be stored in different files and compiled separately. This greatly facilitates the development and testing of large programs. Once a module has been compiled and successfully tested, it need not be recompiled, no matter how many times the main program is recompiled. With languages that lack this feature, all parts of the program must be recompiled whenever any part of the program is changed. This feature will be illustrated later in the chapter.

A simple example of a Modula-2 program is shown in Fig. 11-1. This program simply prints **This is a test.** on the video screen. The first line of the program is a comment, enclosed between the symbols (* and *). It serves to identify the program. The program itself begins with the heading **MODULE Modula1;**.

An illustration of the modular structure of Modula-2 is found in the next line. The basic input and output routines are implemented as procedures in a separately compiled module called **Terminal**. This module resides in the system library. (With most languages, such routines are included in the compiler. The Modula-2 approach improves the portability of the language and keeps the size of the compiler to a minimum.) This program needs the procedures **WriteString** and **WriteLn**, so it must **IMPORT** these procedures from the module **Terminal**, as illustrated.

The main body of the program is contained between **BEGIN** and **END Modula1**. Note that the name of the module follows the **END**, and that a period follows, because this is the end of the program.

```
(*   Figure 11-1:   A Simple Modula-2 Program.   *)
(*                                                *)
MODULE Modula1;
  FROM Terminal IMPORT WriteString, WriteLn;
  BEGIN
    WriteString("This is a test.");
    WriteLn();
  END Modula1.
```

Fig. 11-1. A simple Modula-2 program.

The main body of the program is quite simple, consisting of two statements. There are several points to note, however. First, Modula-2 is case-sensitive. In other words, WriteString is not the same as Writestring. They differ because the letter "s" is capitalized in one instance and not capitalized in the other. All Modula-2 keywords, such as BEGIN and FROM must be written with all capital letters. Procedure and variable names can be upper- or lowercase, or mixed upper- and lowercase.

Second, WriteString can print out exactly one character string. It cannot handle any other data type. It does not even output a carriage return and line feed; WriteLn is needed for that. Similarly, as you will see, separate output procedures are needed for each data type. There is no generic output statement or procedure such as the PRINT statement of BASIC or the WRITELN statement of Pascal.

More details about the structure of Modula-2 programs will be discussed as they are illustrated in subsequent sample programs.

DATA REPRESENTATION

The basic data types in Modula-2 are REAL, INTEGER, CARDINAL, CHAR (character), and BOOLEAN (logical). Character strings can be represented as arrays of type CHAR, but most implementations of Modula-2 also include a STRING type.

The CARDINAL type consists of zero and the positive integers. Many situations call for nonnegative integers; the CARDINAL type allows Modula-2 to verify that no negative integers are used in those situations. The smallest number of type CARDINAL is zero. The largest number of type CARDINAL depends on the system. In most implementations it is 65535. This compares to the usual range for variables of type INTEGER, which is -32768 to $+32767$.

ITC Modula-2 allocates eight bytes of storage to REAL variables, which corresponds to double-precision in many other languages. I have successfully used REAL variables as large as 10^{306}, so the magnitude of real numbers shouldn't be a significant constraint.

Like Pascal, Modula-2 includes a provision for defining new data types. For example, electrical engineers might need a type called COMPLEX; such a type could be easily added in a library module.

Constants

INTEGER and CARDINAL constants are represented in the usual way. The BOOLEAN constants are TRUE and FALSE. REAL constants include a decimal point and an optional exponent. The following are examples of REAL constants:

```
1.0
-9.1
3.2E4
```

The last example is read, "Three point two times ten to the fourth power." Modula-2 requires that the E be in uppercase; a lowercase e is unacceptable.

String constants may be enclosed between either single or double quotation marks. If double quotation marks are used, apostrophes can be used freely within. Similarly, if single quotation marks are used, double quotation marks can be used freely within the string. Here are two examples:

"Don't give up."
'He said, "Hello."'

Symbolic constants can be declared and given values. One advantage of this is that programs can be made easier to read when constants are used. For example, a program that computes sales tax could contain the following constant:

CONST rate = 0.04;

Throughout the program the symbol **rate** could be used wherever the tax rate is needed. Not only does this make the program easier to understand, it makes the program easier to change when the tax rate changes.

A program that uses a symbolic constant is shown in Fig. 11-2. It simply prints out the value of the constant **PI**, which is used in geometry and trigonometry. The program imports **WriteString** and **WriteLn** from the module **Terminal**, as did the previous program. Because **PI** is of type **REAL**, this program must import the procedure **WriteReal** from the module **RealInOut**.

The constant declaration follows the import lists. The only other new item in this program is the **WriteReal** procedure. It requires two arguments; the first is the value to be printed, and the second is the width of the field in which to print it. The number is printed in scientific notation, as follows:

3.141589999999999882E0

The extra fraction at the end resulted from the inability of the computer to store decimal fractions exactly in its internal binary format. (As of version 2.0a, the second parameter of **WriteReal** in the ITC Modula-2 compiler does not work; the number should be only 8 characters wide.)

```
(*  Figure 11-2:  Illustrate Use of Constants.  *)
(*                                            - *)
MODULE Modula2;
  FROM RealInOut IMPORT WriteReal;
  FROM Terminal IMPORT WriteString, WriteLn;
  CONST
    PI = 3.14159;
  BEGIN
    WriteString("PI = ");
    WriteReal(PI, 8);
    WriteLn();
  END Modula2.
```

Fig. 11-2. The use of constants.

Variables

All variables must be declared in Modula-2. Variables may be declared at the beginning of a module or at the beginning of a procedure. (Remember that the main program is a module.) Variables are only "visible" within the module or procedure in which they are declared unless they are specifically exported to another module.

A program illustrating the declaration and use of several variables is shown in Fig. 11-3. This program computes and prints the area of a circle with a radius of five. Two variables of type REAL are declared—area and radius. A variable (i) of type INTEGER is declared for illustration, but it is not used in the program.

THE ASSIGNMENT STATEMENT

The assignment operator in Modula-2 is a colon followed by an equals sign (: =). An example is shown in the program in Fig. 11-3, where the variable radius is assigned the value 5.0. The statement that immediately follows is also an assignment statement.

A variable name always appears on the left side of an assignment statement. On the right there can be another variable, a constant, or an arithmetic expression. (Arithmetic expressions are discussed in the following section.)

Whatever appears on the right side of an assignment statement must be compatible in type with the variable on the left. In other words, a real value cannot be assigned to an integer variable. In those instances where this must be done, Modula-2 provides

```
(*  Figure 11-3:   Illustrate Variable Declarations.   *)
(*                                              *)
MODULE Modula3;
   (*  Compute Area of Circle                  *)
   FROM Terminal IMPORT WriteString, WriteLn;
   FROM RealInOut IMPORT WriteReal;
   CONST
     PI = 3.14159;
   VAR
     area, radius : REAL;
     i : INTEGER;
   BEGIN
     radius := 5.0;
     area := PI * radius * radius;
     WriteString("Radius:   ");
     WriteReal(radius, 10);
     WriteLn();
     WriteString("Area:     ");
     WriteReal(area, 10);
     WriteLn();
   END Modula3.
```

Fig. 11-3. Variable declarations.

the functions TRUNC, to convert a REAL to an INTEGER, and FLOAT, to convert an INTEGER to a REAL.

ARITHMETIC EXPRESSIONS

Arithmetic expressions in Modula-2 use conventional infix notation (see Chapter 2). Modula-2 supports the usual arithmetic operators (+, −, *, and /). The division operator (/) works only for the division of REAL numbers. The division of INTEGER and CARDINAL numbers is handled with the DIV operator. The MOD operator is available to compute the modulus of two INTEGER or CARDINAL numbers (the remainder after integer division).

The operators INC and DEC can be used to increment or decrement, respectively, variables of the INTEGER type. The following examples are illustrative:

Modula-2 Operator	Equivalent Operation
INC(n)	n := n + 1
INC(n,3)	n := n + 3
DEC(n)	n := n − 1
DEC(n,2)	n := n − 2

These operators are quite handy in practice. Of the other languages presented in this book, only C has a similar facility.

Like Pascal, Modula-2 lacks an exponentiation operator. Wirth apparently feels that exponentiation should be performed by repeated multiplication in the case of integers or with logarithms in the case of real numbers. A Modula-2 user who needs to perform exponentiation regularly can easily create a library function to handle the task.

A simple example of an arithmetic expression is shown in the statement that computes the value of the variable **area** in Fig. 11-3.

BOOLEAN EXPRESSIONS

Chapter 2 discussed logical expressions. These are called *Boolean expressions* in Modula-2. Modula-2 supports the usual relational and logical operators as listed in Chapter 2, such as greater than (>) and OR.

Modula-2 permits the use of the pound symbol (#) as a synonym for < >, meaning not-equal-to. The ampersand symbol (&) is a synonym for the logical operator AND.

An advantage of Modula-2 over most other languages is that Boolean expressions are evaluated only far enough to determine the truth or falsity of the expression. For example, suppose M and N are of type INTEGER. The following expression:

(N > 0) AND ((M DIV N) > 5)

would produce an error in Pascal if N had the value 0, because the subexpression (M DIV N) would be undefined. In Modula-2 the falsity of the entire expression would be determined as soon as the subexpression (N > 0) was found to be false; the remainder of the expression would not be evaluated.

INPUT AND OUTPUT

The first three example programs contained examples of the WriteString, WriteReal, and WriteLn procedures. The module InOut also includes the procedures WriteInt and WriteCard, which print variables of type INTEGER and CARDINAL, respectively.

If the variable I is of type INTEGER, and the variable C is of type CARDINAL, they could be printed using the following statements:

```
WriteInt(I, 5);
WriteCard(C, 5);
WriteLn( );
```

These statements would write the values of the two variables on the same line, each in a field of width 5. The WriteLn( ) procedure outputs a carriage return and line feed.

It would be convenient if there were a module in the standard library that provided for printer output. Unfortunately the method of handling printer output varies from operating system to operating system and from computer to computer. A standard module is therefore not practical. One of the beauties of Modula-2, however, is that the user can easily create such a library module that can be imported by any program that requires it.

For the moment, assume that such a module exists and is called PrinterIO. The program in Fig. 11-4 shows how this module can be used to direct output to the printer. How PrinterIO works and is implemented will be explained in the section on separate compilation.

The program in Fig. 11-4 imports the variable out and the procedures PrinterOn, PrinterOff, and CRLF. The variable out is not referred to explicitly, but it is used implicitly when output is diverted to the printer.

As might be expected, PrinterOn diverts output to the printer, and PrinterOff reverts output back to the screen. CRLF is used to send a carriage return and line

```
    (*   Figure 11-4:   Demonstrate Printer Output.   *)
    (*                                                 *)
    MODULE Modula4;
       (*  Demonstrate Printer Output   *)
       FROM InOut IMPORT WriteString, WriteLn, out;
       FROM PrinterIO IMPORT PrinterOn, PrinterOff, CRLF;
       BEGIN
          WriteString("This goes to the screen.");
          WriteLn();
          PrinterOn();
          WriteString("This goes to the printer.");
          CRLF();
          PrinterOff();
       END Modula4.
```

Fig. 11-4. Printer output.

feed to the printer; WriteLn should take care of that but doesn't, apparently due to a bug in ITC Modula-2.

Figure 11-4 illustrates how the output from the procedures in InOut, (WriteString, etc.) can be diverted to the printer instead of the screen. Caution must be exercised to redirect output back to the screen (using PrinterOff) when output must go to the screen again.

Different implementations of Modula-2 tend to differ most in the contents of the supplied library modules, particularly the input and output libraries. Following is a summary of the input and output procedures most frequently used for screen and/or printer output, listed under the name of the library in which they are found in ITC Modula-2:

InOut	Terminal	RealInOut
Read	Read	ReadReal
ReadString	ReadString	WriteReal
Write	Write	
WriteString	WriteString	
WriteLn	WriteLn	
ReadInt		
WriteInt		
ReadCard		
WriteCard		

ReadInt, ReadCard, and ReadReal all read in numbers, each to a variable of the appropriate type. Each ignores leading blanks and control characters and terminates when it encounters a trailing blank or control character. (A carriage return is a good example of a control character.) The corresponding output procedures are, of course, WriteInt, WriteCard, and WriteReal.

ReadString reads in a character string, skipping leading blanks and terminating on a blank or control character. Read reads in a single character at a time, including blanks and control characters. The corresponding output procedures are WriteString and Write.

Procedures from the module Terminal are used, as the name implies, for communicating with the video screen and keyboard. Procedures from the modules InOut and RealInOut, on the other hand, can be used to communicate with the printer as well as the video screen and keyboard. As you will see later, they can also be used to communicate with sequential files.

Note that the input and output procedures in Modula-2 can only handle one data element at a time, and can only handle data elements of a particular type. This is significantly different from the input and output statements of most other languages, such as Pascal and BASIC, which are much less restrictive.

The programs of Figs. 11-5 and 11-6 each emulate an electronic typewriter: what is typed at the console is echoed on the printer. The major difference between the two is that the program in Fig. 11-5 uses string input (ReadString) and output (WriteString), whereas the program in Fig. 11-6 uses character input (Read) and output (Write).

Notice that each program imports a number of procedures from various library modules. One of these is the procedure Clear from the module Screen. Also imported from that module are the type Colors and the variables Fore and Back.

```
(*  Figure 11-5:  Electronic Typewriter, Version 1.   *)
(*                                                     *)
MODULE Modula5;
   (*  Emulate an Electronic Typewriter     *)
   (*      with line-by-line input/output.  *)
   FROM InOut IMPORT WriteString, out;
   FROM Terminal IMPORT ReadString, WriteLn;
   FROM PrinterIO IMPORT PrinterOn, PrinterOff, CRLF;
   FROM SYSTEM IMPORT STRING;
   FROM Screen IMPORT Clear, Colors, Fore, Back;
   FROM String IMPORT Length;
   VAR
      s : STRING[80];
   BEGIN
      (*  First set colors and clear screen  *)
      Fore := White;
      Back := Blue;
      Clear();
      WriteString("Welcome to your Electronic Typewriter.  ");
      WriteLn();
      WriteLn();
      WriteString("Enter your text; blank line ends input.");
      WriteLn();
      WriteLn();
      (*  Now turn on printer and begin main loop  *)
      PrinterOn();
      LOOP
         ReadString(s);
         WriteLn();
         IF Length(s)=0 THEN
            EXIT;
         END;
         WriteString(s);
         CRLF();
      END;
      CRLF();
      PrinterOff();
   END Modula5.
```

Fig. 11-5. Electronic Typewriter, Version 1.

When a type is imported, all the instances of that type come with it. The instances of type **Color** include **Red, White, Blue,** and so forth. The variables **Fore** and **Back** are of type **Color**, as can be seen by examining the ITC Modula-2 documentation. In the program in Fig. 11-5, **Fore** is set to **White**, and **Back** is set to **Blue**. Then, when the procedure **Clear** is called, the screen is cleared to a blue background with white letters. (This assumes a color monitor, of course.)

Because this program uses strings, the type STRING must be imported from the module SYSTEM. The procedure Length is imported from the module String in order to obtain the length of a given string.

As mentioned above, the program in Fig. 11-5 handles text as character strings, a line at a time. This has the advantage that the text can be edited as it is entered; that is, you can backspace over mistakes before they are printed on the printer. The program in Fig. 11-6 handles data a character at a time. The implication is that once an error is typed, it is sent to the printer; there is no chance to correct an error.

Each program contains a loop; one program loops for every line, and the other for every character. The LOOP statement will be discussed in more detail in a later section. Simply put, the loop repeats until an EXIT statement is encountered. In both cases, the EXIT statement is executed when the end-of-input condition is encountered. The program in Fig. 11-5 uses a string of length zero to signal the end of input. The program in Fig. 11-6 uses the <Control-Z> character for this purpose.

There are some subtle differences between the two programs involving the placement of the PrinterOn and PrinterOff procedures, which determine whether output goes to the screen or the printer. In Fig. 11-6 the printer is turned on and off just before and after each printer write. This is always the safest procedure. In Fig. 11-5, the printer is turned on before the main loop and off after the main loop. This is possible because the procedure ReadString inside the loop was imported from Terminal and is therefore unaffected by PrinterOn or PrinterOff. (This is a consideration because ReadString echoes its input to the screen. The version of ReadString from InOut would not echo its input to the screen with PrinterOn in effect.)

LIBRARY MODULES: SEPARATE COMPILATION

The preceding programs assume the existence of a library module called PrinterIO. This module was not furnished with the system; it was created and compiled separately. This section shows how this was done.

There are several advantages to having separately compiled modules. One advantage is that commonly used routines, such as PrinterIO, can be made available to any number of other programs. With separate compilation it is not necessary to compile the module into every program that uses it.

Another advantage is realized during the development cycle of a large program with many modules. Once a module is compiled correctly and tested, it need not be recompiled. Without separate compilation, every module would have to be recompiled every time that any module was recompiled.

To add a module to the library requires the creation and compilation of a *definition module* and an *implementation module*. The definition module establishes the interfaces between modules. It contains declarations and procedure headings for all data, types, and procedures that are to be exported. Viewed another way, a definition module contains all the information that a programmer needs to know to call the module from another module. The definition module for PrinterIO is shown in Fig. 11-7.

The implementation module contains the actual bodies of the procedures to be exported. It may also contain local variables and procedures, and may import data, types, or procedures from other sources. The implementation module for PrinterIO is shown in Fig. 11-8.

```
(*  Figure 11-6:   Electronic Typewriter, Version 2.   *)
(*                                                      *)
MODULE Modula6;
   (*  Emulate an Electronic Typewriter          *)
   (*        with single-character input/output.  *)
   (*        Does not support backspace.          *)
   FROM PrinterIO IMPORT PrinterOn, PrinterOff, CRLF;
   FROM Screen IMPORT Clear, Colors, Fore, Back;
   FROM ASCII IMPORT EOL;
   FROM InOut IMPORT Read, Write, WriteString, WriteLn, out;
   VAR
     c : CHAR;
   BEGIN
     (*  First set colors and clear screen  *)
     Fore := White;
     Back := Blue;
     Clear();
     WriteString("Welcome to your Electronic Typewriter.   ");
     WriteLn();
     WriteLn();
     WriteString("Enter your text; (Control-Z) ends input.");
     WriteLn();
     WriteLn();
     (*  Begin main loop  *)
     LOOP
       (*   Read from keyboard  *)
       Read(c);
       IF c=CHR(26) THEN
         (*  End of keyboard input signalled  *)
         WriteLn();
         PrinterOn();
         CRLF();
         PrinterOff();
         EXIT;
       ELSIF c=EOL THEN
         (*  End of Line.  Handle screen then printer.  *)
         WriteLn();
         PrinterOn();
         CRLF();
         PrinterOff();
       ELSE
         (*  Echo character to printer  *)
         PrinterOn();
         Write(c);
         PrinterOff();
       END;
     END;
   END Modula6.
```

Fig. 11-6. Electronic Typewriter, Version 2.

```
(*   Figure 11-7:   Definition Module for PrinterIO.   *)
(*                                                      *)
DEFINITION MODULE PrinterIO;
   (*   Contains procedures to redirect output to printer  *)
   (*        (using InOut) and to emulate WriteLn(), which  *)
   (*        does not work correctly with a printer.        *)
   EXPORT QUALIFIED PrinterOn, PrinterOff, CRLF;
   PROCEDURE PrinterOn();
   PROCEDURE PrinterOff();
   PROCEDURE CRLF();
   END PrinterIO.
```

Fig. 11-7. The definition module for PrinterIO.

The form of the definition module is relatively straightforward. Note that the heading begins with the words **DEFINITION MODULE**. The rest of the definition module consists of an export list and procedure headings. The export list identifies those procedures, types, and variables that can be imported by another module.

The implementation module in Fig. 11-8 is straightforward. The procedures **OpenOutput** and **CloseOutput** are imported from the module **InOut**, along with the

```
(*   Figure 11-8:   Implementation Module for PrinterIO.   *)
(*                                                          *)
IMPLEMENTATION MODULE PrinterIO;
   FROM InOut IMPORT OpenOutput, CloseOutput, Write, out;
   FROM ASCII IMPORT cr, lf;
   PROCEDURE PrinterOn();
     BEGIN
       OpenOutput("PRN");
     END PrinterOn;
   PROCEDURE PrinterOff();
     BEGIN
       CloseOutput();
     END PrinterOff;
   PROCEDURE CRLF();
     BEGIN
       Write(cr);
       Write(lf);
     END CRLF;
   BEGIN
   END PrinterIO.
```

Fig. 11-8. The implementation module for PrinterIO.

variable out. These procedures allow output to be redirected to somewhere other than the screen. In this case the new destination is the printer, identified as PRN.

Unfortunately, the WriteLn procedure of InOut is not affected by redirection in ITC Modula-2, so I have included the procedure CRLF in PrinterIO to take its place.

The modules that comprise the main programs in the earlier examples are called *program modules*. Another way to refer to the module that imports another module is to call it the *host module*. There are thus three kinds of modules that you need to be concerned with: host modules, definition modules, and implementation modules. You have seen examples of each.

The order of compilation of these three kinds of modules is important. The definition module must be compiled first. This defines the interface between the host module and the implementation module. Once this is done, the other two modules can be compiled in any order.

Modula-2 maintains version control between modules. Once a definition module is compiled, it is assigned a unique version number. That version number is noted by both the host and the implementation modules. When a host module is executed, it checks to make sure that the implementation module it imports has the same version number as the definition module with which the host module was compiled. If it does not, the host module will abort.

This procedure has several implications. First, if the definition module and implementation module are recompiled, possibly altering the interface, then the host module must also be recompiled. This provides protection against unwanted interactions caused by changes to library modules.

The second implication is that if the definition module is not recompiled, then the host module and the implementation module can be recompiled at will. This means that different parts of a complex program can be modified independently as long as the interfaces are not disturbed.

In short, separate compilation of modules makes the development of large, complex programs simpler. The way in which Modula-2 implements separate compilation provides protection against unwanted interactions between different modules.

CONTROL STRUCTURES

Modula-2 supports a wide variety of control structures, more than enough for any occasion. The one control statement it lacks is a GO TO statement. The other control statements provided make a GO TO statement unnecessary.

The control structures of Modula-2 facilitate the modern concept of structured programming. The scope of each control structure is well-defined and delimited by key words. With one exception (REPEAT . . . UNTIL), all Modula-2 control structures are terminated by the keyword END. (Pascal programmers should note that the keyword BEGIN is used only at the beginning of a Modula-2 module or procedure and not in control structures.)

Simple Selection: The IF Statement

The basic form of the IF statement in Modula-2 is as follows:

```
IF condition THEN
   statement(s);
END;
```

The condition may be any Boolean expression, as defined above. There may be one or many statements between the **THEN** and the **END**; the END is required no matter how many or few statements there are in the body of the statement.

Suppose that you have two variables called month and year and that you wish to increment month. Here is one way to do this using a simple **IF** statement:

```
INC(month);
IF month < 12 THEN
   month := 1;
   INC(year)
END;
```

The standard procedure **INC** can be used to increment an **INTEGER** or **CARDINAL** variable. What this **IF** statement does is to check whether or not month has been incremented too far; if it has been, it sets month back to 1 and increments year.

An **IF** statement may also have an **ELSE** part; the format is as follows:

```
IF condition THEN
   statement(s);
ELSE
   statement(s);
END;
```

An **IF** statement with **ELSE** can be used to accomplish the same task as in the previous example:

```
IF month < 12 THEN
   INC(month)
ELSE
   month := 1;
   INC(year)
END;
```

Modula-2 provides for nested **IF** statements through the use of the **ELSIF** clause of an **IF** statement. For example, consider the computation of a weekly payroll. If the hours worked do not exceed 40, then payment is made at the standard rate. If more than 40 but less than 50 hours are worked, the hours in excess of 40 are paid at 1.5 times the standard rate. All hours worked in excess of 50 hours per week are paid at twice the standard rate. This computation could be programmed as follows:

```
IF hours < = 40.0 THEN
   pay := hours*rate
ELSIF hours < = 50.0 THEN
```

```
        pay := 40.0*rate +
            (hours – 40.0)*rate*1.5
    ELSE
        pay := 40.0*rate +
            10.0*rate*1.5 +
            (hours – 50.0)*rate*2.0
    END;
```

Notice that some of the statements are continued to the next line. None of the statements within the body of the construct above end with a semicolon (;) because the semicolon is a statement separator in Modula-2, not a statement terminator. No harm would be done, however, by including the semicolons. (Note that in Pascal the extra semicolons would not be allowed. In Ada or C they would be required.)

Multiple Selection: The CASE Statement

The IF statement provides selection between two alternatives. Nested IF statements can provide selection between more than two alternatives. Another way of providing selection between multiple alternatives (when those alternatives can be enumerated) is the CASE statement.

An example of a CASE statement is shown in Fig. 11-9. This program reads a month number from the keyboard; it then prints the name of the corresponding month and the number of days in that month. February is given special treatment. If the month number is not one of the numbers 1 through 12, the program prints out an appropriate error message. This is accomplished by the ELSE clause. Note that the various cases are separated by the symbol I (vertical line).

Loops

Modula-2 supports four different kinds of loop: the FOR statement, the WHILE statement, the REPEAT . . . UNTIL statement, and the generalized LOOP statement. Each of these is described in the sections that follow.

Counted Loops: The FOR Statement. Chapter 2 includes a simple example program in BASIC that prints out the integers from one to 10. Figure 11-10 contains a Modula-2 program that accomplishes the same thing.

In this program, the variable i serves as the loop counter. It happens to be of type CARDINAL, but it could also be of type INTEGER. (Recall that CARDINAL numbers cannot be negative.) The FOR statement initializes i to one and then checks to see whether or not i exceeds 10 (the upper limit). If it does, control passes to the statement following END; if it does not, the statements between the DO and END delimiters are executed. Following execution of the body of the loop, the counter i is incremented. If i does not exceed 10, the process is repeated.

Note that the FOR statement performs its test for termination *before* the body of the loop is ever executed. Thus the body of the loop may never be executed. The following is a simple example of this possibility:

```
    FOR i := 1 TO 0 DO
        WriteString ('Never happen . . .')
    END;
```

```
(*  Figure 11-9:  The Calendar Program, Version 1.   *)
(*                                                    *)
MODULE Modula9;
  FROM InOut IMPORT Read, ReadCard, WriteCard, WriteString, WriteLn;
  VAR
    month, days, year : CARDINAL;
    reply : CHAR;
  BEGIN
    REPEAT
      WriteLn();
      WriteString("Enter the Month (1..12):  ");
      ReadCard(month);
      WriteLn();
      CASE month OF
        1, 3, 5, 7, 8, 10, 12 :
        days := 31;
      | 4, 6, 9, 11 :
        days := 30;
      | 2 :
        WriteString("Enter the Year:  ");
        ReadCard(year);
        WriteLn();
        IF (year MOD 4 = 0) THEN
          days := 29;
        ELSE
          days := 28;
        END;
      ELSE
        WriteLn();
        WriteString("Sorry, month must be 1..12.");
        WriteLn();
        days := 0;
      END;
      WriteString("Month");
      WriteCard(month, 3);
      WriteString(" has");
      WriteCard(days, 3);
      WriteString(" days.");
      WriteLn();
      WriteLn();
      WriteString("Again?  (y/n)");
      Read(reply);
      WriteLn();
    UNTIL reply # 'y';
  END Modula9.
```

Fig. 11-9. The Calendar Program, Version 1.

In this case the **WriteString** statement will never be executed, because the initial value of i exceeds the limiting value, which is zero.

Conditional Loops. A counted loop repeats a specified number of times. A conditional loop executes as long as a certain condition is true, or until a certain condition

```
(*   Figure 11-10:   Counted Loops:   The FOR Statement.   *)
(*                                                          *)
MODULE Modula10;
  FROM InOut IMPORT WriteCard, WriteLn;
  VAR
    i : CARDINAL;
  BEGIN
    FOR i := 1 TO 10 DO
      WriteCard(i, 3);
      WriteLn();
    END;
END Modula10.
```

Fig. 11-10. Counted loops: the FOR statement.

becomes true. Modula-2 includes two kinds of conditional loops, the WHILE statement and the REPEAT . . . UNTIL statement.

The WHILE statement repeats as long as the stated condition is true. The test is performed at the top of the loop, so the body of the loop may never be executed if the condition is initially false. The body of the loop must contain some logic that will cause the condition to eventually become false; otherwise the loop would try to continue indefinitely.

The program in Fig. 11-11 is a rewrite of the program in Fig. 11-10 using the WHILE statement instead of the FOR statement. The program prints the numbers from one to 10 on the screen. Note that in Fig. 11-11, the counter variable i must be initialized and incremented explicitly; in Fig. 11-10 these functions were taken care of by the FOR statement.

```
(*   Figure 11-11:   Conditional Loops:   The WHILE Statement.   *)
(*                                                                *)
MODULE Modula11;
  FROM InOut IMPORT WriteCard, WriteLn;
  VAR
    i : CARDINAL;
  BEGIN
    i := 1;
    WHILE i <= 10 DO
      WriteCard(i, 2);
      WriteLn();
      INC(i);
    END;
END Modula11.
```

Fig. 11-11. Conditional loops; the WHILE statement.

The function of these two programs is identical. In this case the **FOR** statement is probably more appropriate. There are other cases, however, in which a conditional loop is more appropriate. Such a case is shown in the program in Fig. 11-12.

This program reads in a series of numbers from the console, stopping when the sum of the numbers exceeds 100. It then prints out a count of the numbers entered, their sum, and the number that would have caused the sum to go over 100.

Notice that this program repeats the following statements:

```
ReadInt(num);
WriteLn( );
```

both before the **WHILE** loop and at the bottom of the **WHILE** loop. This is necessary so that the condition can be checked both on the first and on subsequent passes through the loop. (Later you will see how to avoid this duplication using a generalized loop.) The

```
(*  Figure 11-12:   Another WHILE Demonstration.   *)
(*                                                 *)
MODULE Modula12;
  FROM InOut IMPORT ReadInt, WriteInt, WriteString, Write, WriteLn;
  VAR
    num, count, sum : INTEGER;
  BEGIN
    count := 0;
    sum   := 0;
    WriteLn();
    WriteString("Enter a series of numbers:");
    WriteLn();
    WriteLn();
    ReadInt(num):
    WriteLn();
    WHILE (sum + num) <= 100 DO
      INC(count);   .
      INC(sum, num);
      ReadInt(num);
      WriteLn();
    END;
    WriteLn();
    WriteInt(count, 3);
    WriteString(" numbers were read.");
    WriteString("They sum to ");
    WriteInt(sum, 5);
    Write(".");
    WriteLn();
    WriteString("The number ");
    WriteInt(num, 5);
    WriteString(" was not counted.");
    WriteLn();
  END Modula12.
```

Fig. 11-12. Another WHILE statement demonstration.

WriteLn( ) statement is needed immediately following ReadInt( ) because that procedure does not echo the carriage return to the screen.

Notice also that there are two forms of the INC statement within the body of the loop. The following statement:

```
INC (count)
```

simply increments count by one. The statement below:

```
INC (sum, num)
```

is equivalent to the following statement:

```
sum := sum + num
```

The remainder of the program is straightforward.

The other form of conditional loop in Modula-2 is the REPEAT . . . UNTIL statement. This statement repeats until the specified condition becomes true. An example of this construct was seen in the program in Fig. 11-9. In that program the body of the loop was repeated until the user replied something other than y when asked whether he or she would like to repeat the process.

The Generalized Loop. Modula-2 provides a more general form of loop. Its format is as follows:

```
LOOP
    . . .
    IF condition THEN
        EXIT
    END;
    . . .
END;
```

The LOOP . . . END construct by itself is an infinite loop. The EXIT statement within the IF statement provides a means of exiting the loop. The EXIT statement can appear anywhere within the loop. In fact, there may be some rare occasions where no EXIT is desired. An example might be a program to continuously monitor the thermometers in an office building.

If the conditional EXIT statement is the first statement within the body of the loop, then the construct is equivalent to a WHILE statement. If the conditional EXIT statement is the last statement within the body of the loop, then the construct is equivalent to a REPEAT . . . UNTIL statement.

The real usefulness of the LOOP and EXIT combination is that the conditional EXIT may be anywhere within the body of the loop. An example of this was seen in the program in Fig. 11-5.

Another example of the generalized loop construct is shown in the program in Fig. 11-13. This program is a rewrite of the program in Fig. 11-12 using a LOOP statement

```
(*  Figure 11-13:  The Generalized LOOP.  *)
(*                                         *)
MODULE Modula13;
  FROM InOut IMPORT ReadInt, WriteInt, WriteString, Write, WriteLn;
  VAR
    num, count, sum : INTEGER;
  BEGIN
    count := 0;
    sum   := 0;
    WriteLn();
    WriteString("Enter a series of numbers:");
    WriteLn();
    WriteLn();
    LOOP
      ReadInt(num);
      WriteLn();
      IF (sum + num) > 100 THEN
        EXIT;
      END;
      INC(count);
      INC(sum, num);
    END;
    WriteLn();
    WriteInt(count, 3);
    WriteString(" numbers were read.");
    WriteLn();
    WriteString("They sum to ");
    WriteInt(sum, 5);
    Write(".");
    WriteLn();
    WriteString("The number ");
    WriteInt(num, 5);
    WriteString(" was not counted.");
    WriteLn();
  END Modula13.
```

Fig. 11-13. The generalized LOOP.

instead of a **WHILE** statement. The primary difference between the two is that the second version requires only one **ReadInt** statement.

It is the presence of the generalized loop construct with **EXIT** that makes a **GO TO** statement unnecessary in Modula-2.

Procedures

Chapter 2 discusses subroutines. Subroutines are called *procedures* in Modula-2.

A procedure is a more-or-less self-contained unit of a program that performs a particular function. It is defined at the beginning of a module, either within a program module or within a separately compiled module. Once defined, a procedure can be invoked (almost) anywhere within a program. Procedures can be exported from and imported into modules.

Together with the use of modules, the use of procedures in Modula-2 makes it easier to construct a large, complex program from smaller, simpler components. This makes the program much easier to write and maintain.

One purpose of a procedure is to reduce the amount of duplicative coding in a program. Consider a program that must exchange the values of two real numbers in several parts of the program. A procedure can be written to perform the swap. The procedure can be called from wherever in the program it is needed. Such a program is shown in Fig. 11-14.

The program initializes two variables, prints them, exchanges their values, and then prints them again. The process is repeated with two other variables. The point is that a procedure can be invoked in different parts of the program with different inputs.

The procedure that exchanges the variables is called **Swap**. The program also contains a procedure called **Print2**, which prints two variables with appropriate labels. Note the placement of the procedure declarations; they are after the declaration of variables for the main program and before the **BEGIN** of the main program.

Next, note the heading of each procedure. The parameters of each procedure are listed in parentheses following the procedure name.

The parameters of **Swap** are u and v. When **Swap** is invoked in the main program, its arguments are p and q the first time, and x and y the second time. The first time **Swap** is invoked, the values of p and q are exchanged; the second time **Swap** is invoked, the values of x and y are exchanged.

Notice that **Swap** has a local variable called **temp**, declared between the heading and body of the procedure. The scope of **temp** is restricted to that procedure. In other words, the variable **temp** is not accessible from anywhere else in the program.

The procedure **Print2** also has two parameters, u and v. When **Print2** is called using p and q as arguments, the values of p and q are printed.

Notice that the procedure heading of **Swap** contains the word **VAR** and that the procedure heading of **Print2** does not. This affects how the arguments are passed to the procedures. In the case of **Print2** (without **VAR**), only the values of the arguments are passed. In the case of **Swap** (with **VAR**), the arguments themselves are passed to the procedure. This permits **Swap** to exchange the values of these two variables. Without the **VAR**, **Swap** would have no effect on the arguments in the main program (p, q, x, and y). If you have access to a Modula-2 compiler, try running this program with and without the **VAR** in the heading of **Swap**.

Because **Print2** returns no values to the main program, there is no need for **VAR** in its heading.

A procedure can be called from the main program or from another procedure, as long as the procedure being called is in the same module or is imported from another module. A procedure can also call itself in Modula-2. This is called *recursion* and will be discussed in more detail in the following pages.

Functions

A function is similar to a procedure. The difference is that a function has a value attached to its name. A function is invoked by writing its name in an expression, as in the following example:

```
x : = ABS(y)
```

```
(*  Figure 11-14:   The Use of Procedures.   *)
(*                                            *)
MODULE Modula14;
  FROM InOut IMPORT WriteString, WriteLn;
  FROM RealInOut IMPORT WriteReal;
  VAR
    p, q, x, y : REAL;
  PROCEDURE Swap(VAR u, v : REAL);
    (*  Exchange the values of two real variables  *)
    VAR
      temp : REAL;
    BEGIN
      temp := u;
      u    := v;
      v    := temp;
    END Swap;
  PROCEDURE Print2(u, v : REAL);
    (*  Print and label two real variables  *)
    BEGIN
      WriteLn();
      WriteString("First  Variable:   ");
      WriteReal(u, 10);
      WriteLn();
      WriteString("Second Variable:   ");
      WriteReal(v, 10);
      WriteLn();
    END Print2;
  BEGIN
    p := 1.0;
    q := 2.0;
    Print2(p, q);
    Swap(p, q);
    Print2(p, q);
    x := 3.14159;
    y := 2.71828;
    Print2(x, y);
    Swap(x, y);
    Print2(x, y);
  END Modula14.
```

Fig. 11-14. The use of procedures.

Here **ABS** is a standard function supplied with the language; it produces the absolute value of its argument. That value, in effect, takes the place of the function name in the expression.

A procedure call, on the other hand, stands alone; it is not used in an expression. For example, the following statement:

```
INC(n)
```

is a call to a procedure that increments the variable n.

Because a function name returns a value, the function must be given a type (**INTEGER** for example). This is done in the heading of the function. Suppose, for example, that you needed a function to return the value of its argument divided by two. Here is how such a function could be defined:

```
PROCEDURE Half (x: REAL): REAL;
   BEGIN
      RETURN x/2.0;
   END Half;
```

Note that the heading of a function definition in Modula-2 uses the word **PROCEDURE** rather than **FUNCTION**. Modula-2 differs from Pascal in this regard. The : **REAL** following the parenthesized parameter list gives the function a type. The presence of such a type declaration is the easiest way to distinguish a function from a procedure in Modula-2.

A function in Modula-2 must have at least one **RETURN** statement. In this case, the value that is returned is x/2.0. That value is then used in the expression in which the function name appears in the invoking program or procedure. For example, the following could appear in a program:

```
x := Half(y)
```

A simple example showing the use of a function in an actual program is given in Fig. 11-15. This program includes a function that returns the largest of its three integer arguments. The function uses a local variable called **max** and a nested **IF** statement to compute the maximum of the three values; then it uses a **RETURN** statement to return that value to the main program.

Recursion

Another way to control the flow of execution in a program is through the use of recursive procedures and functions. As discussed in Chapter 2, a recursive procedure or function is one that calls itself. Obviously the process must be finite, so the procedure or function must have some provision for terminating the recursion.

Many programming problems can be solved equally well with or without recursion. As an example, consider the program in Fig. 11-16. This program prints a character string, drops the first character, and then repeats the process until there are no more characters to print. A typical output from this program would appear as follows:

```
(*  Figure 11-15:  A Function Demonstration.  *)
(*                                            *)
MODULE Modula15;
  FROM InOut IMPORT WriteString, WriteInt, WriteLn, Read, ReadInt;
  VAR
    i, j, k : INTEGER;
    c : CHAR;
  PROCEDURE Max3(x, y, z : INTEGER) : INTEGER;
    (*  Returns the largest of the 3 inputs  *)
    VAR
      max : INTEGER;
    BEGIN
      IF (x )= y) AND (x )= z) THEN
        max := x;
      ELSIF (y )= x) AND (y )= z) THEN
        max := y;
      ELSE
        max := z;
      END;
      RETURN max;
    END Max3;
  BEGIN
    REPEAT
      WriteLn();
      WriteLn();
      WriteString("You will be asked to enter three integers.");
      WriteLn();
      WriteString("The program will then print the largest one.");
      WriteLn();
      WriteLn();
      WriteString("Enter an integer:  ");
      ReadInt(i);
      WriteLn();
      WriteString("Enter an integer:  ");
      ReadInt(j);
      WriteLn();
      WriteString("Enter an integer:  ");
      ReadInt(k);
      WriteLn();
      WriteLn();
      WriteInt(Max3(i, j, k), 5);
      WriteString(" is the largest of the three.");
      WriteLn();
      WriteLn();
      WriteString("Again?  (y/n)");
      Read(c);
      WriteLn();
    UNTIL (c # 'y') AND (c # 'Y');
  END Modula15.
```

Fig. 11.15. A function demonstration.

```
(*   Figure 11-16:   Demonstrate Recursive Procedure.   *)
(*                                                       *)
MODULE Modula16;
  FROM Terminal IMPORT WriteString, WriteLn, Read, ReadString;
  FROM String IMPORT Length, Delete;
  FROM SYSTEM IMPORT STRING;
  VAR
    s : STRING[80];
    c : CHAR;
  PROCEDURE PrintAndDrop(s : STRING);
    (*  Print a string, drop first character, repeat  *)
    BEGIN
      IF Length(s) > 0 THEN
        WriteString(s);
        WriteLn();
        Delete(s, 1, 1);
        PrintAndDrop(s);
      END;
    END PrintAndDrop;
  BEGIN
    REPEAT
      WriteLn();
      WriteLn();
      WriteString("Type a string:   ");
      ReadString(s);
      WriteLn();
      WriteLn();
      PrintAndDrop(s);
      WriteLn();
      WriteString("Again?   (y/n)");
      Read(c);
      WriteLn();
    UNTIL (c # 'y') AND (c # 'Y');
  END Modula16.
```

Fig. 11-16. A recursive procedure.

```
HELLO
ELLO
LLO
LO
O
```

Notice the call to **PrintAndDrop** within the procedure itself. This is the recursive call. The **IF** statement within the procedure allows the recursion to be continued only as long as there are more characters in the string. The procedure **Delete**, imported from the module **String**, is used to drop the first character from the string after the string has been printed.

There are some problems, however, that naturally lend themselves to recursive solution. Here is an example from mathematics.

The factorial of zero is defined as one. The factorial of a positive integer N is defined as N times the factorial of N – 1. The definition of the function is itself recursive; in other words, the function is defined in terms of itself.

The program in Fig. 11-17 contains a recursive function that computes the factorial of a positive integer. It works for values of N up to 170. (The factorial of 170 is computed to be approximately 7.257 times 10 raised to the 306th power!) For N greater than 170 the program reports **INF** as the result.

The function **Factorial** is invoked by writing its name in a **WriteReal** statement in the main program. Each recursive call computes the factorial of a smaller number; eventually the number reaches zero and the function returns, one level at a time, until the correct result is computed.

The details of the console input and output of this program require comment. The number is read as a **CARDINAL** number. This prevents negative and fractional numbers from being read. (**ReadCard** returns 0 in ITC Modula-2 whenever a negative number is input.) It also allows the user to omit typing a decimal point, as would be required if a **REAL** number were being read. The **CARDINAL** number is converted to **REAL** by the built-in function **FLOAT**.

DATA STRUCTURES

Modula-2 supports a wide variety of data structures, including arrays and records. Further, Modula-2 records and pointer variables can be used to construct more complicated data structures, such as linked lists and trees.

Arrays

Modula-2 uses square brackets to delimit the subscripts of arrays. As in most languages, arrays must be declared before use.

Chapter 2 included an illustration of an array called **POINTS**. In Modula-2 this array could be declared as follows:

```
VAR Points:
  ARRAY [1..10, 1..20] OF INTEGER;
```

This notation means that the first subscript can range from one to 10, and the second subscript from one to 20. **OF INTEGER** means that each element of the array is to be an integer.

An example of the use of arrays in Modula-2 is shown in the program in Fig. 11-18. This program is a calendar program similar to that in Fig. 11-9, except that it uses arrays rather than a **CASE** statement to do the work.

The program uses an array called **DaysIn** to store the number of days in each month and an array called **NameOf** to store the name of each month. The subscript of each array corresponds to the number of the month. Each array is declared in and initialized in a subordinate module called **Initialize**.

Initialize exports the arrays to the main module. The important point to note here is that the body of the module **Initialize** is executed before the body of the main module

```
(*   Figure 11-17   Demonstrate Recursive Function.   *)
(*                                                     *)
MODULE Modula17;
  FROM InOut IMPORT Read, ReadCard, WriteString, WriteLn;
  FROM RealInOut IMPORT WriteReal;
  VAR
    x : CARDINAL;
    n : REAL;
    c : CHAR;
  PROCEDURE Factorial(n : REAL) : REAL;
    (*   Compute the Factorial of a non-negative integer   *)
    (*   Overflow occurs for n > 170.                       *)
    VAR
      f : REAL;
    BEGIN
      IF n <= 0.0   THEN
        f := 1.0;
      ELSE
        f := n * Factorial(n - 1.0);
      END;
      RETURN f;
    END Factorial;
  BEGIN
    REPEAT
      WriteLn();
      WriteString("Enter a non-negative integer:  ");
      ReadCard(x);
      (*   ReadCard() converts negative integers to 0   *)
      WriteLn();
      (*   Convert to REAL for computations              *)
      n := FLOAT(x);
      WriteReal(n, 10);
      WriteString(" Factorial is ");
      WriteReal(Factorial(n), 10);
      WriteLn();
      WriteLn();
      WriteString("Again?  (y/n)");
      Read(c);
      WriteLn();
    UNTIL (c # 'y') AND (c # 'Y');
  END Modula17.
```

Fig. 11-17. A recursive function.

```
(*   Figure 11-18:   The Calendar Program, Version 2.   *)
(*                                                       *)
MODULE Modula18;
  FROM InOut IMPORT Read, ReadCard, WriteCard, WriteString, WriteLn;
  FROM SYSTEM IMPORT STRING;
  VAR
    month, days, year : CARDINAL;
    reply : CHAR;
  MODULE Initialize;
    IMPORT STRING;
    EXPORT DaysIn, NameOf;
    TYPE
      String10 = STRING[10];
    VAR
      DaysIn : ARRAY [1..12] OF CARDINAL;
      NameOf : ARRAY [1..12] OF String10;
    BEGIN
      NameOf[1]  := "January";
      DaysIn[1]  := 31;
      NameOf[2]  := "February";
      DaysIn[2]  := 28;
      NameOf[3]  := "March";
      DaysIn[3]  := 31;
      NameOf[4]  := "April";
      DaysIn[4]  := 30;
      NameOf[5]  := "May";
      DaysIn[5]  := 31;
      NameOf[6]  := "June";
      DaysIn[6]  := 30;
      NameOf[7]  := "July";
      DaysIn[7]  := 31;
      NameOf[8]  := "August";
      DaysIn[8]  := 31;
      NameOf[9]  := "September";
      DaysIn[9]  := 30;
      NameOf[10] := "October";
      DaysIn[10] := 31;
      NameOf[11] := "November";
      DaysIn[11] := 30;
      NameOf[12] := "December";
      DaysIn[12] := 31;
    END Initialize;
  BEGIN
    REPEAT
      WriteLn();
      WriteString("Enter the Month (1..12):   ");
      ReadCard(month);
      WriteLn();
      IF (month > 0) AND (month <= 12) THEN
        days := DaysIn[month];
        IF month = 2 THEN
          WriteString("Enter the Year:   ");
          ReadCard(year);
```

Fig. 11-18. The Calendar Program, Version 2.

```
            WriteLn();
            IF (year MOD 4 = 0) THEN
               INC(days);
            END;
         END;
         WriteString(NameOf[month]);
         WriteString(" has ");
         WriteCard(days, 2);
         WriteString(" days.");
         WriteLn();
       ELSE
         WriteString("Month must be in the interval 1..12.");
         WriteLn();
       END;
       WriteLn();
       WriteString("Again?    (y/n)");
       Read(reply);
       WriteLn();
    UNTIL (reply # 'y') AND (reply # 'Y');
END Modula18.
```

Fig. 11-18. The Calendar Program, Version 2. (Continued from page 369.)

Modula18, so that it can be used to initialize variables and arrays. Also note that a module, unlike a procedure, is not ''called'' by the main program.

The module **Initialize** needs the type **STRING** from the library module **SYSTEM**. Because it is a local module, it has access to the ''outside world'' only through its host module, **Modula18**. The host module imports **STRING** for the local module, and the local module uses a simple **IMPORT** (without a **FROM** clause) to import it from the host module.

The arrays **DaysIn** and **NameOf** are made visible in the host module by means of an **EXPORT** clause in the local module. Note that the host module does not need to explicitly import items exported from a local module.

The main program is straightforward. Note that the value of the variable **month** is validated before being used as an array subscript.

Records

Chapter 2 discusses the need to have a record containing the name of a student and his or her scores on up to 20 tests. Suppose there may be up to 30 students in the class. An array of records will do the job. The following declarations would establish such a data structure:

```
CONST NrOfStudents = 30;
      NrOfTests = 20;
TYPE Entry =
RECORD
     Name: STRING[25];
     Score:
```

```
        ARRAY [1..NrOfTests] OF REAL;
    END;
VAR Student:
    ARRAY [1..NrOfStudents] OF Entry;
```

A new type called **Entry** is declared. Once a type is declared, as many variables as desired can be declared of that type. In this case that type is a record. The variable **Student** therefore ends up being an array of records, as desired.

Suppose that you need to write out the name of the fourth student and the score that student received on the first test. The following statements would print these items:

```
WriteString(Student[4].Name);
WriteString("      ");
WriteReal(Student[4].Score[1], 10);
WriteLn( );
```

The period or dot (.) is used to refer to individual record elements. The second **WriteString** leaves blank space between the name and the score.

Examples of the use of records in actual programs will be presented in later sections of this chapter.

Linked Lists

Chapter 2 explained the concept of linked lists and showed how they could be implemented using arrays. Modula-2 also provides a more advanced means of handling linked lists, using pointers and dynamic allocation of storage space. These advanced topics are, however, not necessary for the understanding of linked lists and so are omitted.

This section explains how linked lists can be implemented in Modula-2 using arrays of records. The methodology is essentially the same as that described in Chapter 2, except that an array of records is used instead of parallel arrays. Also, the value -1 is used to mark the end of a list.

The following declarations will establish the necessary array of records to support the example given in Chapter 2:

```
CONST EndList =  -1;
        MaxSize = 5;
VAR
    First, FirstFree: INTEGER;
    List: ARRAY [1..MaxSize] OF
RECORD
        name: STRING[15];
        link: INTEGER;
END;
```

The name part of the third record of the structure could be printed by the following:

```
WriteString (List[3].name);
```

The subscript of the next record in the list can then be found in this element:

    List[3].link

The comprehensive sample program at the end of the chapter illustrates the use of linked lists in an actual program. That example shows the details of how linked lists can be manipulated and how records can be added to and deleted from a linked list.

FILE HANDLING

For a microcomputer to process data, that data must be input to the program in some way. One way is via the keyboard. If an application requires the same data day after day, it would become rather tedious to reenter the data every day using the keyboard. A better solution is to key in the data once and save it in a file on a magnetic disk.

There are two principle types of files in Modula-2. First is the *text* file. A text file is a sequence of ASCII characters. It is accessed in sequence, from beginning to end. A text file can be a disk file. The printer and console can also be thought of as text files, as the organization is the same (except, of course, that you cannot read from a printer). The standard library module InOut includes procedures for handling text files.

The other type of file in Modula-2 is a sequence of records. Each record may be as simple as an integer or as complex as needed. The RECORD facility described above is useful for defining file records. This type of file, unlike a text file, does not necessarily consist only of ASCII characters. Integers, real numbers, and so on are stored in their binary form.

A file of records can be accessed using either sequential access or direct access. This kind of file is classified as being of type File.

The standard procedures for creating, opening, and closing nontext files are found in the module Files. A file can be created using the procedure Create. Files that previously existed can be accessed using the procedure Open. With each file is associated a variable of type File, called the *file variable*. Both Create and Open establish the connection between the file variable and the name of the external file. The procedure Close terminates access to a file.

Some implementations of Modula-2 include procedures to read and write records to a file. ITC Modula-2 includes such procedures for text files in the module InOut, but it does not include any such procedures in the module Files. It is therefore necessary to resort to the use of the low-level procedures ReadNBytes and WriteNBytes. These procedures must be passed the actual machine address of the variable or record, and its length in bytes.

Fortunately the module SYSTEM includes the functions ADR, SIZE, and TSIZE to compute these values. ADR returns the actual machine address of its argument. SIZE returns the length of its argument in bytes. TSIZE also returns the length of its argument in bytes. The difference is that SIZE takes a variable as its argument, and TSIZE takes a type as its argument.

Examples of file access using these procedures are contained in Fig. 11-19 and in the comprehensive sample program of Figs.11- 20 through 11-28.

Text files are accessed in much the same way as the printer or the console, using the procedures in the InOut module. The difference is that the procedures OpenInput, OpenOutput, CloseInput, and CloseOutput are used to determine whether input comes from and output goes to the console (the defaults), the printer, or a disk file. Examples of the use of this process were given in Fig. 11-8.

Sequential Files

The distinguishing characteristic of a sequential file is that it is accessed from beginning to end, one record at a time. It is impossible, for example, to access the second record of the file without having first accessed the first record.

The program in Fig. 11-19 stores a file of records, each record consisting of a name and an age. The records are read from the keyboard and stored sequentially in the file. After the last record has been written to the disk, the file is closed. It is then reopened and read in from the disk. Each record is written to the console as it is read from the disk.

The program in Fig. 11-19 was written using the file procedures from the module Files. It could also have been written using only the input and output procedures from the module InOut. The problem that would have been encountered, however, is frequent shifting back and forth between console and disk file input and output.

The records are written to the file using the procedure WriteNBytes, and read from the file using the procedure Readnbytes. These procedures were discussed briefly above. Note that each transfers the contents of the entire record in one operation.

The module Files contains a variable called status that is set to reflect the results of each file operation, such as opening or writing to a file. If the operation was successful, status has the value Done. If the operation was not successful, status can have any of a number of other values, depending on what problem occurred. The programmer should make a habit of checking status after each file operation.

Direct-Access Files

There are many applications for which sequential access is inadequate. It is often necessary to access a particular record directly, without first accessing the previous records. An example would be a program at a bank that is designed to lookup the balance of a customer's account. It is certainly desirable to be able to go to that customer's account record without first accessing the account records of many other customers.

The records of a file can be numbered, starting with 1. Each record has associated with it a file position; that is, the point in the file at which that record begins. The problem is to calculate the file position corresponding to a record number and to position the file at that position.

The standard procedure SetPos is used to calculate the starting position for a given record. As input it requires the displacement of the record from the beginning of file in bytes. To calculate the displacement, you need the record number and the size of a record. As mentioned above, the size of a record can be calculated with either the function procedure SIZE or TSIZE, both found in the module SYSTEM (because they are system-dependent).

Once SetPos sets the file at the required position, a subsequent call to ReadNBytes or WriteNBytes will access the desired record in the file.

A program illustrating the use of direct-access files is included as the comprehensive sample program later in this chapter.

```
(*   Figure 11-19:   Sequential File Demonstration.   *)
(*                                                    *)
MODULE Module19;
    (*   Store a file of names and ages.   *)
    (*   Use the module Files.              *)
    FROM InOut IMPORT ReadString, ReadCard, WriteString, WriteCard,
        WriteLn;
    FROM Files IMPORT Create, Open, Close, ReadNBytes, WriteNBytes,
        FileStatus, File, Mode, PathName, status;
    FROM SYSTEM IMPORT STRING, ADR, TSIZE;
    FROM String IMPORT Length;
    TYPE
        ENTRY =
            RECORD
                name : STRING[20];
                age  : CARDINAL;
            END;
    CONST
        FNAME = "AGES.TXT";
    VAR
        R : ENTRY;
        f : File;
        RecSize, BytesRead : CARDINAL;
        str : STRING[1];
        Path : PathName;
    BEGIN
        (*   Create disk file for output.   *)
        Path := FNAME;
        f := Create(Path, Wmode);
        IF status # Done THEN
            WriteString("Unable to create ");
            WriteString(FNAME);
            WriteLn();
            ReadString(str);
        END;
        RecSize := TSIZE(ENTRY);
        (*   Read from keyboard and write to disk.   *)
        WriteLn();
        WriteLn();
        WriteString("Enter Names and Ages; <CR> to quit.");
        WriteLn();
        LOOP
            WriteLn();
            WriteString("Name:   ");
            ReadString(R.Name);
            WriteLn();
            IF Length(R.name)=0 THEN
                EXIT;
            END;
            WriteString("Age:    ");
            ReadCard(R.age);
```

Fig. 11-19. A sequential file demonstration.

```
        WriteLn();
        WriteNBytes(f, ADR(R), RecSize);
    END;
    Close(f);
    (*  Now read the file back and display on the screen.   *)
    f := Open(Path, Rmode);
    IF status # Done THEN
        WriteString("Unable to Open ");
        WriteString(FNAME);
        WriteLn();
        ReadString(str);
    END;
    WriteLn();
    WriteLn();
    WriteString("Here are the contents of the file:");
    WriteLn();
    WriteLn();
    LOOP
        BytesRead := ReadNBytes(f, ADR(R), RecSize);
        IF status = EndOfFile THEN
            (*  End of file encountered.   *)
            EXIT;
        END;
        WriteString("Name:   ");
        WriteString(R.name);
        WriteLn();
        WriteString("Age:    ");
        WriteCard(R.age, 3);
        WriteLn();
        WriteLn();
    END;
    WriteLn();
    Close(f);
    WriteString("All done ...");
    WriteLn();
END Modula19.
```

GRAPHICS

ITC Modula-2 includes procedures to implement graphics in the modules **Screen** and **Geometry**. Because the use of graphics in Modula-2 is implementation dependent, the topic will not be pursued further in this book.

THE COMPREHENSIVE SAMPLE PROGRAM

All of the example programs so far in this chapter have been relatively short. Each has had the purpose of illustrating a particular concept. Unfortunately not all "real" programs are short. In order to illustrate what a "real" Modula-2 program that performs a nontrivial function looks like, a comprehensive sample program is included.

The program maintains a file of names, addresses, and phone numbers in alphabetical order on disk. It also maintains an index file to keep track of the order of all active and

```
(*  Figure 11-20:  Comprehensive Sample Program.  *)
(*                                                 *)
MODULE Modula20;
   (*  A program to create and maintain a file of names  *)
   (*      and addresses.  The file is maintained in      *)
   (*      alphabetical order by name using an index      *)
   (*      consisting of a linked list of pointers.  A    *)
   (*      linked list of vacant (free) records is also   *)
   (*      maintained.                                    *)
   FROM FileIO IMPORT OpenFiles, CloseFiles;
   FROM TextIO IMPORT Menu;
   FROM Lists IMPORT Append, Review, ListFile, Dump;
   VAR
      c : CARDINAL;
   BEGIN
      OpenFiles();
      LOOP
         Menu(c);
         CASE c OF
            1 :
            Append();
         | 2 :
            Review();
         | 3 :
            ListFile();
         | 4 :
            Dump();
         | 5 :
            EXIT;
         END:
      END;
      CloseFiles();
   END Modula20.
```

Fig. 11-20. Comprehensive sample program.

unused records. This program illustrates the use of a direct-access file and is shown in Figs. 11-20 through 11-28.

The organization of the program is illustrated in the structure chart of Fig. 11-29. The chart shows the name of each procedure and the module wherein it resides. The hierarchical structure of the program is displayed using indentation. A procedure is called by a given procedure if it is listed below it and one level of indentation to the right. For example, the procedure GetFree is called by Insert, which is called by Append, which is called by the main program Modula20.

The program is implemented as four modules. The main program is the module **Modula20**, which is shown in Fig. 11-20. The module **FileIO** is shown in Fig. 11-21 (the definition module) and in Fig. 11-22 (the implementation module). The module **TextIO** is shown in Figs. 11-23 and 11-24. The module **Lists** is shown in Figs. 11-25 and 11-26. Finally, the module **Utilities** is shown in Figs. 11-27 and 11-28. The **PrinterIO** module, shown in Figs. 11-7 and 11-8, is also used.

The details of file input and output have been suppressed to the module **FileIO**. This module includes the procedures to initialize files, to open and close files, and to access

```
(*   Figure 11-21:   The FileIO Definition Module.   *)
(*                                                    *)
(*   Supports the Comprehensive Sample Program.       *)
(*                                                    *)
DEFINITION MODULE FileIO;
  FROM Files IMPORT File;
  FROM SYSTEM IMPORT STRING;
  EXPORT QUALIFIED OpenFiles, CloseFiles, GetRec, PutRec, RecType, InBuf,
      OutBuf, Index, EndList, MaxRecords;
  CONST
    MaxRecords = 10;
    EndList = 0;
    FName = "ADDRESS.TXT";
    IName = "INDEX.TXT";
  TYPE
    NameType =
      RECORD
      last, first : STRING[12];
      END;
    RecType =
      RECORD
      name : NameType;
      address : STRING[20];
      city : STRING[12];
      state : STRING[2];
      zip : STRING[10];
      phone : STRING[14];
      END;
  VAR
    InBuf, OutBuf : RecType;
    AddrFile, IndexFile : File;
    Index : ARRAY [-1..MaxRecords] OF INTEGER;
  (*   Note:                                            *)
  (*      Index[-1] is subscript of first free record   *)
  (*      Index[0]  is subscript of first record in use *)
  PROCEDURE OpenFiles();
  (*   Opens Address and Index Files; reads Index file  *)
  PROCEDURE CloseFiles();
  (*   Saves Index and closes Address and Index files   *)
  PROCEDURE GetRec(i : CARDINAL; VAR InBuf : RecType);
  (*   Reads record i of AddrFile into InBuf            *)
  PROCEDURE PutRec(i : CARDINAL; VAR OutBuf : RecType);
  (*   Writes OutBuf to file position i of AddrFile     *)
  END FileIO.
```

Fig. 11-21. The FileIO definition module.

```
(*   Figure 11-22:   The FileIO Implementation Module.   *)
(*                                                        *)
(*   Supports the Comprehensive Sample Program.           *)
(*                                                        *)
IMPLEMENTATION MODULE FileIO;
  FROM Terminal IMPORT WriteString, WriteLn;
  FROM InOut IMPORT WriteCard;
  FROM Utilities IMPORT Pause;
  FROM Files IMPORT Open, Create, Close, Rename, ReadNBytes, WriteNBytes,
      SetPos, FileStatus, Mode, status;
  FROM SYSTEM IMPORT ADR, TSIZE;
  CONST
    BackUp = "INDEX.BAK";
  VAR
    IndexBuf : [0..MaxRecords];
    RecSize : CARDINAL;
  PROCEDURE InitFiles();
    (*   Establish AddrFile and IndexFile.  Initialize    *)
    (*      AddrFile by filling it with blank records.     *)
    (*      Initialize IndexFile as a linked list of       *)
    (*      free records.                                  *)
    CONST
      blank = "    ";
    VAR
      i : CARDINAL;
    BEGIN
      (*   Create Address File   *)
      AddrFile := Create(FName,Wmode);
      IF status # Done THEN
        WriteString("Unable to create ");
        WriteString(FName);
        WriteLn();
        Pause();
      ELSE
        WITH OutBuf DO
          name.last := blank;
          name.first := blank;
          address := blank;
          city := blank;
          state := blank;
          zip := blank;
          phone := blank;
        END;
        FOR i := 0 TO MaxRecords DO
          WriteNBytes(AddrFile, ADR(OutBuf), RecSize);
        END;
        Close(AddrFile);
        (*   Initialize Index File   *)
        IndexFile := Create(IName, Wmode);
        IF status # Done THEN
          WriteString("Unable to Create ");
          WriteString(IName);
          WriteLn();
          Pause();
        ELSE
        (*   First Free Record   *)
```

Fig. 11-22. The FileIO implementation module.

```
            IndexBuf := 1;
            WriteNBytes(IndexFile, ADR(IndexBuf), RecSize);
            (*  No Records in use, so First "Record" is EndList  *)
            IndexBuf := EndList;
            WriteNBytes(IndexFile, ADR(IndexBuf), RecSize);
            (*  Now Complete Free List  *)
            FOR i := 1 TO MaxRecords-1 DO
              IndexBuf := i + 1;
              WriteNBytes(IndexFile, ADR(IndexBuf), RecSize);
            END;
            IndexBuf := EndList;
            WriteNBytes(IndexFile, ADR(IndexBuf), RecSize);
            Close(IndexFile);
          END;
        END;
    END InitFiles;
PROCEDURE OpenFiles();
    (*  Open the Address and Index files; read index file  *)
    VAR
      i : INTEGER;
      NrBytesRead : CARDINAL;
    BEGIN
      AddrFile := Open(FName, RWmode);
      IF status = FileNotFound THEN
        InitFiles();
        OpenFiles();
      END;
      IF status # Done THEN
        WriteString("Unable to open ");
        WriteString(FName);
        WriteLn();
        Pause();
      ELSE
        IndexFile := Open(IName, Rmode);
        IF status # Done THEN
          WriteString("Unable to open ");
          WriteString(IName);
          WriteLn();
          Pause();
        ELSE
          FOR i := -1 TO MaxRecords DO
            NrBytesRead := ReadNBytes (IndexFile, ADR (IndexBuf),
                RecSize);
            Index[i] := IndexBuf;
          END;
          Close(IndexFile);
        END;
      END;
    END OpenFiles;
PROCEDURE CloseFiles();
    (*  Write Index File to Disk and close both files  *)
    VAR
      i : INTEGER;
      index : CARDINAL;
    BEGIN
      Rename(IndexFile, BackUp);
      IndexFile := Create(IName, Wmode);
      FOR i := -1 TO MaxRecords DO
        IndexBuf := Index[i];
```

```
                    WriteNBytes(IndexFile, ADR(IndexBuf), RecSize);
                END;
                Close(IndexFile);
                Close(AddrFile);
            END CloseFiles;
        PROCEDURE Seek(i : CARDINAL);
            (*  Position file at record i of Address File *)
            VAR
                pos : LONGINT;
            BEGIN
                pos := INTEGER((i-1)*RecSize);
                SetPos(AddrFile, pos);
                IF status # Done THEN
                    WriteLn();
                    WriteString("Unsuccessful seek for record # ");
                    WriteCard(i, 5);
                    WriteLn();
                    Pause();
                END;
            END Seek;
        PROCEDURE GetRec(i : CARDINAL; VAR InBuf : RecType);
            (*  Read Record i of Address File into InBuf  *)
            VAR
                NrBytesRead : CARDINAL;
            BEGIN
                Seek(i);
                NrBytesRead := ReadNBytes(AddrFile, ADR(InBuf), RecSize);
                IF status # Done THEN
                    WriteString("File Read Error ...");
                    WriteLn();
                    Pause();
                END;
            END GetRec;
        PROCEDURE PutRec(i : CARDINAL; VAR OutBuf : RecType);
            (*  Write OutBuf to file position i of Address File  *)
            BEGIN
                Seek(i);
                WriteNBytes(AddrFile, ADR(OutBuf), RecSize);
                IF status # Done THEN
                    WriteString("File Write Error ....");
                    WriteLn();
                    Pause();
                END;
            END PutRec;
            BEGIN
                RecSize := TSIZE(RecType);
            END FileIO.
```

Fig. 11-22. The FileIO implementation module. (Continued from page 379.)

particular records of the address file. It also includes the record and type definitions for this particular file structure.

The details of accessing a particular record of a file discussed above are illustrated in the procedures **Seek**, **GetRec**, and **PutRec**, found in Fig. 11-22.

The details of screen input and output and printer output are subordinated to the module **TextIO**. Notice that the interface presented to the main module by the definition

```
(*   Figure 11-23:   The TextIO Definition Module.   *)
(*                                                    *)
(*   Supports the Comprehensive Sample Program.       *)
(*                                                    *)
DEFINITION MODULE TextIO;
  FROM FileIO IMPORT RecType;
  EXPORT QUALIFIED PrintRec, GetEntry, Menu, TEXT;
  TYPE
    TEXT = (Printer, Console);
  PROCEDURE PrintRec(dest : TEXT; i : CARDINAL);
  (*   Print record i on text file dest                *)
  PROCEDURE GetEntry(VAR r : RecType; VAR finished : BOOLEAN);
  (*   Read 1 record from console into record r        *)
  PROCEDURE Menu(VAR c : CARDINAL);
  (*   Display main menu and return selection          *)
  END TextIO.
```

Fig. 11-23. The TextIO definition module.

module of Fig. 11-23 is very simple. All of the tedious details are in the implementation module in Fig. 11-24.

The details of keeping the list in sequence, adding records, deleting records, and so on are suppressed to the module Lists. The module Utilities contains only a procedure to pause and wait for a key to be pressed. This procedure (Pause) is used in so many places that it isn't shown on the structure chart in Fig. 11-29.

A program that is segmented into modules such as this is easier to understand than one that is not. To judge for yourself, compare this program with the Pascal program in Fig. 12-18. The algorithms used are the same. Separate compilation of modules also makes implementation easier. A long program takes longer to compile than a short module; the difference can be significant on a microcomputer.

Using the address file program is simple. It presents a menu of options, including adding a record to the file, reviewing the file one record at a time, listing the file to the screen or printer, and dumping the file to the printer.

When you are adding a record to the file, the program presents a screen to be filled in with the appropriate data. Pressing RETURN at the beginning of the last name field terminates input. When the data has been entered, it is written to disk in the next available location. It is then inserted into the index in the appropriate place. The index is maintained as a linked list, much like the linked list example in Chapter 2.

The review option also allows records to be deleted. When a record is deleted, it is removed from the index of active records and added to the list of free records for subsequent reuse.

The list option lists the file in alphabetical order. The user is given the choice of whether to list it on the video screen or on the printer.

The dump option is provided as a learning tool. It prints all records, active or free, in the order in which they are stored. It also prints the appropriate record pointers. A

```
(*   Figure 11-24:   The TextIO Implementation Module.   *)
(*                                                        *)
(*   Supports the Comprehensive Sample Program.           *)
(*                                                        *)
IMPLEMENTATION MODULE TextIO;
  FROM Terminal IMPORT ReadString;
  FROM InOut IMPORT Write, WriteString, WriteLn, ReadCard, out;
  FROM FileIO IMPORT GetRec, RecType;
  FROM PrinterIO IMPORT PrinterOn, PrinterOff, CRLF;
  FROM Screen IMPORT Clear, SetCursor, Colors, Back, Fore;
  FROM Geometry IMPORT Point;
  FROM String IMPORT Length;
  FROM SYSTEM IMPORT STRING;
  FROM Utilities IMPORT Pause;
  PROCEDURE PrintRec(dest : TEXT; i : CARDINAL);
    (*  Print record i on screen or printer  *)
    VAR
      r : RecType;
    BEGIN
      GetRec(i, r);
      WITH r DO
        WriteString(name.first);
        Write(" ");
        WriteString(name.last);
        IF dest = Printer THEN
          CRLF();
        ELSE
          WriteLn();
        END;
        WriteString(address);
        IF dest = Printer THEN
          CRLF();
        ELSE
          WriteLn();
        END;
        WriteString(city);
        WriteString(", ");
        WriteString(state);
        Write(" ");
        WriteString(zip);
        IF dest = Printer THEN
          CRLF();
        ELSE
          WriteLn();
        END;
        WriteString(phone);
        IF dest = Printer THEN
          CRLF();
```

Fig. 11-24. The TEXTIO implementation module.

```
      ELSE
         WriteLn();
      END;
   END;
   END PrintRec;
PROCEDURE NextField(VAR P : Point);
   (*  Position cursor 2 rows down, same column  *)
   BEGIN
      INC(P.y, 2);
      SetCursor(P);
   END NextField;
PROCEDURE GetEntry(VAR r : RecType; VAR finished : BOOLEAN);
   (*  Read 1 record from console into record r  *)
   VAR
      start, i : CARDINAL;
      P : Point;
   PROCEDURE MarkOff(start, spaces : CARDINAL);
      (*  Mark off data input area with colons  *)
      VAR
         Scrn : Point;
      BEGIN
         Scrn.x := start;
         Scrn.y := P.y;
         SetCursor(Scrn);
         Write(":");
         FOR i := 1 TO spaces DO
            Write(" ");
         END;
         Write(":");
      END MarkOff;
   BEGIN
      Clear();
      (*  Display skeleton record  *)
      start := 14;
      P.x := 1;
      P.y := 5;
      SetCursor(P);
      WriteString("Last Name:");
      MarkOff(start, 12);
      NextField(P);
      WriteString("First Name:");
      MarkOff(start, 12);
      NextField(P);
      WriteString("Address:");
      MarkOff(start, 20);
      NextField(P);
      WriteString("City:");
      MarkOff(start, 12);
      NextField(P);
      WriteString("State:");
      MarkOff(start, 2);
```

```
            NextField(P);
            WriteString("Zip Code:");
            MarkOff(start, 10);
            NextField(P);
            WriteString("Telephone:");
            MarkOff(start, 14);
            (*  Read in each field  *)
            P.x := 15;
            P.y := 5;
            SetCursor(P);
            WITH r DO
               ReadString(name.last);
               finished := (Length(name.last) = 0);
               IF NOT finished THEN
                  NextField(P);
                  ReadString(name.first);
                  NextField(P);
                  ReadString(address);
                  NextField(P);
                  ReadString(city);
                  NextField(P);
                  ReadString(state);
                  NextField(P);
                  ReadString(zip);
                  NextField(P);
                  ReadString(phone);
               END;
            END;
         END GetEntry;
      PROCEDURE Menu(VAR c : CARDINAL);
         (*  Display menu and return choice  *)
         VAR
            Scrn : Point;
         BEGIN
            (*  Set colors and clear screen  *)
            Fore := White;
            Back := Blue;
            Clear();
            Scrn.x := 5;
            Scrn.y := 5;
            SetCursor(Scrn);
            WriteString("1  Add to File");
            NextField(Scrn);
            WriteString("2  Review File on Screen");
            NextField(Scrn);
            WriteString("3  List File to Screen or Printer");
            NextField(Scrn);
            WriteString("4  Dump File to Printer");
            NextField(Scrn);
```

Fig. 11-24. The TEXTIO implementation module. (Continued from page 383.)

```
              WriteString("5)   Quit");
              INC(Scrn.y, 2);
              Scrn.x := 1;
              REPEAT
                SetCursor(Scrn);
                WriteString("Select 1, 2, 3, 4, or 5:   ");
                ReadCard(c);
                WriteLn();
              UNTIL c IN {1..5};
            END Menu;
          BEGIN
          END TextIO.
```

Fig. 11-24. The TEXTIO implementation module. (Continued from page 384.)

good way to learn how the file is structured is to add a few records, dump the file, delete a record, dump the file, and repeat.

The constant MaxRecords in the module FileIO limits the size of the file to 10 names. This conserves paper when you are running the dump option. If this program is to be used to maintain an actual list of names, addresses, and phone numbers, the constant MaxRecords should be increased as appropriate, and the modules recompiled.

Notice that the module FileIO is used by both Modula20 and TextIO. This means that the definition module of FileIO must be compiled before either Modula20 or TextIO is compiled. Because TextIO is used by Modula20, the definition module of TextIO must be compiled before Modula20 can be compiled.

```
(*  Figure 11-25:  The Lists Definition Module.  *)
(*                                                *)
(*  Supports the Comprehensive Sample Program.    *)
(*                                                *)
DEFINITION MODULE Lists;
  EXPORT QUALIFIED Append, Review, ListFile, Dump;
  PROCEDURE Append();
  (*  Add records to the file  *)
  PROCEDURE Review();
  (*  Review records, 1 at a time, on screen  *)
  (*      Option to delete a record.           *)
  PROCEDURE ListFile();
  (*  List file to screen or printer.          *)
  PROCEDURE Dump();
  (*  List file and pointers on printer for     *)
  (*      analysis.                             *)
  END Lists.
```

Fig. 11-25. The Lists definition module.

```
(*   Figure 11-26:   The Lists Implementation Module.   *)
(*                                                       *)
(*   Supports the Comprehensive Sample Program.          *)
(*                                                       *)
IMPLEMENTATION MODULE Lists;
  FROM InOut IMPORT Read, WriteString, WriteLn, WriteInt, out;
  FROM TextIO IMPORT GetEntry, PrintRec, TEXT;
  FROM Utilities IMPORT Pause;
  FROM FileIO IMPORT PutRec, GetRec, RecType, Index, InBuf, EndList,
      MaxRecords;
  FROM PrinterIO IMPORT PrinterOn, PrinterOff, CRLF;
  FROM String IMPORT Compare;
  PROCEDURE GetFree() : CARDINAL;
    (*   Get record number of next free record and   *)
    (*       remove it from the free list            *)
    VAR
      free : CARDINAL;
    BEGIN
      IF Index[-1] = EndList THEN
        RETURN EndList;
      END;
      free := Index[-1];
      (*   Move next free record to head of free list   *)
      Index[-1] := Index[free];
      RETURN free;
    END GetFree;
  PROCEDURE Greater(a, b : RecType) : BOOLEAN;
    (*   Return TRUE if a.name > b.name   *)
    VAR
      i, j : INTEGER;
    BEGIN
      i := Compare(a.name.last, b.name.last);
      j := Compare(a.name.first, b.name.first);
      (*   Compare(str1, str2)   returns ( 0 if str1<str2,   *)
      (*                                   0 if str1=str2    *)
      (*                                 ) 0 if str1)str2    *)
      RETURN (i)0) OR ((i=0) AND (j)0));
    END Greater;
  PROCEDURE Insert(InBuf : RecType);
    (*   Insert record into the index   *)
    VAR
      p, q, free : INTEGER;
      TempBuf : RecType;
    BEGIN
      (*   Locate free record   *)
      free := GetFree();
      (*   Write buffer to file in free location   *)
      PutRec(free, InBuf);
      (*   Find proper place in index   *)
      p := Index[0];
      q := 0;
      LOOP
```

Fig. 11-26. The Lists implementation module.

```
            IF p=EndList THEN
               EXIT;
            END;
            GetRec(p, TempBuf);
            IF Greater(TempBuf, InBuf) THEN
               EXIT;
            END;
            o := p;
            p := Index[o];
         END;
         (*  Make entry in index  *)
         Index[free] := p;
         Index[o] := free;
      END Insert;
   PROCEDURE Append();
      (*  Add records to the file  *)
      VAR
         finished : BOOLEAN;
      BEGIN
         LOOP
            IF Index[-1] = EndList THEN
               WriteLn();
               writeString("No room left in the file ...");
               WriteLn();
               Pause();
               EXIT;
            END;
            GetEntry(InBuf, finished);
            IF finished THEN
               EXIT;
            END;
            Insert(InBuf);
         END;
      END Append;
   PROCEDURE Review();
      (*  Review records, 1 at a time, on screen  *)
      (*       Option to delete a record          *)
      VAR
         o, r : [0..MaxRecords];
         c : CHAR;
         Buf : RecType;
      PROCEDURE PutFree(r : INTEGER);
         (*  Put record r in the free list  *)
         BEGIN
            Index[r] := Index[-1];
            Index[-1] := r;
         END PutFree;
      BEGIN
         WriteLn();
         WriteLn();
         (*  Start with first record in active list  *)
         r := Index[0];
         o := 0;
         LOOP
```

```
            IF r = EndList THEN
              EXIT;
            END;
            WriteLn();
            PrintRec(Console, r);
            WriteLn();
            WriteString("G)et next record, D)elete this record, ");
            WriteString("or Q)uit? ");
            Read(c);
            WriteLn();
            CASE c OF
              'G', 'g' :
              (*  Get next record  *)
              q := r;
              r := Index[r];
            | 'D', 'd' :
              (*  Delete this record  *)
              Index[q] := Index[r];
              PutFree(r);
              r := Index[q];
            | 'Q', 'q' :
              EXIT;
            ELSE
              (*  Do nothing  *)
            END;
          END;
          Pause();
      END Review;
    PROCEDURE List(dest : TEXT);
      (*  List all active records to dest in alphabetical order *)
      VAR
        i : [0..MaxRecords];
      BEGIN
        (*  Start with first record  *)
        i := Index[0];
        IF dest = Printer THEN
          PrinterOn();
        END;
        WHILE i # EndList DO
          IF dest = Printer THEN
            CRLF();
          ELSE
            WriteLn();
          END;
          PrintRec(dest, i);
          i := Index[i];
        END;
        IF dest = Printer THEN
          PrinterOff();
        END;
      END List;
    PROCEDURE ListFile();
      (*  List file on screen or printer  *)
```

Fig. 11-26. The Lists implementation module. (Continued from page 387.)

```
      VAR
        a : CHAR;
      BEGIN
        WriteLn();
        WriteLn();
        WriteString("List to S)creen or P)rinter?   ");
        Read(a);
        WriteLn();
        CASE a OF
          'S', 's' :
            List(Console);
        | 'P', 'p' :
            List(Printer);
        ELSE
          (*  Recursive call *)
          ListFile();
        END;
        Pause();
      END ListFile;
   PROCEDURE Dump();
      (*  List file and pointers on printer for analysis  *)
      VAR
        i : CARDINAL;
      BEGIN
        PrinterOn();
        WriteString("First Record in Use:   ");
        WriteInt(Index[0], 1);
        WriteString("     First Free Record:   ");
        WriteInt(Index[-1], 1);
        CRLF();
        FOR i := 1 TO MaxRecords DO
          CRLF();
          WriteString("Record ");
          WriteInt(i, 1);
          CRLF();
          PrintRec(Printer, i);
          WriteString("Next Record:         ");
          WriteInt(Index[i], 1);
          CRLF();
        END;
        PrinterOff();
      END Dump;
   BEGIN
   END Lists.
```

Fig. 11-26. The Lists implementation module. (Continued from page 388.)

ADVANTAGES AND DISADVANTAGES OF MODULA-2

This chapter has only scratched the surface of Modula-2. It has not discussed, for example, the ability of Modula-2 to handle coprocessing, dynamic storage allocation, or open arrays. Much more space than is available in this chapter is needed to discuss these features of Modula-2. In this section only those features that have been presented will be appraised.

```
(*   Figure 11-27:   The Utilities Definition Module.    *)
(*                                                        *)
(*   Supports the Comprehensive Sample Program.           *)
(*                                                        *)
DEFINITION MODULE Utilities;
  EXPORT QUALIFIED Pause;
  PROCEDURE Pause();
  END Utilities.
```

Fig. 11-27. The Utilities definition module.

As a successor to Pascal, Modula-2 is in the enviable position of having learned from Pascal's mistakes. Perhaps the greatest advantage of Modula-2 over Pascal is the availability of modules and separate compilation.

The availability of the module encourages the proper structuring of programs and provides safeguards against unwanted interference between different parts of programs.

Modula-2 includes an additional control structure, the LOOP . . . END structure with EXIT. This permits increased flexibility in implementing loops.

Modula-2 includes an ELSE clause in its CASE statement. This corrects an apparent oversight in Pascal. The individual cases in Modula-2 can be subranges such as ['A'..'Z']. In Pascal, the equivalent case would have to enumerate each letter 'A', 'B', 'C', and so on through 'Z'.

```
(*   Figure 11-28:   The Utilities Implementation Module.   *)
(*                                                           *)
(*   Supports the Comprehensive Sample Program.              *)
(*                                                           *)
IMPLEMENTATION MODULE Utilities;
  FROM Terminal IMPORT Read, WriteString, WriteLn;
  PROCEDURE Pause();
    VAR
      c : CHAR;
    BEGIN
      WriteLn();
      WriteString("Press (Return) to Continue ....");
      Read(c);
      WriteLn();
    END Pause;
  BEGIN
  END Utilities.
```

Fig. 11-28. The Utilities implementation module.

```
Figure 11-29:   Structure Chart for the Comprehensive
                    Sample Program.


        Main Program                    Fig.  11-20
              OpenFiles()               Fig.  11-22
                    InitFiles()         Fig.  11-22
                    OpenFiles()         Fig.  11-22
              Menu()                    Fig.  11-24
                    NextField()         Fig.  11-24
              Append()                  Fig.  11-26
                    GetEntry()          Fig.  11-24
                          MarkOff()     Fig.  11-24
                          NextField()   Fig.  11-24
                    Insert()            Fig.  11-26
                          GetFree()     Fig.  11-26
                          PutRec()      Fig.  11-22
                                Seek()  Fig.  11-22
                          GetRec()      Fig.  11-22
                                Seek()  Fig.  11-22
                          Greater()     Fig.  11-26
              Review()                  Fig.  11-26
                    PrintRec()          Fig.  11-24
                          GetRec()      Fig.  11-22
                                Seek()  Fig.  11-22
                          CRLF()        Fig.  11-8
                    PutFree()           Fig.  11-26
              ListFile()                Fig.  11-26
                    List()              Fig.  11-26
                          PrinterOn()   Fig.  11-8
                          PrintRec()    Fig.  11-24
                          CRLF()        Fig.  11-8
                          PrinterOff()  Fig.  11-8
                    ListFile()          Fig.  11-26
              Dump()                    Fig.  11-26
                    PrinterOn()         Fig.  11-8
                    CRLF()              Fig.  11-8
                    PrintRec()          Fig.  11-24
                    PrinterOff()        Fig.  11-8
              CloseFiles()              Fig.  11-22
```

Fig. 11-29. Structure chart for the comprehensive sample program.

Modula-2 terminates its control structures (except the **REPEAT . . . UNTIL** structure) with **END**. This eliminates all the extra **BEGIN**s found in Pascal.

On the negative side, the fact that Modula-2 implements its input and output statements as procedures in library modules has some undesirable side effects. Consider the output procedures for example. Separate procedures are needed for writing a character, a string, an integer, a real number, and a carriage return. Furthermore, each procedure can handle only one data item. Thus to write a line containing two character strings, an integer, and a real number would require five separate procedure calls, two to **WriteString** (for the character strings), one to **WriteInt** (for the integer), one to **WriteReal** (for the real number), and one to **WriteLn** (for the terminating carriage return and line feed).

Like Pascal, Modula-2 lacks an exponentiation operator.

AVAILABILITY

Modula-2 is a relatively new language, having been introduced in the 1980s. There are already several implementations available. Besides the Interface Technologies Corporation compiler, other implementations of Modula-2 are available from the following companies: Logitech, Inc., of Redwood City, California; Modula Corporation of Provo, Utah; PCollier Systems of Tucson, Arizona; and Volition Systems of Del Mar, California. A review of four of these compilers can be found in the October 1986 issue of *Dr. Dobb's Journal of Software Tools*.

SUMMARY

Modula-2 is an extremely powerful, yet compact language. It is among the newest of the languages presented in this book. Like C and Ada, its appeal is more to serious programmers than to casual programmers; the latter group will probably be happier with BASIC or Pascal.

Modula-2 has features that facilitate the orderly development of large-scale programming systems. The module structure and the enforced interface standards between modules (including version control) are especially useful when a program is to be developed by a team of programmers.

Modula-2 offers facilities (not discussed herein) for low-level operations, such as manipulating bits and bytes. This makes it suitable for systems programming applications such as operating systems.

Modula-2 is similar enough to Pascal so that Pascal programmers can make the transition to Modula-2 in a matter of a few hours.

Modula-2 encourages good structured programming style. It is an excellent language for general-purpose programming and for the development of large-scale programming systems.

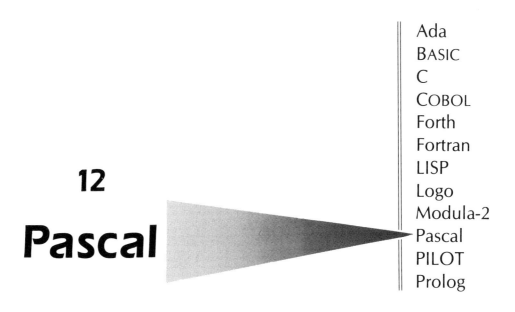

Ada
BASIC
C
COBOL
Forth
Fortran
LISP
Logo
Modula-2
Pascal
PILOT
Prolog

12

Pascal

The Pascal language was designed by Niklaus Wirth of the Eidgenossische Technische Hochschule (Federal Institute of Technology), Zurich, Switzerland. It is based largely on an earlier language known as ALGOL 60. ALGOL 60 was developed between 1957 and 1960 and as such is one of the earliest high-level computer languages. It found favor in Europe, but was used very little in the United States outside of universities. Professor Wirth was associated with ALGOL in the 1960s, both at Zurich and at Stanford University in California.

The late 1960s saw the introduction of a successor to ALGOL 60 known as ALGOL 68. Professor Wirth and others objected to ALGOL 68 as being too unwieldy. His response was to develop (between 1968 and 1970) a more streamlined successor to ALGOL 60, a language he called Pascal. The name Pascal is in honor of the 17th Century French mathematician, Blaise Pascal, who is credited with inventing the world's first digital calculating machine.

Pascal was originally designed as a language suitable for teaching computer programming to students. It has achieved great popularity not only as a teaching language, but also as a general-purpose language. Because of its streamlined design, it is easily implemented on microcomputers. Dr. Kenneth Bowles of the University of California at San Diego (UCSD) deserves special recognition for his early implementation of Pascal on microcomputers.

ALGOL 68, the ''official'' successor of ALGOL 60, has faded quietly into oblivion. Pascal, on the other hand, is probably second only to BASIC in popularity among microcomputer users.

The examples in this chapter were tested using the popular Turbo Pascal compiler running under MS-DOS on a Zenith Z-150 microcomputer. They are adaptations of earlier versions written and tested using the Apple/UCSD implementation of Pascal.

PROGRAM STRUCTURE

A Pascal program consists of a heading and a block. A simple Pascal program that does nothing but print This is a test can be written as shown in Fig. 12-1.

The first line is a comment line. Comments in Pascal are enclosed between braces, { and }, or between the symbols (* and *). Comments serve only to document the program and are ignored by the compiler.

The line that begins with Program is the program heading; it gives the program a name and identifies any input or output files. The file Output means normal console output. (Note that some versions of Pascal make the listing of input and output files in this line optional.) The main body of the program is the block, which begins with Begin and ends with End.

In this case the body of the program consists of a single statement, which writes a message to the console. Statements in Pascal are separated by semicolons. A semicolon need not appear just before an End, however; the last semicolon in Fig. 12-1 is therefore optional. A period must appear after the final End of a program.

A useful feature of Pascal, inherited from ALGOL, is that wherever a statement can appear, so can a block. A block is defined as zero or more statements bracketed by Begin and End. Pascal, for that reason, is sometimes called a *block-structured language*. The significance of this feature will become more clear in subsequent sections of this chapter.

Most implementations of Pascal on microcomputers use *native-code* compilers or *intermediate-code* compilers. Native code is another name for the machine language of a particular computer. Intermediate code (sometimes called *p-code*) resembles the assembly language of a hypothetical computer that may or may not exist anywhere. An intermediate code compiler translates a program from its source language (in this case Pascal) to intermediate code. The intermediate code is then interpreted. The advantage of this scheme is that the compiler need be written only once; only the intermediate-code interpreter need be rewritten to implement the system on another host computer. Most popular implementations of Pascal on 16-bit and 32-bit microcomputers, such as Turbo Pascal and Microsoft Pascal, are native-code compilers. UCSD Pascal, popular

```
(   Figure 12-1:   Simple Test Program.   )

Program Pascal_1(Output);

Begin
      WriteLn('This is a test.');
End.
```

Fig. 12-1. A simple test program.

```
(   Figure 12-2:   Demonstrate Constant Declaration.   )

Program Trig(Output);

    Const
        PI = 3.14159;

Begin
    WriteLn('PI =   ', PI);
End.
```

Fig. 12-2. Constant declaration.

on eight-bit microcomputers such as the Apple *II+* and *IIe*, is an intermediate-code compiler.

Most implementations of Pascal are not case-sensitive, so that WriteLn, WRITELN, and writeln are equivalent. I have chosen to write Pascal keywords and procedure names in upper- and lowercase, user-defined constants in all uppercase, and user-defined variables in all lowercase.

DATA REPRESENTATION

The basic data types in Pascal are real, integer, char (character), and Boolean (logical). Character strings are represented as arrays of characters in standard Pascal, but most versions also incorporate a string type. Some implementations also support a form of binary-coded decimal (BCD) representation. This form of representation is particularly useful for business applications.

An interesting feature of Pascal is that the programmer can define additional types of his or her own description. As a simple example, suppose that a programmer requires a nonnegative integer value. A type can be declared as follows:

```
Type
    cardinal = 0..MaxInt;
```

MaxInt is a predefined constant that represents the largest integer that can be represented on a particular computer. The type cardinal therefore includes all integers between zero and MaxInt.

Constants

Pascal allows constants to be named and declared in a program. A simple example is shown in Fig. 12-2. In this program PI is declared to be a constant and is given a value, which it retains for the duration of the program. This helps to document programs. Although in this case the value of the constant PI is not likely to change, in some cases there are constants, such as the sales tax rate, that remain relatively constant, but may change over time. By naming and declaring such constants at the beginning of the program, the programmer makes subsequent updating of the program much easier. Otherwise the person doing the modification would have to seek out and update each and every occurrence of the value throughout the program.

Representation of numerical constants, integer and real, is conventional, as described in Chapter 2. The two Boolean constants are of course True and False.

Variables

Variables in Pascal must be declared at the beginning of the program. A simple example is given in Fig. 12-3. The program simply computes and prints out the area of a circle of radius 5.0. The integer variable i was not actually used; it was declared simply to display the format for declaring variables of different types.

THE ASSIGNMENT STATEMENT

The assignment operator in Pascal is a colon followed by an equals sign (: =). The example in Fig. 12-3 contains two simple assignment statements immediately following Begin.

The assignment statement is very particular about types. For example, the following statement:

    i := area

in the program in Fig. 12-3 would not compile correctly because i is of type Integer and area is of type Real.

```
{  Figure 12-3:   Compute the Area of a Circle.   }

Program Circle(Output);

    Const
          PI = 3.14159;

    Var
          area, radius:  Real;
          i:             Integer;

Begin
    radius := 5.0;
    area   := PI * radius * radius;
    WriteLn('Radius:  ', radius);
    WriteLn('Area:    ', area);
End.
```

Fig. 12-3. Computing the area of a circle.

ARITHMETIC EXPRESSIONS

Pascal uses conventional infix notation (see Chapter 2) for its arithmetic expressions. It has the usual arithmetic operators (+, −, *, /) with the significant exception of an exponentiation operator. Wirth apparently reasoned that exponentiation can be performed by repeated multiplication (in the case of integer exponents) or by using logarithms (in the case of real numbers), and that it is better to let the programmer decide how it should be done than to let the system decide. Absence of this operator is a minor annoyance.

BOOLEAN EXPRESSIONS

Chapter 2 discusses logical expressions. Pascal calls logical expressions *Boolean expressions.* Pascal has the usual relational and logical operators as listed in Chapter 2 (for example, > and Or.)

A minor difficulty arises when combining simple Boolean expressions to form compound Boolean expressions. Suppose that A, B, C, and D are all real variables. In most languages the following expression:

A > B Or C > D

would be perfectly acceptable. In Pascal you would have to write the following:

(A > B) OR (C > D).

The latter expression is easier to read anyway.

INPUT AND OUTPUT

You have already seen examples of the WriteLn statement in Figs. 12-2 and 12-3. These examples directed output to the system console (video screen). An alternate form of the WriteLn statement allows the output to be directed to the system printer or, as will be discussed in a later section, to a disk file.

How this is done unfortunately varies somewhat from system to system. An example will be given anyway because the topic is too often not covered properly in language manuals. Figure 12-4 shows a simple program that writes to both the video screen and to the printer. The example is valid for Turbo Pascal; the details may vary somewhat for other Pascal implementations.

The standard output file in Pascal is called Output and refers to the video screen. The file Output does not have to be declared explicitly. Note that Output appears in parentheses following the program name at the top of the program. Standard Pascal requires all input and output file names to be so listed. (Some microcomputer versions omit this requirement.) This program introduces another file called Lst.

Note that Lst is also listed in parentheses following the program name. Lst is a standard file that is provided with Turbo Pascal and need not be declared.

The syntax of a WriteLn statement allows the first item inside the parentheses to be the name of a file. If it is not, then the default output file Output is assumed. The first WriteLn in Fig. 12-4 could also have been written as follows:

WriteLn (Output,'This goes to the video screen.').

```
(   Figure 12-4:   Demonstrate Printer Output.   )

Program PrintTest(Output, Lst);

      ( This program writes to the video )
      (    screen and to the printer.     )

Begin
      WriteLn('This goes to the video screen.');
      WriteLn(Lst, 'This goes to the printer.');
End.
```

Fig. 12-4. Printer Output.

In the next **WriteLn**, **Lst** is the first item inside the parentheses. This causes output to be directed to the file **Lst**, which in this case is the printer.

A WriteLn statement always causes a carriage return at the end of the output. If the output device is the video screen, this means that the cursor automatically returns to the first column of the next line. If this is not desired, the **Write** statement can be used instead of the WriteLn statement. Otherwise there is no difference between the two statements.

It is often useful to be able to control the format of the output. In the case of a character string this means the field width of the output. Suppose the character string **s** has the value **Hi**. The following statement:

Write(s:5)

would write **Hi** to the screen, and the cursor would be left three spaces to the right of the letter **i**. The total field width would be five: two columns for the character string and three for trailing blanks. Assuming the letter **H** went in column 1, anything written after this string would begin in column 6.

As illustrated above, character strings are left-justified in the designated field. Numbers are right-justified. For example, if **a** has been declared as an integer,

a := 1;
Write(a:5);

would write "**4 spaces 1**" to the screen, i.e., a one preceded by four blanks.

The user can also control the number of digits to the right of the decimal point in real numbers. For example, if **x** has been declared as real, the following:

x := 3.1;
Write(x:5:2);

would write **3.10** to the screen. The total number of spaces occupied would be five, with two places to the right of the decimal point.

The **Read** and **ReadLn** statements are used for input. The standard input device is the terminal or keyboard and is formally called **Input**. **Input** needs to be mentioned in the parentheses in the **Program** line at the top of the program for all programs containing **Read** or **ReadLn** statements.

The distinction between **Read** and **ReadLn** needs to be studied carefully. When using **Read** with a variable of type **Char** (character), **Read** takes a single character from the file at a time and assigns its value to the variable in the **Read** statement. For example, if **c** is a character variable, the following:

Read(c)

or

Read(Input,c)

would read one character from the **Input** file and assign its value to the variable **c**. When an end-of-line character (a carriage return, ASCII 13) is encountered, **Read** returns a space (ASCII 32) rather than a carriage return.

Another option is to read from the predefined device **Kbd**, which stands for the keyboard. The following statement:

Read(Kbd, c)

behaves slightly differently. A carriage return is read as a carriage return (ASCII 13), not as a space, and characters typed are not echoed to the screen. If the character typed needs to appear on the screen, a **Write** statement must follow the **Read**.

There are two Boolean variables called **EoLn** (End of Line) and **Eof** (End of file) implicit in every program. **EoLn** becomes true when the end-of-line character is encountered by a **Read** or **ReadLn** statement. **Eof** becomes true when the end of the input file is encountered. The end-of-file character is Control-Z (ASCII 26) in MS-DOS. Testing for **Eof** or **EoLn** is inconvenient when reading from the **Input** file. It is better to read from the **Kbd** device and test for the appropriate ASCII value.

When **Read** is used with a numeric variable (**Real** or **Integer**), it skips any spaces or end-of-line characters preceding the number and then reads the digits until it encounters a space, an end-of-line character, or end-of-file character. The next **Read** statement will start looking in the very next position of the same line (unless the previous **Read** was terminated by an end-of-line or end-of-file character).

ReadLn may be used with variables of type **Char**, **String**, **Integer**, **Real**, or (when implemented) **Long Real**. The format is as follows:

ReadLn(v1,v2, . . . ,vN)

or

ReadLn(Input,v1,v2, . . . ,vN).

The difference between Read and ReadLn is that with ReadLn, after the last variable in the list (vN in this case) is read, the remainder of the current input line is skipped. The next Read or ReadLn statement will start looking on the next line.

Most of the time Read and ReadLn produce the same results when used with the standard Input file, but not always. ReadLn is usually preferred, because its results are usually easier to predict.

ReadLn is especially convenient for reading variables of type String from the console (Input). Suppose s is a String variable. The following statement reads an entire line from the console and stores it in the variable s:

ReadLn(s).

The program in Fig. 12-5 serves as an electronic typewriter; it reads line after line from the console, printing each successively to the printer. It uses a ReadLn statement and a string variable. (Note that the use of the WHILE construct, introduced in Chapter 2, is discussed in more detail in a later section of this chapter.)

For comparison, the program in Fig. 12-6 does essentially the same thing using Read (from the Kbd device) and a character variable. The first thing you will note is that the logic is slightly more complex. If you try the two programs, you will note that the program in Fig. 12-5 is much more forgiving; it lets you backspace and correct errors. The program in Fig. 12-6 does not. That alone is sufficient reason for preferring the use of ReadLn and string variables over Read and character variables for console input.

```
(  Figure 12-5:   Pascal Electronic Typewriter, Version 1.  )

Program TypeWriter1(Input, Output, Lst);

     (  Emulates an electronic typewriter using the  )
     (      ReadLn statement with a String variable.  )

     Var
         s:   String[80];

Begin
     WriteLn('Welcome to your Electronic Typewriter.');
     WriteLn;
     WriteLn('Enter your text, followed by blank line:');
     WriteLn;
     ReadLn(s);
     While (Length(s) > 0) Begin
          WriteLn(Lst, s);
          ReadLn(s)
     End;
End.
```

Fig. 12-5. Pascal Electronic Typewriter, Version 1.

```
(  Figure 12-6:  Pascal Electronic Typewriter, Version 2.  )

Program TypeWriter2(Input, Output, Kbd, Lst);

     (  Emulate an electronic typewriter using the  )
     (      Read statement with a Char variable.    )

     Var
         c:  Char;

Begin
     WriteLn('Welcome to your Electronic Typewriter, Version 2.');
     WriteLn;
     WriteLn('Enter your text, followed by <Control-Z>.');
     WriteLn;
     Read(Kbd, c);                        ( Get first character  )
     While (c <> Chr(26)) Begin           ( Test for <Control-Z> )
          If (c = Chr(13)) Then Begin     ( Test for <CR>        )
               WriteLn;                   ( Echo <CR> to screen  )
               WriteLn(Lst);              ( Echo <CR> to printer )
          End Else Begin
               Write(c);                  ( Write c on screen    )
               Write(Lst, c);             ( Write c on printer   )
          End;
          Read(Kbd, c);                   ( Get next character   )
     End;
     WriteLn(Lst);
     WriteLn;
End.
```

Fig. 12-6. Pascal Electronic Typewriter, Version 2.

CONTROL STRUCTURES

Pascal has a rich set of control structures, much richer than that of such languages as Fortran, COBOL, or BASIC. The control structures in Pascal are highly structured in addition to being numerous. What this means is that Pascal control structures follow the fundamental principle that there should be only one entry to and one exit from a control structure. This makes it easier to structure the logic of a program. The result is a program that is easier to read and easier to maintain.

The format of the various control structures rely heavily on the block structure of Pascal. Recall from the discussion above that wherever the language calls for a statement, a block containing several statements can occur, delimited by Begin and End.

Simple Selection: IF-THEN-ELSE

The general format for this statement in Pascal is as follows:

```
If condition Then
     statement1
```

```
Else
     statement2;
```

The **Else** and **statement2** are optional. The condition is understood to be any Boolean expression as defined above. **Statement1** and **statement2** can be single statements or blocks.

Here is a simple **If** statement without an **Else** part. It is intended to avoid division by zero and signal when it would have occurred. **Num, denom,** and **quotient** are real variables, and **flag** is a Boolean variable assumed to be initially false:

```
If denom = 0.0 Then Begin
     denom := 1.0;
     flag := True
End;
quotient := num/denom;
```

In this example the two statements between **Begin** and **End** are treated as if they were syntactically one statement.

Now suppose in the same situation that you could not assume that **flag** was initially false. Here is a solution:

```
If denom = 0.0 Then Begin
     denom := 1.0;
     flag := True
End Else
     flag := False;
quotient := num/denom;
```

In this case **flag** is set to false if the denominator is not zero. This example illustrates another point: There can be no semicolon after the **End** (just before **Else**). A semicolon there would cause the compiler to think that everything between **If** and the semicolon is a single statement. It would then try unsuccessfully to form a new statement starting with the **Else**.

One (or both) of the statements within the **If-Then-Else** construct can also be an **If** or **If-Then-Else**. Suppose that in computing a weekly payroll, time-and-a-half is paid for all hours worked in excess of 40 but less than 50, and double-time is paid for all hours in excess of 50:

```
If hours < = 40 Then
     pay := hours * rate
Else If hours < = 50 Then
     pay := 40 * rate +
          (hours – 40) *
          rate * 1.5
Else
     pay := 40 * rate + 10 *
```

rate * 1.5 + (hours – 50)
      * rate * 2;

This is called a *nested* If. Notice that several statements are continued onto succeeding lines. Remember that statements in Pascal are separated by semicolons; it makes no difference that a statement spills over onto another line.

The CASE Statement

If statements permit two-way selection between alternatives. Nested If statements permit selections among a number of alternatives. The **Case** statement provides another form of selection among multiple alternatives. Whereas nested If statements are perfectly general, the **Case** statement is often more convenient in situations in which the choice to be made depends on the value of a specific variable. That variable must be an **integer, Boolean, character,** or user-defined scalar type. (Note: As mentioned earlier, user-defined types are beyond the scope of this book.)

An example of a Pascal **Case** statement is given in Chapter 2. For another example, suppose that a program needs to calculate the number of days in a month. We all know the old poem, "Thirty days hath September, . . .," but most computers do not. Figure 12-7 gives a short program to handle this problem.

This program reads in the month, and then uses the **Case** statement to decide what value to assign to the variable **days**. Notice that there are only three cases: one case for the 31-day months, one case for the 30-day months, and one case for February. The **Case** statement permits like cases to be grouped together, so this situation is easy to accommodate. In the case of February, the program must also know the year so that it can determine whether or not it is a leap year. The operator **Mod** computes the modulus, or remainder after integer division. Thus if the following is true:

(year Mod 4 = 0),

then the year is evenly divisible by four and is a leap year.

A shortcoming of the standard Pascal **Case** statement is that if the case selector variable is not one of the values listed, the alternative is not defined. In this case that means that there would be no protection against the user asking for the number of days in the 13th month. To guard against such possibilities, the **Case** statement has been enclosed within an If statement to check for such a situation. Many implementations of Pascal extend the language in the form of an "else" or "otherwise" clause in the **Case** statement.

Loops

Pascal provides a variety of control structures for repetition: one kind of counted loop and two kinds of conditional loop.

Counted Loops: The FOR Statement. Chapter 2 contains a simple example in BASIC of a program that prints out the integers from 1 to 10. Figure 12-8 contains a Pascal program that does the same thing using a **For** statement.

In the program in Fig. 12-8, the variable i serves as the loop counter. The variable i is incremented from 1 to 10; during each loop the value of i is printed out on the screen

```
{  Figure 12-7:   The Calendar Program.  }

Program Calendar(Input, Output);

   {  Print number of days in a given month }

   Var
       month, year, days:  Integer;
Begin
   WriteLn;
   WriteLn('Welcome to the Pascal Calendar Program.');
   Repeat
       WriteLn;
       Write('Enter the month (1..12; 0 to Quit):   ');
       ReadLn(month);
       If (month >= 1) And (month <= 12) Then Begin
           Case month of
               1,3,5,7,
               8,10,12:   days := 31;
               4,6,9,11:  days := 30;
               2:              Begin  ( Handle February }
                               Write('Enter the year:   ');
                               ReadLn(year);
                               If year Mod 4 = 0 Then
                                   days := 29
                               Else
                                   days := 28;
                           End;
           End;  { Case }
           WriteLn('Month ', month, ' has ', days, ' days.');
       End
   Until (month = 0);
End.
```

Fig. 12-7. The Calendar Program.

using the **WriteLn** statement. The **WriteLn** statement is the body of the loop. In this case the body of the loop consists of only one statement. If there were a need for more than one statement in the body of the loop, the statements would be surrounded by **Begin** and **End**, forming a block.

Conditional Loops. Conditional loops repeat a sequence of statements until a certain condition is met or as long as a certain condition stays true. The two types of conditional loop in Pascal are the **While** loop and the **Repeat-Until** loop.

The **While** loop repeats as long as the stated condition is true. The test of the condition is performed at the top of the loop, before the body of the loop is performed.

```
{   Figure  12-8:   The  Counted  Loop.   }

Program  TestFor(Output);

    Var
        i:   Integer;

Begin
      For  i  :=  1  to  10  Do
          WriteLn(i);
End.
```

Fig. 12-8. The counted loop.

If the condition is initially false, the body of the loop will not be performed at all. Figure 12-9 shows how the task in Fig. 12-8 can be performed using a While loop rather than a For loop.

Note that the program in Fig. 12-9 is longer than that in Fig. 12-8, even though they do exactly the same thing. A For loop is more efficient than a While loop for this particular application. Nonetheless Fig. 12-9 is useful for pointing out some of the functions performed automatically by the For loop. Note that in the While loop the variable i must be initialized to 1 before the loop begins, and that it must be incremented at the bottom of the loop. These are functions performed automatically by the For loop.

There are other situations, however, in which the While loop is more appropriate than the For loop. Suppose, for example, a program is required to read in integers from the console and add them as long as the sum does not exceed 100. The program must

```
{   Figure  12-9:   The  Conditional  Loop.   }

Program  TestWhile(Output);

    Var
        i:   Integer;

Begin
    i  :=  1;
    While  i  <=  10  Do  Begin
        WriteLn(i);
        i  :=  i  +  1;
    End;
End.
```

Fig. 12-9. The conditional loop.

then print out the sum and the number of integers that formed the sum. The last integer read is not to be counted or summed. Such a program is shown in Fig. 12-10.

A While loop is preferable to a For loop in this situation because it cannot be determined in advance how many times the loop will be executed. A For loop is best when the number of iterations is known in advance.

The program in Fig. 12-10 is slightly more complicated than earlier programs in this chapter. One reason is that the task is more complicated. Another reason is that the program is designed to be interactive, so it contains a number of WriteLn statements intended to prompt the user for input and to explain the output.

In this example the initialization step consists of setting the variables count and sum to zero and reading in the first value of num. The While statement checks to see whether the most recent value of num added to the current value of sum is less than or equal to 100. If it is, the body of the loop is executed. The body of the loop consists of counting the number just read, adding it to sum, and reading in the next value of num. The process is repeated as long as the last value of num would not push the sum over 100. The rest of the program merely reports the results.

```
(  Figure 12-10:   The Sum-Up Program, Version 1.   }

Program SumUp(Input, Output);

    (  Read until sum > 100   }

    Var
        num, count, sum:  Integer;

Begin
    count := 0;
    sum   := 0;
    WriteLn;
    WriteLn('Enter a series of numbers:  ');
    ReadLn(num);
    While (sum + num) <= 100 Do Begin
        count := count + 1;
        sum   := sum + num;
        ReadLn(num)
    End;
    WriteLn;
    WriteLn(count, ' numbers were read.');
    WriteLn('Their sum is ', sum, '.');
    WriteLn('The number ', num, ' was not counted.');
End.
```

Fig. 12-10. The Sum-Up Program, Version 1.

```
{  Figure 12-11:  The Sum-Up Program, Version 2.  }

Program SumUp2(Input, Output);

   {  Read until sum > 100   }
   {  Using Repeat ... Until }

   Var
      num, count, sum:  Integer;
Begin
   count := -1;
   sum   := 0;
   num   := 0;
   WriteLn('Enter a series of numbers:');
   Repeat
      count := count + 1;
      sum   := sum + num;
      ReadLn(num)
   Until (sum + num) > 100;
   WriteLn;
   WriteLn(count, ' numbers were read.');
   WriteLn('Their sum is ', sum, '.');
   WriteLn('The number ', num, ' was not counted.');
End.
```

Fig. 12-11. The Sum-Up Program, Version 2.

The **Repeat-Until** loop repeats a sequence of statements until a certain condition is attained. In contrast to the **While** statement, the **Repeat-Until** statement performs the test at the bottom. In some situations it is preferable to test at the bottom, and in some it is preferable to test at the top. In other situations it doesn't make any difference one way or the other.

The program in Fig. 12-11 performs the same task as that in Fig. 12-10 using a **Repeat-Until** loop rather than a **While** loop. Notice that certain adjustments had to be made because the **Repeat-Until** loop tests at the bottom and therefore must execute at least one time. The variable **count** had to be initialized to −1 and num to 0 so that the first iteration would not throw off the count and the total. Although this works perfectly well, it is less straightforward than the approach taken with the **While** loop. In this case, the **While** loop is preferable to the **Repeat-Until** loop. In other cases the **Repeat-Until** loop may be preferable.

Procedures

Subroutines are called *procedures* in Pascal. A procedure is a more-or-less self-contained module that is defined at the beginning of a Pascal program and can be invoked (almost) anywhere in a program. The use of procedures in a Pascal program usually makes the program easier to design, develop, and maintain. This is accomplished largely by subdividing large, complex tasks into smaller, simpler tasks. These smaller tasks are conceptually much easier to deal with. The advantages of using procedures are discussed further in the section on subroutines in Chapter 2.

Sometimes procedures are convenient merely to reduce the amount of duplicate coding in a program. Consider for example a program in which the values of two real variables must be exchanged at various places in the program. Figure 12-12 shows such a program.

The program in Fig. 12-12 contains two procedures, one to exchange the values of two variables and one to print out two variables with labels. Clearly this program could have been written without any procedures. With such simple tasks the benefit of using procedures is perhaps marginal. Had the procedures consisted of 30 lines each rather than 3 lines each, the savings of not having to place the code "in line" would have been more significant. In either case, however, the main program is simpler to read and understand. This is particularly true when the names of the procedures are descriptive of the tasks to be performed, as in this program.

Several details in Fig. 12-12 need to be pointed out. First, note the placement of the procedure declarations: They are placed after the declaration of variables for the main program and before the **Begin** of the main program. Next, note the heading of each procedure. Following the name of the procedure, the parameters of the procedures are listed in parentheses. The parameters of **Swap** are u and v. When **Swap** is invoked in the main program, its arguments are first p and q, then x and y. The first time **Swap** is invoked, the values of p and q are exchanged; the second time Swap is invoked, the values of x and y are exchanged.

Notice the presence of the word **Var** in the parameter list of the procedure **Swap** and its absence in the parameter list of the procedure Print2. When **Var** is present, any changes made to the parameters in the procedure are reflected in the values of their arguments in the main program. Without **Var**, the values of the arguments in the main program remain unchanged no matter what happens in the procedure. To demonstrate this, try running the program as is; then remove the word **Var** from the parameter list of Swap, recompile the program, and run it again.

The procedure **Print2** is straightforward. Because **Print2** returns no values to the main program, there is no need for **Var** in its parameter list.

Procedures can invoke other procedures in Pascal, and can even be recursive (self-invoking). (Recursion is discussed further later in the chapter.) Because procedures must be defined *before* they are used ("before" means closer to the top of the program), Pascal programs tend to appear upside down. The main program comes last, preceded by the highest-level procedures. The lowest-level procedures come first.

Functions

A function is similar to a procedure. Each is a more-or-less self-contained module that is defined at the beginning of a Pascal program and can be invoked almost anywhere in that program. As explained in Chapter 2, the primary differences between a function and a procedure are in the heading of the definition and in the manner in which the result is returned to the invoking program or procedure.

```
(  Figure 12-12:   Procedures:   The Swap Program.   )

Program SwapEm(Output);

   (  Demonstrate a procedure to exchange   )
   (      the values of 2 variables.        )

   Var
       p,q,x,y:   Real;

   Procedure Swap(Var u,v:   Real);
      Var
         temp:   Real;
      Begin
         temp := u;
         u    := v;
         v    := temp;
      End;   ( Swap )

   Procedure Print2(u,v:   Real);
      (  Print out two variables with labels   )
      Begin
         WriteLn;
         WriteLn('First  Variable:   ', u);
         WriteLn('Second Variable:   ', v);
      End;   ( Print2 )

Begin

   p := 1.0;   q := 2.0;
   Print2(p, q);
   Swap(p, q);
   Print2(p, q);

   x := 3.14159;   y := 2.71828;
   Print2(x, y);
   Swap(x, y);
   Print2(x,y);

End.   ( Program   )
```

Fig. 12-12. Procedures: The swap program.

Pascal has built-in or predefined functions that perform the usual standard mathematical operations such as computing square roots, sines, cosines, and so on. The user can also define functions as necessary.

A function definition begins with the word Function, followed by the name of the function, a parameter list in parentheses, a colon, and the type of the function. A function must have a type; this determines the type of the value returned by the function to the invoking program or procedure.

A simple example that finds the largest of three integers is shown in Fig. 12-13. In this example the name of the function is Max3 and its type is Integer.

The function heading is followed by the declaration of local constants and variables (as in a procedure). In this case there are none. The body of the function follows, enclosed in a Begin-End block. Notice that Max3, the name of the function, is used as a variable in the function. The value returned to the invoking program or procedure will be the value of the variable Max3 at the end of the function.

Notice that, in the example, I have included a comment on the same line as the final End of the function to indicate that this End is the end of the procedure Max3.

```
(  Figure 12-13:   A Function Demonstration.   )

Program GetMax(Input, Output);

   Var
      i,j,k:  Integer;

   Function Max3(x, y, z:  Integer):  Integer;
      (  Returns the largest of the 3 inputs  )
      Begin
         If (x >= y) And (x >= z) Then
            Max3 := x
         Else If (y >= x) And (y >= z) Then
            Max3 := y
         Else
            Max3 := z;
      End;  ( Max3  )

Begin

   Write('Enter three integers separated by spaces:  ');
   ReadLn(i, j, k);
   WriteLn;
   WriteLn(Max3(i, j, k), ' is the largest of the three.');

End.  ( Program  )
```

Fig. 12-13. A function demonstration.

Recursion

As indicated above and in Chapter 2, a procedure or function is said to be recursive if it invokes itself. How this works in Pascal will be illustrated using two simple examples. The first is a recursive function that computes factorials; the second is a recursive procedure that demonstrates simple string manipulation.

The factorial of a positive integer is a mathematical function that is defined recursively. The factorial of zero is defined as one. The factorial of a positive number N is defined as N times the factorial of N – 1. Such a recursive definition (the factorial function is defined in terms of itself) seems to cry for a recursive implementation. Such an implementation is shown in the program in Fig. 12-14.

The recursive function in Fig. 12-14 is appropriately called **Factorial**. It is of type **Real** rather than of type **Integer** because the largest **Integer** value in most microcomputer versions of Pascal is 32767, and the factorial of numbers as small as 8 exceed that value.

Note that there are three possibilities when the function is invoked: N can be negative, zero, or positive. If N is negative, something has gone wrong (probably a meaningless input), so an error message is printed and an impossible value (zero) returned for **Factorial**. If N is zero, **Factorial** is set to one. In either of these cases, the function is not invoked again. In the third case, N is positive, so the recursive definition that N factorial is N times N – 1 factorial is applied.

How this works is better understood after stepping through a simple example. Consider the computation of the factorial of three. When **Factorial** is called with n = 3, the function notes that three is positive and so decides that three factorial is three times two factorial. To compute two factorial, the function **Factorial** is called again with n = 2. The original invocation of **Factorial** is suspended pending the result.

The second invocation of the function notes that two is positive and so decides that two factorial must be two times one factorial. **Factorial** is called again with n = 1. Similarly, the function decides that one factorial is one times zero factorial and **Factorial** is invoked for the fourth time, this time with n = 0.

It is important to note that each of these invocations of **Factorial** is independent and is working with a different value of n. Earlier invocations of the function are suspended waiting for later invocations to return.

Because n equals zero on the fourth invocation of **Factorial**, the function returns the value 1. Now the third invocation of the function can compute one factorial as one times zero factorial, which is one. This value is then returned to the second invocation, which computes two factorial as two times one. The first invocation of the function **Factorial** can now compute three factorial as three times two factorial, or six.

A less mathematical example of recursion is the program in Fig. 12-15, which illustrates how a recursive procedure can be used to manipulate a character string. The procedure takes a string of length N and prints it N times, dropping the first letter with each repetition until there are no letters remaining. The result is sort of a triangle, which can be read horizontally and vertically.

The procedure uses the Turbo Pascal string intrinsics **Length** and **Delete**. **Length** is a function that returns the number of characters in a string. **Delete** is a procedure that deletes a character or characters from a string, in this case one character from the first position of the string.

Each time the procedure **Print__And__Drop** is called, it checks the length of the

```
(   Figure 12-14:   Recursion in Pascal:   Factorials.   )

Program Fact(Input, Output);

    (   Demonstrate a recursive function   )
    (      to compute factorials.          )

    Var
        n:       Real;
        reply:   String[80];

    Function Factorial(n:  Real):   Real;
        Begin
            If n < 0 Then Begin
                WriteLn('Number must be >= 0');
                Factorial := 0
            End Else If n = 0 Then
                Factorial := 1
            Else
                Factorial := n * Factorial(n-1);
        End;  (   Factorial   )

Begin

    Repeat
        Write('Enter a non-negative integer:   ');
        ReadLn(n);
        WriteLn(n:1:0, ' factorial is ', Factorial(n):1:0);
        WriteLn;
        Write('Again (y/n)?   ');
        ReadLn(reply);
        WriteLn
    Until (reply <> 'y') And (reply <> 'Y');

End.  (   Program   )
```

Fig. 12-14. Recursion in Pascal: factorials.

string s. If the length of s is greater than zero, it prints the string, deletes the first character of the string, and calls itself again using the remaining part of the string as its argument. If the string has a length zero, it does nothing, terminating the recursion.

The GoTo Statement

The GoTo statement is not often needed in Pascal programs because of the rich variety of other control statements available. Occasionally, however, it is convenient to exit from a loop when a certain condition is met. There are also times when it is necessary to escape from a deeply nested situation when an error condition is met. Thus, while many programming experts advocate keeping the number of GoTo statements in a program to a minimum, it is not always possible or desirable to eliminate GoTo statements altogether. Care must be taken, however, to avoid their indiscriminate use.

A GoTo statement requires a label as a destination, and the label must be declared. Pascal labels must be integers of up to four digits and must be declared before constants and variables are declared.

The situations described above, which call for the use of a GoTo statement, are difficult to illustrate in a short example. The example given in Fig. 12-16 is therefore a little contrived. The example program contains an input routine that validates the input to be sure it is positive before proceeding. The same result could have been achieved using the Repeat-Until construct.

DATA STRUCTURES

So far the Pascal programs in the examples have used simple data structures. One of the great strengths of Pascal is its ability to handle complex data structures. In fact,

```
{  Figure 12-15:  The Word Triangle Program.  }

Program Recurse(Input, Output);

    Type
        String80 = String[80];
    Var
        s:  String80;

    Procedure Print_And_Drop(s:  String80);
        {  Print a string, drop first character, then repeat  }
        Begin
            If Length(s) > 0 Then Begin
                WriteLn(s);
                Delete(s, 1, 1);
                Print_And_Drop(s)
            End;  {  If  }
        End;  {  Print_And_Drop  }

Begin

    Write('Type a string:  ');
    ReadLn(s);
    WriteLn;
    Print_And_Drop(s);

End.  {  Program  }
```

Fig. 12-15. The Word Triangle Program.

```
(  Figure 12-16:   The GoTo Statement.   )

Program Square_Root(Input, Output);

    (  Compute the square root of positive numbers  )

    Label 1;

    Var
        x, sq:   Real;

Begin

    1:   Write('Enter a Positive Number:   ');
         ReadLn(x);
         If x < 0.0 Then GoTo 1;
         sq := Sqrt(x);
         WriteLn('The square root of ', x:1:5, ' is ', sq:1:5);

End.   (  Program  )
```

Fig. 12-16. The GOTO statement.

Pascal contains the facilities to define data structures of arbitrary complexity.

Arrays

The subscripts of Pascal's arrays are delimited by square brackets.

In Chapter 2 an integer array called POINTS is used. In Pascal this array would be declared as follows:

```
Var
    Points: Array [1 . . 10, 1 . . 20]
        of Integer;
```

The 1 . . 10 indicates that the first subscript can range between 1 and 10, while the 1 . . 20 indicates that the second subscript can range between 1 and 20. The of Integer indicates that each element of the array is of the type Integer.

The usage of arrays in Pascal is similar to that in most other languages. Examples of the proper usage of arrays in Pascal can be found in subsequent sections of this chapter.

Records

In Chapter 2 I talked about wanting to have a record containing a student's name and his scores on up to 20 tests. Suppose there may be up to 30 students in the class.

What is needed is an array of records. It is convenient to define what each element of the array looks like as a type. Here is how the declaration might look:

```
Const
      NR__OF__STUDENTS = 30;
Type
      entry = Record
            name:  String[25];
            score:  Array [1..20] of Real
      End;
Var
      student: Array [1..NR__OF__STUDENTS]
              of entry;
```

Notice that I used a constant for NR__OF__STUDENTS. This makes it easier to change the program at a later date if the number of students increases. I could have done the same thing for the number of scores recorded for each student. I also declared that the name of a student could contain up to 25 characters.

Now suppose that you want to write out the name of the fourth student and the score he or she received on the first test. Here is how it would look:

```
WriteLn(student[4].name, student[4].score[1];
```

The period (.) is used to refer to individual record elements. In the first case the record element referred to was a string (name), and in the second case it was an element of an array (score[1]).

Examples of the usage of records in actual programs will be found in the later sections of this chapter.

Linked Lists

Pascal contains advanced facilities for the handling of linked lists, including the dynamic allocation of space. For the beginner, however, it is probably easier to understand what linked lists are all about without going into pointer variables and dynamically allocated storage. These topics are treated in some of the better texts on Pascal and in some advanced texts on the topic of data structures.

This section discusses how linked lists can be implemented using arrays of records. The methodology is essentially the same as that described in Chapter 2, except that an array of records is used rather than parallel arrays, and the value -1 is used to mark the end of the list.

Here are the declarations to support the appropriate data structure in Pascal:

```
Const
      END__LIST = -1;
      MAX__SIZE = 5;
Var
      first, first__free: Integer;
```

```
list: Array [1 . . MAX_SIZE] of
Record
     name: String[15];
     link: Integer
End;
```

To reference the fourth record of the structure following these declarations, you would write list[4].name and list[4].link.

The comprehensive sample program at the end of the chapter illustrates the use of linked lists in an actual program, showing the details of how elements are added to and deleted from linked lists.

FILE HANDLING

To be useful in a variety of applications a microcomputer programming language must have provision for the storage of data on disk (floppy disks or hard disks).

Standard Pascal, as defined by Wirth, has provision only for sequential files. Most implementations of Pascal have added provision for the handling of direct-access files as well. Unfortunately, not all such extensions are compatible. The following description is applicable to Turbo Pascal. Users of other versions of Pascal should check their compiler documentation to see how direct-access files are handled in their implementations.

Text Files

A file in Pascal may be thought of as a sequence of components, each of which is of the same type. In the simplest form of file, called a text file, each component of the file is simply a character.

Each file has associated with it a file variable of the appropriate type. For text files, the appropriate type is called **Text**. Suppose that f is the file variable of a particular text file. It would be declared as follows:

```
Var f: Text;
```

A file must be opened before it is accessed. Two things must be accomplished in opening a file: the file variable must be associated with the name of file as known to the operating system, and the input/output routines must be properly initialized. In Turbo Pascal the former process is done by the **Assign** procedure, and the latter by the **Reset** procedure.

Here is an example of how a file could be opened in Turbo Pascal:

```
Assign(f, 'EXAMPLE.TXT');
Reset(f);
```

In this example, 'EXAMPLE.TXT' is the name of the file to be read from the disk. Access to text files is gained by using the standard procedures **Read**, **ReadLn**, **Write**, and **WriteLn**. If s has been declared a variable of type **String**, then the following would read a line from the file f:

```
ReadLn(f, s);
```

Pascal treats the keyboard and display as special, predeclared text files called **Input** and **Output**, respectively. If a **Read** or **ReadLn** does not include the name of a file variable, it is assumed to refer to the standard file **Input**. If a **Write** or **WriteLn** does not include the name of a file variable, then it is assumed to refer to the standard file **Output**.

Some versions of Pascal allow a file opened for input using **Reset** to also be used for output. To create a new file, however, the **Rewrite** procedure is needed. If the file 'EXAMPLE.TEXT' did not already exist, it could be created as follows:

```
Rewrite(f, 'EXAMPLE.TEXT');
```

Files are closed using the **Close** procedure.

Files of Records

Recall that in a text file, each element of the file is a character. In a file of records, each element of the file is a record. A record can be something as simple as an integer or as complicated as a Pascal record of arbitrary complexity, as described above in the section on data structures.

Input and output for files of records in Turbo Pascal is performed using the **Read**, **ReadLn**, **Write**, and **WriteLn** procedures. You should note that this is not the case with standard Pascal, as defined by Wirth. Standard Pascal uses procedures called **Get** and **Put** for this purpose. You should consult a standard text on Pascal and the compiler documentation for the correct procedures if you are using a version of Pascal other than Turbo Pascal.

Suppose, for example, you need a file consisting of records containing the names and ages of individuals. This file could be defined as follows:

```
Type
    entry = Record
          name:   String[20];
          age:   Integer
    End;
Var
    g:  File Of entry;
```

Entry was defined as a type consisting of two elements: **name**, which is a string of 20 characters, and **age**, an integer. This record forms the template for one component of the file. The file variable for this file was defined as **g**.

Input and output using files of records are discussed in the sections that follow and are illustrated in Figs. 12-17 and 12-18.

Sequential Files

A disk file is said to be sequential if it is accessed one record at a time, from beginning to end. Figure 12-17 contains a program that illustrates the use of a sequential file to

```
(   Figure 12-17:   Sequential File Demonstration.   )

Program Sequential(Input, Output, f);

    (  Demonstrate use of a sequential file to store     )
    (      a list of names and ages.                      )

      Type
         entry = Record
                     name:  String[20];
                     age:   Integer
                 End;
         Var
            buffer:  entry;
            f:       File of entry;

Begin

    (  Read records from keyboard,          )
    (      then write to sequential file f  )

    Assign(f, 'AGES.TXT');
    Rewrite(f);
    WriteLn;
    WriteLn('Enter Names and Ages; Age 0 to quit.');
    WriteLn;
    Repeat
       Write('Name:  ');
       ReadLn(buffer.name);
       Write('Age:   ');
       ReadLn(buffer.age);
       WriteLn;
       Write(f, buffer)
    Until buffer.age = 0;
    Close(f);

    (  Read the file back and display data  )

    Reset(f);
    WriteLn;
    WriteLn('Here are the names and ages from the file:');
    Read(f, buffer);
    While (buffer.age <> 0) Do Begin
       WriteLn('Name:  ', buffer.name);
```

Fig. 12-17. Sequential file demonstration.

```
        WriteLn('Age:      ', buffer.age);
        WriteLn;
        Read(f, buffer)
    End;  (  While  )
    Close(f);
    WriteLn('All done ...');

End.  (  Program  )
```

store a list of names and ages, and then to print them out again. The program also illustrates the use of Rewrite, Reset, Read, and Write with a sequential file.

The variable buffer serves as a conduit for writing to the file and reading from the file. Notice that it is declared using the same record type (entry) that defines the file (File Of entry).

Rewrite opens the file for output. Once the file is open, the values to be written are stored in the buffer variable. The notation buffer.name means the name component of the record that comprises the buffer variable. The notation buffer.age refers to the age component of that record. When the Write(f,buffer) procedure is executed, the contents of the buffer are written to the file. A subsequent call to Write would output to the file immediately following the previous record.

If Rewrite is used to open a file that already exists, the new file will replace that file.

This program uses age = 0 as a signal to quit reading from the keyboard. Note that this last record is written to the file to serve as a sentinel to indicate the end of the file. After age = 0 is encountered the file is closed.

Reset opens an existing file for input and positions the file pointer at the first record of that file. Read(f, buffer) reads the next record of the file into the buffer. The While loop repeats the input process until the age = 0 sentinel record is encountered.

Direct-Access Files

Suppose a program must access the fifth record of a file. If the file is a sequential file, the first four records must be read before the fifth record can be read. In a direct-access file the program can read the fifth record directly without regard to the first four records.

Direct-access files are not a part of standard Pascal as defined by Wirth. Most microcomputer implementations of Pascal have added this capability. Most versions have followed the lead of UCSD Pascal by implementing direct-access files using the Seek procedure.

For the purposes of the Seek procedure, the file records are assumed to be numbered beginning with zero. To expand a file, it is possible to seek one record beyond the end of a file.

To access the fifth record of the file g, you would write the following:

```
    Seek(g, 4);
```

```
(  Figure 12-18:   Comprehensive Sample Program.  }

Program Address_File(Input, Ouput, Lst, A_File, I_File);

    (  A program to create and maintain a file of names and  }
    (       addresses in alphabetical order.  Order is main-  }
    (       tained using an index.  The index is a linked     }
    (       list of pointers.  A linked list of empty records }
    (       is also maintained.                               }

    Const
        MAX_RECORDS = 10;            ( Modify as required      }
        F_NAME = 'ADDRESS.FIL';
        I_NAME = 'INDEX.FIL';
        B_NAME = 'INDEX.BAK';
        END_LIST   = 0;

    Type
        a_name =
            Record
                last, first:  String[12];
            End;
        entry =
            Record
                name:        a_name;
                address:     String[20];
                city:        String[12];
                state:       String[2];
                zip:         String[10];
            End;

    Var
        address_buffer:  entry;
        index:          array[-1..MAX_RECORDS] of Integer;
                ( array[-1] = pointer to first free record }
                ( array[0]  = pointer to first used record }
        a_file:     File of entry;
        i_file:     File of Integer;
        finished:   Boolean;
        a:          Char;
        c, index_buffer:  Integer;

    Procedure Initialize_Files;
        ( Establish the address amd index files.  Initialize  }
        (      address file by filling with blank records.     }
        (      Initialize index as a linked list of free       }
        (      records.                                        }
```

Fig. 12-18. Comprehensive sample program.

```
    Var
        i:   Integer;
    Begin
        Assign(a_file, F_NAME);    ( Open address file     )
        Rewrite(a_file);
        With address_buffer Do Begin
            name.last    := ' ';
            name.first   := ' ';
            address      := ' ';
            city         := ' ';
            state        := ' ';
            zip          := ' ';
        End;
        For i := 0 to MAX_RECORDS Do
            Write(a_file, address_buffer);
        Close(a_file);
        Assign(i_file, I_NAME);      ( Open index file       )
        Rewrite(i_file);
        index_buffer := 1;           ( First free record     )
        Write(i_file, index_buffer);
        index_buffer := END_LIST; ( No records in use     )
        Write(i_file, index_buffer);
        ( Now complete Free List  )
        For i := 1 to (MAX_RECORDS - 1) Do Begin
            index_buffer := i + 1;
            Write(i_file, index_buffer);
        End;
        index_buffer := END_LIST;
        Write(i_file, index_buffer);
        Close(i_file);
    End; ( Initialize_Files  )

Procedure Open_Files;
    ( Open the address and index files.  Read index file.  )
    Var
        i:   Integer;
    Begin
        ($I-)                          ( Turn off I/O checking  )
        Assign(a_file, F_NAME);
        Reset(a_file);
        ($I+)                          ( Restore I/O checking   )
        If IOresult <> 0 Then Begin    ( New File              )
            Initialize_Files;
            Open_Files;
        End;
        Assign(i_file, I_NAME);
        Reset(i_file);
        For i := -1 to MAX_RECORDS Do
```

```
                    Read(i_file, index[i]);
             Close(i_file);
      End;  ( Open_Files  )

Procedure Close_Files;
   ( Write index file to disk and close both files        )
   Var
       i:  Integer;
       backup:  File of Integer;
   Begin
       Assign(backup, B_NAME);
       ($I-)                            ( Turn off I/O checking )
       Reset(backup);                   ( See whether backup    )
       ($I+)                            (    file exists.       )
       If IOresult = 0 Then Begin
           Close(backup);               ( If so, erase it.      )
           Erase(backup);
       End;
       Rename(i_file, B_NAME);      (  Create new backup    )
       Assign(i_file, I_NAME);      (  Reopen Index  File   )
       Rewrite(i_file);
       For i := -1 to MAX_RECORDS Do  ( Write Index file   )
           Write(i_file, index[i]);
       Close(i_file);               (  Close Index   file   )
       Close(a_file);               (  Close Address file   )
   End;  ( Close_Files  )

Procedure Print_Rec(Var f:  Text;  i:  Integer);
   ( Print record i to device f (Lst or Output) )
   Begin
       Seek(a_file, i);
       Read(a_file, address_buffer);
       With address_buffer Do Begin
           Write(f, name.first, ' ');
           WriteLn(f, name.last);
           WriteLn(f, address);
           WriteLn(f, city, ', ', state, ' ', zip);
       End;  ( With  )
   End;  ( Print_Rec  )

Procedure Dump;
   ( Dump entire file to printer, including empty         )
   (     records and index file entries.  Useful for      )
   (     learning how the program works.                  )
   Var
       i:  Integer;
   Begin
```

Fig. 12-18. Comprehensive sample program. (Continued from page 421.)

```
        WriteLn(Lst, 'First Free Record:  ', index[-1]);
        WriteLn(Lst, 'First Used Record:  ', index[0]);
        For i := 1 to MAX_RECORDS Do Begin
            WriteLn(Lst);
            WriteLn(Lst, 'Record ', i);
            Print_Rec(Lst, i);
            WriteLn(Lst, 'Next Record:  ', index[i]);
        End;  ( For  )
    End;  ( Dump  )

Procedure List(Var f:  Text);
    ( List all active records in alphabetical order on      )
    (    device f                                           )
    Var
        i:  Integer;
    Begin
        i := index[0];           ( First active record       )
        While i <> END_LIST Do Begin
            WriteLn(f);
            Print_Rec(f, i);
            i := index[i];
        End;  ( While )
    End;  ( List  )

Function Get_Free:  Integer;
    ( Return record number of next free record and remove  )
    (    record from the Free List                         )
    Var
        free:  Integer;
    Begin
        free      := index[-1];
        index[-1] := index[free];
        Get_Free  := free;
    End;  ( Get_Free  )

Procedure Put_Free(i:  Integer);
    ( Put record i back into the Free List                 )
    Begin
        index[i]  := index[-1];
        index[-1] := i;
    End;  ( Put_Free  )

Procedure Increment(Var row, col:  Integer);
    ( Position cursor 2 rows down, same column             )
    Begin
        row := row + 2;
        GotoXY(col, row);
    End;  ( Increment  )
```

```
Procedure Get_Entry(Var finished:  Boolean);
    {  Read 1 record from keyboard   }
    Var
        row, col, start:  Integer;
    Procedure MarkOff(start, spaces:  Integer);
        {  Mark off data input area with colons   }
        Begin
            GotoXY(start, row);
            Write(':');
            Write(' ':spaces);
            Write(':');
        End;  {  MarkOff   }
    Begin
        ClrScr;                    { Clear screen }
        start := 14;
        row   := 5;
        col   := 1;
        GotoXY(col, row);
        Write('Last Name:');
        MarkOff(start, 12);        Increment(row, col);
        Write('First Name:');
        MarkOff(start, 12);        Increment(row, col);
        Write('Address:');
        MarkOff(start, 20);        Increment(row, col);
        Write('City:');
        MarkOff(start, 12);        Increment(row, col);
        Write('State:');
        MarkOff(start, 2);         Increment(row, col);
        Write('Zip Code:');
        MarkOff(start, 10);
        row := 5;
        col := 15;
        GotoXY(col, row);
        With address_buffer Do Begin
            ReadLn(name.last);
            finished := (name.last = '');  { Empty string }
            If Not finished Then Begin
                Increment(row, col);
                ReadLn(name.first);
                Increment(row, col);
                ReadLn(address);
                Increment(row, col);
                ReadLn(city);
                Increment(row, col);
                ReadLn(state);
                Increment(row, col);
                ReadLn(zip);
```

Fig. 12-18. Comprehensive sample program. (Continued from page 423.)

```
                    End;  { If }
             End;  { With }
       End;  { Get_Entry  }

Function Greater(Var a, b:  entry):  Boolean;
    {  Returns True if a > b, using name as the key field  }
    Begin
        If (a.name.last > b.name.last) Or
          ((a.name.last = b.name.last) And
           (a.name.first > b.name.first)) Then
                Greater := True
        Else
                Greater := False;
    End;  {  Greater  }

Procedure Insert;
    {  Insert the record in address_buffer into the index  }
    {      and write it to disk                            }
    Var
        p, q, free:   Integer;
        temp_buffer:  entry;
    Begin
        free := Get_Free;      { Put record in next vacant  }
        Seek(a_file, free);    {     slot.                  }
        Write(a_file, address_buffer);
        { Find where it belongs in index                    }
        p := index[0];         { First active record        }
        q := 0;
        If p <> END_LIST Then Begin
            Seek(a_file, p);
            Read(a_file, temp_buffer);
            While (p <> END_LIST) And
              (Greater(address_buffer, temp_buffer)) Do Begin
                q := p;
                p := index[p];
                Seek(a_file, p);
                Read(a_file, temp_buffer);
            End;  { While }
        End;  { If }
        { Insert into linked list }
        index[free] := p;
        index[q]    := free;
    End;  {  Insert  }

Procedure Menu(Var c:  Integer);
    {  Display main menu and return selection              }
    Var
        row, col:  Integer;
    Begin
```

```
        ClrScr;                      (  Clear screen              )
        row := 5;
        col := 5;
        GotoXY(col, row);
        Write('1   Add to File');
        Increment(row, col);
        Write('2   Review File on Screen');
        Increment(row, col);
        Write('3   List File to Screen or Printer');
        Increment(row, col);
        Write('4   Dump File to Printer');
        Increment(row, col);
        Write('5   Quit');
        col := 1;
        row := row + 3;
        Repeat
            GotoXY(col, row);
            Write('Select 1, 2, 3, 4, or 5:  ');
            ReadLn(c)
        Until c in [1..5];
    End;  ( Menu )

Procedure Append;
    (  Add records to the file  )
    Begin
        finished := (index[-1] = END_LIST);
        If finished Then Begin
            WriteLn('No room in the file ...');
            Write('Press <Return> to continue ...');
            ReadLn(a)
        End;

        While Not finished Do Begin
            Get_Entry(finished);
            If Not finished Then
                Insert;
            If index[-1] = END_LIST Then
                finished := True;
        End;  ( While )
    End;  (  Append  )

Procedure Review;
    (  Step through the file.  Allow deletion of record.   )
    Var
        q, r:  Integer;
        c:     Char;
    Begin
        ClrScr;                      ( Clear screen              )
```

Fig. 12-18. Comprehensive sample program. (Continued from page 425.)

```
        r := index[0];                  ( Pointer to first record )
        q := 0;
        Repeat
            WriteLn;
            Print_Rec(Output, r);
            WriteLn;
            Repeat
                Write('G)et Next Record, D)elete This Record ',
                      'or Q)uit?  ');
                ReadLn(c)
            Until c In ['G','g','D','d','Q','q'];
            Case c Of
                'G','g': Begin                   ( Get Next  )
                            q := r;
                            r := index[r];
                        End;
                'D','d': Begin                   ( Delete    )
                            index[q] := index[r];
                            Put_Free(r);
                            r := index[q];
                        End;
                'Q','q':                         ( Quit      )
            End;  ( Case )
        Until (r = END_LIST) Or (c In ['Q', 'q']);
    End;  ( Review )

Procedure List_File;
    ( Find out whether to list file to screen or printer,  )
    (     then call List.                                  )
    Begin
        ClrScr;                              ( Clear Screen )
        Repeat
            Write('List to S)creen or P)rinter?  ');
            ReadLn(a)
        Until a In ['S','s','P','p'];
        If a In ['S','s'] Then
            List(Output)
        Else
            List(Lst);
        WriteLn;
        Write('Press <Return> to continue ...');
        ReadLn;
    End;  ( List_File  )

    Begin
        Open_Files;
        Repeat
            Menu(c);
            Case c Of
```

```
            1:    Append;
            2:    Review;
            3:    List_File;
            4:    Dump;
            5:                    ( Quit )
      End;  (   Case   )
   Until c = 5;
   Close_Files;
End.  (  Program   )
```

Fig. 12-18. Comprehensive sample program. (Continued from page 427.)

Note that 4 appears rather than 5 because numbering starts with zero. After the **Seek**, a **Read** or **Write** will access that record.

When you create a new direct-access file, you must exercise care to allocate enough disk space to accommodate as many records as the file will ever have. For example, if a file is expected to have up to 100 records eventually, but it will have only 10 records the first time it is used, space for the 100 records should be allocated when the file is first opened. Here is a procedure that would allocate space for n records for the file in Fig. 12-17:

```
Procedure Allocate (n: Integer);
     { Assumes that g is declared and }
     { opened in the main program }
     Var
          i: Integer;
Begin
     buffer.name := ' ' ;
     buffer.age := 0;
     For i := 1 TO n Do
          Write(g, buffer);
End; { ALLOCATE }
```

Note that sequential access is used to establish the size of the file by writing n dummy records with the name field blank and the age field zero.

The comprehensive sample program below illustrates the use of direct-access files.

GRAPHICS

Standard Pascal, as defined by Wirth, does not support graphics. Various implementations of Pascal, including Turbo Pascal and Apple/UCSD Pascal, do support graphics. Unfortunately, each implementation of graphics in Pascal tends to differ from every other implementation. For that reason, graphics will not be discussed further in this chapter.

Pascal programmers who wish to use graphics should consult the documentation furnished with their particular implementation of Pascal.

THE COMPREHENSIVE SAMPLE PROGRAM

All the programs so far in this chapter have been relatively short and straightforward, each illustrating a particular feature of the language. There is a need for a more comprehensive sample program in order to convey more fully the flavor of the language.

The sample program is shown in Fig. 12-18. The purpose of the program is to establish and maintain a file of names and addresses. The program provides the capability of adding records to the file, listing the file on the screen or on a printer, and deleting records from the file. The file is maintained in alphabetical order by name, but the file is never explicitly sorted. This is possible because the file is maintained as a linked list, and all names are inserted in the correct order as they are added to the file.

Because the program is relatively long (compared to the other programs given in this chapter), it is difficult to see at a glance how it is organized. Figure 12-19 is a structure chart for the program in Fig. 12-18. The structure of the program is shown by indentation. A module that is subordinate to another module is listed indented below that module. At the top of the chart is the main program. At the next level of indentation are the procedures called directly by the main program: Open__Files, Menu, Append, Review, List__File, Dump, and Close__Files. The procedure Open__Files calls the procedure

```
Figure 12-19:   Structure Chart for the
                Comprehensive Sample Program.


Main Program
    Open_Files
            Initialize_Files
    Menu
            Increment*
    Append
            Get_Entry
                    MarkOff
                    Increment*
            Insert
                    Get_Free
                    Greater
    Review
            Print_Rec*
            Put_Free
    List_File
            List
    Dump
            Print_Rec*
    Close_Files
```

Fig. 12-19. Structure chart for the comprehensive sample program.

Initialize__Files, and so on. Procedures marked by an asterisk (*) are called by more than one higher-level procedure.

Notice that the main program is quite short. This is typical of well-written Pascal programs. Most of the work is done in procedures; the purpose of the main program is to invoke its subordinate procedures in the proper order.

Several other features of the program are worthy of note. First is the way in which the file is kept in alphabetical order. A linked list is used to keep track of disk records in use and those not in use. The discussion earlier in the chapter illustrated the use of linked lists for a similar application. Careful study of the example program will reveal how records are added to and deleted from a linked list. The Dump procedure prints out all the links as well as the data elements to aid in understanding the techniques used.

Another feature of note is the manner in which data is input from the keyboard. The user appears to be filling out a form on the screen. Implementation of this technique requires the GotoXY function, which positions the cursor on the screen. If a particular version of Pascal does not come with this function, you must provide it.

The program as written will accommodate only 10 records. To change this, all that is necessary is to change the value of the constant MAX__RECORDS at the beginning of the program. I recommend that MAX__RECORDS be left small until you have completed using the Dump procedure to analyze how the program works.

ADVANTAGES AND DISADVANTAGES OF PASCAL

Pascal was designed as a language to be used for teaching students how to write good programs. Clarity of expression is therefore its major strength. Pascal is a compact language. It has been implemented successfully on numerous microcomputers. Some of its specific advantages are enumerated in the following paragraph.

Pascal has a large repertoire of control structures, including the For statement, Repeat-Until, the While statement, the Case statement, and recursion. It is therefore possible to express algorithms clearly and concisely in Pascal.

Pascal has the facilities for defining a large variety of data structures. The ability to define new data structures of the user's own design makes the language extremely powerful. The power of Pascal with respect to handling data structures has only been hinted at in this book.

Some colleges have begun to teach their students Pascal as a first language, as a preparation for later courses in COBOL or Fortran. This is because Pascal as a language encourages good programming techniques.

Programs written in Pascal usually execute faster than those written in interpreted BASIC. How much faster depends on the particular version of Pascal.

On the negative side, standard Pascal as defined by Wirth lacks several desirable features. Perhaps most serious is the fact that standard Pascal will not accommodate direct-access files. Most implementations have corrected this omission by adding a Seek procedure.

Standard Pascal also does not support separate compilation of procedures. Many implementations of Pascal have some way of accommodating separately compiled procedures.

Standard Pascal does not have an exponentiation function. The user must solve this problem through repeated multiplication or by using logarithms and antilogarithms.

Some might consider the fact that Pascal is usually implemented as a compiled language as a disadvantage. This means that the user must go through a separate compile step before the program can be run.

AVAILABILITY

There are many implementations of Pascal available to microcomputer owners. Turbo Pascal is by far the most popular, with over 500,000 copies sold. Microsoft also has a version of Pascal. Its version is a more "heavy-duty" model and supports separate compilation and programs larger than those supported by Turbo Pascal. Versions of UCSD Pascal are available for most microcomputers including Apple and the IBM Personal Computer.

Turbo Pascal, by Borland International, is also available for the CP/M operating system.

SUMMARY

Pascal is a compact yet powerful language and is available on most brands of microcomputers. It is the second most popular language (after BASIC) among microcomputer users, although recently it has been losing ground to the C language. It provides many advanced features not available in BASIC, and programs written in Pascal generally run faster than those written in BASIC.

Pascal is an excellent language for learning. It encourages the use of modern structured programming techniques and provides powerful facilities for handling complex data structures. It is an excellent language for the user interested in constructing complex programs.

Ada
BASIC
C
COBOL
Forth
Fortran
LISP
Logo
Modula-2
Pascal
PILOT
Prolog

13
PILOT

PILOT is a special-purpose language, intended for use in the area of computer-assisted instruction (CAI). It was first developed by Professor John A. Starkweather of the University of California in San Francisco in the late 1960s and early 1970s. PILOT is used both for the preparation of CAI lessons by a teacher or author and for the administration of these lessons to a student. The name *PILOT* is an acronym that stands for *P*rogrammed *I*nquiry, *L*earning *O*r *T*eaching.

PILOT is a very simple language. It has relatively few commands, and each is simple. PILOT's commands are tailored to the needs of CAI. An example is the **MATCH** command, which matches a student's response to a list of possible correct answers. PILOT is a tool that can be easily used by subject-matter specialists with no prior programming experience to develop instructional materials. These instructional materials may then be used by students for independent study.

Because PILOT is very different from the other languages discussed in this book, the order of presentation in this chapter varies somewhat from that of the other chapters.

PILOT is quite suitable for implementation on a microcomputer. The PILOT programs in this chapter were tested on an Apple II Plus microcomputer using Nevada PILOT, written by John Starkweather and distributed by Ellis Computing. Nevada PILOT runs under the CP/M operating system.

PROGRAM STRUCTURE

A PILOT program is simply a sequence of PILOT statements. A simple PILOT program that does nothing but print "This is a test" is shown in Fig. 13-1.

```
R:    Figure 13-1:   Simple PILOT Program.
R:
T:    This is a test.
E:
```

Fig. 13-1. A simple PILOT program.

The first two lines of this program are simply remarks. They serve the purpose of documenting the program, but they do not affect the execution of the program. The third line of this program is a **TYPE** statement: it types whatever follows on the screen. The fourth is the **END** statement, which marks the end of a program or subroutine. Most PILOT commands consist of one or two letters followed by a colon.

PILOT is usually implemented with an interpreter. With an interpreter, each line of the program is translated into machine code as it executes. If a particular line is executed five times, it must be translated five times. This implementation scheme is quite adequate for the kinds of programs written in PILOT because execution speed is usually unimportant.

DATA REPRESENTATION

There are two types of data in PILOT: character strings and integers. (Some versions of PILOT may also support real numbers.) Character strings are written without quotation marks. The default maximum length of a character string is 80 characters, but this may be increased or decreased as desired using the **INMAX:** statement.

Constants

Integers may range in magnitude from -32768 to $+32767$. The logical values true and false are represented by the integers $+1$ and 0, respectively. In logical contexts, however, any nonzero number is interpreted as true.

Variables

Variables need not be declared as to type in PILOT. In fact, there is no way to do so. Integer variable names may consist of one letter (A-Z) preceded by the pound (#) sign. There are thus 26 possible integer variables in a PILOT program. The following are legitimate names for integer variables in PILOT:

    #A
    #X

Until given a value, an integer variable has value zero. All integer variables may be reset to zero by the following command:

    VNEW:#

String variable names may consist of up to 10 characters preceded by the $ sign. The following are legitimate names for string variables in PILOT:

```
$NAME
$AGE
```

If more space is needed for string variables, all previous string variables can be erased by one of the following commands:

```
VNEW:$
VNEW:
```

The second command shown also resets all integer variables to zero.

INPUT AND OUTPUT

In Fig. 13-1 you saw a simple example of the **TYPE** statement. It is frequently necessary to write passages consisting of several lines on the screen. These may be background reading for a series of questions or multiline questions. This can be done as follows:

```
T: This is a
T: passage consisting of
T: three lines.
```

A common shortcut is to eliminate the T on the second and subsequent lines, as in the following:

```
T: This is a
 : passage consisting of
 : three lines.
```

A carriage return is automatically output at the end of a line printed using T:. If this is not desired, the **TH:** command can be used instead. TH: stands for **TYPE HANG.** It is named thus because it leaves the cursor "hanging" at the end of the line. This is often desired when you are prompting the user for input. Here is a simple example:

```
TH: Type a number between 1 and 5:
```

As long as the next statement is an ACCEPT statement, the cursor will wait at the end of the line for the user to respond.

The **TP:** command sends output to the printer instead of to the video screen. The program in Fig. 13-2 demonstrates the operation of this command.

Input from the keyboard is accomplished by the **ACCEPT** statement. Consider the following sequence of PILOT statements:

```
TH: Enter a number between 1 and 5:
A:
```

```
R:    Figure 13-2:    Illustrate Printer Output.
R:
TP:   This goes to the printer.
R:
T:    This goes to the screen.
E:
```

Fig. 13-2. Printer Output.

The TH: statement types the prompt to the user, leaving the cursor at the end of the line. The A: (ACCEPT) statement waits for the user to type in a number. When the user does type the number, it is read into the *accept buffer.*

The accept buffer is a special place in memory that can hold one number or string at a time. A value in the accept buffer is available for comparison with other values, as discussed below in the section on the MATCH statement. A value stays in the accept buffer until displaced by another value.

The ACCEPT statement can also be used to read values into a variable. Here is a simple example:

```
TH:    What is your name?
A:     $NAME
T:     Hello, $NAME. I am glad to meet you.
```

In this case the user's response is stored in the variable $NAME. If the user responds by typing "Mary", PILOT will then type, "Hello, Mary. I am glad to meet you."

THE MATCH STATEMENT

The MATCH statement compares the contents of the accept buffer with the values listed in the MATCH statement. If a match is found with any of its arguments, the MATCH statement sets the *yes flag.* If no match is found, it sets the *no flag.* Subsequent statements can then be conditioned on whether the yes flag or the no flag is set. A simple program illustrating this is shown in Fig. 13-3.

In Fig. 13-3, the first new statement is the CH: statement, which clears the screen and "homes" the cursor (i.e., leaves the cursor in the upper-left corner of the screen). After the question is typed, the A: (ACCEPT) statement reads the user's response into the accept buffer. The following statement tries to match the response to the letter b or the name Grant, either of which would be accepted as a correct response. (Note: MATCH does not distinguish between uppercase and lowercase.) If there is a match, the yes flag is set. If anything but b or Grant is entered, the no flag is set. The following statement, TY:, is read as "TYPE YES". It is a TYPE statement that is executed only if the yes flag is set. The TN: statement is a TYPE statement that is executed only if the no flag is set.

You have just seen that the TYPE statement can have a condition between the letter T and the colon. As you will see later, other PILOT statements can have a condition in the same place, and will behave similarly.

```
R:    Figure 13-3:   The TYPE, ACCEPT, and MATCH Statements.
R:
CH:
T:    Who is buried in Grant's Tomb?
 :
 :       a.   Robert E. Lee
 :
 :       b.   Ulysses S. Grant
 :
 :       c.   Groucho Marx
 :
TH:   Select a, b, or c:
A:
M:    b, Grant
T:
TY:   Congratulations!  You are right!
TN:   Sorry, the answer is Grant.
E:
```

Fig. 13-3. The TYPE, ACCEPT, and MATCH statements.

THE COMPUTE STATEMENT

The COMPUTE statement is used to assign a value to a variable. It is also used for all numerical computation in PILOT. For example, the following statement adds two numbers and assigns the result to the variable #X:

    C: #X = 2 + 3

A subsequent statement:

    T: #X

will cause PILOT to show a five on the screen.

COMPUTE is often used in conjunction with the MATCH statement and the yes and no flags to keep track of right and wrong answers. The following statement:

    CY: #N = #N + 1

will add one to the variable #N if the previous MATCH statement set the yes flag.

The arithmetic operators available for use in the COMPUTE statement are +, −, *, /, and %. The slash (/) operator stands for integer division. The percent (%) operator is the modulus function and produces the remainder after integer division. PILOT uses conventional infix notation for all arithmetic expressions. (See Chapter 2 for an explanation of infix notation.)

PILOT also provides a random number generator. The function RND (N) returns a random integer between one and N, where N is less than or equal to 32767. The following example generates a random number between one and 100 and assigns it to the variable #N:

```
C:  #N = RND (100)
```

LOGICAL EXPRESSIONS

PILOT supports the usual relational operators: =, < > (not equal), <, < = (less than or equal to), >, and > = (greater than or equal to). In addition it supports the logical operators \ (not), & (and), and ! (or).

The form of PILOT logical expressions is conventional. For example, the following expression:

```
(#X > 5)
```

tests whether or not the value of the variable #X is greater than five. Because anything other than zero is taken to mean true in a logical context, the expression below:

```
(#X)
```

can be taken as a logical expression that is false if #X has value zero, and true in all other cases.

What is unusual about logical expressions in PILOT is the way that they are used. Recall that it was mentioned earlier that the TYPE statement and some other PILOT statements can have a condition just before the colon. That condition can be any PILOT logical expression. Here are two examples:

```
T(#X>5):  The number is greater than 5.
T(#X):  The number is not zero.
```

The first TYPE statement above is executed only if the value of the variable #X exceeds five. The second is executed in all cases except when the value of #X is zero.

CONTROL STRUCTURES

PILOT offers only two basic ways to alter the flow of execution of a program: the JUMP statement and the USE statement. The JUMP statement is much like the GO TO statement of most other languages, with a few variations. The USE statement is a subroutine call. Nevada PILOT also supports calls to machine language subroutines, but such calls are beyond the scope of this book.

The JUMP Statement

The destination of a JUMP (J:) statement can be a label, the previous ACCEPT statement, the next MATCH statement, or the next PR: statement. Each of these possibilities is explained in the paragraphs that follow.

Any PILOT statement in a program can be preceded by a label. A PILOT label may consist of up to 10 characters preceded by an asterisk (*). A JUMP statement, like most other PILOT statements, can be modified by a condition. Examples of PILOT JUMP statements follow:

```
JY: *NEXT
JN: *AGAIN
J (#X=0): *DEFAULT
```

In the above examples, *NEXT, *AGAIN, and *DEFAULT are all PILOT labels. A program illustrating a JUMP to a label is shown in Fig. 13-4. The label in Fig. 13-4 is called *START.

If a user supplies the wrong answer, it is sometimes desirable to provide another chance. This can be done with a JUMP to the previous ACCEPT statement. The form for this is as follows:

```
J: @A
```

A JUMP to the next MATCH is sometimes convenient if you wish to provide different replies for different responses. This can be done as follows:

```
J: @M
```

If the user gets the correct answer right away, you may wish for him to JUMP immediately to the next problem. The next problem can be marked by PR: and the following JUMP executed:

```
J: @P
```

```
R:   Figure 13-4:   JUMP to a Label.
R:
CH:
TH: What is your name?
A: $NAME
T: This is a math quiz, $NAME.  I hope you have been studying.
 :
*START   T: How much is 2 plus 2?
A: #S
M: 4
T:
TN: Sorry, 2 plus 2 does not equal #S.  Try again.
JN: *START
T:
 : Congratulations!  You are absolutely correct!
E:
```

Fig. 13-4. JUMP to a label.

Illustrations of the use of these three forms of the JUMP statement can be found in the program in Fig. 13-5.

Something new in Fig. 13-5 is the AS: statement, which ACCEPTs a single character. This is useful for multiple choice questions such as these.

The program first asks which state is famous for growing potatoes. If the user selects b, the JY: @P takes him or her to the next problem. If the user selects a, the program says that Iowa is famous for corn, not potatoes. The J: @A then JUMPs to the previous ACCEPT statement to await the user's next choice. If the user at this point did not select a, the JN: @M passes control to the next MATCH statement, which checks for an answer of c. If c is chosen, the user is told why Florida is not the correct answer and then given the chance to pick another answer. If none of the choices is selected, the user is given further instructions and offered another chance.

The second problem is labeled with a PR: to serve as the destination of one of the previous JUMPs. The structure of the second question is similar to that of the first.

The logic in this example could have been simplified and a few of the JUMPs eliminated. It was left as it is in order to illustrate the various kinds of JUMPs. As an exercise, you might want to restructure the program slightly to simplify the logic.

The MATCH JUMP and JUMP MATCH Statements

Two other approaches to handling multiple choice questions are the MATCH JUMP (MJ:) and JUMP MATCH (JM:) statements. The MJ: statement is equivalent to an M: statement followed by a JN: @M statement. In other words, it does a MATCH statement, and if no match is found, it jumps to the next MATCH statement. This is illustrated in the first half of the program in Fig. 13-6. (Figure 13-6 is of course a modified version of Fig. 13-5.)

The second half of the program in Fig. 13-6 illustrates the JUMP MATCH (JM:) statement. This statement allows for multiple selection, and is related to the CASE statement described in Chapter 2. Here is a simple example:

```
A:
M: C1, C2, C3
JM: *CASE1, *CASE2, *CASE3
```

The JM: statement does a JUMP to the first, second, or third listed label, depending on whether the preceding M: statement scored a match on the first, second, or third item in its list. Of course the number of possible matches and possible destinations is not limited to three.

Use of the JM: statement, as in the second half of Fig. 13-6, provides an easy and clean way to handle multiple choice questions.

Subroutines: The USE and END Statement

The USE (U:) statement is used to call a subroutine. The argument of the U: statement is usually a label that marks the beginning of the subroutine. The argument of the U: statement can also be @M or @P, as with the J: statement described above.

The end of a subroutine is marked with an END (E:) statement. This functions like the RETURN statement of BASIC, causing control to return to the statement following

```
R:    Figure 13-5:   More JUMP Statements.
R:
R:    JUMPs to the previous accept, the next match,
R:      and the next problem.
R:
CH:
T: Which state is famous for growing potatoes?
  :
  :     a.   Iowa
  :     b.   Idaho
  :     c.   Florida
  :
TH: Enter a, b, or c:
AS:
M: b
T:
TY: Correct.  Now for another tough question.
JY: @P
M: a
JN: @M
T: No, Iowa is famous for growing corn, not potatoes.  Try another choice.
J: @A
M: c
TY: No, Florida is famous for growing oranges, not potatoes.
TY: Try another choice.
JY: @A
T: Your answer wasn't one of the choices.  Type a, b, or c.
J: @A
PR:
T:
  : Which state extends the farthest west?
  :
  :     a.   California
  :     b.   Alaska
  :     c.   Hawaii
  :
AS: Enter a, b, or c:
M: b
JN: @M
T: Correct.  Alaska's Aleutian Islands extend farther west than any other
  : state, including Hawaii.
J:*END
M: a
JN: @M
T: No, both Alaska and Hawaii extend farther west.  Try another choice:
J: @A
M: c
TY: No.  There is another state which extends farther west.
TY: Try another choice.
JY: @A
T: Sorry, you must select a, b, or c.  Enter your choice.
J: @A
*END E:
```

Fig. 13-5. More JUMP statements.

```
R:  Figure 13-6:  MATCH JUMP (MJ:) and JUMP MATCH (JM:).
R:
CH:
T:  Which state is famous for growing potatoes?
 :
 :     a.   Iowa
 :     b.   Idaho
 :     c.   Florida
 :
TH: Enter a, b, or c:
AS:
MJ: b
T:
T:  Correct.  Now for another tough question.
J:  @P
MJ: a
T:  No, Iowa is famous for growing corn, not potatoes.
T:  Try another choice.
J:  @A
M:  c
TY: No, Florida is famous for growing oranges, not potatoes.
TY: Try another choice.
JY: @A
T:  Your answer wasn't one of the choices.  Type a, b, or c.
J:  @A
PR:
T:
 :  Which state extends the farthest west?
 :
 :     a.   California
 :     b.   Alaska
 :     c.   Hawaii
 :
T:  Enter a, b, or c:
AS:
M:  a, b, c
JM: *CA, *AK, *HI
T:  Sorry, you must select a, b, or c.  Enter your choice again.
J:  @A
*AK  T: Correct.  Alaska's Aleutian Islands extend farther west than any other
 : state, including Hawaii.
J:  *END
*CA  T: No, both Alaska and Hawaii extend farther west.
T:  Try another choice.
J:  @A
*HI  T: No.  There is another state which extends farther west.
T:  Try another choice.
J:  @A
*END E:
```

Fig. 13-6. MATCH JUMP (MJ:) and JUMP MATCH (JM:).

the U: statement. If a subroutine is at the end of a program, there must be two E: statements, one for the subroutine and one for the program.

All variables in PILOT are global; in other words, there can be no variable that is purely local to a subroutine. Consequently there is no passing of arguments from a main program to a subroutine.

One possible use of a subroutine in a PILOT program is to provide additional instructions to the user upon request. An example of this is shown in Fig. 13-7.

PILOT is not designed for recursion, but subroutines can call each other within limits. For Nevada PILOT, this limit is a depth of seven. In other words, no more than seven U: statements can be pending at a given time.

Loops

Loops are possible in PILOT, using the JUMP and COMPUTE statements, but there is very little occasion for their use in ordinary PILOT programs. An example of a loop is nevertheless provided in the program of Fig. 13-8. This program prints out the integers from one to 10.

```
R:    Figure 13-7:    The USE Statement.
R:
CH:
T: Welcome to a Math Quiz.
 :
TH: Would you like instructions?
A:
M: n
T:
UN: *HELP
T: How much is 12 times 9?
A:
M: 108
TN: Try again.
JN: @A
T:
T: How much is 11 times 11?
A:
M: 121
TN: Try again.
JN: @A
T:
 : That wasn't so hard, was it?   Come again some time.
E:
*HELP
T:
 : You will be asked several math problems.   If you do not
 : answer correctly, you will be asked to try again until
 : you get it right.
 :
E:
```

Fig. 13-7. The USE statement.

```
R:    Figure 13-8:   A Loop in PILOT.
R:
CH:
T: This program prints the numbers from 1 to 10.
T:
C: #N = 1
*TOP
T: #N
C: #N = #N + 1
J(#N<=10): *TOP
E:
```

Fig. 13-8. A loop in PILOT.

DATA STRUCTURES

The use of data structures is an easy topic to cover with respect to the PILOT language, because PILOT does not support any data structures more complicated than a simple variable and a character string. There are no arrays, lists, records, trees, or the like, nor is there any convenient way to simulate them. This is not such a bad thing, because in the kind of programs for which PILOT is intended, there is no need for such advanced data structures.

FILE HANDLING

There are many instances in which it is necessary, or at least convenient, to save data from one session to the next. In the case of PILOT, a particular lesson may take more than one session to complete, and it would be convenient to keep a record on disk of the student's progress during each session so that subsequent sessions can begin in the appropriate place and so that the student's overall performance can be evaluated at the end of the final session.

PILOT supports sequential files, but not direct-access files. PILOT provides commands to create a file, open a file, write to a file, read from a file, rewind a file, close a file, and delete a file.

Files are created by the **CREATEF:** command. The argument of the command is the name of the file. The following would create a file called **AGES.TXT**:

CREATEF:AGES.TXT

If the file is to be created on a disk drive other than the default disk drive, the filename may be preceded by the drive designator, as in the following:

CREATEF:B:AGES.TXT

Nevada PILOT permits up to two files to be in use at a given time. Files that are in use are identified within the program by a numeric variable. That variable is associated with the external filename by the OPENF: command. Here is an example:

OPENF:AGES.TXT,F

Normally numeric variables such as F are preceded by the # sign. In many instances in PILOT it doesn't seem to matter whether or not the # is present. Nevada PILOT is quite fussy about the form of its file-handling commands, however. The presence of the # or even of an extraneous space can cause unexpected and unwanted results.

The WRITE: and WR: commands both cause the contents of the accept buffer to be written to a file. The RW: (Remark Write) command behaves like the T: command, except that it writes to the disk instead of the screen. The RW: command can therefore be used to write the contents of a variable or any arbitrary text to a file.

When a file is opened (with the OPENF: command), it is positioned so that the first read or write will take place at the beginning of a file. If a file is closed and then reopened, a subsequent WRITE: will overlay whatever was in the file before. If you want to add something on to the end of a file that has just been opened, the APPEND: command positions the file at its end so that that will occur.

If you wish to intentionally overwrite the previous contents of a file, it is a good idea to mark the new end of the file by issuing an EOF: command. Otherwise, the old and new contents may be inadvertently mixed.

The READ: command reads a line of text into the accept buffer, and if desired, into a string variable.

The CLOSEF: command is used to close a file after the last record has been written. The KILLF: command can be used to delete a file from the disk.

Suppose that you wish to write out some data on a file and then read it back. One way is to write the file, close it, and then open it again. Another way is to use the REWIND: command to reposition the file at its beginning.

In the preceding paragraphs the CREATEF:, OPENF:, WRITE:, WR:, RW:, EOF:, APPEND:, READ:, REWIND:, CLOSEF:, and KILLF: commands have been discussed. The CREATEF: and KILLF: commands require only the filename as an argument. All of the other commands require the numeric file designator (discussed in the paragraph on the OPENF: command) as an argument.

The program in Fig. 13-9 illustrates the use of most of these commands. This program reads a name and age pair from the keyboard, writes it to a sequential disk file, and repeats the process until a / is entered instead of a name. The file is then closed, reopened, and read back in from the disk. Note the use of the numeric file indicator variable F in the file-access commands.

GRAPHICS

Apple PILOT includes excellent graphics facilities. It permits pictures, charts, and diagrams to be used as part of lesson materials. It also includes facilities for producing simple musical tunes.

Nevada PILOT does not support sound or graphics. It can, however, control a video cassette recorder. This opens up a whole new dimension in the preparation of course materials.

```
R:   Figure 13-9:   The Name and Age File.
R:
CH:
T: You will be asked to enter a series of names and ages.
 : Type "/" to quit.
CREATEF:AGES.TXT
OPENF:AGES.TXT,F
*TOP
T:
TH: Name:
A:
WRITE: F
M: /
JY: *OUT
TH: Age :
A:
WRITE: F
J: *TOP
*OUT
CLOSEF: F
T:
  :
  : The file will now be read back from disk:
  :
OPENF:AGES.TXT,F
*LOOP
READ: F,$N
M: /
JM: *END
T: $N
READ: F,$A
T: $A
T:
J: *LOOP
*END
CLOSEF: F
E:
```

Fig. 13-9. The name and age file.

THE COMPREHENSIVE SAMPLE PROGRAM

The sample programs thus far in this chapter have been relatively short. Each has served to illustrate a particular feature of the language. A longer, more comprehensive sample is needed to provide a better picture of what PILOT programs are like.

The comprehensive sample programs for most other languages presented in this book have been programs that maintain an address book. Because PILOT is a special-purpose language intended for use in the area of computer-assisted instruction (CAI), an address book program would not fairly illustrate the nature of a typical PILOT program. Such a program would also be difficult to implement in PILOT because PILOT lacks direct-access files, arrays, and lists. For these reasons, the comprehensive sample program of this chapter will not be an address book program. Instead it will be a quiz covering North American geography.

The program is shown in Fig. 13-10. The program begins by displaying user instructions. The subroutine WAIT is used to keep the instructions on the screen until the user is ready to proceed.

The remainder of the program consists of five questions on North American geography plus a section to compute the final score. This may seem like a lot of program for just five questions. Upon examination of the program, it is apparent that the bulk of the text is taken up with the questions themselves, not with the instructions that administer the quiz.

The hard part of preparing a PILOT program is in the design of the subject matter to be presented. The skills involved in this effort are subject matter skills, not computer skills. The computer skills needed are minimal.

There is little in this program that has not been illustrated in previous examples. One new thing is the addition of the funny looking character (~) at the end of each TH: command. This character does not print on the screen, but it ensures that the preceding blanks do print, so that the cursor "hangs" several spaces beyond the preceding colon.

The screen is cleared (using CH:) before each question is presented, so only one question appears on the screen at a given time. If a user answers a question incorrectly, he or she is given a short message and then given another opportunity to answer. When the correct answer is given, the user is told that it is the correct answer; then the subroutine WAIT is called to hold the display until the user is ready to proceed.

The JM: (JUMP MATCH) command, which was discussed earlier, is used to direct the flow of control to the proper place, depending on the user's response. Erroneous responses (e.g., an x when the choices are a, b, c, and d) are trapped and the user given another chance. As each answer is processed, the variable #R (for number right) or the variable #W (for number wrong) is incremented as appropriate.

After all the questions have been processed, the user's score is calculated as 100 times the number right divided by the total number of responses. The factor of 100 is needed to make the percentage a number between zero and 100, because Nevada PILOT supports only integer arithmetic.

ADVANTAGES AND DISADVANTAGES OF PILOT

Any evaluation of the merits of PILOT as a language must consider that PILOT is a special-purpose language, designed for use in the preparation of computer-assisted instruction (CAI) materials. It was never intended as a general-purpose language.

One advantage of PILOT is its terseness. Its commands are simple (such as T:, A:, M:, and so on), yet they take care of the functions most commonly needed in the preparation of CAI materials. The MATCH (M:) instruction is a good example. It can handle one or several possible answers and can pick answers out of context. For example,

```
R:   Figure 13-10:   North American Geography.
R:
R: This program presents a series of questions concerning North
R:   American geography.  The program provides appropriate feedback
R:   when an incorrect answer is chosen and positive reinforcement
R:   when the correct answer is chosen.  The program keeps track of
R:   the number of right and wrong answers and prints the user's
R:   score at the end.
R:
R: First initialize the number Right and Wrong:
C: #R=0
C: #W=0
CH:
T: Welcome to a quiz on North American Geography.
 :
 : You will be asked a series of questions about various geographical
 : facts about North America.  You will be given an opportunity to
 : answer a question repeatedly until you get it right.  Your score
 : will be the number of correct answers divided by the total number
 : of answers.
 :
U: *WAIT
T: Which of the following is NOT a North American river?
 :
 :      a.   Mississippi
 :
 :      b.   Colorado
 :
 :      c.   Amazon
 :
 :      d.   Mackenzie
 :
TH: Select a, b, c, or d:       ~
AS:
M: a,b,c,d
T:
JM: *Q1a, *Q1b, *Q1c, *Q1d
TH: Sorry, you must type a, b, c, or d:     ~
J: @A
*Q1a
T: No, the Mississippi River is the queen of North American rivers.
TH: Select a river that is NOT in North America:     ~
C: #W=#W+1
J: @A
*Q1b
T: No, the Colorado River flows through the United States and Mexico.
TH: Select a river that is NOT in North America:     ~
C: #W=#W+1
J: @A
*Q1c
T: Correct.   The Amazon River is in SOUTH America.
U: *WAIT
C: #R=#R+1
```

Fig. 13-10. A North American geography program.

```
J: @P
*Q1d
T: No, the Mackenzie River flows north through Canada.
TH: Select a river that is NOT in North America:  ˜
C: #W=#W+1
J: @A
PR:
T: Which of the following rivers flows into the PAcific Ocean?
 :
 :        a.   Columbia
 :
 :        b.   Colorado
 :
 :        c.   Rio Grande
 :
 :        d.   Hudson
 :
TH: Select a, b, c, or d:  ˜
AS:
M: a, b, c, d
T:
JM: *Q2a, *Q2b, *Q2c, *Q2d
TH: Sorry, you must select a, b, c, or d:  ˜
J: @A
*Q2a
T: Correct.   The Columbia River flows into the Pacific Ocean.
C: #R=#R+1
U: *WAIT
J: @P
*Q2b
T: No, the Colorado River flows into the Gulf of California.
TH: Select a, b, c, or d:  ˜
C: #W=#W+1
J: @A
*Q2c
T: No, the Rio Grande River flows into the Gulf of Mexico.
TH: Select a, b, c, or d:  ˜
C: #W=#W+1
J: @A
*Q2d
T: No, the Hudson River flows into the Atlantic Ocean.
TH: Select a, b, c, or d:  ˜
C: #W=#W+1
J: @A
PR:
T: Which of the following mountain ranges is located in North America?
 :
 :        a.   Andes
 :
 :        b.   Pyrenees
 :
 :        c.   Himalayas
 :
 :        d.   Sierra Madre
 :
```

Fig. 13-10. A North American geography program. (Continued from page 447.)

```
TH: Select a, b, c, or d:  ~
AS:
M: a, b, c, d
T:
JM: *Q3a, *Q3b, *Q3c, *Q3d
TH: Sorry, you must select a, b, c, or d:  ~
J: @A
*Q3a
T: No, the Andes Mountains are in SOUTH America.
TH: Select a, b, c, or d:  ~
C: #W=#W+1
J: @A
*Q3b
T: No, the Pyrenees Mountains are in Europe, between France and Spain.
TH: Select a, b, c, or d:  ~
C: #W=#W+1
J: @A
*Q3c
T: No, the Himalaya Mountains are in Asia.
TH: Select a, b, c, or d:  ~
C: #W=#W+1
J: @A
*Q3d
T: Correct.   The Sierra Madre Mountains are in Mexico.
C: #R=#R+1
U: *WAIT
J: @P
PR:
T: Which of the following deserts is located in North America?
 :
 :      a.  Sahara
 :
 :      b.  Gobi
 :
 :      c.  Mojave
 :
 :      d.  Great Sandy
 :
TH: Select a, b, c, or d:  ~
AS:
M: a, b, c, d
T:
JM: *Q4a, *Q4b, *Q4c, *Q4d
TH: Sorry, you must select a, b, c, or d:  ~
J: @A
*Q4a
T: No, the Sahara Desert is in northern Africa.
TH: Select a, b, c, or d:  ~
C: #W=#W+1
J: @A
*Q4b
T: No, the Gobi desert is in Asia, in northern China and in Mongolia.
TH: Select a, b, c, or d:  ~
C: #W=#W+1
J: @A
*Q4c
T: Correct.   The Mojave Desert is in southern California.
```

```
C: #R=#R+1
U: *WAIT
J: @P
*Q4d
T: No, the Great Sandy Desert is in Australia.
TH: Select a, b, c, or d:   ~
C: #W=#W+1
J: @A
PR:
T: Which of the following is the tallest mountain in North America?
 :
 :        a.   Mount Whitney
 :
 :        b.   Mount McKinley
 :
 :        c.   Mount St. Helens
 :
 :        d.   Mount Rainier
 :
TH: Select a, b, c, or d:   ~
AS:
M: a, b, c, d
T:
JM: *Q5a, *Q5b, *Q5c, *Q5d
TH: Sorry, you must select a, b, c, or d:   ~
J: @A
*Q5a
T: No, at 14,495 feet, Mount Whitney is the tallest mountain in
 : the 48 adjacent United States, but there is a taller mountain
 : elsewhere in North America.
TH: Select a, b, c, or d:   ~
C: #W=#W+1
J: @A
*Q5b
T: Correct.  At 20,320 feet, Alaska's Mount McKinley is the highest
 : peak in North America.
C: #R=#R+1
U: *WAIT
J: @P
*Q5c
T: No.  Even before it blew its top, Mount St. Helens was only
 : 9,678 feet tall.  It is now 8,364 feet tall.
TH: Select a, b, c, or d:   ~
C: #W=#W+1
J: @A
*Q5d
T: No, Washington's Mount Rainier is only 14,410 feet in elevation.
TH: Select a, b, c, or d:   ~
C: #W=#W+1
J: @A
PR:
C: #T=#W+#R
T:
 : Number right:  #R      Number wrong:  #W        Total:  #T
C: #P=100*#R/#T
```

Fig. 13-10. A North American geography program. (Continued from page 449.)

```
T:
  : Percent right:   #P
E:
*WAIT
CA: 23,1
TH: Press <RETURN> to continue...
A:
CH:
E:
```

if it is told to match no, it will also match such answers as Not really and Definitely not. To accomplish the same thing in any other language presented in this book would require a significant amount of programming.

PILOT is an easy language to learn and to use. Because the language is so simple, the programmer can concentrate on the subject matter instead of on the mechanics of programming.

On the negative side, PILOT does not support loops or other advanced control structures. Although the simple and conditional JUMP statements permit the emulation of structured constructs, they also permit haphazard programming.

PILOT does not support data structures other than simple numeric variables and character strings. In most cases this is not a problem, but there are instances in which arrays would be welcome.

Nevada PILOT does not support floating-point arithmetic. Limiting numbers to integer values is a serious limitation when mathematical and scientific subject matter must be presented.

PILOT is not at all suited for use as a general-purpose programming language. Of course it was never intended to be used as such.

AVAILABILITY

Nevada PILOT (by Ellis Computing of Reno, Nevada) is available for microcomputers that run the CP/M operating system. Ellis Computing also sells Utah PILOT for PC-DOS and MS-DOS computers (IBM PCs and compatibles). Apple Computer distributes Apple Pilot and Super Pilot for Apple microcomputers. I am not aware of any other microcomputer versions of PILOT that are widely available at this time.

SUMMARY

PILOT is a language designed for use in preparing computer- assisted instruction (CAI) materials. It is a simple, easy-to-learn language, yet it includes commands that greatly simplify the preparation of CAI materials.

PILOT is highly recommended for use in preparing CAI materials. It is not at all recommended for use as a general-purpose language.

Ada
BASIC
C
COBOL
Forth
Fortran
LISP
Logo
Modula-2
Pascal
PILOT
Prolog

14

Prolog

Prolog was developed in the early 1970s by Alain Colmerauer, Philippe Roussel, and their associates in the Artificial Intelligence Group of the University of Marseilles, France. Much of the early development of the language was done in the Department of Artificial Intelligence of the University of Edinburgh, Scotland. In fact, the most popular version of Prolog is the Edinburgh version, as definitized in *Programming in Prolog,* by W. F. Clocksin and C. S. Mellish (Springer Verlag, 1981 and 1984).

The name ''Prolog'' is a blend of words, standing for PROgramming in LOGic. As is custom, the name will be shown in lowercase in this book.

As you have probably surmised by now, Prolog was developed for use in the field of artificial intelligence. Its chief rival language in that field is LISP, described in Chapter 9. Until relatively recently, LISP received by far the most attention in the artificial intelligence field, having become entrenched by virtue of its earlier availability and exceptional flexibility. Prolog has received much attention since 1983, when Japan announced that it had selected Prolog as its language of choice for its ambitious ''fifth generation'' computer project.

The field of artificial intelligence is necessarily beyond the scope of this book. This chapter attempts to illustrate the nature of the Prolog language without delving into artificial intelligence.

In covering so many languages, this book attempts to highlight the commonalities and similarities between and among computer languages such as Ada, BASIC, C, Fortran, Modula-2, Pascal, and so on. Prolog does not fit in the same mold. It is fundamentally different from most other computer languages. This chapter attempts to highlight the differences.

452

Every other language covered in this book is a *procedural* language. The programmer must specify what problem is to be solved *and* the step-by-step procedures to be followed to solve the problem.

Prolog, on the other hand, is a *declarative* or *descriptive* language. The programmer describes the problem to be solved, and declares known facts and relationships between and among those facts. The programmer does *not* specify step-by-step procedures for solving the problem. The Prolog language includes built-in procedures that solve the problem (answer the question) through logical inference. These procedures are collectively called an *inference engine*. In other words, given a description of a problem, Prolog infers the solution or solutions. Simple examples of this process are given in the following sections.

Once a set of facts and rules are declared, Prolog can handle a variety of questions or queries. It is particularly useful for handling ad hoc queries. Prolog's strength lies in its ability to answer queries based on known facts and rules. That is what makes it useful in the field of artificial intelligence. That same strength has the potential to make Prolog useful for database applications.

Prolog can be implemented using either an interpreter or a compiler. (The difference between the two forms of language translation is explained in Chapter 1.) The sample programs in this chapter were tested with the Turbo Prolog compiler by Borland International. Although some purists maintain that Turbo Prolog is not standard Prolog (as defined by Clocksin and Mellish), it is more than suitable for illustrating the nature of Prolog.

PROLOG PROGRAMS

The basic building block of a Prolog program is the *predicate*. A predicate is an assertion that can succeed or fail. If a predicate succeeds, we say that it is true. If a predicate fails, it might be false, or there might be no possible solution given the facts at hand.

A predicate can take the form of a *goal* or of a *clause*. A goal corresponds to the question that the program is intended to answer. A clause can be a *fact* or a *rule*. A fact is simply a statement that something is true. For example, the following is an example of a fact:

John likes Mary.

In Prolog, that fact could be stated as follows:

likes(john,mary).

In Prolog parlance, likes is a *functor*; john and mary are *arguments* of the functor.

A rule is a statement regarding the relationship between various facts and rules. An example might be as follows:

John likes a girl if the girl likes tennis.

In Prolog, this might be stated in the following way:

```
likes(john,Girl) :-
     likes(Girl,tennis).
```

The : – symbol is pronounced "if." (Turbo Prolog permits the use of if in place of : –, but I have stayed with the more standard notation.) Notice that I have shown some arguments of functors in all lowercase letters, and others beginning with a capital letter. In simple terms, constants in Prolog begin with lowercase letters and variables begin with capital letters. Thus john is a known constant, and Girl is an unknown variable.

A Turbo Prolog program consists of several sections, which may include **domains**, **global domains**, **database**, **predicates**, **global predicates**, **goal**, and **clauses**. The shortest Turbo Prolog programs consist of only a **goal** section, but most Turbo Prolog programs have at least a **predicates** and a **clauses** section. In brief, the **clauses** section constitutes the main body of a program and its subroutines, the **goal** section declares what problem is to be solved, and all other sections exist to declare functors and their arguments. Each section will be explained in more detail as it is encountered in an example.

Standard Prolog does not have sections like Turbo Prolog. A standard Prolog program consists of clauses and an external goal without any declarations. There are no section headings in standard Prolog. The section headings were added to Turbo Prolog in order to produce a compiler that executes very quickly and generates relatively fast programs.

A minimal Turbo Prolog program is shown in Fig. 14-1. The program prints **This is a test.** on the screen, followed by a carriage return/line feed sequence (indicated by "\n", as in the C language). The program consists of a single goal, which is the built-in predicate **write**. The object of a Prolog program is to make its goal(s) succeed. By definition, **write** always succeeds, and produces output as a side effect.

Figure 14-2 illustrates a slightly more complicated program that implements a simple database of facts. In this case the data is about the colors of various flowers.

The program has a **domains** section, a **predicates** section, and a **clauses** section. The **predicates** section declares the predicates used in the main body of the program, which is called the **clauses** section. The **domains** section is used to declare the data types of the parameters of the predicates declared in the **predicates** section.

The only predicate in this program is **color__of**. It has two arguments, **flower** and **color**, each of which is declared in the **domains** section to be a *symbol*. A symbol is simply the name of something. The various facts in the **clauses** section give the color of each type of flower.

Because this program has no **goal** section, running it results in a prompt to type

```
/*   Figure 14-1:  Minimal Prolog Program.  */

goal
          write("This is a test.\n").
```

Fig. 14-1. A minimal prolog program.

```
/*   Figure 14-2:   Simple Query.   */

domains
        flower, color = symbol
predicates
        color_of(flower,color)
clauses
        color_of(rose,red).
        color_of(violet,blue).
        color_of(daffodil,yellow).
        color_of(hibiscus,red).
        color_of(lily,white).
        color_of(poinsettia,red).
        color_of(daisy,white).
        color_of(iris,blue).
```

Fig. 14-2. Simple query.

in a goal at the keyboard. Each goal must end with a period. Here are some sample interactions with this program, with Prolog's part of the dialog in bold type:

Goal: color__of(rose,red).
True
Goal: color__of(rose,black).
False

This illustrates that one thing Prolog can do is determine whether a given predicate is true or false. That can be useful, but often it is not enough. Suppose, for example, we want to know the color of an iris. The way to find out is to substitute an unknown variable for the color in the goal. As alluded to above, anything starting with a capital letter can be a variable in Prolog. It need not be declared. The following dialog shows how to find the color of an iris:

Goal: color__of(iris,Y).
Y = blue
1 Solution

As mentioned earlier, Prolog's mission is to try to make a goal succeed. In this case one of the arguments of the goal predicate is an unknown. The only way to make the goal succeed is to search through the various clauses to try to find a value for the unknown variable that will make the goal succeed. In this case Turbo Prolog searches until it finds a fact stating that the color of an iris is blue.

In the above example the name of the flower was known and the color of the flower was unknown. Now suppose you instead want a list of all flowers in the database that are red. The following dialog shows the result:

> **Goal:** color__of(X,red).
> **X** = **rose**
> **X** = **hibiscus**
> **X** = **poinsettia**
> **3 Solutions**

Notice that the program doesn't say anything about the step-by-step process of searching the database for a solution to our goal. Prolog takes care of the details. This example begins to hint at some of the power of Prolog. The goal color__of(X,Y). would produce a list of each flower in the database along with its color, a total of eight solutions.

DATA TYPES

Turbo Pascal supports the following data types: char, integer, real, string, symbol, and file. A **char** is a single character enclosed between two single quotation marks (e.g., 'c'). An **integer** is a 16-bit whole number between -32768 and 32767. A **real** is a floating-point number with optional sign, decimal point, and exponent. Exponents can range from -307 to $+308$, a considerable range. Exponents are indicated by the letter e, as in 0.314159e1.

A **string** is any sequence of characters enclosed between double quotation marks, as illustrated in Fig. 14-1. A **symbol** is a name that stands for itself, not for anything else (in other words, it is not a variable). For example, in Fig. 14-2, red and iris are symbols. A symbol can take one of two forms. It can be a sequence of alphabetic characters, numeric digits, and underscores (no spaces), provided that the first character is a lowercase letter. It can also be just like a character string. It is necessary to use the character string format when there are embedded spaces or when the first character must be uppercase. Clocksin and Mellish use the term **atom** instead of **symbol**.

The **file** data type is discussed in the section of the chapter dealing with files.

Constants

A constant in Prolog can be of any of the above types. A constant can be a symbol, or it can be simply a number, a character, or a string. A constant retains its value throughout the program.

Variables

A variable in Prolog is a name that can have a value, or it can have no value. A variable that has a value is called *bound* or *instantiated*. A variable that has no value is called *free* or *uninstantiated*.

Variable names in Prolog begin with a capital letter or an underscore. A variable can have one of the types described above. Variables in standard Prolog need not be declared in advance. The same is true even in Turbo Prolog. Note, however, that the parameters of a predicate declared in the **predicates** section of a program must be declared in the **domains** section. A variable used in the **clauses** section of a program as an argument of a predicate will take on the type of the corresponding parameter. For example, in Fig. 14-2, the variable X was used to stand for the first parameter of the predicate color__of. Its type is implicitly the same as that of the first parameter of color__of, which is a symbol.

THE ASSIGNMENT STATEMENT

The assignment statement is central to most computer languages. It is a statement in which a value is assigned or given to a variable. In Prolog parlance, it is the process by which a variable becomes instantiated or bound to a particular value. In most languages the assignment statement is quite common.

The assignment statement in Prolog is relatively rare. It does not play a very important role in Prolog programs. Variables usually take on their values as a byproduct of attempting to satisfy a goal, as in the program in Fig. 14-2.

Here is a simple assignment statement in Prolog:

    X = 2.

It looks much like an assignment statement in BASIC or Fortran, but there are differences. For example, I could have just as easily written the following:

    2 = X.

The result would have been exactly the same. Prolog looks at either form of the statement as a goal to be satisfied, and the only way to satisfy the goal is for the variable X to take on the value 2.

The following assignment statement:

    N = N + 1

makes perfect sense in BASIC. Its result is that one is added to the value of N and the result becomes the new value of N. It makes no sense at all in Prolog. Prolog attempts to satisfy the goal by finding a value of N such that both sides of the equation are true at the same time. That is not possible. To increment N in Prolog, one must resort to something like the following:

    N1 = N + 1.
    N = N1.

One can define a simple predicate in Prolog to act in a manner similar to an assignment statement. Here is one example:

    equal(X,Y).

A typical usage of this predicate would be something like this:

    equal(Year,1987).

This would have the same result as this assignment statement:

Year = 1987.

In standard Prolog, a predicate such as **equal** is quite useful. In Turbo Prolog, however, it is less useful because the arguments of the predicate are restricted to a single data type (e.g., integer). In standard Prolog, they could be integer, string, or whatever.

Turbo Prolog is not consistent with standard Prolog in the use of the equal (=) sign. Standard Prolog uses the symbol **is** in the same context as illustrated above. The = sign means something different in standard Prolog. For example, the following statement:

X = 2 + 3.

would result in the message below:

X = 5

in Turbo Prolog, but it would result in the following:

X = (2 + 3)

in standard Prolog. In standard Prolog, one would write this:

X is 2 + 3.

to produce the message below:

X = 5.

ARITHMETIC EXPRESSIONS

Arithmetic expressions in Prolog are usually written using standard infix notation, e.g., 4 + 2. I say infix because the operator (+) is in between the two operands (4 and 2). Arithmetic expressions in Prolog can also be written in a kind of a prefix notation with the operator coming first and the operands in parentheses, but such usage is rare and will not be mentioned again in this chapter.

Prolog supports the usual arithmetic operators (+, −, *, /). Turbo Prolog also supports the operators **mod** (modulus or remainder after integer division) and **div** (integer division). Prolog does not have an exponentiation operator.

A simple example of the use of an arithmetic expression to calculate the area of a circle is shown in Fig. 14-3. Notice that the program has a **domains** section, a **predicates** section, and a **clauses** section.

The **predicates** section declares the predicate **circle**, and the domains section declares that both parameters of **circle** are of type **real**. The **clauses** section declares that the area of a circle can be found by multiplying 3.14159 times the radius times the radius again.

```
/*   Figure 14-3:   Illustrate Arithmetic Expressions.   */

/*   Compute the area of a circle.   */

domains
        radius, area =   real

predicates
        circle(radius,area)

clauses
        circle(R,A) :-
                A = 3.14159 * R * R.
```

Fig. 14-3. Arithmetic Expressions.

Because the program does not contain a **goal** section, the goal must be supplied at runtime. The following sample session illustrates how the program can be used to compute the area of a circle:

Goal: circle(5,A).
A = 78.53975
Goal: circle(1,A).
A = 3.14159.

LOGICAL EXPRESSIONS (PREDICATES)

A logical expression evaluates to the value true or false. In Prolog parlance, it succeeds or fails. Another name for a logical expression is a *predicate*.

In one sense, nearly everything in Prolog is a logical expression or predicate. Often, however, that fact is merely incidental. For example, the **write** predicate is a logical expression that always succeeds, but that is incidental to its primary function, which is to send output to the screen or other output device.

Prolog supports the usual relational operators ($<$, $>$, $<=$, $>=$, $=$, and $<>$). The "not equal" relation can be written as $<>$ or $><$. Some versions of Prolog support $=<$ rather than $<=$ for "less than or equal to."

Turbo Prolog supports the use of **and** and **or** to represent the logical conjunction and disjunction operations. Turbo Prolog allows, and standard Prolog requires, the use of the comma (,) to mean **and**, and the semicolon (;) to mean **or**.

A predicate in Prolog is evaluated only as far as is necessary to determine whether it is true or false. This means that compound predicates joined by commas (the logical **and** operator) are evaluated only until the first failure is found. This is sufficient to determine that the entire predicate has failed. Any part beyond the first failure is not evaluated. The entire predicate succeeds only if all parts succeed.

Similarly, a compound predicate joined by semicolons (the logical **or** operator) is evaluated only as far as the first predicate that succeeds. This is sufficient to determine that the entire predicate has succeeded. Remaining parts are not evaluated. The entire predicate fails only if all parts fail.

Consider, for example, the following predicate:

```
test :-
    10 < 0,
    write("Can't get here!").
```

This is a compound predicate consisting of two parts joined by a comma (the logical **and** operator). The first part immediately fails because 10 is not less than zero. This is sufficient to determine that the entire **test** predicate fails, so there is no point in evaluating the second part (the **write** predicate). Therefore, the message ''Can't get here!'' is never printed.

The program in Fig. 14-4 illustrates the use of a logical expression. The program is based on the program of Fig. 14-2, and uses the same database of information about flowers. The difference is that it introduces a new predicate called **bouquet**. The purpose of **bouquet** is to select the names of three flowers, the first one of which is red, the second white, and the third blue.

```
/*   Figure 14-4:   A Compound Query.   */

domains
        flower, color = symbol
predicates
        color_of(flower,color)
        bouquet(flower,flower,flower)
clauses
        color_of(rose,red).
        color_of(violet,blue).
        color_of(daffodil,yellow).
        color_of(hibiscus,red).
        color_of(lily,white).
        color_of(poinsetta,red).
        color_of(daisy,white).
        color_of(iris,blue).

        bouquet(X,Y,Z)  :-
                color_of(X,red),
                color_of(Y,white),
                color_of(Z,blue).
```

Fig. 14-4. A compound query.

Notice first that **bouquet** is declared in the **predicates** section as having three parameters, each of the domain **flower**, which is in turn a symbol. The predicate **bouquet** is defined in the **clauses** section. There are three parts to the definition, and each is separated by a comma.

As mentioned above, the predicate **bouquet** has three parameters. The first part of the definition says that the color of the flower that matches the first parameter **X** must be red. The second part of the definition says that the color of the flower that matches the second parameter **Y** must be white. The third part of the definition says that the color of the flower that matches the third parameter **Z** must be blue. Because the three parts of the definition are separated by commas (and a comma means **and**), all must succeed before the predicate succeeds.

Here is a sample dialog with the program in Fig. 14-4, showing how it can be used:

Goal: bouquet(rose,Y,Z).
Y = lily, Z = violet
Y = lily, Z = iris
Y = daisy, Z = violet
Y = daisy, Z = iris
4 solutions
Goal: bouquet(rose,Y,iris).
Y = lily
Y = daisy
2 solutions

The goal bouquet(X,Y,Z) will result in a listing of all combinations of flowers in which the first is red, the second white, and the third blue. There are twelve such solutions.

INPUT AND OUTPUT

Prolog has only a few input and output statements. The **write** statement, as in the program in Fig. 14-2, causes output to be sent to the screen. That is because the screen is the default standard output device. To send output to another output device, such as the printer, one still uses **write**, but changes the output device. An example of how this is done in Turbo Prolog is given in Fig. 14-5.

Notice that the goal of this program is contained in the program file. That makes it execute without waiting for any keyboard input.

Turbo Prolog uses the **writedevice** predicate to change the output device. (Standard Prolog instead uses a predicate called **tell** to do the same thing.) The program in Fig. 14-5 alternates sending output to the printer and to the screen.

Input in Turbo Prolog works similarly. The most-often used input predicate in Turbo Prolog is **readln**. The **readdevice** predicate works analogously to **writedevice**. Standard Prolog uses **read** instead of **readln** and **see** instead of **readdevice**.

The program in Fig. 14-6 illustrates string input in Turbo Prolog. It again illustrates redirection of output. The program emulates an electronic typewriter. Everything that is typed on the keyboard is echoed, line by line, on the printer.

The program consists of two predicates, **typewriter** and **type**. The former simply sets things up, redirects output to the printer, calls **type**, and redirects output back to the screen. The actual work of the program is done in **type**.

```
/*    Figure 14-5:   Demonstrate Printer Output.   */

predicates
        testprint

goal
        testprint.

clauses
        testprint :-
                writedevice(printer),
                write("This goes to the printer."),
                nl,
                writedevice(screen),
                write("This goes to the screen."),
                nl.
```

Fig. 14-5. Printer output.

```
/*    Figure 14-6:   Prolog Electronic Typewriter.   */

predicates
        typewriter
        type

goal
        typewriter.

clauses
        typewriter :-
                write("Welcome to Your Electronic Typewriter!"),
                nl,
                write("Enter text, <Ctrl-Break> to end."),
                nl, nl,
                writedevice(printer),
                type,
                writedevice(screen).

        type :-
                readln(S),
                write(S),
                nl,
                type.
```

Fig. 14-6. Prolog Electronic Typewriter.

The **type** predicate reads a line of text into a character string, writes that string on the printer, sends a newline to the printer to get ready for the next line, and calls itself to repeat the process.

The act of a predicate calling itself is called *recursion* and is discussed in more detail in the next section. In this context it serves as a convenient way to repeatedly execute the predicate **type**. In fact, this is an infinite recursion, and will repeat forever, or until the user types < Control-Break >, or turns off the computer, whichever comes first.

The **write** predicate can accept a variable number of arguments, which can be of any of the standard types (real, integer, string, etc.). The **readln** predicate, on the other hand, can accept only one argument, which must be a string or a symbol. In order to read an integer, a real number, or a character in Turbo Prolog, one must use, respectively, **readint**, **readreal**, and **readchar**.

Input and output predicates in Turbo Prolog differ from their counterparts in standard Prolog. Readers using standard Prolog should consult Clocksin and Mellish and the documentation for the implementation of standard Prolog being used.

CONTROL STRUCTURES

In most languages, the flow of execution of statements is usually sequential. In other words, the statements are usually executed in the order in which they appear. In the case of Prolog, the various clauses in a predicate are executed sequentially, but only until the truth or falsity of the predicate is determined.

A predicate in a Prolog program can have more than one definition. For example, the predicate **color__of** in Fig. 14-2 was defined eight times, once for each kind of flower described. What happens in such cases is that Prolog starts with the first definition and if it succeeds, goes no further. If, however, the first definition fails, it tries the next definition in sequence. The process is repeated until Prolog finds a definition that succeeds, or until all definitions have been tried unsuccessfully.

Control structures are the means by which a programmer can alter the flow of execution in a computer program to be other than sequential. In conventional procedural languages the list of control structures usually includes simple and multiple selection, various kinds of loops, and so on. Control structures are usually more alike than different from one language to another. As an example, consider the **for** statement in Pascal, C, Ada, Modula-2, and even BASIC.

Because Prolog is a declarative language, not a procedural language, it does not operate in the same way. (The difference between a declarative language and a procedural language was discussed earlier in this chapter.) Consequently, Prolog does not feature the usual statements for simple and multiple selection and various kinds of loops. This is part of what makes Prolog so different from the other languages covered in this book.

The major means of controlling the flow of execution in a Prolog program are *predicates, recursion, backtracking,* and the *cut.*

Predicates

Predicates were discussed above in the section on logical expressions. I mentioned there that nearly everything in Prolog is a predicate of one sort or another. In the context of control structures, predicates serve in a capacity similar to that of procedures and functions in other languages.

In the program in Fig. 14-6, the predicate type served as a procedure. It was called from the "main program," which was the predicate typewriter. In this case the predicate type did not have any parameters, but you have already seen several examples of predicates with parameters.

Functions in other languages typically return values, such as integers or real numbers. Predicates in Prolog always succeed or fail, so in a sense they return *true* or *false*. In that sense a predicate in Prolog is a function of type Boolean (logical).

Recursion

A recursive predicate is one that invokes itself. An example is the function type in Fig. 14-6.

Recursion is used occasionally in other languages such as Pascal, C, Ada, and Modula-2. In Prolog, recursion is the most common way of repetition, replacing loops. LISP and Logo rely heavily on recursion, but they also provide a loop mechanism. Prolog does not provide a loop mechanism.

Notice that in the predicate type of Fig. 14-6, the last statement of the predicate is the recursive call to type itself. This is called *tail recursion* and is one of the most common types of recursion when the purpose of recursion is simply repetition. Recall that in this example, the recursion was infinite and could be halted only by typing <Control-Break> or turning off the computer. In other cases, the predicate provides a means for terminating the recursion. This is illustrated in the following examples.

The example in Fig. 14-7 shows how a recursive procedure can be used to print out the integers in a given range. For example, typing the following goal:

count(1,10).

would cause the integers from one to 10 to be printed out, one per line.

The first expression within the predicate count is X < = N. Recall that a predicate consisting of expressions joined by commas (logical ands) is evaluated only until any

```
/*   Figure 14-7:   A Counting Program.   */

domains
        start, stop = integer
predicates
        count(start,stop)
clauses
        count(X,N) :-
                X <= N,
                write(X), nl,
                Y = X + 1,
                count(Y,N).
```

Fig. 14-7. A counting program.

```
/*    Figure 14-8:    The Triangle Program.    */

predicates
        triangle(string)
clauses
        triangle(S)  :-
                str_len(S,N),
                N>0,
                write(S), nl,
                frontchar(S,Head,Tail),
                triangle(Tail).
```

Fig. 14-8. The Triangle Program.

subexpression fails. This expression thus serves as the limiting condition; in other words, the predicate fails and stops executing if its first argument (X) is greater than its second argument (N).

The next line of count prints out the value of X followed by a newline (carriage return and line feed). The following line computes a new variable Y to be one more than X. The last line of the predicate count recursively calls itself with Y in place of X. This process is repeated until it reaches N.

The program in Fig. 14-8 is another example of the use of recursion. The program prints a word triangle, as in the following dialog:

Goal: triangle(hello).
hello
ello
llo
lo
o
False

The final **False** response means that the predicate failed because the length of the string was reduced to 0. If the string to be printed begins with a capital letter or contains embedded spaces, it must be enclosed in quotation marks (e.g., "Hi there!").

The predicate triangle repeats recursively until the length of the string S is reduced to zero. The predicate str__len is built into Turbo Prolog and performs the obvious function. The predicate frontchar is also built into Turbo Prolog. It splits the incoming string S into two parts, a head consisting of the first character and a tail consisting of the remainder of the string. The triangle predicate is called recursively with the tail (all but the first letter) of the string as its argument. The result is as shown above.

The factorial function is a mathematical function defined as follows:

factorial(0) is 1.
factorial(n) is n * factorial(n − 1) if n > 0.

This definition is recursive in that the function is defined in terms of itself. A recursive implementation on a computer is fitting. A Prolog version is shown in Fig. 14-9.

This example consists of two predicates, **factorial** and **fact**. The former exists simply to call the latter and to print out the result. Note that there are two definitions for **fact**. The first one says that the factorial of zero is one. If that definition succeeds, Prolog doesn't look any farther. If that definition fails, Prolog looks to the second definition.

The second definition contains a limiting test to be sure that the argument N is greater than zero. If not, the predicate fails and the recursion ceases. This does one of two things. First, it will stop the process immediately if the argument N is less than zero. Otherwise, it will stop the process when the recursion gets down to zero and the result has already been computed. The remainder of the predicate subtracts one from N, recursively calls **fact** with the lesser value, and then uses the result to compute the value of the factorial function.

The preceding discussion of the computation of the factorial function is couched in procedural terms. In other words, the discussion has concentrated on the sequence of the processing. It can also be viewed in declarative terms.

In declarative terms, the **fact** predicate is defined to be true if all of the subexpressions that make it up are true. In the case of the recursive call, the definition must again be analyzed to see whether it is true or false. The process of evaluating the expression continues recursively until a nonrecursive definition (**fact(0,1)**) is encountered.

This demonstrates that Prolog programs can often be viewed in both procedural and nonprocedural (declarative) terms. The temptation of a programmer experienced in procedural languages is to view Prolog only in procedural terms. This temptation should be avoided in order to realize the full potential of Prolog.

```
/*   Figure 14-9:   The Factorial Function.   */

domains
        number,result = real
predicates
        factorial(number)
        fact(number,result)
clauses
        factorial(N)  :-
                fact(N,X),
                write(N, " factorial is ", X),
                nl.
        fact(0,1).
        fact(N,NFact)  :-
                N>0,
                N1=N-1,
                fact(N1,X),
                NFact=N*X.
```

Fig. 14-9. The factorial function.

Whether viewed in procedural or declarative terms, the factorial predicate will find the factorial of numbers from 0 to 170. The following interactive session illustrates its use:

Goal: factorial(0).
0 factorial is 1
True
Goal: factorial(– 1)
False
Goal: factorial(3).
3 factorial is 6
True
Goal: factorial(170).
170 factorial is 7.2574156153E + 306
True

The **True** results simply mean that the predicate succeeded. The **False** result means that the factorial function is not defined for $N = -1$. Note that the factorial of 170 is a very large number. The factorial of 171 is such a large number that it cannot be handled by Turbo Prolog.

Backtracking

The program in Fig. 14-4 provides a good framework for discussing the concept of backtracking. The following goal:

bouquet(X,Y,Z)

produces 12 solutions such that X is a red flower, Y is a white flower, and Z is a blue flower. Why didn't it stop with just one solution? The answer is *backtracking*.

The inference engine of Prolog is designed to find *all* possible solutions to a goal. The backtracking process works roughly as follows: Once a solution is found for X, Y, and Z, Prolog backtracks to see whether other solutions might exist. It does this by first looking for another solution for Z. This process is repeated until no more solutions can be found by varying Z. The next step is to try varying Y. Once varying Y yields no more solutions, the final step is to try varying X. Through this process all possible solutions that satisfy the predicate are found.

The Cut

Sometimes you don't want to find all possible solutions that satisfy a predicate. Sometimes only one solution is sufficient. The backtracking process can be inhibited to limit the number of solutions using the *cut*.

The symbol for the cut in Prolog is the exclamation point (!). The cut symbol means, in effect, "No backtracking beyond this point." For example, the **bouquet** predicate in Fig. 14-4 could be rewritten as follows using a cut:

bouquet(X,Y,Z) : –
        color__of(X,red), !,

```
        color_of(Y,white),
        color_of(Z,blue).
```

This would mean that once a value is found for **X** that satisfies the predicate color_of(X,red), that value of **X** is fixed and cannot be varied during the backtracking process. In this case, that would reduce the number of solutions to four, with each having **X** = **rose**.

Now suppose that the cut is placed after the second predicate, as follows:

```
  bouquet(X,Y,Z) : –
        color_of(X,red),
        color_of(Y,white), !,
        color_of(Z,blue).
```

This would mean that backtracking could proceed only on **Z**, because both **X** and **Y** are defined before the cut. This would limit the number of solutions to two, with only **Z** varying.

Finally, if the cut were placed at the end of the predicate, only one solution would be found. No backtracking at all would occur.

DATA STRUCTURES

The most common data structure in most programming languages is the array. Prolog does not support arrays. Instead, the most common data structure in Prolog is the list. More complex data structures can be built up from lists. Prolog also supports a data type known as the *compound object.* Perhaps the most powerful data structure in Prolog is the *database.*

Lists

Lists in Prolog are written as individual elements separated by commas and enclosed by square brackets. For example, the following is a list of the first five positive integers:

    [1,2,3,4,5]

Given that a list is a sequence of objects, perhaps the most basic operation involving a list is to print those objects in sequence. The program in Fig. 14-10 does just that.

The **domains** section of the program in Fig. 14-10 defines a **name** as a **symbol**, and a **namelist** as a list of zero or more **names**. (The * in **namelist** = **name*** means "zero or more instances.")

The **predicates** section declares the predicates **print** and **printlist**. The actual work is done by **printlist**. The first expression in **printlist** uses the vertical bar (|) operator to separate the list into two parts: **Head** is the first element of the list and **Tail** is the rest of the list. The predicate then writes the first element and recursively calls itself with the rest of the list as its argument. This process repeats with an ever-decreasing list until the list runs out of elements. At that point, **printlist** fails.

The predicate **print** has two definitions. The first definition initializes the list and

```
/*   Figure 14-10:   Print a List.   */

domains
        namelist = name*
        name = symbol
predicates
        print
        printlist(namelist)
goal
        print.
clauses
        print :-
                NL=[charles,sarah,nat,heather,cindy],
                printlist(NL).
        print :-
                write("End of List ..."),
                nl.
        printlist(NL) :-
                NL=[Head|Tail],
                write(Head), nl,
                printlist(Tail).
```

Fig. 14-10. Printing a list.

calls printlist. When printlist eventually fails, that causes print to fail; at that point Prolog executes the second definition of print, which wraps things up.

Because the goal is internal to the program, it executes as soon as the program is executed, without waiting for keyboard input. Here is what the output of the program looks like:

```
charles
sarah
nat
heather
cindy
End of List . . .
```

Structures

Another name for a structure is a *compound object*, an object that consists of various parts, not all of which need be alike. A compound object in Prolog consists of a *functor* and a sequence of subordinate objects, as in the following:

functor(object1, object2, ..., objectN)

A simple example of a compound object is a date:

date(month,day,year)

Another example could be a lecture, defined as follows:

lecture(speaker, topic, date(month,day,year))

This is a more complex object because one of its subordinate objects is itself a compound object. In this manner, compound objects of arbitrary complexity can be constructed.

The program in Fig. 14-11 implements a list of structures. Each structure represents a person and contains the person's first and last names and age, as follows:

person(name(first,last),age)

This can also be represented graphically:

```
                      person
                     /      \
                 name        age
                /    \
            first     last
```

Representation in this fashion highlights the inherent hierarchical nature of the structure.

The program in Fig. 14-11 reads in the first names, last names, and ages of a series of people, and then writes them back out again.

The basic data structure is called a **kidlist**, which is defined in the **domains** section as a sequence of objects of type **kid**. (The * symbol means zero or more occurrences.) A **kid** is defined as a **person(ident,age)**, and an **ident** is defined in turn as a **name(first,last)**. All of these definitions collectively make up the structure described above.

The **readkid** and **writekid** predicates read in and write out, respectively, one instance of the structure. The **readkid** predicate checks to see whether a blank first name is entered; if so, it causes the predicate to fail. This initiates action to stop reading and start writing.

The **readlist** predicate controls the input. This predicate first uses **readkid** to read the head of the list, and then recursively calls itself to read the tail of the list. If **readkid** fails, **readlist** also fails. The cut keeps it from backtracking to another call to **readkid**. Instead it calls the second definition of **readlist**, which simply returns the empty list, terminating the recursion smoothly.

The **writelist** predicate controls the output process. In a manner similar to **readlist** it first calls **writekid** to print out the first element of the list, and then recursively calls itself to print out the rest of the list. The predicate **writelist** eventually fails because it runs out of names to print. The recursion is halted gracefully by the second definition of **writelist**, which returns the empty list.

The above discussion presents just a sample of the many kinds of data structures that can be represented in Prolog.

```
/*    Figure 14-11:    Names and Ages.          */

/*    Demonstrate a structure made up of a      */
/*       list of compound objects.              */

domains
        kidlist = kid*
        kid = person(ident,age)
        ident = name(first,last)
        age = integer
        first, last = symbol
predicates
        readkid(kid)
        writekid(kid)
        readlist(kidlist)
        writelist(kidlist)
goal
        write("Enter a list of names and ages\n"),
        write("Type <Return> to stop.\n"),
        readlist(KL),
        write("\nHere is the list again:\n\n"),
        writelist(KL).
clauses
        readkid(Kid) :-
                nl,
                write("First Name:   "),
                readln(FN),
                FN <> "",
                write("Last  Name:   "),
                readln(LN),
                write("Age:          "),
                readint(Age),
                Kid = person(name(FN,LN),Age).
        writekid(Kid) :-
                Kid = person(name(FN,LN),Age),
                write(FN,"\t",LN,"\t",Age), nl.
        readlist([H|T]) :-
                readkid(H),!,
                readlist(T).
        readlist([]).
        writelist([H|T]) :-
                writekid(H),!,
                writelist(T).
        writelist([]).
```

Fig. 14-11. A names and ages structure.

Databases

The program in Fig. 14-4 contains a set of facts and rules about flowers. All the facts and rules are specified in the program itself and were fixed at the time the program was written. By *fixed*, I mean that no provision was made to add to or subtract from the facts and rules when the program is executed.

Clearly, it is desirable to be able to add to a set of facts and rules after a program is written. Referring again back to Fig. 14-4, it is clear that I have omitted many kinds of flowers from my list.

A set of facts and rules that can be changed at run time is called a *dynamic database* in Turbo Prolog. Several predicates exist for updating dynamic databases. The **consult** predicate reads in facts and rules from a disk file and adds them to the active database. The use of disk files in Prolog is covered in the next section of this chapter.

The **asserta** predicate adds a fact to the beginning of the active database. The **assertz** predicate adds a fact to the end of the active database. The **retract** predicate removes a fact from the database. To modify a fact, first retract it, and then add the revised fact to the database.

A database, as I have been using the term, resides entirely in memory and is therefore limited in size by the amount of available memory. In fact there are ways to maintain databases limited only by the amount of disk storage available. One such way is explained in the Turbo Prolog documentation and will not be discussed here.

Turbo Prolog requires that dynamic databases be declared in the **database** section, which must come just before the **predicates** section of a Turbo Prolog program. A **database** declaration is otherwise similar to any other predicate declaration.

The program in Fig. 14-12 illustrates the use of a dynamic database in Turbo Prolog. The program maintains a database in memory of first names and ages. It queries the user for a name. If the name is in the database, the program reports the age. If the name is not in the database, the program asks the user for the age and enters the name and age into the database using the **assertz** predicate. A subsequent query about that name will find the age.

Note the **database** section of the program. The **goal** section prints introductory remarks, reads the first name, and then turns control over to the **run** predicate. The first definition of the **run** predicate in the **clause** section uses the predicate **person** to determine whether or not the name is in the database. If it is, the predicate succeeds, the program prints out the name and age, calls **getname** to read another name, and calls **run** recursively to continue.

If, on the other hand, the predicate **person(N,A)** fails, that causes **run** to fail. Prolog looks for another way to make **run** succeed. It tries the second definition of **run** in the **clauses** section. This definition queries the user for the age, then uses **assertz** to add the new fact to the database. It then gets a new name and calls **run** recursively. Prolog will go to the first definition of **run** and continue the process.

If the user presses the return key instead of typing a name, the predicate **getname** fails (because of the predicate **Name < > ""**). This causes **run** to fail. Because **run** and **listall** are separated by a semicolon (logical **or**) in the **goals** section, Prolog continues to attempt to satisfy the overall goal by trying the predicate **listall**.

Had there been a comma (logical **and**) instead of a semicolon before **listall**, the predicate **listall** would never have been executed. This is because, as discussed above,

```
/*   Figure 14-12:   Dynamic Database Demonstration.   */

domains
        name = string
        age  = integer
database
        person(name,age)
predicates
        run(name)
        getname(name)
        listall
goal
        write("Type a first name,"),nl,
        write("and I will tell you the age."),nl,
        write("Press <Return> to exit."),
        nl,nl,
        getname(Name),
        run(Name);
        listall.
clauses
        run(N)  :-
                person(N,A), !,
                write(N," is ", A), nl, nl,
                getname(Name),!,
                run(Name).
        run(N)  :-
                write("I give up.  "),
                write("How old is ", N, "?  "),
                readint(A),
                assertz(person(N,A)),
                nl,
                getname(Name),!,
                run(Name).
        getname(Name) :-
                write("Enter a name:  "),
                readln(Name),
                Name <> "",!.
        listall :-
                person(N,A),
                write(N, " is ", A),
                nl,
                fail.
```

Fig. 14-12. A dynamic database demonstration.

the failure of run when there is no more input is sufficient to determine the failure of the entire goal. Another way to handle this situation would have been to use not(run(Name)) instead of run(Name) in the goal, and to separate it from listall with a comma. This would succeed when the input ran out, and execution would proceed to listall.

The listall predicate simply lists all active facts in the database. Notice the use of fail at the end of listall. This causes listall to fail. This initiates backtracking, so person tries to find another solution. When there are no more names in the database, person also fails, causing listall to fail, and the program terminates.

Note the use of cuts (!) to inhibit backtracking in various places in the run and getname predicates.

Once the program terminates, all the data is lost because no provision was made to save it on disk. The next section discusses how to save data on disk.

The following is a sample session, with Prolog's side of the "conversation" shown in bold:

Type a first name,
and I will tell you the age.
Press <Return> to exit.

Enter a name: Nat
I give up. How old is Nat? 16

Enter a name: Heather
I give up. How old is Heather? 12

Enter a name: Cindy
I give up. How old is Cindy? 3

Enter a name: Nat
Nat is 16

Enter a name: <Return>
Nat is 16
Heather is 12
Cindy is 3

Obviously the "conversation" could continue ad infinitum. The point is that the program only has to be told a given fact once. The **assertz** predicate adds the new fact to the database, where it remains until the program is terminated. Note that the program prints out a summary of all active facts before it terminates.

FILE HANDLING

The previous section illustrated the utility of being able to store and retrieve data. It also illustrated the limitations of being able to do so only in memory, in which case all data added to the database during the program is lost once the program terminates. This section will show how to use disk files to store data more permanently.

Database Files

Storing data from a dynamic database into a disk file is very simple in Turbo Prolog. The predicate **save** stores the current database to disk. The program in Fig. 14-13 illustrates how this can be done.

This data input portion of this program is almost identical to the corresponding part of Fig. 14-12. The **listall** predicate is replaced by the built-in predicate **save**. The argument of **save** is the name of the file where the database is to be stored.

The database is saved as a series of facts. For example, the file might contain these three facts:

```
person("Nat",16)
person("Heather",12)
person("Cindy",3)
```

A file created using **save** can easily be read into a dynamic database using the **consult** predicate. Fig. 14-14 shows how this can be done.

As you can see, the program in Fig. 14-14 is very short and simple. All the work is done by the **consult** predicate. The data is printed to the screen using the **listall** predicate. Figure 14-14 shows how this can be done.

Sequential Files

Prolog also provides the means to create sequential files other than database files. The basic principle is that a predicate is used to divert output to a file, and then ordinary output predicates such as **write** are used. The procedure is similar to the method illustrated earlier in this chapter for printer output.

The details of file input and output differ between standard Prolog and Turbo Prolog. For this reason, and because of space limitations, further details are omitted from this chapter.

Direct-Access Files

Standard Prolog, as defined in Clocksin and Mellish, does not support direct (random) access to files. Turbo Prolog provides a predicate called **filepos**, which operates much like the **fseek** function of the C language, enabling direct file access. Further details are omitted from this chapter.

GRAPHICS

Standard Prolog does not support graphics. Turbo Prolog, however, does offer point and line graphics and turtle graphics. Turtle graphics are discussed in the Logo chapter. Further details are omitted.

THE COMPREHENSIVE SAMPLE PROGRAM

The sample programs shown thus far in this chapter have been relatively short, and each was intended to illustrate a single facet of the language. The purpose of the comprehensive sample program in each chapter is to show a more substantial program in the language, thereby giving a more realistic portrayal of the language.

```
/*   Figure 14-13:   Save a Database on Disk.   */
domains
        name = string
        age  = integer
        file = datafile
database
        person(name,age)
predicates
        run(name)
        getname(name)
goal
        write("Type a first name,"),nl,
        write("and I will tell you the age."),nl,
        write("Press <Return> to exit."),
        nl,nl,
        getname(Name),
        not(run(Name)),
        write("Saving to disk ...."), nl,
        save("NAMES.DAT"),
        write("Done."), nl.
clauses
        run(N)  :-
                person(N,A),  !,
                write(N," is ", A), nl, nl,
                getname(Name),!,
                run(Name).
        run(N)  :-
                write("I give up.  "),
                write("How old is ", N, "?  "),
                readint(A),
                assertz(person(N,A)),
                nl, getname(Name),!,
                run(Name).
        getname(Name)  :-
                write("Enter a name:  "),
                readln(Name),
                Name <> "",!.
```

Fig. 14-13. Saving a database on disk.

The program in Fig. 14-15 creates and maintains an address book. Each entry in the address book consists of a name, an address, and a telephone number. The program permits entries to be added, viewed, printed, and deleted.

The entries are maintained in a dynamic database, as illustrated in Figs. 14-12, 14-13, and 14-14. The program first uses the consult predicate to read in the database from disk. During the course of the program, the database is maintained in memory. At the

```
/*    Figure 14-14:    Read a Database from Disk.    */

domains
        name = string
        age  = integer
database
        person(name,age)
predicates
        listall
goal
        write("Here is the data from the file NAMES.DAT."),
        nl, nl,
        consult("NAMES.DAT"),
        listall.
clauses
        listall :-
                person(N,A),
                write(N, " is ", A), nl,
                fail.
```

Fig. 14-14. Reading a database from disk.

termination of the program, the **save** predicate is used to store the database, as modified, back to disk.

The **clearall** predicate at the end of the program deletes the database from memory before the program terminates. If this were not done when running the program from within Turbo Prolog, running it a second time consecutively would result in the database from disk being added to the database left in memory from the previous run. The result would be the duplication of every entry in the database.

Unlike the corresponding program in most other chapters, this program does not maintain the records in alphabetical order. Prolog provides two predicates to add a record to a dynamic database. The **asserta** predicate adds the record to the beginning of the database, and the **assertz** predicate adds the record to the end of the database. Although it would be possible to maintain a dynamic database in alphabetical order, it would require a method beyond the scope of this book. Other possible options would have been to use the implementation-specific direct-access facility of Turbo Prolog, or to have maintained the data in a list, as in Fig. 14-11. The result of using a list would have been a program very similar to the program in Fig. 9-14.

The program in Fig. 14-15 introduces the use of windows for text input and output in Turbo Prolog. The predicates that make this easy are makewindow, clearwindow, shiftwindow, and cursor.

There is no dump option in this program, as there is in most of the corresponding programs in other chapters. The purpose of such an option is to display the details of the linkages between entries in the database. This is not necessary in this program because Prolog itself takes care of the details of maintaining the linkages, and they are not accessible to the programmer.

```
/*   Figure 14-15:   Comprehensive Sample Program.   */
/*                                                    */
/*      Maintain a list of names, addresses,          */
/*      and telephone numbers on disk.  Allow         */
/*      addition of new records, deletion of          */
/*      existing records, review of file, and         */
/*      printing of file.  Records are not            */
/*      maintained in alphabetical order.             */

domains
        choice   = integer
        filename = string
        name     = string
        address  = string
        city     = string
        state    = string
        zip      = string
        phone    = string
database
        entry(name,address,city,state,zip,phone)
predicates
        setup
        window1
        window2
        window3
        menu(choice)
        getfile(filename)
        run
        alternative(choice)
        append
        review(name)
        option(char,name)
        list
        list_next_record(name)
        choose(char)
        clearall(name)
goal
        setup,
        run,
        clearall(N).
clauses
        setup :-
                makewindow(1,15,15,"Address Book Program",
                        0,0,25,80),
                window1,
                makewindow(2,15,15,"Data Input Screen",
                        5,5,15,70),
                window2,
                makewindow(3,15,15,"Main Menu",
                        5,5,15,70),
                window3,
                getfile("ADDRESS.DAT").
```

Fig. 14-15. Comprehensive sample program.

```
window1 :- !.
window2 :-
        cursor(2,10), write("Name:"),
        cursor(4,10), write("Address:"),
        cursor(6,10), write("City:"),
        cursor(6,35), write("State:"),
        cursor(8,10), write("Zip Code:"),
        cursor(8,30), write("Phone Number:").
window3 :-
        cursor(2,10), write("1    Add to file"),
        cursor(4,10), write("2    Review file on screen"),
        cursor(6,10), write("3    List file to screen or printer"),
        cursor(8,10), write("4    Quit").
getfile(Name) :-          /*  Read file from disk  */
        existfile(Name), !,
        consult(Name).
getfile(_) :- !.
menu(C) :-                /*  Display main menu    */
        shiftwindow(3),
        cursor(10,5),  write("Select 1, 2, 3, or 4:       "),
        cursor(10,28), readint(C),
        C >= 1, C <= 4.
menu(C) :-
        menu(C).
run :-
        menu(Selection), !,
        shiftwindow(1),
        alternative(Selection).
alternative(1) :-
        append,
        run.
alternative(2) :-
        review(_),
        run.
alternative(3) :-
        shiftwindow(1),
        clearwindow,
        write("List to S)creen or P)rinter?  "),
        readchar(D), write(D),
        nl, nl,
        choose(D),
        list,
        run, !.
alternative(4) :-
        deletefile("ADDRESS.DAT"),
        save("ADDRESS.DAT").
choose('S') :-
        writedevice(screen).
choose('s') :-
        writedevice(screen).
choose('P') :-
        writedevice(printer).
choose('p') :-
        writedevice(printer).
```

```
choose(_) :-
        alternative(3).
 append :-                     /* Add a record to the file */
        shiftwindow(2),
        clearwindow,
        window2,
        cursor(2,21), readln(Name),
        cursor(4,21), readln(Address),
        cursor(6,21), readln(City),
        window2,
        cursor(6,43), readln(State),
        cursor(8,21), readln(Zip),
        window2,
        cursor(8,45), readln(Phone),
        assertz(entry(Name,Address,City,State,Zip,Phone)).
 review(N) :-                   /* Review one record at a time */
        shiftwindow(1),
        clearwindow,
        list_next_record(N),
        write("G)et next record, D)elete this record, or Q)uit?  "),
        readchar(C), write(C),
        option(C,N).
 review(_) :- !.
 option('G',_) :-                      /* Get next record */
        clearwindow,
        !, fail.
 option('g',_) :-
        clearwindow,
        !, fail.
 option('D',Name) :-                   /* Delete record    */
        retract(entry(Name,_,_,_,_,_)), !.
 option('d',Name) :-
        retract(entry(Name,_,_,_,_,_)), !.
 option('Q',_) :- !.            /* Quit            */
 option('q',_) :- !.
 option(_,_).
 list  :-
        list_next_record(_),
        fail.
 list :-
        flush(printer),
        writedevice(screen),
        write("Press <Return> to continue ..."),
        readchar(_).
 list_next_record(Name) :-
        entry(Name,Address,City,State,Zip,Phone),
        write(Name), nl,
        write(Address), nl,
        write(City,", ",State," ",Zip), nl,
        write(Phone), nl, nl.
 clearall(N) :-
        retract(entry(N,_,_,_,_,_)),
        fail.
```

Fig. 14-15. Comprehensive sample program. (Continued from page 479.)

ADVANTAGES AND DISADVANTAGES OF PROLOG

Prolog was designed for use in the field of artificial intelligence, and any consideration of its advantages and disadvantages should be made with that in mind. Nevertheless, it is interesting to compare the features of Prolog with those of other languages described in this book.

First, it is worth noting that the comprehensive sample program written in Prolog is considerably shorter than the corresponding program written in any of the other languages of this book. This is partly due to the fact that it does not maintain its names and addresses in alphabetical order, but it is also partly due to the ease with which Prolog maintains dynamic databases.

Prolog is very strong in the area of data structures. It is very easy to define data structures of arbitrary complexity in Prolog.

Prolog is also very strong in its ability to show the relationships between and among data. This is particularly useful in the creation of databases that store knowledge as opposed to just facts and figures.

Prolog is easy to use in an interactive environment. The example program in Fig. 14-4 illustrated how easy it is to use *ad hoc* queries in Prolog. Most of the other languages in this book were designed to be used in a batch environment.

A noteworthy strength of Prolog is its built-in inference engine. As discussed earlier in the chapter, the language itself has the power to analyze given facts and rules and to draw appropriate conclusions. With any of the other languages in this book, including LISP and Logo, it is up to the programmer to provide the logic for making inferences.

On the negative side, the input and output features of Prolog are relatively primitive. The extensions provided by Turbo Prolog help, but they are nonstandard.

Prolog is not well-suited for many programming tasks such as arithmetic computation, file maintenance, and business data processing.

Programming in Prolog is sufficiently different from programming in other languages, such as BASIC, C, and Pascal, that it is relatively difficult for a person who has programmed in one or more of these other languages to learn to program well in Prolog. My own opinion is that Prolog is inherently difficult to learn, but once learned becomes a very powerful tool.

AVAILABILITY

There are a number of Prolog implementations readily available for microcomputers that run the MS-DOS or PC-DOS operating systems, at prices ranging from $9.95 up to $895. Automata Design Associates (A.D.A.) offers a public domain version called PD Prolog, which is offered for sale at $9.95. It can also be legally copied from a friend or downloaded from an electronic bulletin-board system. It is complete enough to provide a good introduction to programming in Prolog.

Other Prolog implementations are available from the following companies:

A.D.A. Prolog	Automata Design Associates Dresher, PA
Prolog-86 Plus	Solution Systems Norwell, MA

micro-Prolog	Programming Logic Systems, Inc. Milford, CT
Turbo Prolog	Borland International Scotts Valley, CA
MProlog	Logicware Inc. Newport Beach, CA
Arity Prolog	Arity Corp. Concord, CA
Prolog II	Expert Systems International Philadelphia, PA

SUMMARY

Prolog is a very powerful language intended principally for use in the field of artificial intelligence. It is also useful for tasks that require the manipulation of complex data structures, such as natural language processing.

Prolog includes powerful facilities for maintaining dynamic databases, including a built-in ad hoc query capability.

Programming in Prolog requires a different way of thinking than programming in most other languages. This is because it is a *declarative* rather than a *procedural* language. In Prolog, facts, relationships between facts, and rules form a knowledge base. Prolog has the ability to draw inferences from the declared knowledge base. The programmer does not need to provide the procedural steps for doing so.

Prolog is not suitable for all programming applications, but it is a very powerful tool for working in the field of artificial intelligence.

15

Microcomputer Languages Compared

Ada
BASIC
C
COBOL
Forth
Fortran
LISP
Logo
Modula-2
Pascal
PILOT
Prolog

Twelve microcomputer languages have been covered in this book:

Ada	LISP
BASIC	Logo
C	Modula-2
COBOL	Pascal
Forth	PILOT
Fortran	Prolog

A chapter has been devoted to each language, describing the features of that language. Each language has been described in isolation, independent of the other languages. This has given you the freedom to read the language chapters in any order, skipping those languages not of interest.

The purpose of this chapter is to examine the languages as a group, considering the strengths and weaknesses of each in relation to the others. This is intended to make it easier for you to select an appropriate language for a particular application.

Which language is most suitable for a particular application depends on the nature of that application. There is no one universal language that is best for all applications. A language that is excellent for one application might be terrible for another. As an example, PILOT is an excellent choice for the preparation of computer-assisted instruction programs, but a terrible choice for programs involving extensive numerical computations.

Figure 15-1 contains a chart comparing the 12 languages in various performance categories. The performance categories are listed down the left side and the languages across the top of the chart.

The numerical ratings for each language in each performance category are on a scale of 1 to 5, with 1 meaning very poor and 5 meaning excellent. The rating scale is described in more detail in the figure. Within each category, the score of the top-ranking language is marked with an asterisk. In several cases, two languages are tied for the top rating in a particular category.

The ratings are discussed by performance category in the paragraphs that follow.

NUMERICAL COMPUTATION

This performance category refers to the ability of the language to support applications involving extensive numerical computations. The traditional leader in this area is Fortran. This should not be surprising, inasmuch as Fortran was designed to support numerical computations; in fact, number-crunching is Fortran's reason for existence.

Although Fortran is the oldest of the languages covered in this book, it is still the overwhelming favorite of engineers and mathematicians. Fortran compilers usually include a large library of predefined mathematical functions for operations such as finding the secant of an angle. Most implementations also include functions for handling complex numbers. (If you aren't mathematically inclined, you might not know what secants and

	Ada	Basic	C	Cobol	Forth	Fortran	LISP	Logo	Modula-2	Pascal	PILOT	Prolog
Numerical computations	5*	4	4	2	2	5*	2	3	4	4	3	2
Character handling	4	5*	5	4	3	2	5	5	4	4	3	5
Data structures	5*	3	5	5	2	3	4	4	5*	5	1	4
Control structures	5*	3	5	3	4	3	3	4	5*	5	2	2
Console input/output	5	5	4	5*	3	4	2	4	5	5	5	3
File input/output	4	4	4	5*	3	4	2	2	4	4	2	3
Subroutine interface	5*	2	3	2	3	4	4	4	5*	4	2	3
Low-level operations	4	3	5*	2	5	2	2	2	4	3	1	2
User Friendliness	3	5	3	3	2	3	4	5*	4	4	5	3

Rating scale: (* indicates best in category)

5 = Excellent
4 = Good
3 = Fair
2 = Poor
1 = Very poor

Fig. 15-1. Microcomputer languages compared.

complex numbers are. The point is that Fortran is one of the few languages that directly support such mathematical operations.)

Although Fortran is still the most popular language for scientific applications, Ada also has very strong abilities in this area. In several areas, Ada surpasses Fortran in technical features, such as the ability to specify numerical precision more precisely. The disadvantage of Ada in this area is that Ada subroutine libraries are not yet as extensive or as widespread as Fortran subroutine libraries. This may be a temporary disadvantage. I predict that Ada will become more and more popular for numerical applications.

Other possible choices for applications involving numerical computations include BASIC, C, Modula-2, and Pascal. BASIC supports most of the basic operations needed for numerical operations, but it is usually rather slow in execution.

Modula-2, Pascal, and C are fast enough for numerical operations, but each lacks an operator for performing exponentiation. The structure of these languages, however, permits the creation and use of user-defined functions to perform exponentiation and other mathematical operations.

Each of the other languages supports simple arithmetic operations, but they are rated lower. COBOL is rated low because its verbosity makes numerical computations tedious. LISP is rated low because it uses prefix notation. Forth is rated low both because it uses postfix notation and because it requires the programmer to most of the work of analyzing and evaluating arithmetic expressions. Prolog is rated low because its declarative nature is not conducive to specifying numerical computations.

CHARACTER HANDLING

Most of the languages covered handle characters very well. BASIC is the winner in this category based on ease of use. Logo and LISP are actually more powerful in that they offer greater flexibility in the handling of characters, but they are not as easy to use. C also has excellent character handling facilities. For heavy-duty character-handling applications, such as writing a text editor, C is probably the language of choice.

COBOL, Modula-2, and Pascal are rated just slightly lower in this category because they require the maximum length of a character string to be declared in advance. Forth also requires the maximum length of the string to be declared in advance, plus it requires the programmer to do more of the work, such as keeping track of how many characters there are in each character string. Ada provides fairly good character handling.

Many versions of Fortran do not even support a character type directly, requiring that characters be stored as integer variables. This omission has been corrected with the latest version, Fortran 77.

Pilot supports character strings, but offers little in the way of operators to manipulate them.

DATA STRUCTURES

To earn a high rating in the data structures category, a language must support advanced structures such as records, lists, and so forth, as well as traditional data structures such as arrays. Several languages earn the top rating: Ada, C, COBOL, Modula-2, and Pascal. The distinction of best of category is shared by Modula-2 and Ada, as they allow data structures to be isolated in modules or packages, insulating the main program from the details of the data structure.

LISP, Logo, and Prolog do an excellent job of supporting advanced data structures, and would have earned the top rating except that they do not support arrays.

Fortran and BASIC support arrays, but little else in the way of data structures. Advanced data structures in these languages must be simulated using arrays. Forth can support many data structures but, as usual, it makes the programmer do most of the work. PILOT does not support any data entities beyond simple variables and character strings.

CONTROL STRUCTURES

To earn the top rating in the category of control structures, a language must support an **IF-THEN-ELSE** statement, a **CASE** statement (or its equivalent), a counted loop, one or more kinds of conditional loop, functions and/or subroutines, and recursion. Only Ada, C, Modula-2, and Pascal win the top rating.

COBOL lacks recursion and a **CASE** statement. Until the COBOL 85 standard, it also lacked in-line loops (**PERFORM** statements). Forth lacks a **CASE** statement. Fortran lacks a **CASE** statement, conditional loops, and recursion. BASIC lacks a **CASE** statement and recursion. The LISP **COND** statement is a very powerful variation of the **IF** statement, but LISP is lacking in the loop category. LOGO has a counted loop, but no conditional loop. Prolog is particularly poor in its support of the traditional control statements, relying on recursion and alternate definitions of predicates to control the flow of execution.

PILOT has only simple conditional statements and jumps (similar to the **IF** and **GO TO** of other languages).

The winners in this category are Ada and Modula-2. They are rated higher than Pascal and C on the strength of the generalized **LOOP** statement (with **EXIT**) and on the completeness of their **CASE** statements.

CONSOLE INPUT/OUTPUT

This category covers the ease of reading data from the console and writing data to the console. It includes the ability to control the appearance of the output, such as the width of a print field and the number of decimal places for real numbers. The languages covered vary widely in this category.

I have rated COBOL tops in this category because it supports the input and output of a full screen at a time, using the **ACCEPT** and **DISPLAY** verbs. The programmer has full control over the format of the screen.

BASIC also rates high in this category. (Those versions of BASIC, such as Applesoft, that lack a **PRINT USING** statement do not rate as high.) Ada, Modula-2, Pascal, and PILOT are also rated high.

LISP is downgraded in this category because it cannot easily distinguish the end of a character string in the input stream. This may be a problem only with this particular implementation, however.

FILE INPUT/OUTPUT

This category covers the ease of reading data from and writing data to disk files. COBOL is the clear winner in this category. This should not be a surprise, as COBOL was designed for applications that consist primarily of maintaining data files.

A high rating in this category requires the ability to handle sequential files and direct-access files, and to perform the read and write operations easily. An advantage COBOL has over all the others is the ability to easily control the format of the data being stored. For example, the number 734 could be stored by a COBOL program as a binary integer, as a binary-coded decimal number, or as ASCII characters.

Most implementations of BASIC and C do very well in supporting file input and output. Standard Pascal lacks direct-access files, but most implementations include this feature.

Forth supports a unique file structure, in which the data as organized as ''screens'' of 1024 characters. Forth treats the disk as if it were an extension of memory. The major disadvantage of many implementations of Forth is that Forth files are not compatible with any other kind of files.

PILOT supports data files, but limits what can be written to a file to what has been read in. For example, you cannot write the results of a computation to a PILOT file. Logo does not support the storage of data in files except as part of a workspace. LISP supports files, but to read in data, that data must have been written out in the form of a program. Prolog is more flexible, but standard Prolog does not support direct-access files.

SUBROUTINE INTERFACE

The covered languages vary greatly in the way in which data are passed to and from subroutines and functions. The clear winners in this category are Ada and Modula-2, which are very similar in this area.

The superiority of Ada and Modula-2 in this category lies in the way in which they implement separately compiled packages or modules. Ada and Modula-2 control the interface between modules, insuring that changes made in one module do not adversely affect another module.

Most implementations of Fortran also support separately compiled subroutines. LISP, Logo, and Pascal also have very good interface mechanisms between programs and subroutines. Prolog's interface mechanism is a bit ambiguous, as Prolog allows several alternate definitions of a subroutine.

Forth communicates with subroutines using the stack. This works well, but requires careful planning by the programmer.

The C language has an adequate interface between subroutines (functions), but requires explicit reference to the passing of pointers for variables that are to have their values changed in the subroutine.

BASIC and PILOT support subroutines, but they have no provision for the passing of data between programs and subroutines. All values are global in these languages; that is, all values are equally accessible from anywhere in the program. The disadvantage of this is that it is difficult for a subroutine to operate on more than one set of data. (For example, a sort subroutine could only sort one specific array.)

LOW-LEVEL OPERATIONS

Operations on bits and bytes are called low-level operations. They are often required for interfacing directly with computer hardware, such as in writing a driver routine for a serial interface to a modem.

Low-level operations have not been discussed much in this book, as this book concentrates on high-level operations. Nevertheless, for the sake of completeness, the languages are rated on their abilities to handle low-level operations.

The winner in this category is C. Evidence of its suitability for low-level operations is the fact that the UNIX operating system is written in C. (Operating systems typically require numerous low-level operations.) C has also become the language of choice for the development of commercial software for microcomputers, partly because of its ability to easily control low-level operations on a microcomputer. Forth also has excellent provisions for low-level operations. Ada and Modula-2 support low-level operations, but not as easily.

Pascal supports low-level operations, but not without resort to various programming tricks. The **PEEK** and **POKE** operations of BASIC can be used to provide direct access to the hardware, and some versions of BASIC provide some bit manipulation operators. The other high-level languages covered provide little or no support of low-level operations.

USER FRIENDLINESS

User friendliness is a much-abused term, but it generally refers to the ease of use of a software product. It includes such factors as how easy it is to compile and execute a program, how easy it is to understand the language as a whole, and how easy it is to write a program in that language.

The clear winner in this category is Logo. Logo is so user-friendly that it can easily be taught to young children as soon as they can read. BASIC and PILOT are also very easy to use, partly because they do not require a separate compile step.

LISP is a remarkably consistent language. Because it is so different from most other languages, it at first appears foreboding. Once a few basic concepts are mastered, LISP is actually a very easy language to learn and use.

Ada, Modula-2, and Pascal are not quite as friendly, but because they are strongly typed languages, they do provide good error diagnostics and excellent protection against careless mistakes. C and Forth provide no such protection. C and Forth are powerful tools in the hands of experts, but can be frustrating to beginners.

I personally find Prolog to be not very friendly, probably because it is so different from the other languages discussed. It is difficult to learn well, but once learned, it provides a lot of power with less effort than most other languages.

MATCHING THE LANGUAGE AND THE APPLICATION

Life would be simple if there were one language that was best for all applications. Unfortunately life is not that simple.

Of the languages covered in this book, five best fit the description of general-purpose languages: Ada, BASIC, C, Modula-2, and Pascal. In theory at least, any program can be written in any one of these languages. A programmer having a wide variety of applications and wishing to do all of his or her programming in only one language would do well to choose one of these languages.

Not all programmers, however, are faced with a wide variety of applications. For a particular set of applications, some other language may be better.

For business applications the language of choice is COBOL. COBOL rates high in support of data structures and in file handling. In addition, COBOL can perform exact arithmetic in the decimal system, as is often required for business applications. Other possible choices for business applications include the general-purpose languages (Ada, BASIC, C, Modula-2, and Pascal) and Fortran.

For scientific applications involving numerical applications, Ada and Fortran are the languages of choice. My personal preference would be Ada. As an alternative, one of the general-purpose languages could be used.

For developing computer-assisted instruction, PILOT is the language of choice. Other possible choices for this type of application are Logo, LISP, and Prolog. BASIC would be a distant fourth choice.

For applications involving artificial intelligence or knowledge-based systems, the best choice is Prolog. LISP is also a strong contender, but Prolog's built-in inference engine sets it apart.

For applications involving character manipulation, the best choices are BASIC and C. For simple character applications, I recommend BASIC. For heavy-duty character applications, I recommend C. Logo, LISP, Pascal and Modula-2 would also be acceptable choices. Fortran should be ruled out.

For applications involving bit and byte manipulations, the best choices are C and Forth, with C being my personal preference.

For teaching children to program, the first choice is clearly Logo. Logo has been successfully used with children in kindergarten, although second grade is a more common starting level. Second choice for children is BASIC. Sixth grade is probably a good time to start children with BASIC.

For real-time applications, Ada and Modula-2 are superior. Forth is excellent for control applications, such as use in robots, telescopes, and other instruments. The features that support such applications, however, are not discussed in this book.

CONCLUSIONS

The purpose of this book has been to describe a wide variety of high-level languages available for microcomputers. Illustrative sample programs have been presented in each language. Some of the sample programs have been the same from language to language, making it easier to compare the features of each language.

Many of you will have purchased this book because you know one language and want to see what other languages are like. You might be planning to buy another language compiler and need help in deciding which one to choose.

The one inescapable conclusion to be drawn is that, despite the availability of general-purpose languages, some things are easier to do in one language than in other languages. The clear implication is that it is an advantage for a programmer to be able to program in more than one language.

A cabinetmaker learns to use a variety of tools so that he or she can make better cabinets. It is a matter of using the right tool for the right job. Similarly, a programmer should learn to use a variety of languages so that he or she can write better programs. Again, it is a matter of using the right tool for the right job. I hope that you will be motivated to learn at least one more language.

Index

Index

498

Other Bestsellers From TAB

☐ **TURBO PASCAL® FOR THE MAC: PROGRAMMING WITH BUSINESS APPLICATIONS—Dr. Leon A. Wortman**

Speed on demand . . . powerful syntax . . . a full range of built-in functions . . . these are just a few of the advantages that have earned Borland International top acclaim for its Turbo Pascal compiler. For Mac users who have been anxious to try Turbo Pascal's power, the time is now! It's a simplified learning manual that includes numerous useful examples and in-depth discussion of the program applications for Turbo Pascal 3.0 and 3.1. The hands-on, learn-by-doing technique demonstrated in this book is all you need to master programming in the high-level Turbo Pascal language. 288 pp., 83 illus.

Paper $17.95   **Book No. 2927**

☐ **POWER PROGRAMMING WITH ADA® FOR THE IBM PC®—John Winters, Ph.D.**

This excellent new guide puts Ada programming within easy understanding. Whether you'd simply like to find out how Ada works or you need a fundamental knowledge of Ada to compete more effectively in the Defense Department-related marketplace, John Winters leads you easily and effectively through the principles of Ada programming. He even includes an extensive glossary filled with sample code that's an ideal programming reference. 220 pp., 153 illus.

Paper $16.95   **Hard $24.95**
Book No. 2902

☐ **PRODOS® INSIDE AND OUT—Dennis Doms and Tom Weishaar**

This introduction to programming with BASIC.SYSTEM gives practical tips and how-to advice on everything from booting your system to assembly language programming with ProDOS. You'll even cover such hard-to-find topics as subdirectories and their use, programming examples for the Field and Byte options of text files, the use of BSAVE and BLOAD parameters to save disk space, and more! 270 pp., 113 illus.

Paper $16.95   **Hard $24.95**
Book No. 2745

☐ **CLIPPER™: dBASE® COMPILER APPLICATIONS—Gary Beam**

Going well beyond the standard user's manual, this book provides you with a treasury of programming techniques and applications examples that allows you to take maximum advantage of Clipper's program development potential. Whether you are a novice Clipper user trying to master this compiler's many special functions and features or an experienced program developer looking for new techniques, this book is a must. 190 pp., 37 illus.

Paper $16.95   **Book No. 2917**

☐ **ASSEMBLY LANGUAGE SUBROUTINES FOR MS-DOS® COMPUTERS—Leo J. Scanlon**

This collection of practical, easy-to-use subroutines is exactly what you need for performing high-precision math, converting code, manipulating strings and lists, sorting data, reading user commands and responses from the keyboard, and doing countless other jobs. If you consider your time a valuable asset, you won't want to miss this handy quick-reference to a gold mine of subroutines. 350 pp., 43 illus.

Paper $19.95   **Hard $27.95**
Book No. 2767

☐ **MACINTOSH™ ASSEMBLY LANGUAGE PROGRAMMING—Jake Commander**

Delve below the surface-level capabilities of your Macintosh and discover the incredible power that assembly language can add to your programming practice. You'll learn all about the fundamentals of machine code . . . gain an understanding of editors and assemblers . . . and tap into the 68000's addressing modes and instruction set. It's a book no Mac owner can afford to miss! 208 pp., 31 illus.

Paper $16.95   **Hard $24.95**
Book No. 2611

*Prices subject to change without notice.

Look for these and other TAB books at your local bookstore.

TAB BOOKS Inc.
Blue Ridge Summit, PA 17294

Send for FREE TAB Catalog describing over 1200 current titles in print.

OR CALL TOLL-FREE TODAY: **1-800-233-1128**
IN PENNSYLVANIA AND ALASKA, CALL: **717-794-2191**